- Please return items before closing time on the last date stamped to avoid charges.
- Renew books by phoning 01305 224311 or online www.dorsetforyou.com/libraries
- Items may be returned to any Dorset library.
- Please note that children's books issued on an adult card will incur overdue charges.

Dorset County Council
Library Service

DL/2372 dd05450

The Luftwaffe

A Study in Air Power 1933–1945

The Luftwaffe

A Study in Air Power 1933–1945

'ooton

S S I C

rint of
ublishing

The Luftwaffe: A Complete History 1933-45
E. R. Hooton

First published 2010

ISBN 978 1 90653 718 0

Published by Classic Publications

an imprint of Ian Allan Publishing Ltd, Hersham, Surrey KT12 4RG.
Printed in England by Ian Allan Printing Ltd, Hersham, Surrey KT12 4RG.

Visit the Ian Allan Publishing website at www.ianallanpublishing.com

Project Editor: Robert Forsyth / Chevron Publishing Limited

The editor would like to thank Mr Eddie Creek for his kind co-operation in regard to the provision of photographs in this book.

Contents

FOREWORD

This is the fifth book I have written about the *Luftwaffe* and brings to an end nearly 15 years of research into the evolution and development of German air power during the first half of the 20th Century.

I began because I was dissatisfied with the treatment of the subject which seemed to follow a particular course and which, by the 1990s, was clearly outdated as demonstrated by a raft of specialised works. I had the opportunity, through the efforts of my fellow author, Mr Mike Gething, to examine and to revise the Luftwaffe's history with the help of many friends, who are listed below, as well as studying numerous works and documents. My understanding was further assisted by the opportunity to revise my manuscript on air operations over the Western Front which was published by Ian Allan Publishing as *War Over the Trenches* in early 2009.

The German Air Force did not die at the end of the Great War; on the contrary, it expanded briefly and from 1920 covert development gathered pace not only in Russia, but also in Germany. By 1932 the German Defence Ministry had decided to reform an air force which would be equal in status to the traditional services and this was the scheme which the Nazis inherited and expanded substantially. The *Luftwaffe*'s shadow lay over Europe in the 1930s and its successes in the early years of the war were a combination of focusing upon Operational and Tactical level (army group and army) missions using balanced task forces against enemies who were often in the midst of re-equipment and with fragmented command and control.

But the *Luftwaffe*'s technological foundation was flawed, and under growing pressure, its leaders increasingly reverted to a pattern of Tactical operations with echoes of their Great War experience. The bomber forces never possessed an adequate instrument for Strategic (beyond army group) missions partly because the Nazis were more interested in quantity rather than quality, while industrialists were allowed numerous flights of fancy which made no contribution to the war effort. By the end of the war the *Luftwaffe*, despite possessing some sophisticated aircraft including jet fighters and bombers, was itself making no contribution to the war effort.

An interesting aspect of my research was to discover the impact of individuals and relationships upon *Luftwaffe* operations. In part this reflected the 'Devil Take the Hindmost' philosophy of the Nazis of which the development of 'aces' was another aspect. What is clear is that the *Luftwaffe*'s decline was in direct proportion to Göring's growing intervention and is exemplified by the decision taken in the immediate aftermath of the July Plot to scrap the four-engined bomber force in the summer of 1944. It was also a combination of Göring's megalomania and Raeder's conservatism which hamstrung Luftwaffe maritime co-operation.

Apart from Alfred Price's account, there had been little attempt to examine the last year of *Luftwaffe* operations. Yet there is a mass of material which, I believe, I have been able to exploit to produce a comprehensive account of this period of continuous decline. Yet this decline is full of interest and may well reward a new examination of the period.

Restrictions of space have meant that this account has had to make a more empirical approach than my earlier works. I have focused less on day-to-day operations and individuals and more upon the broad sweep of campaigns and the relationships within the *Luftwaffe* leadership. Much still remains to be written especially on operations over the Eastern Front and here I greatly benefited from Mr Christer Bergström's work which has made him the air equivalent of the late Professor John Erickson and Colonel David Glantz through his excellent studies of Soviet operations. My own studies on the Soviet Air Force and the *Luftwaffe* have greatly benefited from the World Wide Web which gives access to much information, although some care must be taken with this. But it has allowed me to produce a far more detailed examination of air operations in the East and has provided much understanding of the problems faced by Soviet air power as well as allowing me, for my own interest, a monthly Soviet Air Force Order of Battle to the end of the war.

Information on the web permits even more detailed studies on the Luftwaffe and its operations – but for me this must come later. Nevertheless, I would welcome other historians making the effort. While my name is on the title page, this book, and all my others, owes a colossal debt to dozens of specialist writers and to people who have helped me personally with information thus putting me eternally in their debt. These include William Green, José Ignacio González-Aller Hierro, Caroline Hooton, Jennifer Hooton, Jörg Huthmann, the late Admiral Gert Jeschonnek, Hans-Eberhard Krüger, Ken Munson, Dr Richard Osborne, Martin Pegg, the late *Herr* Steffen Papsdorf, J. Richard Smith, Martin Streetley, Alex Vanags-Baginskis, David Wadman, and Peter Waller, (Publisher, Books at Ian Allan Publishing).

I must also thank Dr H. Amersfoort of the Netherlands Army's Military History Section, Mr Frits Gerdessen, Mr T. H. Holm of the Norwegian Armed Forces Museum, Mr Jörg Huthmann, Mr Etienne Reunis, Attaché/Air & Space Department in the Belgian Museum of the Army and Mr Martin Streetley. I have had to research in numerous archives and libraries so I am happy to acknowledge the debt I owe to the Bundesarchiv-Militärarchiv in Freiburg, the Imperial War Museum, the UK National Archives, the US National Archives, the Service Historique de Défence, the Armée de l'Air, The Library of the Royal United Services Institute, the Cuartel General del Ejercito del Aire, the Servicio Historico y Cultural Instituto de Historia y Cultura, Institutio de Historia y Cultura Naval, the Heeresgeschichtliches Museum, Vienna and Langley Library, Slough through which I have ordered many works.

Above all I would like to pay a special tribute to Mr Robert Forsyth who has driven this and my last two titles and has been unfailingly supportive as well as providing much information. In producing this book I would like to thank his editorial and production team at Chevron Publishing as well as my publisher, Ian Allan Publishing.

Finally, I would like to thank my wife Linda for her tremendous patience while I have been 'with the *Luftwaffe*'.

E. R. Hooton
Langley, 2010

Glossary of Terms

Aéronautique Militaire (AéMI)	Belgian Air Force
Armee	Army
Armée de l'Air	French Air Force
Aufklärungsstaffel	Reconnaissance squadron
Beobachterstaffel	Observer Squadron
Beobachterlehrstaffel	Observer Demonstration Squadron
Chef des Ausbildungswesens	Chief of Training Resources
Chef der Luftwehr	Chief of Air Defence
Deutschen Luftfahrt-Verband eV (DLV)	German Aviation Organisation
Deutschen Luftsportverband e.V	German Air Sport Association
Dunkelnachtjagd	Dark Night Fighting
Ergänzungsgruppe	Operation training Gruppe
Erprobungskommando	Test Command
Gefechtsverband	Battle Formation
General der Aufklärungsflieger	General of Reconnaissance Arm
General der Flakartillerie	General of Flak Artillery
General der Jagdflieger	General of Fighter Arm
General der Kampfflieger	General of Bomber Arm
Generalluftzeugmeister	Chief of Procurement
Geschwader	Wing
Grenzschutz Fliegerabteilungen (GFA)	Volunteer Border Protection Air Unit
Fallschirmjäger	Paratroop
Fallschirmjägerarmee	Parachute Army
Fernaufklärungsstaffeln	Long-Range Reconnaissance Squadrons
Fernkampfführer	Long-Range Bomber Commander
Flakscheinwerferdivision	Searchlight Divisions
Fliegerdivision	Flying Division
Fliegerführer	(Regional) Air Commander
Flieger Ersatz Abteilung-FEA	Air Replacement Battalion
Fliegerkorps	Flying Corps
Fliegerstaffel	Flying Squadron
Fliegertruppe	Flying Force
Fliegerverbindungsoffizier – Flivo	Air Liaison Officer
Fluglehrschule	Flying Instructors' School
Flugmeldedienst	Air Reporting Service
Freikorps	Free Corps
Freiwilligen Fliegerabteilungen (FFA)	Volunteer Flying Units
Fühlungshälter	'Shadowing' aircraft or contact-keepers for night fighting purposes
Hellenachtjagd	Bright Night Fighting
Heeresgruppe	Army Group
Heereswaffenamt	Army Ordnance Board
Inspekteur	Inspector
Inspekteur der Flieger (Idflieg)	Inspector of Flying Forces (WW1)

Inspekteur der Jagdflieger	Inspector of Fighter Forces
Inspizient	Inspecting Authority
Jabo (Jagd-Bomber)	Fighter-Bomber
Jagdabschnittsführer	Fighter Sector commander
Jagdfliegerführer (Jafü)	Area Fighter Commander
Jagdgeschwader	Fighter Wing
Jagdgruppe	Fighter Group
Jagdkorps	Fighter Corps
Jagdstaffel	Fighter Squadron
Jagdlehrstaffel	Fighter Demonstration Squadron
Jägerschreck	'Fighter Fear'
Kampfgeschwader	Bomber Wing
Kampfgruppe	Bomber Group
Kampfzerstörer	Combat Destroyer
Kombinierte Nachtjagdgebeite	Combined Night Fighting Zones
Kommandierende General der	
Deutschen Luftwaffe in…	Senior Luftwaffe General in …
Kommandeur	Commander of a Gruppe
Kommandeur der Luftwaffe (Koluft)	Luftwaffe Commander (tactical co-ordinator)
Kommodore	Commander of a *Geschwader*
Kriegsministerium	Prussian War Ministry
Lehrgeschwader	Operational Training Wing
Luftflotte	Air Fleet
Luftgau	Air District
Luftkommandoamt	Air Command Directorate
Luftkriegschule	Air War School
Luftkreis	Air Region
Luftnachrichtenwesen	Air Signal Service
Luftschutz Amt	Air Defence Department
Luftschutzkommando	Air Defence Command
Luftsportlandesgruppen	Air Sport Regional Groups
Luftstreitkräfte	Military Air Arm (WW1)
Lufttransportführer	Air Transport Commander
Lufttransportchefs Land	Chief of Land-Based Air Transport
Luftüberwachungsabteilung	Airborne Protection Battalion
Luftversorgungsstab	Air Supply Staff
Luftwaffenführungsstab	Air Command Staff
Luftwaffengeneralstab	*Luftwaffe* General Staff
Luftwaffengruppenkommando	Air Group Command
Luftwaffehelferinnen	*Luftwaffe* Female Auxiliaries
Luftwaffenkommando	Air Force Command
Luftwaffenpersonalamt	*Luftwaffe* Personnel Office
Oberbefehlshaber	Commander-in-Chief
Oberkommando des Marines (OKM)	Naval High Command
Oberkommando der Wehrmacht (OKW)	Armed Forces High Command
Militaire Luchtvaart (ML)	Dutch Air Force
Nahaufklärungsstaffel	Corps/Short-Range Reconnaissance Squadron
Nachtjagddivision	Night Fighter Division

Nachtjagdraumführer	Area Night Fighter Commander
Nachtjagdversuchskommando	Night Fighting Trials Unit
Nachtjagdwaffe	Night Fighter Force
Nachtschlachtgruppe	Night Ground-Attack Gruppe
Nahkampfführer	Close-Support Commander
Panzerjägerkommando	Tank-Hunting/-Busting Command
Panzerjägerstaffel	Tank-Hunting/-Busting Squadron
Polizei-Fliegerstaffel	Police Flying Squadron
Regia Aeronautica	Italian Air Force
Reichsmarine	Navy
Reichsminister für die Luftfahrt	Reich Minister for Aeronautics
Reichswehrministerium (RWM)	Armed Forces Ministry
Ritterkreuz	Knight's Cross
Schlachtflugzeug	Assault or Ground-Attack Aircraft
Schlachtgeschwader	Ground-Attack Wing
Schlachtgruppe	Assault or Ground-Attack Group
Schnellbomber	Fast-Bomber
Schwarzemänner	'Black Men': Luftwaffe slang for ground crews on account of their black overalls
Seeluftstreitkräfte	Naval Air Corps
Seetransportabteilung	Sea Transportation Organisation
Sondergruppe/-staffel	Special Task Group/Squadron
Staatssekretär	Secretary of State
Staffel	Squadron
Staffel zbV ObdL	Luftwaffe Commander-in-Chief's Special Employment Squadron
Störangriffe	Harassment/Nuisance Attacks
Störkampfgruppe	Harassment Gruppe
Sturmstaffel / -gruppe	Close Assault Squadron/Group
Stürzkampflugzeug (Stuka)	Dive-Bomber
Technisches Amt	Air Ministry Technical Office
Transportgruppe	Transport Gruppe
Truppenamt	Troop or Military Office/Department
Versuchstelle für Höhenflüge	Experimental Establishment for High-Altitude Flight
Viermot	*Luftwaffe* slang term for 'four-motor' – a four-engined bomber
ground*Unternehmen*	Military Operation (as in 'Operation *Bodenplatte*')
ground*Wehrkreis*	Military District
Wilde Sau	'Rogue Elephant' – method of free-range night fighting
ground... *zbV*	Unit or individual designated for Special Employment
Zahme Sau	'Pet Lamb' – method of 'tame' night-fighting
Zerstörer	Destroyer or Heavy Fighter
Zerstörergruppe/ -geschwader	Destroyer or Heavy Fighter Group or Wing
Zielfinder	Target Marker

Luftwaffe Ranks and Flying Units

Ranks

The table below lists the wartime *Luftwaffe* ranks together with their equivalent in the Royal Air Force and the US Army Air Force:

Luftwaffe	Royal Air Force	USAAF
Generalfeldmarschall	Marshal of the RAF	Five Star General
Generaloberst	Air Chief Marshal	Four Star General
General der Flieger	Air Marshal	Lieutenant-General
Generalleutnant	Air Vice-Marshal	Major-General
Generalmajor	Air Commodore	Brigadier-General
Oberst	Group Captain	Colonel
Oberstleutnant	Wing Commander	Lieutenant-Colonel
Major	Squadron Leader	Major
Hauptmann	Flight Lieutenant	Captain
Oberleutnant	Flying Officer	First Lieutenant
Leutnant	Pilot Officer	Lieutenant
Oberfähnrich	(leading cadet)	(leading cadet)
Fähnrich	(cadet)	(cadet)
Stabsfeldwebel	Warrant Officer	Warrant Officer
Oberfeldwebel	Flight Sergeant	Master Sergeant
Feldwebel	Sergeant	Technical Sergeant
Unterfeldwebel	-	-
Unteroffizier	Corporal	Staff Sergeant
Hauptgefreiter	-	Sergeant
Obergefreiter	Leading Aircraftman	Corporal
Gefreiter	Aircraftman First Class	Private First Class
Flieger	Aircraftman	Private

In addition, the *Luftwaffe* used the term '*Hauptfeldwebel*'. This was not a rank. A *Hauptfeldwebel* (colloquially called '*Spiess*') was the NCO administrative head of a company or corresponding unit (*Staffel*, battery, etc). His rank could be anything from *Unteroffizier* to the various *Feldwebel*.

Flying Units

The basic *Luftwaffe* flying unit was the *Staffel* or squadron which was normally made up of between 9 and 12 (later 16) aircraft. It was led by a *Staffelkapitän* who normally had the rank of *Hauptmann* or *Oberleutnant*. The *Staffel* was always identified by an Arabic number - for example, the *5.Staffel*. The dot which followed the number had the same meaning as 'th' in English – this is the Fifth *Staffel* in the above example. Apart from the aircraft and aircrew, the *Staffel* had a ground organisation of various vehicles and about 150 men.

Three or four *Staffeln* could be combined together to form a *Gruppe* or Group. This could be autonomous, usually in the case of reconnaissance units, (when it was identified by an Arabic numeral), or as part of a *Geschwader* or Wing (when it was identified by a Roman number). For example, *Nahaufklärungsgruppe 6* or the *III.Gruppe* of JG 27. The *Gruppe* also contained a *Stab* (literally 'staff') or Headquarters Flight which included such persons as the as the *Gruppen Kommandeur* (usually a *Major* or *Hauptmann*, the *Gruppe Adjutant* and the *Gruppe Technische Offizier* (Technical Officer).

As with the *Staffel*, three, four or occasionally five *Gruppen* could be combined together to form a *Geschwader* or Wing. These were always identified by an Arabic numeral. Like the *Gruppe*, the *Geschwader* contained a *Stab* made up of the *Geschwader Kommadore*, (usually an *Oberst, Oberstleutnant or Major*) and other personnel such as *Adjutant*, TO, Ia (operations officer), Ic (intelligence officer), and *Nachrichten Officer* (signals officer).

When the Second World War began, the make-up of a typical *Geschwader* was as follows:

Geschwader Stab

I. Gruppe	II. Gruppe	III. Gruppe
1.Staffel	4.Staffel	7.Staffel
2.Staffel	5.Staffel	8.Staffel
3.Staffel	6.Staffel	9.Staffel

During the autumn of 1944 (and in the case of JG 2 and JG 26 the summer of 1943) many Fighter Wings *(Jagdgeschwader)* were expanded to have four *Gruppen* of four *Staffeln* each. The typical fighter *Geschwader* of this period would appear thus:

Geschwader Stab

I. Gruppe	II. Gruppe	III. Gruppe	IV. Gruppe
1.Staffel	5.Staffel	9.Staffel	13.Staffel
2.Staffel	6.Staffel	10.Staffel	14.Staffel
3.Staffel	7.Staffel	11.Staffel	15.Staffel
4.Staffel	8.Staffel	12 Staffel	16.Staffel

The major type of *Geschwader* were:

German	English	Written as
Jagdgeschwader	Day Fighter Wing	JG
Kampfgeschwader	Bomber Wing	KG
Kampfgeschwader (Jagd)	Bomber Wing on Fighter operations	KG
Nachtjagdgeschwader	Night Fighter Wing	NJG
Schnellkampfgeschwader	Fast Bomber Wing	SKG
Schlachtgeschwader	Ground Attack Wing	SG
Sturzkampfgeschwader	Dive Bomber Wing	St.G
Transportgeschwader	Transport Wing	TG
Zerstörergeschwader	Destroyer Wing	ZG

Common types of autonomous *Gruppen* were:

Aufklärungsgruppe	Reconnaissance Group	Aufkl.Gr.
Fernaufklärungsgruppe	Long-Range Reconnaissance Group	FAG
Nahaufklärungsgruppe	Short-Range Reconnaissance Group	NAG
Nachtschlachtgruppe	Night Ground-attack Group	NSG

Other *Luftwaffe* units mentioned in this work include the *Erprobungskommando* and the *Kommando*. These were both experimental tests units, the former charged with developing a particular aircraft, weapon or weapons, the latter with developing operational tactics. *Erprobungskommando* were identified by an Arabic numeral, a *Kommando* either by its commander's name or codename.

Chapter One

Died in War – Born in Peace

The Armistice of 11 November 1918 marked both an end and a new beginning for German air power which blossomed briefly in the chaos of the post-war world. German air power enjoyed a renaissance and began the post-war peace in the same way it helped to end it, in more ways than one – fighting the Poles.

In the winter of 1918/1919 Germany faced internal and external threats. Internally, 'Red' (Socialist and Communist) factions of differing hues sought by force of arms to create a new state which many hoped would emulate the Bolsheviks in Russia. Externally, the Bolsheviks were extending their power westwards towards the Baltic States and Poland, but it was the efforts by Poland to secure more of the German Reich which was the most pressing problem. [1]

The *Kriegsministerium* (Prussian War Ministry) in Berlin responded by supporting the creation of volunteer units (*Freikorps*) from both troops returning from the battlefronts, and recruits who had just missed the conflict. These they equipped and despatched against their foes as the basis of the future army, with many having air support through a new department under the former the chief of staff of the *Luftstreitkräfte*, *Oberst* Hermann von der Lieth-Thomsen. There was no problem equipping them; under the direction of *Major* Wilhelm Haehnelt, who had led Germany's first air campaign over Verdun in 1916 and who had succeeded *Oberstleutnant* Wilhelm Siegert as *Inspekteur der Flieger* (*Idflieg*) – effectively director of air production, German factories worked on raising the inventory between January and March 1919 from 6,000 to 9,000 aircraft, including trainers and reserves. [2]

Thomsen could equip the *Freikorps* with the latest aircraft including the Albatros D.Va, the Fokker D.VII, the Fokker D.VIII 'Flying Razor', the all-metal Junkers D.I and the Siemens-Schuckert D.IV fighters, the Halberstadt C.V and LVG C.V/C.VI corps (single-engine, multi-role, two-seat tactical) aircraft as well as close-air support (*Schlacht*) machines including the Halberstadt CL.II/CL.V, the Hannover CL.V and the all-metal Junkers CL.I. There were hundreds of bitter and disgruntled airmen to fly them and Thomsen was able to create some 35 squadrons with up to 300 aircraft; these comprised *Freiwilligen Fliegerabteilungen* (*FFA*) to meet the internal threat and *Grenzschutz Fliegerabteilungen* (*GFA*) to protect the eastern borders, although such distinctions were not rigid.

It was the 14 squadrons (80 aircraft) supporting *Generaloberst* Johannes (Hans) von Seeckt's *Grenzschutz Nord* (Northern Border Patrol) in East Prussia and *Grenzschutz Ost* (Eastern Border Patrol) in Silesia which were first into action against the Poles from 7 January 1919. As with most *Freikorps* squadrons their missions largely took the form of reconnaissance and ground-attack flights, although *Oberleutnant* Oskar *Freiherr* von Boenigk, the 26-victory ace who had formerly commanded *Jagdgeschwader* (*JG*) II, did bring down an enemy aircraft. He would later become a general in the *Luftwaffe*, and other future *Luftwaffe* worthies who fought alongside him included *Hauptmann* Erhard Milch and *Hauptmann* Hugo Sperrle, who commanded the *Grenzschutz Ost* squadrons.

From mid-January *Freikorps* squadrons supported operations against 'Red' forces in many of Germany's urban centres including Berlin, Munich and Hamburg as well as the industrial Ruhr. [3] The largest concentration was in Bavaria where seven squadrons (50 aircraft) fought against the Socialist Republic of Bavaria which fell in early May. Among those who participated in these operations were future *Luftwaffe* generals *Hauptmann* Ulrich Grauert and *Leutnant* Otto Hoffmann von Waldau. Conspicuously absent from the fray were four of the *Luftwaffe's* key figures; *Hauptleute* Hermann Göring and Robert *Ritter* von Greim, who were living in Munich as students, together with *Oberleutnant* Ernst Udet and Wolfram *Freiherr* von Richthofen. [4]

A large *Freikorps* presence acted at the Allies' insistence as an advance guard against the Bolsheviks invading the Baltic States of Latvia, Lithuania and Estonia. Seeckt supported the force of some 50,000 men (which included future *Panzer* leader *Leutnant* Heinz Guderian) under *General* Gustav-Adolf Rüdiger *Graf* von der Goltz, with some 130 aircraft, including two heavy bombers and six seaplanes, and which eventually reached some 11 squadrons (including future *Luftwaffe* General Bruno Loerzer). [5] The aircraft helped Goltz stop any Bolshevik threat, but then he turned from crusader to conquistador and tried to create his own kingdom.

He was defeated and an Allied blockade helped deplete his materiel resources, leading to his resignation in the summer of 1919. He was succeeded on 12 October by *Generalleutnant* Walter von Eberhardt, the *Fliegertruppe* commander at the beginning of the Great War, who now led the *Freikorps* including three air squadrons on an epic march back to the Fatherland, reaching East Prussia in December 1919. Some of these squadrons were earmarked for Germany's post-war air force by the *Reichswehrministerium* (*RWM* or Armed Forces Ministry) with planning assigned to *Hauptmann* Helmuth Wilberg, who had commanded German squadrons around the Ypres salient from August 1918. [6]

During the early summer of 1919 Wilberg and Thomsen began converting a number of *Freikorps* squadrons into *Fliegerstaffel*, usually designated *Truppen-Fliegerstaffel*. They also had to attend the peace conference at Versailles and were present when the bombshell of terms was dropped. [7] Berlin had anticipated losing territory and paying an indemnity but the Allies, especially the French who had suffered terribly during the war, were determined that no further threats to the continent's security would emerge from its heart. The draft peace treaty published on 25 April 1919 shocked all Germany, which was to be emasculated, its armed forces becoming little more than a *gendarmerie* deprived of military aircraft with severe restrictions on its industry and aircraft manufacture as well as the establishment of an Inter-Allied Aeronautical Control Commission (IAACC) to ensure the country did not evade these restrictions.

The *Reichswehr* fought a desperate rearguard action, disbanding Thomsen's department on 11 August 1919 and while he went into retirement, *Idflieg* survived four more months with Haehnelt hanging around the *Reichsheer* for another year as an 'officer with special duties'. After demobilisation Haehnelt remained prominent in civil aviation, becoming vice president of the German Aero-Club until 1935 when he became Germany's official air war historian, joined the *Luftwaffe* and finally retired in

March 1942 as a *General der Flieger*. After the war he was taken prisoner by the Russians and died in the former Sachsenhausen concentration camp in March 1946.

German air power was now in the hands of *Hauptmann* (*Major* from 1 June 1921) Helmuth Wilberg who continued planning a post-war air force to meet internal threats and a potential conflict with Poland from within the camouflaged General Staff known as the '*Truppenamt*'. In January 1920 he proposed the creation of seven air bases and three independent squadrons but the Allies rejected even this and the Germans were forced to bend with the wind. From September 1919, the *Reichswehr's* surviving squadrons were converted into 10 *Polizei-Fliegerstaffeln* including a maritime squadron at Kiel. [8] These were turbulent times and in March 1920 the *Polizei-Fliegerstaffeln* helped to crush a right-wing rebellion led by *Doktor* Wolfgang Kapp with reconnaissance, ground-attacks and leaflet drops. Their swansong was to help suppress a left-wing insurrection in the Ruhr, with the last sorties being flown on 4 April in an operation which cost four aircraft (two in a collision) and three men killed.

But the police squadron collars were felt by the IAACC which informed the Allies who put intense diplomatic pressure on Berlin. The Germans converted the *Polizei-Fliegerstaffeln* into an air traffic control and airport police force known as the *Luftüberwachungsabteilungen* on 30 June 1921. Their ranks included several future *Luftwaffe* generals including Karl Koller who would become Chief of the Operations Staff in 1943. By the end of the year the IAACC would report: 'The aerial disarmament of Germany may be regarded as virtually accomplished.'

Austria's armed forces suffered a similar state of emasculation following the Treaty of St Germaine-en-Laye, signed on 10 September 1919. But in Austria too there was a brief flare of post-war air power as the *Deutschösterreichische Fliegertruppe*, established on 6 December 1918 under *Hauptmann* Anton Siebert, supported militias defending the southern province of Carinthia (Koroška) and its capital Klagenfurt (Celovec) from Serbian/Yugoslav incursions. Some 20 aircraft were used and the defenders were able to win a plebiscite in which the province opted to remain with Austria. [9] Siebert also tried to secure some air support through three *Polizei-Flugstaffeln* but diplomatic pressure caused their disbandment in December 1920. Paramilitary squadrons were created to help protect Vienna, but these too were disbanded in March 1921 and Austria's military aircraft were quickly disposed of, either to foreign buyers or the scrap heap.

With no immediate prospect of squadrons, the German and Austrian armed forces would spend the next decade focusing upon developing an organisational and doctrinal foundation for an air force as well as developing a cadre of air crew and leaders. In Germany the early part of the decade was dominated by Seeckt, a taciturn and enigmatic character who was by turns both radical and conservative. He insisted that 180 (5.5%) of the *Reichsheer's* 3,800 active officers would be airmen including 10 per cent of those responsible for developing military equipment in the Army Ordnance Board (*Heereswaffenamt*), the latter including former air ace *Hauptmann* Kurt Student, who evaluated foreign equipment. Seeckt also demanded the *Reichsheer* be 'air minded' with a cadre of air staff officers created in each *Wehrkreis* (Military District) as *Referenten zbV* (experts for special employment) who held their own war games early in each year and, like a mother hen, he shielded his airmen from external interference. [10] Yet these officers also had to serve in front-line units on traditional duties, Wilberg (an *Oberstleutnant* from 1 April 1927) being transferred to an infantry regiment in 1928 and not renewing his aviation activities until the Nazis took power.

By contrast the *Reichsmarine* (navy) was dominated by conservatives and only 20 of its 1,500 front-line officers (1.5%) had aviation experience and a third of them were airship experts. *Kapitänleutnant* Walther Faber headed the aviation desk at the *Reichsmarineamt* (Admiralty), but at the end of March 1923 he too resumed a conventional career specialising in torpedoes and mines and heading the science department of the *Oberkommando des Marines* or *OKM* (Naval High Command) until almost the end of the war. [11] He managed, by some sleight-of-hand, to retain six Friedrichshafen FF.49 floatplanes at Norderney and Holtenau and used them for second-line duties – indeed they were still in service in 1934! Faber also played an important part in the clandestine development of anti-aircraft guns, for the navy was permitted to retain a few such weapons at Königsberg allowing improvements to types such as the 8.8cm flak, 18 which would become the formidable flak 18/36.

Surprisingly, some German manufacturers continued to produce military aircraft openly – and with Allied support. Ernst Heinkel sold his submarine-borne floatplanes to both Japan and the United States, which also acquired Dornier flying-boats and fighters. The Japanese market would prove a valuable legitimate outlet for Heinkel's military designs in the coming decade. [12] But Allied hands remained firmly on the throat of the aero-industry, restricting production and aircraft performance so that by the end of 1921 all the great wartime aircraft manufacturers had vanished.

Yet Seeckt was able to exploit civil aviation with *Hauptmann* Ernst Brandenburg, wartime leader of the *Englandgeschwader* strategic bombing unit and the *Reichsheer*'s candidate, being given a key role in the development of civil aviation. Ultimately, Brandenburg became *Ministerialdirigent der Reichsamt für Luftfahrt* (Ministerial Director for the Transport Ministry's National Air Travel Department) until 1933. This allowed him to supervise the *Deutschen Luftfahrt-Verband eV-DLV* (German Aviation Organisation) established in 1920 to foster young peoples' interest in aviation. It focused upon gliding to encourage embryo flying training as well as the study of aerodynamics and airframe construction with gliding events supported by Wilberg and often visited by army officers. The most famous event was the annual meeting in the Rhön Mountains east of Fulda which had the enthusiastic support of both Student and his wife. [13]

While Wilberg was trying to learn the wartime lessons of air operations, command and production, Berlin's caution was almost overcome when France and Belgium invaded the Ruhr in January 1923 as Germany's Slavic neighbours in Poland and Czechoslovakia made threatening noises. In response, the *Reichsheer* secretly mobilised and swelled its ranks with former *Freikorps* militias. As a shield against French bombers President Friedrich Ebert authorised the covert acquisition of aircraft and with money from Ruhr industrialist Hugo Stinnes, an order was placed (ostensibly by Argentina) with Fokker for 100 fighters, half D.XI and half D.XIII. Some German military aircraft were ordered, including 53 Dietrich DP IIa (a development of the Fokker D.VII) for fighter training, while Student ordered reconnaissance aircraft from Heinkel, although the first did not appear until 1924 after the crisis had passed. [14] With 2,500 men the veteran airmen's organisation, *Ring Deutscher Flieger* under former *Idflieg Major* Wilhelm Siegert, could provide a ready-made pool of experienced manpower. Siegert selected some 100 former fighter pilots and the *Wehrkreise Referent zbV*s organised refresher training for them at private air schools and basic training for reconnaissance crews on Albatros B.II trainers. The navy acquired 10 Heinkel HE 1 seaplanes, although their 'Brazilian' owners assembled and based them across the Baltic in Stockholm.

The situation was diffused by the conciliatory approach of the new German Chancellor, Gustav Stresemann, who was appointed in August 1923 as the German economy went into meltdown with hyper-inflation. Stresemann later became Foreign Minister and in 1924 negotiated the Dawes Plan which matched reparations with Germany's ability to pay them, while opening the country to substantial American investment. He also convinced the Allies that not only had Germany disarmed but also that she was no longer a threat to European peace which led to the dismantling of the Allied monitoring organisation. His final triumph was the Treaty of Locarno signed on 1 December 1925 which guaranteed Germany's western borders and ended any further threat of French military action while guaranteeing the Rhineland would remain demilitarised when France withdrew in 1930. This would be underlined when he accepted the Young Plan in 1929 which not only reduced reparation payments but set a deadline of 30 June 1930 for the evacuation of the Ruhr.

The Ruhr Crisis accelerated Seeckt's attempts at a long-term solution to his strategic problems. The eastern borders remained menaced by Poland and Czechoslovakia for most of the decade, and the *Reichsheer* regarded them, France and Belgium as the prime threats to German security, especially Poland which was like the bullying child of over-indulgent parents, its position guaranteed by France. [15]

Seeckt was a political conservative whose downfall in 1926 came because he invited the exiled Crown Prince Wilhelm to observe *Reichsheer* manoeuvres. However, he was prepared to sup with the Bolsheviks if it would help neutralise Poland. His priority was to develop the military technologies banned by Versailles and contact was established with Moscow which sent an emissary, Viktor Kopp, to assess what was on offer. The Russians were especially interested in Junkers all-metal aircraft which they had encountered when fighting Goltz. Dr Hugo Junkers, whose business was hovering on the brink of bankruptcy despite every effort at diversification, was interested in an agreement.

As early as July 1921, *Major Dr* Oskar Ritter von Niedermeyer, who was leading a delegation to the Soviet Union to examine the Russian armament and aircraft industry asked whether or not Junkers was interested in collaboration with the Bolsheviks. Junkers was more than willing to support the *RWM*'s aims as the Russians and Germans began to hammer out details of their military co-operation during the autumn using the Berlin apartment of Kurt von Schleicher, founder of the *Freikorps* who fought the Bolsheviks' German allies! Following a visit to Junkers' works at Dessau, there was a verbal agreement by which Junkers would build aircraft and aero-engine factories in Russia in return for government funds and a share of the profits. [16] Early in 1922 the Chancellor/Foreign Minister Joseph Wirth allocated the army RM150 million ($2.8 million) to support collaboration with the Russians. He also opened negotiations with Moscow to formalise diplomatic and commercial relations leading, on 16 April, to the Treaty of Rapallo which renounced war reparations, improved trade relations and provided for what would later be described as technology exchange.

A *Sondergruppe R* was established under Seeckt's former adjutant *Major* (later *Oberst*) Veit Fischer who had outline agreements with both Albatros and Junkers in mid-March 1922 to establish factories in the Soviet Union, the latter in return for a down-payment of RM40 million ($746,000) and RM100 million ($1.86 million) in capital. The Albatros deal collapsed for unknown reasons, but other manufacturers were interested in working in Russia and one of them, Friedrich ('Fritz') Siebel, represented the Foreign Ministry in negotiations.

The pace now grew and on 22 November 1922 Junkers signed an agreement with the Russians in which he would establish factories in Russia to build his aircraft and aero-engines in return for Moscow's guarantee of work. Barely a week later, on 4 December, the Russians ordered 100 aircraft although Moscow did not actually ratify the order until February, by which time the French occupation of the Ruhr was giving new urgency to the Soviet-German talks on collaboration.

A high-level meeting in February 1923 saw a liaison office, *Zentrale Moskau* (*ZMo*), established under the *Truppenamt* and led by Thomsen who arrived in Moscow in November. *ZMo* supervised not only the creation of an air-training and aircraft development establishment but also chemical warfare and armoured vehicle facilities. Governmental support remained half-hearted, Stresemann believing it would undermine his attempts to regain Germany's international political standing. Many begrudged any form of military expenditure, but the position eased following the formal *rapprochement* with Russia in the Treaty of Berlin in April 1926. Although assisted by seven officers acting as advisors and instructors to the Soviet Air Force, including future *Luftwaffe* General *Hauptmann* Martin Fiebig, ZMo was a demanding position and it undermined Thomsen's health; he may have been suffering from diabetes, and was steadily losing his sight. In 1929 he was forced to hand over to Niedermeyer but lived on until August 1942, becoming an honorary *General der Flieger*.

The Germans placed a priority on covert air training and aircraft development and rejected Odessa because it was a major port but then both sides agreed, on 15 April 1925, to establish a base at Lipetsk, some 500 kilometres south-west of Moscow. A disused factory on the outskirts became the heart of the establishment which was gradually expanded to include two runways, hangars, repair shops, an engine test bed and a hospital – indeed after the Germans departed it remained in Soviet Air Force hands and even at the beginning of the 21st century it remains a major base. [17]

The Ju 22 was to have been the backbone of activities at Lipetsk but it was extremely unstable and prone to spinning. Fortunately the 50 Fokker D.XIII acquired during the Ruhr Crisis were still available and they were shipped in crates from Stettin to Leningrad in May then railed to Lipetsk for re-assembly. Only a third were used at any one time, two replacements being received, and extensive rotation meant that when the last Germans departed in September 1933 some 40 aircraft remained airworthy.

The German army assigned between 60 and 70 staff under *Major* Walter Stahr, *Kofl 7.Armee* during the Malmaison offensive of October 1917, to the Lipetsk establishment which was designated the *Wissenschaftlichliche Versuchs- und Prüfanstalt für Luftfahrzeuge* (*Wivupal*) or Aviation Scientific Experimental and Testing Establishment. It would cost Germany RM 2 million ($478,000) a year but proved a lifeline for German air power, initially providing operational training within a few weeks of its establishment. The instructors were nominally civilians on contract either from civilian flying schools or from airlines and, for security reasons, were paid in US dollars.

Each summer until 1927 *Wivupal* received 30 veteran fighter pilots ('Old Eagles') for a course lasting up to 22 weeks operating in a *Jagdstaffel* (fighter squadron) and a *Jagdlehrstaffel* (fighter demonstration squadron) with the highlight being a dogfight between two squadrons of nine aircraft equipped with camera guns. By the time Lipetsk closed some 120 fighter pilots had been either trained or received refresher training at the base. The excellent safety record meant there were only three fatalities: two in a mid-air collision and the third being 35-victory ace *Leutnant* Emil Thuy, killed in the vicious Albatros L.76 in June 1930.

From 1927 the emphasis switched to 'Young Eagles' and Lipetsk attracted not only would-be fighter pilots but also artillery observers for a six-month course in an *Beobachterstaffel* (observer squadron) and *Beobachterlehrstaffel* (observer demonstration squadron), their training culminating from 1928 in live firing with Russian batteries at Voronezh. The aircraft included six or seven Heinkel HD 17 corps aircraft later augmented by a similar number of Albatros L.76/78, but in 1930, thanks to Stresemann's diplomatic efforts, observer training returned to Germany.

Lipetsk had few facilities; newcomers were met by a sign declaring 'A warm welcome to the world's arse' ('*Herzlich Willkommen am Arsch der Welt*'), but parties and receptions provided some form of social life and occasionally there were movies. While Moscow might have been enthusiastic about Russo-German fraternal relationships, the Germans had little contact with the general population apart from the pretty maids with whom many relationships went beyond the fraternal.

Training was vital because the numbers of potential aircrew in Germany were slowly declining; some 'Old Eagles' died or were killed in accidents (notably Lothar von Richthofen, brother of the 'Red Baron') while others had to keep body and soul together with work outside aviation. By 1926 only 100 members of the army were eligible for flying duty and, despite the endeavours of the Lipetsk facility, by November 1930 the 'flying officers' list had only 168 names against a target of 180, although 77 of these would later become generals in the *Luftwaffe*. Only 6 per cent of the army officers holding a pilot's licence actually flew in their spare time while the number of officers seeking flying training dropped from six in 1926 to three in 1931 due to the *Reichswehr*'s low pay rates which meant few officers without private means could afford to fly.

Yet the *RWM* subsidised civilian flying training organisations to help with clandestine military air training. Basic flying training was provided by half-a-dozen private flying schools, including that of Ernst Udet, and by *Sportflug GmbH* which was established in 1924 by Siebel. The *Sportflug* concern operated seven small schools while the associate *Aerosport GmbH* at Warnemünde used war-surplus floatplanes for seaplane training. Each *Sportflug* school was conveniently close to a *Wehrkreis* (Military District) headquarters which sent officers for initial pilot and observer training, but when the Allies discovered the subsidies they compelled *Sportflug*'s closure [18]. Most of its assets were absorbed by the *Deutschen Verkehrsfliegerschule GmbH* (*DVS*) which was established at Berlin-Staaken in 1925 as an international centre of excellence for advanced air training including instrument training. The school was placed under the command of *Major* Alfred Keller, a famous bomber pilot (whose nickname was '*Bombenkeller*' or 'Bombshelter') and holder of the *Pour le Mérite*, who oversaw a significant expansion during the late 1920s matching that in civil aviation which itself was boosted by *DVS* aircraft orders. Schools were opened at Schleissheim (near Munich) and in Brunswick while the organisation received secret *RWM* subsidies.

Wilberg arranged with Brandenburg for 40 *Offizieranwärter* (officer candidates) each year to train at DVS Schleissheim while from 1928 DVS Berlin-Staaken and Brunswick were used for clandestine observer training, the latter providing practical training from 1931 and qualifying some 80 officers, including *Major* Student, in the next two years. The best students at Brunswick went to Lipetsk for fighter training and upon joining the army they received refresher training courses at a new training organisation *Luftfahrt* (later *Deutsche Luftfahrt*) *GmbH*.

Lipetsk also helped to train a core of ground crews, some 450 by 1933, who gained experience in the very latest all-metal airframe technology. They could also practise on a wide variety of aero-engines including Napier Lions as fitted to the Fokker D.XIII and HD 17 which were originally returned to England for overhaul until the Germans became sufficiently confident to perform this task themselves at Lipetsk.

From 1928 Berlin also began evaluating new combat aircraft at Lipetsk with technicians, scientists and military observers swelling the numbers at *Wivupal* to an average 200 men, which rose to 300 in 1931. Single-engined aircraft were flight-tested in Germany, dismantled, shipped to Leningrad and then railed to Lipetsk for re-assembly and testing with weapons, bomb racks and sights. Multi-engined aircraft posed as part of a civil airline, such as the Russo-German *Deruluft*, and were flown from Königsberg to Velikiye Luki, which would be the scene of an epic siege involving *Luftwaffe Transportgruppen* between November 1942 and January 1943. [19]

Yet despite the most stringent security precautions, British and French intelligence built up a comprehensive picture of activities in Lipetsk; French military intelligence monitored the situation while the British Secret Intelligence Service produced two reports in November 1929 and August 1932. The British noted the disappearance and reappearance of army officers from the active list and deduced this was for flying training. The Ambassador, Sir Horace Rumbold, noted on 29 May 1931 that 66 officers had gone through the process and named seven who had 'returned to the fold'. In fact six were on a secret list drawn up in 1930 of officer airmen and they included *Rittmeister* Pflugbeil and *Oberleutnant* Schulze-Heyn who would become *Kommodore* of *KG 51* in August 1940. [20]

The great loser in Germany's Russian adventure was Junkers whose new factory at Fili lost money because he had no orders from Berlin and few from Moscow. On 1 March 1927 Fili was taken over by the Russians and placed under Andrei Tupolev whose designs for several years reflected the Junkers influence. Junkers sued both governments but lost the cases and German officials forced him to accept his airline being absorbed in the *Deutsches Luft Hansa AG* or *DLH* (more commonly *Lufthansa*) which was created on 6 January 1926. Its Operations Director (Commercial Director from 1929) was Erhard Milch, a former Junkers man and *Polizeiflieger*, as well as being a friend of Wilberg, both men having Jewish fathers. The baby-faced Milch was a shrewd manager who recognised that the way to make the new airline profitable was to keep its aircraft in the air as long as possible, and he expanded the multi-engined aircraft fleet, later including the Ju 52/3m which could also be used as a bomber. [21]

For maximum flying time, even at night and in bad weather, he introduced a system of visual and radio navigation beacons as well as providing landing aids at all his main airports to ensure that by 1929 all *Lufthansa* pilots were instrument rated. This philosophy would have an impact upon *Luftwaffe* bomber development the following decade, allowing it to make a quantum leap beyond its rivals. The commander of the RAF's air defence of Great Britain observed in October 1934 that *Lufthansa*'s nightly service between Cologne and Croydon had been cancelled on only four occasions in the previous year, a capability which the RAF could not match. [22]

By contrast planning for the future air force was extremely conservative and Wilberg's first proposals, in June 1927, focused upon fighter and corps squadrons augmented by a small heavy (night) bomber force. But reformers, led by the *Truppenamt*'s head of operations, *Oberst* Werner von Blomberg, recognised the importance of air power and from 1924 expanded Wilberg's organisation into a full department with operations, air defence, Intelligence, personnel, technical and administration desks to create an embryo air staff. These were available to Wilberg's successors, *Major* Hugo Sperrle and then *Hauptmann* Helmuth Felmy, who had been Wilberg's planning officer. The *Heereswaffenamt* aircraft and equipment development organisation was re-organised and on 1 October 1929. *Hauptmann* Helmuth Volkmann became responsible for both development/testing and acquisition/economic planning but was then replaced by Bavarian 'Old Eagle' *Major* Wilhelm Wimmer under whom almost all of the *Luftwaffe*'s wartime combat aircraft were developed. The increasing status of air power was reflected in the decision to rename the *Inspekteur der Waffenschule* on 1 October 1929 the *Inspekteur der Waffenschulen und der Luftwaffe* which was of equal status to the remaining *Truppenamt* departments under the *Generalmajor* Hilmar *Ritter* von Mittelberger. With these changes, by April 1930 the *Reichsheer* was envisaging an air force of which two-thirds of its squadrons would be fighters and bombers. [23] Most of the *Luftstreitkräfte* officers whom Seeckt had inserted into the *Reichsheer* were still alive by the early 1930s and they had been augmented by some 550 potential air crew who had been through either Lipetsk or the *Sportflug/DVS* organisations. Curiously a high proportion of air officers – up to 20 per cent – tended to be attached to the cavalry divisions. [24]

With the new decade the international situation had improved to such a degree that the *RWM* prepared to resuscitate German air power barely 11 years after the Versailles *Diktat*. Three *Reklamestaffeln* ('Skywriting Squadrons') were created on 1 October 1930 in *Wehrkreise I* (Königsberg), *II* (Berlin) and *III* (Nuremberg) each with 11 men (including recalled instructors from Lipetsk) and four Albatros L 75a/L 82 biplane trainers. Ostensibly owned by *Luftfahrt GmbH*, they were cadres for corps squadrons with qualified observers but would also tow targets for the anti-aircraft batteries. [25]

This was the first stage of a careful programme to create a German air force; the next stage was a meeting on 29 November 1930. It was convened by the Defence Minister Wilhelm Groener (a former *Generalleutnant* and last wartime army chief of staff) and attended by Foreign Minister Julius Curtius and Transport Minister

Theodor von Guerard with expert advice provided by Brandenburg and Mittelberger. The participants reluctantly accepted Curtius' argument that there should be no open defiance of the Versailles Treaty but agreed to begin production of military aircraft and equipment developed at Lipetsk for storing at secure facilities. [26]

Within a month Mittelberger was espousing the cause of an autonomous air force to the fury of his more stiff-necked colleagues led by *Oberstleutnant* Wilhelm Keitel, Head of Organisation (and future leader of *Oberkommando der Wehrmacht-OKW* or Armed Forces High Command), who feared the airmen would fight a private war and abandon the army, an argument identical to that used by opponents to the Royal Air Force (RAF) in 1917. They wished to re-create the wartime army air force (*Luftstreitkräfte*) but Mittelberger skilfully diverted their wrath by assuring his colleagues the airmen would never abandon their comrades. Mittelberger convinced the newly appointed *Truppenamt* leader, *Generalleutnant* Wilhelm Adam, and on 21 April 1931 (the 13th anniversary of the Red Baron's death) Adam stated the airmen and the anti-aircraft forces should be unified and later he faced down a rebellion by some of the departmental heads on this issue. Mittelberger's victory was secured when Adam's predecessor and now the *Reichsheer* commander, *Generalleutnant* Kurt *Freiherr* von Hammerstein-Equord, stated on 24 February 1932 that the air arm would be a separate service equal in status to the army and the navy. Six months later one of Mittelberger's officers, *Hauptmann* Hans Jeschonnek, made the logical proposal that an air ministry based upon Brandenburg's organisation be established for the new service. [27]

While Keitel's old department endorsed the plan in October there remained some dissenters, the most notable being training chief, *Oberstleutnant* Walther Wever, who described the idea as 'nonsense'. On 28 October 1932 the *Truppenamt* decided to sell the idea to the government but the politicians were more concerned with the deepening political crisis, although the appointment of the former *Truppenamt* operations chief Blomberg as defence minister in December 1932 was a straw in the wind.

Felmy was already champing at the bit to begin German aerial re-armament and demanded the creation of 22 *Staffeln* with 280 aircraft and Adam formally made the request when he met new Defence Minister and *Freikorps* father Kurt von Schleicher on 11 July 1932. Adam wanted to complete the plan by 1936 and also to create a training organisation of seven units with 140 aircraft and 4,600 men. After pondering the programme for three days Schleicher rubber-stamped it on 14 July (Bastille Day) as well as authorising the creation of anti-aircraft gun (*Fliegerabwehrkanone-Flak*) batteries from October 1933. But Felmy was already looking to the future and in February 1932 proposed an 80-*Staffel* force (720 aircraft) from 1938 of which more than half would be bombers at the disposal of general headquarters and this would form the basis for the next generation military aircraft. [28] On 27 January 1933, three days before Adolf Hitler became chancellor, Hammerstein-Equord informed the *Reichswehr* leadership that the training of air- and ground-crews would have absolute priority.

By contrast, German naval aviation, having sailed through the storms of scandal, by the early 1930s was in the doldrums. [29] In June 1925 Faber's organisation was incorporated under the *Allgemeines Marineamt* (naval administration) *Seetransportabteilung* (sea transportation organisation) and assigned to *Kapitän zur*

See Rudolf Lahs, a destroyer commander at the Battle of Jutland who retired in September 1929 as a *Konteradmiral* and became head of the *Reichsverband der Deutschen Luftfahrtindustrie-RDLI* (National Association of the German Aviation Industry). The naval organisation then came under *Kapitän zur See* Konrad Zander in October 1929; he was replaced three years later by former U-boat ace *Fregattenkapitän* Ralf Wenniger, who had no knowledge of aviation and was selected purely for reasons of seniority.

The Navy's covert armament activities during the mid-1920s were under the head of the *Seetransportabteilung*, *Kapitän zur See* Günther Lohmann, but he lost control of covert investment which caused a RM26 million ($6.19 million) loss. When revealed the scandal swept away Lohmann, the navy commander (who was replaced by *Admiral* Erich Raeder) and even the defence minister, leaving Groener to resolve the crisis by winding up Lohmann's organisations.

This had an impact on pilot training, all of which was performed within Germany with *ab initio* work at a yacht club near Lübeck. Most training was performed by *Seeflugzeug-Versuchsabteilung GmbH* (*Severa*) which naval fighter ace Theo Osterkamp had established at Kiel-Holtenau in 1924 ostensibly as a civilian air freight organisation with a contract to tow targets for navy gunnery training. *Severa* provided air- and ground-crew training and provided a cover for the naval air bases which were established during the next five years at Norderney, Wangerooge and Wilhelmshaven-Rüstringen. The last closed in the wake of the Lohmann scandal when *Severa* was officially disbanded, although it re-emerged as *Luftdienst GmbH* and continued its overt and covert activities unhindered until absorbed by *DVS* in 1933.

The navy exploited the Paris Agreement of 1926 to begin ordering seaplanes and flying boats. Evaluation was performed at Travemünde and in 1928 the first nine Heinkel HE 5 were acquired and 10 HE 9 the following year while six Dornier R *Superwals* were also acquired 'for *Severa* and *Lufthansa*.' Because they operated in Germany they were unarmed, although from the late 1920s, as the navy began to evaluate fighter designs, Lipetsk was used in the weapon development process while sea trials were conducted either on Swiss lakes or in Scandinavian fjords. In 1932, for example, a Swedish-registered Ju 52ce was used for torpedo-bomber trials in Oslo Fjord using Norwegian navy torpedoes.

Work began on developing land-based torpedo-bombers in 1928 but an increasingly cost-conscious government sought rationalisation of the two services' air programmes. Raeder and most of his senior officers were battleship men and to secure funding for the first of the new light battleships (*Panzerschiffe*) they agreed on 1 October 1929 (the day of Zander's appointment) to rationalise aircraft development, the army being responsible for landplanes and the navy for seaplanes. This innocuous agreement would set the navy on the slippery slope which would eventually end in losing all control of air power.

Landlocked Austria also covertly re-established its air arm during the late 1920s despite severe funding problems. [30] Vienna regained control of national aviation with a separate Paris Agreement signed on 27 October 1927 and this included a provision that a maximum of 12 soldiers might hold civilian pilot's licences over the next seven years. The task of covertly creating an air force was assigned to *Oberst* Alexander Löhr, a staff officer and 'Old Eagle' who promptly created a training organisation. His officially authorised pilots were to be the instructors and were trained in Switzerland as well as by *DVS*, while a school nominally owned by the national airline, *ÖLAG*, was established at Graz-Thalerhof.

Army cadets could volunteer for the school where instruction with *DVS* support began in 1930 using war-surplus Brandenburger C.Is augmented by Hopfner HS 8–29 and Phönix L2cs. Despite cash shortages the school was slowly expanded and by 1932 Löhr had 46 airmen. The previous year an operational unit had been created under *Major* Yllam with a single Junkers A 35b which was augmented by six Fiat-Ansaldo A120 corps aircraft. From May 1930 police airmen were trained at Graz-Thalerhof and a *Polizei-Fliegerstaffel* was created with 12 war-surplus aircraft.

Vienna's financial resources were stretched to the limit and it proved impossible to expand the miniature air force during 1932; indeed by the end of the year two of the Fiat-Ansaldos had to be grounded to save money. Germany maintained links with the new air force and during 1931 Sachsenberg gave lectures on air warfare while Wimmer visited the country.

The catalyst for the renaissance of German, and ultimately Austrian, air power was the appointment of Adolf Hitler as chancellor of Germany on 30 January 1933. The Nazis' siren song of defiance to the *Versailles Diktat* was sweet music to the *Reichswehr*, many of whose aristocratic leaders otherwise regarded the movement with disdain. Many middle-class officers were more sympathetic, including Defence Minister Blomberg who had enjoyed a close relationship with the party when he commanded the East Prussian military district (*Wehrkreis I*).

But the Nazis offered a dynamic solution to the nation's social, economic and strategic problems. Many 'Old Eagles' were either Party members or sympathisers including the deputy *Führer* Rudolf Hess (who had flown with the *Freikorps*), Greim (who had taken Hitler on his first flight), Heinrich Müller (who would later run the *Gestapo*) and former air ace Bruno Loerzer (who commanded the Party's aviation organisation, the *SA Fliegersturm*) while future *Luftwaffe* general Günther Korten had been linked early with the Party and participated in the farcical Munich *Bierkeller Putsch* in 1923 which brought Hitler to prominence.

But the aviation spokesman was Hermann Göring, the scion of a judge and former governor of a colony, who held the *Pour le Mérite* and was Manfred von Richthofen's heir to command *JG I*. He came into contact with the Nazis while studying in Munich after the war and headed their *Sturm Abteilung* (SA) bully-boys, but was seriously injured in the *Bierkeller Putsch* and was left a lifelong drug addict on 'hard' and then 'soft' drugs. These further warped his personality and caused his weight to balloon until by 1933 he weighed some 20 stone (125 kilogrammes) and while Göring regarded himself as 'The Iron Man' (*Der Eiserne*) his weight led to the less flattering nickname of 'The Fat Man' or 'Fatty' (*Der Dicke*).

Yet this gave him the bluff, good-humoured *persona* which was more acceptable to the Great and the Good. In reality he remained a thug and blustering bully; he was the first head of the Prussian *Gestapo* and would control the national telephone interception service whose headquarters would be installed in the basement of the *Reichsluftministerium-RLM* (Air Ministry). He was also corrupt and as a parliamentary deputy he supplemented his income by acting as part-time agent for both Heinkel (although uneasy at the designer's Semitic appearance) and BMW while receiving bribes from Milch, who was seeking *Lufthansa* subsidies. [31] Göring was eventually receiving RM50,000 ($11,900) a year at a time when a night out with a meal, beer and a visit to the cinema cost only RM5.00 ($1.19).

The Party's pledge to create an air ministry controlling all aspects of aviation fuelled Göring's megalomania and in January 1933 he became *Reichskommissar für die Luftfahrt* (National Commissar for Aviation) within Brandenburg's organisation but with Milch as his deputy. In March the *Reichsluftfahrkommissariat* began the flight to independence by moving to Behrenstrasse and during that month Göring visited the German flight test centre at Rechlin to demand greater progress on military aviation although he never gave any thought to air power applications.

To supervise the reformation of the German air force, Göring wanted to use the most senior representative of the aircraft industry, *Konteradmiral* Lahs. But Lahs recognised that the *RLM* would be a poisoned chalice and politely declined. Brandenburg was too conservative and too stubborn, so Göring proposed Milch, who proved so useful in the early months, as *Staatssekretär der Luftfahrt* (State Secretary for Aviation) and Blomberg sanctioned this on 19 October 1933 by promoting him to *Oberst*, Göring having been promoted to *General der Infanterie* on 31 August.

The fact that Milch and Wilberg had Jewish fathers posed an ethical problem for the new regime, but Göring himself once stated he would decide who was, or was not, Jewish and he (unlike Milch) shielded many people, partly influenced by his second wife Emmy. Given the value of both Milch's and Wilberg's experience (and the fact their mothers were not Jewish so neither were they) Göring signed a degree making them *kosher* Aryans. Yet Party influence remained strong in the clandestine organisation and the *Deutscher Grüss* (Party salute) remained the norm with the *Luftwaffe* until it was unveiled on 1 March 1935 while both Hitler and Göring had wanted this adopted by the other services. [32]

Substantial funds were made available for the new air force and one of the few Nazi cabinet meetings approved the expenditure of RM40 million ($9.52 million) on the rapid expansion of the force. Göring would ensure that the *Luftwaffe*'s share of the defence budget would rise from 10 per cent (RM 76 million or $18.1 million) in 1933 to 38 per cent (RM2.23 billion or $897 million) in 1936. In dollar terms this compares with British expenditure of $66.5 million (15.6% of the defence budget) to $247.2 million (26%) in the same period and French expenditure of $5.8 million (12.7%) and $17.4 million (18.5%).

In the meantime, Göring's control over aviation became absolute. On 25 March the *DLV* absorbed all private aviation organisations and remained as the *Deutschen Luftsportverband e.V* (German Air Sport Association) under Göring's pre-war friend, Loerzer. Its 12 (later 16) *Luftsportlandesgruppen* retained the ethos of the original *DLV* but added paramilitary training together with subtle political indoctrination for boys as young as 10. As the *RWM* was already espousing the idea of an air ministry, it did not object to the Nazis' actions but it did wish for a civilian overlord, even one with so distinguished a war record. Mittelberger now made his last contribution to German air power and at his suggestion all military and naval aviation, as well as *Flak*, were to be merged into the *Luftschutz Amt* (Air Defence Department) on

1 April 1933 while the *Heerswaffenamt* remained responsible for development and production. Mittelberger then retired and spent a decade advising the Turkish government and instructing at its war academy then became head of the liaison staff in Ankara, returning to Germany in 1943 and dying a decade later.

But Göring and Milch were already outflanking the army and navy, aided by Blomberg. Instead of assigning the *Luftschutz Amt* to Milch's old friend Felmy, as the army intended, it went to *Oberst* Eberhardt Bohnstedt, a wartime *Flak* officer due to retire in September and described, probably unfairly, by Reichenau as a 'stupid clot'. Felmy was transferred to an infantry regiment and while Milch hypocritically expressed surprise, he wrote in his diary following a meeting with Blomberg on April 25: '*We get the lot!*' [33] Two days later Göring became *Reichsminister für die Luftfahrt*, nominally under Blomberg who curtly informed Bohnstedt a fortnight later that the *Luftschutz Amt* would be transferred to the *RLM* on 15 May, which became the *Luftwaffe*'s official birthday. [34] Göring would play little further part in the development of the *Luftwaffe* until 1936 and Milch was *de facto* air minister until the autumn of 1937. Initially he directly controlled Bohnstedt's and Brandenburg's departments which became separate directorates responsible for military and civil aviation and were joined on 1 October 1933 by Wimmer's organisation from the *Heereswaffenamt*.

Bohnstedt and Brandenburg quickly faded from the picture and with Wimmer's arrival the former's old organisation was renamed the *Luftkommandoamt* (Air Command Directorate) under *Oberstleutnant* (*Oberst* from April 1934) Bernhard Kühl, who would later play a major role in wartime training. The naval air organisation was absorbed with Wenniger and his deputy, *Korvettenkapitän* Ulrich Kessler then sidelined as air attachés covering London, Brussels and The Hague. The organisation remained unchanged for a year when in June 1935 the expanded *Luftkommandoamt* created a *Luftwaffenführungstab* (Command Staff), with intelligence and administrative elements, as an operational headquarters under Kühl who handed over to *Oberst* Wilhelm Mayer in October 1935.

More important than the air force organisation were the men who ran it. Blomberg had available some 550 officers with flying experience but between 1933 and 1934 transferred only 182 soldiers and 42 sailors, the majority (175, or 78%) being reserve officers. The Defence Minister clearly, and understandably, had no intention of undermining the expansion of the traditional services but what they lacked in quantity was compensated by the quality and they helped lay a firm foundation for the new service. [35]

First to arrive, on 1 July, was *Oberstleutnant* Hans-Jürgen Stumpff, the congenial, yet self-effacing Pomeranian who became head of the *Personnelamt* (personnel department) having once run the army personnel department. He possessed considerable vision and ability while also having the confidence of both Blomberg and Göring but appears to have preferred administrative to operational work while proving a capable front line leader. [36] In October he appointed *Oberst* Albert Kesselring head of administration but a month earlier made the decisive appointment of *Oberst* Walther Wever, who had opposed the concept of an independent air force only a year earlier, as Bohnstedt's replacement.

To gain operational freedom the stocky, open-faced officer, who resembled a senior manager, was happy to become the *eminence grise* and he deftly avoided confrontation with his masters who gave him *carte blanche*. He was blessed with intellectual curiosity and, unlike many modern managers, he was willing to listen to his subordinates, testing their arguments by playing devil's advocate and accepting a well-reasoned argument even when not fully convinced.

Working in harness with Milch he remorselessly drove the *Luftwaffe's* expansion and when subordinates complained there were only 24 hours in the day he would curtly advise them: 'Work at night!' Wever was willing to work behind a desk but, following the Prussian tradition of setting an example, he learned to fly although in three years he had only 200 hours, less than many new *Luftwaffe* pilots. Yet he would often fly out to his growing empire to discuss matters informally in the German tradition of coffee and cake, usually providing the cake himself. [37]

Wever's greatest contribution was to combine wartime experience with imagination to develop a unique air doctrine. [38] During the Great War defensive power was the king based upon artillery which became queen of the battlefield by delivering accurate fire at long ranges and at high volumes to create barriers of fire and steel. During 1918 tactical level (division and army corps) breakthroughs became routine, but exploitation at what the Germans termed the operational (*Operativ*) level (army and army group operations) proved fleeting as the defenders could easily reweave their webs by exploiting undamaged road and rail systems. Seeckt believed the keys to deeper operational level exploitation were improved command and control and motorisation but, like most generals, he still believed in the ultimate power of the defence. Revolutionaries in the German Army, and these apparently included Wever, believed that motorised units spearheaded by tanks could move so quickly that they could break through the defensive crust and envelop whole armies.

Many generals, including *Generalleutnant* Ludwig Beck who was chief of the *Truppenamt* and later the General Staff until 1938, believed air power should focus upon supporting tactical level operations. Reconnaissance and close air support were the prime roles, executed mostly by the corps aircraft shielded by fighter screens, a view underlined by post-war doctrinal documents from September 1921 and repeated during the 1920s. Bombers were to act as long-range guns engaging targets such as supply dumps and railway marshalling yards, although a counter-air element was included with attacks on airfields and army headquarters. [39]

At the other end of the air power spectrum was a doctrine based upon the bomber which reduced the traditional services to little more than spear carriers. The disciples of the Italian air power theorist Giulio Douhet believed wars would be decided by striking the enemy's industrial heartland to deprive their forces of the sinews of war. Wartime experience appeared to show that exposure to air attack demoralised civilians and Douhet believed that future attacks upon cities would be heavier and force a terrified populace to sue for peace. The siren song of air power supremacy provided the rationale for autonomous air forces, notably the RAF, which followed it unquestioningly. The image of bomber fleets razing cities to the ground, most strikingly shown in the British 1936 film *Things to Come*, loomed large in the public mind fed by ever-more apocalyptic visions in fiction, much as the horrors of nuclear war were highlighted after the Second World War. In February 1932 the

World Disarmament Conference, attended by Blomberg and Brandenburg, vainly proposed a total ban on bombers.

The German army was aware of Douhet's ideas; indeed *Hauptmann* Wolfram von Richthofen, who would soon head technical development, was attached to the embassy in Rome between April 1929 and September 1932 partly to discover as much as possible about them and their importance to the Italian Air Force. [40] His future boss, Wimmer, had long advocated a strategic bombing force and in February 1932 argued the future belonged to those nations which could strike fear in the civilian population. A month later Felmy wrote that bombers were the only means of neutralising the air threat to Germany, indeed Mittelberger had sought a heavy bomber based upon the Dornier *Superwal* (super whale) flying boat.

The day Hitler came to power, the *Heereswaffenamt* issued a directive for a *Langstrecken-Grossbomber* (long-range heavy bomber) capable of reaching targets in northern Scotland or the Urals, the latter earning the nickname of 'Ural Bomber.' Milch was closely in tune with the wishes of his political masters and knew they desired an air force which could cow its neighbours. But he also recognised that German industry at that time could not produce a fleet of heavy bombers so his industrial plans focused upon medium bombers which could be produced quickly and strike at targets within 300 miles (500 kilometres) of the border. [41]

With air power debates polarised between the conservatives and the radicals it was Wilberg who had suggested a middle way in May 1926. [42] This envisaged an opening attack upon the enemy heartland to hinder mobilisation and strategic movement, then striking enemy air forces and rear areas to impede their operational level movement and finally an all-out assault upon logistics, units and reserves throughout their tactical and operational depth in support of friendly operations.

Wever, who read voraciously about air power, was probably aware of this document from his time as head of training, but he was also aware of moves to create mechanised mobile formations and the air operations proposed by Wilberg offered him a means of squaring the circle and supporting the army spearheads. He tested the concepts in two war games on 27 September 1934 and between 6 November and 11 December 1934, and they brought the enemy to their knees. Referees concluded the *Luftwaffe* had suffered 80 per cent losses but Wever brow-beat them into reversing their views. [43] The experience was rapidly incorporated into a new doctrine, drawn up by a committee headed by Wilberg, published within months of the exercise as *Luftwaffedienstvorschrift 16: Luftkriegführung* (Luftwaffe Regulation 16: '*The Conduct of the Air War*'). [44] This accepted the general doctrine that the destruction of the enemy armed forces was the primary goal while Paragraph 10 stated: '*The mission of the Luftwaffe is to serve these goals by combining the war in the air within the framework of combined operations.*'

This would be achieved by securing air superiority then hamstringing enemy mobile forces. This meant attacking road and rail communications between the supply dumps and the front line, especially 'choke points', communications centres and any troop concentrations encountered. At sea they would strike the enemy fleet and its bases, or at ports if the navy was attacking enemy maritime commerce. This doctrine was accepted by all but the most reactionary staff officers, although they included Beck. But as a 'concession' Wever gave them operational control of

Nahaufklärungsstaffeln (corps squadrons) and some *Fernaufklärungsstaffeln* (long-range reconnaissance squadrons) which actually denied them any excuse for interfering in the *Luftwaffe*'s operations.

Wever also used his war games' success to play for higher stakes. He recognised the strategic potential of air power but, unlike many air leaders, he believed this should be harnessed to an integrated war strategy. Operational level support could be used as an interim step towards developing a long-range strategic bombing force and *Luftwaffedienstvorschrift 16* anticipated the existence of such a force. Indeed, as early as May 1934 Wever confirmed a seven-year development programme for the 'Ural Bomber'.

The strategic element in Operational Level support was clearly described in Paragraph 21 which noted: '*It is more effective to set the air force against a distant target if, by its destruction or closure, it can decisively influence the fighting power of the enemy army or navy.*' It added: '*Even during combined operations with the army and navy, the air force should not give up the campaign against the sources of enemy power. One stipulation should be to select targets so that the air force's battle will have a rapid effect upon the ground and sea battle.*' The document frequently used Operational terms which had strategic interpretations.

But without infrastructure and aircraft these were mere words. When the Nazis came to power the army was just beginning to implement Felmy's 22-*Staffeln* plan but a *Truppenamt* meeting on 9 March 1933 amended this to 32 *Staffeln* within two years. Hitler, Göring and Milch had no time for army caution and within two months Milch revamped the plan to a 51-*Staffeln* force by August 1936 with a strong bomber element. [45] Milch drafted a RM170 million ($40.5 million) production plan to support this programme which began on 29 June 1933 and focused on off-the-shelf designs, some from Lipetsk and others already being marketed. He organised funding for the expansion of existing production facilities and for expansion through the acquisition of related facilities to create production complexes with cost-plus contracts, industrial manpower rising from some 17,000 at the end of 1933 to nearly 125,000 by mid-1936.

The Lipetsk-developed Arado Ar 64/65 and Heinkel He 51 fighters, together with the Heinkel He 45/46 reconnaissance aircraft, would equip many of the squadrons but the Arado proved delicate, the He 51 would prove inferior to its contemporaries while the He 46 vibrated badly. The Dornier Do 11C 'freighter' was selected as the foundation of the bomber force but proved structurally weak and was dubbed the 'Flying Coffin' by its luckless crews. Strengthened versions – the Do 11D and Do 13 (Do 23 from 1935) – proved little better. Fortunately the robust and reliable Junkers Ju 52/3m airliner and *Behelfsbomber* (auxiliary bomber), universally dubbed *Tante Ju* (Aunty Yu)' by the *Luftwaffe*, proved an adequate substitute. From 1934 the Technical Office (*Technisches Amt*) under Wimmer was responsible for aircraft development. New aircraft development was under Richthofen, who was well aware that the infant *Luftwaffe* was poorly equipped but argued: 'Better to have second-rate equipment than none at all.'

He was commenting at a turning point in aviation technology, for in the late 1920s the US aircraft industry revolutionised aircraft design. The traditional airframe was made of alloy tubes and spars strengthened internally and externally with steel rigging wires and covered in fabric, light wood or alloys. It was usually a biplane design to provide greater aerodynamic lift, although the early 1930s saw the appearance of more monoplanes with wings braced by fuselage struts. Both biplanes and monoplanes usually had open cockpits and fixed undercarriages.

But the Americans developed semi-monocoque or stressed-skin construction which reversed the traditional concept and which was usually incorporated into a monoplane design. Airframes were now based upon metal skins with some internal stiffening while wings were formed around a steel spar which ran through fuselages. The lightweight structure increased the power-weight ratio to make these aircraft faster than traditional machines and speed was further increased through the introduction of enclosed crew compartments and retractable undercarriages. The increased internal volume provided greater fuel and payload capacity but the technical sophistication of the new aircraft was reflected in their increased price. The Martin 139 bomber was the first combat aircraft to use the semi-monocoque construction technique and enter volume production. It was capable of outrunning even the fastest fighter and underlined the message of British Premier Ramsay MacDonald that 'The bomber will always get through.'

In July 1932 the *Heereswaffenamt* issued a specification for a high-speed twin-engined medium bomber leading to the development of the Dornier Do 17, the Heinkel He 111 and the Junkers Ju 86, although development was plagued by the difficulty of developing high-power engines, a legacy of the Versailles Treaty, and the Junkers' Jumo 205 diesels would prove unreliable. Yet Wimmer and Richthofen recognised the need for a complementary heavy bomber and accelerated the 'Ural Bomber' programme during 1935 leading to the Do 19 and Ju 89 prototypes appearing in 1936 although both proved under-powered. Consequently, Wever issued a new heavy bomber requirement in April 1936 for 'Bomber A' with a range of 6,700 kilometres (4,160 miles) with a 900 kilogramme (2,000 lb) bomb load, the 'Ural Bomber' programme being down-graded to one of evaluation. [46]

For tactical air support a requirement was issued in May 1934 for a multi-role twin-engined aircraft but within a month this was revised with the reconnaissance role assigned to the Do 17 and close air support assigned to both light and heavy dive-bombers, the former renamed *Schlachtflugzeug*, while the latter became the *Stürzkampflugzeug* or 'Stuka'. The former was a single-seat aircraft carrying light bombs and the He 50 was augmented by fighters until the Henschel Hs 123 arrived. The latter led to a slightly revised requirement in January 1935 for a two-man aircraft with longer-range and capable of carrying a heavier bomb load, although Richthofen remained dubious about the whole concept. [47]

Oberst Ernst Udet, the *Inspekteur der Jagd- und Sturzkampfflieger* (Inspector of Fighters and Dive-Bombers), made his most significant contribution to the *Luftwaffe* through the development of the Messerschmitt Bf 109 fighter. The first generation of German fighters reflected a traditional fighter design philosophy emphasising manoeuvrability for dogfights and an open cockpit for all-round vision. But the second generation were bomber interceptors and this required designs emphasising speed and firepower which drove the requirement for semi-monocoque construction. A fighter requirement was issued in December 1933. While he was no intellectual, Udet made a significant mental leap to appreciate the advantages of the Bf 109 which was designed by his friend Willi Messerschmitt. He 'sold' the Bf 109 at a demonstration before Göring and Blomberg on 3 July 1936 when he combined his own flying skills and the aircraft's superb performance to 'shoot down' not only a bomber formation but also its He 51 fighter escort. However, it is worth noting that the Bf 109 B-1 was a matron with a facelift for, like most biplane fighters, it featured only two rifle-calibre machine guns which had to be cocked manually as well as a wooden propeller, but variable pitch propellers and 20mm cannon were soon introduced.

Messerschmitt also met another requirement, issued in March 1934, for a 'heavy' fighter. The Germans had sought two-seat long-range fighters since the mid-1920s and a requirement was issued in August 1932 for a 'heavy' fighter which was quickly renamed 'combat destroyer' (*Kampfzerstörer*). The idea fascinated Göring and in a rare moment of exuberance, Wimmer let his imagination run free and the roles were expanded from long-range escort and interception to reconnaissance, ground-attack and high-speed bombing. While Wever opposed what he called 'a forlorn hope', he could not dissuade Göring and the outline requirement was redrafted in May 1934 to seek a twin-engined, multi-role aircraft armed with cannon.

Richthofen managed to head off the stampede to mediocrity in January 1935 by splitting the requirements into a heavy fighter, a high-speed reconnaissance bomber and a fast-bomber (*Schnellbomber*). Although Udet was still a civilian at the time, he is reported to have influenced selection of the Bf 110 for the heavy fighter requirement with the prototype flying in May 1936, while the *Schnellbomber* shortlist, including the Junkers Ju 88, appeared at the end of 1936.

There remained deep concern about bombing accuracy; indeed, even in 1937 an elite unit with the most modern aircraft could put barely 2 per cent of its bombs within a 200-metre (220-yard) diameter target from 4,000 metres (13,000 ft). Greater accuracy could be achieved by diving on the target and Heinkel had been developing dive-bombers for the Japanese Navy. Their accuracy impressed the *RLM*, which ordered 111 He 50s, and the popularity of the concept led to two Curtiss Hawks being bought by dive-bomber enthusiast Ernst Udet with *RLM* funds and they were demonstrated at Rechlin in October 1933. [48]

In an effort to kick-start German military aviation Göring, who had maintained close links with Italy's Fascist Party since 1923, returned to Rome in mid-April 1933 to seek Mussolini's help with aircraft and training. Despite promises, no aircraft were provided but in July Pflugbeil led some German pilots, including future *Inspekteur der Jagdflieger* Adolf Galland, to Italy for fighter training. They qualified in the autumn but no more followed because the DVS Schleissheim proved more suitable. In fact Italy's attitude to Germany was ambiguous. In the late 1920s it had ignored diplomatic convention and allowed Richthofen to become a de facto air attaché. But Italy also feared a resurgent Germany and as late as the summer of 1936 the *Regia Aeronautica* (Italian Air Force) and the *Armée de l'Air* (French Air Force) were negotiating joint action against Germany. [49] For this reason Italy preferred to provide military aid to its northern neighbour, and former sworn enemy Austria.

The Austrian air force slowly expanded and in 1933 added two squadrons of fighters and corps aircraft at Graz in March 1934 together with a primary training squadron. Administration was under *Lehrabteilung III* at Vienna which also controlled an advance training squadron, and by March 1934 the Austrian air service had 30 aircraft and 440 men. In May 1934 the *Luftschutzkommando* (Air Defence Command) was created and between July and December it flew its first operational missions, the first against Austrian Nazis who had murdered Chancellor Engelbert Dollfus, and the second against Socialists who had rebelled against his right-wing successor, Kurt von Schuschnigg. [50] Hitler's public revelation of the *Luftwaffe* on 1 March 1935 encouraged Vienna to follow suit on 19 June. Under *Generalleutnant* Löhr, by the end of the year, the *Österreichische Luftstreitkräfte* had 78 aircraft and 686 men. But expansion was slow because of the country's parlous financial situation and by the summer of 1936 it had 1,000 men with orders for Fiat CR 32bis fighters and Caproni Ca 133 bombers.

By contrast, the *Luftwaffe's* expansion was dramatic but until conscription was introduced in March 1935 it relied largely upon volunteers, although the *Wehrkreise* were assigned quotas for transfer. Some 2,000 soldiers and sailors, including some 300–400 aircrew, were transferred in 1933. The police, *Lufthansa* and *DVS* provided more, including some 100–200 aircrew, while an increasing number of 'Old Eagles' were persuaded to join the fold, most notably Udet. [51]

Loerzer's *DLV* provided a growing stream of young men and also began training reservists, and by October 1935 it had some 28 training centres. Regular training was centralised from November 1933 when the naval air ace *Oberst* (*Generalmajor* by 1937) Friedrich Christiansen was appointed *Inspekteur der Schulen der Luftwaffe* with six *DVS* schools, but from October 1935 a process of decentralisation began when each *Luftkreis* (air region) created a *Flieger Ersatz Abteilung-FEA* (air replacement battalion), later *Flieger Ausbildungs Regiment-FAR*, to provide basic training. *Fliegerschulen* were attached to each unit to provide basic and advanced flying training and were augmented by specialist schools. [52]

At the same time, Milch exploited his *Lufthansa* experience to create a network of 36 well-equipped bases by 1936. Each had accommodation for man and machine, workshops, storage facilities, an extensive communications system with radios, telephones and teletypes together with radio and visual navigation aids. Seeckt had encouraged the development of modern communications; Guderian's rise within the armoured forces began because he was a signaller, and the importance of communications led to the creation, in December 1933, of the *Luftnachrichtenwesen* (Air Signal Service) under one of the original qualified aviators, *Oberstleutnant* Wolfgang Martini. He and Milch exploited the navigation aids to improve bomber performance. Unlike most of their European contemporaries each German bomber had a direction-finding (DF) antenna and was supposed to have a fully-qualified navigator to ensure they could operate both in cloudy weather and at night. From November 1933 *Lufthansa* organised blind-flying training, initially under the guise of *Reichsbahnstrecken* (state railway extensions), which continued until the outbreak of war. The navigation system technology would be further exploited later in the decade to create electronic bombing aids allowing specialised aircraft to strike targets even on the darkest nights or in the densest cloud.

As men and machines arrived the *Luftwaffe* began to expand. On 1 March 1934 it had only 77 aircraft rising to 800 within a year and by April 1936 the figure was nearly 2,700, including 1,000 bombers. The *Flak* arm, which was an army organisation initially came under the *Luftwaffe's* operational control, but in February 1935 Göring assumed absolute control of the arm, although the army would later re-create its *Flak* batteries. Initially the handful of squadrons were concentrated from 1 April under Sperrle's *Fliegerdivision 1* because Sperrle was one of the most experienced air commanders in the *Reichsheer* and, therefore, the *Luftwaffe*.

At the same time the *Luftwaffe* created its equivalent of the *Wehrkreise* as *Luftkreise* with the Kiel-based *Luftkreis VI* being a purely naval organisation. Initially these were largely administrative, logistics and training organisations but as the squadrons and *Flak* batteries expanded from October 1935, they were given an operational role with a *Höhere Fliegerkommandeur* and *Höhere Kommandeur der Flakartillerie* (senior air and flak commanders). For greater efficiency, the administrative and routine work was devolved into *Luftgaue* (air districts) from April 1936 and this organisation would remain substantially unchanged for the next two years. There was no air commander in either the East Prussian or Naval regions, the latter (now under *Konteradmiral* Zander) having instead a *Führer der Seeluftstreitkräfte* (Naval Air Corps Leader) who was former *Fregattenkapitän* Hermann Bruch.

All units were given cover names, most purporting to be part of *DVS*, *DVL* or *Lufthansa*. This deceived neither the French nor the British, both of whom received what the British called 'secret information' which included details of the 51-*Staffeln* plan. The British air attaché, Group Captain J. H. Herring, was actually told by Milch's assistant, Carl Bolle, in June 1933 that Germany had begun air re-armament. It was an open secret even within Germany and a week after Bolle's admission Herring observed two unknown 'express postal aircraft' (one a He 51 fighter) at an air display at Tempelhof. He asked the senior air official sitting beside him about the aircraft but before he could answer his bored wife indiscreetly responded: 'Oh, those will be two of the new single-seat fighters, I suppose.' [53]

The Allied response when Hitler revealed the *Luftwaffe* was therefore muted, encouraging Berlin to accelerate the expansion programme. A degree establishing the new service was signed by Hitler on 26 February (he preferred the title *Reichsluftwaffe* but this was soon formally reduced to *Luftwaffe*), its uniform based upon that of *DLV*, and as the third element of the *Reichswehr* which would be renamed the *Wehrmacht* on 1 June 1935. To facilitate expansion, the ever-helpful Blomberg provided 6,000 technically-trained men, including 4,300 air crew volunteers, between May and September but with the German Army itself expanding, this was 'Fatty's' last favour.

The urgent need for strategic reconnaissance led to the use of an aerial photography company under *Flugkapitän* Theodor Rowehl, a former naval air observer, known as *Hansa-Luftbild GmbH*, which began operations over Poland in 1933. The following year the *Luftwaffe* created its own *Staffel zbV ObdL* (Luftwaffe commander-in-chief's special employment squadron) flying 'civil' He 111s. However, in January 1935, *Hansa-Luftbild* appears to have absorbed the *Staffel* to become the *Versuchstelle für Höhenflüge* under Rowehl, who became first a *Hauptmann* and then a *Major*. Ostensibly part of *Lufthansa*, *Kommando Rowehl* or *Fliegerstaffel zbV* would roam the skies of Europe on 'route-proving' trials and would supply the *Luftwaffe* with the foundation of its target folders. The covert reconnaissance was extended over the Soviet Union and Great Britain from 1936 and his command became *Aufklärungsgruppe Rowehl* or *Kommando Rowehl*. [54]

Its growing importance was underlined when the *Luftwaffe* was committed for the first time a year after its existence was revealed. On 2 May 1935 France signed a mutual assistance pact with the Soviet Union, which had a first-line strength of 6,672 aircraft. Right-wing opposition delayed French parliamentary ratification of the agreement until 11 February 1936 and this was completed only 16 days later. Hitler ordered the reoccupation of the Rhineland on 11 February and Blomberg drafted the directives on 28 February for what was officially called the *Winterübung* ('Winter Exercise').

On 7 March German troops marched into the Rhineland shielded by the Ar 65s of *III./JG 134* and He 51s of *I./StG 165* and some *Flak* batteries, the aircraft initially lacking ammunition and operating with neither guns nor sights harmonised. To give the illusion of strength the aircraft switched airfields frequently and were hastily painted with new markings. Although France partially mobilised there was no political will to fight the re-occupation but fear of potential French bomber attacks reportedly led to *KG 253* being alerted to attack Paris. [55]

The occupation of the Rhineland led the *Luftwaffe* to expand the *Luftkreis IV* and *V* infrastructure across the Rhine. From April 1936 there was a further expansion frenzy with an 18 per cent increase in aircraft strength with 54 'daughter' *Staffeln* being created from 'Mother' *Geschwader* and *Gruppen*. But within three months of the Rhineland success the *Luftwaffe* suffered its greatest tragedy.

On 3 June Wever flew his He 70 to Dresden to lecture officer cadets at the *Luftkriegschule* but he was anxious to return to Berlin for a state funeral. In his haste he neglected pre-flight checks, forgot to release the aileron lock and the 3-tonne Heinkel crashed at the end of the runway, killing him and his flight engineer. When he heard the news Göring reportedly burst into floods of tears, for Wever had been unique, a fact which was to become only too apparent in the following years.

Chapter Two

A Sword over Europe

Wever's death left the *Luftwaffe* flying without a pilot in the years leading to the outbreak of war and within a week of his death it suffered an even greater disaster, although this was not recognised for years. [1]

Wever's loss occurred as the *Luftwaffe* became a major instrument in German foreign policy, feeding Göring's megalomania and his desire for a greater say in 'his' service. Before 1936 he rarely visited the *RLM* more than four times a year but his promotion to *Generaloberst* on 20 April 1936 dictated a more active role as he moved from Minister to *Oberbefehlshaber* (commander-in-chief). Milch, also promoted on 20 April to *General der Flieger*, saw himself as Wever's replacement but Göring had no intention of making his rival any stronger and the two would now fight for control of German air power.

Blomberg proposed the Bavarian *Generalmajor* Franz Halder as a replacement for Wever, but Halder elected to remain in the Army where he became Chief of the Army Staff two years later. Göring opted for another Bavarian, his administrative chief, *Generalleutnant* Albert Kesselring, to head the *Luftkommandoamt*, which was the *Luftwaffe's* general staff. Milch retained overall administrative authority for the *Luftkommandoamt* and out of pique he began sniping at Kesselring, interfering on every possible occasion. On one occasion, following a series of accidents Milch wished to court martial his former adjutant, *Major* Hans Jeschonnek, now *Kommodore* of the *Lehrgeschwader Greifswald*. Kesselring slapped him down, leaving Milch to add Jeschonnek to his long list of enemies by means of a personal reprimand. Yet even the usually optimistic Kesselring tired of the constant petty struggles and resigned on 1 June 1937 to assume, no doubt with great relief, command of *Luftkreiskommando III*.

The struggles with Milch limited Kesselring's impact upon *Luftwaffe* development with the *Staatssekretär* opposing development of a *Bomber B* heavy bomber successor until the day after Kesselring's departure when *RLM* pettily authorised a programme using the Heinkel He 177 design. Yet Kesselring strengthened the *Luftwaffe's* supply organisation in order to support the anticipated rapid advances of mechanised forces and in April 1937 also took the first steps to creating night fighters by producing a manual on the subject. [2] Before he departed, Kesselring fired a Parthian shot by playing on Göring's vanity in an attempt to persuade him to place the *Luftkommandoamt* under his personal control and finally to rename it the *Luftwaffengeneralstab* (*Luftwaffe* general staff). Its reluctant first *Chef* was *Generalmajor* Stumpff who was appointed on 1 June. He retained the post until the end of January 1939 but achieved little except to hold the line, although he did oversee the *Luftwaffe's* part when it contributed more than 62,000 men and 1,337 aircraft to the *Wehrmacht's* largest peacetime exercise which involved several *Panzer* divisions in September 1937. [3]

Not only was there a leadership vacuum at this point, but the game of musical chairs at the *RLM* saw a disastrous decision within days of Wever's funeral. On the morning of 9 June 1936 Richthofen went to see Wimmer to express doubts about the *Stuka* concept and to recommend its abandonment. But that very day, after 'flying a desk' so successfully for so many years, Wimmer was given command of *Luftkreis III* and was replaced not by the experienced Richthofen but by the *Stuka* enthusiast, the stocky, balding Ernst Udet. [4] He was one of the last 'Old Eagles' to join the colours, in 1935, attracted to a great extent by a steady income, although Göring also promised to let him pursue his fascination with dive-bombers. He knew little about aircraft development; his 'test flights' involved throwing an aircraft around the sky, and although he was one of the few senior members of the *Luftwaffe* who was a Party member (from 1933) the *Gestapo* watched him, partly because he had anti-Nazi friends.

However, Udet was reluctant to accept greater responsibilities and told Göring: 'This isn't for me. I don't know anything about production and big aircraft.' It was probably because of Udet's technical ignorance that Göring appointed him as he would not show up the *Luftwaffe* commander's own ignorance while he was confident that the organisation Wimmer had built would carry its new boss by making all the technical decisions. The Nazis believed that the strong should rule the weak uninhibited by moral or legal considerations; indeed it was brawn rather than legality which defined the leadership of Party organisations from top to bottom. Udet had been a close friend of Milch, and Göring wanted to turn them against each other to counter-balance the *Staatssekretär* as relations between the two surviving members of the *Luftwaffe* triumvirate deteriorated. There were heated rows over the telephone which Milch would often end by slamming the receiver down, and knowing that the *Staatssekretär*'s ego was harnessed to control of aircraft production, the new appointment undoubtedly gave Göring much private enjoyment. In turn Milch soon began to exploit Udet's inadequacies in intrigues which gradually grew in effectiveness until in November 1941 Udet shot himself, leaving a note which blamed 'the Jew Milch.'

The engineers in the *Technisches Amt* also followed Göring's 'divide and rule' policy. To improve their status, and to permit them to indulge their interests in technical discussion and development, they got Udet to rubber-stamp a re-organisation between March and May 1938 into 13 highly specialised departments. In practice this blinkered the various departments and increased development times because manufacturers had to deal with numerous private little empires whose activities Udet could not co-ordinate. [5]

Despite his inadequacies Udet developed ambition late in life and proposed an air production ministry in all but name similar to the wartime *Flugzeugmeisterei*. On 29 January 1939 *Generalmajor* Udet (he had been promoted in April 1937) became the *Generalluftzeugmeister* controlling the *Technisches Amt* supply and economic directorates, the Industrial Group and numerous development establishments. Milch must have been green with envy that his former friend was holding the position he coveted but even he would have found it hard controlling an organisation of 19 departments.

Ritter von Greim replaced Stumpff at the *Luftwaffenpersonalamt* and, while both he and Udet were placed nominally under Milch, by mid-July 1937 Göring was meeting them without bothering to inform the *Staatssekretär*. In September 1937, when he learned what was happening, Milch replaced the acting head (since April) of the *Luftwaffenführungsstabes*, and *de facto* deputy *Luftwaffe* Chief of Staff, *General* Paul Deichmann with *Generalmajor* Kühl, who would be its first 'official' head, and he would remain until 28 February 1939. Greim retaliated by placing *Oberstleutnant* Jeschonnek as head of the *Luftwaffenführungsstabes* Operations. [6]

For Milch, 1937 was the *annus horribilis* in which he lost not only power but also his appendix, and even the following year began badly. It was clear the *Luftwaffe* was becoming too unwieldy for Milch and the *RLM* to control directly and, on 1 February 1938, it was re-organised with Udet and Greim formally becoming Göring's subordinates. The remaining administrative departments were placed under the *Chef der Luftwehr* (Chief of Air Defence), 55-year-old *General der Flakartillerie* Otto Günther Rüdel, leaving Milch, now appointed *Generalinspekteur der Luftwaffe*, in a largely ceremonial role although he did share with Stumpff responsibility for the 10 inspectorates.

The new organisation lasted less than a year for it was too unwieldy for any one man to control, especially the lazy Göring whose fat fingers were in far too many other pies. He was forced to recognise Milch's administrative skills and another re-organisation took effect on 1 February 1939. Essentially it followed the wartime principle of splitting leadership between the operational and administrative/industrial elements with Göring taking control of the former while Milch controlled the latter (aping *Kogenluft* and *Idflieg* in the Great War).

The operational element consisted of the *Generalstab der Luftwaffe* whose chief now controlled the *Führungs-* (Operations), *Fremde Luftmächte* (Intelligence) and *Taktischeabteilungen* (Support) directorates, leaving the *Organization-*, *Quartiermeister-* (Supply), and *Rüstungsabteilungen* (Replacements) departments under a separate *Generalquartiermeister*. Milch now controlled the organisations of Udet, Rüdel (who replaced Greim in the *Personalamt*), and Martini as well as the inspectorates which were combined under Kühl, who had been promoted *General der Flieger*, as chief of training resources (*Chef des Ausbildungswesens*) but who had become redundant following the disbanding of the *Luftwaffenführungsstabes*. Kühl, whose first chief of staff was *Oberstleutnant* Deichmann, would hold this position until July 1943 and gradually centralised training until he retired in October 1943.

Of equal importance was the appointment on the same day of *Oberst* Hans Jeschonnek, who had been Milch's first adjutant in 1933, as Chief of Staff. Unfortunately Jeschonnek shared Milch's ability to make enemies, for while he possessed a near-English reserve, he was also capable of sarcastically berating his subordinates and making comments which were deeply wounding. They had fallen out and in October 1935 Jeschonnek was appointed *Kommandeur* of *Fliegergruppe Greifswald (II./KG 152)* to get him out of the way. In April 1937 this *Gruppe* became part of the newly created *Lehrgeschwader Greifswald* set up to develop new operational techniques with Jeschonnek as its *Kommodore*.

From October 1937, as head of Operations within the *Luftwaffenführungsstabes*, Jeschonnek's influence grew because he drafted operational requirements and his concern about bombing accuracy grew as a result of his experience with the *Lehrgeschwader*. This fostered in him a special interest in dive-bombing which he applied to the He 177 heavy bomber – but he was not alone. The contemporary Royal Air Force Specification P.13/36 for a new medium bomber included a similar requirement and led to the Avro Manchester (which became the Lancaster) and Handley Page Halifax. While the dive-bomber requirement was abandoned it meant the Lancaster and Halifax were strong enough to make surprisingly violent manoeuvres without threat to their airframes. [7]

Milch's enmity helped propel Jeschonnek into the chief of staff role. In October 1938, Hitler demanded a huge expansion of the *Luftwaffe* and on 9 November Jeschonnek produced a plan for 10,700 first-line aircraft by New Year's Day 1942. Although wiser heads in the *RLM*, including the Organisation head, *Oberst* Josef Kammhuber, believed only a 4,000-strong force was possible, Jeschonnek retorted: 'In my opinion it is our duty to support the *Führer* and not oppose his wishes.' Milch mockingly raised the issue with Göring to humiliate his former friend but underestimated both Fatty's loyalty to Hitler and dislike of his *Staatssekretär*. Göring supported Jeschonnek and soon propelled him to the heights of *Luftwaffe* leadership while Kammhuber promptly requested transfer to a front line command and, after a few months, became chief of staff of Felmy's *Luftflotte 2*. Göring selected Jeschonnek partly because he anticipated less opposition from younger, and less experienced, officers although, as happened in this case, such officers tended to defer to older and wiser heads and lacked the seniority to override them.

Jeschonnek appointed his friend *Oberst* Otto Hoffmann von Waldau to replace him as operations chief. It was a good choice, for Waldau was a perceptive staff officer, but he would not hold his tongue and the two men, who had once addressed each other by their Christian names, quickly clashed over plans for the Ju 88. Soon the relationship between them became icily correct. In April 1942 Waldau became *Fliegerführer Afrika* then commander of *Fliegerkorps X* and when he died in an air crash in May 1943 his former friend refused to attend the funeral.

Jeschonnek's professional failings, above all his lack of experience, overshadowed his personal ones, for he was promoted far beyond his capabilities. Like many *Luftwaffe* leaders he held technicians in low esteem; indeed, less than five per cent of *Luftwaffe* generals and staff officers actually held technical degrees, for most came from classically biased schools (*Humanistische Gymnasien*) rather than the technical schools (*Realgymnasien*). The impact of technical developments such as radar were therefore underestimated and there was also a tendency to neglect both intelligence and supply. Jeschonnek also had a tendency towards short-term solutions and when shortfalls occurred, especially in transport, he tended to raid the training organisation. However, even as operations chief he recognised the need to provide stronger support for the mechanised forces and it was apparently his decision to create a dedicated strike force or *Nahkämpfkorps* (Close Air Support Corps), the *Fliegerdivision zbV*, in August 1938, renamed *Fliegerführer zbV* on 19 July 1939 under Richthofen.

The decision, and Richthofen's appointment, came after experience in Spain where the civil war raged for four years following a failed military coup on 19 July 1936. Rebels under *General* Emilio Mola controlled a large slice of northern Spain, there was a bridgehead around Seville in southern Andalucia, while General Francisco Franco held the Canary Islands and the colony of Morocco with the Army of Africa, Spain's only professional troops. The remainder of the country was under nominal government hands although the real power was held by left-wing militias. Both sides sought foreign military aid; Madrid from socialist France and even from Germany (it sought He 51 fighters), Mola looked to Italy while rebel supporters in Morocco turned towards Berlin and here serendipity would play a part.

A passing *Lufthansa* Ju 52 was commandeered and two Nazi businessmen then used the aircraft to fly to Berlin to persuade Hitler to aid the rebels. Yet diplomatic protocol meant Berlin continued to recognise the Madrid government and *Lufthansa* would operate commercial flights through Barcelona until 8 August. Hitler met the delegation on 25 July at Bayreuth where he had been intoxicated with a performance of Wagner, but he was cautious. Arguing, correctly, that Communist power was growing in the government (later Republican) area but unwilling to intervene directly for fear forcing France into premature intervention, he authorised covert military support for the rebels (who would soon be called Nationalists), although only to Franco.

The priority was to tip the balance of power by getting the Army of Africa across the Straits of Gibraltar and over the Republican Fleet. Blomberg and Göring thrashed out the details in a meeting which continued into the early hours of Sunday, 26 July, to provide air transport facilities with a self-defence capability. Blomberg was enthusiastic while Göring's initial reluctance (he had wanted to use *Lufthansa* aircraft rather than erode *Luftwaffe* strength) was rapidly overcome upon hearing of Hitler's support for the project which the *RLM* would control.

Ostensibly everything would be run by a Spanish organisation, the *Hispano-Marroqui de Transportes SL (HISMA)* and all German personnel would wear its white uniform. Milch was summoned to Bayreuth, briefed and as church bells summoned the faithful to prayer, he tackled the project with the verve of a hell-fire preacher. The programme was dubbed *Unternehmen 'Feuerzauber'* (Operation 'Magic Fire') and operational control was assigned to Wilberg and his newly created *Sonderstab W* (Special Staff W) as the *RLM* ignored the day of rest. [8]

The new policy was based on transports which could be used as bombers, a popular concept in the 1920s and early 1930s. Three *Kampfgruppen* each supplied three Ju 52/3mg3e while two *Jagdgruppen* provided He 51 B-1 fighters. HISMA chartered a ship for them in Hamburg and 91 men, many of whom were 'volunteered' by their commanding officers after signing declarations of secrecy before being told the good news; they included future aces *Leutnant*s Hans Trautloft and Hans-Joachim 'Hajo' Hermann. They changed into civilian clothes and travelled as a *Kraft durch Freude* (Strength through Joy) tourist group, meeting their commanding officer, *Major* Alexander von Scheele, in Hamburg shortly before departure. Scheele was a *Schlasta* veteran who had emigrated to Latin America after the war and returned to the Fatherland after the Nazis took power [9].

Scheele's was purely a transport and training mission, forbidden to participate in combat missions although the Heinkel fighters could escort the transports until Spanish pilots could master them. The 'tourists' sailed out of the Elbe on 1 August while another 11 demilitarised Ju 52 bombers painted in *Lufthansa* colours flew to the Nationalist enclaves via San Remo in Italy, although one accidentally landed at a Republican airfield, its crew being released from a Madrid jail after German diplomatic pressure. By the time the *'Feuerzauber'* team reached Seville on 6 August, the airlift was actually under way. Franco had six aircraft, but it was the reluctant *Flugkapitän* Alfred Henke (whose comandeered Junkers had flown the Nazis to Germany days earlier) who flew the first German mission on 28 July with some 35 men sitting on the floor with their knees drawn to their chins. He flew several flights a day, joined by a second *Lufthansa 'Tante Ju'* and over a fortnight they transported 2,489 men.

The airlift, which soon placed under *Hauptmann* Rudolf 'Bubb' *Freiherr* von Moreau, concluded on 11 October with the delivery of 13,900 men and 270 tonnes of equipment including 36 guns. The effort involved 868 sorties and only one aircraft was lost with the deaths of two men. As Hitler rightly said: 'Franco ought to erect a monument to the glory of the Junkers 52. It is this aircraft which the Spanish Revolution has to thank for its victory.' [10]

The *'Feuerzauber'* team began to train the Spanish to fly German aircraft, but while combat operations were *'verboten'*, Scheele interpreted his orders to authorise bombing of Republican warships since opposition anti-aircraft guns forced Moreau's transports to fly high. The battleship *Jaime I* based at Malaga posed an especially serious threat and on 13 August Moreau and Henke flew two Junkers fitted with crude racks and loaded with 250kg bombs to attack her, but only the *Lufthansa* pilot found her and struck her with two bombs which severely damaged her upper deck and killed 47 of her crew. The battleship promptly withdrew to Cartagena. [11]

Gradually, the Germans were sucked into the conflict and in October were reinforced to create *Gruppe Eberhardt* with 14 fighters, and *Gruppe Moreau* with 20 bombers and a pair of He 70F reconnaissance aircraft together with some seaplanes. The Germans returned to the fray during the second half of October becoming an aerial fire brigade, a role which was to become familiar in the *Luftwaffe*. But as Franco's forces approached Madrid in late October, Stalin opted to support the Republican government and Soviet merchantmen began unloading large quantities of military equipment. This included the nimble I-15 biplane fighter, dubbed *Chato* ('Snub Nose'), and the fast I-16 Type 5/6 monoplane fighter nicknamed both *Mosca* ('Fly'), because of its whining engine noise, and *Rata* ('Rat') because of its manoeuvrability. Also arriving were the elegant, modern, twin engine SB (*Skorostnoi Bombardirovshchik* or Fast Bomber) 2M-100A 'frontal' bomber, which was nicknamed *Katiuska* (Katy) or *Martin* because it was confused with the Martin 139 and was 110 km/h (70mph) faster than the He 51! The Russians were grouped under Yakov Smushkevich, an air commander with political credentials, who would become a senior leader in the Soviet Air Force in 1939 and then be succeeded by Pavel Rychagov, who was the Chato unit commander in Spain. The Russians were augmented by Spanish and mercenary air crew, including Germans *emigrés* and Austrians, but it was the newcomers who quickly proved superior to the Germans and Italians.

Fears of Russian intervention saw an expansion of the German presence as Berlin formally recognised Franco's Nationalist government. German participation in the Spanish Civil War now fell under the auspices of *Winterübung 'Rügen'* (winter exercise 'Rügen') whose operational elementwas originally dubbed first *Eiserne Rationen* ('iron rations') then the *Eiserne Legion* ('Iron Legion') but finally, and at the animal-loving Göring's insistence, the *Legion Condor*. [12] It was formed on

7 November by expanding Scheele's force, the *'Feuerzeuber'* commander becoming Air Attaché with the Nationalist Government until January 1939. Tragically, he and eight other veterans were killed when their Ju 52 crashed at Roubilon in France in February that year. Henke was more fortunate and with the re-organisation finally left Spain to become associated with the new four-engined Focke-Wulf Fw 200 *Condor* airliner. In August 1938 he again teamed with Moreau to set a non-stop record from Berlin to New York in 24 hours and 36 minutes, but within two years they were both dead; Moreau testing a Ju 88 on 4 April 1939 at Rechlin while Henke's *Condor* crashed while taking off from Berlin-Staaken on 22 April 1940.

Given his experience as a senior air commander during the Great War, it was logical that *Luftkreis V*'s Hugo Sperrle, now a *Generalmajor*, would command the *Legion* and he flew into Seville, via Rome, on 5 November after a six-day journey. His chief of staff was *Oberstleutnant* Alexander Holle who, while very capable, appears to have had trouble delegating authority and to have reacted pessimistically to adversity. The *Legion Condor* consisted of two *Gruppen*; *Kampfgruppe K/88* and *Jagdgruppe J/88*, while Moreau's reconnaissance aircraft were absorbed into *Aufklärungsstaffel A/88* with corps and reconnaissance *Kette*, and the floatplane-equipped *Küstfliegerstaffel AS/88*. A variety of maintenance, base protection and transport units were also created but against an establishment of 5,500 it had only 5,000 Germans. The remainder were Spaniards acting as 'hewers of wood and drawers of water' manning a network of airfields, depots and signal centres throughout the Nationalist zone. While much equipment came by sea from the west, the largest aircraft flew via Italy.

Most of the men, volunteers and usually bachelors, sailed to Cadiz and Seville from Stettin and Swinemunde wearing civilian clothes until they entered Spanish territorial waters where they received a uniform similar to that of the *Reichsarbeitsdienst-RAD* (National Labour Service) but with Spanish insignia. Their mail would be sent 'care of *Herr* Max Winkler', who was the Junkers representative in Spain, and upon arrival the volunteers would often find themselves promoted by a grade. Pay was excellent and, even with the excesses of the young, there were special arrangements in which the men marched down to selected brothels. Veterans would return tanned and with enough savings to buy a motor car. [13]

The superior Russian aircraft quickly eroded Sperrle's 120 aircraft as they supported Franco's final assault upon Madrid, the dead including Eberhardt who was replaced by *Major* Hubertus von Merhardt. He informed Sperrle he would not send his pilots against such overwhelming odds [14]. The shield of *J/88* became so leaky that Fuchs temporarily abandoned daylight raids upon Madrid on 26 November. By January Sperrle had lost 20 per cent of his front line strength and by the end of the month *K/88* had only 26 Ju 52s. Morale plunged and only the Germans' own professionalism and Sperrle's leadership prevented a collapse. *J/88* was reduced to a bomber escort role and the *Legion Condor* began 1937 operating on fronts were Russian opposition was weakest. On 6 February Sperrle returned to the Madrid front to support a new Nationalist offensive south of the city, in the Jarama valley, and sought to interdict roads, but the air battles merely confirmed the inferiority of German aircraft with He 51 escorts having to shelter behind the guns of *K/88* bombers!

The *Legion Condor* needed modern aircraft urgently. In December the development unit received three Bf 109 prototypes, which returned to Germany in February, but accompanying them was Richthofen who supervised their operational evaluation. The Spanish conflict had stirred his blood and when he returned to Berlin before Christmas he began pulling strings to get a permanent posting away from the dilettante Udet. On 6 January a top-level conference involving Milch, Kesselring, Udet and Wilberg apparently agreed the *Legion* should get modern aircraft and also that Richthofen should replace Holle who departed on 22 January. Sperrle found he had merely replaced the thorn in his side. He and Richthofen had had many disputes about the quality of aircraft in 1934 and, perhaps as a reflection of his own feelings of social inferiority, he may have regarded Richthofen as an aristocratic snob. For his part Richthofen disliked his fastidious gourmet superior's table manners and coarse wit and yet, despite the tensions, they formed a working partnership helped by a mutual interest in cards. However, Richthofen had linguistic skills including Italian which eased relations with the *Aviación Legionaria*, Mussolini's equivalent of the *Legion Condor*. He also learned Spanish which helped him to develop quickly a good working relationship with Franco, allowing Sperrle to leave daily affairs in his capable hands.

Richthofen was followed by a stream of new aircraft including 12 Do 17 E-1, He 111 B-1 and Ju 86 D-1 and 16 Bf 109 B-1. The last were under *Oberleutnant* Günther 'Franzl' Lützow. A scion of a very distinguished military family and Lipetsk veteran, Lützow now took a leaf from the book of the wartime ace Boelcke, by keeping his 'cubs' out of the firing line until they had familiarised themselves with their new aircraft. He also appears to have introduced the tactic of operating in pairs or *Kettehunde* ('Tethered Dogs') rather than in trios. [15]

Their debut came on a quieter front. Having failed to seize Madrid, Franco decided to eliminate the Republic's northern enclave along the Bay of Biscay based upon Bilbao, Santander and Gijon whose conquest would provide him with a much-needed industrial base, as well as manpower and minerals to trade for foreign weapons. Richthofen was briefed by the Nationalist air force commander, General Alfredo Kindélan, who would nominally control 150 German, Italian and Spanish aircraft, and promised that if he provided integrated air and artillery bombardments and close air support they would exploit the attacks. In the past they had watched German fighters strafe and bomb enemy positions and emerged from their trenches only to applaud! [16]

Sperrle's headquarters transferred to Vitoria while 62 aircraft had moved to Burgos by 21 March 1937. The enemy had only 30 aircraft and to prevent reinforcement the *Legion Condor's* bombers, including Heinkels and Dorniers, struck airfields. The main offensive began on 31 March with Sperrle providing both battlefield interdiction and close air support around Orchandiano. [17] But despite Kindélan's promise they were not exploited while Mola seemed uninterested in these missions and demanded attacks on Bilbao's factories leading to a bad-tempered exchange on 2 April with Richthofen who regarded such attacks as 'nonsense'.

A face-saving compromise saw continuation of the close-air support missions while Richthofen promised to strike an explosive factory during a lull. The Germans were already irritated with Mola; Sperrle disliked his step-by-step attacks and was also annoyed that a bombing raid which the Spaniard had requested upon enemy reserves reported assembling at Durango proved a propaganda disaster. The reserves had gone by the time *K/88* struck and the 750 casualties were all civilians, a waste of resources in Sperrle's book! Sperrle protested to protest to Franco and vainly pressed his Spanish allies to conduct a battle of envelopment which German air power could influence. By 25 April Richthofen had moved his command post to Durango and could see an opportunity developing some 15 kilometres to the north-west.

The Republican centre was being driven towards the River Oca and to reach safety would have to pass over the bridge running from Rentaria into the town of Guernica on the west bank. But first they would have to pass through the 'choke point' town of Guerricaiz (which Richthofen called Guernicaiz in his diary), 9 kilometres from Rentaria, and here his bombers could annihilate them and, by destroying the Rentaria bridge, he could bottle the defenders up on the wrong side of the Oca. Although the Astra-Unecta small arms factory lay in south-eastern Guernica with a rail station to the north, there was no target folder on the town. Indeed when Richthofen asked if any of his staff knew anything about the town they all shook their heads. On the evening of 25 April Richthofen decided to strike Guerricaiz. [18]

But the following morning *A/88* reported the assembly of large enemy forces (actually they were civilians on their way to the market) around Guernica. Richthofen saw an opportunity to use air power to isolate and destroy these 'reserves' and rushed to see Mola's Chief-of-Staff, *Coronel* Juan Vigón, who gave him permission to abandon other missions and strike the new target. *VB/88* and *K/88* (together with Italian bombers whom he roped in for the mission) were to strike roads immediately east of Guernica, the nearby suburbs and the Rentaria Bridge while *J/88* and *A/88* interdicted the roads to herd the defenders into the Guerricaiz killing ground.

There was confusion communicating the modified concept from Durango 160 kilometres over mountains to Burgos and the message was interpreted as an attack *upon* Guernica. That afternoon 52 aircraft appeared over the town, dropping nearly 8 tonnes of bombs around the bridge and 37 tonnes into the centre and south of the town, setting ablaze an olive-oil plant and creating dense clouds of smoke which confused the later waves. Between 250 and 1,500 people were killed or wounded, some being strafed by the fighters as they tried to flee the holocaust. The small-arms factory and convents used by two Republican battalions were unscathed as were the town's two hospitals. Guernica's destruction horrified the world and provoked a storm of controversy – the Republicans claiming it was an attempt to terrorise the Basques and the Nationalists claiming the defenders had blown up the town. In fact Richthofen had no time for 'terror' attacks and he was initially bewildered by the town's destruction.

When Nationalist troops occupied the town on 29 April they learned the truth, and a furious Mola banned further attacks upon towns or villages. For propaganda reasons the Germans denied bombing the town. Meanwhile, once across the Oca, Mola's troops closed upon Bilbao whose defences, the *Cinturón de Hierro* (Ring of Iron), were pounded by the *Legion Condor's* bombers which dropped 681 tonnes of bombs by 10 May, sometimes flying three sorties a day. The ground crews, called

Schwarzemänner ('Black Men') because of their black, often oil-streaked, overalls, made this possible and ensured serviceability rates of up to 90 per cent and the final assault from 11 June saw some airmen fly seven sorties a day. Appropriately, the city surrendered on 19 June to the *Legion*'s liaison officer, *Leutnant* Gockel, ending an 11-week campaign which had cost the Germans eight aircraft and 25 men, including nine aircrew of whom two were executed at Orchandiano on 6 April. Fuchs was now replaced at *K/88* by *Major* Karl Mehnart, while at the beginning of July, Merhardt was relieved at *J/88* by *Major* Karl Hermann Gotthard Handrick, who had won the Modern Pentathlon Gold in the 1936 Olympic Games, and joined the Legion as it returned to the Madrid front.

Here, on 6 July the Republic tried to envelop the enemy salient pointing into the heart of the capital. The northern attack took the town of Brunete close to the Nationalist supply line then halted, allowing General José Enrique Varela to contain them. Sperrle, whose *nom de guerre* was 'Sanders', immediately despatched two squadrons but, as the scale of the operation became apparent, he assumed command of German and Nationalist units as *Grupo Aéro Sanders* which incorporated the whole of the *Legion Condor*. Establishing a command post close to Varela, he assumed command of all Nationalist air power over the battlefield – some 161 aircraft of which he provided half – while facing some 250 in opposition.

From 8 July he maintained pressure upon the enemy bridgehead using small formations of bombers to interdict communications and to strike troop assemblies. Corps aircraft roamed the battlefield and called down the modern bombers such as the Do 17 and He 111 (the Ju 86 was withdrawn in June while the He 70 of *A/88* were replaced by Do 17F) on targets of opportunity along the roads, a tactic first used by the British during the autumn of 1918. Fighter-bombers struck enemy positions, including anti-aircraft batteries, while under blazing skies and during the oppressively hot nights the older bombers (including Ju 52s) struck 'choke points' and supply dumps. The new Bf 109s had now overcome their teething troubles and established superiority over the *Chatos* and *Moscas*. Sperrle also provided powerful air support for Varela's counter-offensive on 18 July which regained most of the lost ground after six days of ferocious fighting. Sperrle's campaign cost the Nationalists 23 aircraft, the *Legion* lost eight and nine aircrew, but the Republic lost about 100 aircraft and *2.J/88*'s Bf 109s claimed 16. [19]

Sperrle returned to the north without replacing his losses for four months leaving him with only 68 aircraft, and with *J/88* down to 27 fighters it was little wonder that *Oberleutnant* Douglas Pitcairn, *Staffelkapitän* of *3.J/88* observed: 'We had a feeling we had been sent to Spain and then deserted.' The *Schwarzemänner* kept serviceability rates high, although sometimes they had to cannibalise wrecked aircraft. For the advance on Santander, which fell on 27 August, the Bf 109s and He 111s penetrated deep into enemy air space and the former proved a match for the *Ratas*, tightening Nationalist air dominance. The northern campaign, which consumed 2,500 tonnes of bombs, ended on 21 October with the fall of Gijon. Ground fire proved deadlier than fighters, accounting for half the losses. [20]

Ten days after Gijon fell, Sperrle returned to Germany, having fallen out with Richthofen who was refused permission to make a farewell address at a ceremony to mark his commander's departure. Sperrle spent the next three months on leave and writing reports before becoming commander of *Luftwaffengruppenkommando 3* on 4 February 1938. His replacement was being considered as the Brunete battle raged, with Blomberg wanting to send Kesselring, who would certainly have been a good choice. But the former chief of staff had just assumed command of *Luftkreiskommando 3* and Göring wisely decided against a sudden change in command. Instead he decided to send his chief military administrator, *Generalmajor* HelmuthVolkmann who needed a front line command after 'flying a desk' for three years and appears to have been 'ticket punching' [21].

When he assumed command on 1 November he retained Richthofen for three months to ensure continuity. Richthofen handed over to *Major* Hermann Plocher on 11 January 1938 and departed Spain at the end of the month. Volkmann's arrival also marked Hitler's renewed commitment to the Nationalist cause with the delivery of new aircraft and equipment. The *Legion's* strength rose to 100 aircraft with *K/88* receiving two He 111 *Staffeln*, while *J/88* had a second Bf 109 *Staffel* with the He 51s used for ground-attack durities. However, the new aircraft required 100-octane fuel, when most aircraft in Spain relied upon 87-octane, and the *Reich* provided only a trickle, so that fuel economy was a major element in Volkmann's planning. He arrived as the *Legion* concentrated around Soria ready to support alternate strategies; Franco wanted to assault Madrid while his allies preferred striking eastwards into Aragon. Enemy air power had been boosted by the arrival of the I-152 or *Super Chato*, but this proved less formidable than fog and snow which disrupted operations and caused both a Bf 109 and a He 111 to force-land behind enemy lines during the first half of December. The Republican government permitted its French and Russian friends to evaluate the aircraft which were then shipped to the Soviet Union. [22]

On 15 December the Republic pre-empted the strategic argument by attacking at Teruel, 180 kilometres south-east of Soria, but a week elapsed before Franco reluctantly abandoned plans for his Madrid offensive and took up the gauntlet. He reinforced the Teruel front despite advice from his allies, including Volkmann, and at a planning conference attended by Richthofen (who returned to Spain at the beginning of the month), he announced that a counter-offensive would begin on 29 December. [23] Volkmann's headquarters moved to Bronchales, 35 kilometres north-west of Teruel, which confirmed its reputation as the coldest city in Spain; the mechanics had to build temporary shelters to warm aircraft engines before take-off and operations were further hampered by snow until the counter-offensive was buried by a blizzard on 31 December.

It resumed on 17 January forcing the Republicans to strip troops north of the city in the Alfambra valley, which was then captured on 7 February in a day-long offensive. The *Condor Legion* softened up the defences and, each day for four days, flew 100 sorties and dropped 120 tonnes of bombs. In the face of overwhelming air superiority the Republican defence collapsed, exposing Teruel which fell on 17 February, when *K/88* and *A/88* dropped 65 tonnes of bombs, although *Leutnant* Eckehart Priebe's He 51 just missed a tank carrying the famous Republican general Valentín González, better known as *El Campesino* ('the Peasant'), to safety. The same day also marked the debut of the Ju 87B, a trio of which had been transferred from *Lehrgeschwader Greifswald* in mid-January. They were used for precision attacks upon strong points and demonstrated their ability to put bombs within five metres (5½ yards) of the target. This brought a triumphant conclusion to the *Legion*'s Teruel campaign which had cost it only five aircraft and 10 dead.

Teruel decimated the Republican forces and Franco decided to exploit the situation with a series of successive thrusts into Aragon north of Teruel, these lasting until resistance grew too strong and then being renewed on nearby sectors in the classic late 1918 tradition. With 460 aircraft (220 Italian and 100 German), the Nationalists achieved air superiority over the 550 Republican aircraft, including the latest I-16 Type 10. Franco's air support consisted of both Tactical and Operational-level missions, the latter striking reserves and communications deep in the enemy rear and arousing great fear in the Republican ranks. [24]

The campaign began south of the River Ebro on 9 March when *K/88* dropped 88 tonnes of bombs to leave the surviving defenders shell-shocked and unable to resist, leading to the collapse of the front. The *Legion* rapidly assumed the traditional role of cavalry with *K/88* dropping 45.5 tonnes on communications, the *Stukas* flying 12 sorties while *J/88*'s Bf 109s strafed the enemy to help the He 51s wreck every enemy counter-attack, bringing the total tonnage of bombs on the first day to 210 – a record for the Civil War. Within a week *A/88* was unable to locate useful targets and Volkmann switched his effort north of the Ebro, leaving support south of the river to the lumbering He 59 floatplanes of *AS/88*.

The air support ensured steady progress, allowing the Nationalists to reach the sea and split the Republic on 15 April. The *Luftwaffe* then conducted *Unternehmen 'Neptun'* against the Republican Fleet's bases, involving 59 sorties and 82.5 tonnes of bombs for the loss of one aircraft. This was a brief interlude because from 22 March Volkmann, despite bad weather, supported operations north of the Ebro. From 25 April the Nationalists swung southwards into the Levante towards Valencia and for two months crawled forward against fierce resistance; the *Legion Condor* suffered severe attrition from a resurgent enemy air force.

Volkmann was recalled to Berlin late in May but was left to cool his heels until a meeting at the *RLM* on 10 June. He told his masters he had lost 20 per cent of his strength since 9 March with 20 aircraft destroyed and seven badly damaged, while 38 crew were dead or missing. Only 16 Bf 109s remained serviceable and the He 51s could barely fly. He demanded either reinforcement or withdrawal but received no decision and when he returned to Spain he warned his commanders on 16 June that operations might have to be restricted. He was already under a cloud for expressing his fears of isolation if a general European conflict erupted – the first time after the *Anschluss* in March and again during the summer in the Sudetenland crisis.

The *Anschluss* crisis saw Wilberg replaced at *Sonderstab W* on 1 April by *Generalleutnant* (*General der Flieger* from June 1) Karl-Friedrich Schweickhard. In addition to Volkmann's want of nerve, Berlin was also concerned about friction between him and Franco and with the Sudetenland crisis, the *RLM* was slow to respond – apart from despatching a band! On 17 June Berlin decided to make *J/88* a complete Bf 109 unit, new fighters especially benefiting *3.J/88* under *Oberleutnant* Werner '*Vati*' ('Daddy') Mölders as the *Jagdgruppe* began to conduct sweeps of up to 32 fighters and usually proving triumphant in air battles.

While *AS/88*'s floatplanes were used briefly over land during March, their greatest contribution during the spring and early summer was interdicting the

Republic's maritime communications. Created under *Major* Karl-Heinz Wolff purely as a reconnaissance force, it began to carry torpedoes (nicknamed 'Eels') from January 1937 and *Oberleutnant* Werner Klümper (*Kommodore* of the torpedo-bomber-equipped *KG 26* in 1943–1944) damaged the 1,253 GRT freighter *Delfin* on 30 January. There was then a lull of several months before an anti-shipping campaign began during the second half of 1937 with the He 59s using bombs and 20mm cannon rather than torpedoes; most of the attacks were around Cartagena and Valencia.

With the arrival in November 1937 of *Major* Martin 'Iron Gustav' Harlinghausen, the campaign intensified with up to 16 sorties a day being flown by August 1938. Under Harlinghausen, ships were usually attacked in the approaches to ports whose facilities were also bombed. The He 59s *Zatapones* ('Big Shoes') sank 23 ships (55,161 GRT) during the Spanish Civil War and many small sailing vessels and fishing boats but 12 were lost in 1938 and 1939 including three to night fighters. [25]

As the Sudetenland crisis intensified, Volkmann had more pressing problems. During July *A/88* began bringing disturbing images of Republican preparations for an offensive across the Ebro towards Gandesa but Franco's headquarters ignored the warnings. On the night 24/25 July the enemy crossed the river supported by 260 aircraft and Gandesa was quickly under threat. Reinforcements, including 434 aircraft, were despatched and from 6 August the Nationalists, through limited offensives, waged a battle of attrition which began in stifling heat and ended with the last Republican troops withdrawing through falling snow on 18 November. [26]

With its forward bases under threat Volkmann immediately committed the *Legion's* 70 aircraft. During the first week the airmen were flying two or three sorties a day with 587 bomber sorties by *K/88* and *A/88* who dropped more than 566 tonnes of bombs while the *Stukakette* flew 77 sorties and dropped 37.5 tonnes of bombs. The bridges were the prime target and in August alone the Republican umbilical received more than 1,564 tonnes of bombs from *K/88* supported by the *Stukas*, although *A/88* reverted to a pure reconnaissance role (This air offensive mirrored the Allied operations on the Marne in July 1918.). The Germans alone would drop 1,713 tonnes of bombs during the campaign but while they hindered the movement of enemy supplies, and forced the Republicans to build bridges just under the water, Nationalist air power failed to isolate the battlefield. Fighter sweeps quickly established air superiority over the bridgehead although the *Katiuskas* would make occasional attacks upon their bases, destroying or damaging five Bf 109s at La Cenia on 4 October.

With the Sudetenland crisis bringing Europe to the verge of war, Volkmann was ordered to strip his squadrons to supply the *Reich* and 246 experienced aircrew returned to German shores. This robbed him of both his *Kommandeure*, Handrick being replaced by *Hauptmann* Walter Grabmann in *J/88*, while Mehnart was replaced by *Major* Fritz Härle at *K/88*. Having lost half his fighter pilots and bomber crews as well as a quarter of his reconnaissance and seaplane crews, Volkmann was forced to replace them with Spanish airmen who, luckily, proved very capable. However, this enforced situation led him to pen a highly critical and pessimistic letter to Berlin about the Spanish conduct of the war. For the *RLM* this was the final straw but it waited until the Munich Agreement was signed before recalling him on 13 November.

He was briefly replaced by Plocher, who supervised the final stages of air support for the Ebro battle aided by the arrival of five Ju 87 B which entered the fray on 30 October. The Ebro campaign cost the *Legion* ten aircraft, most to accidents, while 14 were badly damaged and there were 18 aircrew casualties. There was then a brief respite and, with the end of the Sudetenland crisis, reinforcements of men and machines arrived to replace many of the Spanish airmen as the *Legion* expanded to 96 aircraft, a fifth of total Nationalist air strength, including Bf 109 E, He 111 E/J and the Hs 126.

Volkmann's replacement on 1 December was *Generalmajor* Richthofen, accompanied by *Oberstleutnant* Hans Seidemann who replaced Plocher in what became a military marriage. They had three weeks to plan the next campaign, the occupation of Catalonia, which began on 23 December 1938. The Republican air force had lost 150 aircraft over the Ebro but remained aggressive and elusive to the end until *A/88* discovered its bases leading to devastating attacks. The bombers and *Stukas* focused their fury on communications, striking targets around Figueras at hourly intervals and contributed to the Nationalists' rapid advance, despite snow, with the French frontier reached on 9 February. [27]

Losses were heavy – 11 aircraft, or nearly 11.5 per cent of strength, and some 30 airmen of whom 21 were German, mostly due to accidents. Richthofen then moved to Toledo for the final assault upon Madrid. Fighter sweeps sought out the last remnants of Republican air power and *Oberleutnant* Hubertus von Bonin, commander of *3.J/88* since the Ebro battle, shot down a *Chato* over Alicante for the Legion's 314th and last aerial victory on 5 March. But the previous day Härle, *Kommandeur* of *K/88*, was killed when his He 111 exploded in mid-air over Madrid, apparently the victim of a faulty electric fuze in the bombs. Three *K/88* '*Schwarzemänner*' were killed by two explosions during the Bilbao campaign and during 1938 two aircraft suffered the same fate as Härle's. Indeed it was a problem which plagued the *Luftwaffe*, accounting for at least 12 aircraft and 24 lives between September 1939 and May 1940.

Yet the Spanish Civil War ended in farcical anti-climax, with the Republic collapsing in internecine fighting and surrendering to Franco on 26 March 1939. Tragically, before the *Legion's* final parade on 26 May, there were several fatal accidents but on that day 5,136 men departed from Vigo taking with them some 700 tonnes of equipment including all their modern aircraft.Some 19,000 men served in the *Legion Condor* which lost 226 dead (including 41 aircrew) and 139 wounded, while 449 had been injured in accidents! The materiel losses were 232 aircraft, 72 to enemy action, and the expenditure of munitions may be gauged from the fact *K/88* alone dropped more than 21,000 tonnes of bombs. The small training mission had produced 500 Spanish aircrew within Spain while another 40 pilots were trained in Germany. [28]

While the experience in Spain apparently confirmed the supremacy of the high-performance bomber, as well as the value of dive-bombing, it also showed the need to strengthen defensive armament which influenced Ju 88 development. Experience also led Udet to increase the fighter-to-bomber production ratio from 25 per cent to 33 per cent while strengthening armament through the introduction of the 20mm Oerlikon *MG FF/M* cannon. [29] The need for a long-range fighter underlined development of the Bf 110, although none was sent to Spain. There was also a requirement for an armoured ground-attack aircraft issued in December 1937 leading to the Henschel Hs 129, while in Moscow a similar requirement a few months later led to the Ilyushin Il 2.

Yet some of the after-action reports included words of caution. Lützow noted: 'The fact that we suffered only slight losses despite being outnumbered is due to the inadequate training and erratic leadership of the enemy airmen, and to the greater speed of out own fighters….' Another noted: 'It proved impossible to inflict lasting damage on, or to put out of action completely, any enemy air force ground installation. It also proved impossible to knock out enemy air forces on the ground because of the high degree of flexibility of enemy formations.' Both these statements would prove prophetic in the coming months.

Richthofen also recognised the problem of providing air support for mechanised formations striking deep into enemy territory. Upon his return to Berlin in 1937 he had campaigned for the *Luftwaffe* to address this problem, but with little initial success, although *Wehrmacht* exercises that year demonstrated his perception. [30]

Meanwhile, the *Luftwaffe* continued to expand from 84,000 officers and men by the summer of 1937 to 220,500 a year later (see Table 2-1) as conscription took hold, although there were many volunteers. [31] The expansion of the *Luftwaffe* required more generals and led to a wry story circulating in the *Luftwaffe* about a caged lion which Göring was supposed to keep in the *RLM*. One evening the lion managed to open the lock, strolled around the *RLM*, encountered a general, gobbled him up then returned to the cage and reset the lock. Every few days he would unlock his cage and find another general to eat but it was six months before anyone noticed!

Table 2–1: Luftwaffe expansion in Staffeln, 1937–1939

Type	1937	1938	1939
Fighter	42	54	73
Bomber	94	90	95
Stuka/Schlacht	15	19	29
Reconnaissance	17	14	24
Corps	17	23	34
Transport	6	9	9
Naval	10	16	18
Total	201	227	282

All strengths on April 1 of each year. It should be noted that these figures include *Staffeln* raised on that date.
Collins and Miller web site, Holm's web site, Schliephake Appendix G. Völker.

A mixture of motives spurred recruitment; there was the glamour of aviation, the promise of a less rigid relationship between the ranks while spearheading the resurgence of national pride. Many were also encouraged by the prospect of learning to drive because the *Luftwaffe* was the only fully motorised service and driving was as much a dream of young men then as now. There were also plenty of inducements to join the *Luftwaffe* including special labour certificates, subsidies and loans and the prospect of remaining in aviation once a man was demobbed. It was worth noting that senior *Luftwaffe* officers, like those in the other services, received bribes to stay 'loyal' with even 'C' List Richthofen receiving RM4,000 ($950.00) in 1943. [32]

While the closer relationship between the ranks reflected the Nazi ethos of dissolving class barriers, at this time relatively few of the junior officers, NCOs and enlisted men were Nazis, although future fighter ace (258 victories) Walter 'Nowi' Nowotny regularly wore a Party pin. The *Luftwaffe* was certainly associated with the Nazis; conservatives referred to the Royal Army, the Imperial Navy and the Party Air Force, but it appears to have been no more committed to the Party than the remainder of the *Wehrmacht*. However, every recruiting draft included one or two *HJ Quex* who were asked to report on their comrades by the authorities (see note 33). There also remained some army traditions such as officers' committees in which senior officers vetted not only their juniors but also their fiancées. One officer who faced such a veto was future air ace *Major* Helmut Wick, who was the top *Experte* (56 victories) when he was killed in November 1940. [33]

Providing aircrew proved a taxing problem with the emphasis upon quantity rather than quality hindered by a chronic lack of instructors with one for every six pupils instead of one for every four. This was one reason for what Göring called a 'plague' of accidents with 108 aircraft destroyed and 1,290 damaged in 1937 at the cost of 147 men killed and 2,422 injured. Of course this also reflected an increase in flying hours, especially by the squadrons, from 603,000 in 1935 (40,000 by squadrons) to 750,000 in 1936 (290,000 by squadrons), and the technical sophistication of the new generation of aircraft and wheels-up landings undoubtedly accounted for the 75 Bf 109s, He 111s and Do 17s damaged in 1937.

However, the chronic unreliability of the Ju 86's Jumo 205 diesels was also a factor and 'The Flying Coffee Grinder' as it was called, was involved in 56 accidents during 1937 although the leaders tended to blame the pilots rather than the aircraft. [34] The devolution of flying training to semi-operational commands did not help and while, as has been mentioned, in February 1939 a *Chef des Ausbildungswesens* (chief of training resources) was created under Kühl to co-ordinate the inspectorates, it was primarily interested in operational training. Responsibility for flying training was devolved to the *Luftgaue* which in turn devolved this to newly-established *Höhere Fliegerausbildungskommandos* (senior flying training commands).

Operational and administrative command was split between seven *Luftkreiskommandos*, but the need for better operational control saw Stumpff re-organise them into three *Luftwaffengruppenkommandos* (air group commands): Kesselring's Berlin-based *Luftwaffengruppenkommando 1* in the east; Felmy's *Luftwaffengruppenkommando 2* in the north-west; and Sperrle's *Luftwaffengruppenkommando 3* in the south-west. Geography and roles dictated that two autonomous commands remained: Keller's *Luftwaffenkommando Ostpreussen* in East Prussia and Zander's naval *Luftwaffenkommando See*.

The aircraft were the *Luftwaffe*'s sword while its shield was the *Flak* arm which also expanded steadily with personnel strength rising from 46,140 in October 1937 to 98,600 in July 1939 (see Table 2–2). The *Flakwaffe* had not only an excellent range of weapons from the 8.8cm *Flak 18* and *36*, through the 3.7cm *Flak 18* and *36* to the 2cm *Flak 30*, all of which were supported by electro-mechanical fire control computers.

Table 2-2: Flak expansion in batteries, 1937–1939

Type	1937	1938	1939
Gun batteries	147	192	321
S/L batteries	40	55	49
Total	187	247	370

Sources: Table 2-1.

Such was Göring's confidence that he famously claimed that if any bombs fell on Germany then people could call him by the Jewish name 'Meyer'. Curiously enough, when civilians raised this point during the war he never took offence. Nevertheless he had good cause for his confidence for an anti-aircraft barrier was built parallel with the Rhine from June 1938 as part of the *West Wall* defences, to be known as *Luftverteidigungszone West* under *Generalleutnant* Karl Kitzinger. It was some 600 kilometres long, 10–30 kilometres deep with 1,300 guns in some 1,500 concrete positions.

Hitler's confidence in the *Luftwaffe* was such that on 5 November 1937 he informed his military leaders that the *Reich* would be expanded into Austria and Czechoslovakia even if this meant war. Many Army leaders, including Blomberg, protested and Hitler decided to purge the 'defeatists'. He did so on 4 February 1938 and Göring, who helped execute the purge against the Army leadership which included Blomberg, extended it to remove those within the *Luftwaffe* who were more 'old' than 'eagle'. These included Wilberg, who returned to the colours when war was imminent and given a training command (*Höhere Fliegerausbildungskommando 4*) which he held until his death in an air crash on 20 November 1941.

The Old Eagles had barely departed when Hitler returned to his Austrian homeland. The Austrian Nazi party under Dr Arthur Seyss-Inquart instigated a crisis and the chancellor, Dr Kurt Schuschnigg, visited Berchtesgaden in February to defuse the situation. He was coerced, with the aid of Sperrle's brooding presence, into accepting Seyss-Inquart as the interior minister, but on 9 March decided to lance the *Anschluss* boil with a plebiscite, an announcement which provoked Hitler to new heights of fury. He demanded military intervention which had already been anticipated in *Sonderfall 'Otto'* (contingency plan 'Otto') with the mobilisation of *8. Armee*, Sperrle's *Luftkreis 5* and Kesselring's *Luftkreis 3* which were to seize the country after a telephone ultimatum to Schuschnigg. While some bombers were to be kept in reserve, it was expected the *Luftwaffe* would merely support the advance, capture airfields and drop leaflets. Göring recalled Milch from a skiing holiday and briefed him personally so he could smooth the logistical arrangements for Sperrle. [35]

The *Österreichische Luftstreitkräfte* (*LStrKr*) was in no condition to oppose the *Luftwaffe*. In January 1936 it had only 151 aircraft and while Löhr had ambitious plans for some 15 and later 20 *Staffeln*, by March 1938 it had only six *Jagdstaffeln* with Fiat CR 20bis/30/32, two *Bombenstaffeln* with Caproni Ca 133 and two *Aufklärungsstaffeln* with Fiat A 120 and Romeo Ro 37. While most of these aircraft were from Italy, German aircraft had been evaluated and the He 112 and Ju 86 selected but limited funds reduced the numbers of both aircrew and spares so that on 11 March Löhr had only 210 aircraft of which only 33 were serviceable. [36] Sperrle had the active role of assembling a *Jagdgruppe*, three *Kampfgruppen* and five *Aufklärungsstaffeln*, most of which were assigned to *Generalmajor* Ludwig Wolff's *Höhere Fliegerkommandeur 5* apart from three corps *Staffeln* which were assigned to *Stabsoffizier der Flieger (Stofl) 8.Armee*. Kesselring's role was purely support and he raised three *Transportgruppen* with the aid of *Lufthansa* Ju 52s to fly in troops and equipment.

Aerial demonstrations – threatening massed flights of aircraft to demonstrate German might – began on 10 March as Schuschnigg resigned in favour of President Wilhelm Miklas who rejected Hitler's call to appoint Seyss-Inquart chancellor. The following morning Löhr ordered day and night reconnaissance flights along the border, but that afternoon there were ominous reports of German aircraft flying over Austrian territory. The blustering Göring directed a barrage of telephone calls upon the unfortunate Miklas who capitulated that evening and in the midst of attending a diplomatic ball, Milch was ordered to begin the *Luftwaffe* occupation the following morning.

Ironically, trainers of *Oberst* Vierling, Sperrle's training commander, were the first over Vienna on 12 March dropping leaflets, followed by Do 17 Es on a similar mission, one of the bombers then landing at the city's Aspern airfield. The bomber was quickly followed by Wolff with two infantry companies to secure the airfield. As leaflets rained down on Austrian towns other transports followed bringing in some 2,000 troops. By the end of the first day nine *Luftwaffe Staffeln* landed unopposed at Austrian air bases being not only welcomed, but actively assisted, by the *Luftstreitkräfte*. Austria was quickly secured and on 15 March there was a massive fly-past of 720 German and Austrian aircraft led by one carrying Wolff with Löhr in its co-pilot's seat. Although only three aircraft were lost in accidents during '*Otto*' the operation demonstrated serious weaknesses within the *Wehrmacht*. Staff work was poor and this especially hindered the mobilisation of reservists and, despite Milch's best efforts, civilian vehicles had to be impressed to transfer fuel in large drums due to the lack of petrol bowsers [37].

The *Luftwaffe* learned from its mistakes and received a substantial reinforcement when it absorbed nearly 4,100 *Luftstreitkräfte* and Austrian army flak and administrative personnel on 12 April. However, many senior officers were dismissed including the veteran Yllam (see Chapter One) who retired to die amid his memories at Klagenfurt in January 1942. [38] Löhr, now a *Generalleutnant*, provided continuity by assuming command of the new *Luftwaffenkommando Ostmark* (or *Österreich*) whose terrestrial infrastructure was under the newly created *Luftgau XVII*. However, he was given a German chief of staff in the shape of the Nazi sympathiser, *Oberstleutnant* Günther Korten.

Hitler now turned on Czechoslovakia which was, with Poland, a key eastern strategic threat. He decided to destroy the stronger Czechs first by using the Sudetenland, with its largely German populace, as the wedge, partly because the Czech equivalent of the Maginot Line ran through this region. From the *Luftwaffe*'s viewpoint it was especially important because France had arranged in 1934 to station bombers and 400 tonnes of bombs in Bohemia (western Czechoslovakia) while the Soviet-Czech mutual assistance pact of March 1935 provided the Czech air force with Tupolev SB bombers which became the Avia B.71. [39]

As Goebbels propaganda shrilled claims of Czech persecution, Hitler called his military leadership to a conference on 28 May and announced that he wanted the country 'wiped off the map.' Preparations were to be complete by 1 October and while Czechoslovakia was the prime target, no-one was under any delusions that France, and possibly Britain, would not become involved. Army contingency plans were updated as *Planstudie 1938* and with *Luftwaffengruppenkommando 1* on the Czechs' northern border in June 1938, Kesselring began drafting a support plan which was published on 11 July as *Planstudie Grün* ('Study Plan Green') with detailed planning assigned to the *Höherer Fliegerkommandeuren* (*Fliegerdivisionen* from 1 August) and the *Luftgaue*. Later planning was extended southwards to Sperrle and Löhr. [40] The *Luftwaffe* sought a knock-out blow to destroy the Czech air force then provide direct and indirect support of the Army's advance, but on 30 May the sword was stayed by Hitler's order to spare industrial centres where possible which could support the *Reich*. A notable feature of the later stages of the campaign was the creation, probably on 1 August, of *Fliegerdivision zbV* using three *Schlachtfliegergruppen* of Hs 123 light dive-bombers while another two, with He 45 close-air support aircraft, were assigned to Sperrle, these *Gruppen* being created by *Oberleutnant* Adolf Galland who exploited his experience in Spain. [41]

The *Luftwaffe* also planned its first airborne operation, when paratroop units were created as part of *Regiment General Göring* from October 1935. Kesselring encouraged their development and used them in the 1937 *Wehrmacht* manoeuvres. Fittingly they were now assigned to Kesselring who assigned them, on 1 September, under the newly created 7. *Fliegerdivision* led by the *Luftwaffeninspkteur der Luftlande und Fallschirmtruppe Generalmajor* Kurt Student with six *Transportfliegergruppen* to augment the two active *Gruppen*. The division was to be used in Exercise (*Übung*) 'Freudenthal' with paratroops dropped 250 kilometres (150 miles) behind the Czech fortifications. [42]

The Czech Air Force was not regarded as a major problem; indeed, Jeschonnek referred to '…those ridiculous Hussites.' With 54 squadrons and 800 largely obsolescent aircraft it was a slender reed as was its potential ally, the Russian *VVS-RKKA* which was numerically strong (some 7,000 aircraft) but had been ravaged by Stalin's purges which had decimated its leadership. But on 12 August Hitler discovered the *Luftwaffe*'s feet of clay when he received a *Wehrmacht* survey.

On 1 August the *Luftwaffe* had an impressive 2,928 aircraft, including 81 transports, with the latest Bf 109 D, He 111 H and Do 17M/P entering service, but total production of these modern aircraft was less than 500 aircraft a month. While the *Kampfgruppen* mostly had modern aircraft, including some Ju 86 'coffee grinders', the *Jagdgruppen* had not received the Bf 110 – indeed the heavy fighter groups (*Jagdgruppen, Schwere*) were not formed until 1 November. Most *Jagdgruppen* had Bf 109s but they were under strength, averaging only 26 aircraft, many of which lacked radios; seven (31%) had biplanes (mostly Ar 68) and the recently formed *IV/JG 132* was equipped with requisitioned Japanese He 112s. From training formations two *Staffel*-sized *Reservejagdgruppen* were created and assigned to Sperrle. Low spares production cut serviceability to 57 per cent; 60 per cent of aircraft required an overhaul, while maintenance depots held engine stocks which could support only 4–5 per cent of front line strength. It was later estimated the supply of spares and tools would have supported barely a month's operations. The serviceability rate was raised by 26 September to 94 per cent due to careful organisation and a severe reduction in flying hours, which hit training badly. Worse was the problem of inexperienced aircrew. The *Luftwaffe* had only two-thirds of the men it was supposed to have and of 2,577 aircrew barely a third (1,432) were fully qualified. Effectively this reduced the *Kampfgruppen* to 378 aircraft and the *Jagdgruppen* to 537, 32.5 per cent and 83.5 per cent of their strength.

Undaunted by its problems, the *Luftwaffe* leadership accelerated preparations for *Fall Grün*, the invasion of Czechoslovakia, whose main blow would come from the north and the north-west supported by 1,200 aircraft of Kesselring, whose Silesian, Saxon and Thuringian airfields were shielded by two borrowed Naval *Freya* radars. Kesselring would also be responsible for the airborne assault by 7. *Fliegerdivision* which had 400 transports although there was considerable opposition from the Army leadership to '*Freudenthal*'. Sperrle would support *12. Armee's* attack from the south-west with 650 aircraft, while Löhr had 180 aircraft to support *14. Armee's* attack from the south. The western defences were stripped to 400 aircraft (excluding *Luftwaffenkommando See*) mostly under Felmy, who had only 175 bombers. Some 500 fighters were assembled for *Grün*, but a third were assigned home defence duties.

Fortunately for the *Luftwaffe*, its opponents in Great Britain and France were even weaker. The British front line strength on 1 October was 1,606 aircraft with a 25 per cent reserve, while the French had 1,454 with a 50 per cent reserve. But of the allies' combined 700 fighters only 71 were modern. In March, London and Paris audited their air forces and their chiefs-of-air staff, Marshal of the Royal Air Force Sir Cyril Newall and Général Joseph Vuillemin, stated that their bomber forces were incapable of effective offensive operations. In his annual report on 10 March Air Chief Marshal Sir Edgar Ludlow-Hewitt commented '…our bomber force is, judged from a war standard, practically useless. [43]'

Both had an accurate picture of *Luftwaffe* strength, which they estimated at 3,000, and the French certainly had detailed orders of battle. Vuillemin assessed the accuracy of his intelligence 16–21 August during his famous tour of the German aircraft industry. Although his report was later dismissed as defeatism, aggravated by fear, it was actually an extremely pragmatic assessment which led to an acceleration of French aerial re-armament. [44] But the politicians and the general public were also influenced by Jeremiahs such as the famous aviator, Charles A. Lindbergh. As the Sudetenland crisis grew, the dread of aerial bombardment and the knowledge of their national military unpreparedness influenced the British and French politicians and led to Chamberlain's first flight to Munich on 14 September in a desperate effort to negotiate a peaceful solution.

But six days later the German *Gruppen* moved to their operational airfields as Europe seemed poised upon another bloody war. Göring's nerves were hardly soothed by pessimistic reports from Felmy about the prospects of an air war against Great Britain. Astonishingly it was not until the *Anschluss* crisis that Felmy, whose command was closest to the British Isles, was asked to investigate the problem and he concluded that without bases in the Low Country his *Kampfgruppen* could not strike in September; Göring promptly reprimanded Felmy, planning to replace Felmy's British industry until they received heavy bombers. [45] This report arrived on 22 September with his old friend *Oberst* Ulrich Kessler who was deputy air attaché in London to put more backbone into *Luftwaffenkommando 2*. But when Kessler met Göring in Carinhall on 17 September he begged him to avoid war with the British and in November he became *Kommodore* of *KG 152*.

Chamberlain was willing to betray the Czechs and signed the Munich Agreement on 30 September, giving Berlin control of the Sudetenland. The unopposed occupation spanned 1–10 October, supported by 500 aircraft, some of which demonstrated over

Czech cities at the cost of four aircraft; three in accidents and one courier aircraft shot down by trigger-happy *Flak* gunners in Vienna. From 13 October the *Luftwaffe* began to stand down and the ad hoc *Gruppen* which augmented its strength were mostly disbanded apart from the Hs 123 units. But the *Luftwaffe* demonstrated its growing proficiency in airborne operations when some 300 aircraft and gliders landed in the Sudetenland in front of Hitler on 6 October, although civilians had earlier cleared the landing zone of all obstacles.

To allow the *Luftwaffe Oberbefehlshaber der Luftwaffe* (*ObdL* – commander in chief) to focus upon operational/strategic operations in the aftermath of Munich, the other services were given limited tactical control of the squadrons supporting them. *Luftwaffe* generals with army and navy headquarters (*Luftwaffe Generale beim Oberbefehlshaber das Heeres* (*ObdH*) and *Oberbefehlshaber der Kriegsmarine* (*ObdM*) were established under former gunner *Generalmajor* Rudolf Bogatsch and former seaplane pilot *Generalmajor* Hans Ritter respectively but Göring held tightly to the most important elements of air power and the navy lost its fighter squadrons.

Although Hitler claimed he had no further territorial ambitions after the Munich Agreement, his warped mind felt cheated by Chamberlain. He encouraged the Slovaks in the east of Czechoslovakia to demand independence by March 1939 and the elderly Czech president, Emile Hácha, went to Berlin on 14 March to seek a negotiated solution. Instead he found Göring threatening to bomb Prague, although with flying conditions deteriorating with every hour, 'Fatty' knew this was an increasingly hollow threat. Hácha reluctantly signed away his country's independence on 15 March, and the Slovaks confirmed their independence but quickly became a 'protectorate' of the *Reich*. German troops promptly occupied western Czechoslovakia, supported by 500 aircraft drawn largely from Sperrle who lost a pair of aircraft and seven men in accidents. The *Luftwaffe* gained vital strategic air bases while the Army swelled by a third by gorging on looted military equipment. Three days later Germany occupied the former German port of Memel (Klaipeda), with *Luftwaffenkommando Ostpreussen* demonstrating over the city for an hour to dissuade resistance. The German aggression now steeled hearts in both Paris and London where military support was pledged for Poland if it was similarly threatened. Chamberlain warned publicly on 31 March that aggression against Poland would lead to war. [46]

The following day the *Luftwaffe* was again re-organised. Kesselring's, Felmy's and Sperrle's *Luftwaffengruppenkommandos* were renamed *Luftflotten* while Löhr's was upgraded to *Luftflotte 4*. The same day Rowehl's secret strategic reconnaissance unit was renamed *Aufklärungsgruppe ObdL* with a second *Staffel* as the *Luftwaffe* began planning operations against Great Britain. However Felmy's latest pessimistic appreciation, *Planstudie 1939*, further irritated Göring. To help Felmy interdict Britain's sea lanes, *Generalmajor* Joachim Coeler was appointed *Führer der Luftstreitkräfte* (air corps commander) to conduct minelaying operations while *Generalleutnant* Hans Geisler became *General zbV der Luftflotte 2* (general for special employment with *Luftflotte* 2) for bombing and torpedo attacks. During the early summer British radar monitored Geisler's North Sea exercises, with one *Gruppe*-sized formation approaching Norfolk but it turned back some 10 kilometres away.

Only now did the *Luftwaffe* General Staff finally receive a proper air intelligence organisation with the creation of a *Fremde Luftmächteabteilung* (Foreign Air Power

Directorate) under lizard-eyed *Oberstleutnant* Josef 'Beppo' Schmid. Previously *Luftwaffe* intelligence had a low status, largely relying upon the army's organisation, the *Abwehr*, and it was not until June 1935 that the *Luftwaffenführungstab* created an intelligence office under *Oberst Freiherr* von Bülow. However it was manned by reservists and civilians and its activities consisted of assembling newspaper clippings. Furthermore, it had no access to Martini's seven communications intelligence (Comint) stations or Rowehl's photographs and no reports from diplomatic attachés.

Schmid was poorly qualified for the post: he was not an airman, he had no intelligence experience and spoke no foreign languages, but he was a friend of Göring. Yet the new intelligence organisation retained its lowly status for Schmid's opposite number in the Royal Air Force was equivalent to a *Generalmajor*! His staff training helped him recognise the weaknesses of the intelligence organisation and he defined his role, established priorities and began acquiring information. The *Abwehr* provided him with spy data augmented by reports from the attachés and he received input from both Martini's comint organisation and Rowehl. Schmid had good relations with Milch, who would provide industrial insight, and regarded himself as an expert on the British, but *Luftwaffe* technical intelligence remained weak until the end of the war; indeed it was apparently on Martini's initiative that three inconclusive signals intelligence missions were flown in the retired commercial airship, *LZ 130 Graf Zeppelin II*, to investigate British radar activity [47].

Martini was slower to develop radar and by September 1939 was still evaluating a naval *Freya* (*FuMG 39*) search radar; two were on order while a contract for two *Würzburg* (*FuMG 62*) anti-aircraft fire control radars had been signed. But Martini had provided the *Luftwaffe* with an electronic precision bombing system in the '*X-Gerät*' which was based upon radio navigation technology and this had equipped an operational unit, *Luftnachrichtenabteilung 100*, for nearly a year while another system, '*Y- Gerät*', was at an advanced stage of development when war broke out.

The *X-Gerät* would soon see action. Schmid produced three detailed studies on enemy air power in Poland (*Studie Grün*), France (*Rot*) and Great Britain (*Blau*), the latter being updated until the end of the war with input from specialists and academics. *Studie Grün* was especially relevant, for two days after the *Luftwaffe* re-organisation, Hitler began planning an invasion of Poland known as Contingency White (*Fall Weiss*). It was to support '*Weiss*' that Jeschonnek created the *Fliegerführer zbV* which was not a purely tactical command (like the ad hoc *Fliegerdivision zbV*) but an Operational-level one with *Stukagruppen* and long-range reconnaissance aircraft.

As the beautiful summer of 1939 reached its peak, the *Luftwaffe* prepared to go to war as Goebbels' propaganda machine shrieked once more about the persecution of Germans by the evil Slavs. While thousands of *Luftwaffe* men hoped against hope for another peaceful solution, their leaders were less optimistic and waited with bated breath. Göring, who had made every effort to establish good relation with Poland's leaders, was appalled but when he tried to dissuade his *Führer* he was called 'an old woman.' He would seek a political agreement through backdoor links almost to the moment when the first shots were fired, and his ultimate commitment to military action was largely due to German Foreign Minister Joachim Ribbentrop negotiating a non-aggression agreement with the Soviet Union on 25 August.

Chapter Three

The Shadow of Douhet

Poland

Over the next 12 months the *Luftwaffe* helped to ensure the *Reich*'s dominance of Europe, demonstrating that Douhet had been right in forecasting the importance of air operations in military campaigns. Yet a year's operations would leave its weaknesses only too apparent.

ObdL's initial strategy, *Planstudie Grün* of 1 March 1939, envisaged a defensive strategy in the West and an offensive one in the East. The *Oberkommando des Heeres* (*OKH* – Army High Command) plans for what became *Fall 'Weiss'* (Contingency 'White') drafted two months later, formed the framework for *Luftwaffe* planning against Poland and benefited from Schmid's inputs.

With Germany now occupying territory around Poland, a network of 74 comint stations assessed the *Polskie Lotnictwo Wojskowe- PLW* (Polish Air Force) order of battle and intentions, while *Abwehr* (Intelligence) agents supplemented the information. Rowehl's *AufklGr ObdL* began to assemble key photographic images about the same time, but it was not until July that the *Fernaufklärungstaffeln* began penetrating Polish air space, flying up to 160 kilometres beyond the German frontier to build up a detailed picture of Poland's communications system and industrial base. [1] Yet Schmid over-estimated *PLW* strength at 740 aircraft (315 fighters, 130 bombers) when it was, in fact, 494 aircraft, of which 392 were combat aircraft.

The *Wehrmacht*'s battle plan envisaged *Generaloberst* Fedor von Bock's *Heeresgruppe Nord* occupying northern Poland, while the main blow would be launched from Silesia by *Generaloberst* Gerd von Rundstedt's *Heeresgruppe Süd*, whose spearhead would be *General der Artillerie* Walter von Reichenau's *10. Armee* using mechanised corps to drive some 500 kilometres north-eastwards to Warsaw, ignoring their flanks and rear to reach the Vistula before the enemy could retreat across the river. Bock would be supported by Kesselring's *Luftflotte 1* and Rundstedt by Löhr's *Luftflotte 4*, representing a total of 2,315 aircraft including more than 70 per cent of the *Luftwaffe*'s 1,176 bombers, and all its *Stuka*- and Schlachtgruppen. In accordance with *Luftwaffe* doctrine the aerial campaign would open with a pulverising double blow, the most important being the destruction of the *PLW* on the ground, followed by a massive attack upon Warsaw to be known as *Unternehmen 'Wasserkante'* (Operation 'Seaside') intended to erode both Poland's industrial base and its political will.

Once these operations were complete the *Luftwaffe* would provide the army with unlimited Tactical and Operational support. Kesselring's subordinates, who received a verbal briefing on 31 August, were *Generalleutnant* Ulrich Grauert's *1. Fliegerdivision*, *Generalmajor* Helmuth Förster's *Lehrdivision* and *Generalleutnant* Wimmer's *Luftwaffenkommando Ostpreussen* in East Prussia. Löhr had *Generalmajor*

Loerzer's *2. Fliegerdivision*, to which Richthofen's *Fliegerführer zbV* was attached to support *10. Armee* under the Anglophile *Nazi* (and International Olympic Committee member) Reichenau, whom Richthofen met shortly before the campaign together with his colourless chief of staff, *Oberst* Friedrich Paulus, who would later command the renamed *6. Armee*.

From July the pace of preparation increased with more intensive reconnaissance and the stocking of 155 airfields and airstrips. There was also a last-minute 30 per cent expansion of the fighter force through the creation of 26 *Staffeln*, including 12 *Nachtjagd* (night fighter) and three *Zerstörer*. It was easier to create *Zerstörerstaffeln* than to equip them; indeed on 1 September there were only 102 Bf 110 in service and *Major* Walter Grabmann, *Kommandeur* of *I.(Z)/LG 1* (and last *Kommandeur* of *J/88*), later noted that many *Staffeln* had only seven serviceable aircraft due to a spares shortage. [2] Only three of the 10 *Zerstörergruppen* were genuine units with the others flying false colours using the Bf 109 *Dora* (Bf 109D) leading to them receiving temporary *Jagdgruppe* designations.

Most *Jagdgruppen* had their full establishment of Bf 109E (*Emils*), but to preserve them the *Doras* were used for training until mobilisation and *3./JG 54* reportedly used former Czech Avia B.534 biplanes until just before '*Weiss*' began. To support the advance the *Luftgaukommandos* on the Polish border created *Luftgaustaben zbV* (Special Employment Air District Staffs) to provide logistics, communications and air defence, but Richthofen, whose *Fliegerführer zbV* would be reined to the mechanised forces, had well-founded concerns about their effectiveness. Jeschonnek had anticipated the problem and two days earlier created a new transport *Geschwader*, *KGzbV 2*, to support Löhr while *KGzbV 172* would support Kesselring with some 270 aircraft, including a proportion of *Lufthansa*'s 147-strong fleet. However, these moves proved to be little more than an aspirin to cure pneumonia.

With only the 1937 exercise to demonstrate the validity of *Luftwaffe* doctrine, the generals took counsel of their fears and in late August demanded a greater degree of air support at the start of the campaign. Hitler backed them on 31 August leaving a grumbling Jeschonnek to make major last-minute revisions of *ObdL*'s plans, which saw a diversion of half the strike force to hit enemy communications. '*Wasserkante*' now slipped to the latter part of *A-Tag* (A-Day), the German equivalent of D-Day, but was now augmented by *LnAbt 100*'s night precision attacks. The *Luftwaffe* planned to open the campaign by striking the *PLW* at its air bases, although it was aware on 25 August that the Poles had dispersed their squadrons to guard against this eventuality. In the event, it would work to the Germans' advantage for the command of the *PLW* was already fragmented and the dispersal of the squadrons would aggravate problems of command, control and logistics.

The campaign began on 1 September but was hampered by morning fog and mist which meant only five of Kesselring's 15 *Kampf*- and *Stukagruppen* took off on schedule and led to the postponement of '*Wasserkante*'. There were scattered aerial clashes and the first German air victory went to *Oberleutnant* Frank Neubert of *I./St.G 2* whose gunner blew apart the P.11c fighter of Captain Mieczyslaw Medwecki. [3] Counter-air missions rapidly declined in the face of weak Polish air opposition and the *Luftwaffe* adopted a policy of seeking out and swooping on occupied 'nests'.

The prime role of the *Luftwaffe* was to provide direct and indirect support for the army's advance and this created a synergy which benefited both greatly. Through striking communications, the *Kampf-* and *Stukagruppen* hamstrung enemy movement, allowing German mechanised forces to advance deep into enemy territory overrunning airstrips and the early warning network, while also disrupting command, control and logistics. By 6 September the *PLW* squadrons were running out of supplies, forcing the abandonment of numerous aircraft and on 18 September the surviving 98 combat aircraft withdrew to Rumania.

With the decline in enemy air power the *Luftwaffe* could increase support for the army and help accelerate its advance. Surprisingly, in the first two days the emphasis was upon tactical air support but then the emphasis switched to operational support and Loerzer despatched reconnaissance aircraft with radio links to the *Kampfgeschwader* which had rapid-response forces, each of one or two *Ketten*, ready to set-off at a few minutes' notice to interdict retreating Polish troops whose columns were frequently struck by low-level bombers. [4]

But the speed of the advance posed serious problems of command and control for, as in France two decades earlier, army headquarters lost touch with their forward units. Each army and army group (*Armee Oberkommando* and *Heeresgruppe*) had a *Kommandeur der Luftwaffe* (*Koluft*) who commanded army *Fern-* and *Nahaufklärungsstaffeln* (long-range reconnaissance and short-range corps squadrons) and were supposed to co-ordinate air-ground operations. But they were only advisors and had neither direct contact with, nor tactical control over, the fighter and strike units. These latter were controlled by the *Fliegerverbindungsoffizier - Flivo* (air liaison officer) who were responsible not to the army but to the *Luftwaffe*, keeping their own commanders constantly informed of the situation on the ground through radio-equipped vehicles; indeed there was no common radio frequency with *Koluft* units. [5]

Richthofen suffered worst of all and as early as 3 September commented in his diary that the army headquarters never seemed to know the location of the front line. From *A-Tag* he began committing units according to his own interpretation of the situation inevitably leading to 'friendly fire' incidents and actually preventing the crossing of the Vistula when *Stukas* demolished a bridge on 8 September unaware a *Panzer* division was about to cross [6]! Loerzer was useless. Richthofen, however, wanted to be in the thick of the action and he flew personal reconnaissance missions in a Fi 156 *Storch* (Stork), seeking to co-ordinate air and ground operations by reporting to army command posts, although his claims were not always believed. This also exposed him needlessly; indeed, *Major* Werner Spielvogel, his *Schlachtgruppe Kommandeur* was killed when his *Storch* fell to anti-aircraft fire over Warsaw on 9 September [7].

Even the *Luftwaffe*'s formidable signals network was brought to the verge of ruin. Each *Fliegerdivision* seemed well-endowed with signals support – a telephone company, five liaison platoons, two radio aircraft as well as telephone/teleprinter units –but the system was designed to follow an army advancing at a pedestrian seven kilometres a day. The *Panzer* divisions advanced at an average 40 kilometres a day with the result that land-line communication collapsed and the increasing demands on the radios meant messages were taking up to three hours to get through! [8] Where possible the Germans had to exploit the surviving elements of the Polish communications network which they had previously sought to wreck.

The logistics system was also unable to keep pace with the advance and by 11 September, despite fuel conservation, Richthofen's *Stukas* which had flown three sorties a day on *A-Tag* were reduced to one. Milch roamed the battlefield trying to help but the situation eased only from 13 September when a force of 21 *Staffeln* was assembled for Löhr who subordinated them to the *ad hoc Geschwader zbV Ahlefeld.* [9] On occasion the desperate Germans were forced to scavenge enemy supply depots to survive, just as in 1918.

The rapid German advance meant thousands of Polish troops were left behind the front line and from 8 September, just as the assault began on Warsaw, the isolated troops tried to break out near the forests around Ilza, south of Radom, and at the River Burza. This led to a confused series of battles lasting nine days in which *Flak* batteries were often the backbone of German resistance on the ground. But it was the aerial onslought from Richthofen and Grauert which doomed the Poles, although communications were not always reliable and on one occasion Löhr's chief of staff, *Oberst* Korten, had to intervene to ensure support for *8. Armee.* Reconnaissance aircraft usually discovered Polish columns which were blasted by the *Kampf-* and *Stukagruppen*, those who fled into the forest being literally smoked out by incendiary bombs and on 17 September the last survivors surrendered. Göring later enthused to the *Luftwaffe*: 'If you perform in the West as you did in Poland, then the British too, will run.' The implications of this success and statement did not become apparent until eight months later.

Only Warsaw held out: the city had been under sporadic air attack since 8 September. Just after midnight on 12/13 September, Jeschonnek telephoned Löhr with orders for an afternoon incendiary raid by Grauert and Richthofen upon northern Warsaw, centred upon the Ghetto which was due north of the main railway station. There was no time to co-ordinate what were undoubtedly terror attacks and several German units narrowly avoided 'friendly bombs' while the dense smoke prevented any form of damage assessment leading a furious Richthofen to confront Göring at Radom. [10] He demanded unified command for air operations over Warsaw, and strongly hinted he was the best man for the job, although he did not get his wish until 21 September and then, the following day, *ObdL* divided responsibility; Kesselring was to strike the north while Löhr was to attack the west and south, the east escaping because it was scheduled to be occupied by the Russians. *ObdL*'s growing preoccupation with preserving the strike force for the Western campaign proved a major irritant for it deprived Richthofen of the He 111 *Kampfgeschwader* and replaced them with Ju 52s of *IV./ KGzbV 1.*

On 22 September Richthofen signalled *ObdL*: 'Urgently request exploitation of last opportunity for large-scale experiment as devastation and terror raid...' ominously adding '...every effort will be made to eradicate Warsaw completely.' Two days later the air and artillery bombardment began, the former hindered by low cloud. Only when the weather cleared on 26 September did the full weight of the *Luftwaffe* fall upon the city with 400 aircraft from five *Stukagruppen*, a transport *Gruppe* and a *Kampfstaffeln* flying 1,150 sorties for the loss of three aircraft, two of them Ju 52s. Some 560 tonnes of high explosive and 72 tonne of incendiaries fell on the city, many of the latter carried by the transports. Accuracy was impossible, especially with the incendiaries, many of which were pushed from their nominal targets by a strong north-easterly wind, and this led to more than half the city's buildings being hit with 40,000 casualties. [11]

Some bombs hit German positions and the smoke cloud rose to 5,500 metres (18,000 ft) concealing targets from the gunners. *General der Infanterie* Johannes Blaskowitz, the *8. Armee* commander, was furious and, as Richthofen indignantly noted in his diary, when they met: 'I was treated in an extraordinarily unfriendly manner. Neither Blaskowitz … nor *Generaloberst* (Walther) von Brauchitsch, *Oberbefehlshaber des Heeres*, took any notice of my reports or offered me their hand.' Only Rundstedt was his usual courteous self and laughingly reproved him as: 'You old firebug (*Sie alter Kokelfritze*).' [12] Blaskowitz took his complaints to the top and demanded an end to the air assaults, but Hitler told Richthofen to carry on. Pettily, Göring told Richthofen to support only those missions which Blaskowitz requested. On 27 September Warsaw surrendered and avoided another drenching in bombs which was being planned even as the envoys entered German lines.

Richthofen and his staff flew to Berlin three days later as the *Staffeln* either returned to their peacetime bases in eastern Germany to lick their wounds or flew to new bases in the West. *OKW* directives had anticipated the transfer to the West as early as 9 September (*Weisung Nr 3*). By 24 September the two eastern *Luftflotten*, but mostly Löhr's *Flotte*, controlled only the *Lehrdivision, 15 Gruppen* and five *Aufklärungsstaffeln*. It was decided to leave three *Jagdgruppen*, four *Kampfgruppen* and two *Aufklärungsstaffeln* to secure Poland from Russian interference and for 'police actions'.

The Polish campaign demonstrated the soundness of *Luftwaffe* doctrine and tactics making the *Lehrdivision* redundant. The *Luftwaffe* now created dedicated *Erprobungskommando* (test commands) to test new designs under service conditions and to develop tactics. The writing was on the wall during the spring when an *Erprobungskommando 88* was created for the new Ju 88 *Schnellbomber* (high-speed bomber). Much was expected of the new aircraft, despite prolonged development problems, and although only 60 were delivered by the end of 1939, a major re-equipment programme was expected for the *Kampfgruppen*. To facilitate this, Förster's headquarters was disbanded on 30 September and was assigned to Milch's staff as *General zbV*. [13]

Poland had been annihilated thanks greatly to the *Luftwaffe*, typical activity being that of *Stab* and *II./ KG 26* together with the attached *I./ KG 53* which flew a total of 430 sorties for the loss of four bombers with 18 damaged out of 72. Only 285 aircraft were lost and 279 suffered damage in excess of 10 per cent while aircrew casualties amounted to only 539 (413 dead and missing) out of a *Luftwaffe* 'butchers' bill' of 759. By contrast the *PLW* lost between 327 and 335 aircraft, of which some 66 per cent fell to the *Luftwaffe* which accounted for many of the 140 aircraft which crashed on landing. [14]

'Sitzkrieg'

In contrast to the air war in Poland the *Luftwaffe*'s activities in the West were restricted until the spring, during a period that was quickly dubbed the 'Phoney War' or *Sitzkrieg*, with no aerial action permitted west of Germany's border in the early days. Yet there was nothing 'phoney' about the airmens' war and when it ended on 9 April the *Luftwaffe* had suffered 460 aircrew killed or missing in operations, while a further 547 had died in accidents which injured another 202. [15]

The western shield was split between Felmy's *Luftflotte 2* in the north and Sperrle's *Luftflotte 3* in the south. Felmy had *Fliegerdivision 3* under *Generalmajor* Richard Putzier and *Fliegerdivision* 4 under the old bomber ace, *General der Flieger* Alfred Keller. They were joined on 3 September by *General der Flieger* Geisler's anti-shipping command, *Fliegerdivision 10*, which was upgraded from *General zbV der Luftflotte 2*. Sperrle had *Fliegerdivision 5* under Greim and *Fliegerdivision 6* under *Generalmajor* Otto Dessloch. The offensive strength of these commands was depleted by transfers to Poland but even when strike forces were restored, they spent most of this period undertaking training flights and dropping leaflets, although training was disrupted by one of the harshest winters of the century. Only Geisler's command conducted any bombing missions by seeking to erode Royal Navy strength, but with little success.

With the arrival of units from the East there was inevitable re-organisation and Grauert's *Fliegerdivision 1* was assigned to Sperrle. One of the first lessons learned was the need to expand the signals and logistical organisations of the *Fliegerdivisionen* and when this occurred from 2 October they were renamed *Fliegerkorps*; Richthofen's *Fliegerführer zbV* was briefly designated *Fliegerdivision 8*. The exceptions were the airborne forces of Student's *Fliegerdivision 7* and *Fliegerdivision 6* which became *Flakkorps II* under Felmy, while *Luftgaukommando III* created *Flakkorps I* under Sperrle, Poland having shown the need for better command and control of *Flak* in the field.

The *Luftwaffe* fighter force, whose *Zerstörergruppen* gradually re-equipped with the Bf 110 C, flew the only other offensive action in the West, sweeping over the Maginot Line and West Wall and frequently clashing with the Allies. In the first eight months of the war, 45 Allied fighters were shot down compared with 38 German (including six Bf 110), and during the spring the *Luftwaffe* began probing even deeper behind the Maginot Line although the situation was evenly balanced.

Meanwhile, the German high command considered its options for 'Fall Gelb' ('Contingency Yellow'). The original strategy was to repeat the 1913 Schlieffen Plan with the German Army swinging like a door hinged on Luxembourg and using Belgium as the doormat, but no one was happy and there was constant tinkering. The first radical change was the decision, made at Göring's insistence, that the neutral Netherlands be invaded to shield the Ruhr and to provide more bomber bases to strike at Great Britain. On 10 January 1940 it was decided to use *Fliegerdivision 7* as the spearhead for this task.

Ironically, the same day a German Bf 108 light aircraft crash-landed at Maasmechelen (Mechelen-sur-Meuse) north of Maastricht in neutral Belgium. The passenger in this aircraft was a liaison officer at *Fliegerdivision 7* who breached security by carrying orders for the original airborne assault near Ghent, orders quickly recovered by the Belgians. News of the 'Mechelen Incident' broke the next day leaving Göring aquiver – and with his weight ballooning again, there was much to quiver. Hitler's wrath was justifiably ignited by a security lapse which reflected badly on the diplomacy of the Third Reich and as a birthday present to himself Göring on 12 January sacked Felmy, and then vindictively had him cashiered.

During the summer not only was Felmy under a cloud but also, given the paranoia of totalitarian regimes, so were his sons and brother Gerhard, a *Luftwaffe Oberst* who had served with him in Palestine and later in *Lufthansa*. Milch sought to replace Felmy as *Luftflotte 2* commander but he was thwarted by Jeschonnek's enmity and the experienced Kesselring was transferred from *Luftflotte 1* to team with his former *Luftflotte 1* chief of staff, Speidel, who provided continuity after Felmy's dismissal.

The incident forced the Germans to revise their strategy completely and the main blow now would be a massive armoured thrust through the Ardennes to emerge at the French town of Sedan then split the Allies in two. Irrespective of the planning, the *Luftwaffe* continued its reconnaissance efforts as *OKW* gradually eased restrictions on air operations beginning on 13 September when Göring permitted Sperrle 'unobtrusive, long-range reconnaissance at extreme altitudes' without *OKW* authority. The first missions on 21 September were performed by *1./AufklGr ObdL*. Only on 25 September did *OKW* formally allow reconnaissance flights beyond Germany's borders and by October *Luftflotte 2*'s cameras began to cover the neutral Low Countries with *Fernaufklärrungsstaffeln* augmented by *Kampfgeschwader Stäbe* who were familiarising themselves with their potential targets. However, meteorological flights were being flown over France and also the British coast.

Until blizzards blotted out operations during the winter, some *Luftwaffe* units were flying up to six sorties a day and this pace picked up during the spring. The Germans flew nearly 900 reconnaissance sorties during the first eight months of the war and lost 56 aircraft but by the beginning of May they had full target folders of their enemies' airfields, industrial sites and communications, one of the most important contributions being the discovery that what were thought to be bunkers at Sedan were actually half-complete works. [16] In addition the *Luftwaffe*'s excellent comint (radio interception) organisation also contributed greatly to building up a picture of the enemy order of battle and intentions. Established by Martini in 1934 it was consolidated into III./*Luftnachrichtenregiment* ObdL in September 1939 under *Hauptmann* Kohlmorgen who was replaced in April 1940 by *Major* Frunewald. [17]

Scandinavia

When the 'cold war' turned 'hot' from 9 April it was not in Western Europe but in Scandinavia because of the German Navy. Where Göring had wished to violate Dutch neutrality to support air operations, *Grossadmiral* Raeder wished to support his service's mission by seizing Norway using Denmark as the door.

Hitler approved and planning accelerated from a feasibility study to an operation dubbed *Weserübung* (Weser Exercise). [18] Rowehl flew high-altitude photographic missions over Norway but the northernmost objective, Narvik, was too far for his workhorses and he had to use one of the precious four-engined Fw 200 *Condors* (even in May 1940 there were only four Fw 200s in *KG 40*). Bizarrely, *ObdL* was kept out of the planning loop until a directive was published on 1 March although more than 100 *Luftwaffe* officers including Milch were involved in the *Weserübung* planning process.

Göring, still smarting over the Mechelen Incident, was furious and after protesting to Hitler, he was given a nominal role in detailed planning but continued to act like a dog in a manger until the *Führer* finally banned him from any planning meetings. [19] But 'Fatty' did make one malevolent contribution by successfully demanding that the destroyers escorting the northernmost task convoy remain in Narvik Fjord until the merchantmen (half of their capacity carrying *Luftwaffe* supplies) were unloaded – a demand Hitler rubber-stamped on 2 April.

In view of the naval background for the offensive it was logical that the *Luftwaffe* contribution should be under former sailor Geisler, and his *Fliegerkorps* X. He was reinforced with *Jagd-* and *Zerstörergruppen*, *Stukas* (including some long-range Ju 87R) and *Kampfgruppen* including the precision-bomber unit *KGr 100*, (as *LnAbt 100* has been renamed,) but for conventional bomber operations. Geisler had 527 combat aircraft, including 314 bombers and 39 *Stukas*, but there was a separate and substantial transport force under *Lufttransportchefs Land* (chief of land-based air transport) established on 12 March from the *Kommando der Blindflugschulen* (instrument training schools' command). Its leader was *Oberstleutnant* Karl August, *Freiherr* von Gablenz who simply changed hats from trainer to transporter and had 533 aircraft, including most of *Lufthansa's* four-engined fleet, with some being used to carry *Fallschirmjäger* (paratroops) for seizing key objectives while most would carry up to 18 per cent of the servicemen assigned to *Weserübung* together with vital equipment to operate and to protect captured airfields.

Weserübung illustrated Clausewitz's dictum that no plan survives first contact with the enemy. [20] The invasion of Denmark went like clockwork with the enemy airforces being caught on the ground and the *Fallschirmjäger* making their long-delayed combat debut, having suffered a frustrating month of postponed operations during the Poland campaign. In Norway surprise was lost when a German transport with *Luftwaffe* personnel was sunk off the coast on 8 April, the survivors cheerfully telling their rescuers what was to happen, allowing Oslo to begin mobilisation.

Consequently, on the first day there were mixed fortunes and while bridgeheads were established, the *Luftwaffe* often had to suppress the defenders. In Oslo it snatched victory from the jaws of defeat although the Norwegian government escaped the capital. Despite this setback, by the end of the first day the *Reichsbanner* flew over all of Norway's major ports and airfields into the latter of which a stream of transport aircraft brought men and materiel to support incoming *Staffeln*, many aircraft staging through Aalborg airfield in Denmark while Gablenz flew to Oslo to organise transport operations. During *A-Tag* the *Luftwaffe* flew 280 combat and 400 transport sorties, suffering 43 aircraft destroyed or severely damaged (including 4 seaplanes in warships), but destroying or capturing most of Norway's combat aircraft in the process and leaving the rump living on borrowed time without adequate logistic support.

Geisler's duel with the Royal Navy began on *A-Tag* and quickly established that Britannia no longer ruled the waves when her ships were within range of German land-based aircraft and lacked adequate air cover. The Royal Navy had believed that air attacks could be thwarted by a combination of armour plate, anti-aircraft guns (six cruisers were converted to the anti-aircraft role) and manoeuvre but quickly found that fighters were the best shield, the first ship lost in the Norway campaign being the destroyer HMS *Gurkha* whose commander had been a strong advocate of guns against aircraft.

The Royal Navy would return with carriers but they were used mostly to strike shipping in harbours; indeed an attempt was made to neutralise Stavanger-Sola airfield with shells from the cruiser HMS *Suffolk* which inflicted some damage on the night of 16/17 April but was nearly sunk by vengeful *Kampfgruppen*. The carriers would be used to ferry two fighter squadrons to Norway, but the British aircraft were usually overwhelmed in combat. Weak air support was provided by Coastal Command's No 18 Group which had only 90 serviceable aircraft on 9 April, including 11 entirely inappropriate Tiger Moths, and by Bomber Command which would fly 576 bomber- and a number of minelaying sorties up to the night of 7/8 May at the cost of 31 aircraft, before being diverted to deal with *'Gelb'*.

Despite its successes against the Royal Navy, the *Luftwaffe* was unable to break the British blockade which isolated many of the German bridgeheads. Advances from Oslo would eventually relieve the garrisons but in the meantime they relied upon the *Luftwaffe* both for support and succour. At Trondheim two *U-boats* brought in 245 tonnes of aviation fuel and six tonnes of bombs. It was certainly essential at Stavanger where the British monitored the build-up of fuel stocks; 110,000 litres on 21 April at Trondheim-Vaernes, 115,000 litres the next day but only 5,000 litres by 6 May. [21]

The situation grew more acute when the Allies landed north and south of Trondheim at Namsos on 14 April and Åndalsnes on 17 April. Geisler promptly created a forward command to meet the threat under his chief of staff, *Oberstleutnant* Martin Harlinghausen, as *Fliegerführer Drontheim* (Air Commander Trondheim) on 17 April, later making the *Kommodore* of *KG 26, Oberst Dpl.Ing* Robert Fuchs, the *Fliegerführer Stavanger* (Air Commander Stavanger). This was Geisler's last independent command decision for the crisis made a re-organisation essential as well as the creation of a *Luftflotte* headquarters. In a rare moment of putting the national interest ahead of his own, Göring willingly nominated his deputy Milch to lead it. However, although the courtier Milch knew *'Gelb'* was imminent and wanted to participate, 'Fatty' was happy to assure him that Norway was only a temporary assignment; no doubt having lined him up as a scapegoat if the campaign was a failure.

Luftflotte 5 was duly created on 12 April but it was not until 16 April that Milch, accompanied by *Generalmajor* Helmuth Förster, the former *Lehrdivision* commander, as his chief of staff, finally flew into Oslo then flew to Stavanger-Sola where he was awoken by HMS *Suffolk*'s shells. Before leaving Germany Milch met Göring and Jeschonnek at Carinhall and and persuaded them to strengthen reconnaissance, communications and infrastructure, especially at Trondheim-Vaernes which was to be the main centre for air support. He also received 160 aircraft, including a *Kampfgruppe*, and the permanent assignment of *1./KG 40*'s Fw 200 C while the transport force was expanded. Milch immediately shook up his command, expanding the signals network and creating a maintenance/repair facility established in Oslo together with a repair organisation from civilians. [22]

Operationally Milch focused upon the threat to central Norway and from *OKW* received the uncompromising instruction on 19 April: *'By order of the* Führer *the towns and rail junctions of Namsos and Åndalsnes are to be destroyed without consideration for the civilian population; the rail line and roads near these junctions are to be interrupted for a considerable period.* [23]*'* So intense were the succeeding attacks that within two days the Allied land commander, Major-General Sir Adrian Carton de Wiart VC, informed London it was pointless sending any further supplies because unless German air attacks were stopped there was little prospect of a successful offensive. A Gladiator squadron was flown in and promptly annihilated, leading to the evacuation of central Norway which was completed on 4 May.

By now the imminence of *'Gelb'* meant *ObdL* reclaimed many of the *Staffeln* temporarily assigned to Norway with seven *Kampf-*, a *Zerstörer-* and most of the *Transportgruppen* flying south in early May, the latter causing transport sorties to drop from a daily average of 30 to about six. [24] Milch also returned to Germany on 7 May and received a well-deserved *Ritterkreuz*. He was replaced by the *Luftwaffe's* one-time Chief of Staff, *Generaloberst* Hans-Jürgen Stumpff, who arrived from *Luftflotte 1* (which was assigned to *General der Flieger* Wilhelm Wimmer) bringing with him a pair of night fighter and seaplane squadrons to give a total of some 375 aircraft by 10 May. He made no changes to the existing organisation but brought in his *Luftflotte 1* chief of staff, *Generalmajor* Ulrich Kessler, to take his place temporarily since Harlinghausen, his nominal chief of staff, was otherwise engaged. When the situation eased around 20 May, Kessler and Harlinghausen swapped places, although the former took over *Fliegerkorps* X headquarters, which was now providing overall operational co-ordination in Trondheim. [25]

A long-running crisis began to lurch into disaster just as Stumpff arrived when the threat to the garrison led by the Bavarian *Generalleutnant* Eduard Dietl began to grow. Because of Göring's interference, the naval task force carrying Dietl's troops was trapped and destroyed in Narvik Fjord between 10-13 April, leaving the garrison isolated in the Arctic Circle. Hitler was in despair over Dietl's fate because the general had been in the 1923 *Bierkeller Putsch* while, to the chagrin of Milch, *Luftwaffe* support was restricted by a combination of distance and the limited facilities at Trondheim-Vaernes.

When the Allies landed in central Norway they also established a forward base at Harstad on an island just off Narvik Fjord, then landed on the mainland and edged towards Narvik, pushing Dietl back towards the port and the Swedish border. They built an airfield on the mainland at Bardufoss, north of Narvik, and moved in two fighter squadrons which were used to support the land advance. With central Norway secure, a German relief force supported by Harlinghausen and spurred on by Hitler set out on a long, exhausting journey over mountains and down valleys which often lacked roads.

The *Luftwaffe* was able to harass the Allies around Narvik but its effort was noticeably reduced in April as it focused upon the threat to Trondheim. Dietl felt especially abandoned, pointedly commenting to *OKW* on 4 May about the lack of supplies with no air drops over the previous five days. With the threat to Trondheim fading and Milch's hard work beginning to show results, the *Luftwaffe* began focusing upon Narvik and during May flew some 485 bomber sorties. These sank or damaged many ships but the Bardufoss fighters, supported by the radar-equipped anti-aircraft cruiser, HMS *Curlew*, took a steady toll of the attackers. The cruiser was sunk by *KGr 100* on 26 May and Bf 110s with long-range fuel tanks sought to regain air superiority but proved no match for the nimble Gladiators and Hurricanes.

Despite the *Luftwaffe's* efforts the Allies retook Narvik on 28 May and Dietl faced the ignominy of being driven across the Swedish border into captivity. On 2 June a row broke out between Stumpff, Geisler and Kessler, with the *Luftflotte* commander obeying Hitler's specific orders to ease pressure upon Dietl and supporting the demands of the army commander-in-chief in Norway, *General der Infanterie* Nikolaus von Falkenhorst for direct air support. Geisler and Kessler wished to pursue the *Luftwaffe's* traditional doctrine of indirect support by gaining air superiority and striking the enemy's communications, the latter later complaining of Stumpff's 'fawning' on Falkenhorst whom, he alleged, was his former commanding officer.

In fact the paths of Stumpff and Falkenhorst seem barely to have crossed and the heart of the dispute may have been the more traditional rivalry between armies and navies, for the *Fliegerkorps* X leaders were both former sailors. On 2 June Kessler despatched a mission to strike Bardufoss airfield, but Stumpff recalled it *en route* so the aircraft might be used for a direct support mission. This wasted fuel and ordnance, which had to be dumped for a safe landing, and a furious Kessler resigned.[26] For the next two years he would cool his heels as chief of staff to the training command before succeeding Harlinghausen as *Fliegerführer Atlantik* in 1942.

In fact the Allies had already decided to abandon Norway and wished to seize Narvik only to destroy its iron-ore loading facilities. Shielded by carrier-borne fighters they began to evacuate Narvik on 3 June in an operation which lasted six days, unimpeded by *Luftflotte 5* which was grounded by bad weather until 6 June, allowing the Allies to take 24,500 troops with all their artillery, equipment, ammunition and most of their stores.

Gablenz's sterling work organising transport had already seen him promoted *Lufttransportsführer bei Generalquartiermeister* (air transport leader with the General Quartermaster) on 5 May, where he remained until October 1941. By then, concern over *Luftwaffe* development and production saw Milch ordered to re-organise Udet's *Generalluftzeugmeister* organisation and Gablenz was brought in to direct planning. Later, in his suicidal anguish, Udet would blame both Milch and Gablenz as influencing his decision to end his life. Gablenz remained in office until he was killed when his transport crashed in a thunderstorm at Mühlberg near Leipzig on 21 August 1942, a similar fate befalling Dietl in June 1944.

The conquest of Norway secured mineral supplies for the Reich and provided it with submarine and air bases to prosecute the war against Great Britain at a cost of 5,300 casualties including nearly 3,700 dead and missing, while the Allies lost some 3,800 on land and 2,500 at sea. Ironically one of the new air bases was Banak, 320 kilometres north of Narvik, which the British had been building as a bomber base but which the *Luftwaffe* would occupy and use to deadly effect over the coming years.

The cost of the campaign to the *Luftwaffe* was 260 aircraft, including 86 transports, while the butcher's bill was 1,130 air crew, of whom 341 were killed and 448 missing. The *Luftwaffe* destroyed 93 of the 169 British aircraft lost in the campaign (43 were lost in HMS *Glorious*) with 43 destroyed in air combat, 24 by *Flak* and the remainder on the ground. The *Luftwaffe* sank a cruiser, six destroyers and sloops, 12 smaller warships and 21 merchantmen (58,600 grt) together with many fishing craft.

The *Luftwaffe* had contributed much to the victory less through its senior leaders such as Milch and Stumpff and more due to the middle-ranking officers such as

Fuchs, Gablenz and Harlinghausen but the contribution of junior officers should also not be ignored. The investment in the transport arm paid dividends: it flew 3,018 sorties to bring in 29,280 men, 2,376 tonnes of supplies and 1,179 tonnes litres of fuel – indeed the German presence in Norway often depended upon this airlift. The Allies had much to learn, especially about improving protection against air attack. The aggressive use of carriers against land targets gave a tantalising taste of things to come but the Royal Navy would not be in a position to demonstrate this for three years.

The West

On the morning of 10 May the *Wehrmacht* began rolling westwards to execute '*Fall Gelb*' which was to be rather like a boxer jabbing with his right while preparing to deliver the knock-out punch with his left. While the mouths of everyone – from Hitler down to the lowest private – were dry with tension, the omens looked especially good for the *Luftwaffe*. [27]

Facing them in Europe were 2,065 aircraft (about 1,550 serviceable), while the Royal Air Force (RAF) could commit up to 1,072 (643 serviceable) from the British Isles. Even excluding the fighter defences of north-western Germany, Coeler's minelayers and the navy's seaplanes, the German army could count on the support of 3,984 combat aircraft, of which 2,877 were serviceable. The odds were further weighted in the Germans' favour because enemy air power was fragmented in terms of command and control. There were four air forces: the French *Armée de l'Air* and *Aéronavale*, the British RAF, the Dutch *Militaire Luchtvaart* (ML) and the Belgian *Aéronautique Militaire* (AéMI). In all except the *Aéronavale* squadrons were split between air and army headquarters, with the French especially weak not only because their bomber squadrons were still receiving modern aircraft, but also because the politicians who drove the creation of the *Armée de l'Air* in 1936 had expected its ageing leadership to genuflect towards Douhet.

In reality they were all apostates who followed the old religion of army support and on 26 February 1940, *Général d'Armée Aérienne* Joseph Vuillemin, the commander of the *Armée de l'Air* received a new directive which '…placed the air forces and anti-aircraft defence forces at the permanent disposal of the major land units on the north-eastern front.' [28] This meant he answered to *Général* Jacques Georges who headed the *Théatre d'Opérations de Nord-Est* (North Eastern Operational Theatre), which controlled the army groups and the British Expeditionary Force (BEF), at whose behest squadrons were scattered among every level of military command from army corps upwards. By contrast, the *Luftwaffe* was organised into balanced aerial task forces – the *Fliegerkorps*, although fighter operations were co-ordinated by the *Jagdfliegerführer* (*Jafü*), which between them controlled 3,511 aircraft. However, barely 71 per cent (2,489) were serviceable, for German industry could still not provide the level of spares and tools needed to maintain full operational strength, but the *Schwarzmänner* would prove force multipliers by generating high sortie rates.

The opening hours of '*Gelb*' provided mixed success for the *Luftwaffe*, which had wanted to herald the offensive with its own offensive against enemy air power. Hitler vetoed this plan so that he could achieve strategic surprise, forcing the *Kampfgruppen* simultaneously to neutralise enemy air power while striking communications, logistics and troop concentrations to aid the army. The effectiveness of the counter-air campaign therefore depended upon a careful assessment of enemy dispositions or potential dispositions.

Against the Dutch, and especially the Belgians, Kesselring and *Luftflotte 2* had considerable success, accounting for 210 aircraft (340 were claimed) including trainers and liaison aircraft. The ML continued to harass the *Luftwaffe* like wasps until the Dutch capitulated on 15 May, but apart from a single bomber strike, the Belgian AéMI would spend the campaign flying from airfield to airfield and contributed little to Belgian defence. By contrast *Luftflotte 3*'s campaign against the British and French failed because Sperrle's intelligence organisation literally took a hit-or-miss approach to targeting with the result that most fighter and bomber fields escaped unscathed with 40 first-line aircraft destroyed against claims of up to 490.

On the first day the *Luftwaffe* flew some 5,000 fighter and bomber sorties compared with 585 by the Allies, and while neither the level nor the ratio could be maintained, the following weeks saw the Germans exploit their advantages through intense activity. The *Luftwaffe*'s daily average was 2,000–3,000 sorties a day, the single-engined crews flying up to five or six, while during the crucial first five days the Allies averaged less than 800, partly because they were holding back their bombers until they could discern the main axis of advance, and gradually they lost control of the skies.

Kesselring was the more heavily committed, supporting Bock's *Heeresgruppe B*'s advance into the Low Countries, with Putzier's *FlFü zbV* (254 combat aircraft) underpinning the attack on the Netherlands while 937 aircraft of Keller's *Fliegerkorps IV* and Richthofen's *Fliegerkorps VIII* backed the advance into Belgium. Paratroops and airborne troops were a feature of operations in the Low Countries with a full airborne assault upon the Netherlands by 436 transport aircraft carrying Student's *Fliegerdivision 7*, a glider-borne attack upon Fort Eben Emael, whose guns covered the key bridges across the Maas at Maastricht, and an ad hoc airborne operation in the Ardennes using a fleet of *Storch* light aircraft. The glider attack was an outstanding success, the Ardennes operation a farce and the Dutch operation a Pyrrhic victory. The Dutch airfields were heavily defended, most alternate landing sights (including roads) were covered in obstacles and the remainder were polder (land reclaimed from the sea) which bogged down the heavy Ju 52 transports. The campaign ended in tragedy with the bombing of Rotterdam by *KG 54* in which 800 died and 78,000 were rendered homeless when the message cancelling the mission failed to get through. In the subsequent confusion Student was seriously injured and replaced by Süssman who had to begin rebuilding the airborne forces; a third of *Fliegerdivision 7*'s paratroops became casualties as well as 20 per cent of the airborne troops.

In Belgium the Germans achieved their strategic aim of enticing the Allied motorised forces of *Général* Gaston Billotte's *1er Groupe des Armées* northwards, harassed by the *Luftwaffe* all the way from the French frontier to their new line. By contrast there were few attacks upon German columns and an attempt to destroy the Maastricht bridges was thwarted by nine *Jagdstaffeln* under Ibel's *Stab JG 27* and the guns of *Generalmajor* Dessloch's *Flakkorps II*. In the three days from 10 May, the Allies flew 74 sorties against the bridges and lost 33 bombers, while Ibel's men flew 340 sorties and claimed 35 victories for the loss of five fighters. But of far greater concern to the Germans was the progress of the main armoured force, *Gruppe Kleist*, with 41,140 vehicles and 134,370 men which was driving through the narrow Ardennes valleys and whose poor march discipline caused huge traffic jams. They were shielded by *Oberstleutnant* Harry von Bülow-Bothkamp's *JG 2* supported by 43 *Luftwaffe Flak* batteries who usually held the French reconnaissance squadrons at arm's length although it was inevitable that some aircraft returned to report the wrath to come. Fortunately for the Germans, these reports were ignored or under-estimated and late on 12 May the spearheads reached the Meuse, having suffered only one air attack the previous day, and, in error, that by 25 *Luftwaffe Stukas*! The advance encountered serious resistance only once and used a considerable amount of anti-tank ammunition which was replaced by an air-drop from Ju 52s. [29]

Overall co-ordination of the air cover was provided by Loerzer's *Fliegerkorps II* but *ObdL* recognised that with only 400 aircraft the *Korps* was not strong enough to support the crossing of the Meuse. It was planned to reinforce Loerzer with Richthofen's *Fliegerkorps VIII* comprising some 500 aircraft. Unfortunately, a major lapse in staff work meant that no one had informed Richthofen, who was furious when he learned on 12 May that he was supposed to move 100 kilometres south by the next day! Commitments to Generaloberst Walther von Reichenau's *6. Armee* (formerly *10. Armee*) in northern Belgium meant that Richthofen was forced to split his command to support two axes for several days.

The Meuse was crossed at Sedan on 14 May with the *Luftwaffe* flying some 2,700 sorties and stunning the defenders. As motorised units crossed the river, the defence rapidly collapsed, allowing engineers to throw bridges across, but these were quickly detected by Allied reconnaissance aircraft. The next day the Allied bomber force was unleashed, although it had already been weakened by Sperrle's counter-air campaign of the previous days. The Allies flew 128 bomber and 93 fighter sorties but Massow's *Jafü 3* had arranged strong fighter cover (814 sorties) augmented by 27 *Flak* batteries which between them destroyed 48 bombers and 21 fighters.

With his supply line secure, *General der Panzertruppe* Heinz 'Fast Hans' Guderian's *XIX. Motorisiertkorps* tore up the rule book and was soon driving down the Somme valley to the Channel. This time there was no problem with air support, for Richthofen had supplied radio-equipped forward liaison officers in their own armoured command vehicles; they could bring in the *Stukas* to disrupt any strongpoints within 45 to 75 minutes and in the case of the Henschel Hs 123A (known as *Ein Zwei Drei*), within 10 minutes! With such support Guderian reached the Channel on 20 May and then turned north to strike Billotte from the rear.

The advance greatly helped the *Luftwaffe* by overrunning or threatening Allied airbases, forcing their squadrons to waste time finding new nests, while the French had to abandon 420 damaged or unserviceable aircraft between 10–20 May. In turn, the German airmen helped the *Landsers* (the German equivalent of 'Tommies' or 'Doughboys') by striking enemy road and rail communications, 174 rail targets being struck between 13–24 May, keeping the enemy off balance. But it was not easy as the *Luftwaffe* had great problems finding forward airfields and then supporting them with fuel, ammunition and spares, the air transport force being strained to breaking point. Milch had a roaming commission to alleviate the bottlenecks and although his organisational abilities undoubtedly smoothed the flow of supplies, he could not achieve miracles.

Allied air activity actually increased with 376 bomber sorties from 16–20 May, but German fighters and *Flak* inflicted heavy losses. Yet *ObdL* had no grounds for optimism and by the time the Channel coast was reached, it had lost 20 per cent of its first-line strength in both man and machine, some 485 combat aircraft destroyed or with more than 60 per cent battle damage and 1,887 aircrew casualties. The replacement system for man and machine was collapsing while the perennial shortage of spares halved serviceability in many units. However, the *Luftwaffe* kept up the pressure as Billotte's forces, pressed from the east by Bock and from the south by Rundstedt, retreated towards the Channel. The biggest air threat to the *Wehrmacht* came from the RAF flying across the Channel but by this point the German High Command were taking counsel of their fears. The Allies were holding waterlogged ground criss-crossed with canals and ditches bringing the prospect of the *Wehrmacht*, exhausted by their recent exertions, fighting a bloody battle of attrition. Although Sperrle was virtually single-handedly holding off the enemy south of the Somme, Hitler and his generals still feared a relief effort.

On 24 May Kleist reined in his tanks and Hitler rubber-stamped the decision. The previous day Göring, remembering the *Luftwaffe's* success against the Ilza and River Burza pockets in Poland, begged: 'My *Führer*, leave the destruction of the enemy surrounded at Dunkirk to me and my *Luftwaffe*.' Both Richthofen and Kesselring protested against Göring's decision, but were overruled and Richthofen was ordered to support the final assault on the Allied pocket together with Grauert's *Fliegerkorps I*. [30]

While the *Luftwaffe* inflicted heavy losses in men and materiel on the Allies they were unable, significantly, to interfere with Operation 'Dynamo', the evacuation of troops from Dunkirk which began on 27 May and concluded on 3 June. Both air forces were fighting at a disadvantage virtually close to the limit of their operational radii, many *Kampfgruppe* were down to 15 serviceable aircraft and supply problems meant they often flew only one sortie a day. There was also a lack of interest; Göring was scouring the Netherlands for Dutch Masters, Sperrle was focused upon covering the southern flank and mentally, while most of the *Luftwaffe* leadership were pondering the next campaign, '*Fall Rot*' ('Case Red'), which would capture northern and western France, it was not until 30 May that the Germans recognised a major evacuation was under way and by then the weather was closing in. There was no attempt to interdict shipping or strike disembarkation ports; indeed the *Luftwaffe* was more interested in supporting the army, although it did sink or damage 89 merchantmen (126,518 grt) while the Royal Navy had 29 out of 40 destroyers sunk or damaged.On 28 May the Belgian Army capitulated and a week later, so did the surviving troops in the Dunkirk pocket. The *Luftwaffe* had flown some 4,000 sorties and lost 100 aircraft but it destroyed 106 British fighters, bringing total British fighter losses during the campaign to some 450 aircraft. It was not just the loss of machines (at the end of June Fighter Command had only 384 Spitfires and Hurricanes) and scarce pilots which alarmed the RAF staff but also precious VHF radios whose production was so low that on 26 May Dowding withdrew them all and replaced them with HF radios.

Planning for *'Rot'* began on 20 May and *OKW Weisung Nr 13* of 24 May stated that the *Luftwaffe's* task was to support the army. Kesselring was to support Bock's *Heeresgruppe A* in the west, with Grauert's *Fliegerkorps I*, Keller's *Fliegerkorps IV* and Richthofen's *Fliegerkorps VIII* and, to prevent another maritime evacuation, Coeler's *Fliegerdivision 9*. Sperrle was to support Rundstedt's *Heeresgruppe B* with Loerzer's *Fliegerkorps II* and *Fliegerkorps V*. A colossal amount of administrative work was necessary, not only to prepare new airfields and weave new communications nets but also to turn both the communication and logistics networks, which had extended westward from the German border, to face south. In this the *Luftwaffe* was a victim of its own success in cutting roads and railways as well as dropping bridges. The nearest railhead was Brussels and the roads were clogged with traffic forcing the *Luftwaffe* to call again upon its exhausted *Transportgruppen* – indeed by 31 May IV./KGzbV 1 was down to 11 serviceable transports.

Poor weather in late May reduced the tempo of operations allowing the *Schwarzmänner* time to catch up on much needed maintenance and when *'Rot'* began on 5 June serviceability was about 70 per cent. But there were fewer aircraft; by the end of the month *Oberst* Stefan Fröhlich's *KG 76* of *Fliegerkorps I* based around Bonn and Cologne, which had 110 aircraft and 89 per cent serviceability on 10 May, was down to 85 bombers of which 58 (68%) were serviceable. [31] Kesselring had some 600 aircraft for the campaign but he also had to shield the Low Countries, and Sperrle had 1,000 augmented by 300 *Heeresflieger* reconnaissance aircraft. Their numerical margin of superiority was low for, despite the loss of 787 aircraft to 5 June, *Armée de l'Air* strength had risen to 2,086 aircraft augmented by an unknown number of corps aircraft. Tragically, component production did not match that of airframes and engines, with severe shortages of everything from tyres to propellers as well as spares and only 29 per cent (599 aircraft) were operational, while the British could add 121 aircraft. [32] In an attempt to wreck French war production on 3 June almost every German fighter and bomber was committed to an assault on factories around Paris, *Unternehmen P (Paula)*. The operation was compromised by faulty signal security but although anticipated by the French their attempt at interception misfired. They suffered a 19 per cent loss rate (15 fighters) and shot down only 10 attackers although their victims included the *Kommodore* of *KG 51*, *Oberst* Josef Kammhuber, and the *Jafü 3*, Oberst Gerd von Massow.

'Rot' began under clear skies two days later and the *Luftwaffe* quickly established air superiority to aid the rapid advance into central and western France. But operations were hamstrung by a lack of supplies although this increasingly ceased to matter as enemy air resistance evaporated like the morning dew. On 14 June Paris fell and three days later a new French government under Great War hero *Maréchal* Henri Pétain requested an armistice. Germany's terms were presented by Hitler and Göring on 21 June using the same railway carriage in which the Allies had forced Germany to accept an armistice in 1918. Within a day they were accepted and from 23 June the *Luftwaffe* began to wind down, Sperrle ordering his *Jagdgruppen* to give a third of their pilots a six-day rest and rebuild their strength. In the final days some sporadic air fighting continued until 24 June when a Bf 109

secured the campaign's last victory, a Potez 63-II at Montélimar, while *Oberleutnant* John of *5.(H)/13* was shot down in an Hs 126 near Marchelidon and killed; he was the *Luftwaffe*'s last fatal casualty of the western campaign.

Germany had won a stunning victory. *Luftwaffe* casualties were 6,653, including 4,417 aircrew and 83 *Schwarzmänner*, with the aircrew losing 1,092 killed and 1,930 missing, although many of the latter such as Kammhuber and Massow were soon liberated from French prison camps. Materiel losses included 28 per cent of the *Luftwaffe*'s initial strength (1,428 aircraft) and, if damaged aircraft are included (488 aircraft), the figure rises to 36 per cent (see Table 3-1). Of these 1,129 were lost to enemy action and when compared with strength at the beginning of the campaign the far-roaming *Zerstörergruppen* suffered worse with nearly 32 per cent losses closely followed by the *Stuka-* and *Kampfgruppen* with 26–24 per cent.

Table 3-1: Losses in the air, 12 May – 22 June 1940

Week	German	French	British
May 12–18	314	163	189
May 19–25	155	101	155
May 26 – June 1	126	50	138
June 2–8	111	127	65
June 9–15	75	74	76
June 16–22	38	14	20

For the *Luftwaffe* the Western campaign was a textbook operation which saw it achieve air superiority while simultaneously supporting the army which greatly benefited from its assistance. But it was a symbiotic relationship, for by easing the soldiers' advance, the *Luftwaffe* gained the disruption of the enemy air forces' infrastructure and this was related in the weekly losses (Table 3-1) which steadily declined through both campaigns. This required a massive effort and while detailed records no longer exist, fragmentary evidence suggests the average *Kampfgeschwader* flew a total of 1,500 sorties while the *Jagd-* and *Stukageschwader* flew 3,000. [33]

Battle of Britain

The *Luftwaffe*'s last campaign of 1940 would be the nearest any air force would approach to Douhet's ideals. That summer represented the zenith of the Third Reich, but Hitler's fears of a long, bloody, war had dissipated with peace seeming only weeks away. The feeling was reflected by the popular song of the time *Auf dem Dach Welt* ('On Top of the World').

But to Berlin's surprise, London dismissed Hitler's peace overtures and reluctantly he began planning an invasion of England, this being published as *Unternehmen 'Seelöwe'* (Operation 'Sealion') on 16 July. *OKH* was confident the army would overrun England rapidly once ashore but *OKM* was only too aware that the Norwegian campaign had left barely half the fleet operational. Yet, as Hitler informed Raeder, *'Seelöwe'* was more a matter of last resort than a full-scale amphibious assault, while on 30 June *OKW* Operations chief, *Generaloberst* Alfred Jodl described an invasion as a *coup de grâce* once the *Luftwaffe* had reduced the enemy defences. [34]

Everything depended upon the *Luftwaffe* which would also counter-balance the Royal Navy as the invasion fleet crossed the Channel. As early as 24 May *OKW Weisung Nr* 13 had directed *Luftwaffe* attacks 'in the fullest manner' as reprisals for British attacks upon the Ruhr and there had been some night harassing attacks, mostly aimed at British bomber bases, which ended when *Fall 'Rot'* began. On 27 June *ObdL* ordered an extensive aerial reconnaissance of Great Britain and three days later issued a blueprint for the forthcoming campaign. [35] This envisaged a carefully co-ordinated assault, preceded by attacks upon industrial targets, especially the aircraft industry, but Göring demanded '...every effort should be made to avoid unnecessary loss of life among the civilian population.' The main effort would fall upon the RAF's infrastructure with the U-boat blockade augmented by air attacks upon the ports. Yet there remained tremendous uncertainty, for while its objective remained the disruption of the enemy throughout his Operational depth, the *Luftwaffe* would have to achieve this on its own.

The campaign did not start until early August, some 40 days after the fall of France. Battered squadrons, now at half strength, had to be rebuilt while the combat efficiency of newly qualified aircrew was improved through new *Ergänzungsverbände* (supplemental formations). Simultaneously, and despite a severe shortage of trained staff officers, the *Luftwaffe* began moving forward 1,000 kilometres and the signals system, vital to efficient air operations, had to make its third major change in less than two months having been extended first eastward into the Low Countries, then south into France. It was now was expanded along the Channel and Atlantic coasts while the web of navigation aids had to be rewoven. [36]

Units moved to new bases which then had to receive all the sinews of war; food, fuel, spares, ammunition and (of course) forms to requisition them, but these often had to come over road and rail systems needing urgent attention as a direct result of having received *Luftwaffe* attention. When France surrendered on 25 June the *Luftwaffe* supply system had been stretched to breaking point; by 8 July only 20 of 84 railway tanks with fuel had reached Le Mans, while the *Transportgruppen* were unable to take up the slack and barely kept units running. [37]

On 11 July *ObdL* demanded intensified operations to destroy the RAF and its infrastructure but it pessimistically informed the Army that this would take up to a month. Meanwhile, the *Luftwaffe's* preparations for the air campaign moved at glacial pace and an outline plan of campaign was produced only at the end of July. There remained sharp differences about the best way to defeat the RAF, not only between Sperrle and Kesselring, but also within Kesselring's command. Grauert wanted mixed formations of fighters and bombers to trail their coats, thereby tempting the enemy fighters who would then be ambushed by massed *Jagdgruppen*. Loerzer proposed striking at London to force the enemy into combat, using the metropolis as an anvil for the fighters' hammer despite Hitler's ban on attacking London.

Within the *Luftwaffe* leadership there was a tendency to enjoy the fruits of conquest rather than prepare for another hard campaign. Kesselring moved to Brussels while the gourmet Sperrle, whose personal transport had a refrigerator to keep wines cool, was delighted when he moved his headquarters to Paris. On 19 July celebrations continued when most of the *Luftwaffe* leadership was promoted at least one rank, Göring becoming *Reichsmarschall*, while Kesselring and Sperrle were appointed *Generalfeldmarschall*. On the same day Jeschonnek was at a strategy conference in Berlin during which Hitler commented that Stalin was showing signs of unfriendliness and predicted: 'Thoughtful measures must be made.' A few hours later the first steps were taken to planning an invasion of the Soviet Union.

Much of Sperrle's attention was focused upon plans for a massive victory parade in Paris, which was not officially postponed until 12 July, but as late as 3 August Keller asked whether or not it would be taking place. [38] The previous day, Sperrle brought in the *Luftgau* VII band (*Stabsmusikkorps und Spielmannszug*) and planned to bring in up to nine more. [39] More seriously Göring and his subordinates, who had moved *ObdL* to Beauvais, 60 miles (90 kilometres) south-east of Paris, boycotted joint-service planning meetings although *ObdL* did produce an operational concept, Operation 'Eagle' (*Unternehmen 'Adler'*). When Hitler reviewed preparations on 31 July, however, the *Luftwaffe* did not even have a representative.

Jodl slipped in the knife by noting that his liaison officer with *ObdL* was reporting Göring's indecision on the operational plan. The following day a teleprinter message clattered into Beauvais. 'The *Führer* has ordered that preparations for the great attack against England should be completed immediately and with great despatch so that it may commence within 12 hours of the *Führer* issuing the orders.' On the same day *OKW Weisung Nr 17 'On the conduct of air and sea warfare against England'* was published and noted the intensification of the air war would begin about 5 August with the invasion *A-Tag* set for 15 September.

'Fatty' was forced to break off his Crook's Tour for the looting of art treasure and hastily called a conference on '*Adler*' in The Hague garden of former naval air ace *General der Flieger* Friedrich Christiansen, *Wehrmachtsbefehlshaber in der Niederlande* (Armed Forces Commander in the Netherlands) on 2 August. [40] It was agreed to opt for a 13-day three-phase campaign which would first strike at Fighter Command's bases, starting with those up to 90 miles (150 kilometres) south and east of London, then to work closer to the metropolis until the bases only 30 miles (50 kilometres) away were in the bomb sight. Simultaneously there would be a round-the-clock offensive against the British aircraft industry, which both Kesselring and Sperrle would have preferred to destroy through a night-bombing campaign.

A stroke of a crayon marked the boundaries between Kesselring and Sperrle with the former responsible for operations north of the Seine and eastern England, while Stumpff's *Luftflotte 5* with 170 aircraft would be responsible for attacking Scotland and north-eastern England. Kesselring had Grauert's *Fliegerkorps* I, Loerzer's *Fliegerkorps II*, Döring's *Jafü 2* and Coeler's *Fliegerdivision 9*, while Sperrle had Greim's *Fliegerkorps V*, Richthofen's *Fliegerkorps VIII* and Keller's *Fliegerkorps IV*. Total strength rose from 2,502 aircraft on 20 July (excluding reconnaissance machines) of which 1,841 (73.5%) were serviceable, to 2,849 (1,344 bombers) by 13 August with 79 per cent (2,256) serviceable.

Not only was this a formidable threat facing the British shield provided by Air Chief Marshal Sir Hugh Dowding's Fighter Command, but Germany's victories had eroded Dowding's strength and compromised his strategy, which was based upon a threat largely from unescorted bombers flying from the east. Dowding developed complex tactics, exploiting the quadrupling of fighter firepower to eight rifle-calibre machine guns in its modern interceptors, the Hawker Hurricane and Supermarine Spitfire. These would be augmented by the single-engined Boulton-Paul Defiant whose quadruple gun turret was designed to fire on the vulnerable undersides of the bombers – a tactical concept developed later for *Luftwaffe* night fighters as *Schräge Musik* ('Jazz Music'). Dowding's minimum requirement against the threat of weakly escorted German bombers was 46 squadrons, but now he faced threats from escorted bombers along a massive arc covering the whole north-western European coast with 48 operational single-engined fighter squadrons including Defiants. [41] Of the 261 Hurricanes despatched for operations in France, only 66 had returned, and he was forced to adopt a new defensive strategy with a 'reconnaissance' mission by two Spitfires on 9 July as his last official offensive activity. [42]

He had the advantage of interior lines and a long-established, smoothly-functioning, organisation of group and sector headquarters which could track enemy formations and direct interceptors. The development of radar, the Chain Home (CH) and Chain Home Low (CHL), provided longer detection times than visual observer networks and they aided interception but they were no panacea because the immaturity of radar technology meant it was far from perfect in terms of warning time and accuracy. The CH (later Type 1) was a high frequency (30 MHz) sensor while the CHL (later Type 2) was a very high frequency (200 Hz) one, but both had a single wavelength, often detecting aircraft only when they were around the Franco-Belgian coast. Furthermore, the estimates of target height and strength were often unreliable, while CH was vulnerable to jamming. Controllers could place the interceptors only within three to five miles (five or eight kilometres) of the enemy formations while radar gave No 11 Group shielding London no more than 15 minutes' notice of incoming raids. Two to four minutes might be lost getting the fighters airborne and some 13–20 minutes lost while they climbed to reach the bombers, by which time a *Kampfgruppe* flying from France would be halfway across Kent. Massed formations further complicated the defenders' problems because each sector could track no more than four formations. [43]

Despite capturing some British HF radars in France, the *Luftwaffe* was ignorant of both the radar chain and the organisation, and the captured sensors were dismissed by the German electronics' industry which had developed VHF and ultra-high-frequency (UHF) radars. Between May and August 1939 *Generalmajor* Wolfgang Martini, head of *Luftwaffe* communications, flew three signals intelligence (Sigint) missions using the airship *Graf Zeppelin II* and recorded signals but the airship's metallic framework created interference which made it difficult to determine British activity. It was concluded that the British were still at the experimental stage although when war broke out Martini regarded the matter as 'not proven'. In fact the CH system had detected and tracked the airship without difficulty and at one point operators considered sending a correction when the airship sent a wrong navigation reading! Shortly after the occupation of France the *Reichspost-Zentralamtes* (Central Department of the National Postal Service) established a number of receiver stations covering 75–300 MHz along the coast with a *Beobachtungs- und Auswertestelle* (Observation and Analysis Centre) near Calais. It appears that it was this organisation, which was established to augment the comint facilities of the *Luftnachrichtenregimenter*, which first detected, catalogued and analysed British radar signals. [44]

Schmid, who underestimated enemy air strength, made no attempt to seek out the *Armée de l'Air* liaison officers who had written numerous reports on the British air defence system and could have provided personal experience. [45] He also repeated his error before 'Gelb' by failing to assess the roles of British airfields by examining the aircraft on them, with the result that much effort would be wasted on those operating bombers, the Fleet Air Arm and even trainers! Martini's *Funkhorchdienst* (Radio Interception Service) should have been able to locate the sector headquarters and careful photographic analysis of the airfields might have been able to discover their exact location. While focusing upon order of battle information, the service quickly determined that British fighters were being accurately guided to German formations. The Germans concluded that the orders were being transmitted from the network of HF transmitters they could observe along the coast.

First the *Luftwaffe* gained control of the waters of the Channel through the *Kommodore* of *KG 2*, *Oberst* Johannes Fink, who acted as *Kanalkampfführer* (Channel Combat Leader). Under Loerzer's overall direction, Fink, aided by a naval *Freya (FuMG 80)* surface search radar covering the Straits of Dover, flew about 1,000 sorties and expended almost 1,400 tonnes of bombs sinking 24,000 tons of shipping from 3 July until 9 August, at which point he was re-assigned. He forced the British to divert trans-Atlantic convoys to the northern ports but coastal convoys continued until CW 9 was savaged on 8 August, after which they ceased until the end of the year. Simultaneously Grauert struck the Dover area and drove the British destroyer flotillas away from the White Cliffs and north of the Thames Estuary. The relatively light shipping losses were due to Fighter Command flying up to 80 per cent of its patrols over the sea but it was hamstrung by operating only in squadron strength, on the periphery of radar coverage. The *Jagdgruppen* usually kept these patrols at arm's length and the *Luftwaffe* loss rate was only 2–3 per cent or some 30 aircraft.

On 4 July the *Jagd-* and *Zerstörergeschwader* began sweeps (*Freijagd*) over southern England to erode Fighter Command and the strength of the German formations and their superior tactics usually gave them the edge in these clashes which accounted for 28 per cent of Fighter Command's losses in the first five weeks of the conflict to 11 August. The *Luftwaffe* lost 42 fighters to 4 August, a gratifying loss rate of 1.25 per cent, but the limitations of the *Zerstörer* in the face of modern fighters were becoming all too apparent. The *Zerstörergruppe Kommandeure* were slow to develop the obvious tactic of high-level swoops which would exploit the formidable forward armament of twin 20mm cannon and four 7.9mm machineguns which could blow apart an enemy fighter. Even more disturbing was the effectiveness of the British air defences against lone reconnaissance aircraft, and in the five weeks from 1 July, 49 aircraft were lost. Inland bomber missions were restricted to *Störangriffe* (harassing attacks) which were classified as missions in which less than 50 tonnes of bombs were dropped and were usually flown by individual aircraft or small formations.

The *Zerstörer*'s inadequacies hindered the deployment of large bomber formations which depended upon the limited operational radius of 186 miles (300 kilometres) and endurance (90 minutes) of the Bf 109E, which was confined to 20–30 minute operations south of the Thames. With an ideal ratio of two fighters for every bomber, major daylight attacks were restricted to no more than 450 bombers and while moulded-plywood drop tanks to double the operational radius were produced there were never enough, they often leaked and restricted manoeuvrability. With their shield weakened, Sperrle's *Kampfgruppen* increasingly turned to night missions augmented by some of Kesselring's strike force.

A conference at Carinhall, Göring's lavish residence, set *'Adler'* for 10 August but the adverse British weather prevented the full blow from falling until the 'Weather Frogs' (meteorologists) could guarantee *ObdL* three days of fine conditions. Consequently, *'Adler'* got into its stride only from the afternoon of 13 August, seeking the destruction of Air Vice-Marshal Keith Park's No 11 Group in the south and south-east and the eastern sector of Air Vice-Marshal Sir Christopher Quentin Brand's No 10 Group through attacks upon their bases. On 12 August the *Luftwaffe* began a campaign against what it believed was the enemy communication system by striking radar stations along the coast. On the first day three radars were out of action for six hours but Martini's comint stations continued to monitor radio signals and the campaign was soon abandoned. In any event, on 19 August Dowding had sufficient VHF radios to abandon the HF ones although dummy signals continued to be sent.

From 13 to 15 August the *Luftwaffe* flew some 2,500 sorties, of which 1,485 were on *'Adler Tag'*, but poor co-ordination by staff meant that on several occasions bomber formations were unescorted and Dowding's fighters inflicted a 7 per cent loss rate. The *Kampfgruppen* leaders demanded better fighter support and an abandonment of *Freijagd* although this type of fighter mission could be very destructive and Dowding ordered sector controllers to ignore enemy fighter sweeps and hit bomber formations. Poor quality German intelligence and photographic analysis was reflected in the dispersion of effort. Between 13 and 15 August some 450 tonnes of bombs were dropped on British airfields but only 219 tonnes hit Fighter Command bases, of which 80 tonnes hit the key sector headquarters. Nearly half the tonnage expended on Fighter Command bases was on the three forward airfields of Hawkinge, Manston and Lympne which were peripheral to the defensive effort. It would appear the daylight operations accounted for between 2,300 and 2,500 tonnes of bombs of which 1,015 tonnes (some 40–45%) were on airfields. [46]

Thursday, 15 August, saw a new disaster when the loss rate leapt to 10 per cent due to Stumpff's lone daylight contribution from *Luftflotte 5* and Schmid's poor intelligence which grossly under-estimated the number of fighters in northern Britain. A 17 per cent loss rate stopped Stumpff's daylight campaign in its tracks, news of the disaster arriving as Göring met his *Luftflotten* commanders again at Carinhall. This conference concluded the assault on enemy 'radio stations' had little effect, that the *Zerstörer* had to be conserved and that the *Stukas*, which would suffer a 21 per cent loss rate three days later, would also be held back.

As a result of the meeting it was decided to pay greater attention to Fighter Command's bases which were already under attack. Park's sectors felt the brunt of it, suffering 53 attacks, the majority on Hornchurch [24] and Biggin Hill, [15] while No 10 Group's neighbouring Middle Wallop sector suffered six raids, but there remained a disproportionate effort against the three coastal airfields, which suffered 14 attacks. During this period 119 aircraft were destroyed on the ground, of which only 45 were fighters including five night fighters, the greatest successes being at Detling [22] on 13 August and Brize Norton on 16 August where the British lost 46 aircraft, but most were trainers.

Yet the Germans were learning from their mistakes. On 20 August another conference was held at Carinhall with Göring commenting that: 'We have reached the decisive period of the air war against England.' The strike force had been cut by a fifth following the down-grading of the *Stukas*, although serviceability in the *Kampfgruppen* was maintained at 70 per cent. In the *Jagdgruppen* however, it dropped from 85 per cent to 75 per cent by 4 September. Staff work also improved and there was a changing of the guard with the most senior casualty being Keller who was kicked upstairs to command *Luftflotte 1* in the East and was replaced by *Generalleutnant* Curt Pflugbeil.

Luftflotte 3's participation in the day battle was declining because few of Sperrle's *Jagdgruppen* could support the bombers, so seven *Jagd-* and *Zerstörergruppen* were transferred to Kesselring as the bombers turned to night operations. The last week in August and the first in September saw the *Luftwaffe* reach a peak of activity with some 11,000 sorties (including reconnaissance aircraft) with an overall loss rate of some 3 per cent. Strike force losses dropped significantly from 6.5 per cent in the first week to 2.5 per cent in the second as the *Luftwaffe* began to establish air superiority over south-eastern England in a battle of attrition, pounding Park's bases. From 24 August to 6 September Dowding, who was desperately short of pilots, lost 103 killed and 128 wounded, or about a quarter of his strength. This was partly because the radar network could not give Park adequate warning time and *Freijagd* missions eroded his strength. A growing irritation for both Dowding and Park were the machinations of Air Vice-Marshal Trafford Leigh-Mallory of 12 Group, north of London, who was advocating massed formation ('Big Wing') attacks which could be devastating but required time to assemble. This was a luxury Park did not have and the best he could do was to pair squadrons to meet *Jagdgruppen* with some degree of equality.

By the beginning of September six out of Park's seven sector stations together with the telephone communications network was badly damaged while by 3 September Schmid had concluded that since 8 August the RAF had lost 1,115 aircraft and that 18 airfields had been destroyed with another 26 damaged. But the escorts lost an average 2.6 per cent of aircraft as 230 fighters, a quarter of them *Zerstörer*, failed to return. Yet Fighter Command was clearly not defeated and for *ObdL* the dilemma was bringing Dowding's fighters to battle. However, the apparent failure of attacks upon the RAF infrastructure left *ObdL* with only the strategy of striking directly at central London which Hitler had banned. Hoffman von Waldau's Operations Department now suggested an offensive against the British aircraft industry and on 1 September selected some 30 prime targets, but the attacks had barely begun when Hitler changed his mind about London. The city was hit accidentally on the night of 24/25 August and in retaliation Churchill ordered raids upon Berlin. This led Hitler, on 30 August, to authorise a major reprisal attack but he stipulated that it was not to be a *Terrorangriff* ('terror attack') on residential areas, although domestic and business property in London lived cheek by jowl.

Another conference at The Hague on 3 September decided on a massed attack upon the London Docks and four days later an armada of 348 bombers and 617 fighters roared over Cap Gris Nez watched by Göring who acted to the newsreel cameras by pretending to be deafened by the noise, putting his hands over his ears.

Park was wrong-footed into believing his airfields were again the target and although he committed 21 squadrons, they failed to prevent the Germans reaching central London. Leigh-Mallory assembled a 'Big Wing' to support him but this was bounced by *Jagdgruppen* which shot down five of his fighters. The raid was extremely destructive, causing 1,600 civilian casualties and damaging 107,400 grt of shipping at the cost of eight bombers (less than 2.3% of the formation) and 20 fighters (3.24%), although more than a third were *Zerstörer*. Dowding lost 29 aircraft (the *Luftwaffe* claimed 93) while in London uncontrollable fires acted as beacons for 247 night bombers which added to the chaos.

Yet the change in goals ended a battle of attrition which ultimately the *Luftwaffe* had been bound to win, although whether or not it would have been in time for *Seelöwe* is a matter of doubt. Of 3,309 tonnes dropped during daylight operations in September only 337 tonnes fell on airfields. [47] Moreover, increasing restrictions were placed by Göring who insisted the *Jagdgruppen* provide close escorts but they were feeling the strain as much as their enemies, probably more. Where the RAF abhorred the concept of *Experte* ('aces') the *Luftwaffe* embraced it and encouraged the accomplishment of high-scoring, 20 'kills' earning a *Ritterkreuz*. Many *Experte* thrived because their hard-pressed *Rottenhunde* (wingman of a pair) kept them safe and were often simply 'bullet catchers'. However, as they and the *Experte* fell, their replacements lacked both combat and flying experience, Milch noting on 26 August that some had flown their *Emils* only 10 times before joining the units. [48]

Clouds and showers prevented the Germans exploiting their success but on 9 September *ObdL* confirmed that London would continue to be the prime target. During the assault upon the British airfields Martini had finally recognised the enemy did have a radar network and the *Luftnachrichtenregimenter* carefully pinpointed locations and frequencies. But it lacked a transmitter powerful enough to jam the sensors and so turned to the *Reichspostzentralamt* (National Postal Office) which established a special detachment, code-named *Nachtfalter* ('moth'), under *Luftnachrichtenregiment 2* near Wissant. *Nachtfalter* took nearly a month to establish but came on line on 9 September. While the jammer degraded CH and CHL performance, the former used a crude anti-jamming device which meant the British were never blinded, yet Martini lacked high-power valves which would have finished the job.

A small attack on London on 14 September left the Germans with the impression the defences were on their last legs. This was partly because Fighter Command controllers were still unsure whether or not the capital was the prime target and tended to hold back squadrons to defend airfields. Göring decided to launch a knock-out blow on 15 September, but Dowding had been given time to prepare and he gave Park a dozen fresh squadrons to replace those exhausted in the bitter fighting. As a result Dowding responded to Göring's knock-out blow with some 450 sorties including a 'Big Wing', which inflicted an 18 per cent loss rate on the *Kampfgruppen*, allowing the British to regain control of their skies.

On 16 September Göring met his *Luftflotten* and *Fliegerkorps* commanders at Boulogne and was outwardly optimistic. The following day, however, Hitler indefinitely postponed '*Seelöwe*' rather than gamble Germany's newly gained prestige, especially in the face of a sceptical Stalin. In the last days of the Battle of Britain the bombers became tethered goats for the *Jagdgruppen*, but their operations proved to no avail and in early October cloud and rain gave *ObdL* the excuse to abandon large-scale daylight raids on 7 October. At this point the Battle of Britain effectively ended. By now overall bomber strength had dropped to 800 aircraft, from a peak of 1,100, with some 50 per cent serviceability. Fighter strength had dropped from a peak of 950 to 600 aircraft with 68 per cent serviceability and many *Jagdgruppen* were now distributed among *Luftgaue* on defensive missions.

The 14-week daylight campaign which was the Battle of Britain had cost the *Luftwaffe* 1,200 aircraft and some 3,140 casualties including 2,800 killed or missing, of whom 750 were prisoners, the casualties including three *Kommodore* and 21 *Kommandeure*. The British success owed much to its combination of sophisticated technology and practical organisation but they were greatly aided by *Luftwaffe* weaknesses. Intelligence was a major problem and Schmid's failure once again illustrated that the most significant element was not acquiring data but analysing it and this would remain a fundamental problem. Criticism of the failure to strike Britain immediately after the fall of France misses the point that the *Luftwaffe* was in no position to conduct a major campaign westward. Its logistical and communications systems had to be rebuilt and supplies built up in the West before it could move and this took the best part of July.

A more legitimate criticism is the failure to analyse the enemy defensive system and then to press attacks. Instead *ObdL* hopped from one strategy to another, like a flea on a hot plate, striking first the infrastructure, then the radar network, then the infrastructure again and finally London. Ultimately it was a failure of staff work, for while the RAF staff worked with near Prussian efficiency, the *Luftwaffe* staff were plagued with British amateurism.

Table 3-2: The Battle of Britain week-by-week

Week	Luftwaffe		Fighter Command	
	Bomber/Stuka	Fighter/Jabo	Total	Interceptions
Jul 1–7	245 (18)	750 (3)	2,581 (9)	1,634
Jul 8–14	540 (31)	1,140 (26)	4,028 (23)	2,464
Jul 15–21	300 (12)	800 (9)	3,637 (21)	2,013
Jul 22–28	340 (13)	700 (19)	3,876 (15)	2,137
Jul 29 – Aug 4	230 (18)	460 (2)	3,836 (6)	2,106
Aug 5–11	720 (26)	1,995 (40)	3,516 (45)	1,681
Aug 12–18	1,620 (134)	3,925 (150)	5,653 (122)	3,680
Aug 19–25	750 (44)	2,030 (41)	4,030 (47)	2,627
Aug 26 – Sep 1	1,060 (58)	5,260 (105)	5,165 (119)	3,641
Sep 2–8	1,200 (28)	4,090 (121)	4,911 (132)	3,813
Sep 9–15	970 (64)	1,900 (54)	3,369 (93)	2,489
Sep 16–22	750 (22	1,200 (14)	3,625 (26)	2,479
Sep 23–29	1,170 (18)	1,340 (64)	4,825 (73)	3,236
Sep 30 – Oct 6	560 (30)	1,270 (44)	4,217 (27)	3,158

Based upon USNA T971 Roll 8. Amended by Mason. Luftwaffe figures rounded out to nearest 10. Fighters – second figure is *Jabos*.

British figures based upon Air 24/526–529 (July–October 1940). Figures in brackets are losses.

Chapter Four

Gripping the Throat

Europe's nightmare in the 1930s was of cities reduced to scorched, gas-tainted rubble by armadas of bombers leaving the terrified survivors in a state of barbarity, a nightmare shown in the early part of the 1936 movie *Things to Come*. During the Second World War the prophecy was partly fulfilled especially in Germany and Great Britain, yet the strategic bombing campaigns were not born but, rather like Topsy in *Uncle Tom's Cabin*, '…just growed.'

The apocalypse was delayed because during the *Sitzkrieg* neither side had the political will, aircraft, support systems and bomb reserves for strategic bombing. The bombers were used for maritime support operations but air defence systems quickly contained the threat and, by chance, the *Luftwaffe* system caused a major re-evaluation of British bombing policy within months. *Flak* was the foundation of the *Reich*'s air defence but, unlike Great Britain, there was no central organisation and instead the *Luftgaue* were responsible for protecting targets within their boundaries. To improve fighter control over the north-west German coast, *Luftgau XI* (Hannover) and *Luftflotte 2* agreed to the establishment of *Jagdfliegerführer* (*Jafü*) *Deutsche Bucht* (Fighter Commander, Heligoland Bight) on 12 November under *Oberstleutnant* Carl-August Schumacher.

Normally the *Jagdgruppen* made their own arrangements with ground-based observer networks but Schumacher, a former naval officer, learned of the Navy's chain of *Freya* coastal radars, realised they could provide early warning of approaching enemy aircraft and wove a signal system between them and his airfields. This proved devastating against British bomber formations in December 1939, destroying half the 34 Wellingtons despatched and dashing the RAF's hopes of daytime operations by medium bombers. The success led to the creation of *Jafü* with similar organisations, the acquisition of more *Freya* search radars by the *Luftwaffe* and forced the RAF to switch to night-bombing with a desultry campaign against offshore seaplane bases.

Tragically, the greatest loss of German life occurred in daylight on 10 May 1940 when a formation from *III./KG 51*, using radio navigation to fly in thick cloud, became confused and struck the town of Freiburg causing 158 casualties. During the spring and summer of 1940 the *Kampfgruppen* focused upon Operational missions, but their failure in British skies by October forced the reluctant *Luftwaffe* to begin a strategic campaign to destroy the enemy's means and will to continue the conflict. The *Luftwaffe* had long had aspirations to strategic bombing but the first generation of aircraft proved under-powered and hopes now rested with a new four-engined heavy bomber, the Heinkel He 177, but this was still at the prototype stage by the autumn of 1940.

Despite this hurdle, the *Luftwaffe* was far better prepared for strategic bombing at the outbreak of war than the RAF for whom this role was the *raison d'etre*. The *Kampfgruppen* were always equipped with multi-engined aircraft with inherent advantages in terms of speed, range and payload; the He 111, for example, had a range and bomb load which bore favourable comparison with Britain's Armstrong-Whitworth Whitley 'heavy bomber.' The *Luftwaffe* also had large bombs, up to 1.80 tonnes (3,970 lbs), at a time when the RAF had nothing larger than 0.22 tonnes (500 lbs), and the *Lotfe* (*Lotfernrohr*) 7 stabilised bomb sight.

But the *Luftwaffe's* greatest advantage was its superior navigation capability. The RAF expected bomber pilots to navigate their aircraft, as in the Great War, but the Germans provided each bomber with a trained navigator supported by a chain of radio beacons. The beacons allowed bombers to fly in poor visibility and at night and they led to bomber support systems; FuSAn 721 *Knickebein* ('Dog-Leg'), X- and *Y-Verfahren* (X- and Y-systems), the latter invented by *Dr* Hans Plendl and sometimes referred to as the Plendl System. *Knickebein* equipped every bomber and could be used through the Lorenz blind-approach receiver, but *X*- and *Y-Verfahren* required specialist crews and the lack of high-power valves meant their coverage reached only into the Midlands, later extending to north-western England. Night attacks upon ports, industrial targets as well as airfields began on 17/18 June, although actually authorised the following day during a conference at Dinant. [1] Sperrle advocated concentrating upon night-bombing operations but the campaign lacked focus until the first Hague conference of 2 August when the enemy aero-industry became the prime target. It was initially spearheaded by Greim's *Fliegerkorps* V and Coeler's *Fliegerdivision* 9, later joined by Pflugbeil's *Fliegerkorps* IV which included *Hauptmann* Kurt Aschenbrenner's *KGr 100* which had flown its first *X-Verfahren* mission on 13/14 August displaying great accuracy.

Until the last week of August the *Luftwaffe's* night offensive was really a series of *Störangriffe* (less than 50 tonnes of bombs) but then the effort doubled as the western ports were pounded by 448 sorties (629 were despatched) and 455 tonnes of high explosive, plus some 45 tonnes of incendiaries, were dropped over four nights (see Table 4-1).

Table 4-1: Luftwaffe night bombing, July 1940–June 1941

Month	Bomber sorties	Fighter Command sorties
July 1940	553	407 (excl Jul 1–9)/-
Aug 1940	2,210	1,502 (-)
Sep 1940	3,680	1,186 (-)
Oct 1940	6,537 (23)	811 (-)
Nov 1940	6,117 (48)	935 (-)
Dec 1940	3,453 (44)	641 (-)
Jan 1941	2,035 (22)	584 (3)
Feb 1941	1,441 (18)	589 (-)
Mar 1941	4,267 (46)	1,027 (1)
Apr 1941	5,259 (58)	1,697 (4)
May 1941	5,376 (55)	2,357 (10)
Jun 1941	1,840 (22)	1,650 (2)

USNA T971 Roll 8. UKNA Air 16/1037. UKNA Air 16/1036. UKNA Air 41/17 Appendix 14.

The attacking force included some four-engined Fw 200 of *I./KG 40* which flew 25 sorties against west coast ports to 28/29 November. The defences forced the *Kampfgruppe* high and made accurate bombing impossible while jamming caused some bombers to get lost but casualties were light.

Between 5/6 September and 16/17 November central London suffered major attacks on 70 nights involving some 11,870 sorties, the *Luftwaffe* dropping 15,000 tonnes of bombs. The raids severely damaged the docks (and the surrounding housing) and disrupted rail traffic, especially the distribution of coal, partly due to the use of delayed-action bombs which often did not detonate because moisture interfered with the electrical fuzes. This problem grew steadily worse during the Blitz, the Germans calculating that 5–10 per cent of bombs failed to detonate while the British calculated it was 20 per cent. The Germans failed in their objective, partly because the British had anticipated the impact of bombing upon production and distribution and had appointed regional commissioners with plenipotentiary powers to restore communications and organise the distribution of supplies.

Until mid-September Sperrle carried the burden of the night bomber offensive while Kesselring focused on daylight operations, but with London the prime target from 7 September, a decision confirmed by *ObdL* two days later, *Luftflotte* 2 was increasingly diverted to night operations both on the metropolis and the eastern towns. At the Boulogne conference of 16 September, Sperrle was also ordered to join the night assault upon London but otherwise concentrated upon Southampton and the western ports. A disturbing feature of this conference was the decision to allow Coeler's *Fliegerdivision* 9 (*Fliegerkorps IX* from 16 October) to drop naval mines upon London, starting on 17/18 September. The mines could level whole streets but, inevitably, some did not explode and revealed their secrets to the Royal Navy, allowing it to reduce the impact of Coeler's maritime operations. By the night of 19/20 April 1941, Coeler had dropped 3,984 mines on land targets, representing 35 per cent of the total delivered since 17 April 1940. [2] Their use against London reflected a subtle change in *Luftwaffe* targeting policies. The folders of *Luftwaffe* (and RAF) bomb-aimers showed specific industrial or utility targets which were to be hit by high-explosive bombs, with incendiaries used against large area targets.

But decisions apparently taken at *Luftflotte*- or *Fliegerkorps*-level meant attacks on individual targets were gradually replaced by what was, in all but name, an area attack concept or *Terror Angriff* (Unrestricted 'Terror' Bombing). Meteorological conditions, including ground haze, together with industrial pollution made night navigation and bombing harder, for it was difficult to distinguish specific targets. *Knickebein* was supposed to help but from July the British created an electronic counter-measures (ECM) unit under Wing Commander Edward Addison as No 80 Wing. In addition to jamming the electronic support systems with varying degrees of success (*X-Verfahren* remained effective throughout the Blitz), Addison also produced false radio navigation signals by re-transmitting the originals, a technique known as masking beacons (meacons). [3]

Yet legitimate targets and homes were so close to each other in British cities – often in the same road – that it was impossible to be certain the bombs would land on legitimate targets. The impact of variables such as wind and atmospheric density compounded the problem and the *Luftwaffe* night assault quickly declined from precision to area attack due to tactical expediency rather than strategic decision. The suggestion that this was partly because German bombers could not carry adequate ordnance loads to British targets seems self-evidently wrong because heavy bombs and mines were delivered all over the British Isles throughout the Blitz.

The move from precision to area attack is illustrated by the activities of *KGr 100* which flew 1,130 sorties between late August and the end of December. In August the unit dropped some 142 tonnes of bombs including 19 tonnes of incendiaries (13%) but during September half its missions were precision attacks and the remainder part of the general assault upon London. During October, 28 per cent of the 370 tonnes *KGr 100* dropped on British targets consisted of incendiaries which were inherently inaccurate because the *Gruppe* became a *Beleuchter-* or *Anzündergruppe* (Firelighter, or Fire-Raiser Group), although the first operation may have been during raids on Merseyside in late August. The *Y-Verfahren*-equipped *III./KG 26*, soon joined by *II./KG 55*, switched from using parachute flares as route-markers to target-markers as well as dropping very heavy bombs such as SC 1000 'Hermann', SC 1400 and SC 1800 'Satan' to augment Coeler's mines.

The new tactic was called *Feuerleitung* ('blaze control') and had the objective of creating *Brandbombfelde* (incendiary fields), a task assisted shortly before Christmas by the introduction of the monster SC 2500 'Max'. But the use of incendiaries, together with the small size of the target-marking force and the failure to produce dedicated flares meant that soon after a raid began, the target marker fires were obliterated by blazes caused by the main force's incendiaries. [4] During December 92 per cent of the 169 tonnes of bombs dropped by *KGr 100* were incendiaries although this was the peak, and the percentage dropped to 54 in April and less than 25 in May. Homes became kindling for the *Brandbombfelde* whose effects could not be controlled owing to the scale of attacks; indeed on 11 November the British overheard a prisoner from *KG 1* talking about plans for future missions in which workers' homes were the target. [5]

The lengthening nights of winter slashed *Kampfgruppen* combat losses by two-thirds but the accident rate rose; in October 142 bombers were lost on operations, of which 78 were in accidents such as crashes on landing, while the November and December figures were 71/57 and 120/58 respectively. The accident rates reflected reductions in instrument training time and the failure to expand training facilities, and thus it was usually new crews who fell. During October the number of night bomber sorties was more than double that of the day raiders with attacks nearly every night. But the *Luftwaffe's* perennial shortage of spares meant that only 700 aircraft were available at any one time while serviceability rates remained at a constant 50 per cent throughout the Blitz.

The overall aircraft loss rate was about 1 per cent, reflecting the threadbare nature of the night defences, although this was due less to neglect than the slow pace of re-armament, which forced unwelcome compromises. Although anti-aircraft guns were the backbone of their defence, the British began to consider the night defence problem in March 1940. A committee which included Air Vice-Marshal Sir Christopher Quentin Brand, the commander of No 10 Group, and the top scientists, concluded that because the day defences were so good the *Luftwaffe* would be forced to go over to a night-bombing offensive. [6]

In the Great War night fighting was usually performed by single-seat fighters who would orbit visual beacons (the British called them lighthouses) placed across the bombers' likely approach route, searchlights tracking the targets and attracting the fighter. Against the slow bombers of the day, these tactics were effective, indeed Brand was a night fighter 'ace'. The most significant change between the wars was the use of 'heavy' or twin-engined fighters for the night role, but the 'Mark 1 eyeball' remained the prime sensor. Dowding wished to adapt his day interception system to night-fighting and he recognised the value of airborne radar as the night fighter's sensor.

He requested that the Air Ministry build a network of inland CH stations but his request was rejected and he was left to rely upon the airborne radar, which had its first success on 23/24 July when Flying Officer Glynn Ashfield, Pilot Officer Geoffrey Morris and radar-operator Sergeant Reginald Leyland in a Blenheim IVF shot down a Do 17 of *2./KG 3*, *Leutnant* Kahlfuss' crew being captured. But the second radar 'kill' was not until 19 November, for the hand-built AI (Airborne Interception) Mk III radars were temperamental, difficult to maintain, had inexperienced operators and had a range of only 330–5,300 yards (300–4,800 metres) making it difficult to acquire the target until it was within gun range. Significantly, the next kill was by one of the new Bristol Beaufighters equipped with new AI Mk IV radar with increased detection range and a minimum range of 140 yards (130 metres). [7]

Focusing upon the day campaign, Dowding neglected the night menace just as a whispering campaign grew against him. It originated in Leigh-Mallory's No 12 Group and had begun over 'Big Wings' and then been fuelled a feud with No 11 Group's Park. Dowding, long-overdue for retirement, failed to rein in his warring subordinates, or to meet the machinations of Lord Trenchard 'The Father of the Royal Air Force' and his successor Salmond. His failure to meet the night threat damned him in the politicians' eyes and on 25 November he was removed in a shoddy manner which reflected badly on all the participants from Churchill down, Park being forced to hand command to Leigh-Mallory on 18 December. [8]

Air Vice-Marshal Sholto Douglas replaced Dowding and brought the dynamism which the politicians were seeking. He created more night fighter squadrons (although even in February 1941 there were only 87 pilots or half their establishment), and removed VHF (176 MHz) Gun Laying (GL) radars from sector station control, where Dowding had put them, to create a threadbare 'carpet' covering the southern counties. This was augmented by six dedicated VHF (192–209 MHz) GCI (Ground-Controlled Interception) radars with a 50-mile (80-kilometre) range to support the night fighter force in a system similar to the German *Dunkelnachtjagd* ('Dark Night Fighting') being developed simultaneously. Single-seat fighters and a variety of desperate measures were deployed including aerial minelayers and flying searchlights.

Meanwhile, *ObdL* on 9 October ordered the *Luftflotten* to strike London in the middle of the month when the moon was full, partly because *Knickebein* was compromised, but ports were to be attacked. Yet *ObdL* planning lacked coherence and on 20 October, Sperrle was ordered to despatch 250 sorties a night, of which 100 would be against the Midlands and western ports, while Kesselring would reduce his effort against London to no more than 50 sorties a night (assisted by Italian bombers), all the attackers using 'Plendl equipment.' *Fliegerkorps IX* would augment its mining activities with conventional bombing on targets in Lincolnshire as well as dropping naval mines over land targets.

But within three weeks, on 7 November, new orders were issued giving the Midlands priority, with Wolverhampton the original target. When it was realised the city's anti-aircraft defences had been strengthened, Coventry was subsequently selected. On the moonlit night of 14/15 November both *Luftflotten* despatched 449 aircraft supported by both *X*- and *Y-Verfahren* to deliver 545 tonnes of high explosives and incendiaries. The *Kampfgruppen* replaced the tight *Gruppen* with looser formations in a more flexible stream which the Germans called *Krokodile* ('Crocodiles'). These formations were 20 kilometres apart, flying on a 10-kilometre-broad front at 9,800–11,800 feet (3,000–3,600 metres) forcing the night fighters to search vast areas of airspace. [9] They turned Coventry city centre into a blazing inferno which could be seen by follow-up crews from the other side of the Channel, although an amazing 18 per cent of crews failed to reach the target! The British despatched 125 night fighter sorties but only one bomber was shot down, and that by anti-aircraft fire. The city centre was wrecked; 21 factories were severely damaged while the loss of utility services (electricity, gas and water) prevented nine others working, disrupting production for months. The following day's OKW communique noted: '*After this large-scale attack …the English invented a new verb "to coventrate".*' Coventry would certainly mark a watershed in strategic bombardment for the devastation, which far exceeded *ObdL*'s expectations, had been achieved by accident but the British believed it was deliberate and took careful note. [10]

Coventry marked a changing of the guard at *ObdL* as Milch was given an opportunity to indulge his desire for operational command, but in splendid isolation as Göring and Jeschonnek (the latter one of a long line of *Luftwaffe* officers who loathed Milch) went on leave until late January, the former occasionally dictating orders down the telephone. Milch's tenure came at a time when the *Luftwaffe's* night offensive began to have some impact upon the phlegmatic British population and in Southampton thousands of people 'trekked' out of the city with civic leaders at their head, a demonstration of declining morale. [11] November saw the Blitz reach its zenith with the *Luftwaffe* flying more than 6,000 sorties to deliver 23 major (more than 100 tonnes of bombs on a single target) and 2 heavy (more than 50 tonnes) attacks, but the effort halved during December with 11 major and 5 heavy attacks.

The weather, with low cloud, now conspired to reduce the *Luftwaffe* offensive, the freezing temperatures and snow during January and February slashing the total effort over two months to a total of seven major and eight heavy attacks. In January the *Luftwaffe* had only 1,214 bombers of which 551 were serviceable, a 25 per cent drop in three months. Only the most experienced crews, *Altere Häse* ('Old Hares'), could be despatched and the use of *Stukas* on the night of 15/16 January suggests Milch was becoming desparate. [12]

The relative lull in January gave the British an opportunity to improve their defences. Six sectors with GCI radars were deployed in an arc from the Humber to the Avon covering the approaches to both London and the Midlands. But by mid-February there were still only two Beaufighter squadrons, although radar-equipped fighters were growing increasingly proficient. In January 1941 they flew 84 sorties and achieved 44 contacts of which two ended in combat, while by May there were 643 sorties achieving 204 contacts with 74 combats. Yet even in May, 67 per cent of all night fighter sorties were visual ('cat's eye') missions and while the radar-equipped fighters accounted for only 43 per cent of contacts they produced 61 per cent of combats. [13]

With the return of Göring and Jeschonnek in late January the *Luftwaffe* joined *OKW*'s overall review of the war against Great Britain leading to *OKW Weisung Nr 23 'Directions for operations against the British war economy'* which was published on 6 February and replaced *Weisung Nr 17* to conclude that ports should have priority. *ObdL* anticipated this with its directive of 1 February, the German decision driven by two interesting conclusions; firstly, the difficulty of estimating the impact of the air offensive upon British war production and, in the Germans' own words, *'The least effect of all (as far as we can see) has been made upon the morale and will to resist of the English people.'* The air offensive would now focus upon ports, the aircraft industry and factories producing anti-aircraft guns and explosives, while other targets would be struck only if weather or operational conditions prevented the prime targets being attacked.

There was also a very significant paragraph towards the end of *OKW*'s directive: *'Until the beginning of the regrouping of forces for "Barbarossa" (the invasion of the Soviet Union), efforts will be made to intensify air... warfare, not only to inflict the heaviest possible losses on England, but also to give the impression that an attack on the British Isles is planned for this year.'* Yet the *Luftwaffe* was unable to pursue this objective in February, partly due to meteorological conditions over Britain, partly due to water-logged airfields through rain and partly because 18 *Kampfgruppen* had been temporarily withdrawn for rest and re-equipment.

Improvements in the weather during March, together with a return of *Kampfgruppen* to the front, saw the *Luftwaffe* effort during March quadruple to more than 4,000 sorties, including 12 major and three heavy attacks. The electronic war was intensified but until April the *Kampfgruppen* flew major attacks upon inland targets only on moonlit nights, ports being attacked more frequently because they were easier to find. To confuse the enemy strict radio silence was imposed until the first bombs fell while X- and *Y-Verfahren* beams were placed over false targets and switched to the real ones at the last minute. Rapid frequency changes were also introduced for the *X-Verfahren* whose wider band of frequencies and greater tactical flexibility ensured it remained effective at a time when selective jamming was degrading the effectiveness of *Y-Verfahren*.

During March the *Luftwaffe* began striking targets, usually west coast ports, several nights in succession. Once again these attacks hit civilian morale, with streams of people 'trekking' out of the cities beforehand, but the *Luftwaffe* effort eased in the last 10 nights as seven *Kampfgruppen*, were transferred to the Balkans. The shortage of bombers might explain why 50 *Stukas* and *Jabos*, officially 'light bombers' (*Leichte Kampfflugzeuge*') and unofficially '*Leichte Kesselringe*' ('Light Kesselrings'), joined the campaign. The defences failed to inflict heavy casualties but did help prevent the *Kampfgruppen* concentrating their bombs and on some occasions only a third of the ordnance despatched reached the target. [14]

During April a total of more than 5,000 sorties were flown, 75 per cent by Sperrle, with raids every night, mostly in the Midlands but extending to Belfast on 15/16 April in one of 16 major and five heavy attacks flown against Great Britain. Western ports were again struck, but the worst attacks were on London where more than 1,200 tonnes of bombs were dropped on 19/20 April as a 'birthday present' for the *Führer* following some 1,080 tonnes two nights earlier. However, such a level of effort was exhausting just at the time that more *Kampfgruppen* were being sucked into the Balkans. The remaining crews had to fly at least two, and sometimes three, sorties a night using forward airfields to reload and refuel. The aircraft were noisy and often vibrated badly, while tension and exhaustion would further drain the crews and while flying his 50th mission against Portsmouth on 28/29 April, Peter Stahl of *KG 30* fell asleep at the controls. [15] He awoke in good time, but many crews were not so lucky and *Luftwaffe* losses rose.

With the imminent departure of most *Kampfgruppen* eastwards, and the weather improving, the *Luftwaffe* assault in May reached a new intensity with some 3,800 sorties including 100 by '*Leichte Kesselringe*'. There were 11 major and three heavy attacks during the first half of the month and the British Minister of Home Security, Mr Herbert Morrison, warned that sustained bombing might cause a collapse in provincial morale. The campaign reached a crescendo on 10/11 May (the night Rudolf Hess landed in Scotland after a flight from Munich) with 507 bombers striking London and dropping 820 tonnes of bombs in the last major raid for three years. A smaller raid followed the next night and, uniquely, it was accompanied by 63 fighters reflecting the defence's growing effectiveness, although the loss rate in May was only 1.4 per cent, compared with 1.1 per cent the previous month. A post-Blitz analysis by the RAF noted that all towns and cities recovered at a rate of 2–3 per cent, measured by a variety of indices with cities generally taking between 10–15 days to recover from major attacks. [16]

The *Luftwaffe* dropped 45,000 tonnes of bombs during the Blitz disrupting production and transport, reducing food supplies and shaking British morale. It also helped to support the U-boat blockade by sinking some 58,000 grt of shipping and damaging 450,000 grt. Yet overall British production rose steadily throughout this period although there were significant falls during April, probably influenced by the departure of workers on their Easter holiday. The British official history on war production noted the greatest impact was upon the supply of components rather than complete equipment. [17]

Between 20 June 1940 and 31 March 1941 the *Luftwaffe* lost 2,265 aircraft in operations against the British Isles – a quarter fighters and a third bombers. No fewer than 3,363 men were killed, 2,641 were missing and 2,117 were wounded. More might have been achieved if *ObdL* had sought to exploit a weak spot, such as the Allies would do later when concentrating upon transportation and oil production. But this would have required an economic-industrial analysis of which the *Wehrmacht* was incapable, thanks to Seeckt's decisions not to provide the new generation of staff officers with industrial awareness. Instead *ObdL* sought clusters of targets which suited the latest policy and disputes within the leadership were about tactics rather than strategy; indeed this led to the departure of Kesselring's operations chief, *Major* Viktor von Lossberg, who would later become a night fighter expert influencing developments during the second half of 1943. By the second half of May it did not matter, for Kesselring had departed for Warsaw and the majority of the *Kampfgruppen* followed him eastward leaving Sperrle with *KG 2* to continue a token offensive.

The relieved British began to assess the impact and in August 1941 the air staff analysed the effects of the Blitz to improve their own bombing offensive, concluding that bombers should strike a single target each night and use more incendiaries because they had a greater impact on production than high explosive. They also noted that regional production was severely disrupted when city centres were devastated through the loss of administrative offices, utilities, transport and small workshops. The results arrived as the RAF was reviewing the first year's bombing campaign against Germany. It was obvious the precision attack policy had failed because most crews could not find the targets and with so much investment in strategic bombing, the RAF needed a new strategy. With a remorseless logic on a par with that of the famed German Army General Staff, the RAF staff concluded that the most effective use of bombers was to ape the *Luftwaffe* and to launch concentrated raids which used largely incendiaries to saturate the target. This would be called 'area attack' and would form the foundation of both RAF and USAAF strategic bombing during the latter war years. In developing this concept the *Luftwaffe* was sowing the dragons' teeth, but it was the German people who would reap the whirlwind.

The threat to the *Reich* grew steadily as Bomber Command became the instrument of retribution, not only for the British Empire, but also occupied Europe, although at a terrible cost: of the 125,000 men, one boy, one woman and one dog who flew with the Command over Western Europe during the war, more than 57,000 were shot down, about one-third of them in the 18 months before D-Day. [18] Although most aircrew were white, a number of black West Indians shared the danger, as well as men drawn not only from the Empire and Occupied Europe but also from the United States and even from Germany itself, the last flying in 'ABC' ('Airborne Cigar') Comint jamming missions from late 1943. [19]

The campaign began on the night of 10/11 May 1940 and the first 18 months would be wasted effort because the absence of navigators, navigation aids and bombing aids meant the British crews could neither hit a barn door nor even find the barn (see Table 4-2). Until 1942 the average British bomber struck homes and fields rather than German industry, leading the Germans to assume that these raids were *Terror Angriffe*, although Goebbels did not use this phrase until March 1942. Despite the trivial military damage the *Luftwaffe* naturally wished to protect the population and restore its prestige. However, the *Reich*'s night defences were not strengthened until after the fall of France with measures which mirrored those of the British, although the *Luftwaffe* was slower developing both GCI techniques and airborne radar. [20]

Table 4–2: Night bomber offensive against the Reich, July 1940–June 1943

Quarter	Sorties	Lost	Percentage	N/F claims
Q3 1940	4,227	107	2.53	17
Q4 1940	3,735	64	1.71	11
Q1 1941	3,008	48	1.59	22
Q2 1941	5,582	151	2.70	81
Q3 1941	7,630	281	3.74	130
Q4 1941	3,840	150	3.90	57
Q1 1942	2,862	102	3.56	69
Q2 1942	8,359	378	4.52	271
Q3 1942	8,512	417	5.02	288
Q4 1942	2,752	151	5.49	101
Q1 1943	7,151	254	3.55	194
Q2 1943	14,765	701	5.06	564

Sources: Middlebrook and Everitt. UKNA Air 14/2666–75). Figures in Q3 1941, Q3 1942 and Q2 1843 include Russian but their losses in 1942 and 1943 are unknown.

Flak was the Reich's shield by both day and night, the batteries increasingly supported by *Würzburg* radar which claimed its first victory in September 1940, although even at the end of 1942 only 25–30 per cent of batteries had radar fire control. The number of batteries rose from 756 (423 heavy) in 1940 to 932 (537) the following year and 1,182 (744) in 1942, while command and control improved with the creation of *Luftverteidigungskommandos* or *LvKdo* (Air Defence Commands) before the war renamed on 1 September 1941 *Flakdivisionen* (anti-aircraft artillery divisions). [21] At the outbreak of war a few *Nachtjagdstaffeln* existed with obsolete single-engined fighters, relying upon searchlights to detect their targets in *Hellenachtjagd* ('bright night fighting') but they were quickly absorbed into the *Jagdwaffe* (day fighter force) units.

The rebuilding of the *Nachtjagdwaffe* (night fighter force) from the spring of 1940 owed much to the efforts of junior officers although Milch may well have been the *eminence grise*. One of Schumacher's pilots and a signals specialist, *Leutnant* Hermann Diehl, proposed to *ObdL* that radar be used for night GCI, but nothing was done until, in April 1940, the *Kommandeur* of I./ZG 1, *Hauptmann* Wolfgang Falck, intercepted some enemy aircraft with the aid of *Würzburg*. He too alerted *ObdL* and, possibly at Milch's instigation, on 22 June his *Gruppe* was transferred to Düsseldorf to become I./NJG 1 and he was promoted *Kommodore*. He was given operational control of a searchlight regiment and began a modified form of *Hellenachtjagd* but was confined to *Luftgau VI*. [22]

The need for a more comprehensive organisation was rapidly becoming apparent and led to the formation, on 17 July, of *Nachtjagddivision 1* under *Oberst* Josef Kammhuber (the former *Kommodore* of KG 51 and one of the most experienced *Luftwaffe* officers, who had recently returned from a French prison camp). Auspiciously, three nights after Kammhuber's appointment, *Oberleutnant* Werner Streib, the

Kommandeur of I./*NJG 1*, on 20/21 July claimed the first of his 66 victims and the following night five more were claimed, including a second by Streib. [23]

Kammhuber, who became *Inspekteur der Nachtjagd*, expanded Falck's concept over the next eight months, creating a *Scheinwerfergürtel* (searchlight belt) of six *Scheinwerfer-Grossräume* (large searchlight sectors) each with a searchlight regiment subdivided into 17 battalion *Räume* originally 30 kilometres long and 20 kilometres deep from Lübeck to Liège, with a separate *Raum* in Schleswig-Holstein covering Kiel. They were supported by a dedicated signals system and 12 purpose-built night fighter bases usually equipped with cramped and crudely converted Bf 110s fitted with flame dampers, but they were supplemented by other *Zerstörer* including the roomy Ju 88C and the underpowered Do 17Z-6/10 *Kauz* ('Screech Owl') I/II and even some Bf 109s for a short time. Manpower was more difficult to obtain, as the British discovered, and despite using retrained *Zerstörergruppen* augmented by men drawn from *Kampf-* and *Fernaufklärungsstaffeln, Transportgruppen, Lufthansa* and the training schools, by the New Year there were only 60 operational aircrew in 16 *Nachtjagdstaffeln* [24].

However, *Hellenachtjagd* could operate only to 5/10ths cloud conditions because the searchlights were unable to penetrate the vapour. *Würzburg* was added to the searchlight battalions from October, but Kammhuber initially was sceptical about radar. He did establish six *Kombinierte Nachtjagdgebeite* (Combined Night Fighting Zones) around prime RAF targets where fighters were supposed to co-operate with *Würzburg (FuMG 62A)*-supported *Flak*, but success was limited as there was no long-range radar. Diehl gave Falck a demonstration of *Freya* and recommended incorporating it into the night defence system. Kammhuber received the memorandum on 19 August (his 44th birthday) and reluctantly he assigned Diehl a zone south of the Ijssel Meer (Zuider Zee) linking a *Freya* with a searchlight in what was called a *Parasitanlage* ('Parasite Installation'). This became operational on 26 September but it was in the zone of the second, established on 2/3 October, where *Leutnant* Ludwig Bekker opened the score book. [25]

Designated *Dunkelnachtjagd*, the system was expanded into six coastal *Gebiete* some 140 kilometres in front of the *Scheinwerfergürtel* from the Danish border to the Scheldt estuary. Expansion proved painfully slow due to production delays with *Freya* and a shortage of experienced ground controllers. For his part, Kammhuber had become interested in airborne sensors, and the failure of *Spanner* ('Peeping Tom') infra-red searchlights led him in the autumn of 1940 to consider radar. Despite opposition from Göring he found Martini and *RLM* more supportive. Telefunken had developed a derivative of a radio altimeter known as *Lichtenstein B/C*, and by the summer of 1941 experiments with this sensor were proving extremely promising.

The re-organisation of Germany's night defences took its toll and pushed British loss rates between July 1940 and June 1941 to twice those of the *Luftwaffe* during the Blitz, despite a smaller scale of operations. The longer distances flown by British pilots, the inadequacies of many bomber designs, especially with regard to endurance, and the RAF's pre-war neglect of navigation proved just as deadly as Kammhuber and Falck. During the second half of 1940 more than 170 British aircraft failed to return from night-bombing operations against the Reich (excluding minelaying sorties), yet the defenders claimed only 72 (30 by *Flak*). While the shortfall may be explained partially by 'winged birds' (damaged aircraft) which later succumbed to their injuries, it is clear that many aircraft simply ran out of fuel and crashed.

There was some improvement in defence command and control with the formation of *Luftwaffe Befehlshaber Mitte*, intended to reinforce the defences of Berlin, on 24 March 1941 originally with *Luftgaue III* (Berlin) and *IV* (Dresden) and under the former's air defence commander, *Generalmajor* Hubert Weise. To provide depth, in May Weise extended his empire into *Luftgaue VI* (Münster) and *XI* (Hanover) when Kesselring's *Luftflotte 2* moved eastwards, but Sperrle refused to relinquish control of his *Luftgaue VII* (Munich) and *XII/XIII* (Wiesbaden) and would later retain 'his' *Nachtjagdgruppen*. Weise also assumed command of Kammhuber's *Nachtjagddivision*, but his organisation was still inferior to RAF Fighter Command, for there were four autonomous observation organisations under the *Luftwaffe* (*Flugmeldedienst*), the Navy, the Nazi Party and the *Reichsbahn* (State Railway) whose reports were uncoordinated and which provided less information than the enemy's Royal Observer Corps, specifically about aircraft types. The organisation was further refined on 1 August 1941 when Kammhuber's command was expanded into *Fliegerkorps XII* responsible for both the night and day defence of the *Reich*.

The threat by day was minor; just over 200 sorties in the second half of 1940, almost twice as many in 1941 and 464 in 1942, most of these directed against ports or mounted on cloudy days (see Table 4-3). A few *Jagdgruppen* were retained but day defence largely relied upon *Flak* and ad hoc fighter units formed by schools and aircraft factories with operations locally co-ordinated by *Jafü Deutsche Bucht* and *Jafü Mitte* (created from *Jafü 1* on 1 April 1941), the latter under *Generalmajor* Eitel-Friedrich Roediger von Manteuffel. On 1 September a *Jafü Berlin* was created and Manteuffel's command (under *Generalleutnant* Kurt-Bertram von Döring from 1 October 1941) was subordinated to *Fliegerkorps XII* but it controlled the other *Jafü* and *Jafü Holland-Ruhrgebiet* when it was created on 1 February 1942. [26] These defences inflicted an overall loss rate of 6.37 per cent or nearly three times that of night operations.

Table 4-3: Day bomber attacks upon the Reich, July 1940–June 1943

Quarter	Sorties	Lost	Percentage
Q3 1940	170	18	10.6
Q4 1940	37	2	5.4
Q1 1941	5	1	20.0
Q2 1941	227	12	5.3
Q3 1941	153	23	15.0
Q4 1941	5	1	20.0
Q1 1942	18	–	–
Q2 1942	36	9	25.0
Q3 1942	259	21	8.1
Q4 1942	151	10	6.6
Q1 1943	415	23	5.5
Q2 1943	1,437	122	8.5

Sources: Freeman, *Mighty Eighth War Diary*. Middlebrook and Everitt; Day Bombing Raid Sheets (PRO Air 14/3361-4).

Kammhuber's organisation was certainly having an impact upon Bomber Command operations and quarterly figures showed that during 1941 and 1942 the percentage of British losses rose steadily, clearly due to the expanding *Nachtjagdwaffe*. The Germans claimed 421 victories in 1941 and 729 the following year – two-thirds of Bomber Command's casualties. A German report noted that in the second quarter of 1941 *Hellen-* and *Dunkelnachtjagd* each claimed 36 victories, while *Kombiertnachtjagd* claimed only nine, all in June. [27] On 27/28 June 1941 Bomber Command first recorded 'intense night fighter attacks' and a third of the 35 Whitleys despatched were lost together with three Wellingtons; on 7/8 November 12.4 per cent of the mission against Berlin was lost, although the night's overall loss was 9.4 per cent partly due to severe icing conditions. [28]

Nevertheless the weight of bombs falling on German soil grew as the ratio of heavy bombers steadily increased from 4 per cent of sorties in July 1941 to 84 per cent by December 1942. The new generation of British bombers (Halifax, Lancaster, Manchester and Stirling) could often fly higher and faster than the Bf 110, but they were plagued by mechanical problems, giving the *Luftwaffe* time to adjust to the threat. Four-engined bombers also struck from the East when the Russians staged a brief campaign against Berlin from 7/8 August to 3/4 September at which point their bases had to be abandoned. [29]

The leading night fighter ace in 1941 was Streib (22 victories), who exploited *Dunkelnachtjagd* as the most efficient defence, even without airborne radar: it required less than nine sorties to achieve a victory in the final quarter of 1941 (52%of all victories), compared to 41 with *Hellenachtjagd*. [30] His successes, like that of his fellow *Experten*, owed as much to his status as *Kommandeur* of *I./NJG 1* as to his own skills (and those of his controllers), for he could select when, where and with whom to fly. The *Experten* could 'poach' active areas, leaving less favoured crews futilely orbiting beacons in fallow sectors, with the result that a small number of crews accumulated great experience at the expense of the majority. [31] The inevitable losses of *Experten* had an impact out of all proportion to their numbers, yet there were always ambitious pilots in both the *Nacht-* and *Tagjagdwaffe* who suffered *Halsweh* (a sore throat), meaning that they wanted a *Ritterkreuz*, which was worn around the neck, and only 12 of 118 night fighter *Ritterkreuz*-holders joined after July 1942. [32]

The growing British threat forced Kammhuber to expand his system in the west and to develop a line of *Hellenachtjagdräume* and *Dunkelnachtjagdgebiete* to protect Berlin. Each *Hellenachtjagdraum* received two *Würzburgen* to control searchlights, and a *Freya* to detect approaching targets and from the autumn of 1941 the *Raum* control posts increasingly used the radars as the prime sensors with *Seeburg* automated plotting tables in a system designated *Himmelbett Verfahren* ('four-poster bed procedure'). Improved sensors arrived from the autumn of 1942 including *Würzburg-Reise (FuMG 65)* and improved *Freya AN, while* long-range (200–300km) radars began to appear in the spring of 1942 including *Mammut (FuMo 51)* and *Wassermann (FuMG 402)*. [33]

Shortage of aircraft was a major problem for Kammhuber, whose strength dropped from 263 on 9 September 1941 to 223 on 1 July 1942 (Sperrle did have another 30), the total being only 63 per cent of establishment. Numbers gradually rose but Sperrle's empire-building meant that by the beginning of December 1942 he had 107 and Kammhuber 247 while generally only two-thirds were serviceable. There was the continued demand for *Zerstörer* from the Eastern and Mediterranean fronts while during the summer of 1941, Messerschmitt AG ran down the Bf 110 production line to ensure acceptance of the diabolical Me 210. This policy was reversed only in the late autumn of 1941, leading to the Bf 110G which entered service during the summer of 1942.

The *Nachtjagdwaffe* did not escape unscathed and the bombers' much criticised 7.7mm (0.303 inch) machine guns accounted for most of the 103 fighters destroyed or badly damaged due to enemy action over the *Reich* between April 1942 and June 1943 (see Table 4-4) while Sperrle lost another 24 and accidents accounted for another 175 and another 42 in Luftflotte 3. Wear and tear on aircraft meant that 179 had to return to factories and aircraft parks for overhauls, but 619 aircraft arrived new from the factories (others were transferred between units) to help expand *Fliegerkorps XII* to 349 aircraft by the beginning of July 1943.

Table 4-4:Luftwaffe night fighter activity, April 1942–June 1943

Quarter		Losses		Overhaul	New aircraft
		Enemy action	*Accident*		
Q2 1942	Reich	35	18	15	70
	Lfl 3	4	9	-	3
Q3 1942	Reich	16	39	53	124
	Lfl 3	2	3	-	9
Q4 1942	Reich	5	17	20	84
	Lfl 3	6	-	8	24
Q1 1943	Reich	23	42	39	160
	Lfl 3	2	9	5	24
Q2 1943	Reich	24	59	52	181
	Lfl 3	10	21	10	70

Source: BA MA RL 2 III/874 - 879.

The beginning of 1943 saw a slight surplus in night fighter crews as losses were reduced and more students completed their course. By then Bomber Command was growing in effectiveness as navigation became a recognised profession and electronic navigation aids such as Gee (resembling *Knickebein)* and Oboe (known to the Germans as *Bumerangverfahren*, or Boomerang Procedure) entered service. RAF electronic intelligence gradually developed a detailed picture of what they called the 'Kammhuber Line', and mission planning sought either to avoid it or reduce the attackers' exposure. The radical overhaul of Bomber Command was symbolised by the appointment of Air Chief Marshal Sir Arthur Harris as its commander-in-chief on 22 February 1942. Harris, a fighter squadron commander in the Great War, was one of the Douhet crusaders who believed that aerial bombardment almost alone would defeat Germany. [34]

The British turned towards area attacks based upon their Blitz studies at a time when Harris inherited a directive from his predecessor to strike at civilian morale, especially industrial workers. He decided to strike German city centres and his operational research section addressed the problem of assuring higher bomb concentrations and reduced exposure to the defences. The bombers would now fly in a tight stream, similar to the *Krokodil* tactics, up to 60 miles (100 kilometres) long and 25–30 miles (40–50 kilometres) broad by the spring of 1944, which could saturate any night fighter sector. [35] The bomber force would focus upon one target per night rather than several, although for much of 1942 Harris concentrated on re-equipping his forces and developing tactics.

The new strategy began with a short campaign against Essen from 8/9 March 1942 and although it did not inflict the damage anticipated it did slash casualties to 2.86 per cent. On the night of 28/29 March 1942 Harris' bombers outflanked the Kammhuber Line to strike the medieval streets of Lübeck using 400 tonnes of bombs, including 266 tonnes of incendiaries, burning out the heart of the Hanseatic city and causing 200 million Reichsmarks' worth of damage (equivalent to $500 million at the 1939 exchange rate), at the cost of 12 aircraft (5.12% of the attacking force). This was followed by four attacks upon Rostock from 23/24 April to 26/27 April which demonstrated that Lübeck had not been unique. According to Goebbels the raids virtually ended any form of community. There were vain attempts to repeat the success in the Ruhr and Hamburg, and pressure grew on the RAF to transfer bomber squadrons both to overseas theatres and to the Battle of the Atlantic. To counter this, Harris planned a publicity stunt using a thousand bombers to wipe out a German city. By mobilising operational training units (which provided a third of his strike force), he despatched 1,047 aircraft against Cologne on 30/31 May. Harris expected to lose 50 aircraft, but Bomber Command actually lost only 41 (3.9%), more than on any previous mission, with about half falling to night fighters, of which 25 made contact. However, the centre of Cologne was devastated and industrial activity paralysed for a week, although within six months the city had recovered. [36] Similar attacks were carried out against Essen and Bremen during June, but Harris could not maintain the momentum and during the rest of the year smaller attacks were made, although in growing strength.

Harris' strategy accelerated radical reforms in the defence beginning with a major re-organisation on 1 May in which *Fliegerkorps XII* sub-divided the West between three fighter commands: *Jagddivision 1* (formerly *Nachtjagddivision 1*) at Deelen under Döring; *Jagddivision 2* (formerly *Flakscheinwerferdivision 2*) at Stade under *Generalleutnant* Walter Schwabedissen, and *Jagddivision 3* formed as a new command at Metz under *Generalleutnant* Werner Junck. On 17 August they would be joined by *Jagddivision 4* under *Generalleutnant* Joachim-Friedrich Huth at Döberitz, the former *Jafü Mitteldeutschland* formed to shield Berlin six months earlier. Between them they controlled eight *Nachtjagdgruppen* and seven signal regiments. The demise of both *Flakscheinwerferdivision* (searchlight divisions) and the dispersal of their batteries to the cities, largely as a result of Party demands, signalled the demise of *Hellenachtjagd* in favour of radar-based systems.

But the *Räume* could control only one fighter at a time and tracking was difficult until the introduction of *FuG 25 Erstling* IFF systems, when it became possible to hold a second fighter in reserve orbiting a radio beacon. The problem was eased by allowing a 50 per cent overlap in radar coverage and adding more *Räume* which from July 1942 were grouped under *Nachtjagdraumführer*, each responsible for a

Himmelbettraum and a pair of *Dunkelnachtjagdgebieten* on either side of it. Each division was assigned at least three *Nachtjagdraumführer*. By the beginning of 1943 there were 24 and a further two or three more would be added later in the year controlling 149 *Räume* by the end of June. To improve the defences, Kammhuber demanded another 150,000 men, 600 *Würzburg-Reisen* by September 1942 and the creation of three more *Nachtjagdgeschwader*. Although justified, these demands revealed an obsession bordering on arrogance, stirring further resentment against *'Wurzelsepp'* ('Bavarian Turnip Head'), as some called Kammhuber. These feelings were partly due to his abstemious behaviour and his critics' views; RAF intelligence commented that he was *'a small, insignificant-looking man ... of the type who does not drink or smoke much because he cannot stand it.'* [37]

In the longer term, Kammhuber sought new ground and airborne radars but encountered opposition from both Göring and Jeschonnek, who regarded his demands as excessive. Subsequently, he went around them by appealing to the Nazi Party's organisations for manpower, and by August 1942 he had 30,000 male and female auxiliaries in his signals establishment, which was expanded as the *Dunkelnachtjagdgebieten* were added behind the *Himmelbett* line to provide a total of 96 signal companies, each supporting one night fighter station. However, during the Cologne raid many crews were uncommitted and subsequently there was a groundswell of opinion seeking more flexible tactics. Kammhuber preferred to improve co-ordination on the ground and the policy appeared to pay off: from August 1942 until December the RAF's main attacks were losing an average of 5.76 per cent per month compared with 3.98 per cent from January to July, while in December the figure rose to 7.14 per cent, the RAF attributing half of these losses to fighters. [38]

This partly reflected the growing use of airborne radar which the Germans had been slower to develop than the British while suffering similar problems; indeed their unreliability was one reason why these sensors remained unpopular for a long time. A prototype *Lichtenstein* was installed in a Do 215B and flown by *Oberleutnant* Ludwig Bekker, who claimed five victories between 8/9 August 1941 and 1/2 October when his radar became unserviceable and could not be repaired. [39] His success encouraged the instalation of radars into the Bf 110s of *NJG 1*, but shortages of technicians at Telefunken delayed production of *FuG 202 Lichtenstein B/C* and only in February 1942 were the first four Bf 110s of *II./NJG 1* so equipped. The sensor proved unpopular because the 'antlers' ('antenna') reduced speed by 40 km/h (25 mph), the set was temperamental and there were no victories for four months.

Gradually, more sensors became available and from two aircraft out of 218 with radars on 1 March 1942 within eight months more than half (152) of the 247 night fighters had received the new sensors. By January 1943 nearly two-thirds of Kammhuber's fighters had radar and by the beginning of June 1943 nearly 82 per cent of the 276 aircraft had 'antlers' but many were old aircraft; indeed the Do 215B-5 in which Ludwig Bekker achieved his first radar victory in August 1941 was still in service during the spring of 1944. [40]

There were many problems caused by the Nazis' failure to expand the electrical and electronics industries. Low production standards resulted in many radars being returned to the manufacturers for repairs, while the shortage of spares (especially valves) meant that serviceability was low. [41] Kammhuber's solution was to expand the night fighter force from 18 to 72 *Gruppen*, with 2,100 first-line aircraft and he received Göring's approval in May 1943 but the task proved to be a poisoned chalice. During a formal presentation to Hitler on 25 May, Kammhuber was cut off in mid-sentence when Hitler stated the proposals were unnecessary as he was overestimating the enemy's air strength. The Bavarian's star began to wane when Göring afterwards accused him of being a megalomaniac.

Yet during the spring of 1943 Kammhuber was inflicting loss rates approaching 6 per cent upon individual major attacks and in the second quarter of 1943 his fighters claimed 80 per cent of the British bombers shot down. With the prospect of all his night fighters being radar-equipped by the end of 1943, Kammhuber faced the future with confidence; his system covered the western and northern approaches to Germany and almost encircled Berlin. The growing threat from the Russians, who mounted 212 sorties during the summer of 1942 and 920 in April 1943, caused him to extend the system into East Prussia with 18 *Räume* and he planned to add another 40 along the Baltic coast and from Belgium down the Rhône valley. [42]

The suspicions of Kammhuber's rivals about his ambition may have had an element of truth. In the face of a growing daylight threat from the US Army Air Force (USAAF), on 23 May Kammhuber had suggested creating a full equivalent of Fighter Command. On 21 June he produced for Hitler more detailed proposals with a *Luftflotte* based on the *Fliegerkorps XII* organisation and featuring a central command post and two *Jagdkorps* controlling day and night operations in both the *Reich* and Western Europe. But this would have meant taking over *Luftflotte 3*'s fighters and as Sperrle had good relations with both Hitler and Göring, while Kammhuber's position was on the wane, the idea was rejected. [43] It was a measure of Sperrle's influence that comint early warning of major attacks from England, such as the testing of aircraft radios, first had to pass through *Funkhorchdienst-West* headquarters in Paris before being passed to *Fliegerkorps XII*. [44]

By early 1943 Kammhuber's system was being criticised for inflexibility and in April *Oberleutnant* (later *Oberst*) Lossberg, now head of night fighters in the *RLM Technische Amt* and a protegé of Milch, noted the success of a few pilots in exploiting *Himmelbett* to enter the bomber stream which they then pursued using *Lichtenstein*. He proposed adopting these tactics when the improved *FuG 212 Lichtenstein SN-2* radar was introduced and gained Göring's approval in principle on 30 April. Kammhuber, however, doubted that the fighters could stay in the stream without ground control and feared 'friendly fire' casualties. Yet he was not against flexibility and in February 1943 introduced a modified *Y-Verfahren* system which allowed *Himmelbetträume* to have two fighters in aerial reserve with a third engaging the enemy, while by the summer he was also examining automated control for the fighters' semi-active radar guidance and radar data links between the command posts and sensors. [45] Another straw in the wind came from bomber *Experte Major* 'Hajo' Hermann, who noticed that the increase in searchlight batteries around the cities, together with illumination created by British pyrotechnics, silhouetted the bombers and he proposed using day fighters to intercept them. In April 1943, he persuaded the *General der Jagdflieger*, Adolf Galland, to authorise experiments with an *ad hoc* force of pilots 'moonlighting' from the *Fluglehrerschule* (Flying Instructors' School) at Brandenburg-Briest, and this led to the creation of a *Nachtjagdversuchskommando* in late June.

There was one other cloud on the horizon, namely a growing threat to the radar system: while the British had anticipated such a threat from the moment they began building the CH system, the Germans were in denial. Kammhuber and Martini were half aware of the enemy's growing electronic threat, for during a raid upon Mannheim on 6/7 December 1942, the British jammed both *Freya* radars and the night fighter radio system. The former was overcome by stretching radar operating frequencies and the defenders took refuge in complacency, congratulating themselves that *Würzburg* was unaffected and that their lead in radar remained. [46] To strengthen this lead *Dr* Plendl had become responsible for radar research in November 1942 and secured a *Führer* order to release 1,500 scientists from the services for special research centres. Yet even as the order went out, Telefunken abandoned research into centimetric radars because its scientists concluded that nothing could be achieved except at very great cost and resources which were more urgently needed to improve the existing family of sensors.

Surprisingly neither Milch nor Martini were willing to accept full responsibility for radar development and the lack of clear leadership bedevilled the *Luftwaffe* until Milch became radar supremo on 6 July. German complacency was pricked when a Pathfinder Stirling was shot down at Ilendrik-Ido-Ambracht near Rotterdam and its 10 cm (3 GHz) H2S navigation radar, with cavity magnetron, was recovered intact by *Luftwaffe* intelligence. Dubbed *'Rotterdamgerät'* ('Rotterdam Device'), it proved startlingly advanced when tested by Telefunken in Berlin, and although the original was destroyed when the factory was bombed out on 1/2 March another was found the following morning in a wrecked Halifax. By now Martini had established the *Arbeitsgemeinschaft Rotterdam* (Rotterdam Commission) to investigate the technology and develop ESM systems, the first being *FuG 350 Naxos Z*, which could home on H2S, but after studying the first report in May, Göring commented, 'We must frankly admit ... the British and Americans are far ahead of us. I expected them to be advanced but, frankly, I never thought that they would get so far ahead.' The *Luftwaffe* would soon discover how advanced the British were.

Kammhuber was not content to remain on the defensive observing: 'If you want to render a swarm of wasps harmless it is better to destroy the nest along with the wasps.' *Kampfgruppen* harassed RAF airfields at night but Kammhuber wanted a dedicated intruder force and in mid-August, *Major* Karl-Heinrich Heyse's *I./NJG 2* began probing sorties over eastern England (see Table 4-5). Heyse was lost on 9/10 October and replaced by *Hauptmann* Karl Hühlshoff and on 24/25 October came the first successes. [47] The impact was more moral than physical for the attacks added greater psychological strain to tired returning bomber crews and disrupted night-flying training. The only major physical success came on 10/11 February 1941 when the *Gruppe* claimed five enemy aircraft, although two were damaged and a third, denied permission to land and running low on fuel, was abandoned. Initially encouraged by the success, Göring ordered the creation in December 1940 of three intruder *Geschwader* but this ran into fierce opposition from Jeschonnek, *ObdL* and several *Fliegerkorps* commanders. Jeschonnek believed Kammhuber was empire-building and refused to replace Hühlshoff's losses with the result that the *Gruppe* slipped from 15 aircraft in November 1940 to seven in January 1941 although it was later expanded. On the opposite side of the Channel Fighter Command began its own night intruder campaign on 21/22 December, initially bombing the airfields.

Table 4-5: NJG 2 intruder campaign, October 1940–October 1941

Month	Sorties	Losses (accident)	Claims	Victories	Reich claims
Oct 1940	36	5 (5)	2	2	5
Nov 1940	111	4 (1)	3	-	4
Dec 1940	61	2 (1)	5	-	2
Jan 1941	56	1 (-)	-	3	2
Feb 1941	25	2 (1)	2	6	5
Mar 1941	53	3 (-)	6	2	15
Apr 1941	205	2 (1)	12	12	14
May 1941	216	1 (-)	5	4	23
Jun 1941	245	6 (-)	23	1	44
Jul 1941	223	4 (-)	15	8	43
Aug 1941	187	2 (1)	20	8	56
Sep 1941	104	2 (-)	16	3	31
Oct 1941	81	1 (-)	14	3	24

Sources: IWM AHB 6 Tin 29, fr.2798 Einsatz gegen England. USNA T321 Roll 176 Luftkrieg gegen England. Parry, Appendices. Foreman et al, *Luftwaffe Night Fighter Victory Claims.*

A whispering campaign began accusing Hühlshoff's men of exaggerating their successes, which had some truth, for 125 victories had been genuinely claimed to the end of September 1941 although only 49 aircraft had been shot down. The rumours reached Hitler and when he raised them with *ObdL*, Jeschonnek did nothing to contradict them while Göring was silent. From the German perspective the shield was more effective than the sword for from August 1940 to October 1941, the *Reich*-based units were credited with 278 victories, which could all be verified, while the intruders were credited with 127, which could not. [48] Hitler ordered intruder operations curtailed, arguing it was better to shoot down bombers over Germany to raise national morale, this decision being conveyed to Hühlshoff's men by Kammhuber at a parade on 12 October.

One last mission was flown that night then the *Gruppe* was sent to Sicily for conventional night fighter operations. It returned in August 1942 with plans for renewed intruder operations, but in November returned to Sicily. Sperrle's *Kampfgruppe* carried out occasional intruder operations, flying 210 sorties in November and December 1941. By conceding the night skies over Great Britain, the *Luftwaffe* helped to fuel Bomber Command's expansion and to forge a sword which would be plunged into the heart of the Reich. Yet there remained a significant opposition to intruder operations within the higher echelons of the *Luftwaffe* even after Kammhuber's departure in 1943.

As the scale of British bombing increased, the *Luftwaffe*'s bombing efforts upon Great Britain, directed by Coeler's *Fliegerkorps IX*, declined. [49] With the departure of the *Kampfgruppen* to the East, Coeler had only 63 bombers (38 serviceable) at the end of July, although these could be augmented by nine *Ergänzungsgruppen* and even the occasional *Fernaufklärungsstaffeln*. The defences were growing in strength, and benefited from 17 mobile GCI stations by July which supported six squadrons of radar-equipped Beaufighters with another two squadrons converting to this aircraft. The growing effectiveness of the defences was shown against *KGr 100* which continued precision attacks before it went East on 19 July and lost 10 aircraft. [50] Two months later No 80 Wing was controlling 85 interceptor, jammer and meaconing sites as well as 150 decoy sites. [51]

Jeschonnek and Milch discussed the most efficient use of this tiny force and concluded that it should be to mine harbours and to attack coastal shipping, but on 26 July *ObdL* ordered Sperrle to fly reprisal attacks upon London following raids upon Berlin. During 1941 there were only three major (100 tonnes or more of bombs) raids (see Table 4-6) but the inexperience of the crews meant a smaller proportion of aircraft reached the target, relying less on electronic navigation aids and more on dead reckoning (*Koppelnavigation*) techniques. There was a growing reluctance to despatch raids against inland targets; indeed of 33 raids involving the dropping of more than 30 tonnes of bombs only nine were against inland targets and the rest were against ports. [52]

Table 4-6: Luftwaffe night operations against Great Britain, July 1941–June 1943

Quarter	Sorties	Lost	Percentage	Fighter Command	Losses
Q3 1941	938	76	8.1	3,367	1
Q4 1941	586	53	9.0	2,557	2
Q1 1942	208	4	1.9	1,307	2
Q2 1942	2,249	40	1.8	3,297	4
Q3 1942	881	53	6.0	4,214	3
Q4 1942	163	13	7.9	1,733	-
Q1 1943	902	47	5.2	2,893	4
Q2 1943	942	29	3.1	3,508	3

IWM Tin 29, fr 2826. UKNA Air 16/1036. Balke *KG 2* Vol 2 pp.74–183.

The Germans also launched sporadic daylight attacks usually by individual bombers or very small formations but, like the night raids, they rarely inflicted much damage and were largely harassing operations, dubbed *Seeräuber/Pirat-angriffe* ('Pirate Raids'). The only advantage was to tie down British resources and by the beginning 1942 Sperrle, with 274 bombers was holding down some 2,000 fighters (including 450 night fighters), 600,000 personnel and some 2,800 AA guns. [53]

On 21 March 1942 Göring, Milch and Jeschonnek discussed the possibility of a destructive attack upon Great Britain and the feasibility of a retaliatory attack upon London. Jeschonnek rejected the latter idea arguing it would be dependent upon the weather and that there were not enough bombers in the West, indeed *Fliegerkorps* IX had only 98 bombers (43 serviceable). But it was decided to withdraw *2./KG 100* from the Eastern Front in April and use it to form a 'Plendl' bomber unit with *X-* and *Y-Verfahren* as *Erprobungs und Lehrkommando* 100, later *Erprobungskommando* 17. [54] But Harris' devastating raids during the spring saw Party officials baying for vengeance, and Hitler's headquarters ordered *ObdL* on 14 April to give the air war against England 'a more aggressive stamp', adding, '…when targets are being selected, preference is to be given to those where attacks are likely to have the greatest possible effect on civilian life.' Minelaying was to be replaced by what were described as '…terror attacks of a retaliatory nature.'

The backbone of the offensive remained *Oberst Dr* Georg Pasewaldt's *KG 2*, which was reinforced by two *Kampfgruppen* from Sicily, anti-shipping and *Ergänzungsgruppen* (the last under *Stab KG 111*), to give 429 bombers by 30 April, of which half were serviceable. Attacks began on 23/24 April 1942 but navigation was poor and while fighter-bomber (*Jabo*) attacks increased in intensity they could do little damage. Following an attack upon Rostock, Hitler declared in a speech on 26 April that he would eradicate all British cities for each RAF attack, and the German press referred to selecting targets from a Baedeker's Tourist Guide and marking off each destroyed British city. That night the first of the 'Baedeker Raids' was made on poorly defended Bath, where the attackers flew as low as 600 feet (180 metres) to cause tremendous damage through the use of greater concentrations of incendiaries including the use of the new AB 500 with 140 kilogrammes of bombs although the attacks rarely lasted more than 30 minutes. [55] Such success, repeated on British cities of Lübeck's vintage such as Exeter, Norwich and York, achieved higher levels of concentration because crews flew double sorties. *EprKdo 17* joined the offensive on 27/28 April, later being used to mark targets. Both *X-* and *Y-Verfahren* were used, operating at various frequencies to reduce the risk of jamming, and the targets were marked with flares by *KG 2* and *3.(F)/123*.

The need to keep the enemy off balance meant shuttling between bases, increasing wear upon man and machine, while the defences coped with the threat and by inflicting a 5.3 per cent loss-rate (38 aircraft), helped conclude the offensive on 8/9 May after 716 sorties and the dropping of 2,000 tonnes of bombs, with 16 of the lost aircraft coming from the *Ergänzungsgruppen*. Sharp blows continued to fall at night upon British cities until the autumn, notably a series of tit-for-tat raids in late July upon Birmingham after attacks upon Hamburg, but there was an air of desperation about these operations, reflected in the use *III./KG 26*, which had barely completed a torpedo-bombing course. By the end of the year, Coeler had flown some 2,400 night bomber sorties against British targets for the loss of 244 aircraft (10.16%), many of them from the *Ergänzungsgruppen*.[56] The policy of tit-for-tat raids was opposed by the anti-shipping commander, *FlFü Atlantik Generalleutnant* Ulrich Kessler in his letter to Jeschonnek of 5 September 1942, when he demanded more bombers for the anti-shipping campaign than for what he described (in a phrase more common in Germany before 1945 than afterwards) as 'You thrash my Jew and I'll thrash your Jew', arguing that the ship was 'The British Jew'.

The British defence – now based upon 28 GCI stations, 10 Beaufighter squadrons and 1,960 heavy guns – had successfully contained the threat. In April 1942 the first Mosquito night fighter squadron with AI Mk V entered service, joined later by the centimetric AI Mk VII, and it had its first success against a Do 217E-2 of 8./KG 2 on 5/6 April. [57] The British augmented their GCI sensors with the 'Smack' system, splitting southern and central England into Fighter boxes averaging 14 miles (22.5 kilometres) wide and 32 miles (51.5 kilometres) deep, in the middle of which was a searchlight beacon around which the night fighter orbited. The first 19 kilometres were searchlights, often radar-controlled, in an indicator zone while more powerful searchlights would illuminate targets when they entered the killer zone. The system, which was similar to Germany's *Hellenachtjagd* and the later *Wilde Sau* could be used by night fighters relying upon 'cat's eyes' (visual) detection as well as radar so that GCI and 'Smack' remained operational until the end of the war. [58]

During May 1942 the first steps were taken to augment Sperrle's strike force with the creation of *Stab KG 6* at Dinard with an *Ergänzugsstaffel* (later the cadre for *IV./KG 6*.) joined in September by a new *Kommodore*, *Oberstleutnant* Walter Storp. A further three *Kampfgruppen* from other units and three separate *Staffeln* were also created: *14./KG 6* with Ju 86P/R high-altitude reconnaissance aircraft; *15./KG 6* formed from *EprKdo 17* as pathfinders and *16./KG 6* formed from *Erprobungskommando* Me 210 which became *11./ZG 1*. Allied landings in North Africa in November 1942 saw two of the new *Kampfgruppen* transferred to the Mediterranean: *KG 2* was involved in the occupation of Vichy France while *15./KG 6* was sent East to fly supplies into Stalingrad. It returned in the spring of 1943 to become a Pathfinder *Gruppe* as *I./KG 66*. At the end of the year Coeler went into the *Führer* reserve and would later command the transport force (*Fliegerkorps XIV*) and he was replaced by *Generalleutnant* Stefan Fröhlich. The Ju 86Rs had earlier been used for experimental daylight high-altitude raids from 24 August 1942 when two such machines assigned to the *Versuchsstelle für Höhenflüge* each dropped a 250kg bomb on Camberley and Southampton from 40,000 feet (12,200 metres). A few more sorties were flown until 12 September, when the approach of a vengeful, modified Spitfire forced the abandonment of both this and subsequent missions. [59]

Bomber Command's campaign against the Ruhr early in 1943 and especially a raid upon Berlin on 1/2 March, struck a nerve in Hitler. Göring was in Rome when, on 6 March, Jeschonnek received a teleprinter message from *Oberstleutnant* Nicholas von Below, Hitler's adjutant and the nephew of a First World War army commander, demanding he appoint an officer to co-ordinate attacks upon the British Isles. Jeschonnek wanted to use the *Stuka* 'ace', *Oberst* Oskar Dinort, who was overdue a front line command but deeply involved in technical trials, so *ObdL* proposed the *General der Kampf- und Sturzkampfflieger*, *Oberstleutnant* Dietrich Peltz. He was selected on 24 March 1943 but did not officially take up his command as *Angriffsführer England* (England Attack Commander) until the morning of 1 April, setting up his headquarters at Le Coudray en Thelle, south of Beauvais but dual-hatting his original position until 3 September. In planning attacks upon Britain, Peltz' prime strike force was still Fröhlich's *Fliegerkorps IX*, which had 186 bombers (109 serviceable). Peltz had seen growing Allied industrial might during operations over the western Mediterranean during the previous winter and later claimed this had ended any belief in a German victory; he thus sought to use bombing as a means of securing a negotiated peace. [60] Peltz recognised that the defences were too formidable to be tackled during daylight and concentrated upon developing night operations.

The new appointment was not accompanied by any significant increase in resources for he had only *Oberstleutnant* Walter Bradel's *KG 2* and Storp's *KG 6*, whose total strength by 31 March was only 205 (55% serviceable) with 175 crews. He was, however, given control of *SKG 210*'s Fw 190 *Jabos* although their potential contribution in night operations were clearly limited but he did receive the Pathfinder I./KG 66 although only one *Staffel* was operational during the summer.

Peltz' offensive opened on 14/15 April and began inauspiciously when only 73 of 101 aircraft sent against Chelmsford reached the target, while six aircraft were lost. [61] Two nights later 28 *Jabos* were sent against London in ideal conditions; a full moon and no cloud but three were lost in a collision on take-off and six during the mission, three landing at RAF airfields! Other raids failed, for the *Jabos*' Achilles Heel was the direction-finding system and the British were already preparing a jammer to counter it. However, by the time it became operational in June, the *Jabos* were confining themselves to daylight missions. [62]

The *Kampfgruppen* struck throughout England and Scotland with nine raids of 60–75 aircraft in May and June, the strongest being 85 sorties again against Chelmsford on 13/14 May. They would cross the Channel at 165–330 feet (50–100 metres) in order to reduce the risk of radar detection, then climb in a spiral to 13,000 feet (4,000 metres) to make a dive-bomber attack, usually eastwards so the speed would help them to escape the defences. Pathfinders would line up on visual beacons to make a low-level approach and drop flares to mark turning points for the main bomber force. The *Zielfinder* (Target Marker), who would usually be a *Kommandeur* and never less than a *Kapitän*, would be supported by aids such as FuSAn 700 *Elektra*. Once the *Zielfinder* had hit the target a trio of *Beleuchter* (illuminators) would drop flares and incendiaries to guide in the main force. The offensive was supported by *Y-Verfahren* on a case-by-case basis, for its vulnerability to jamming was recognised, while a new version of *Knickebein* was introduced with a receiver covering 34 frequencies instead of the previous three. Also used was *FuSAn 701 Sonne* ('Sun'), a new electronic navigation system established from 1941 along western Europe from Stavanger in Norway to Seville in neutral Spain and dubbed Consol (Spanish for 'with sun') by the Allies. It was so good it remained in service for 30 years after the war. [63]

Peltz' offensive involved a total of 557 bomber sorties and approximately 730 tonnes of bombs. Some 24 bombers were lost although the *Angriffsführer England* made no attempt at penetrating deep into British air space, partly because the British 'Aspirin' jammers were quickly adapted to the improved *Knickebein*. During 1943 the GCI stations began to receive the Type 21 radar while night fighters, increasingly using the formidable Mosquito, received the American-made AI Mk X. [64] The smaller *Luftwaffe* effort made it difficult for the British defences to intercept its bombers yet from July 1942 to March 1943 they inflicted a higher percentage of losses than the German defences upon Bomber Command.

By contrast, Peltz' force slowly declined from 113 bombers (82 serviceable) in mid-May to 66 (49 serviceable) nearly a month later, for *ObdL* refused to invest resources. Towards the end of the offensive, the *Kampfgruppen* dropped a large number of SD-2 anti-personnel munitions on Humberside which earned the name 'Butterfly Bomb'. Their shape made them especially attractive to the curiosity of children, many of whom were killed or maimed. There was some re-equipment, with KG 2 receiving Do 217M while the new Me 410A-1 *Hornisse* ('Hornet'), which was to be the German equivalent of the Mosquito, arrived in April and by June equipped a whole Gruppe (V./KG 2).

On 18 June Peltz met Milch to review progress and complained that while pathfinders were marking targets, many crews simply could not reach them. Two-thirds of his losses were due to accidents which he noted were especially prevalent on return trips, a sad commentary on *Luftwaffe* training. [65] Yet Peltz soon had other concerns, for Hitler was now desperate to shore up his Italian ally, Mussolini, and was diverting a substantial part of the *Luftwaffe* to the Mediterranean, including *Stab* and I./KG 6 which were briefly sent to the Mediterranean. On 20 June, Peltz joined the exodus to become *Fernkampfführer Luftflotte 2*, also *Fernkampfführer Mittelmeer* (Long-Range Bomber Commander, *Luftflotte* 2 or Mediterranean) and Fröhlich was left to maintain the illusion of an offensive..

Chapter Five

Duel in the West

B ombing was not Germany's only strategic option in the war against Great Britain. The submarine (U-boat) had brought Britannia to the verge of ruin in 1917 and, with *Luftwaffe* support, Hitler could hope for greater success in the new war. [1]

His hopes would be dashed however, for the implementation of such a strategy depended upon *Grossadmiral* Erich Raeder, commander of the *Kriegsmarine* (Navy), and upon Göring and these were the slenderest of reeds. Like virtually all admirals, Raeder measured naval strength in the number of large-calibre guns that his ships carried, he had little interest in air power and to assure funds for his nascent battle fleet he agreed in 1932 to abandon land-plane development and to merge naval and military aviation, leaving himself with only seaplanes. [2]

The agreement was signed as land-plane performance significantly improved, but Raeder was slow to recognise the implications and only after realising he had deprived himself of a modern strike force, did he attempt to reverse the decision. His requests fell upon the breakwater of Göring's stubborn determination to control all aviation, reinforced by a streak of personal antipathy between the two men. Raeder regarded 'Fatty' as a posturing buffoon, while Göring saw in the admiral all the bourgeois features which the Nazis were pledged to remove from German society. His contempt for the Navy was barely concealed. In return for a pledge of support to expand the battle fleet (Plan Z), Raeder struck his colours on 27 January 1939, leaving himself with a *Seeluftstreitkräfte* of a few hundred seaplanes to provide tactical air support under the *Führer der Seeluftstreitkräfte (FdL)* led by the former naval officer *Generalmajor* Hermann Bruch.

But this was not obvious at the beginning of the war when naval air power in the West consisted of *Generalmajor* Joachim Coeler's *Fliegerführer der Seeluftstreitkräfte West* with 10 seaplane squadrons. At the start of the war *Luftflotte 2* commander Felmy realised high performance land-based aircraft were needed to augment this force and on 5 September formed *Fliegerdivision 10 (Fliegerkorps* from 2 October) under *General der Flieger* Hans Geisler based upon *KG 26* later augmented by the newly raised *Wunderbomber* (Ju 88) unit *I./KG 30 (Hauptmann* Helmut Pohle). From November Geisler benefited from having *Luftflotte 2's* Operations Officer, Harlinghausen, who became his chief of staff.

Göring dreamed of his airmen destroying the Royal Navy and wanted a mass attack upon the Home Fleet's base at Scapa Flow at the outbreak of war. Hitler rejected the plan for fear of retaliatory attacks on the *Reich* but as compensation, encouraged attacks at sea as British Home Fleet task forces were engaged in the North Sea on 26 September and 9 October. No damage was inflicted, and the *Luftwaffe* had the embarrassment of Goebbels' triumphant (but premature) boast to have sunk the aircraft carrier *Ark Royal* which was compounded on 16 October when a raid on warships in the Firth of Forth unexpectedly encountered British fighters who shot down Pohle.

The attack, came immediately after a U-boat penetrated Scapa Flow and sank the battleship HMS *Royal Oak*, shaking British confidence, and thus the Home Fleet sheltered in western ports until its bases had stronger defences. [3] It was a timely decision, for the following day *Fliegerdivision 10* sent seventeen bombers to Scapa Flow. Sporadic attacks in *Staffel* strength would continue throughout the winter with the most successful on 16 March damaging the cruiser HMS *Norfolk* and the gunnery training ship HMS *Iron Duke*, a decommissioned battleship which had been the flagship of the Grand Fleet when the German High Seas Fleet was scuttled in 1918. The strengthening of Scapa Flow's defences, including the provision of radar and three fighter squadrons made further daylight attacks extremely hazardous, but the *Fliegerkorps* ceased operations in early April to rest units before '*Weserübung*'.

The task of interdicting the sea lanes was initially left to Coeler whose lumbering seaplanes sought to cut British trade with neutral Scandinavia and Britain's extensive coastal traffic. The latter was an important element of British war industry for the rail system had lacked investment between the wars with infrastructure, locomotives and rolling stock all ageing. To relieve the strain on the system large, bulky cargoes and especially coal were carried by coasters, coal being the foundation of European energy requirements for both industrial and domestic use.

But Coeler was hamstrung by the slow seaplanes of the *Küstfliegerstaffeln*, who suffered from the weather, mechanical failure and even from attack by British Ansons and Hudsons. On 29 November they suffered 29 per cent losses and by 24 December the War Diary of the Naval Staff Operations Division described the seaplanes as '… *in every respect inferior*' to the British aircraft. [4] On 25 October the *Gruppen* were re-organised to ease their administrative and maintenance problems while *KüFlGr 706* replaced its biplanes with He 111J bombers (described by the Naval Staff as 'antiquated'). However, the re-organisation brought no significant improvement in seaplane operations, which were further disrupted from late November when sea ice closed most bases for several months.

Geisler willingly joined in the North Sea offensive with armed reconnaissance missions from 17 October initially targeting lone ships but on 1 November he was permitted attacks on convoys although with limited results. Indeed, *KG 26* failed to sink any vessels until 17 December (For Allied shipping losses to the Luftwaffe see Table 5–1).

Despite this, in December Geisler was informed he might attack convoys to Norway and on 23 December received permission to attack all shipping within 30 nautical miles of the British coast. [5] Spearheaded by *KG 26*, during the first quarter of 1940, the anti-shipping campaign inflicting a growing stream of losses mostly on independently sailing vessels or fishing boats, reaching a peak in March with attacks upon 57 merchantmen and 38 trawlers, seven of the former and one of the latter being seriously damaged. But there was a disaster on 22 February when *KG 26* bombed a German destroyer task force (the navy having failed to notify the *Luftwaffe* of the presence of its vessels), sinking one. Hitler was furious: 'I would not say anything if all the Navy were sunk in battle with the enemy, but it is inexcusable that this happens because of a failure in co-ordination.' The incident strained relations between the two services just as they were planning for '*Weserübung*' and provided Göring with an excuse not to place his *Gruppen* under naval control. [6]

Table 5-1: Luftwaffe campaign against shipping, October 1940–December 1942

Quarter	Home Waters	Atlantic	Mediterranean	Arctic
Q 4 1939	2 (714)	-	-	-
Q 1 1940	13 (30,949)	-	-	-
Q 2 1940	34 (189.932)	6 (18,398)	2 (28,962)	
Q 3 1940	41 (123,535)	4 (24,819)	-	-
Q 4 1940	13 (41,234)	16 (74,534)	-	-
Q 1 1941	25 (85,869)	41 (171,724)	28 (112,537)	-
Q 2 1941	40 (99,825)	18 (69,855)	46 (200,191)	-
Q 3 1941	14 (32,286)	5 (10,686)	3 (11,650)	-
Q 4 1941	12 (29,000)	1 (2,473)	2 (8,861)	-
Q 1 1942	6 (13,755)	1 (1,757)	8 (45,359)	2 (11,823)
Q 2 1942	2 (6,650)	2 (1,831)	10 (37,851)	15 (83,615)
Q 3 1942	3 (3,352)	-	6 (59,932)	23 (126,904)
Q 4 1942	-	-	8 (62,482)	1 (7,925)

Sources: UKNA Adm 186/804. UKNA Air 41/47 App. 17.

Notes: Figures in parenthesis are gross registered tons (grt). Home Waters are defined as those within 40 miles (64 kilometres) of a British-based fighter airfield (of Q2 western Europe has been included while Norway has been included in the Atlantic. Trawler losses are excluded. No figures for Q2 1940 because ships sunk in this period were during support of land operations. The Q4 1940 figure includes two ships (46,550grt) shared with U-boats and counted as half-kills.

From 27 February British coastal convoys received permanent fighter cover which inflicted casualty rates of 27 per cent and 40 per cent upon two missions, but at the beginning of March *KG 26* was confident enough to strike into the eastern English Channel, to attack at night and to engage convoys. Every convoy sailing between Norway and Great Britain from 20 March until 9 April was struck but only the first suffered casualties thanks to the provision of strong escorts, including a radar-equipped anti-aircraft cruiser and fighter patrols. Bombs remained the preferred weapon against ships; torpedoes were used by naval seaplanes but the weapons were too slow and none hit their targets. [7]

Bombing aids were also harnessed for anti-shipping operations with *Knickebein* used to strike convoy HN.20 in March 1940, while *X-Gerät* was used by *KGr 100* in occasional armed reconnaissance from 6 December 1939 until 3 April – some into the eastern Channel. It is astonishing that the *Luftwaffe* staff permitted the exposure of such a specialised unit to this sort of mission and it reflected both the shortage of dedicated anti-shipping forces and the growing trend towards short-term expedience. Luckily, while aircraft equipped with both systems fell into enemy hands, the British did not discover their secrets.

A more effective means of interdicting British seaborne trade was the mine, and Germany had developed such weapons fitted with magnetic sensors. But production was slow and only in mid-November were there adequate numbers delivered and even then only by ancient He 59s, with Jeschonnek rejecting Navy demands for Do 17 Zs and even the new Do 217. The campaign began on the night of 18/19 November with the deadly 'eggs' being laid off British East Coast ports and Dunkirk, France's prime port in the Channel. A mixture of poor weather, poor navigation and ageing aircraft meant the campaign proceeded in fits and starts leading the navy to conclude it would be better to deliver the mines by ship or U-boat. Worse still, within weeks the British recovered a mine and developed counter-measures including degaussing. At the end of November the *Luftwaffe's* liaison officer with the navy *(General der Luftwaffe beim ObdL)*, *Generalmajor* Hans Ritter, protested strongly against operations which he felt were sapping the *Luftwaffe's* strength to no good purpose. It was a view with which Göring sympathised.

On 8 December Hitler attended a conference on naval matters including aerial minelaying and Göring promised to provide a *Kampfgruppe*, and later three minelaying *Geschwader*, while it was agreed to create a reserve of mines in anticipation of a major operation against Scottish ports during the New Year.

Despite, or because of, Raeder's opposition, Göring persuaded Hitler to authorise a renewed *Luftwaffe* minelaying effort in the spring. In anticipation of this, *Fliegerdivision 9* was created under Coeler in February 1940, with *KG 4* (He 111P-4s) and *KüFlGr 106*, although *FdL* was also permitted to lay mines. [8] But Coeler's triumph was short-lived, for on 10 February, *I./KG 4* was assigned to *Luftflotte 2* for training on aerial resupply missions and its replacement, *I./KG 1*, returned to conventional bombing ten days later together with *III./KG 4*, which converted to the Ju 88 A. *KG 4* became a conventional anti-shipping unit attacking targets with bombs and did not begin minelaying until mid-June. Coeler did receive *KGr 126* (formerly *III./KG 26*) at the end of March, but by the beginning of the month only 566 mines were in stock, with 700 added during the next two months.

In anticipation of *'Weserübung'* it was decided to try to neutralise Scapa Flow, and on 5 April both *Fliegerkorps X* and *Fliegerdivision 9* were ordered to mine the base and bomb its facilities. [9] However, *Fliegerdivision 9* did not commence operations until the night of 17/18 April with attacks on British east coast ports using He 111 bombers for the first time – although having to fly high-performance aircraft slow and low over the sea was a challenge. The new minefields were far more successful while *Luftwaffe* losses were sharply reduced, but the diversion of *KG 4* to *'Weserübung'* blunted the offensive and within a month *Fliegerdivision 9* was reduced to supporting *'Gelb'*. [10]

With the successful conclusion of what Telford Taylor called 'The March of Conquest', the strategic campaign against Britain's sea trade entered a new era. Air and U-boat bases in Norway and France meant the Germans could range deeper into the Atlantic beyond the continental shelf straining the Royal Navy's escort forces to breaking point. Furthermore, the British now needed to provide ships with higher endurance and better anti-aircraft armament. As the U-boats gradually adopted tactics of mass attack ('wolfpacks') the British were faced with the problem of providing more high endurance escorts as well.

In the aftermath of victory, the *Kampf-* and *Stukagruppen* harassed shipping in British Home Waters, including the Western Approaches, 250 nautical miles (465 kilometres) west of the British Isles. The bombers flew lone or *Kette*-strength armed reconnaissance missions against targets of opportunity and *Oberst* Alfred Bülowius'

LG 1 distinguished itself by claiming nine ships sunk or damaged during the first half of July. These attacks merged with preparations for *'Seelöwe'*, for which the Channel's closure was an essential prerequisite. The British Admiralty's desire to avoid congestion in western ports by running convoys to the eastern ones along the south coast meant that this 'operational' requirement accidentally merged into the 'strategic' anti-shipping campaign that opened on 4 July when Richthofen's *Stukas* attacked convoy OA.178 in Portland.

Richthofen was responsible for the Western Channel, while the Straits of Dover was the responsibility of Fink as *Kanalkampfführer*. The combined strike forces flew some 1,300 anti-shipping sorties (representing 67% of the total strike effort against Britain from 1 July to early August), while more were flown by Bruch's airmen. Although Fighter Command was committing up to 80 per cent of its patrols over the sea, convoy OA.178 was the twenty-sixth convoy to be savaged, for combat air patrols over the ships were weak, rarely more than 12 aircraft, and they operated on the periphery of the radar screen with no radio link to their charges. The bombers' escorts usually kept them at arm's length, and the *Luftwaffe* loss rate on these missions was 4 per cent. The savaging of convoy CW 9, half of whose ships were hit and of which three, amounting to 3,581grt, were sunk, (although the German airmen claimed to have sunk 8,500 grt) ended coastal traffic in the Channel on 11 August for several months. [11]

However, *Obdl's* goal was air superiority over England, and with the *'Adler'* offensive there was a dramatic drop in anti-shipping sorties mounted by *Kampfgruppen* although Geisler's *Fliegerkorps X* and *Küstfliegerstaffeln* continued to harass shipping off the Scottish and Tyneside coasts sinking 67,000 grt between September and December 1940, until Coeler lost several *Kampfgruppen* to Kesselring. [12] Much of the success here, and later, reflected the weak fighter shield and the merchantmen's poor anti-aircraft armament, so the effect of the relatively small numbers of aircraft committed '… was out of all proportion to the force employed'. Lightships were also attacked, together with fishing boats, which the *Luftwaffe* regarded as legitimate targets in contrast to Coastal Command, which sanctioned attacks only if the vessels fired on British aircraft. [13]

The subordination of the campaign was clearly indicated by *OKW Weisung 17* of 1 August 1940 on *'The conduct of air and sea warfare against England'*. This stated that *'…air attacks upon enemy warships and merchant ships may be reduced except where some particularly favourable target happens to present itself, where such attacks would lend additional effectiveness (to continuing the air war against ports) or where such attacks are necessary for the training of aircrew for further operations.'* Although attacking ships in harbour seemed the equivalent of shooting fish in a barrel, only 20 vessels (71,566 grt) were sunk between July 1940 and July 1941. However, 148 vessels (693,446 grt) were damaged; indeed, the *Luftwaffe* may have been responsible for up to a third of enemy shipping damaged and immobilised and awaiting repair early in 1941. The *ObdL* directive of 20 October ordered Sperrle to use his *Stukas* (reinforced by *KGr 606* and *806*) against shipping in the Channel 'which has appeared again during the last few days', while Fw 200 *Condors* were to be used in the northern Irish Sea. The *Stukas* flew about 100 sorties against shipping in the mouth of the Thames during October and November, but were quickly neutralised by a dynamic defence, and in

December Richthofen was transferred to Rumania. His departure and Geisler's the following month for Sicily left the anti-shipping campaign in the doldrums.

The *Kampfgruppen* returned in force to British coastal waters during February, to familiarise crews with daylight operations, such missions having declined sharply since October. However, on 6 February *OKW* published *Weisung 23 'Directions for operations against the British war economy'*, which belatedly recognised the validity of the navy's argument that the merchant fleet was Britain's Achilles heel. There was even a rare hint of *Führer* fallibility, for the directive began: '*Contrary to our former view, the greatest effect of our operations against the British war economy has been the heavy losses in merchant shipping inflicted by sea and air operations.*' A stronger U-boat campaign was expected to lead to the collapse of British resistance, but Hitler warned that '*...we are unable to maintain the scale of our air attacks as the demands of other theatres compel us to withdraw increasingly large forces from operations against the British Isles'*. The *Luftwaffe* was to concentrate upon ports as well as shipping, with priority given to the latter, while there was also to be an increase in the minelaying effort. There was an upsurge in activity aided by improving weather, with nearly 1,100 sorties by the western *Kampfgruppen* and Stumpff until the withdrawal of units during the spring (as *Weisung 23* had warned) brought much needed relief to the British. The relief may have been shared by the *Luftwaffe*, for, as convoys received stronger fighter protection, improved communications with the growing number of escort vessels and increased anti-aircraft armament, the *Kampfgruppen* were increasingly forced to operate at dusk and dawn, using the sun to outline their targets. In the first quarter of 1941 some 60 per cent of ships were sunk in daylight, but in the following quarter this dropped to 24 per cent.

The U-boat remained the prime weapon of strategic blockade but the 'view from the conning tower' was obviously restricted and the *Befehlshaber der Unterseeboote* or *BdU* (submarine commander), *Konteradmiral* Karl Dönitz (*Vizeadmiral* from 1 September and *Admiral* from 14 March 1942) had foreseen the need for very long-range reconnaissance aircraft and exercises during May 1938 had demonstrated the feasibility of such support. The elegant four-engine Do 26 flying boat was selected and in October 1939 a *Transozeanstaffel* of Do 26 flying boats was created. Simultaneously a *Fernaufklärungsstaffel* (later *1./KG 40*) was formed under *Major* Edgar Petersen using the Fw 200C-0, which originated as a Japanese navy requirement for a maritime reconnaissance version of the Fw 200B airliner. It was never more than a stop-gap for the *Luftwaffe* intended using the He 177 *Greif* ('Griffon') four-engine bomber for long-range maritime operations, but was mobilised due to the *Greif*'s prolonged development problems. The Fw 200C, operating under *AufklGr ObdL* supported U-boat operations in the Western Aproaches, flying as far west as Iceland and the Faeroes, but the *Staffel* was hampered by a shortage of aircraft and, together with the Do 26 *Staffel*, it was diverted to support *Weserübung*.

Most of the Do 26s were lost in Norway but the *Transozeanstaffel* was reformed and the few survivors resumed their original role from Brest on 16 August, but it was disbanded at the end of January 1941 and after a brief attachment to *I./KG40* the Do 26s returned to Germany in March. [14] In July 1940 the *Condors* were also transferred to Brest and flew 12 minelaying sorties under *Fliegerkorps IV*, but a 16.6 per cent loss rate led *Kommandeur Major* Edgar Peterson to telephone a protest to Jeschonnek at the end of the month and the *Gruppe* was then assigned the long-range armed reconnaissance role. [15] The first sorties from Bordeaux-Mérignac were flown on 8 August, flights being extended to Aalborg in Denmark three days later in a 1,900 nautical-mile (3,500-kilometre) journey lasting up to 13½ hours as far west as 20°W (325 nautical miles/600 kilometres) from the British Isles, carrying six or eight 250-kilogramme bombs. The return trip was made the following morning, but, to avoid exhaustion, Peterson restricted crews to three sorties a fortnight. There were rarely more than two a day and their reports proved of little value to Dönitz, having passed first through *Fliegerkorps IV* and the naval command in France, *Marine Gruppe West*. [16] Despite its relatively low speed, the *Condor* proved to be a potent weapon, especially against unarmed independents (representing 14% of all transatlantic trade at this time) or stragglers.

The first success was on 25 August in the Western Approaches, but within a month emboldened *Condor* pilots struck convoys, beginning with OA.218. They would approach at 200–400 metres (660–1,300 feet), then make a shallow dive attack with bombs and automatic weapons to as low as 150 metres (500 feet), the SS *Svien Jarl* being hit 256 times by 20mm cannon fire. The highlight came on 26 October when *Oberleutnant* Bernhard Jope set ablaze the liner *Empress of Britain* (42,348 grt), which had carried King George and Queen Elizabeth on their North American tour in June 1939. She was later finished off by a U-boat and was the largest liner to be sunk during the war. [17] By the end of the year the *Condors* had sunk 15 ships (74,543 grt), which represented 37 per cent of the total tonnage sunk by air attack and led Churchill to call them the 'Scourge of the Atlantic'. [18]

The operations were mostly with the delicate early-production *Condors*, whose backs sometimes snapped through the weight of bombs, and it was not until November 1940 that the main production version, the Fw 200C-3, with a stronger structure, became available. As they entered service Raeder secured a brief victory in his campaign for closer co-operation between the U-boats and *Condors*, for which he received some sympathy from Jeschonnek, who had two brothers in the Navy. [19] During 'Fatty's' prolonged leave, Hitler succumbed to naval pressure and on 6 January gave Dönitz operational control of *I./KG 40*, but this stimulated the furious Göring into some dextrous political manipulation. A month after Hitler's decision, Göring requested the *Gruppe's* return in exchange for an air command in the Atlantic and, despite Raeder's objections, the *Führer* agreed on 28 February, also ordering the creation of what became *Fliegerführer Atlantik*. 'Fatty' thwarted navy ambitions and had not just clipped Raeder's feathers, but also plucked him completely of all means of independent air support by confining *Generalleutnant* Hermann Bruch's *FdL* to the North Sea leaving the Atlantic divided between the new command and Stumpff's *Luftflotte 5*. [20]

Göring was already weakening *FdL*, converting *Küstfliegergruppen* into *Kampfgruppen* then 'borrowing' them but never returning them; Bruch lost two more *Gruppen* through his *FlFü Atlantik* agreement, while the declining numbers of seaplane *Staffeln* gave Jeschonnek the excuse in January 1941 to disband the three *Fliegerführerschulen (See)*. Without sufficient major warships to justify an air arm, in early 1941 Raeder channelled officers away from the *Küstfliegergruppen* towards the

U-boats and many *Seeluftstreitkräfte* officers joined this arm and several became U-boat commanders. On 7 April 1942 *FdL* was subordinated to *Luftflotte 3* and in mid-July was assigned three of Coeler's *Kampfgruppen*, initially for attacks upon Great Britain but from 6 August, he was also responsible for anti-shipping operations in the event of an Allied landing. As autumn storms dispersed the prospects for an invasion, *FdL* was disbanded on 7 September, with its last two *Gruppen* formally absorbed into *Kampfgeschwader* to complete the Navy's defeat. Ritter (now a *General der Flieger*), who had been appointed in 1939 to command all naval aviation including carrier-borne units, recognised by March 1941 that he was little more than a liaison officer and proposed dissolving his position but this would not be implemented until August 1944 when *Generalmajor* Karl-Hennig von Barsewisch, the *General der Aufklärungsflieger*, assumed responsibility for seaplanes. [21] Ritter's last success was on 1 April 1941 when two *Aufklärungsgruppen* (*See*) were created for miscellaneous seaplane units. In July 1943 Ritter re-organised them into six *Seeaufklärungsgruppen* (*SAGr 125-130*) and added *SAGr 131* the following month.

Formernaval officer *Oberstleutnant* Martin Harlinghausen, the *Luftwaffe's* leading anti-shipping specialist, became *FlFü Atlantik* with added responsibilities for Fleet support, meteorological missions and even coastal protection, although he had barely 100 aircraft, including Ar 196 floatplanes! His commitments to the Mediterranean theatre meant he was unable to assume his new command until 31 March. Dönitz wanted the *Condors* to detect and to shadow convoys supplementing his comint organisation, the *B-Dienst* and Harlinghausen agreed to this symbiotic relationship, with hopes of co-ordinated assaults upon the convoys. On 8 February 1941 *U-37* discovered HG.53, allowing *KG 40* to sink five ships (9,201 grt), although 29,000 grt was claimed, while at the end of the month a 'wolfpack' savaged OB.288 which was discovered by *Condors*. [22] Chill reality swiftly overcame the warm glow of anticipation, for inadequate maritime navigation training, exacerbated by out-of-date meteorological data, created errors in location reports of up to 450 kilometres (280 miles), while 19 per cent of all reports gave errors in course up to 90°. [23]

For their part, U-boats were often unable to take sun or star sightings to provide accurate fixes, and, even when convoys were located, the submarines rarely homed-in bombers because their short-range radio transmitters were too weak (although loud enough to alert the vengeful British). Harlinghausen was irritated when his aircraft transmitted accurate locations and the U-boats failed to respond, but only when he complained to Dönitz did he discover *BdU* had failed to inform the *Luftwaffe* there were no submarines in the vicinity. By the end of March Dönitz bowed to the inevitable and abandoned plans for close co-operation in favour of a more flexible arrangement, his War Diary cynically noting that enemy radio signals of air attacks would help his *B-Dienst* to locate the convoys.

During the first quarter of 1941 the *Condors* continued to prowl the Western Approaches and sank 171,000 grt, the majority of the victims being lone ships, although in a sustained attack upon convoy OB.290 on 26 February *KG 40* claimed nine vessels (49,865 grt). However, with rarely more than six operational aircraft, this was an exception. [24] At first *Condor* casualties were light, but the Golden Age was coming to an end as British merchantmen received anti-aircraft guns, while the Germans soon encountered Fulmar and Hurricane fighters carried by catapult aircraft merchant (CAM) ships and work had started on the first auxiliary aircraft carrier, HMS *Audacity*.

By May 1941 *KG 40* had a base at Oslo-Gardemoen in Norway, with a staging base at Stavanger, and the *Geschwader* could fly three sorties daily to, and from, Bordeaux, yet its inadequacy as a long-range strike force was vividly demonstrated almost immediately. On 24 May the battleship *Bismarck* and cruiser *Prinz Eugen* fought their way into the North Atlantic, sinking the pride of the Royal Navy, the battlecruiser HMS *Hood*. [25] The two ships separated, but almost immediately *Bismarck* was damaged by carrier-borne aircraft and the following day, as she sailed towards the sanctuary of a French base, Göring ordered Stumpff and Harlinghausen to shield her. Harlinghausen was reinforced with five *Kampfgruppen* as air reconnaissance discovered the British Home Fleet closing on *Bismarck*, which was trapped on 27 May some 200 nautical miles (370 kilometres) beyond the effective range of the bombers. In the next two days they flew 158 sorties, near-missing a cruiser, sinking one destroyer and severely damaging another but by then *Bismarck* had been sunk. Her consort, the heavy cruiser *Gneisenau*, was able to reach the security of Brest harbour, joining her sister ship the *Scharnhorst*.

In June 1941 the enemy's growing anti-submarine strength forced Dönitz to operate west of 20°W, beyond the range of the *Condors*, which now interdicted the sea lanes between Great Britain and Gibraltar, the aircraft being concentrated at Bordeaux from the end of July. Dönitz's decision irritated Harlinghausen, who had planned a major offensive in the summer, and relations between the two men briefly cooled. They recovered, partly because, as ships became more effective in protecting themselves, the *Condors* had to revert to the reconnaissance role, attacking only when there was cloud cover. With Gibraltar traffic easier to monitor, the *Condors* flew *Fächer* ('fan') search patterns between 45°N and 34°S and out to 19°W (sometimes 25°W) and found prey for the 'wolfpacks', which savaged convoys OG.69, OG.71, HG.73 and HG.75 between July and October 1941 to achieve 45 per cent of their total success in tonnage terms.

The attack on OG.76 in September 1941, saw four U-boats lost, partly because of the presence of the carrier *Audacity*, whose fighters shot down two *Condors*. The *Condors* became more cautious and their success rate declined during the second half of 1941: losses rose to 13 aircraft, 10 to enemy action, as resistance increased. With production low, crews were ordered to return to base if even slight damage was suffered, while new aircraft were collected immediately they had been accepted at the factory. To add a new iron to the fire, Harlinghausen sent a few *Condor* crews on a torpedo-bomber course during the summer of 1941. The first unsuccessful attack took place on 30 December 1941, a ship escaping three 'eels' from a single bomber, before the need to assign a *Condor Staffel* as transports in the Mediterranean provided a face-saving means of abandoning this bizarre experiment. [26] The *Condor* was no stranger to the Mediterranean, for in August six had been sent to assist the maritime war in this theatre with nine He 111 torpedo-bombers as *Kommando Petersen*. The unit arrived in Athens on 26 August to interdict traffic in the Gulf of Suez, but Petersen barely had time to unpack before he was appointed Director of Research with special responsibility for the He 177 and replaced by *Oberst Dr* Georg Pasewaldt, later *Kommodore* of *KG 40*. [27]

Pearl Harbor was the decisive blow to co-operation between the U-boats and the *Luftwaffe*, for the apparent destruction of the US Pacific Fleet encouraged Hitler's declaration of war upon the United States in the belief that the Americans would concentrate in the Pacific and have difficulty supporting operations in Europe. To hamper the Americans further he supported Dönitz' plans for a U-boat campaign off the American coast which meant there were fewer submarines to co-operate with the *Luftwaffe*, although there was a swansong against HG. 76 from 14 December 1941 during which HMS *Audacity* was sunk by a U-boat after her fighters had despatched another *Condor*. Dönitz's six-month offensive in the Western Atlantic and Caribbean began in January 1942 and he committed most of his boats. Between 1 August 1940 and 31 December 1941 the *Condors* had 41 contacts with convoys, of which 18 were exploited by U-boats that sank 48 merchantmen (129,771 grt), two destroyers, a corvette and *Audacity*. [28]

Harlinghausen was in hospital when HG.76 was attacked, having been forced to ditch after attacking a merchantman. [29] But beforehand he had agreed with Coeler that their shortage of resources meant it was more operationally effective to divide British coastal waters between them, with *Fliegerkorps IX* responsible for eastern waters, although little was achieved. The coastal campaign in 1942 was largely restricted to night operations, apart from *Jabos* which sank two ships (1,460 grt), with the *Kampfgruppe*'s prime objective to provide operational training. Consequently, from October 1942 until the Normandy invasion in June 1944, the *Luftwaffe* failed to sink a single ship in British waters. The only effect of the campaign was to pin down Fighter Command, but as the campaign faded away so the British were able to reduce their activity.

Harlinghausen would spend several months in hospital and was formally replaced on 5 January 1942 by *Generalleutnant* Ulrich Kessler, a former deputy air attaché in London, who arrived from a training command but had briefly been Geisler's Chief of Staff during May and June 1940. Kessler's reign proved unhappy for he also was denied the resources he needed and in the first half of 1942, *FlFü Atlantik* was in the doldrums, able neither to support the U-boats on the other side of the Atlantic nor to interdict the convoy routes while the focus of anti-shipping operations turned to the Arctic and Mediterranean.

For these operations the *Luftwaffe* was able to to deploy the torpedo for stand-off attacks since the *Regia Aeronautica* had made a considerable investment in this form of attack and its torpedo-bombers *(aerosiluranti)* earned respect from friend and foe. The *Luftwaffe* used the standard Italian high-performance torpedo (as the F5a) and when these were delivered they ended Göring's dependency upon the navy and led him to plan a three-*Gruppen* torpedo-bomber force based on *KG 26*. Harlinghausen was a strong advocate of the weapon and in January 1942 became both *KG 26's* new *Kommodore* and *Bevollmähtigten für das Lufttorpedowesen* ('Plenipotentiary for airborne torpedoes'). In March 1942 the torpedo-bombers were transferred to Norway to attack Russian convoys. They returned to the Mediterranean to engage the Allies' North African beach-heads in November 1942 when Harlinghausen and *Stab KG26* were renamed *Führer der Luftwaffe in Tunis (FdL Tunis)*. [30]

The U-boats renewed their assault upon the convoy routes only in the late summer of 1942 when the weather was deteriorating, and consequently during the whole year there were just three attempts at co-operation between the services, the only success being against HG.84 in June. There was also an embarrassing incident on 21 July when a *Condor* hunting a convoy earlier reported south-west of Eire, mistakenly sank three Spanish trawlers. Then in November 1942 Dönitz had to divert many boats to cut the Allied sea lanes to North Africa following the Operation 'Torch' landings but he anticipated focusing upon the North Atlantic during the spring and early summer and returning to a new Golden Age.

Radar might have helped detect convoys in greater safety, but progress was at a snail's pace. A 136-MHz Fu*G Atlas* was installed in a Fw 200C-3/U3 in July 1941 and the similar *FuG Neptun-S* was later trialled off Norway, but both proved disappointing, and when the latter was compared in July 1942 with the equivalent British metric (200MHz) ASV (air-to-surface vessel) Mk II, from a crashed Hudson in Tunisia, the British sensor was found to be far superior. By this time *FuG Rostock*, operating at 120-MHz and with a 16-nautical mile (30-kilometre) range, was under development, but production was so slow that by November 1942 only five Fw 200C-4/U3s in the West had radars, and one of these was the captured set! During the autumn, development began of a fourth sensor, the high-resolution *FuG 200 Hohentwiel*, operating at 550 MHz and with a range of 43 nautical miles (80 kilometres). Its smaller antennas did not degrade aircraft performance, and it entered service in August 1943 in the Fw 200 C-6, but Kessler's low priority meant that even by December 1943 only 16 of 26 Condors in *III./KG 40* had radar. [31]

Although his men claimed to have sunk 13 ships (43,000 grt), a destroyer and an auxiliary cruiser, Kessler was in despair and, after learning that he was to lose *KG 6* he proposed to Jeschonnek on 5 September the disbandment of *FlFü Atlantik*, which he described as 'a living corpse [32].' He peevishly noted that not only had his command not been expanded into a *Fliegerdivision*, but also some units were being used to bomb Britain. 'If we succeed in reducing enemy tonnage by several hundred thousand a month, then American and British armament potential will be irrelevant.' [33] Despite Dönitz's support, Kessler's letter had no effect. During the summer the admiral pressed for the introduction of the He 177 into the Atlantic battle. Milch informed him on 28 October 1942 that Hitler had ordered that the Eastern Front would have priority on this bomber, but nevertheless *I./KG 50* was soon created at Brandenburg-Briest to work up He 177s for operations over the Atlantic.

Unfortunately, the need to supply Stalingrad led to its transfer eastwards for transport operations, where it was joined by 20 *Condors* which formed *KGr zbV 200*.

An ominous feature of 1942 was the provision Kessler had to make for defensive operations, for enemy aircraft in growing numbers were intercepting U-boats crossing the Bay of Biscay even on the darkest night. In May Dönitz sought *Luftwaffe* protection, and although no night fighters could be spared, Kessler did receive six Ju 88 C-6s, which arrived in Bordeaux on 10 June and began patrols a fortnight later, becoming *a Zerstörerstaffel* (later *13./KG 40*). [34] Two Wellingtons were claimed on 20 July and by the end of August seven victories had been recorded, encouraging representations from Raeder which led Hitler to demand a *Zerstörergruppe* (Coastal Command lost a total of 26 aircraft in the Bay during this period). A *Stab V.(Z)/KG 40* was formed under *Hauptmann* Korthals at the beginning of September, but two months elapsed before it reached establishment, and even by the end of the year there were only 27 aircraft (8 fell to enemy action).

As a stop-gap, the nimble Ar 196 floatplanes were pressed into service, claiming eight victories to 6 September. The British reacted by introducing two squadrons of Beaufighters, the heavyweights first clashing on 8 September. The greatest threat to the Beaufighters came from the Fw 190s of *8./JG 2*, which claimed most of the 17 Beaufighters Coastal Command had lost by December, despite Fighter and Army Co-operation Command sweeps over *JG 2's* bases, leading Coastal Command to seek P-38 Lightnings. During the second half of 1942 the pace of battle quickened, with the *Luftwaffe* intercepting Coastal Command aircraft on some 70 occasions and claiming 22 victories. The Command's total losses in this period were 98 aircraft.

Both sides realised that 1943 would be decisive on the convoy routes, especially Dönitz, who now had a first-line strength of some 200 boats. He became commander-in-chief of the Navy following Raeder's resignation on 30 January, but he continued to act as *BdU* and exploited Hitler's high personal regard in order to secure better air support. When he met Göring on 25 February he demanded 12 reconnaissance sorties a day and more very long-range aircraft, but he was informed that the He 177 would not be available until the autumn, while the four-engine Me 264 'Amerika Bomber' had made its maiden flight only two months earlier. The following day Hitler intervened and ordered the transfer of three six-engine Bv 222 *Wiking* ('Viking') flying boats from transport duties to Kessler, who, with Dönitz, dreamed of using them for 24-hour missions over the central Atlantic, and refuelling them from U-boat tankers off the Azores. However, Jeschonnek prevaricated and the Bv 222s did not become available until the summer. As compensation, on 8 March, *ObdL* did agree to provide Dönitz with 10 Ju 88 Hs for reconnaissance and some four-engine Ju 290s, both equipped with FuG 200 *Hohentwiel*. These were heady days for Kessler, with Sperrle talking of expanding his command to 22 *Gruppen* and renaming it *Fliegerkorps III*, while the *Condor* force was increased in size to 39 aircraft by mid-March to fly more than 100 sorties a month. In a spurt of optimism Kessler informed Sperrle that with all *Luftflotte 3's* bombers he could sink 500,000 tonnes a month. [35]

The pace of operations accelerated during the spring, and in March Dönitz came close to winning the Battle of the Atlantic by sinking 108 ships (627,377 grt), of which only 8 per cent were with *Luftwaffe* assistance. During the first quarter of 1943 only six convoys were shadowed, but of the 74,954 grt sunk in co-ordinated air/U-boat operations during the year, 85 per cent were sunk during this period, mostly in actions against SL. 126 and XK.2 during March. [36] After March 1943 *FlFü Atlantik* detected only 14 convoys, while during June 1943 none was attacked in the North Atlantic, allowing Coastal Command to reinforce its ASW sweeps in the Bay of Biscay. Meanwhile by exploiting 'Ultra' intercepts, the British re-routed convoys to ensure that Gibraltar traffic passed beyond *Condor* range.

Meanwhile, the growing power of ASW forces inflicted 30 per cent casualties on the U-boats in May, while the introduction of new ciphers effectively neutralised the *B-Dienst*, making aerial reconnaissance vital to Dönitz. The admiral sought to withdraw from the Atlantic but was told unequivocally by Hitler on 31 May, 'There can be no let-up in the U-boat war. The Atlantic, Admiral, is my first line of defence in the West.' Nevertheless, he sympathised over the inadequate air support and falsely blamed the *Luftwaffe's* insistence on a dive-bombing capability for the delay in introducing the He 177. The *Condors* continued their tedious patrolling, but often flew in formation to and from their sectors for protection not only against Beaufighters but also against Liberator, Fortress and Sunderland ASW aircraft. [37] In fact Dönitz' attempt to withdraw his U-boats from the central Atlantic was a tacit admission that he had lost the Battle of the Atlantic.

By 1942 the focus of *Luftwaffe* naval support operations had turned northward to help cut the flow of Allied supplies to Murmansk. [38] Until then Stumpff's *Luftflotte 5* had been a backwater, contributing a small force to support army operations in the Arctic Circle following a British raid on the Lofoten Islands in December 1941, which increased Hitler's paranoiac fears of an invasion. The garrison was substantially reinforced with men, warships (including the new battleship *Tirpitz*) and torpedo-bombers, the last sent on the *Führer's* specific instructions, while six *Condors* arrived at Stavanger-Vaernes to extend reconnaissance. [39] Yet during the winter crisis on the Eastern Front, the German Navy sank only one of the 103 ships carrying supplies to north Russia, snapping Hitler's patience and on 11 March 1942 he demanded Stumpff and the navy launch intensive attacks upon Russia-bound convoys.

On paper the task was easy, for the polar ice ensured that enemy shipping sailed no more than 240 nautical miles (445 kilometres) from the *Luftwaffe's* chain of bases within the Arctic Circle, but the region's capricious weather and frequent mists hindered operations. A strike force of 115 aircraft was assembled under *FlFü Lofoten (Oberst* Ernst-August Roth) although *I./KG 26* soon lost its *Kommandeur (Oberstleutnant* Hermann Busch) and staff, who became *FlFü Nord (West)*. By now *KG 26* was being converted into a torpedo-bomber unit, the *Luftwaffe* being influenced by the success of the Italian Air Force (*Regia Aeronautica*) *aerosiluranti* (torpedo-bomber) units, and many of the crews had just come from training in the Mediterranean. [40]

Air reconnaissance between Iceland and Spitzbergen would detect and track a convoy which would be attacked only on Stumpff's command once he had squadrons assembled at Bodø, Bardufoss and Banak under Roth. When the enemy convoy passed the line Spitzbergen-North Cape, *FlFü Nord (Ost)*, under *Oberst* Holle would take over with strike forces moving to Kirkenes or Petsamo. During 1942 the *Luftwaffe* had a series of successes, notably against PQ 17 after it dispersed fearing attack by the battleship *Tirpitz*. *Luftwaffe* analysis judged the torpedo to be the most effective means of sinking ships, with one vessel sunk for every eight sorties (compared with 19 bombing sorties), and it was estimated that nearly a quarter of the 340 torpedoes released struck a target. Just as the forces were preparing for a new campaign, in November 1942 they were sent south to extinguish the 'Torch' landings and the Mediterranean became the centre of anti-shipping operations until mid-1944.

Coeler's mundane minelayer operations were overshadowed by his colleagues. Göring had demanded a major minelaying effort in mid-July 1940 and 20 October 1940, but while Coeler had 1,000 mines he lacked aircraft, despite receiving both *KG 4* and *KG 30*, and his efforts were further compromised by the diversion of both to the Blitz, which consumed a third of his ordnance. [41] Between July 1940 and May 1941 some 6,100 mines were laid but the invasion of Russia – '*Barbarossa*' – reduced Coeler (promoted to *General der Flieger* on New Year's Day 1941) to three or four

Kampfgruppen which were increasingly used for conventional bombing, and there were squabbles with Harlinghausen over anti-ship operations with *FlFü Atlantik* laying mines while Coeler's thinly stretched *Gruppen* were used for anti-shipping sweeps.

Because *Fliegerkorps IX* became a general-purpose command Greim's *Fliegerkorps V* was transferred from Russia to Brussels on 30 November 1941 to control minelaying operations. It seems likely that Greim would have been transferred, possibly to replace Jeschonnek, but in the event half of *Fliegerkorps V* staff were sent to help contain a crisis in the Crimea and the remainder went East in the late spring to become *Luftwaffenkommando Ost*. Increasingly the minelaying campaign was diluted, especially during the 'Baedeker' campaign of 1942, despite Sperrle's protests to *ObdL* and *OKW* with *Luftflotte 3*'s anti-shipping effort in 1942 no better than the latter half of 1941. Although *Fliegerkorps IX*'s air strength doubled (from 103 aircraft on 30 April 1942 to 205 on 31 March 1943), minelaying – under the leadership of Fröhlich since December 1942 – virtually ended and British losses to airborne mines dropped from 24 ships (41,324 grt) in 1942 to seven (19,542 grt) in 1943. [42] Fröhlich's appointment was intended not to boost the anti-shipping campaign but rather the air offensive against Britain. In April 1943, however, *Fliegerkorps IX* was assigned to Peltz who would actually command it from September 1943.

In the 46 months from July 1940 the *Luftwaffe* sank 1,988,841 grt of merchantmen, mostly in the West, where 1,228,104 grt were sunk and 1,953, 862 grt damaged, while partial figures indicate that in 1942 and 1943 another 60,866 grt were sunk by *Luftwaffe* mines. [43] Even these substantial figures merely underline the half-hearted nature of the effort, and hint at what have been achieved with wholehearted support. By contrast, the RAF offensive against the smaller German mercantile marine, with grossly inferior aircraft, destroyed 278,863 grt in west European and Scandinavian waters while minelayers sank 462,605 grt. To meet the threat from magnetic mines, the *Luftwaffe* formed *Sonderkommando Ju 52 (MS)* with Ju 52 (and a few Do 23) *Mausi* ('Mice') carrying degaussing rings. [44] The importance of *Mausi* grew, and in October 1942 *Minensuchgruppe 1* was formed with five *Staffeln* but 16 months later the *Gruppe Stab* was disbanded and the *Staffeln* became independent.

By the time Fröhlich arrived the campaign against British coastal shipping had ceased to be a strategic one and had become an Operational one and part of a defensive strategy designed to prevent or delay an Allied invasion of Western Europe. This defensive strategy was heralded soon after Leigh-Mallory assumed command of No 11 Group when, just after noon on 27 December two Spitfires of No 92 Squadron strafed targets at Abbeville. Under Leigh-Mallory, Fighter Command, supported by No 2 Group of Bomber Command, assumed a more aggresive role in the New Year of 1941 in a 'leaning forward' policy to erode the German war machine and *Luftwaffe* strength. There were low-level fighter sweeps, later designated 'Rhubarbs'; from 10 January there were 'Circus' operations with a small bomber formations sent out to attract enemy fighters to their large fighter escorts and these were soon followed by 'Rodeo' massed fighter sweeps by 'Big Wings' equal to *Jagdgruppe* strength as well as 'Ramrod' fighter escort missions for bombers (see Table 5-2 for offensive operations into Western Europe).

Table 5–2: Allied air offensive against Western Europe, October 1940–December 1943

Quarter	Day		Night	
	Fighter	*Bomber*	*Fighter*	*Bomber*
Q 4 1940	2 (-)	153 (3)	28 (-)	1,277 (15)
Q 1 1941	1,683 (26)	224 (4)	83 (4)	1,142 (14)
Q 2 1941	5,192 (86)	962 (33)	192 (1)	2,465 (25)
Q 3 1941	15,385 (298)	1,144 (80)	219 (4)	1,199 (11)
Q 4 1941	5,110 (118)	262 (22)	92 (1)	1,489 (28)
Q 1 1942	3,320 (63)	499 (6)	139 (-)	1,688 (17)
Q 2 1942	19,409 (232)	508 (10)	744 (20)	1,089 (19)
Q 3 1942	12,999 (231)	706 (19)	581 (17)	39 (2)
Q 4 1942	8,999 (71)	1,534 (59)	297 (4)	46 (1)
Q 1 1943	8,921 (113)	1,711 (59)	418	3,122 (37)
Q 2 1943	20,395 (184)	2,209 (100)	1.187	768 (9)

Sources: Freeman, *Mighty Eighth War Diary*. UKNA Air 16/1036. UKNA Air 14/3361-3364. UKNA Air 14/2666-2675. UKNA Air 24/100 Appendix UKNA Air 241101 Appendix. UKNA Air 41/49 Apps 19, 28. UKNA 24/1496.

Notes: Bomber Command night sorties exclude minelaying and leaflet operations. Army Co-operation Command 'Rhubarb' and bomber sorties are included with Fighter and Bomber Command figures. Figures in parentheses are failed to return.

Leigh-Mallory was repeating Trenchard's offensive patrol policy of the Great War which meant that the RAF was effectively making wild swings like early bare-knuckle boxers, while the *Jagdgruppen* responded like the more scientific boxers and in the mindset of the great Manfred van Richthofen, striking when they wished to inflict a constant stream of losses, often without response. The RAF's only significant success occurred on 15 May when Grauert, the commander of *Fliegerkorps I*, whose reputation had been built in Poland, met his nemesis when Polish pilots from No 303 Squadron shot down his transport near Aire.

During June the scale of the offensive increased massively, yet Leigh-Mallory's assumption that the *Jagdgruppen* would automatically meet the challenge proved to be wishful thinking, with the scales further tipped against him by qualitative inferiority. None of his single-engine aircraft, even the Spitfire IX introduced in 1942, had an operational radius beyond 190 miles (300 kilometres), and if the pressure grew too great (as in 1944), the *Jagdgruppen* could have been withdrawn beyond that. However, this was unnecessary, for having learned the advantages of radar-based air defence, the Germans used them to outweigh their numerical inferiority. Early in 1941 they began augmenting the *Flugmelde-* and *Funkhorchdienst* with a radar network which by March 1942 extended from Heligoland to the Biscay coast, with 32 *Freya* and 57 *Würzburg* sets in a command and control system headed by the *JaFü* headquarters with *Flugwachkommando* reporting centres. [45] When *Luftflotte 2* was withdrawn it left behind Osterkamp's *JaFü 2*, responsible for the sector from the Schelde to the Seine, while *Oberst* Werner Junck's (then *Oberst* Max-Josef Ibel's) *JaFü 3* defended air space to the west being joined by *JaFü Holland-Ruhrgebiet* on 1 February 1942. Each *JaFü* controlled a *Jagdgeschwader*, from south to north *JG 2* '*Richthofen*', *JG 26* '*Schlageter*' and *JG 1*, but re-equipment and rest meant that the shield was weak: in July 1941, for example, *II./JG 26* began converting from the Bf 109E-7 to the Fw 190A-1 *Würger* ('Shrike') while *7./JG 26* was in Sicily. [46] During the good flying months of the summer and early autumn, most of their missions were *Alarmstarts* ('scrambles') which accounted for up to 93 per cent of all sorties, but as the weather deteriorated they flew more patrols and intercepted fewer missions.

Early warning of major operations came from the *Funkhorchdienst*, whose detection of pre-flight testing of radios gave clues to the imminence and scale of the attack, leading to radar stations being placed on higher alert. The *Freyas* would observe formations assembling and alert both *Jagdführer* and *Geschwader*, the latter placing their *Gruppen* on standby. Once the attackers' direction was known, the *Jagdgruppen* would take off and, while observing radio silence, receive a running commentary, often by the *Geschwader* signals officer, using *Freya* and *Flugmeldedienst* information with *Würzburg* giving the altitude. The *Kommandeure* would break radio silence to place formations in an advantageous tactical position, then lead the attacks, which the *Jagdfliegerführer* and *Stäbe* followed through radio chatter and ground observer reports. [47]

The odds against the 'Tommies' were further stacked by the *Luftwaffe's* qualitative superiority, first with the introduction of the Bf 109F in March 1941 and then by the Fw 190A in July 1941, the latter proving superior in every respect to the newly introduced Spitfire V. But design faults meant the Fw 190 was plagued by engine problems which *JG 26* had to resolve and it did not become fully operational until September, after which it began to demonstrate its superiority. [48] By the end of the year *JG 26* had completely re-equipped with the Fw 190. Mention should also be made of the formidable *Flakwaffe*, whose numbers halved in the summer but were still adequate to take a steady toll of the attackers.

The British suffered badly during 1941: Fighter Command's daytime loss rate was around 2 per cent, while Bomber Command's (largely No 2 Group) was nearly 7.7 per cent, excluding anti-shipping missions, with ominous increases during the last quarter. From 14 June 1941 until the end of the year, Fighter Command lost 411 aircraft over the Channel, 14 during the last 'Circus', and although its pilots claimed 731 victories, the *Jagdgruppen* lost only 103, leading a post-war RAF staff study to observe that every *Luftwaffe* aircraft destroyed cost the RAF 2.5 pilots. [49] By contrast the *Jagdgruppen*, whose loss rate was less than 1 per cent, destroyed four fighters for every one they lost, and many *Experten* honed their skills over Western Europe, including the diminutive *Oberleutnant* Josef 'Pips' Priller, who claimed 19 aircraft (17 Spitfires) in 26 days from 16 June 1941, with a his 20th victory on 14 July bringing his total to 40. Yet, curiously, when the RAF Air Staff began to conserve resources from October by reducing the scale of the offensive, morale in Fighter Command apparently declined, especially when 'Rodeos' and 'Circuses' were abandoned at the end of the year as the over-stretched RAF faced demands not only from the Mediterranean but also from the new Far Eastern theatre.

During 1941 Bomber Command occasionally risked its growing four-engined bomber force in small-scale surprise daylight raids on French harbours, notably Brest, but rarely with any success, while the majority of night attacks on Western

European targets were conducted by crews who were completing their operational training. The need to protect Brest was a major headache for Sperrle because it became the refuge of the battlecruisers *Scharnhorst* and *Gneisenau* as well as the cruiser *Prinz Eugen*. As part of a campaign to prevent these ships from returning to the Atlantic, Bomber Command began a 10-month offensive on 29 March 1941 which involved 2,928 sorties, 171 of them in daylight, but at great cost, increasingly from *JG 2*. Night bombing was safer in the absence of night fighters and the night of 7/8 December saw the first use of the Oboe electronic navigation aid. Raeder pressed for the ships' return to German waters, Hitler agreeing because he wanted them to underpin the defence of Norway, and it was he who advocated exploiting the short winter days for a dash through the Channel, *Unternehmen 'Cerberus'*. [50]

ObdL was uneasy, with Jeschonnek remarking to *Inspekteur der Jagdflieger Oberst* Adolf Galland (the former *Kommodore* of *JG 26*) that if *'Cerberus'* failed the *Luftwaffe* would be made the scapegoats. Galland was given executive power for the *Luftwaffe* operation, *Unternehmen 'Donnerkeil'* ('Thunderbolt') and worked out the details with *Oberst* Karl Koller, Sperrle's Chief of Staff, although to assemble sufficient strength they had to mobilise some training units. Coeler's *Fliegerkorps IX* (with five *Ergänzungsgruppen* in reserve) would bomb British bases in south-west England and support naval forces in the eastern Channel, while *FAGr 123* and Bruch divided responsibility for reconnaissance in the west and the east respectively. As the task force sailed north, each *Jafü* would cover it in its sector but but to ensure local control *Oberst* Max-Josef Ibel (who had defended the Maastricht bridges as *Kommodore* of *JG 27* in May 1940) embarked in *Scharnhorst* as *JaFü Schiff. Jagd-* while *Nachtjagdgruppen* would keep pace with the task force as it made its way up the Channel, flying under enemy radar until the enemy detected the ships, with the 'black men' refuelling and re-arming the fighters within 30 minutes.

Anticipating *'Cerberus'* through 'Ultra' intercepts, the British assembled 100 bombers and several torpedo-bomber squadrons to thwart it, but their hopes were dashed through a combination of bad luck, bungling and inertia. The bad luck was that a bomber raid delayed the task force's departure on 12 February for three hours, then airborne radar malfunctions prevented Coastal Command aircraft from detecting the ships rounding Brittany. As the task force entered the Straits of Dover in the mid-morning the jammers of the *Funk-technisches Untersuchungskommando* (*FTU*) *Breslau* began blinding British radars, leading Fighter Command to send a pair of Spitfires to investigate. However, when they returned with reports of the task group, Leigh-Mallory was slow to alert either the Royal Navy or Coastal Command (whose anti-shipping forces had stood down). Eventually the British hornets' nest was stirred and 248 strike and 416 fighter sorties were flown in deteriorating visibility which led to 'friendly fire' incidents, but by midnight the warships were in German naval bases.

'Donnerkeil' was a tremendous success which Galland later described as the greatest hour in his career. [51] The *Luftwaffe* flew more than 300 fighter and 40 bomber sorties and lost 22 aircraft – some 5-6 per cent of sorties – and it shot down 41 enemy aircraft (60 were claimed) of which 7 per cent were by *Flak*. But within a fortnight *Prinz Eugen* had been torpedoed by a submarine and *Gneisenau* had been crippled during a bombing raid on Kiel

'*Donnerkeil*' also proved to be a watershed in electronic warfare. *FTU* had controlled radio and radar jamming from its headquarters near Calais using land-based emitters, while three He 111 using *Ballstöranlage* emitters simulated large air formations to divert British attention supported by 15 Do 217 of *III./KG 2*. Another 10 aircraft struck Plymouth harbour and airfield. But the use of jammers, which proved useless against 3–4 GHz sensors, removed British inhibitions concerning the use of ECM against the German defensive system and paved the way for the devastating debut of 'Window' chaff in June 1943. From 6 April, the British began occasional airborne jamming ('Moonshine') although this was not apparently recognised by the *Luftwaffe* until September. [52] The Germans, too, used offensive jamming to support new *Jabo* operations against southern England designed to maintain pressure upon the enemy, who described them as 'a real menace'.

Six months later the *Luftwaffe* supported another German success on the Channel coast. With the Russians seemingly on the verge of collapse and to test invasion tactics, the British launched Operation 'Jubilee' on 19 August, intended to seize and briefly hold the small port of Dieppe. An alert defence contained the main thrust on the beach where half the assault force became casualties, but the lessons learned ensured the D-Day landings two years later would be a success. [53] For Leigh-Mallory 'Jubilee' provided the opportunity he had long sought to bring the *Luftwaffe* to battle in conditions of absolute numerical superiority, with 65 squadrons which flew 2,604 operational sorties (including 120 by the USAAF). Although he succeeded, the results nowhere matched his optimism, for the *Jagdgruppen* whose pilots flew three or four sorties a day continued to pick-off his pilots. By the end of the day the *Luftwaffe*, which had flown 945 sorties, had lost 48 aircraft (a 5% loss rate) and destroyed 99 British and American aircraft (3.8% of sorties, although the USAAF loss rate was 6.7%) as well as eight American.

Dieppe demonstrated that the Allies had a long way to go before they won air superiority against the determined efforts of *JG 2* and *JG 26*. Fighter Command leader Douglas, probably at Leigh-Mallory's urging, sent his fighters eastwards '…to restore morale' ignoring an Air Staff ban on offensive operations which was not lifted until 13 March 1942. [54] 'Circus' operations were resumed to erode *Luftwaffe* strength, but in the first fortnight of April they saw the RAF suffer four times the losses of the *Luftwaffe*. Within a month Douglas (who had lost many experienced pilots to overseas theatres) abandoned deep-penetration 'Circus' operations, but on 24 April he opted for bigger 'Super Circus' missions but it did nothing to change the situation.

Douglas consoled himself with the belief that he was inflicting equal casualties, but the *Jagdgruppen* usually escaped unscathed and only during June did the unwelcome truth began to dawn. On 13 June the Air Ministry informed Douglas that the balance of casualties was turning against against him: in the four months to the end of June, Fighter Command's losses were 264 while the *Jagdgruppen* lost only 58, largely because most of their 332 fighters were the superb Fw 190. Only on 17 July did Douglas admit his inferiority. This followed trials with a captured Fw 190 and a Spitfire V which concluded that the British pilots' best chance was to circle as close as possible to the English coast until the enemy pilots ran short of fuel and with-drew! Douglas received the superior Spitfire IX from July 1942 and eventually would overcome the development difficulties with the Hawker Typhoon but continued bloody deep-penetration missions against Air Ministry advice until August.

American influence on the west European air battle grew during 1942, partly through the replacement of No 2 Group's Blenheims with excellent bombers such as the Douglas Boston (A-20) and North American Mitchell (B-25) as well as the mediocre Lockheed Ventura (B-34).

The Eighth US Air Force arrived in England during the year and flew its first mission in borrowed Bostons on 29 June, but the Americans had to equip their fighter squadrons with Spitfire Vs pending the arrival of the new generation of fighters, including the twin-engine Lockheed P-38 Lightning, the massive Republic P-47 Thunderbolt and the Allison-powered North American P-51A Mustang, for their older aircraft were inferior even to the Spitfire V. [55] The USAAF began its heavy bomber campaign on 17 August when B-17 Flying Fortresses were used for the first time in a strike on the marshalling yards at Rouen/Sotteville: they posed a serious problem for they flew at 7,600 metres (25,000 feet), the limit of the Fw 190's effective performance and the *Luftwaffe* had to place greater reliance on the recently delivered Bf 109 '*Gustav*'. The *Ami* (American) *Viermots* ('Four-Motors') or *Möbelwagen* ('Furniture Vans') were formidable opponents, not only because of their armament but also because of their size, which filled the gun sights before the bombers were in range, leading many pilots to break off attacks too early. Conventional beam and stern attacks meant running the gauntlet of numerous machine guns – one pilot likened it to opening a wasp's nest – but head-on attacks, which began on 23 November, proved an effective tactic which claimed four bombers on the first clash. [56] However, the 'green' leadership of the USAAF believed the gunners in its bombers were devastating the *Jagdgruppen*, shooting down six fighters for every bomber lost.

The Eighth Air Force slowly expanded to 296 bombers and 128 crews on 31 October, 10 days after it opened a new campaign against U-boat bases in France. Then many Eighth Air Force units were transferred to the Mediterranean to support the landings in North Africa and by the end of the year it had only 219 bombers with 176 crews as men and aircraft were transferred to the Mediterranean to join the Twelfth Air Force. [57]

In the aftermath of 'Jubilee', Fighter Command operations were more restricted pending re-equipment with the Spitfire IX. Douglas was replaced on 28 November by Leigh-Mallory, but by the end of the year the two of them, through a combination of poor tactics and operational directives had been partly responsible for the loss of 587 fighters, the equivalent of more than 30 squadrons, as well as many veteran pilots, while total *Jagdgruppen* losses were 198. [58] Moreover, during the year *Jagdgruppen* strength increased to 457 in September with 71 per cent serviceability, and it benefited from improved command and control thanks to the introduction of IFF into formation leaders' fighters, but a new challenge was emerging.

The diversion of squadrons to support 'Torch' eased the pressure on *Luftflotte 3* during the early months of 1943, but the Americans steadily replaced the squadrons and began to build up a formidable 'tactical' air force as part of Eighth Air Force. The RAF also replaced its squadrons and re-equipped; more fighter squadrons received the Spitfire IX and later models, which were superior to the Fw 190 and Bf 109, while the Typhoon became more reliable. The bomber squadrons had all received modern American aircraft and by the summer the Allies were ready to return to Western Europe in force and with a greater degree of confidence in their ability to achieve air superiority, an essential prerequisite for the opening of the Second Front. Sperrle's *Tagjagdwaffe* strength rose from 199 aircraft on 1 January 1943 to 322 in 1 June but losses in the first half of the year were heavy, with 189 destroyed or badly damaged, some on the ground.

Sperrle did not confine himself purely to defensive operations and from the winter of 1941/1942, after flying only 15 daylight bomber sorties in the second half of 1941, sought to pin down the RAF through daylight strike missions (see Table 5-3 for *Luftwaffe* daylight operations over Great Britain).

Table 5-3: Luftwaffe day operations over Great Britain, January 1942–June 1943

Month	Bombers	Fighters/Jabos	Defence
Q1 1942	142 (4)	26 (1)	19,290 (9)
Q 2 1942	262 (4)	189 (9)	20,741 (19)
Q 3 1942	286 (13)	193 (7)	25,559 (25)
Q 4 1942	293 (8)	156 (5)	18,082 (15)
Q1 1943	123 (2)	321 (18)	18,661 (12)
Q 2 1943	12 (1)	359 (26)	24,853 (6)

Sources: IWM Tin 29, fr 2826. UKNA Air 41/49 p.187, Appendix 19. UKNA Air 16/1036. Balke *KG 2* vol 2, pp.74–183. Goss, Cornwell, Raubach App. 8.

Note: Defensive sorties 1943 include USAAF.

The *Kampfgruppen* continued surprise harassing raids, or *Seeräuber/Pirat-angriffe* ('Pirate Raids'), upon factories and harbours, but they were over-stretched with commitments to night-bombing, anti-shipping and minelaying operations. In the aftermath of the Battle of Britain, many fighters were converted to fighter-bombers (*Jagdbomber* or *Jabo*) and harassed the enemy in missions involving up to 300 sorties a day. At the end of 1941 Sperrle revived the idea creating a *Jabostaffel* in *JG 2* and this unit began raiding the British coast during December using under-the-radar tactics but was then reined in to lull the enemy into a false sense of security before '*Donnerkeil*'. [59]

The *Jabostaffel* returned to the fray on 10 March 1942 and a similar unit was formed in *JG 26* initially with Bf 109 F-4/Bs carrying a single 250 kilogramme bomb or four 50 kilogramme bombs, but these loads were doubled from July when the *Staffel* re-equipped with the Fw 190. The offensive was a mixture of harassment and precision bombing and it accelerated British development of the centimetric Chain Home Extra Low (CHEL) radars (initially naval and army coast defence sensors augmented by the Type 13/14 height-finding radars all in 2–4 GHz frequency) which could detect aircraft flying at only 50 feet (15 metres) at distances of up to 40 miles (65 kilometres). The scale increased following a message to *ObdL* on 14 April: '*The* Führer *has ordered that the air war against England is to be given a more aggressive stamp. Accordingly, when targets are being selected, preference is to be given to those where attacks are likely to have the greatest possible effect on civilian life. Besides ports and industry, terror attacks of a retaliatory nature are to be carried out against towns other than London.*'

JG 2 initially focused upon coastal shipping with 20 ships (63,000 grt) claimed sunk, while *JG 26* focused upon industrial targets east of Brighton, a deep penetration raid on 31 October against Canterbury by 111 aircraft succeeding because *FTU* jammed the enemy radars. Fighter Command was rarely able to intercept them and the British tried to counter the raiders by strengthening the anti-aircraft defences of 11 coastal towns although there was a general shortage of the deadly Bofors 40mm guns. During September Fighter Command switched tactics establishing an all-day fighter screen along the Channel with no success. By the end of the year the *Jabos* were tying down 1,500 fighters, 2,800 anti-aircraft guns and some 600,000 personnel and had neutralised the home defence system which Dowding had built up.

From the autumn the *Jabos'* objectives turned increasingly from industrial to civilian targets in reprisal missions. These were augmented by strafing attacks by the *Jagdgruppen* whose pilots were told repeatedly and specifically in briefings that they were to attack public transport, any gathering of people and even herds of cattle and sheep, while farm buildings and even haystacks felt the wrath of the German people! The *Jabo* force was expanded with the establishment on 1 December of *Schnellkampfgeschwader* ('fast bomber wing') 10 (SKG 10) at St André under *Major* Günther Tonne. The unit was to operate by both day and night and was assigned some highly experienced officers with a pilot cadre selected from flying school instructors augmented by their students. Training included preparation for the usual nap-of-the-earth operations together with instrument training for flights at night or in bad weather.

But the defence had been strengthened with the CHEL system expanded, more 40mm batteries deployed, improved reliability for the Typhoons and the introduction of the Spitfire XII. A growing number of raids were intercepted with 5.6 per cent losses inflicted during the first quarter of 1943 and during April Tonne was largely involved in night missions. A return to daylight attacks from 7 May brought no reprieve and in the second quarter of 1943 the loss rate rose to 7.24 per cent. With the Allied landings in Sicily in June, *SKG 10* became part of the great rush to the south and while one *Gruppe* remained, the *Jabo* offensive was effectively over.

Despite everything Sperrle's *Kampfgruppen* maintained pressure on the British during 1942 with daylight *Pirätanflüge* exploiting bad weather or poor visibility and flying more than 980 sorties, but losses began to rise during the latter half of 1942 and during the first half of the following year only 135 sorties were flown. [60] The introduction in April of the light bomber version of the Me 410 *Hornisse* ('Hornet'), the Me 410A-1, brought the prospect of a German equivalent to the de Havilland Mosquito, but the the crisis in Sicily saw *Kampfgruppe* strength drop from 229 on 1 July to 197 on 1 August.

Reconnaissance was also reduced by the growing effectiveness of the British defences. During the second half of 1941 the *Aufklärungsstaffeln* flew an average 184 sorties a month over the British Isles but by the first half of 1943, this had dropped to 21. Greater use was made of single-engined aircraft but this was no panacea and they lacked the range to reach the enemy's industrial heartland. Some very high-altitude missions conducted at over 46,000 feet (14,300 metres) were flown by converted Ju 86s of the *Versuchsstelle für Höhenflüge* (High-Altitude Flight Test Centre) during the summer and autumn of 1942, but these were a rarity.

By the summer of 1943 Allied pressure was increasing, the anti-shipping war over the British Isles had ceased and maritime support of the U-boats was largely defensive. While the *Luftwaffe* could still control the skies over Western Europe, this would soon be very severely challenged and an ominous hint of the future was the decision forced Sperrle to withdraw SKG 10 back to Amiens to avoid the full force of enemy air power. The situation would deteriorate sharply over the next six months.

Chapter Six

Icarus

From 1941 until early 1944 the bulk of the *Luftwaffe* was concentrated either in the Mediterranean or the Eastern Front. From *ObdL's* viewpoint the two fronts were intertwined like a lover's embrace, ultimately with fatal consequences.

At the outbreak of war the *Luftwaffe* had no plans for the Mediterranean but they began when Mussolini suddenly joined the war in June 1940 hoping, like a hyena, to feed off the colonial carcasses of France and Great Britain. Italy's industrial weakness quickly made Mussolini the junior partner in the Axis, his status undermined almost on a weekly basis. Italy's offensive into Egypt ground to a halt after barely crossing the border and an unprovoked attack upon Greece from Albania (occupied in April 1939) turned into a humiliating defeat which provoked the despatch of British air forces to Greece. British carriers raided the Taranto naval base and crippled the Italian battle fleet on the night of 11/12 November and on 9 December the British began an offensive which, in two months, drove the Italians out of Egypt then out of Cyrenaica (the eastern part of Italian Libya) and reached the borders of Tripolitania (the western part).

Within hours of the Taranto debacle *OKW* issued *Weisung Nr* 18 which focused upon the western Mediterranean. The objectives were diplomatic: to ensure that the Iberian nations were either friendly neutrals or allies but the directive also foresaw a *Luftwaffe* presence in North Africa to attack the Suez Canal and the Alexandria naval base. Hitler's prime concern was shielding the Ploesti oil fields in Rumania both from British bombers and a Russian invasion. Plans were already well advanced for an invasion of the Soviet Union the following May, in what would become *Unternehmen 'Barbarossa.'* It was now necessary to occupy mainland Greece to deprive the British of bomber bases and Göring was to prepare to send *Luftwaffe* units to the 'south-eastern Balkans' [1].

In late 1940, *Generalfeldmarschall* Wilhelm List's 12. *Armee* and *Generaloberst* Ewald von Kleist's *Panzergruppe* 1 were sent to secure Rumania and on 10 October Kesselring's former Chief of Staff, *Generalleutnant* Wilhelm Speidel, arrived to become head of the *Deutschen Luftwaffenmission in Rumänien* (German Air Force Mission to Rumania) where he remained until June 1942 ostensibly to modernise and to train the *Forţele Aeriene ale Romaniei* (Royal Rumanian Air Force or FARR) but his mission was also to help defend the oil fields as well as preparing the infrastructure for operations against Greece and Russia. [2]

The *Luftwaffe's* first step into the Mediterranean theatre was the establishment of *Verbindungsstab der Luftwaffe bei der Italienischen Luftwaffe in Rom - Italuft* (Luftwaffe Liaison Staff to the Italian Air Force in Rome) with the *Regia Aeronautica* (Royal Air Force) under the watchful eye of *Generalmajor* (*Generalleutnant* from 1 August) Maximilian *Ritter* von Pohl after Italy entered the war. Pohl was soon sending a stream of critical reports back to Berlin about the *Regia Aeronautica* whose formidable international pre-war reputationwas undermined by inadequately trained pilots, a weak aero-engine industry and an airframe organisation unable to master mass production techniques. [3] The first *Luftwaffe* operation in the theatre was assisting an airlift into Albania, deploying a *Transportgruppe* which flew a total of 4,028 sorties and ferried 28,871 men with 5,680 tonnes of materiel into Tirana and returned with 10,740 men including 7,911 sick and wounded from Foggia between 9 December and 31 March 1941. [4]

Meanwhile, Pohl was urging Jeschonnek to send aircraft to North Africa but nothing happened until the British threatened Tripolitania. Hitler promised Mussolini support and on 25 November Milch led a high-level delegation including Jeschonnek and Hitler's *Luftwaffe* liaison officer, *Generalleutnant* Karl Bodenschatz, to Rome. [5] The trio assessed their allies' air requirements and opted to send a strong anti-shipping force with Geisler's *Fliegerkorps* X, nominated on 4 December because it was not committed to '*Barbarossa*.' On 10 December Hitler rubber-stamped this plan and informed Geisler that he was going to Sicily for the '...elimination of English air power on Malta.'

But Greece remained on Hitler's mind and three days later, OKW *Weisung Nr* 20 was published, envisaging an offensive by List and Kleist from Bulgaria, to be known as *Unternehmen 'Marita'* and intended to occupy mainland Greece, securing Germany's southern flank before '*Barbarossa*' with troops being transferred from Rumania during March. The *Luftwaffe's* role was to support the Army, to destroy enemy air power and to secure Rumania, but where possible it was to '...seize English bases in the Greek islands with airborne forces.' Air support would be provided by *Fliegerkorps VIII* and, on 8 January, Richthofen and List met Hitler for a personal briefing. *Fliegerkorps VIII* began to arrive in Rumania from 23 January moving 290 aircraft to Bulgaria after Sofia joined the Tripartite Pact or Fascist Axis on 1 March, being joined towards the end of the month by *Generalleutnant* Wilhelm Süssman's airborne *Detachement Süssman* in anticipation of airborne operations against the Greek isles, as heralded in *Weisung Nr* 20.

At the other end of the Mediterranean, the despatch of *Fliegerkorps X* was executed with the legendary German efficiency after Milch and *Generalmajor* Otto Hoffmann von Waldau, the *Luftwaffe's* head of operations, completed arrangements with the Italians on 6 December. *Staffeln* began arriving before Christmas but by the first week of 1941 Geisler had only 95 aircraft and 14,389 men in Sicily. On 9 January he detected a convoy carrying supplies for Malta and Egypt and the opportunity was so great that he persuaded *ObdL* to give him four *Stukagruppen* of *Fliegerkorps VIII* giving him 255 aircraft (179 serviceable) by mid-January including a strike force of 209 bombers and *Stukas*. [6] On 10 January the *Stukas* made a spectacular debut planting six bombs on the aircraft carrier HMS *Illustrious*, but these attacks temporarily emptied the bomb dumps. The carrier limped into Valletta, Malta, for emergency repairs and immediately became a magnet for German bombers who faced 56 aircraft, including 20 fighters supported by radar, with a strike force of Wellingtons and Swordfish operating from Luqa (called Lucca by the Germans). Geisler flew 200 strike sorties for the loss of eight aircraft, but failed to inflict mortal damage upon the carrier, which departed for Alexandria on 23 January and a year's repairs in the United States.

Above: A Halberstadt CL.II close-air support aircraft (*Schlachtflugzeug*) from 1917, one of several types with which *Oberst* Hermann von der Lieth-Thomsen equipped the early post-war *Freikorps* air squadrons, many of them formed of often bitter and disgruntled airmen – veterans of the First World War.

Left: Hauptmann Helmuth Wilberg had commanded German squadrons around the Ypres salient in August 1918 but went on to become one of the fundamental architects of post-war German air power. He planned an air force that would meet internal threats and potential conflict with Poland and would later command a *Luftkreisschule*. In the late 1930s, he became involved with German military aid to Spain during that country's civil war.

Below: A line-up of Fokker D XIIIs photographed in the early 1930s at the covert German training facility at Lipetsk, 500 kilometres southeast of Moscow, which operated from April 1925 to September 1933 and through which some 225 German airmen passed, including 77 future *Luftwaffe* generals.

Left: The able and far-sighted *Generalleutnant* Walther Wever, the *Luftwaffe's* first chief of staff who championed the notion of an independent air force in 1934 and later proposed the construction of a four-engined strategic bomber which was to be '… capable of flying around Britain under combat conditions.' His death in an air crash in June 1936 effectively left the *Luftwaffe* flying without a pilot in the years leading to the outbreak of war.

Below: Heinkel He 51s of the *Reklamestaffel Mitteldeutschland* at Döberitz attract attention from a group of visiting Nazi troopers. By the autumn of 1933 three *Reklamestaffeln* (skywriting squadrons) had been established which were, in reality, clandestine fighter units.

Below left: Adolf Hitler shakes hands with the newly promoted Commander-in-Chief of the *Luftwaffe* in 1938, *Generalfeldmarschall* Hermann Göring. Since Hitler's rise to power, Göring's control over aviation in Germany had become absolute.

Below right: Three leading personalities who introduced invention, discipline, egotism and conflict into the *Luftwaffe* during the first phase of its development. Here the aircraft designer *Professor* Willi Messerschmitt presents new plans to *Generaloberst* Ernst Udet (to Messerschmitt's left) and *Generalfeldmarschall* Erhard Milch (to Messerschmitt's right). The ambitious and ruthless Milch took over the post of *Generalluftzeugmeister* following Udet's suicide in November 1941.

Left: Spain – the first test: a flight of Dornier Do 17s of the German *Legion Condor* in formation over mountains in northern Spain during the Spanish Civil War. In conformity with standard practice, the aircraft carry standard Spanish Nationalist insignia.

Right: Strike commanders: *General der Flieger* Albert Kesselring (right) commanded *Luftflotte* 1 at the time of the invasion of Poland, while *Generalmajor Dr.-Ing.* Wolfram *Freiherr* von Richthofen, a distant cousin to the famous 'Red Baron', led the close-support command, *Fliegerführer zbV*. Richthofen, a former chief of staff of the *Legion Condor*, assured *ObdL* that '...every effort will be made to eradicate Warsaw completely.' Both men would be appointed *Generalfeldmarschall* later in the war but, with different temperaments, they would suffer a fractious working relationship.

Below: The pilot of a Henschel Hs 123 biplane of the ground-attack unit, II.(*Schlacht*)/LG 2, leans nonchalantly against his aircraft's wing strut as it is re-armed in its wooded revetment during the campaign in France in 1940. The unit's Hs 123s would be phased out in June 1940 for the new Messerschmitt Bf 109 E.

Above: Ground crew carry bombs out to Junkers Ju 87 dive-bombers – the feared Stukas – of *I./St.G 1* at Insterburg, East Prussia at the time of the invasion of Poland in September 1939.

Right: Generalfeldmarschall Hugo Sperrle, commander of *Luftflotte 3* on the Western Front for most of the war. Experienced and intelligent, but abrasive and bombastic, he had served as an aviator during the First World War and as commander of the *Legion Condor* in Spain. Sperrle enjoyed a taste for the good life: during the campaign against England in the summer of 1940 he arranged to have his personal transport fitted with a refrigerator to keep his requisitioned wines cool.

Below: Air and ground crews relax under a Scandinavian sun in April 1940 while a Messerschmitt Bf 110 D *Zerstörer* (destroyer or heavy fighter), probably of ZG 76, is refuelled. The large central fuselage fairing visible on this aircraft housed the '*Dackelbauch*', a supplementary fuel tank intended to extend combat range.

Above: Fighting to close the Channel: *Oberstleutnant* Harry von Bülow-Bothkamp, *Geschwaderkommodore* of JG 2 stands close to his Messerschmitt Bf 109 E in readiness for another flight over the English Channel and an encounter with RAF Fighter Command, while a member of his ground crew assists in tying his life vest, an essential item of personal equipment, in the summer of 1940.

Below: The founding fathers of the *Nachtjagdwaffe*: *Generalmajor* Josef Kammhuber (centre with fur collar) and *Major* Wolfgang Falck in a photograph believed to have been taken on 22 January 1942 while on a visit to the Heinkel factory at Rostock/Marienehe during which they observed test flights of the He 219 advanced night fighter, at that time still under development. To the far right of the picture is the aircraft designer, Ernst Heinkel.

Above: Under the glow of powerful lights, the pilot of a Messerschmitt Bf 110 G night-fighter of an unidentified *Nachtgeschwader* watches from the cockpit as ground crew prepare the machine for take-off on another nocturnal sortie. The aircraft carries the distinctive '*Englandblitz*' emblem of the night fighter arm and is fitted with an under-fuselage gondola carrying a pair of 20mm MG FF cannon for use against the massed bombers of RAF Bomber Command.

Right Kammhuber Line: an early ground radar station comprising a '*Freya*' (centre) and two '*Würzburg*' D model radar installations. Such technology formed key elements of the German night air-defence system.

Left: In following the shifting pattern of Allied air attacks, German flak guns mounted on railway flat wagons were moved rapidly with their crews, ammunition and stocks of essential supplies, to protect threatened areas. Here, a battery of 105mm guns is seen in action during a night raid over Germany.

Below: A Heinkel He 111 H-6, belonging to *6./KG 26* and converted to carry torpedoes, stands ready for a mission against Allied shipping at an airfield in southern France in 1942. Such aircraft were deployed in operations against the Allied beachheads in North Africa.

Left: Focke-Wulf Fw 200 C-3 *Condors* of KG 40 outside the hangars at Bordeaux-Merignac in western France from where they engaged on long-range anti-shipping missions. The aircraft in the foreground is undergoing a routine check to its four BMW-Bramo 323R-2 *Fafnir* radial engines which were rated at 1,000hp at sea-level and 1,200hp at take-off with the aid of methanol-water injection.

Above: German *Fallschirmjäger* jump from their Junkers Ju 52 transports. The paratroops leapt from the exit door of the aircraft with both arms outstretched and fell past the horizontal before the static line opened their parachutes. They therefore landed unarmed, relying on accurate drops of weapons and ammunition containers, and were often subject to injury when hitting the ground.

Above: General Kurt Student, commander of 7. *Fliegerdivision* and, in 1941, commander of *Fliegerkorps XI*, the *Luftwaffe's* parachute command. Student planned the airborne assault on Crete and, after persuading Hitler and Göring of the feasibility of the plan, was given 22 days in which to make the necessary preparations.

Right: Generalleutnant Ulrich Kessler became *Fliegerführer Atlantik* in January 1942 after the post was held temporarily by *Generalmajor* Wolfgang von Wild, formerly *Fliegerführer Ostsee*, due in turn to the wounding of *Fliegerführer Atlantik*, *Oberstleutnant* Martin Harlinghausen. Kessler was previously leader of KG 1 during the Polish campaign.

Above: Armourers load ammunition into the cowl guns of a Messerschmitt Bf 109 E-7 *Trop* of I./JG 27 in North Africa in late 1941. By the end of March 1942 – five months after the flying elements of *I.* and *II./JG 27* had become operational in Africa – the two *Gruppen* should have received some 1,200 ground personnel and about 400 support vehicles, but only about 110 personnel had arrived and none of the units' transport had made it across the Mediterranean, a situation which was not to improve until April.

Below: *Generalmajor* Hans Seidemann (left), the *Fliegerführer Tunis* discusses operational plans over the wing of a Focke-Wulf Fw 190 with *Oberleutnant* Kurt Bühligen of *II./JG 2*, the highest-scoring German pilot in Tunisia with 44 victories, at Kairouan, Tunisia, in January or February 1943. A pre-war sports aviator and veteran of the *Legion Condor*, Seidemann would hold a number of tactical command positions and lead *Fliegerkorps VIII*.

Left: A view inside the cockpit of a Heinkel He 111 carrier aircraft as its bomb-aimer operates the small joystick on the radio-control unit which transmitted guidance signals to an Hs 293 glider bomb as it made its way, in a shallow dive, towards a ship target. Carried by He 111s, Fw 200s and Do 217s, the Hs 293 carried a warhead of 500kg and was powered by a liquid-fuel rocket motor producing speeds of about 600km/h.

Below: Generaloberst Hans Jeschonnek, the chief of staff of the *Luftwaffe* from February 1939 until his suicide in August 1943. Before the launch of *Barbarossa*, he had warned army commanders that the wide battlefront in Russia and the limited resources available to the *Luftwaffe* meant that air support would be guaranteed only along the key axes of advance and that it was unlikely the *Luftwaffe* would achieve complete air superiority or be able to offer German ground troops sufficient protection.

Above: A pilot of the night-harassment unit, NSG 9, uses a field telephone to receive information at a forward dispersal in Italy in the late spring of 1944. One of NSG 9's Junkers Ju 87s can be seen in the background. These aircraft were deployed in the ground-attack role against Allied targets in the Anzio-Nettuno beachhead area.

Above: Spring rains turned airfields on the Russian Front into quagmires. Here a Heinkel He 111 ploughs through slush and rainwater as it taxies out for a bombing sortie. One German pilot wrote of Russia: '… the mud is indescribable.'

Left: For many German fighter pilots, the Eastern Front brought opportunities for fame and glory. One such typical case was that of *Feldwebel* Alfred Grislawski of *9./JG 52*, who for most of 1941 and early 1942 flew as wingman to the leading *Experte* Hermann Graf. Grislawski claimed his first victory on 1 September 1941, but in the Crimea in late April 1942 increased his tally from 18 to 42 in four weeks. Here, Grislawski is decorated with the *Ritterkreuz* awarded on 1 July 1942.

Right: *Generalmajor* Friedrich-Wilhelm Morzik, the *Luftwaffe's* senior transport commander, was a World War I aviator and former *Kommodore* of KGzbV 1, who was awarded the *Ritterkreuz* on 16 April 1942 for his work during the Demyansk airlift operation. A competent commander, he always fought against slender resources and continual splits in his organisational infrastructure brought about by the huge demands on transport from the Mediterranean and Russian Fronts.

Above: Ground crew work in appalling conditions and freezing temperatures to keep open a runway for Ju 52 transports in Russia in the winter of 1942/43. Such were the conditions during the Stalingrad airlift that apart from wear and tear, operations were disrupted by Soviet ground- and air-attacks and frequent, blinding snowstorms. Often aircraft were grounded for days at a time, requiring large numbers of men to dig them out.

Left: Oberst Hajo Herrmann was a protagonist. A veteran bomber pilot of the Spanish Civil War and the campaigns in Poland, Norway, France and the Mediterranean, from mid 1942 he became involved in night-fighting, devising the *'Wilde Sau'* method of employing single-engined fighters as night fighters. Herrmann shot down nine bombers using this method. He ended the war with the Knight's Cross, Oak Leaves and Swords.

Left: An Fw 190 day fighter of *JG 300* runs up its engines in preparation for a night sortie against RAF Bomber Command.

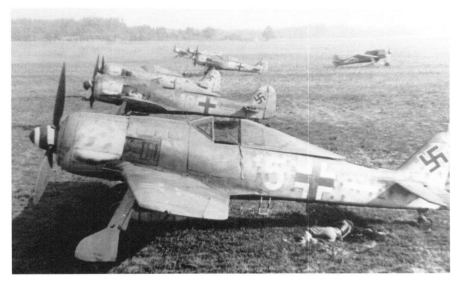

Above: Heavily armed and armoured Focke-Wulf Fw 190 A-8s of the *Sturmgruppe,* II./JG 300, seen at Holzkirchen in late August 1944. Intended for close-range destructive work in the daylight defence of the Reich against the heavy bombers of the USAAF, external armour plate has been fitted to the sides of the fighters' fuselages as well as armoured glass panels on the windscreens.

Left: Former Stuka and bomber ace *Generalmajor* Dietrich Peltz commanded a bomber training and development school before playing a leading role in anti-shipping operations from September 1942. Late in 1942, he was appointed *General der Kampfflieger* and in March 1943, the *Angriffsführer England*, responsible for attempting a new bombing campaign against Britain.

Above: Heinkel He 177 A-3 '*Helga*' of I./KG 100 with temporary black paint applied to its sides and under-surfaces, is bombed up in readiness for a night-bombing mission over England as part of Operation '*Steinbock*' in early 1944. With its troublesome, coupled engines, Hitler described the supposed strategic bomber as '…the biggest load of rubbish that has ever been built.' It is believed that the aircraft seen here was lost in a raid on Portsmouth on 27 April 1944.

Right: A Junkers Ju 87 G-1 fitted with two 37mm flak 18 anti-tank cannon beneath its wings. The emblem carried on the aircraft's nose, a crude depiction of a Russian tank, is that of the 1. *Staffel/ Versuchskommando für Panzerbekampfung*, a specialist tank-destroyer unit which first flew operations during the battle of Kursk in July 1943.

Generaloberst Robert *Ritter* von Greim (right) commanded *Luftlotte 6* in the East from mid-1943 until almost the end of the war. Greim oversaw a dogged withdrawal from the East and subsequently a tenacious air defence campaign of Poland and East Prussia, operating with limited human and materiel resources and fuel against a vastly superior enemy. In the final weeks of the war he was appointed *Generalfeldmarschall* and the last commander-in-chief of the *Luftwaffe*. He is seen here talking with *Generaloberst* Alfred Keller, one-time commander of *Fliegerkorps IV* and later *Luftflotte 1*.

Right: Between September 1943 and 26 April 1945, *Generaloberst* Otto Dessloch at various times commanded both *Luftflotte 4* and, briefly, *Luftflotte 3*. An aviator during the First World War, he also flew in the *Freikorps* under von Epp. Working alongside von Greim, Dessloch fought to defend the airspace over the southern and south-eastern sectors of Eastern Front in 1944 and 1945. He eventually assumed command of *Luftflotte 6* on 27 April 1945 when Greim was summoned to Hitler in Berlin.

Below: A Henschel Hs 129 B-2 purpose-built ground-attack aircraft, a type used to considerable effect in Russia from early 1942 by the *Schlachtgeschwader*, but seen here fitted with a wooden mock-up of the formidable PaK 40 BK 7.5cm cannon and fairing intended for anti-tank work, probably at the *Erprobungsstelle für Seeflug* where it conducted over-water trials in the Baltic. As the Hs 129 B-3 version, the cannon did eventually see limited use in the East, with limited success, with *12.* and *13.(Pz)/SG 9*.

Left: A *Mistel* pilot of 6./KG 200, clad in a life vest, taps the side of his head in a gesture directed at the photographer at Burg in early 1945. Many pilots considered it a bad omen to take photographs immediately before a mission. Behind the pilots can be seen the formidable sight of Fw 190/Ju 88 *Mistel* composite combinations, fitted with hollow-charge warheads, apparently prior to an aborted raid intended to strike at Antwerp docks.

Above: A Fi 103 flying-bomb (what would become known as the 'V-1') is air-launched from a He 111 during a test-flight at Karlshagen on 7 September 1943. Throughout the late summer and autumn of 1944, the He 111s of III./KG 3 and KG 53 carried out a limited campaign of air-launching V-1s against the British Isles. The Heinkels launched 1,287 missiles to the beginning of March 1945, of which only 235 broke through the defensive belt, with accuracy poor due to jamming and meaconing of their radio navigation systems.

Below: Too little, too late: a Messerschmitt Me 262 A-2a jet-bomber of 2./KG 51 is towed out of its forested shelter at Rheine in late 1944. At this time KG 51's jets were flying intensive missions against Allied troops and strongpoints in northwest Germany, Holland and Belgium.

On 20 February Geisler began what *OKW* described as 'the elimination of English air power on Malta', destroying or driving out the island's bomber force and reducing the threat to Axis North African supply lines. [7] Yet he flew less than 700 sorties in three months and was unable to finish off Malta because his own supply situation was parlous. On 22 April he informed *ObdL* that most of his bombers were unserviceable, forcing him to use the minelayers of *KG 4* and *Stukas* for night bombing ,while the quality of the replacements was so disturbingly low that he intended to stand down the *Kampfgruppen* to concentrate upon crew training (see Table 6-1). He was also having to provide air cover for convoys which accounted for another 40 per cent of his sorties between February and April, the situation being aggravated by the Italian Navy's announcement on 29 April that it could not guarantee the safety of convoys.

Table 6-1: Fliegerkorps X operations against Malta, January–May 1941

Month	Strike	Fighter	Reconn	Total	Losses
January	285	152	14	451	21
February	158	204	25	387	17
March	236	253	22	511	10
April	383	224	30	637	11
May	403	311	41	755	6
Total	**1,465**	**1,144**	**132**	**2,741**	**44**

Source: Gundelach p.123.

Geisler also had to support the German Army in North Africa in its commitment of a mechanised force soon named *Deutsches Afrika Korps*-DAK (German African Corps) under *Generalleutnant* Erwin Rommel whose function was to shore up the Tripolitania] front ordered by OKW *Weisung Nr 22* on 11 January. Geisler delegated the task to his chief of staff, *Major* (*Oberstleutnant* from 30 January) Martin Harlinghausen as *Fliegerführer Afrika* (air commander, Africa). Harlinghausen supported Rommel's raids into Cyrenaica which secured Tripolitania until relieved on 20 February by Austrian *Generalmajor* Stefan Fröhlich. [8]

Both Harlinghausen and Fröhlich were handicapped by remaining subordinate to Geisler and although ordered to provide 'the greatest support' to DAK, they were still subject to the whims of *Fliegerkorps X's* headquarters while also at the end of a 2,000-kilometre-long supply line. Fröhlich had 154 aircraft (117 serviceable) on 22 February but demanding conditions quickly wore out aircraft while only a trickle of supplies reached the African shores partly because Göring refused to weaken preparations for *'Barbarossa.'* A shortage of fuel and lubricants meant Fröhlich often had to depend upon captured stocks although *III./KGzbV 1* helped ease the crises. Fortunately, the RAF was dispersed across the Middle East and Greece leaving less than 100 aircraft in North Africa.

The *Luftwaffe's* limited air support quickly strained relations with Rommel, whose antipathy to Austrians might date from his experiences during the Caporetto offensive in 1917. He deeply resented Fröhlich's limited air support while being too blinkered to comprehend the reasons. Rommel was a brilliant tactician with little time for staff work, making co-ordination between the air and ground forces difficult and, as a darling of the Nazi Party, although never a member, he could count upon political support.

On 24 March he struck again, driving back the British to reach the Egyptian border on 13 April, the British tracking him through comint interception of Fröhlich's ciphered communications. [9] But the port of Tobruk held out in Rommel's rear, dividing Fröhlich's forces until the arrival of a *Jagdgruppe* drove the RAF out of Tobruk, while the German supply situation was eased by Hitler's diversion of two *Lufttransporttruppen* from Bulgaria on 26 April. [10] Fröhlich's strength rose to 177 aircraft (108 serviceable) but with logistic priority going to the nascent Russian Front, the resurgence of Malta meant that the supply stream became a trickle forcing Rommel to pause for breath by the beginning of May as the British Western Desert air forces grew in strength. [11]

By then the focus of operations had switched to the eastern Mediterranean and the Balkans where Germany was persuading or coercing governments to join the Tripartite Pact. The little countries duly signed on the dotted line, but Yugoslavia's accession on 25 March 1941 proved so unpopular that within two days a coup by General Dušan Simović, the chief of staff of the *Jugoslovensko Kraljevsko Ratno Vazduhplovstvo – JKRV* (Yugoslav Air Force) established a new government in the name of the young King Peter. This repudiated the agreement and a furious Hitler immediately issued *OKW Weisung Nr 25* extending *'Marita'* to Yugoslavia.

List, Kleist and Richthofen retained their original *'Marita'* assignments but half their forces would now strike westward into Yugoslavia while *Generaloberst* Maximillian, *Freiherr* von Weichs's *2.Armee* assembled in Austria and Hungary to strike southwards. There was also an ominous paragraph in *Weisung Nr 25*: *'As soon as sufficient forces are available and the weather allows, the ground installations of the Yugoslav Air Force and the city of Belgrade will be destroyed from the air by continual day and night attack.'* The assault on Belgrade would quickly become a separate operation known as *Unternehmen 'Strafgericht'* ('Judgement Bench' or 'Seat of Justice').

The Germans organised things with their legendary speed and ruthlessness, taxing the Vienna-based *Luftgau XVII* to the limit as 18 *Gruppen* flew in – 14 of them from France – between 28 March and 4 April, while Löhr transferred his command post to near Graz. [12] Some of the newly arrived *Gruppen* would live a hand-to-mouth existence because they lacked vehicles and there was little time to build up reserves of fuel, ammunition and spares. Yet of 955 combat aircraft assembled, a very credible 84 per cent (809) were serviceable which reflected not only the efforts of the the the *'Schwarzmänner'* (ground crews) but also the working 'marriage' of Löhr and Korten who had been together since 1938.

Planning was completed on 1 April and Richthofen remained the dominant air commander with 372 combat aircraft. Löhr retained a 205-bomber strike force but created two task forces from the *Stäbe* of *St.G 3* and *St.G 77*, *Oberstleutnant* Torsten Christ becoming *Fliegerführer Graz* in Austria with 110 aircraft, while *Oberstleutnant* Clemens *Graf* von Schönborn-Wiesentheid became *Fliegerführer Arad* in Hungary with 255 aircraft. German aircraft were augmented by 666 Italian and 96 Hungarian machines but Bulgaria, while helping to 'plan the robbery' drew a moral line at participation and refused to commit its airforce. Also in theatre, but retained under *ObdL* command, was *Generaloberst* Kurt Student's *Fliegerkorps XI*, created on New Year's Day, with the airborne troops of Süssman's *Fliegerdivision* 7 and *Generalleutnant* Hans *Graf* von Sponeck's 22. *Infanteriedivision* (*Luftlande*) (Infantry Division, Airborne) but its seven *Transportgruppen* under *Oberst* Rüdiger von Heyking's *Stab KGzbV 2* would support the spearheads. The *JKRV* had 468 aircraft but it was fragmented and, scattered among a range of of muddy dispersal fields many of them known to the Germans thanks to a Croatian defector! Yugoslavia's allies could offer only moral support; the *Elleniki Vassiliki Aeroporia – EVA* (Greek Air Force) had only 41 operational, but obsolete, aircraft while Air Vice-Marshal John D'Albiac's RAF force had 152 Hurricanes, Gladiators, Blenheims and Lysanders in Greece, half of them serviceable. [13]

Enemy airpower was the *Luftwaffe's* prime target although it would also provide its usual mix of operational- and tactical-level air support to the army. [14] But Löhr, whose Austro-Hungarian Army background and Croatian parentage undoubtedly provided some antipathy towards the Serbian-based country, also planned '*Strafgericht*'. Whether this was an attempt at decapitation or punishment is a moot point; Löhr's orders of 31 March certainly focused upon government centres within Belgrade which were assigned to experienced bomber crews as well as to the crews of von Schönborn-Wiesentheid's *Stukas*. Hitler rubber-stamped the order on 5 April and the decision to use both incendiaries and even mines suggest a darker motive to punish what Hitler called: 'The Serb traitor clique.' Significantly, *Luftwaffe* operations in Croatia were restricted to tactical air support with bombing authorised only in special circumstances. [15]

On 6 April (Palm Sunday), and before an official declaration of war, the *Luftwaffe* flew 800 counter-air sorties destroying a third of the *JKRV* strength while Belgrade attracted some 825 sorties and the delivery of 360 tonnes of ordnance. [16] The city centre was left in flames with 47 per cent of the buildings destroyed or damaged and a death toll of up to 4,000. In 1947 a Yugoslav court would execute Löhr for war crimes. Yet the bombing forced Simović's government to quit Belgrade and cut its communications with the remainder of the armed forces who were left to fight private wars. [17] The *Blitzkrieg* then followed its usual pattern and while the *JKRV* flashed defiance the end was inevitable and the Yugoslav Army surrendered on 17 April.

In Greece, Richthofen was handicapped by having to divert part of his forces into Yugoslavia, but Geisler's *Fliegerkorps X* literally started things with a bang when it hit, and set ablaze two ammunition ships which blew up in the prime port of Piraeus causing the loss of a total of 11 ships (41,789 grt) as well as wrecking the facilities. Richthofen supported the advance, aided by four *Gruppen* from Löhr and with the imminent fall of Yugoslavia, *OKW Weisung Nr 27* on 13 April gave priority to the destruction of enemy forces in northern Greece.

The *Luftwaffe* was ordered '...*to support the new ground operations with all possible strength*' while Geisler was ordered to prevent a Dunkirk-style evacuation by bombing and mining ports. *ObdL* substantially reinforced Richthofen with eight *Gruppen* bringing his strength to 653 aircraft (511 serviceable) by 15 April and despite shortages of fuel and ammunition, he gave the *coup de grâce* to Allied air power in Athens five days later. From 25 April the British began evacuating their forces under Operation

'Demon', despite tremendous air pressure, with 100 aircraft daily pounding Piraeus, the Germans sinking four destroyers and 18 merchantmen (89,187 grt) yet the British evacuated some 80 per cent (50,672) of their troops by 28 April by dispersing the evacuation points and concealing the men during daytime. With little resistance the *Wehrmacht* occupied the Morea (the southern part of Greece) by 28 April.

Operations in Greece and Yugoslavia cost the *Luftwaffe* 181 aircraft (18 in accidents) and 292 aircrew while their allies lost 17.However by contrast, the *JKRV* lost 400 aircraft (including trainers and transports), the Greeks 162 (130 on the ground) and the RAF lost 127 (55 on the ground) with another 82 abandoned. Although overwhelming strength undoubtedly contributed to the *Luftwaffe* success, the high quality of leadership at all levels was another major contribution in the face of formidable difficulties. The atrocious road conditions lacerated vehicle tyres; indeed, a third of *Fliegerkorps VIII's* 2,700 vehicles were out of action at any one time, and the problem was exacerbated when the Germans began withdrawing troops from Greece for '*Barbarossa'* for there was only a single rail link to the north and many vehicles had to drive back to their new deployment areas. [18]

Only Crete remained under the Greek flag and airborne operations seemed the ideal way to seize the island. An airborne operation in the Mediterranean had been under consideration since the end of October 1940 and resurfaced when Löhr and Student met with Göring in Vienna on 15 April who was champing at the bit to seize Crete. Strategically, it would remove the threat to Ploesti of a potential bomber base and provide a springboard for operations in the eastern Mediterranean and beyond. On 21 April Göring despatched Student and Jeschonnek to *Führer* headquarters at Mönichkirchen to outline the concept and four days later 'Fatty' too was singing the siren song before a receptive Hitler. The only opponent was *OKW* chief, *Generalfeldmarschall* Wilhelm Keitel, who sagely advocated taking Malta, but it was a measure of Hitler's regard for '*Lakeitel'* ('Lackey-Keitel') that on 25 April *OKW Weisung Nr 28* called for Crete's occupation in *Unternehmen 'Merkur'* ('Mercury').

With '*Barbarossa'* dominating everything, and postponed by the Balkans operations, the *Führer* brooked no further delays so *Weisung Nr 28* set a deadline of 16 May. Löhr and Student began work, assisted by Jeschonnek who apparently flew down to Athens on a 'busman's holiday,' but '*Merkur'* faced innumerable hurdles and inevitably missed its deadline. Merely assembling the forces was a Herculean task with the routes out of Greece choked with traffic. The 22. *Luftflande* Division under von Sponeck, was left in Rumania and Student replaced them with mountain troops. Süssman brought *Fliegerdivision* 7 headquarters to Athens, but many of *Fliegerkorps* XI's units and logistical organisation were in Germany where much of the '*Tante Ju'* transport force went for overhaul, returning with units and vital supplies. [19]

There were few airfields but the most serious shortage was petrol, despite the capture of a substantial supply of British fuel outside Athens, and the operation turned on the last minute delivery of 9,000 tonnes to be delivered by ship on 19 May. Richthofen and Student completed operational planning, although there was friction, with Richthofen showing early signs of his penchant for being an armchair general. Filled with foreboding, and ever critical of the groundlings, Richthofen bitterly commented in his diary on 16 May: 'Student plans his operations based upon pure suppositions and preconceived notions.' Yet there was little tactical intelligence: it was *estimated* the British had withdrawn most of their men leaving a garrison of some 5,000 (there were actually 42,000 including 10,500 combatants), and even information on the terrain was limited.

Richthofen had 552 combat aircraft (398 serviceable) augmented by 51 Italian machines. Löhr contributed 51 aircraft and *Fliegerkorps XI* had 516 (422 serviceable) of which 504 were transports (418 serviceable) together with 71 gliders. Richthofen's forebodings were well founded, for Major-General Bernard Freyberg, the British commander in Crete, had dispersed his troops into carefully camouflaged positions, covering most of the potential landing sites. Freyberg was alerted to the prospects of an airborne assault through decrypted messages (Ultra intercepts) on 25 April but failed to comprehend the main blow would come from the air and compromised his defence by placing too much emphasis upon repelling an amphibious assault.

The *Luftwaffe* began probing Crete from 29 April. From 3 May it began to interdict the sea lanes to Crete sinking eight (50,197 grt) out of 15 ships while only 15,000 tons of supplies out of 27,000 tons were unloaded. The air campaign began in earnest on 14 May and within five days the last of some 40 British aircraft withdrew. The airborne assault began the following day but en route to Crete, Süssman's glider crashed, killing the general and his staff. *Kampf-* and *Stukagruppen* pounded the defence, creating a murk of haze, dust and battle smoke into which the first gliders descended. For the glider- and paratroops the next few hours were a nightmare as they came under fierce fire from concealed positions which severely wounded many of the senior commanders, leaving the troops fighting for their lives.

An airlift into Maleme helped to stiffen their resistance and the *Fallschirmjäger* began to advance, but cramped conditions at the airheads which remained under enemy fire meant many transports were wrecked. Reinforcements arrived by sea, despite the best efforts of the Royal Navy, and the Germans rapidly tightened their grip on northern Crete leading to the British decision to evacuate the island on 27 May. By lucky chance the sole aircraft carrier, HMS *Formidable*, was severely damaged by *Stukas* and, lacking air cover, the British were sitting ducks with the *Luftwaffe* sinking three cruisers and six destroyers as well as damaging two battleships, a carrier and 16 other warships effectively neutralising the British Mediterranean Fleet. But the Germans were slow to realise the British were withdrawing southwards which allowed the British to evacuate 16,500 troops by the time the evacuation was completed on 1 June.

Yet the *Luftwaffe* was in no state to exploit its success in Crete; indeed, for *Fliegerdivision 7* it was the second Pyrrhic victory in a year for it suffered some 4,500 casualties including 3,022 dead and missing. When Hitler presented many well-deserved *Ritterkreuze* to the '*Merkur*' survivors he commented that, 'The day of the paratrooper is over…' and the 12-day campaign undoubtedly influenced his strategic decisions in the Mediterranean later. Löhr and Richthofen lost 138 aircraft (25 in accidents) while *Fliegerkorps XI* lost 121 transports of which 48 were to accidents, the *Luftwaffe* suffering a total of 311 dead and missing aircrew. While the Balkans adventure was a dramatic example of *Blitzkrieg* which secured the Rumanian oil fields it was also a costly waste of resources when Germany was on the verge of a major new campaign, for which Richthofen had promptly to fly north to Poland. The *Luftwaffe* might have used Crete as a dagger thrusting into Egypt and the Middle East, but when *ObdL* moved Geisler to the eastern Mediterranean he was too weak to exploit the situation and his departure eased pressure upon Malta, weakening the Axis situation in the Mediterranean.

The decision to transfer Geisler was made on 18 April, although Waldau planned to leave some 60 aircraft in Sicily. *ObdL* recognised this was merely a token presence and on 4 May informed the Italians all the aircraft would go. Rome protested and, with Pohl's support, retained some *Zerstörer* at Trapani to escort the convoys. Geisler's transfer to Kifissia, north of Athens, was officially confirmed on 17 May in *OKW Weisung Nr 29* and executed four days later with 365 combat aircraft and 53 transports. Over Malta Geisler had flown 2,741 sorties between January and May, compared with 4,887 Italian, and lost 44 aircraft although his airmen shot down 62 aircraft. [20] On 26 May, with the imminent capture of Crete, *ObdL* and the *Regia Aeronautica* divided the Mediterranean between them roughly along the line 20° East which ran roughly from Corfu, off western Greece, to Derna in North Africa. The Italians controlled air operations west of the line while Geisler was responsible for operations to the east.

The *Regia Aeronautica* proved a slender reed and on 21 May Malta received Hurricanes from carriers. It was also soon a base for torpedo-bombers which prowled the sea lanes. The island was used as a staging post to reinforce Egypt and from July to December 1941 717 aircraft arrived and 514 departed, mostly eastwards. [21] By early August 1941 Malta had some 75 serviceable fighters and 230 anti-aircraft guns, while a second squadron of Blenheims had joined the strike force. [22] They helped submarines sink 108 ships (300,000 grt) between June and September and during November submarines and aircraft slashed cargo deliveries by 62 per cent. [23] The Italians maintained a desultory offensive against Malta, but their leadership failed to provide either a sharp sword or a strong shield.

Meanwhile, Geisler was ordered on 5 June 1941 to focus upon Egypt by striking at the British infrastructure and mining Alexandria and the Suez Canal. By the end of August, his *Kampfgruppen* had flown 494 sorties, mostly against Nile Delta targets, but also including 157 sorties against the Suez Canal, with his most spectacular success occurring on 10/11 July when 100 aircraft at the RAF's Abu Sueir depot were destroyed. Another 229 sorties were flown in September but on 17 September, under pressure from the German Navy, Hitler ordered *Fliegerkorps X* to resume shielding convoys bound for North Africa, although under Göring's persuasion the order was limited to those Tripoli-bound convoys which Geisler regarded as the most important. [24] Geisler received a *Lufttorpedostaffel* reinforced by *Sonderkommando Petersen* with six Fw 200 *Condors* under *Major* Edgar Petersen, the latter flying from Crete and Greece, also occasionally using Derna as a forward airstrip for missions into the Red Sea. [25] But in September the *Condors* were withdrawn followed by the *Torpedostaffel* on 7 October.

By then Geisler's scepticism of Italian ability to protect Rommel's supply lines had proven only too well-founded. In June 1941 the Italians unloaded 125,000 tonnes of supplies (37,800 for the *Wehrmacht*) in Tripoli but the figure declined to 83,000 tonnes (27,300) in August and by November it was 29,800 tonnes (5,100). [26] As shipping losses grew, German protests became ever more strident and on 12 August *ObdL* told *OKW* it was considering returning Geisler to Sicily, but the Germans backed down following vigorous Italian protests. However, on 6 October Geisler did extend his aerial shield westwards into the Italian sector to cover the main route from Naples to Tripoli. To underline *ObdL* concern in October *Italuft* was upgraded to *General der deutschen*

Luftwaffe beim Oberkommando der Königlichen-Italienischen Luftwaffe (Luftwaffe General with the Royal Italian Air Force Headquarters) retaining the *Italuft* acroynm.

The supply situation was embarrassing for both sides and any solution needed to meet Italian sensitivities. On 2 October, the *Regia Aeronautica* commander, General Francesco Pricolo, met Göring, who displayed surprising delicacy discussing Italian inadequacies while preparing the way for *Luftwaffe* reinforcements. Shortly afterwards Hitler was apparently persuaded to give greater priority to the Mediterranean and the elmination of Malta. [27] A month earlier, Jeschonnek planted the seed of sending *Luftflotte 2*'s ever-optimistic commander, *Generalfeldmarschall* Albert Kesselring, from Russia to the south and this bore fruit in Göring's mind for on 20 October he proposed transferring 16 *Gruppen* from the Russian Front where the *Wehrmacht* was closing in on Moscow and the 'Bolshevik' collapse was anticipated by winter. [28]

OKW decided to send *Luftflotte 2*'s headquarters, together with *General der Flieger* Bruno Loerzer's *Fliegerkorps II*, with Göring also hoping to make Kesselring supreme German commander in the Mediterranean theatre, but this ran onto the rocks of inter-service rivalry. On 10 November Kesselring received his orders and told Hitler the island of Malta must be stormed. Hitler curtly retorted there were no forces available. [29] He added that *Luftflotte 2* headquarters would be brought out of the line in the East, rested for a fortnight in Germany and then despatched south. In fact the situation was changing rapidly, beginning on 9 November when the Italians suspended convoys to Tripoli. [30]

In North Africa Fröhlich helped to contain two abortive British offensives during the summer but both sides recognised the need to improve air-ground co-ordination. When Rommel's command was upgraded to *Panzergruppe Afrika* on 15 August, *Oberst* Otto Heymer was appointed *Koluft Libyen*. But of greater significance was the appointment on 1 July of Air Marshal Arthur Tedder as head of RAF Middle East Command followed, on 30 July, by Air Vice-Marshal Arthur Coningham who assumed command of squadrons in the desert which became the Western Desert Air Force on 21 October. Coningham, with Tedder's approval, established a joint headquarters with the Army to integrate operations at both Operational and Tactical Levels which became as good as, and then superior to, similar *Luftwaffe* operations. Surprisingly, the army's attitude proved the biggest obstacle to co-operation but the problems were resolved in a year and visiting US Air Force officers would regard this as a blueprint for their own air-ground co-operation. [31]

Coningham and Tedder prepared for a major offensive, Operation 'Crusader', and began their campaign on 14 October by striking six *Luftwaffe* airfields pin-pointed through Ultra intercepts. Attacks extended to Axis communications and airfields while Malta increased the scale of its efforts against maritime communications. On 12 November Tedder, with 650 aircraft (550 serviceable) including some 300 fighters, began a six-day night-and-day campaign upon the Axis infrastructure. [32] By contrast Fröhlich had only 160 combat aircraft, of which half were serviceable compared with two-thirds of the 5a *Squadra Aerea*'s 420 inferior aircraft. Geisler had 206 aircraft (118 serviceable) including a strike force of 118 bombers and *Stukas*, 21 seaplanes and 25 transports. [33]

Despite their airfields being flooded at the start of the campaign, the Axis air forces performed well in the face of supply problems, but they were never able to overcome enemy air superiority. [34] By late November Fröhlich was down to some 40 combat aircraft and supplies of all kinds were running out. Kesselring had by now arrived in theatre and urged *ObdL* to support the hard-pressed *FlFü Afrika*, but on 27 November Rommel began to retreat under unrelenting British air attacks and the *Luftwaffe* had to abandon 228 machines, bringing total Axis losses since 'Crusader' began to 460. Fortunately the British were exhausted by their exertions and stopped after taking Benghazi. The respite allowed the *Luftwaffe* to consolidate its infrastructure in the Gulf of Sirte, although the dearth of airfields meant many *Gruppen* were transferred to Crete or even Sicily.

Kesselring's arrival was heralded by the establishment of *FlFü Sizilien* under *Oberst* Ernst-August Roth with five *Gruppen* (three *Kampf-*) which held the ring until 12 January when Loerzer's *Fliegerkorps* II arrived in Taormina. Roth then moved to Norway. Kesselring's headquarters moved to Frascati, some 20 kilometres south-east of Rome, on 1 December and the following day, *OKW Weisung Nr* 38 appointed him *Oberbefehlshaber Süd- OBS* (Southern Commander-in-Chief) nominally under Mussolini but '…in all *Luftwaffe* matters *Oberbefehlshaber der Luftwaffe* (Göring) will deal directly with *Oberbefehlshaber Süd*.' The *Luftwaffe* reinforcements were despatched '… *in order to secure and to extend our own position in the Mediterranean and to establish a focus of Axis strength in the central Mediterranean*.'

The need to establish an infrastructure and fill supply depots meant Kesselring's offensive began only on 20 March, although Roth had begun striking Malta from 5 December (see Table 6-2). By the end of March the *Luftwaffe* had flown some 3,400 sorties against the island while the *Regia Aeronautica* flew 2,455 between February and April. Between 20 March and 28 April the *Luftwaffe* flew 11,819 sorties against Malta, dropped 6,557 tonnes of bombs and lost 173 aircraft. Another report noted that from January to April 1942 the *Luftwaffe* flew 19,462 sorties against Malta dropping 8,366 tonnes of bombs and destroying 251 aircraft for the loss of 60 German aircraft; indeed, *KG* 77 had to be withdrawn to France for a two-month rest. Kesselring slowly built up his strength and by early April had 720 aircraft (435 serviceable). [35]

Table 6-2: Fliegerkorps II operations against Malta, January–November 1942

Month	Strike		Fighter		Reconn	Total
	Day	*Night*	*Escort*	*Attack*		
January	248	216	541	429	34	1,468
February	284	167	964	488	32	1,935
March	859	330	1,958	1,110	43	4,300
April	4,082	256	2,681	1,654	115	8,788
May	277	133	1,029	946	91	2,476
June	2	291	424	180	59	946
July	328	191	1,030	216	54	1,819
August	8	54	552	210	38	862
September	-	-	150	229	12	391
October	394	149	1,651	619	55	2,842
November	-	10	51	39	3	103
Total	**6,482**	**1,797**	**10,975**	**6,133**	**536**	**25,940**

Source: *L'Aeronautica Italiana nella Seconda Guerra Mondiale*, vol 2, p. 295.

Frequent sweeps by *Jagdgruppen*, often 30 minutes before the strike force arrived, reduced the defending fighters from 80 to 23 serviceable aircraft by mid-March and 13 by mid-April and they were thus ordered to avoid the enemy fighters and attack the bombers. [36] Spitfires were flown in from the American aircraft carrier USS *Eagle* but poor reception arrangements meant many were lost almost as soon as their tyres touched earth and the erosion of the island's shield continued with only 358 fighter sorties in April and 18 defenders shot down. [37] Kesselring also blunted Malta's sword with the island's squadrons flying 83 offensive and 41 reconnaissance sorties between 24 February and 24 March, figures which dropped to eight and 16 respectively in the 30 days to 21 April while over the next 30 days to May 19 were 25 offensive and 22 reconnaissance sorties. [38] More Spitfires were flown in on 20 April but most were lost on the ground and with Malta on the verge of destruction *ObdL* pushed for an airborne assault, *Unternehmen 'Herkules'*. [39] But Hitler, mindful of '*Merkur*', was reluctant and with Germany on the verge of a new offensive in Russia, *OKH* feared the loss of transport aircraft needed to support armoured spearheads there. Hitler prevaricated, then decided to postpone '*Herkules*', claiming the the Italian Fleet would not bring in reinforcements. He also hoped Rommel would remove the need to take Malta by occupying the North African coast with his planned offensive *Unternehmen 'Theseus'* by June.

On 9 May more Spitfires were flown into Malta and this time the airfields were given fighter cover. As the reinforcements landed they were guided to selected revetments, refuelled and re-armed, ready to enter the fray. [40] Yet, almost immediately, Kesselring ended his offensive – fortunately for the British who discovered that Fighter Command had palmed off worn-out or poorly repaired aircraft on the island together with green pilots many of whom had never fired their guns in anger. As German pressure eased Malta returned to the offensive and from 20 May to 2 June, airmen flew 21 strike and 56 reconnaissance sorties from the island with 161 strike and some 140 reconnaissance sorties during the remainder of June, growing in July to 320 offensive and some 140 reconnaissance sorties [41]. The *Luftwaffe's* offensive operations against the island were increasingly confined to night bombing which was responsible for nearly a third of the 703 strike sorties during May and June. Loerzer returned to the offensive at the end of June, but had barely 150 aircraft although they flew 1,819 sorties including 519 strike missions. [42] But he now encountered one of the best defensive air commanders of the war, for on 15 July Air Vice-Marshal Keith Park took over in Malta and ironically, given the reasons he lost 11 Group in 1940, he adopted 'Big Wing' tactics which inflicted a 5.8 per cent loss rate on the *Kampfgruppen* during the latter part of the month, forcing Loerzer to rein in his men. However, by the end of July only 80 of 275 Spitfires delivered since the beginning of March were operational.

Geisler barred the door to resupply from the east, sinking five destroyers and two merchantmen (12,915 grt) in what the Royal Navy dubbed 'Bomb Alley' during the first half of 1942 so a new effort was made in August from the west in Operation 'Pedestal'. [43] The convoy was subjected to four days of intense air attack, totalling 270 sorties to sink five ships (52,416 grt), but the survivors reached the island to bring much-needed supplies including aviation fuel. [44] Loerzer had shot his bolt and during August there were only 62 strike sorties against Malta, allowing the island's forces to dominate the sea lanes. Renewed Navy and *OKW* pressure from late September forced a reluctant Jeschonnek to order Loerzer to resume his attacks upon the island although only three reinforcing *Gruppen* were sent. Loerzer had barely 300 aircraft, half of them serviceable, while the *Regia Aeronautica* received 120 reinforcements and when the offensive was renewed from 11 October it was a disaster. [45] The *Kampfgruppen* suffered a 7.5 per cent loss rate to Park's 'Big Wings' and after six days Loerzer cried off as the deteriorating situation in North Africa absorbed all the *Luftwaffe's* spare capacity in the Mediterranean. Kesselring's efforts to crush Malta from 19 December 1941 to 7 November 1942 had cost the *Luftwaffe* 249 aircraft destroyed and 26 badly damaged while the RAF lost 293 fighters. [46]

The only reliable means of transporting Axis supplies was by air and *Oberst* Rudolf Starke was appointed *Lufttransportführer Mittelmeer* (Air Transport Commander, Mediterranean) with six *Transportgruppen* operating in *'pulks'* of up to 25 aircraft. These formations flew 4,425 sorties from Athens-Tatoi or Heraklion to Benghazi by the end of June delivering 28,200 men and 4,400 tonnes of supplies. [47] An extra burden on the *Gruppen* until the fall of Tobruk was the need to fly up to 1,000 men and 25 tonnes of materiel daily to Rommel's troops as well as 300 tonnes of fuel to Waldau's airmen. [48]

Meanwhile, the *Luftwaffe's* early success against Malta gave Rommel the logistical boost he needed to drive the British to the outskirts of Tobruk, the RAF having lost many aircraft sent to prop up the Far East front, but was then held by a fortified position called the Gazala Line. [49] Rommel's cavalier attitude both to staff work and army-*Luftwaffe* co-operation during this advance strained relations with Fröhlich to breaking point and Kesselring relieved the Austrian on 10 April. He was replaced two days later by former Luftwaffe Operations Chief Waldau, himself fleeing a broken relationship with his old friend Jeschonnek with whom he had quarrelled over the war's direction. Rommel did not change his attitudes, and relations with the new *FlFü Afrika* remained tense but Waldau was no doormat and the two services developed at least a working relationship. [50]

Rommel launched *'Theseus'* on 26 May to outflank the Gazala Line, by-passing its southern anchor, the Free French-held Bir Hacheim some 90 kilometres south of Tobruk. [51] An epic struggle developed with Waldau flying some 1,400 sorties and dropping 140 tonnes of bombs before the French abandoned their strong point; this was a serious diversion of resources for, from 25 May to 1 June, in total the *Luftwaffe* flew 2,422 sorties dropping 548 tonnes of bombs and claiming 75 enemy aircraft (55 were actually lost) for the loss of 14 (see Table 6-3 for Luftwaffe operations in North Africa in 1942). On 9 June, the British began their Flight into Egypt but, more ominously for the Axis, the RAF under Coningham and Tedder began interdicting communications and airfields, then striking the battlefield in unprecedented strength day and night. As the Eighth Army retreated, the RAF (assisted by the US Army Air Force) intensified its operations to provide a valuable rearguard with some 6,000 sorties in June and more than 10,000 the following month. [52]

Rommel took Tobruk on 21 June, then entered Egypt, which earned him the baton of a *Generalfeldmarschall*, but the British established a new defensive line near El Alamein. Tobruk now became Starke's southern terminus, with Brindisi the northern one, because of superior Italian rail communications. In mid-August Starke had only 161 aircraft, half of them serviceable, but by 19 November they had flown 11,500 sorties to deliver 42,000 men and 15,000 tonnes of supplies while evacuating 9,000 and wounded.

Table 6-3: Luftwaffe operations over North Africa, January–December 1942

Month	Strike	Jabo	Fighter	Fernaufkl.	Total
January	765	65	1,210	105	2,145
February	365	245	590	80	1,280
March	365	180	740	65	1,350
April	265	160	1,080	65	1,570
May	1,250	155	2,060	105	3,570
June	2,225	550	3,410	140	6,325
July	1,500	175	3,060	145	4,880
August	255	195	2,055	100	2,605
September	635	615	2,550	100	3,900
October	370	575	1,870	125	2,940
November	510	355	1,100	70	2,035
December	385	115	470	50	1,020
Total	**8,890**	**3,385**	**20,195**	**2,770**	**33,620**

Source: *L'Aeronautica Italiana nella Second Guerra Mondiale*, vol 2, p.357. Gundelach Appendix 8.

Despite their efforts and the capture of 7,000 tonnes of supplies and 2,000 vehicles in Tobruk, Waldau was at the end of his tether and by 3 July was down to 22 serviceable fighters and 18 *Stukas*. His airfields were under heavy attack. Sortie levels dropped from more than 6,300 in June to less than 5,000 in July and 2,600 in August. The strain on aircraft may be gauged by the fact between 26 May and 26 July, 134 fighters were lost or damaged of which 91 were due to enemy action (66 destroyed or with damage in excess of 60 per cent) while nearly a third (43 aircraft) were destroyed or damaged in accidents. [53] Total losses since the beginning of 'Theseus' were 271 aircraft, of which 191 were destroyed or suffering at least 60 per cent damage. At the beginning of August Waldau had less than 61 tonnes of fuel.

He was also handicapped by the lack of *Kampfgruppen* to perform the traditional *Luftwaffe* role of Operational Level interdiction. Geisler occasionally raided British communications at night in *Staffel* strength, but the introduction of GCI with radar-equipped Beaufighters made such operations hazardous with 30 Ju 88s shot down between May and September, a third in September over Egypt.On 24 August, Geisler became a *General zbV* ('General with special duties') at *ObdL* and *RLM*, a sinecure pending his retirement on 31 October. He was replaced by Waldau on 31 August and *Generalmajor* Hans Seidemann, Kesselring's former chief of staff, became *FlFü Afrika*. Seidemann sought to support Rommel's first attempt to take the Alamein Line (Battle of Alam Halfa), but he had only 290 aircraft (175 serviceable) facing 674 serviceable RAF aircraft and was unable to stop the air assault on Rommel's communications. By the end of the offensive Seidemann was down to 72 tonnes of fuel and and a *Kampfergänzungsgruppe* had to fly fuel from Italy.

On 22 September Rommel returned to Germany for medical treatment and was replaced by *General der Panzertruppe* Georg Stumme whose command was renamed *Deutsches-Italienische Panzerarmee* two days later. The new British commander,

Lieutenant-General Bernard Montgomery, was preparing a set-piece battle which would cater to the British strengths and this was launched on the night of 23/24 October. The Allies had overwhelming numerical superiority not only on the ground but also in the air, the RAF having 1,301 combat aircraft (996 serviceable) in Egypt on 23 October including 629 serviceable day fighters/fighter-bombers, 272 day bombers and 95 night bombers. [54] In addition Coningham's Western Desert Air Force could count on Major-General Lewis H. Brereton's Ninth US Air Force with some 180 aircraft, including 110 bombers and 70 fighters. By contrast Seidemann had only 324 aircraft of which 167 were serviceable, supported by 250 Italian aircraft and Waldau's bombers from Crete.

The Allied air offensive began on 19 October and proved as effective as Coningham's during 'Crusader' while Axis air power was ineffective, the *Luftwaffe* flying only 100 sorties on the first day and never dropping more than 45 tonnes of bombs per day. [55] Rommel hastily resumed command, but it was like France in 1940 with every Axis counter-attack hammered by Allied air forces which provided both Tactical and Operational level air support. Fuel stocks were halved to 760 tonnes within two days and this meant that from a peak of 242 sorties on 31 October, Seidemann's efforts quickly fell off to 175 by 2 November. The following day the Italians were withdrawing under intense air attack (the Allies mounted 1,300 sorties in 24 hours) and the British finally broke through the defences, leading Rommel to sound retreat. [56] Seidemann was down to 160 tonnes of fuel by 8 November, while many aircraft with minor defects or damage had to be abandoned due to the lack of spares, reducing German assets to 194 aircraft, less than half serviceable, by 20 December.

On 8 November British and American forces landed in French North Africa, as Operation 'Torch', and the Axis forces sought a bridgehead in Tunisia. A resurgent Malta meant much depended upon air transport and Starke organised two *ad hoc Geschwader Stäbe*; *KGzbV S (Sizilien)* and *N (Neapal)* with five *Gruppen* assembled, partly by mobilising schools and even *Mausi* (Mousey) magnetic mine sweeper aircraft to raise *Luftwaffe* Mediterranean transport strength to 514 aircraft. In '*pulks*' of up to 100 transports, the formations rushed troops to Tunisia, which was occupied on 9 November, bringing in 41,768 men and 10,086 tonnes of materiel to 31 December. Supplies for Rommel became the responsibility of *Oberst* Wolfgang von Wild who established *Lufttransportführer I (Südost)* on 1 November with a couple of *Transportgruppen* supplemented by bombers. But the retreat westward took the Axis forces beyond the range of Wild's aircraft and they were transferred to Italy together with the painfully assembled supplies, the command being disbanded on 8 December. [57]

To secure the Mediterranean Hitler ordered the occupation of Vichy France on 11 November, contingency planning having begun in December 1940 with *OKW Weisung Nr 19* for *Unternehmen 'Attilla'* (renamed *'Anton'* in May 1942) whose *Luftwaffe* element was *Unternehmen 'Stockdorf.'* This began on 12 November and involved every spare aircraft under Sperrle's command but, fortunately, the operation was unopposed and provided a useful springboard for the new anti-ship force, Fink's *Fliegerdivision 2* (newly arrived from the Russian front) while also demonstrating the paucity of *Luftwaffe* resources. [58]

In Tunis the Germans created *Generaloberst* Jürgen von Arnim's *5. Panzerarmee* and a defensive web was woven along Tunisia's borders which, together with Allied exhaustion and heavy rain, brought a stalemate that lasted until the early spring. Rommel was given command of all forces in North Africa as *Heeresgruppe Afrika* but a renewed British offensive forced him to retreat in the south from 26 March as Franco-American forces pressed from the west. Arnim replaced Rommel at the head of *Heeresgruppe Afrika* as the British and Americans met on 6 April then advanced upon Tunis, which fell on 7 May. Two days earlier Hitler recognised that Tunisia was lost, but only half-hearted attempts at evacuation were made as the surviving Axis forces retreated to Cape Bon. When Arnim surrendered on 13 May only 800 of his 200,000 men had escaped.

'Torch' led to substantial reinforcements in the western Mediterranean with Kesselring's combat strength rising from 630 on 1 November to 850 a month later – excluding transports and seaplanes. *Luftflotte 4* lost *six Gruppen* which fatally compromised the Russian Front at its most vulnerable point and time while *Luftflotte 5* was stripped of its anti-shipping force The *Regia Aeronautica* assembled 288 aircraft (excluding tactical reconnaissance types) in Tunisia by 15 November, with another 379 in Sardinia and Sicily (excluding seaplanes), representing 47 per cent of its combat strength. [59]

Harlinghausen was appointed *Führer der Luftwaffe in Tunis (FdL Tunis)* on 9 November to provide tactical air support with about 140 aircraft as the *Luftwaffe* established forward bases in central Tunisia at Caabes (Qabes) and Sfax. By the end of the year he had flown 4,620 sorties (1,200 strike) for the loss of 126 aircraft while the *Stukas* growing vulnerability meant a growing reliance on *Jabos*. The Allies had 600 aircraft in French North Africa (drawn from the US Twelfth Air Force, RAF Eastern Command and the *Armée de l'Air*) in addition to the Western Desert- and US Tenth Air Forces, but this ᵃᵀᴴ. numerical superiority was offset by a shortage of airfields, the inexperience of the aircrews and the obsolescence of most of the aircraft, especially the American fighters.

But soon after the Germans arrived in Tunisia their bases and communications came under remorseless air attack which inflicted heavy losses, disrupted the supply organisation and led to a sharp decline in serviceability. [60] Harlinghausen's options were restricted by shortages of spares, supplies and motor transport as well as the poor infrastructure; serviceability dropped to 50 per cent. Nevertheless he handled his aircraft aggressively in support of German probing operations, flying 3,142 sorties (475 strike) in January.

The *Luftwaffe's* problem was the fragmentation of air power between Fink's *Fliegerdivision 2*, Loerzer's *Fliegerkorps II*, Harlinghausen as *FdL Tunis* and Seidemann as *FlFü Afrika* with *FlFü Sardinien* established by Wild on 9 December. Limited airfield space in Tunisia largely restricted the *Luftwaffe* to Tactical air power (fighters, *Jabos*, *Stukas* and *Heeresflieger*) while for Operational missions the *Kampfgruppen* had to operate from the major islands. The bombers interdicted the Algerian sea lanes and in the first week Loerzer claimed 183,000 grt of shipping sunk and 234,000 grt damaged, but the Allies lost only five ships (55,305 grt) and resistance was so fierce that by Christmas his bomber strength had dropped by a quarter. Loerzer's haphazard direction of bombing operations so infuriated *Major* Werner Baumbach, the *Kommandeur* ofI./KG 30, that he protested to Jeschonnek on 12 December and was promptly relieved of his command, returning to Berlin to direct special operations. [61] By New Year's Day *Kampfgruppen* strength had dropped to 270, of which 55 per cent was serviceable, while poorly trained replacement crews could not find Algerian ports so many had to be used to escort maritime convoys. Between December and May, Loerzer's bombers attacked the sea lanes on only 68 out of 182 days; indeed a third of all sorties involved convoy escort, allowing the Allies to ship in men and supplies. Loerzer's incompetence, and possibly corruption, finally led to Kesselring replacing him with Harlinghausen on 6 February and Loerzer became head of personnel at *RLM* until the end of the war. *FdL Tunis* was disbanded on 12 February when Seidemann's *FlFü Afrika* headquarters was renamed *Fliegerkorps Tunis*.

Only as Rommel began to retreat in late March did bomber tactics change at Kesselring's insistence, with the *Kampfgruppen* now concentrating upon the enemy rear, partly to prevent Göring pilfering them for a new bombing offensive against Great Britain from which he may have hoped to seek political kudos from the *Führer*. During April the *Kampfgruppen* had only 180 bombers, but they flew 1,332 sorties, of which 45 per cent were in support of the Army support or attacks against airfields and 31 per cent were convoy escort; the remainder were against shipping or harbours (see Table 6-4 for *Luftwaffe* strength in the western Mediterranean). Even the *Fernaufkärungsstaffeln* were pressed into anti-shipping and convoy escort missions while bombers were used to bring in fuel.

Table 6-4: Luftwaffe strength in the Western Mediterranean, October 1942–July 1944

Date	Fighters		Strike		Aufkl	Total
	Jagd	Zerstörer/ Nachtjagd	Kampf	Stuka/Jabo/ Nachtschl		
1 Nov 1942	199	23	230	115	63	630
1 Dec 1942	298	77	284	117	74	850
1 Apr 1943	316	139	263	94	112	924
1 Jul1943	456	118	428	138	75	1,215
1 Oct 1943	136	-	254	65	37	492
1 Jan 1944	191	-	182	29	218	620
1 Mar 1944	263	-	262	68	33	626
1 Jun 1944	145	23	125	98	35	426

Sources: BA MA RL 2 III/875–881 and information very kindly provided by Mr Nick Beale.

Note: *Aufklärung* excludes *Seeaufklärung*.

This reflected the strain upon Kesselring's airlift which became more important; Allied attacks on the sea lanes had cost the Axis 67 per cent of their supplies leading to Great War ace *Generalleutnant* Theodor Osterkamp's belated appointment as *Jafü Sizilien* on 7 April, whose command fielded a maximum of 148 aircraft and which flew 3,521 sorties during April alone. Nevertheless, despite the loss of 22 fighters, Allied aircraft sank 70,000 grt of shipping. Kesselring's airlift was hamstrung by the need to support Stalingrad with three *Transportgruppen* being sent to *Luftflotte 4* in Russia and reducing the strength of *Luftflotte 2* from 551 aircraft on 30 November to 172 on 31 January. To co-ordinate operations, *Generalmajor* Ulrich Buchholz was appointed *Lufttransportführer II, Mittelmeer* on 15 January, but only when transport requirements in the East eased was he able to expand his force to 185 aircraft on 10 March, 209 a month later and 426 by the beginning of April. They concentrated on bringing fuel and ammunition and for security travelled in *'pulks'* of 80–120 aircraft at 45 metres (150 feet) but 'Ultra' intercepts gave the Allies detailed knowledge of enemy air traffic and were the basis for a massive offensive, Operation 'Flax', to cut the air lanes completely. Bad weather postponed 'Flax' until April when *'pulks'* were intercepted six times bringing total losses during the month to 123 Ju 52s, four S.82s and 14 Me 323s, forcing the hapless transports to operate individually at night when they were harried by night fighters.

Seidemann had some 300 aircraft in mid-February divided between three *Fliegerführer: Tunis, Mitte* and *Gabès* but the Allies had nearly 2,000 and re-organised their squadrons into the North-West African Air Force under Major-General Carl A. Spaatz and divided into Strategic (General James H. Doolittle), Tactical (Air Marshal Sir Arthur Coningham) and defensive Coastal (Air Vice-Marshal Sir Hugh Lloyd) Air Forces. As Rommel retreated these air forces began the usual pounding of enemy communications and as the Axis bridgehead was compressed onto the Tunis plain on 15 April, Seidemann took direct control of air operations, withdrawing the *Fliegerführer* staffs. It was a forlorn hope and as the troops began to surrender wholesale, Kesselring began withdrawing combat units, the last transport mission being flown on 4 May and the pilots often bringing their *'Schwarzemänner'* – even in the cramped fuselages of single-seat Bf 109 fighters. *JG* 77's *Leutnant* Ernst-Wilhelm Reinert, for example, claimed his 51st African victory on 8 May while carrying two passengers. By 11 May Osterkamp's *JaFü Sizilien* was given responsibility for tactical air support in the ebbing bridgehead and the following day, Arnim surrendered.

North Africa was a disaster for the *Luftwaffe*, for, in addition to thousands of trained and experienced men, it lost 2,422 aircraft there between 1 November and 30 April (see Table 6-5 for *Luftwaffe* losses in the Western Mediterranean). Yet there was to be no respite, and Harlinghausen's desire to rest and rebuild his *Kampfgruppen* was overruled by Göring, leading to a month-long night offensive from mid-May involving some 1,300 sorties. But the navigational skills of the crews showed no improvement and when Harlinghausen complained to Kesselring, he was relieved of his command on 16 June and went into limbo for a year being replaced on 26 June by *Generalleutnant* Alfred Bülowius.

Table 6-5: Luftwaffe losses Western Mediterranean, October 1942–July 1944

Date	Losses		Overhaul	New aircraft
	Enemy action	*Accidents*		
Q4 1942	423	489	148	615
Q1 1943	448	471	209	1,054
Q2 1943	677	461	461	1,432
Q3 1943	1,114	578	378	1,408
Q4 1943	261	129	157	461
Q1 1944	458	162	213	681
Q2 1944	421	162	218	580

Sources: BA MA RL 2 III/875–881 and information very kindly provided by Mr Nick Beale.
Notes: Figures exclude seaplane and transport units. Overhaul and new aircraft sections in 1944 exclude *Nachtschlacht*.

This was Kesselring's Parthian shot, for the same day Richthofen reluctantly assumed command of *Luftflotte 2*, telling Göring that: 'This is a theatre where I can lose my honour and reputation.' [62] He established amiable relations with Kesselring, now totally preoccupied with his responsibilities as *OB Süd*, but Richthofen was evidentially Göring's watchdog on 'Smiling Albert', to whom, in his own words, 'the whole *Luftflotte* still pays homage'.

To establish his authority Richthofen began to replace men in key commands: *Generalleutnant* Alfred Bülowius took over *Fliegerkorps II* on 26 June and on the same day, Wild, the *FlFü Sardinien*, was replaced by the *Jabo* specialist *Oberstleutnant* (*Oberst* from 1 July) Hubertus Hitschhold, Wild having clashed with Richthofen during the Sevastopol campaign. [63] Two *Inspekteur* also arrived in theatre at this time: Oberst Otto Weiss, the *Inspekteur der Schlacht und Zerstörerflieger*, who joined his superior, the *Inspekteur der Jagdflieger*, Adolf Galland, to monitor and to support operations.

Galland clearly desired a more 'hands-on' role, first passing some of his staff burden onto *Oberst* Günther 'Franzl' Lützow by appointing him *Inspekteur der Jagdflieger* (*Süd*) on 17 May and then replacing Osterkamp as *JaFü Sizilien* on 22 June. [64] His opposite number for bombers was the former *Angriffsführer England Oberst* Dietrich Peltz, who had helped Richthofen re-organise *Luftflotte 4*'s bombers in the East during January and now became *Fernkampfführer Luftflotte 2* (also *Fernkampfführer Mittelmeer*), probably reflecting *ObdL's* tacit agreement with Harlinghausen about the *Kampfgruppen*, leaving Bülowius to control a Tactical force of fighters and *Jabos*. [65]

The early summer saw *Luftwaffe* combat strength in the western Mediterranean increase by nearly 50 per cent from 812 on 1 April to 1,215 by 1 July while serviceability improved from 52 per cent to 60 per cent. Peltz oversaw a substantial increase in the strike forces, but the vulnerable *Stukagruppen* were transferred to the Balkans. Peltz attempted to disrupt the imminent invasion with a few attacks on harbours using the low-level approach tactics he had used against England, but lacking experienced crews and with barely half the bombers serviceable, the effects were weak and casualties high, amounting to nearly 13 per cent on the last mission leading Richthofen to carp at Peltz' failure. [66]

The Allies had 3,400 aircraft (including transports), of which 2,500 were serviceable. They were soon attacking mainland and offshore Italy, flying 42,147 sorties over the western Mediterranean between 16 May and 9 July and destroying 325 *Luftwaffe* aircraft in the air and 122 on the ground for the loss of 250 of their own. The *Kampfgruppen* were driven into central Italy and southern France, leading one German historian to comment that *ObdL* should have anticipated the impossibility of a successful air defence of Sicily. [67] Galland anticipated a decisive confrontation with the Allies and stripped the Reich of fighters, while Milch diverted to the theatre 40 per cent of total production between 1 May and 15 July. When the Allies landed in Sicily on 10 July, the *Luftwaffe* had some 282 fighters and *Jabos* on the island, but barely half were serviceable due to the loss of spares and tools in Africa, while the *Regia Aeronautica* had 620 aircraft (387 fighters), but was a broken reed, having lost 2,190 aircraft between 2 November and 30 June 1943. The air assault on Sicily was a strain for the *Luftwaffe* leaders with Kesselring's optimism grating certain nerves, while the *Jagdgruppen's* failure depressed Galland who would tongue-lash unsuccessful pilots. Galland's predicament was aggravated by pressure from Göring, who sent hysterical and insulting teleprinter messages. Having lost 70 fighters since the beginning of the month, a furious Galland was summoned to Berlin on 9 July to explain his 'failure'. [68]

That evening *Luftwaffe* reconnaissance discovered convoys sailing to Sicily but they were unchallenged and by dawn were unloading off the beachheads. *Jabo* attacks directed by *Major* Günther Tonne's *Gefechtsverband Major Tonne*, later joined at night by *Kampfgruppen*, struck first at the western (American) beachhead and then the eastern (British) one, the bombers using both bombs and circling torpedoes. The Allied fighter shield proved very effective, destroying 27 enemy aircraft (16 German), for the loss of 25 on the first day. The Axis failed to disrupt the flow of supplies, sinking only seven merchantmen and auxiliaries (48,685 grt), a destroyer and six smaller vessels during July. Richthofen spent long hours on the telephone with Göring and Jeschonnek demanding more anti-shipping units and reinforcements, and he eventually received seven *Gruppen*, including Fink's air-to-surface missile units. Four were from Fiebig's *Fliegerkorps X* whose strength had been doubled before 'Husky' because deception measures had convinced the German High Command that the landing would be in Greece. [69]

In Sicily, Italian resistance collapsed as the Allies expanded their beachheads, screened daily by 1,100 fighter sorties, and within three days these fighters were operating from Sicilian airfields forcing Kesselring to begin an evacuation. Richthofen's *Gruppen* were pushed into southern Italy, staging through airfields in north-east Sicily during the day, but on 14 July Bülowius flew his last serviceable aircraft to the mainland. The same day, no doubt with the encouragement of Richthofen, Galland was recalled to Germany, leaving *Oberst* Carl Vieck in charge of fighter operations. Richthofen's strength dissolved from 120 aircraft (30 serviceable) in Sicily on 16 July, to barely 12 operational aircraft two days later. By dawn on 22 July, the day Palermo fell, the *Luftwaffe* had lost 273 aircraft (the Italians 115) since the invasion and the Allies only 100. Consequently the week-long evacuation, *Unternehmen 'Lehrgang'* ('Instruction Course'), which began on 11 August was largely shielded by *Flak*, although Bülowius provided 74 Bf 109s which flew up to 150 sorties a day, the rearguard being supported by 50 *Jabos* and 50–60 fighters from the 'toe' of Italy, but they averaged only 60 sorties a day. The Allies were slow to respond, and the Germans managed to evacuate 39,569 men (including 4,444 wounded), 17,075 tonnes of supplies and other equipment including 47 tanks to ensure an effective defence of Italy.

It was a small consolation in a disastrous campaign for the *Luftwaffe*. Between 10 July and 17 August, *Luftflotte 2* flew 7,354 sorties over Sicily, including 2,971 (41%) fighter and 2,411 (33%) bomber, losing more than 600 aircraft (262 in the air), while *Fliegerdivision 2* lost another 106 in southern France and the *Regia Aeronautica* lost 400, including 136 in the air. In the same period the Allies flew some 27,400 sorties and lost 140 aircraft (a 0.5% loss rate compared with 3.5% for the *Luftwaffe*). Throughout the Sicily campaign, Richthofen's airfields in Italy were attacked with devastating effect upon the operations of his *Kampfgruppen* and new bases were designed to accommodate no more than two *Gruppen* with well-dispersed aircraft.

In Italy Mussolini was arrested on 25 July and German sceptism about pledges by the new government under Marshal Pietro Badoglio led to a contingency plan, *Unternehmen 'Achse'* ('Axle'), to disarm their allies. Kesselring and Richthofen frequently discussed the situation with Jeschonnek, who was also concerned with the deteriorating situation over Germany and in the East. On 1 August, the *Kampfgruppen* had a rare victory, wrecking Palermo's main dock, but follow-up raids failed to have any effect and while Peltz claimed 516,850 grt sunk or severely damaged, the actual figure was only 54,306 grt. The egocentric Richthofen was increasingly irritated by the *Fernkampfführer's* failure, but it proved difficult to replace Peltz, who was one of Göring's favourites, although eventually *Oberst* Walter Storp relieved him on 6 August.

Storp was reinforced and by the beginning of September he had seven *Kampfgruppen* based on the complex of airfields around Foggia under *Führer des Gefechtsverbandes Foggia*, *Major* Volprecht Riedesel, *Freiherr* von und zu Eisenbach, where he tried to improve crew training, but almost immediately the Allies landed in southern Italy. During the last fortnight of August, communications and airfields in southern Italy came under a systematic attack involving 3,500 sorties, which left fewer than half of Richthofen's 579 aircraft serviceable by 31 August. On 20 August Storp was ordered to launch pre-emptive attacks on shipping but casualties were heavy, at 5–10 per cent per mission, and after 10 days Storp rested his crews, especially new ones who had suffered the worst.

With the invasion of Italy imminent, Richthofen had dissolved *Italuft* and Pohl became *General der Flakartillerie Süd*. Sicily's loss made Calabria untenable, and the *Luftwaffe's* forward elements moved to Puglia (the 'heel' of the country) as five *Gruppen* were withdrawn either for refitting or to defend the *Reich*. By 3 September *Luftwaffe* strength in the theatre had dropped to 880 aircraft in just two months, and that day, the British Eighth Army landed in Calabria. Richthofen had only 170 fighters and *Jabos* immediately available at inadequate airfields, while the Allies had 2,721 combat aircraft, but Kesselring demanded an intense rearguard action, only for Richthofen to refuse to risk his exhausted men's lives because he believed the main landing would be on Sardinia. Rather than flout Kesselring's instructions he 'interpreted' them by limiting the size of attacks. [70]

Richthofen's action was justified when a new invasion force was spotted heading towards Naples on 5 September, and three days later Operation 'Avalanche' began with a landing at Salerno, south of Naples, as the Allies broadcast the news that Rome had secretly signed an armistice. *'Achse'* was implemented, controlled by *Fliegerkorps XI's* headquarters when those of Kesselring and Richthofen were rendered *hors de combat* by bombing. The occupation was largely unopposed and involved some small airborne operations in one of which Mussolini was rescued and became head of a pro-German government nominally ruling the north. This period saw a spectacular success for Fink's *Fritz-X* anti-ship missiles, first used in Sicily on 21 August and now used against Italian warships defecting to the enemy. On 9 September missiles hit the battleships *Italia* and *Roma*, the latter exploding with most of her crew including Admiral Carlo Bergamini. [71]

Salerno was at the range limits of Allied air power, but fighters from British escort carriers, as well as long-range tanks for Spitfires and P-38s provided a shield which the *Luftwaffe* could not dent. [72] Richthofen was now making the concentrated attacks he had long wanted, but serviceability was only 58 per cent and in the first 24 hours he mounted only 260 sorties against the beachhead. For 10 days Bülowius' *Jabos* attacked daily – and sometimes twice a day – with a peak of 100 *Jabo* sorties on 10/11

September, while the *Kampfgruppen* crews flew two sorties a night but never reached more than a total of 100. Fink's missile *Gruppen* joined the fray from 11 September, in daylight, with no more than five sorties per mission but they posed a serious threat because their weapons were launched beyond anti-aircraft gun range into crowded anchorages. They maintained a daily offensive until 17 September, crippling the battleship HMS *Warspite* and sinking a hospital ship (6,791grt), but they suffered 20 per cent losses while conventional anti-shipping forces sank only two merchantmen (14,326grt). Attacks on Foggia from 16 September eroded Richthofen's campaign and the following day Kesselring broke off the Salerno battle and withdrew into fortifications south of Rome, where he held the Allies throughout the winter. The retreat received only token *Luftwaffe* support with barely 30 *Jabo* sorties a day as the *Kampfgruppen* flew to winter bases in northern Italy while single-engine *Gruppen* withdrew to central Italy as autumn rains restricted flying.

On 28 September the enemy occupied the Foggia airfields and promptly began creating heavy bomber bases; indeed, within three days American bombers flew from there to Wiener-Neustadt in Austria. Richthofen now became responsible for protecting the southern approaches to Austria, delegating the task to *Major* Johannes 'Macki' Steinhoff, who had only 149 fighters by the end of October. His lack of success irritated both Richthofen and Göring, the latter expressing his displeasure with the usual stream of hysterical teleprinter signals, and he was replaced on 13 December as *JaFü Oberitalien* by Richthofen's preferred candidate *Oberstleutnant* Günther, *Freiherr* von Maltzahn. It became clear the pilots were suffering physical exhaustion and combat fatigue while the morale of poorly-trained new pilots collapsed when they realised that they had been thrown in at the deep end. [73] Richthofen ordered thorough retraining of all *Jagdgruppen* with the intention of gradually committing them into morale-building set-piece battles and under Maltzahn the policy appeared to bear fruit.

During October and November Richthofen received only 309 replacement aircraft for his battered units but was concerned about the 'extremely questionable morale' of the *Schlachtgruppen* leading to a visit by the *Inspekteur der Tagsschlachtflieger, Oberst* Alfred Druschel. Richthofen had only 290 combat aircraft in Italy (including 82 bombers and 111 fighters), of which 60 per cent were serviceable. [74] With the *Reich* unable, or unwilling, to support him, Richthofen authorised the creation on 23 November of an air force (*Aeronautica Nazionale Repubblicana*, or *ANR*) for Mussolini's puppet state. The *ANR* was to have fighter, torpedo-bomber and transport groups, but, on Hitler's instructions, it was to receive only Italian equipment. Its Macchi MC.205s flew their first patrol on 2 January 1944. Three fighter groups and a fighter squadron, a bomber group, a torpedo-bomber group and two transport groups were eventually created but they were under strength and even in mid-May 1944 there were only 5,000 men.

In the aftermath of the Salerno landings, Kesselring briefly occupied Corsica but on 18 September he ordered the evacuation of the 30,000-man garrison by sea and by air in *Unternehmen 'Schlussakkord'* ('Final Contract'). [75] The latter task was the responsibility of *Transportfliegerführer 1* (*TFF 1*), as Buchholz's *Lufttransportführer II, Mittelmeer* had been renamed on 15 May. This command had 156 aircraft, including 21 of the big, six-engined Me 323 *Gigants*. Despite interdiction by Beaufighters which forced the transports to operate at night, by 2 October 23,192 men and 618 tonnes of materiel had been flown out in 1,580 sorties for the loss of 32 transports. Buchholz continued to control some 240 transports until *TFF 1* was disbanded on 30 January 1944 to meet a new crisis in the East.

The bomber force returned to the fray from 10 October, urged on by a *Führer* directive two days later which demanded an offensive against harbours and shipping. Between 10 October and 5 December it flew about 800 sorties with 10 major night attacks, mostly on Naples (where the Allies were unloading 9,000 tonnes of supplies a day), but night fighters inflicted heavy losses – 13 per cent in the first major raid on Naples on 12/ 13 October and even the use of *'Düppel'* chaff (the German equivalent of `Window') from 23/ 24 October had no effect. Both *Fernkampfführer* having failed him, Richthofen suddenly abolished the position on 28 October, profoundly offending Storp. [76]

Bülowius now controlled most of *Luftflotte 2*'s diminished strength excluding tactical air support, for which was the responsibility of *Oberst* Hitschhold as *Fliegerführer, Luftflotte 2* (later *FlFü 2*). Bülowius planned heavy, short-duration attacks but by the end of November, only 75 of 222 crews were 'Old Hares' and a third were rated 'not combat worthy'; indeed his first raid, against Bari on 2/3 December, saw only 88 of 105 aircraft find the target, although they achieved a rare but spectacular success. They set ablaze an ammunition ship whose detonation caused the loss of 16 ships (69,712 grt) with 38,000 tonnes of supplies and damaged another seven (26,2l7grt). The ammunition ship was carrying poison gas shells and the deadly fumes killed 1,000 people in what the British naval historian described as a 'most serious blow'! [77]

The bombers had barely touched down when *ObdL* informed Richthofen he must hand them to his *bête noir*, Peltz, for a new offensive against England, while three *Gruppen* were sent north for conversion into heavy bombers and torpedo-bombers. A few days later, on 11 December, *Fliegerkorps II* was transferred to *Luftflotte 3* leaving Richthofen with only 243 aircraft by the New Year, his strike force reduced to 28 *Jabos* and *Nachtschlacht* aircraft, although Fink continued to attack Mediterranean convoys. With little else to occupy him, Richthofen spent almost a month on leave returning on 22 January 1944 to learn that the Allies had landed at Anzio. [78]

Operation 'Shingle' was intended to outflank the German defences at Monte Cassino and was accompanied by the US Fifth Army's renewed assault upon the German right, against which Hitschhold's replacement, *Major* Georg Dörffel, threw 158 *Jabo* sorties. [79] It was heralded by a six-day air offensive against communications and airfields involving 1,500 bomber sorties by what became, on 10 December, the Mediterranean Allied Air Force (formerly Mediterranean Air Command and NorthWest African Air Forces) and Mediterranean Allied Tactical Air Force (formerly North West African Tactical Air Force), now under General Ira C. Eaker, with 2,500 combat aircraft. Richthofen's fighters flew 221 sorties against them, claiming only 13 victories, while reconnaissance was difficult in the face of such immense Allied air superiority and bad weather. [80] The *Luftwaffe* had only 291 combat aircraft, of which two-thirds were serviceable, on 20 January while the Allied air forces had 1,100 in western Italy, with 850 in the Naples area.

Initially, the Germans flew 100 sorties a day against the Anzio beachhead as Richthofen brought three *Gruppen* closer to the front line. He received operational control of Fink's *Fliegerdivision 2* but the missile *Gruppen* were slow into action because their airfields had been bombed. Fortunately, the ultra-cautious Allied commander failed to exploit his success, giving the Germans time to rush in troops who sealed the beachhead to dash the Allies' hopes. Kesselring, urged on by Hitler, decided to crush the beachhead culminating in a four-day counter-offensive, *Unternehmen 'Fischfang'* ('Fishtrap') from 16 February, but all efforts withered in the face of Allied fire power, the air forces flying 17,000 sorties on 17 February alone. [?]

Richthofen provided as much air support as possible but the shortage of *Schlachtgruppen* due to a crisis in the East, and waterlogged airfields, hamstrung operations. [81] For *'Fischfang'* Richthofen's strength rose to 479 aircraft and serviceability to nearly 64 per cent; fighter numbers rose to 213 (33 Italian), while the strike forces had 165 bombers and 54 *Jabos* who flew 520 sorties on the first two days. [82] More reinforcements arrived giving Richthofen 607 aircraft by the end of February, of which 75 per cent were serviceable, but quantities of fighters were sent to the *Reich* to meet the USAAF's 'Big Week' offensive, which reduced activity over the beachhead to 120 sorties and Dörffel had also to support troops around Monte Cassino flying up to 150 sorties a day.

Fliegerdivision 2 (under *Generalmajor* Hans Korte on 22 February) spearheaded the assault on the invasion force shipping, staging through Piacenza and Bergamo with operations co-ordinated in a command post established in the old *Fliegerkorps II* headquarters in Merate, while *Oberstleutnant* Joachim Helbig controlled the remaining *Kampfgruppen* based around Udine. By sinking the cruiser HMS *Spartan* on January 27 the missile *Gruppen* forced the cruisers to withdraw from the beachhead every afternoon; but then 'an inexperienced and over-excited crew' attacked three British hospital ships, brightly illuminated in accordance with the Geneva Convention, on 24 January, damaging two and sinking the third. [83] To neutralise the threat the Allies deployed three electronic warfare ships, with ESM and ECM systems, which gradually took the measure of the missiles and reduced their effectiveness, although Korte's men did sink an American destroyer and two freighters (14,327 grt).

Torpedo-bomber missions were hampered by a shortage of 'eels' and these *Gruppen* reverted to conventional bombing but losses were heavy. Despite regular Axis attacks upon the port of Anzio, the Allies landed a daily average of 3,400 tonnes of supplies; indeed, by 29 March there was almost no more space to store supplies. From late February Helbig's bombers could manage only harassing attacks on battlefield targets, rarely with more than 10–15 aircraft, using radio target beacons dropped by reconnaissance aircraft, while *Nachtschlachtgruppe 9* exploited *Egon* radar control. [84] In late January, the USAAF struck Korte's and Helbig's bases, overwhelming the defences and destroying 140 aircraft in the air and on the ground for the loss of nine.

The failure to destroy the beachhead saw Richthofen returning to the shadows. Korte was transferred to Sperrle costing Richthofen 279 aircraft and by the end of March he was down to 394 aircraft (63% serviceable). His decline occurred as the Allies launched Operation 'Strangle' in mid-March to cut the German communications system throughout Italy and soon daylight movements virtually ceased behind the German lines, while the lack of any air threat meant that the Allies' rear zones pulsated with life. Maltzahn did his best with only 125 fighters (including 62 Italian) but by the end of the month Richthofen was describing the situation as 'extremely difficult'. At the beginning of April as the weather improved and Allied air superiority grew, he reorganised his forces, giving Pohl command of a new *Nahkampfkorps* for tactical operations. There was a brief resurgence of *Luftwaffe* activity around Anzio, but while on an inspection tour, Richthofen's limousine was twice attacked by fighter-bombers on 7 May.

He never completed his inspection, for on 11/12 May the Allies began to break through the German mountain defences and advance on Rome, their aircraft crushing the defences and preventing the *Nahaufklärungsflieger* gaining a clear picture of the battlefield situation. At the start of the offensive Richthofen had 408 combat aircraft with 69 per cent serviceability and Pohl struck back with up to 80 sorties a day, but the *Jagdgruppen* suffered such heavy losses that Richthofen had to withdraw them northwards on 14 May. On 13/14 May Helbig led personally a long-planned bomber mission against Allied air bases in Corsica which destroyed 23 aircraft and damaged 90, but Allied retaliation was swift and devastating and that day the *Luftwaffe* was bombed out of Piacenza then Viterbo, with heavy losses.

Monte Cassino fell on 18 May and the next day Richthofen requested a conference with Korten to discuss the *Luftwaffe's* future in Italy. He was extremely pessimistic, agreeing with Steinhoff that *Flak* would have to bear the burden of defence because the air battles were too weighted in the enemy's favour. When the conference began on 22 May, Richthofen demanded to be relieved of his command or that his command be disbanded unless he received more aircraft and supplies. The following day Richthofen met Hitler and Göring, who smoothed his ruffled feathers by assuring him that the theatre remained important, yet during May he received only 134 replacement aircraft. [85]

The Allies now broke out of the Anzio beachhead and Kesselring's demands for increased *Schlachtflieger* effort were countermanded by Richthofen on 25 May, Dörffel being lost the following day on his 1,004th sortie. Richthofen retained the *Kampfgruppen* only because *OKL* feared new Allied landings behind the retreating armies and also to act as a reserve for rapid transfer to France. Hitler further demanded they be used for tactical air support causing heavy losses over the next three weeks. They and *NSGr 9* flew 50–60 sorties a night, but the front collapsed and on 6 June American troops entered Rome as the Allies landed in Normandy. [86]

Throughout this period, the eastern Mediterranean was a *Luftwaffe* backwater although on New Year's Day 1943, Waldau's *Fliegerkorps X* staff became *Luftwaffenkommando Südost*, with a new *Fliegerkorps X* to support Löhr's *OB Südost* and also to defend the Ploesti oilfields. Tragically Waldau was killed in a plane crash on 15 May, depriving the *Luftwaffe of* one of its best staff officers. He was succeeded a week later by Fiebig, who was also responsible for supporting the air forces of Germany's allies as well as counter-insurgency and the operational training commands such as *Luftwaffenstab Kroatien*. To direct operations, *Oberst* Wolfgang von Chamier-Glisczinski established *FlFü Südost Kroatien* on 1 April 1943 and after his death in an air crash, it was renamed *FlFü Kroatien* on 26 August under *Generalmajor Dipl.-Ing.* Wolfgang Erdmann.

Fiebig's greatest crisis was in September when Italy's defection threatened to give the enemy control of the Greek islands and while the Germans secured the major islands, the British began landing on Kos and Leros near Rhodes on 13 September. Hitler, fearing the effect upon Turkey, demanded prompt action. Air support came from *Luftwaffen Stab Griechenland*, established on 15 June in Athens under Holle (now a *Generalmajor* and also commander of *Fliegerkorps X*) and reinforced from the *Reich* and France to supply it with 114 aircraft by 30 September. The Dodecanese Islands were at the limit of the range of British air power but well within German air range, allowing Holle to dominate the skies and to help to take Kos on 3 November and Leros by 12 November assisted by small airborne operations. Holle and Fiebig flew some 2,500 sorties and lost 45 aircraft in a campaign which cost the British 4,800 men, 115 aircraft, five destroyers (two to the new Hs 293 missiles) and a merchantman. [87]

The theatre then reverted to a backwater and Fink was brought in on 10 February 1944 as *Kommandierender General der deutsches Luftwaffe in Griechenland*, being promoted to *General der Flieger* on 1 April the same day that Holle and *Fliegerkorps X* moved to France. A few days earlier, on 25 March, Fiebig supported an attempt to decapitate the Communist guerrillas through an airborne assault on their leader's headquarters, but Marshal Josip Tito escaped through a back door. Simultaneously Fiebig had to divert forces northwards for all three of Germany's Balkan allies were uneasy at the prospect of the Russians reaching their borders. Hungary's loss threatened to sever communications between the German army in Rumania and the *Reich*, as well as the loss of Hungarian oil production. Hitler authorised occupation in *Unternehmen 'Margarethe'* on 19 March with the *Luftwaffe* relying upon the fighters of *JaFü Balkan* (created under *Oberst* Douglas Pitcairn on 7 February), *Kampfgruppen* from *Luftflotte 3* and some training units assembled in Austria with operations directed by the *General der deutschen Luftwaffe in Ungarn*, the Attaché in Budapest *Generalleutnant* Kuno Heribert Fütterer. There was no opposition; the Hungarian Air Force came under German command and on May Day the *Kommandierende General der deutschen Luftwaffe in Ungarn* (Fütterer) and *Jagdabschnittsführer Ungarn* were incorporated in *Luftflotte Reich* as part of *JaFü Ostmark*. [88]

The strengthening of the Balkan defences was timely, for from the beginning of the year the Allies exploited Foggia to increase their pressure upon the production and distribution of Rumanian oil, with side-swipes at Hungarian (and Yugoslav) industry (see Table 6-6). The first attempt had been on 1 August 1943 and proved a disaster for the Americans who lost 51 of 163 Liberators making a daring low-level raid on Ploesti, but from January the enemy returned in force and with fighter escorts. Pitcairn's strength rose from 289 German fighters (117 *Zerstörer* and night fighters) on New Year's Day 1944 to 392 by 1 June, reinforced by up to 230 allied fighters, but they were no match for the Americans and the forces defending the Danube valley lost 444 day fighters in the first half of the year. They were unable to prevent the Americans smashing the refineries, while British bombers mined the Danube to reduce traffic by 60 per cent in May, despite 46 *Mausi* sorties. The campaign continued until the Red Army took Rumania in August to find the oil industry wrecked. The scale of the destruction was a major factor in the Russian decision to develop both nuclear weapons and their own post-war strategic defensive system. [89]

Table 6-6: Strategic campaign in Danube valley, January 1944–August 1944

Month	Day		Night		Luftwaffe losses			
	Bomber	*Fighter*	*Bomber*	*Mines*	*Day*			*Night*
Jan 1944	554 (11)	433 (11)	65 (2)		17	44	1	2
Feb 1944	–	–	30 (1)		–	–	–	3
Mar 1944	367 (5)	120 (1)	258 (12)		43	37	–	1
Apr 1944	3,642 (71)	1,719 (15)	319 (6)	55 (11)	143	77	8	5
May 1944	1,987 (33)	998 (10)	304 (13)	31 (-)	108	40	–	2
Jun 1944	4,676 (61)	2,129 (26)	539 (9)	–	75	35	3	5
Jul 1944	5,169 (122)	2,930 (36)	597 (10)	126 (4)	52	38	5	7
Aug 1944	3,359 (94)	1,946 (16)	394 (24)	27 (-)	8	2	2	1

Source: UKNA Air 24/937–939, 945–948. BA MA RL 2 III/875–881.

Note: Luftwaffe losses, first and third columns are due to enemy action and other columns losses due to accidents.

Chapter Seven

Crusade in the East

Even as planning began for the air campaign against England, Hitler's thoughts were turning to the East and a crusade against the Bolsheviks. Despite their August 1939 agreement, Stalin's Russia and Hitler's Germany did not trust each other, although the former's food and raw materials were exchanged for the latter's manufactured goods including aircraft. The equivalent of a *Jagdgeschwader* shielded Berlin and the Leuna synthetic oil plants, ostensibly from British air attack, but just as equally from Russian, while *Luftflotte 1*'s headquarters moved to Berlin in October.

The Nazis' antipathy to Communism was further fuelled early in 1940 when Stalin exploited Germany's pre-occupation with the West to occupy the Baltic States and seize part of Rumania. At an *OKW* conference on 1 August 1940 Hitler announced he would strike the Soviet Union the following spring and by October *OKW* and *OKH* were planning the offensive. For his part, Stalin was desperate to avoid war, at least until 1942, and his land-grab was an attempt to put as much distance as possible between the heart of the Soviet Union and its potential Nazi enemy, to some extent because his Purges from 1936 onwards had produced an inexperienced military leadership. To secure this glacis, Stalin moved large numbers of troops westwards leading Germany to respond; *Generalfeldmarschall* Wilhelm, *Ritter* von Leeb's *Heeresgruppe C* transferred to East Prussia while *Generalfeldmarschall* Fedor von Bock's *Heersgruppe B* returned to Poland.

The outline of the offensive plans was published on 18 December as *OKW Weisung Nr 21* for *Unternehmen 'Barbarossa'* whose objectives were the destruction of the Red Army in western Russia and its pursuit eastwards until the *Wehrmacht* reached a point from which enemy bombers could not reach the *Reich*. Bock's forces, renamed *Heeresgruppe Mitte* (Army Group Centre), would spearhead the assault, driving into Belorussia before assisting Leeb, (whose forces were renamed *Heeresgruppe Nord* [North]), in their drive through the Baltic States to Leningrad, while *Generalfeldmarschall* Gerd von Rundstedt's *Heeresgruppe Süd* (South) drove into the Ukraine and took Kiev. There would then be an advance to a line from Archangel in the Arctic Circle to the River Volga and from airfields west of this line the *Luftwaffe* would pound the surviving Russian factories in the Urals.

As usual the *Luftwaffe* would provide support at the Tactical and Operational levels for army operations but, unlike *Fall 'Gelb'*, it would give priority to destroying the Soviet air force or *Voyenno-Vozdushnyye Sily Raboche-Krestyanskaya Krasnaya Armiya* (Military Aviation of the Workers' and Peasants Red Army or VVS-RKKA, often abbreviated to VVS). Vague plans for long-range bombing existed as part of the Operational Level concept but only during lulls in ground operations and *Weisung Nr 21*'s comments that they would be '...concentrated first on the Urals area' suggest this was vague. There were ambitious plans for Student's airborne force, *Fliegerkorps XI*, which *Weisung Nr 21* envisaged using to cut the enemy rail network by seizing key locations such as river crossings. But the decimation of the airborne troops in Crete dashed these hopes and German airborne operations were confined to special forces. [1]

There was unease in the *Wehrmacht* as news of the new strategy permeated through the command layers, especially in the overstretched *Luftwaffe* and Göring briefly confronted Hitler over the matter. [2] Soon, however, he became an enthusiastic supporter of the enterprise and even produced a hare-brained scheme for an assault by *Fliegerkorps XI* on the Baku oil fields in the Caucasus, a scheme whose madness briefly infected Keitel until saner counsels prevailed and it was abandoned. [3] On 27 February Jeschonnek warned Halder that the wide battlefront and the limited resources available meant that air support would be guaranteed only along the key axes leading *OKH* to warn the *Heeresgruppen* and *Armee* commanders that it was unlikely the *Luftwaffe* would achieve complete air superiority and that they could expect greater exposure to air attacks than in the earlier campaigns.

The *Luftwaffe* leadership was officially informed of Hitler's intentions on 13 January with Milch and Operations Chief Waldau worried about the prospects, the latter's friendship with Jeschonnek cooling as the chief of staff dismissed his concerns in a reflection of the *Führer*'s optimism that the campaign would last only six weeks. [4] Intelligence chief 'Beppo' Schmid provided an accurate forecast of Russian tactical aviation (VVS) and long-range bomber aviation (DBA) in western Russia at 7,300 aircraft (it was actually 7,850), although the figures ignored the air defence (PVO) and navy with 1,500 and 1,445 aircraft respectively. He estimated the Russians had another 5,000 aircraft (the actual figure was 4,140) but failed to determine enemy dispositions or the quality of the new generation of aircraft. [5] His reports were based on information from the comint network based extended into Finland and Hungary as well as *Oberst* Theodor Rowehl's *AufklGr ObdL*. Rowehl had been taking clandestine photographs of the Soviet Union since 1934 and intensified his activities from October after he met Hitler, although a systematic reconnaissance of the Soviet Union was authorised only on 21 September 1940. [6] Flying up to 12,000 metres (36,500 feet), Rowehl's airmen flew some 500 sorties, first probing the frontier areas then flying as far east as the line Murmansk-Moscow-Rostov. [7]

VVS and PVO leaders recognised these flights heralded an offensive but Stalin was so desperate to delay such an attack and paranoid about 'provoking' the Germans that he banned any attempt to interfere with them. Ironically, this policy helped decapitate the leadership of Soviet aviation on the verge of war when a *Lufthansa* aircraft landed without permission in Moscow on 15 May. Stalin was already concerned about Russian air power and especially the high accident rate, his criticism drawing a hysterical reaction from the VVS commander, Lieutenant-General Pavel Rychagov. Now an incident which owed more to a bureaucratic lapse than treason saw him purge the air force leadership with Rychagov actually arrested on 24 June and replaced by Lieutenant-General Pavel Zhigarev. Rychagov and his colleagues would be tortured and on 28 October they were executed. [8]

Luftwaffe preparations for 'Barbarossa' accelerated in March 1941 and exploited facilities created for the *Fliegerführerschule* which had moved east a year earlier. Signal facilities were expanded and supplies built up, but it was only in May that headquarters moved east; Keller's *Luftflotte 1* quit Berlin for Norkitten near

Insterburg; Kesselring's *Luftflotte 2* arrived in Posen (Poznan) on 22 May and in June, Löhr's *Luftflotte 4* left Vienna for Jasionka near Rzeszow in Poland. For security reasons the *Fliegerkorps* did not arrive until June and *ObdL's* implied confidence in their ability to conduct such moves efficiently was amply repaid. Keller was joined by *Fliegerkorps I*, Löhr received *Fliegerkorps V* in Poland and *Fliegerkorps IV* in Rumania, while Kesselring retained *Fliegerkorps II* and received *Fliegerkorps VIII*. But Richthofen's *Korps* took three weeks to reach Kesselring leaving behind much transport and signals equipment in Greece while there had been no time to rebuild the *Staffeln* after its Balkan adventures. [9] In addition to the *Fliegerkorps*, Keller was given an anti-shipping and naval co-operation force under *Oberst* Wolfgang von Wild who became *Fliegerführer Ostsee*.

The *Fliegerverbände* began arriving from May and by 22 June the three *Luftflotten* had 2,252 aircraft (see Table 7-1) augmented by 570 from the *Heeres-* and *Marinestaffeln*, while the eastern *Luftgaue* had a further 237 fighters to shield the *Reich* from Russian bombers. Löhr would be augmented over the next two months by some 200 Slovak, Hungarian and Italian aircraft but for the eastern crusade the *Luftwaffe* had only 838 bombers, half the size deployed to support 'Gelb' due to unreplaced losses and commitments to Western Europe and the Mediterranean. [10]

Table 7-1: Barbarossa strengths, 22 June 1941

Luftflotte	Germans	Russians
Luftflotte 1	607	2,212
Luftflotte 2	1,448	1,881
Luftflotte 4	810	4,085
Total	**2,865**	**8,178**

Balke, *KG 2* pp 416–419; Gordon p.30, 36; Kopański p.13. Luftwaffe includes *Heeresflieger* but excludes home defence, Rumanian defence and seaplane units. Russians are VVS, DBA and navy but excludes PVO.

The fragmented Soviet air forces were just receiving new aircraft but few aircrew were familiar with them, and most regiments retained the aircraft which the *Luftwaffe* had encountered in Spain. The leadership was still recovering from the Purges of the 1930s and in June 1941 91 per cent of the major formation commanders had been in place less than six months. While some, such as the Leningrad District aviation chief, Major-General Aleksandr Novikov, would distinguish themselves in the years to come, many would answer with their lives for their inexperience and Stalin's refusal to prepare. One aspect which would greatly benefit the *Luftwaffe's* opening operations was the practice of crowding aircraft onto a few bases, presenting tempting targets of which the *Luftwaffe* was only too well aware. Jeschonnek and Waldau wanted to strike Russian airfields after the Army's guns began firing at dawn but *OKH* feared that by then the alerted 'birds' would have flown. Hitler agreed with *OKH* and decreed air strikes at dawn, although many new air crew had limited instrument-flying skills. However, the wily *Luftflotten* overcame the problem by focusing the initial attacks on fighter bases, which would be struck by *Ketten* of experienced crews who would cross the border at high altitude then swoop on their prey. [11]

As the sun rose in the East on 22 June the VVS star faded. Two-thirds of *Luftwaffe* offensive air strength – 637 bombers and Stukas – swooped on 31 airfields and massacred the enemy aircraft. [12] Only two attackers failed to return but it was estimated that the strike force had destroyed 1,800 aircraft, the supersensitive SD-2 bombs proving especially effective against aircraft. [13] The second wave claimed 700 aircraft but lost 33, with total *Luftwaffe* losses on the first day being 78 aircraft. Yet, like angry hornets, the Russians tried to retaliate, flying some 6,000 sorties (including over the Finland front), but their bomber formations, often flying unescorted, were massacred and by 1 July the Russians opposite Kesselring had lost some 1,200 combat aircraft. *ObdL* calculated the Russians had lost 4,990 aircraft compared with 179 German aircraft and between 22 June and 5 July, the *Luftwaffe* lost 491 aircraft destroyed and 316 damaged. [14] The Russians calculated that in three weeks they lost about 3,600 aircraft, of which 75 per cent were on the ground, although the collapse in communications suggests this might be a conservative figure.

By 25 June the lack of targets led the *Luftwaffe* to switch to army support missions, but the VVS and DBA continued to be extremely active and often scored minor tactical successes throughout the year. But the Soviet infrastructure was eroded by the rapid German advance which also threatened production facilities that were hastily moved eastwards. The move, and the shortage of skilled workers, meant that production was disrupted for months and quality declined. To maintain volume, production focused upon single-engined designs which meant that the VVS became a largely tactical-level force with limited operational level capability due to the lack of long-range multi-engine aircraft. The Russians would operate for the rest of the war with designs either in service in 1941 or their evolutionary developments with only one successful war-time multi-engine aircraft, the Tupolev 2 medium bomber, whose production suffered a one-year hiatus between 1942 and 1943 due to Stalin's intervention.

The *Luftwaffe* assault on the Red Army's infrastructure and communications was as succecssful as in the previous campaigns, and the Russians quickly learned to restrict daylight movements to small groups which would seek the safety of brooding woods and forests, making it even more difficult for their own commanders to discover their location and devise plans. Richthofen reprised his well-oiled tactics, giving each mechanised division a radio-equipped *Fliegerverbindungsoffizier* (*Flivo*) so the *Panzer* divisions could confidently expect the first *Stukas* to dive within two hours of a request for support. [15] The other *Fliegerkorps* had to rely upon the *Kampfgruppen* for close air-support and battlefield interdiction and losses from ground fire rose, *Fliegerkorps I* losing 18 bombers on the second day, mostly to this cause. [16]

The mobility of the campaign was such that in the first three weeks, five of Richthofen's *Gruppen* were 600 kilometres east of their initial airfields; *St.G 3* moved that distance in a month, while *Fliegerkorps VIII* headquarters would move 18 times by December. [17] The constant moves forward and the difficulties of supplying forward units had a significant impact upon the *Luftwaffe*, reducing its sortie rates; *Luftflotte 2* flew 2,272 sorties on *A-Tag*, 1,027 on 26 June, 862 the next day and 260 on 29 June, while the number of serviceable aircraft fell from 1,752 on 22 June to 960 a week later. [18] Loerzer again supported Guderian, but the fluid situation proved too difficult for him and Guderian was soon complaining. Kesselring soothed ruffled feathers by appointing *Generalmajor* Martin Fiebig as *Nahkampfführer II* to organise air support – a task made more difficult by a shortage of radios. This was not the only display of army peevishness and on 1 July Halder met Waldau and came away from the meeting feeling that the *Luftwaffe's* plans were '…in an absolute muddle.'

Hitler aggravated Halder's despair through his strategic incoherence; for while *OKH* wished to continue the advance on Moscow, *OKW Weisung Nr 21* laid down that once the Russian forces in Belorussia were destroyed, Leeb's advance on Leningrad would have priority. *OKW Weisung Nr 33* of 19 July confirmed this strategy, but demanded Kesselring fly retaliatory attacks on Moscow and, as a result, that day he received three of five *Kampfgruppen* transferred from the West, the others going to Keller. Attacks on Moscow began on 21/22 July and 358 sorties were flown by the end of the month, forcing Stalin's headquarters into specially prepared tunnels in the metro system. The raids, 11 in daylight, declined in intensity with the last on 5/6 April 1942, the 76th night raid, by which time Stalin was long back in the Kremlin. [19]

Hitler's eyes were increasingly drawn to the huge Russian force exposed in the Ukraine and on 30 July *OKW Weisung Nr 34*, while confirming the basic strategy, authorised Rundstedt to advance upon Kiev. Yet on 3 August, Richthofen's *Fliegerkorps VIII* was transferred to Keller's *Luftflotte 1* with nine *Gruppen* (262 aircraft), leaving two *Stukagruppen* with Kesselring who had only 600 aircraft as the Russians temporarily barricaded the road to Moscow. [20] *ObdL* was not as generous as they appeared; Richthofen was to support only *Generaloberst* Georg von Küchler's *18. Armee* as it advanced along the coast until it isolated Leningrad (now St Petersburg), but none of this was communicated to the *OKH* commander, *Generalfeldmarschall* Walther von Brauchitsch, to Leeb or to Keller. The vigour of Richthofen's operations shocked Leeb, and probably Keller, for his more dynamic, professional and therefore effective air support tactics led some to describe his prosecution of air warfare as 'heartless.' His attack began on 6 August and over the course of 12 days *Fliegerkorps VIII* flew 4,742 sorties and dropped 3,351 tonnes of bombs, helping to drive *18. Armee* into Leningrad's suburbs at the price of 27 aircraft shot down and 143 damaged.

On the coast Wild struck the retreating Baltic Fleet in late August, sinking four transports (13,038 grt) and even acting as minesweepers by bombing minefields. [21] To support the capture of Russian-held islands off Estonia, *Unternehmen 'Beowulf I/II'*, Wild assigned units to Keller's chief of staff, Generalmajor Heinz-Hellmuth von Wühlisch, as *FlFü B*, in operations which included a glider-borne assault by commandos who were supplied by four Me 321 *Gigant* ('Giant') gliders. With the Baltic Fleet trapped in its base at Kronstadt, Wild's command was redundant and it was disbanded on 27 October although the staff were kept together and moved first to Berlin and early in the New Year to the Crimea as *FlFü Süd*. [21]

Yet as Leningrad faced isolation Hitler changed direction. *OKW Weisung Nr 35* on 6 September gave priority to the destruction of the Soviet forces in the Ukraine, the capture of Kiev and the securing of a line along the River Dnieper. On Bock's right Guderian had already begun advancing southwards on 23 August but as a concession to Brauchitsch and Halder, an advance upon Moscow, *Unternehmen 'Taifun'* ('Typhoon'), would follow. In the north Keller had 1,004 aircraft, with 481 serviceable, and was ordered to transfer half, along with *Fliegerkorps VIII*, back to Kesselring by 15 September. [22]

Leeb telephoned *OKH* on 12 September in a last-ditch attempt to retain Richthofen but was told that '*Taifun*' had priority although as a sop Keller was allowed to retain *Oberst* Oskar Dinort's *St.G 2* to pick off the Baltic Fleet at Kronstadt. Ten ships, including two battleships and a submarine, were sunk or damaged. [23] The loss of *Fliegerkorps VIII* began a slow decline for *Luftflotte 1* whose forces helped tighten the siege of Leningrad during October by supporting Küchler's advance to Tikhvin, some 175 kilometres east of Leningrad. The isolation of this sector led to the establishment of *FlFü* Tikhvin under *Oberst* Hans Raithal, but his forward airfield was crude and exposed, as were the German positions which were abandoned on 12 December. [24]

Meanwhile, it quickly became obvious the supply organisation could not hope to meet the *Luftwaffe*'s requirements for 14,000 tonnes a day; indeed a British intelligence document, probably based upon Ultra intercepts, noted that *Luftgau zbV 4* reported that average daily fuel consumption per month between July and October was 50, 167, 111 and 85 tonnes. [25] Long distances were aggravated by a dirt-track road system dissolved by rain into swamps; indeed, during the autumn and spring a combination of rain and thaw created a season known to the Russians as *Rasputitsa* ('time without roads'). The *Wehrmacht*'s motor vehicle fleet was unable to cope, leaving railways the only reliable all-weather transport system; but the Russian system was a different gauge to Western European railways and needed converting from the *Reichsbahn*. When 'Barbarossa' began only four *Transportgruppe* were available, to be joined by five more, but their combined strength was barely 450 aircraft and could support only the spearheads, forcing the *Luftflotte* to use *Kampfgruppen* for resupply missions. [26] Overall *Luftwaffe* serviceability declined to 1,544 on 10 July, 1,654 a month later and 920 by the end of August while losses between 6 July and 31 August were 1,008 aircraft. [27]

By 6 September the three *Luftflotten* had only 1,005 aircraft serviceable between the Baltic and the Black Sea as the Battle of Kiev opened. Since the beginning of '*Barbarossa*' Rundstedt had steadily driven the Russians eastwards, reaching the River Dnieper by 10 July and engulfing some 100,000 Russians around Uman on 2 August. Reducing the pocket was hampered by limited air support due to heavy rain and Greim's *Fliegerkorps V* was so overstretched that Greim refused to support *Generalfeldmarschall* Walter Reichenau's *6. Armee* holding the northern side of the pocket, but Rundstedt and a conciliatory Löhr resolved the matter. *Oberstleutnant* Günther Lützow, became *Nahkampfführer Nord* with three *Gruppen* who helped Reichenau hold the line until Greim came to the rescue, despatching every available aircraft despite low cloud, rain and high winds in a campaign which ended with the Russian defeat by 9 August.

Rundstedt then occupied the whole Dnieper line and prepared to envelop the Kiev salient with an armoured thrust which would meet Guderian from the north. Kesselring had only 251 serviceable aircraft on 6 September but was reinforced by Richthofen, while Löhr was down to 273. [28] The Germans were soon driving deep into the salient, Greim flying 846 sorties between 15 and 19 September against weak air resistance. [29] Stalin refused to sanction a withdrawal, the two German spearheads met on 16 September and within 10 days the pocket and 627,000 troops were mopped up. Greim's air support was hampered by lack of supplies and Löhr lacked the *Transportgruppen* to assist him, but the *Luftwaffe* still maintained air superiority. The scale of operations may be judged from Greim's report in which he flew 1,422 sorties between 12–21 September, dropping some 600 tonnes of bombs for the loss of 17 aircraft and 14 damaged. [30]

With the collapse of the Kiev pocket, the *Wehrmacht* was poised to complete the destruction of the Soviet Union. But the balmy summer breezes were cooling and the autumn rains provided a heavenly shield for the Godless Soviet regime as the *rasputitsa* slowed the flow of supplies to a trickle. It slowed Rundstedt's drive towards Rostov and the Crimean Peninsula with the Black Sea Fleet's base at Sevastopol, the former supported by Greim and the latter by Pflugbeil. Supply problems meant that for a month the advance on Rostov was covered by three single-engined *Gruppen* under *Major* Clemens *Graf* Schönborn-Wiesentheid as *Nahkampfführer Süd*, while Greim kept the multi-engined units closer to their supply depots until they could move forward to the former Russian air base at Taganrog. Pflugbeil had shorter supply lines and despite vigorous air opposition he helped *General der Infanterie* Erich von Manstein's *11. Armee* take the whole of the Crimean Peninsula except for Sevastopol by 16 November.

Three days later Rundstedt took Rostov, but a Russian counter-offensive retook the city within a week leading to Rundstedt's dismissal and replacement by *Generaloberst* Walther von Reichenau. There was little that Greim could do because *Fliegerkorps V* was steadily milked of units with five *Kampfgruppen* withdrawn for rest and re-equipment leaving Schönborn to his own devices. *Fliegerkorps* V headquarters was withdrawn to Brussels on 30 November to become a minelayer force, but it soon returned. On 26 December, the Russians established a beachhead around Kerch in the eastern Crimea. Pflugbeil needed to concentrate his limited resources on 'mainland' threats to the north so Greim was told on 2 January 1942 to return to the East. He took half his staff to the Crimea where they became *Sonderstab Krim* and took control of Wild's *FlFü Süd* on 15 January.

The Crimea was one of series of crises during the winter of 1941/42, yet in early October *ObdL* prepared plans for a *Luftwaffe* winter garrison of 18 *Gruppen* in the East and Jeschonnek would inform Richthofen that he and his *Fliegerkorps* would winter in Bavaria and Austria, although for his part, Richthofen was less optimistic. [31] The last offensive, 'Taifun', against Moscow, saw Kesselring's strength raised to 1,320 aircraft, or half the *Luftwaffe's* Eastern Front strength, including Fiebig's *Nakafu II*, while the Russians had 708 of which 344 were Moscow's air defence shield. [32] The offensive started well on 30 September, encircling thousands of troops at Bryansk and Viazma, although the subjugation of the pockets took most of a month. Kesselring provided his usual high level of support, 2,358 sorties on 2–3 October, but as the rain turned roads and airfields into swamps sortie levels dropped to 600 a day, although this respite allowed the 'Schwarzmänner' to reduce the maintenance backlog to push up sortie levels when the weather improved. [33]

The Germans now prepared to take Moscow but on 5 November Kesselring informed Loerzer that he and most of his units would soon depart for the Mediterranean. When Bock was informed he was appalled and vigorously protested to Halder that it would demoralise his tired troops, yet on 11 November he received formal notice that Kesselring's units would begin departing within a week. He desperately attacked to exploit whatever air support was available but his initiative faded before his eyes; indeed, Loerzer handed over his sector to Fiebig on 12 November, who was soon placed under Richthofen, and took 13 *Gruppen* westward. On 29 November Kesselring set out for Rome and the following day Richthofen moved into Smolensk to support Bock's advance on Moscow. Progress was slow due to German exhaustion, Russian resistance and rapidly deteriorating weather conditions with Siberian winds chilling the air to -46°C and dense snow blotting out all features. As the temperature dropped, the rutted surfaces of airfields froze, making them hazardous obstacle courses, and the average level of operations was reduced to some 300 sorties a day. By contrast the VVS was able to exploit all-weather airfields around Moscow and was extremely active, but by the time '*Taifun*' ended in failure on 6 December it had lost 293 aircraft, having flown 51,300 sorties.

Both sides were now exhausted; the Germans had suffered heavy losses in both men and materiel, the *Luftwaffe* losing 489 aircraft destroyed and 333 damaged since 28 September, and a brief hiatus ensued. On 8 December (when Richthofen's *Korps* flew a mere 44 sorties) Hitler issued OKW *Weisung Nr 39*, ordering the *Wehrmacht* to go onto the defensive owing to '…the severe winter weather which has come surprisingly early.' The savage losses inflicted on the Russians – their own records show 2.5 million dead and missing and 6,100 combat aircraft lost since the German invasion – meant no substantial enemy action was anticipated. The *Luftwaffe* was also to create a defensive infrastructure and to ensure the enemy did not attack, to disrupt him 'as far as possible.'

But Hitler's hopes were already being dashed, for Stalin was determined not to wait like a sheep to be slaughtered and determined upon an active defence despite the exhaustion of his own forces. Counter-attacks to save Moscow began on 5 December supported by 1,376 aircraft (859 serviceable) which flew an average 400 sorties a day and these contributed to the cancellation of '*Taifun*' the following day. To their own surprise the Russians made rapid progress as German resistance collapsed because little air support was available, Richthofen flying only 388 sorties on 12–14 December. [43] Bock's forces began to withdraw, bringing down the neighbouring fronts like a house of cards and the wings of panic beat in many headquarters. On 16 December Hitler issued his 'stand fast' order and three days later replaced *Generalfeldmarschall* Walther Brauchitsch as Commander-in-Chief of the Army. More practically, *ObdL* provided Richthofen with four *Kampfgruppen* and, to supply isolated or retreating troops, five *Transportgruppen* under *Oberst* Friedrich-Wilhelm 'Fritz' Morzik, the *Lufttransportführer beim Generalquartiermeister der Luftwaffe und Kommando der Blindflugschule* or *LTF* since 1 October 1941. *Flak* batteries often formed the backbone of the defence and *Flakkorps II*'s *General der Flakartillerie* Otto Dessloch also acted as *Nahkampffliegerkommando Nord* on the *Heeresgruppe Nord* and *Mitte* boundary using elements of Richthofen's *Fliegerkorps VIII* and flying more than 5,000 sorties between January and March. Richthofen himself had to juggle the resources of 10 understrength *Gruppen* to shield the *Landsers* (soldiers) in the central sector where the fate of the whole Eastern Front was being decided.

The year ended with the *Wehrmacht* in retreat despite the *Führer* order; in fact during the winter of 1941/42 both dictators were driving the war on 'empty', with virtually no reserves of men and materiel. Strength of will alone kept the front aflame as gangs of desperate, hungry, exhausted men under the banners of divisions and brigades fought on. The situation was reflected on the battle maps with the front, especially west of Moscow, evolving into a series of exposed salients which neither side had the strength to eliminate. The survival of so many Germans depended upon the *Luftwaffe* which was hamstrung by a shortage of aircraft because, from the beginning of the campaign to 1 November, its average monthly losses in the East were 741 aircraft and 318 aircrew and neither factories nor schools could keep pace with these losses. [35]

Keeping the remaining aircraft airworthy in the Arctic winter conditions was a new labour of Hercules: metal tools became brittle and not even pre-heating them made them reliable, engine oil froze, hydraulic fluids became like glue, while rubber in seals and tyres crumbled. Engines had to be turned over regularly, especially at night, consuming the limited stocks of petrol and oil or they were enclosed in heated sheds or 'alert boxes'. The *Wehrmacht* lacked winter clothing and with the supply lines in chaos little of this reached the front in time, but Milch rose to the occasion and ensured *Luftwaffe* supplies were assembled and despatched quickly.

Milch's star was rising and with the suicide of the *Generalluftzeugmeister* Ernst Udet on 17 November, he finally took control of aircraft production, bringing order out of chaos through a ruthless rationalisation which saw him pay off some old scores, notably against the aircraft designer, Willy Messerschmitt. The downside was that the 'Great and Good' were summoned to Ernst Udet's funeral and, in the process, *General der Flieger* Helmuth Wilberg, who had laid down the foundations of the *Luftwaffe*, and the *Inspekteur der Jagdflieger* and fighter *Experte,Oberst* Werner Mölders, were killed in air crashes. Mölders was replaced by *Oberstleutnant* Adolf Galland, the *Kommodore* of JG 26 who received his appointment at the graveside on 28 November. [36]

Yet the most significant air operation took place on *Heeresgruppe Nord*'s vulnerable right from 9 February 1942 when the Russians isolated *Generalleutnant* Walter *Graf von* Brockdorff-Ahlefeldt's *II. Armee Korps* with some 95,000 men at Demyansk and 5,000 men at Kholm, south-west of Demyansk. The latter was in the more dire predicament and *KG 4* was immediately ordered to fly in supplies, but no airlift was envisaged until Halder made a formal request to Jeschonnek on 13 February. The previous day *Luftflotte 1* commander Keller, on his own initiative, began using his *Transportgruppe* to fly in supplies, but Hitler now promised him 337 transports within a week although this meant robbing *Fliegerkorps VIII*. On 18 February Hitler ordered Morzik to take his transports to join *Luftflotte 1* where he swiftly established his headquarters at Pskov-West (as *Lufttransportführer Ost*), although there was some initial friction with Keller over responsibility for the new airlift. Within three weeks Morzik expanded his force to 15 *Gruppen* by mobilising schools while Brockdorff-Ahlefeldt helped organise airfields within the pocket. The pocket held out for nearly three months, being relieved on 29 April but the air transport effort continued at a reduced rate from 18 May until the pocket was evacuated on 18 March 1943 by which time the *Luftwaffe* had flown in a total of 64,844 tonnes and 30,500 men and moved out 35,400 sick and injured. The Kholm pocket was supplied by gliders until it was relieved on 5 May. [37]

The relief of the pockets boosted both *Luftwaffe* and army morale after a grim winter but they would have fatal consequences within nine months. From Hitler downwards the *Wehrmacht* was convinced that determined, isolated garrisons could hold out against the 'Bolshevik hordes' if they were supported by an airlift. The Germans were unaware of Red Army weakness during the winter of 1941/42, nor could they anticipate how this would change and the enemy grow in strength by the following winter. *ObdL* should have paid more careful attention to the successes in the pockets and recognised they were achieved in unique conditions, including an unprecedented concentration of *Transportgruppen*. Jeschonnek might also have considered the impact the operation had upon the training organisation which had lost aircraft, instructors and promising students to undermine the bomber force.

With the spring *rasputitsa* the crisis in the East was over and with *Luftwaffe* aid, the *Wehrmacht* had weathered the storm. While the Army preferred close air support it was the interdiction of Russia's over-stretched transport system which was probably the greatest hurdle for Stalin's generals who suffered a perennial shortage of heavy weapons and supplies. But the *Luftwaffe* paid a terrible price for this success. Between 7 December and 8 April the Eastern Front units lost 859 aircraft destroyed and 636 damaged and by 30 March it was left with only 1,766 aircraft including 920 strike, 602 fighters and 335 reconnaissance. [38] The immediate need was to re-organise the *Gruppen*, replace lost aircraft and aircrew, give the exhausted survivors a spot of leave and prepare for the summer campaign. In the course of these preparations Göring deftly tightened his control of the squadrons by hoovering up the weakened *Heeresflieger* into *Fern-* and *Nahaufklärungsgruppen*. [39]

A blueprint for operations in the East, OKW *Weisung Nr 41*, was published on 5 April although even Hitler was forced to recognise that the losses of the previous months meant he had to cut his coat to suit his cloth. The front line was to be smoothed out as far as possible to economise in manpower, but the *Wehrmacht* would quickly return to its old vigour. On the Crimean peninsula Manstein was to eliminate the enemy bridgehead on the Kerch Peninsula (*Unternehmen 'Trappenjagd'* or 'Bustard Hunt') and then take the Black Sea Fleet's main base at Sevastopol. To the north Bock, who had replaced Reichenau, was to eliminate the Russian salient around Izyum whose northern edge was a mere 50 kilometres from Kharkov, the lynchpin of the Ukrainian rail network. The task was assigned to *General der Panzertruppe* Friedrich Paulus' *6. Armee* and *Armeegruppe Kleist* (*1. Panzer* and *17. Armee*) in *Unternehmen 'Fridericus'* supported by *Fliegerkorps IV* and *VIII*. [40]

Once the stage was cleared, the main advance would lead to the occupation of the Caucasian oil fields to compensate for declining production in Rumania. *Fall 'Blau'* would take the *Wehrmacht* via a series of envelopment operations to the Don at Rostov and the Volga at Stalingrad. The former would act as a springboard for an advance into the Caucasus while the latter would cut oil supplies to the main Russian forces. With the oil fields in German hands, Manstein and Richthofen would be transferred north to help Küchler storm Leningrad. Richthofen would play a major role in the new offensive in which the *Luftwaffe* would carry out its usual range of tasks. However, Hitler added the proviso that: 'The possibility of a hasty transfer of *Luftwaffe* units to the central and northern fronts must be borne in mind, and the necessary ground organisation for this must be maintained as far as possible.'

The drive for oil was because '*Barbarossa*' had shown that this was the *Wehrmacht*'s Achilles heel. The major source was Rumania, augmented by smaller supplies from

Hungary and the *Reich* itself, where synthetic oil production facilities were established. For the *Luftwaffe* overall fuel consumption in 1940 did not exceed supply, which included substantial captured stocks but operations during 1941 saw this trend substantially reversed (see Table 7-2) and *ObdL* began cutting back on non-operational flying times to reduce consumption. In one way these moves were extremely successful and during 1942 production exceeded consumption by 156,000 tonnes but it was *General der Flieger* Bernhard Kühl's training organisation which suffered worst. Flying training hours averaged 250 to September 1942 but then slipped to 200, while fighter training time was cut from some 75 hours to 50 [41]. By the end of 1942 the declining standard of bomber crews was becoming all too apparent in the Mediterranean and Western Europe and the loss of both instructors and advanced students at Stalingrad would exacerbate the situation.

Table 7-2: Luftwaffe fuel situation, January 1941–December 1942

Quarter	Production (*tonnes*)	Consumption (*tonnes*)
Q1 1941	183,000	193,000
Q2 1941	217,000	372,000
Q3 1941	236,000	409,000
Q4 1941	274,000	300,000
Q1 1942	281,000	272,000
Q2 1942	333,000	388,000
Q3 1942	417,000	412,000
Q4 1942	441,000	354,000

Source: United States Strategic Bombing Survey, Overall report (European War), 30 September 1945. Chart No 16.

With the ground drying and the *Reichsbahn* having converted the Russian railway lines, supplies could be assembled for the forthcoming offensive. The *Luftwaffe* withdrew units to Germany to receive new aircraft and replace the gaps in aircrews while, with no immediate demands on the remaining *Kampfgruppen*, there was a half-hearted attempt at strategic bombing during April. Attacks were conducted as far east as Stalingrad but, with only a handful of aircraft available for each mission, they achieved little. After the war Plocher wrote revealingly: '*Since none of these attacks resulted in the actual destruction of the source of enemy power, it would have been far more advisable to have committed these few plans in support of the Army. Because these unsystematic attacks made no tactical impact whatever at the front, they were literally senseless and could be considered a typical example of inefficiency and waste in military operations.*' [42] Many of the sorties were flown by Greim, who took *Sonderstab Krim* to the Moscow front (transferring the aircraft to Wild) and rejoined the rest of his *Fliegerkorps* staff to establish *Luftwaffenkommando Ost* on 1 April, replacing *Fliegerkorps VIII* which departed for Germany on 10 April for a well-earned leave. Two days later Greim split his command between Fiebig's *1. Fliegerdivision* at Dugino in the north and *2. Flieger Division* derived from *Nahkampfführer II* in the south at Briansk under Fröhlich, newly arrived from North Africa.

Richthofen enjoyed only a short leave, with some compensation when he lectured Hitler on the importance of air power in the forthcoming assault and made the *Führer* such an ardent convert that he informed a shocked Manstein during a conference on 16 April that he would oversee air support personally. Jeschonnek's faith in the *Führer's* judgement was further tested when he was informed that Richthofen's *Fliegerkorps VIII* would no longer be used to support '*Fridericus*' but would be transferred to the Crimea to aid Manstein. Manstein was no doubt delighted at the prospect of what the *XXX Armeekorps* war diary would describe as '...*concentrated air support the like of which has never existed.*' His enthusiasm was curbed when Richthofen arrived and began behaving like an armchair general with little attempt by *ObdL* to prevent him tinkering with Manstein's preparations. Richthofen established his headquarters in Feodosia on May Day and assumed command of Wild's *FlFü Süd* which now reverted to the anti-shipping role. What Löhr felt about the new arrangements is not recorded, but it left him with just Pflugbeils' *Fliegerkorps IV* on the 'mainland' in the north. [43]

On 1 May Pflugbeil had 507 combat aircraft and some transports (for strengths and casualties from May 1942 to May 1943 see Tables 7-3 and 7-4) but soon had to give 360 machines to Richthofen who had 740 and a few seaplanes to clear the Crimea Peninsula. The first stage was to wipe out the Kerch bridgehead in '*Trappenjagd*', an operation named after the abundant Great Bustards in the area. Although Richthofen denied Manstein direct access to the *Luftwaffe* airmen he provided sufficient support for the whole of the Kerch Peninsula thrust, which was regained by 20 May with 3,800 sorties flown on the first two days and the 400 defending aircraft brushed aside. [44]

Table 7–3: Luftwaffe Eastern Front, May 1942–May 1943

Month	Lft 1	LwKdo Ost	Lft 4	Total
May 1942	506	354	920	1,806
Jun 1942	416	383	1,525	2,324
Jul 1942	250	496	1,758	2,504
Aug 1942	356	473	1,509	2,338
Sep 1942	289	571	1,282	2,142
Oct 1942	517	463	1,090	2,070
Nov 1942	325	459	1,250	2,034
Dec 1942	365	460	853	1,678
Jan 1943	305	330	889	1,524
Feb 1943	257	327	883	1,467
Mar 1943	247	378	946	1,571
Apr 1943	315	462	1,000	1,777
May 1943	332	534	1,204	2,070

Source: BA MA RL 2 III/874–877.

But now a major crisis developed around the Izyum salient where, six days before the Germans planned to launch '*Fridericus*', the Russians beat them to the punch. The VVS had become more active from late April but the Germans thought this was an attempt to disrupt '*Fridericus*'. On the morning of 12 May the Russians, supported by 926 aircraft, broke out of the salient to strike behind Paulus, who also faced a thrust on his left. '*Trappenjagd*' had left Pflugbeil with some 140 aircraft comprising a *Stuka Gruppe*, fighters and reconnaissance aircraft, and once convinced of the seriousness of the situation, Hitler ordered Richthofen not only to return Pflugbeil's *Gruppen* but also to dispatch 150 of his own including his *Stuka* wing, *St.G* 77. Pflugbeil, now reinforced, had 650 aircraft which began interdicting the battlefield, as the Germans decided to exploit a weakness in the Russian advance which left them vulnerable to a thrust from the south by *Generaloberst* Ewald von Kleist. The details were arranged at a conference on 15 May and two days later, under clear, bright skies, Kleist began driving north with massive *Luftwaffe* support from *Gefechtsverband Süd* with 11 *Gruppen* and Richthofen's *III./KG 55* with some 20 aircraft flying four missions (52 sorties) and dropping nearly 59 tonnes of bombs. [45] Two days later the rest of Pflugbeil's squadrons joined Paulus' thrust south the spearheads linked on 24 May, wiping out the pocket within three days to take 170,000 prisoners. Pflugbeil had flown 15,648 sorties and dropped 7,700 tonnes of bombs (and 383 supply canisters) for the loss of 49 aircraft (the Russians lost 615) and 110 aircrew, transport aircraft flying in 1,545 tonnes of supplies to forward airfields and isolated troops. [46]

Table 7-4: Luftwaffe losses in the East, May 1942–May 1943

Month	Lft 1		LwKdo Ost		Lft 4		Total	
	EA	*Accid*	*EA*	*Accid*	*EA*	*Accid*	*EA*	*Accid*
May 1942	90	118	17	23	122	86	229	227
Jun 1942	54	47	44	48	158	139	256	234
Jul 1942	17	15	67	37	233	210	317	262
Aug 1942	51	35	142	52	199	178	392	265
Sep 1942	28	25	95	50	223	133	346	208
Oct 1942	44	36	30	25	143	99	217	160
Nov 1942	27	11	38	34	139	141	204	186
Dec 1942	28	13	50	26	147	91	225	130
Jan 1943	31	20	34	60	199	71	264	111
Feb 1943	44	20	28	16	154	124	226	160
Mar 1943	42	17	70	75	138	128	250	220
Apr 1943	27	15	26	39	94	114	147	168
May 1943	42	34	56	50	200	138	298	222

Source: BA MA RL 2 III/874–877.

German eyes now turned to the Crimea although *Weisung Nr 41* offered no strategic justification for taking the peninsula. It was understood that its capture would eliminate a thorn in the German side yet despite this secondary aim the peninsula became, as one observer noted, a focal point of German operations with a full-scale assault planned upon Sevastopol as *Unternehmen 'Störfang'* ('Sturgeon Trap'). Richthofen's *Gruppen* returned to give him no fewer than 443 aircraft on 1 June, with the *Fliegerkorps* providing Tactical air support while Wild would have the

Operational Level role interdicting Soviet shipping. Richthofen's airmen were reduced to the role of substitute artillerymen when the preparation began from 2 June and would drop 20,528 tonnes of bombs and fly 23,751 sorties by the time the last defender fell on 4 July, only 31 German aircraft being lost. The level of effort (up to eight sorties a day) owed much to the dedication of the '*Schwarzmänner*' who ensured a serviceability rate of 64 per cent. Yet the success would prove a poisoned chalice raising army expectations for similar levels of support which the *Luftwaffe* could not match exacerbating relations between the two services in the future [47].

Richthofen was not present when Sevastopol fell, the imminence of '*Blau*' causing *Fliegerkorps VIII* headquarters to be transferred to Kharkov on 23 June, leaving Wild in charge of the dying Crimea battle. '*Störfang*' demonstrated that Richthofen was overdue for promotion and he was subsequently appointed commander of *Luftflotte 4*. On 28 June, his predecessor Löhr was assigned *12. Armee* in the Balkans, where the former Austrian officer could exploit his familiarity with the region and his linguistic skills. He later became *Oberbefehlshaber Südost* (*OB Südost*) but had little direct contact with the *Luftwaffe* for the rest of the war, although Richthofen did palm off on him the defence of Rumania's oil refineries. Löhr's departure was badly timed, for it was on the day that '*Blau*' (now renamed '*Braunschweig*') began and Richthofen was forced to remain with *Fliegerkorps VIII* supporting the initial phase with Tactical missions while Pflugbeil flew Operational ones, the long days meaning that even bomber crews were flying five sorties a day. [48] A week elapsed before Richthofen was able to hand over to Fiebig and assume command of the *Luftflotte* on 4 July but it was operating in the capable hands of its chief of staff, Korten.

For the new campaign the *Luftwaffe* assembled its largest concentration in the East since '*Barbarossa*', and one never later equalled, with 2,690 aircraft (including *Staffeln* from Spain and Croatia), while the VVS had a total of 2,800 front line combat aircraft (including 700 Polikarpov Po-2 and R-5 night bombers) and 900 aircraft in reserve, as well as 1,200 PVO fighters. German Tactical air support was strengthened through the creation of *Schlachtgeschwader*, with *Jabos*, supplemented by the twin-engined Hs 129 dedicated ground-attack aircraft, some in *Luftflotte 4*, which had 52 per cent (1,400) of the *Luftwaffe's* Eastern Front strength. This force would be supplemented by 265 Hungarian, Italian, Rumanian and Slovak combat aircraft, which faced 23 per cent of the VVS (640 aircraft) in the South-Western Theatre. [49]

To the north Greim, with nearly 500 aircraft, helped *Heeresgruppe Mitte's* deception operation, *Unternehmen 'Kreml'* ('Kremlin'), to convince the Russians that the main thrust would be towards Moscow. There was an extensive building programme to produce new airfields and expand existing ones, while from mid-June Greim was active over the front and increased reconnaissance flights around Moscow [50]. Yet the number of Russian air regiments (each of some 20 aircraft) around Moscow dropped from 35 on May Day to 25 by 1 July, augmented by 22 PVO regiments while the Soviet General headquarters (Stavka) increased its reserve from 32 regiments to 46 in the same period. Opposite *Luftflotte 4*, VVS strength rose from 100 regiments to 159 between May and July, although many of the latter were under strength [51].

Fiebig was forced to divert aircraft to Voronezh because Stalin's fears for the safety of Moscow meant the Russians placed heavy pressure upon the boundary between *Heeresgruppen Mitte* and *Süd*. Fierce air battles brought Russian losses in the Voronezh operation to 783 aircraft by 24 July without the compensation of saving the city, but Fiebig's commitment to the next phase of the offensive (*Unternehmen 'Clausewitz'*) from 9 July made it increasingly difficult for him to continue operations around Voronezh. On 2 August Richthofen created *Gefechtsverband Nord* under Bülowius, with *Nahaufklärungs-, Jagd-, Stuka-* and *Kampfgruppen* on an *ad hoc* basis being joined later by Hungarian and Italian squadrons as their armies entered the line along the Don south of Voronezh. Meanwhile the Russians sought to exploit the German pre-occupation with the south and sought to envelop the Rzhev Salient from 30 July in a series of poorly co-ordinated attacks which rumbled on until early October. Kluge's *Heeresgruppe Mitte* held out, but its survival owed much to Greim's support which was aided by good command and control with *Luftwaffenkommando Ost* juggling his handful of units between the *Fliegerdivisionen* in Tactical operations. [52]

To the south the *Wehrmacht* swept down the west bank of the Don during July but took few prisoners, for on 6 July Stalin ordered his troops to retreat. Fiebig and Pflugbeil continued to support the spearheads providing Tactical- and Operational-level support respectively, Fiebig's *Fliegerkorps VIII Gruppen* leap-frogging forward so rapidly that their new airfields were sometimes under artillery fire. But the usual combination of extreme activity and lengthening supply reduced sortie levels and, as a result, the *Transportgruppen* remained active, flying more than 200 tonnes of fuel to the Panzer divisions on 12 July alone. [53]

With the northern flank almost secure Hitler prepared to achieve his strategic objectives, publishing *Weisung Nr 45* on 23 July for which he had set the scene nearly a fortnight earlier by splitting *Heeresgruppe Süd*, under *Generaloberst* Maximilian von Weichs. Weichs controlled the northern flank as *Heeresgruppe B*, shielding the advance of *Generalfeldmarschall* Wilhelm List's *Heeresgruppe A* into the Caucasus where he would secure the Black Sea coast then seize Caucasian oilfields. But to strengthen the northern shield Weichs had to advance to the Volga and take Stalingrad supported by Fiebig, while Pflugbeil (and Wild) would support List. The directive noted: '*The early destruction of the city of Stalingrad is especially important…*' but attacks on the oil industry infrastructure were permitted '*…only if the Army make them absolutely essential.*'

Richthofen bitterly complained to *ObdL* about having to support two diverging *Heersgruppen* with inadequate resources. In June and July *Luftflotte 4* lost 740 combat aircraft destroyed or badly damaged, 391 to enemy action, while 177 aircraft were sent back for overhauls. Only 668 replacements were received leaving Richthofen with barely 1,500 aircraft but he received no substantial reinforcements for the *Luftwaffe* was already overstretched. [54] German total losses in the East rose from 350 in June to 438 and 436 in the next two months and then dropped to 200 and 224 throughout October and November. [55] Richthofen focused upon the advance to Stalingrad, probably because it was easier to support, with the result that Pflugbeil became the poor relation in supporting List. On 20 August Richthofen regretfully informed List that he was transferring most of his aircraft to Stalingrad on Hitler's orders, and when List's Chief of Staff, *Generalleutnant* Hans von Greiffenberg asked *OKH* on 28 August when the *Heeresgruppe would* receive air support he was told tersely, 'When Stalingrad is taken or given up as impossible'.

On 21 August Paulus thrust towards Stalingrad and within two days his northern spearhead, with 1,600 *Luftwaffe* sorties and 1,000 tonnes of bombs, reached the Volga sustained by air-supplied fuel and ammunition. A brief pause followed as Hungarian and Italian troops were brought to hold the the 500-kilometre Don line south of Voronezh but they never had more than 150 aircraft and to secure the line Richthofen brought in *Fliegerkorps I* headquarters on 26 August. This became *Luftwaffenkommando Don* which absorbed *Gefechtsverband Nord* (which retained a semi-autonomous status until disbanded in November) and was placed under Korten, although Richthofen would have preferred Pflugbeil. [56] With only 151 aircraft on 1 September, Korten had to rely on brains rather than brawn and command posts established at each end of his sector proved useful during October when the Russian probes pushed back allied forces in many places. [57]

To the south the assault upon Stalingrad heralded on 3 September with an unremitting 24-hour bombardment by Fiebig and Pflugbeil, who dropped thousands of incendiaries from as low as 2,000 metres (6,600 feet), turning the log-cabin suburbs into a forest of stone chimneys. As German troops fought their way into the city against fierce resistance, Fiebig established a command post with a panorama of the battlefield, while a neighbouring army observation battalion helped to provide an up-to-the-minute picture of the situation. Air power became an artillery substitute and on 1 November Richthofen wrote in his diary that bombers were dropping bombs within grenade-throwing range. [58] He seized every opportunity to criticise Paulus's leadership and to play the armchair general, and even persuaded *OKH* to despatch five combat engineer battalions claiming they would turn the tide of battle. As late as 16 November he was complaining about Paulus to Army Chief of Staff *Generaloberst* Kurt Zeitzler, who had replaced Halder on 25 September. [59]

The open steppes made it easy for Fiebig to build airstrips for his fighter and close air support units while the *Kampfgruppen* operated from Morozovskaya and Tatsinskaya, 200–250 kilometres from Stalingrad. The VVS fiercely contested the skies over Stalingrad but to little effect due to poorly trained aircrew and between 17 July and 18 November lost 2,063 aircraft. Richthofen's burden was eased from mid-September with the arrival of the Rumanian Air Corps (180 combat aircraft) to support the 3rd Rumanian Army and interdict Russian communications north-west of Stalingrad. [60]

By 6 October Paulus had secured central and southern Stalingrad, but he was exhausted and awaited reinforcements. *Luftwaffe* strength in the East had now dropped by more than 17 per cent after four months of continuous operations while four *Gruppen* returned to the Reich or were transferred to the Mediterranean theatre in September and October. *ObdL* had nothing to spare, so Richthofen, displaying the child-like wilfulness so prevalent in German officers, went south to support *Heeresgruppe A* until Paulus renewed his attack. Göring promptly issued a directive re-emphasising the supremacy of the Stalingrad front, but Richthofen stubbornly refused to return. This stimulated a discussion about *Luftwaffe* resources, leading to a meeting with Hitler on 15 October involving Göring, Jeschonnek and Richthofen. A good-humoured *Führer*, who directed operations in the Caucasus personally following List's resignation on 9 September, rubber-stamped Richthofen's decision, partly because he believed that the Stalingrad battle was in its last phase. Pflugbeil's units were overstretched and hard-pressed to maintain pace with the spearheads while Richthofen's armchair-general tactics meant his views of the Army's prospects decided where air power was to be focused. [61] Mountainous terrain and heavy rain meant that the *Panzer* units could not exploit *Luftwaffe* attacks and, in a fit of pique, Richthofen refused to increase air support. [62]

As the autumn the evenings grew chillier and rain showers became more common, on 14 October Paulus renewed his assault upon Stalingrad. Richthofen returned with most of his *Gruppen* to find that Soviet pressure along the whole front was forcing him to shuffle units to meet real or imagined threats, giving them no time to rest. [63] Nevertheless, *Luftwaffe* support helped to ensure that by 7 November the Russians were left with their legs dangling in the Volga, though this effort created a German supply crisis. On 1 November Richthofen proposed to Weichs and Paulus that railway space for Army ammunition be relinquished, because with fighting at such close quarters '... the *Luftwaffe* cannot be very effective any more'. He was, in fact, better served than the Army, being supported since 10 August by up to ten *Transportgruppen* (506 aircraft on 1 September) initially under Morzik's *Lufttransportführer Ost*, established on 11 June. On 20 October three *Gruppen* (some 135 aircraft) were transferred to the Mediterranean, and it would appear Morzik's command was broken up and the remaining *Gruppen* scattered with Fiebig receiving four under *Stab KGzbV 1*. By mid-November the airlift in support of the German advance had brought 42,630 tonnes of supplies and 27,044 personnel while evacuating 51,018 casualties. Most of these supplies were for the *Luftwaffe*, which received 20,173 tonnes of fuel and 9,492 tonnes of bombs and ammunition, allowing Richthofen to build up what proved to be a very valuable reserve, but 9,233 tonnes were for the Army, half of it vehicle fuel. [64]

Russian air activity was growing as the VVS benefited from organisational and leadership reforms initiated by Colonel General Novikov, who replaced Zhigarev on 11 April 1942 (Zhigarev was sent to command the Far Eastern air forces). Frontal aviation was re-organised into well-balanced air armies of fighter, attack-bomber and light-bomber divisions, each roughly equivalent to a *Geschwader*; while in the *Stavka* reserve from 10 September, units were increasingly concentrated into air corps. Novikov spurred the development of more modern tactics and improved both the maintenance and logistic organisations which might have had a far greater effect, while improved aircraft such as Lavochkin La-5 and Yakovlev Yak-9 fighters as well as a two-seat version of the Il-2 '*Ilyusha*' attack bomber emerged from factories augmented by aircraft from Russia's allies,

But the heavy losses in the two summers meant most aircrew were inadequately trained and horrifyingly vulnerable to the more experienced Germans. Consequently while Novikov had numerous regiments in the rear military districts nominally recovering from losses or being formed, many do not appear to have received aircraft for months, although some were awaiting Lend-Lease aircraft. [65] On 1 November 1942 there were 92 regiments with an establishment of 2,000 aircraft in the Moscow, Volga Military Districts and the rear of the Caucasus while four months later, despite the desperate need at the front for units, 53 of them were still non-operational. Obsolete aircraft such as the SB, the I-153 and Su-2 continued to be used into 1943 and even 1944. [66]

The U-2 trainer (later Po 2), augmented by the surviving R-5 and R-Z, would prove an important influence upon the *Luftwaffe*. From October 1941 these were used to harass the German rear at night, bombing dumps, headquarters, batteries and even individual vehicles while the British using Fleet Air Arm Swordfish and Albacore biplanes for similar duties over the Egyptian desert. The damage inflicted was limited but they were such a problem that on 7 October 1942, the *Luftwaffe* authorised similar units to operate up to 60 kilometres behind enemy lines. Most commands created *Behelfskampfstaffeln* with trainers, corps and liaison aircraft including Fw 58s, Go 145s, He 46s, Hs 126s and Junkers W34s, but Richthofen assigned the task to *Verbindungs-Staffeln*. A month later the *Staffeln* were organised into *Störkampfgruppen*, with one assigned to each major command although Korten's *1. Behelfskampfstaffel, Luftflotte 4* had 70 aircraft. [67]

However, Korten had been steadily milked of forces and by 1 November was down to 140 combat aircraft, but his long-range strike force consisted of a single He 111 of *Stab KG* 27 and on 7 November his 39 fighters (from *II./JG* 77) were transferred to the Mediterranean, although replaced by Fiebig's *I./JG* 52. During November Richthofen lost six *Kampfgruppen* (155 aircraft) transferred to the Mediterranean or withdrawn for rest including all of *Major* Ernst Bormann's *KG* 76. While the Germans dissipated their strength, Stalin conserved his, feeding the fire within the city which bore his name, while his staff prepared a double envelopment, *Operatsiya 'Uran'* (Uranus), to exploit the enemy's exposed position. The Germans were at the tip of a long salient whose flanks were held by allied forces whom the Russians recognised were of dubious effectiveness. *'Uran'* was approved at the end of September, and in the following weeks forces assembled, shielded by rain, sleet and snow showers together with fog, which sharply reduced *Luftwaffe* activity.

Reconnaissance information provided by *FAGr 4* produced evidence that a major blow would strike the 3rd Rumanian Army, which arrived on Paulus's northern flank in October with some 20 corps aircraft, but Fiebig was unable to respond to Hitler's demands for major air strikes, especially after losing Bormann. Richthofen prepared a contingency plan for Pflugbeil to move north in the event of a crisis, leaving Caucasian air support under the commander of *I. Flakkorps, General der Flakartillerie* Otto Dessloch, but signs of a threat to Paulus's southern flank were ignored. By the beginning of November Fiebig had 487 aircraft and Pflugbeil 484, but when 'Uran' began on a snowy, overcast 19 November with low cloud and in temperatures just above freezing, Fiebig had 441 aircraft (219 serviceable) and Pflugbeil 297 (196 serviceable), augmented by 150 in the Rumanian Air Corps, facing 1,170 Russian aircraft.

The Russians struck the Rumanians, who quickly collapsed and the bad weather restricted the *Luftwaffe* reaction, allowing some of its forward airfields to be overrun. On 23 November the Russians isolated *6. Armee* with 250,000 men (including 13,000 Rumanians and 19,800 Russian *Hiwis*) in a pocket 50 kilometres long and 40 kilometres wide which included 12,000 *Luftwaffe* personnel. The Germans cobbled together a line along the Chir behind which the *Luftwaffe* regrouped using the stocks assembled through Richthofen's foresight to fly numerous sorties once the weather improved. [68]

6.Armee's isolation stunned the German High Command, but national prestige and the previous winter's experience created a consensus that Paulus should await relief, although this view was opposed by Manstein when he was hastily brought down from the Leningrad front to relieve the pocket with the new *Heeresgruppe Don* (one of Paulus's corps commanders was *Generalmajor* Walter von Seydlitz-Kurzbach, whose corps had relieved Demyansk). As at Demyansk, everything depended upon an airlift, but when Paulus raised this prospect with Fiebig on the evening of 21 November he latter replied with considerable perception: 'Impossible! Our aircraft are heavily engaged in Africa and on other fronts. I must warn you against exaggerated expectations.' [69]

Hitler's decision was underlined by Göring's assurances, evidently following discussions with Jeschonnek and *General der Flieger* Hans-Georg von Seidel, the *Generalquartiermeister*, who convinced him that the airlift was indeed practicable. [70] Paulus demanded 300 tonnes a day, but half the *Transportgruppen* were in the Mediterranean and the total number of transports in the East on 1 November (including *Fliegerkorps Transportstaffeln*) was 429. Morzik calculated the task required 1,050 aircraft but on 25 November Richthofen had only 298, and to make up the shortfall two *Transportgruppen* returned from the Mediterranean while 600 aircraft were mobilised from the *Fliegerschulen* and even *I./KG 50* whose He 177 were scheduled for use over the Atlantic.

The history of the Stalingrad airlift has been told many times and will not be repeated in detail. By the time the last German troops surrendered on 3 February 1943 the *Luftwaffe* had delivered 8,250 tonnes of supplies and evacuated some 11 per cent of the German troops, 24,700 wounded and 5,150 key personnel or experts. It was an impressive effort but amounted to only 19 per cent of Paulus's requirements; indeed on only four days was this target reached. The cost was high, with a 5.72 per cent loss rate (279 aircraft destroyed or failing to return, including 174 Ju 52); a further 215 were damaged, while personnel losses were also heavy (114 between 28 December and 5 January alone, including many advanced students and their instructors). The difficulties of supplying some 230,000 troops compared with the 95,000 at Demyansk were formidable enough even if operations had not been plagued by bad weather, a shortage of aircraft and an inadequate infrastructure but most importantly there was a failure to provide strong, co-ordinated leadership. The Nazi dog-eat-dog political philosophy meant no senior officer with the status to bring order out of chaos was appointed until 18 January when Milch was selected (no doubt in Göring's mind to be a scapegoat) but even his remarkable organising skills and energy in were used too late although by 29 January he had assembled 363 aircraft.

While Richthofen gave Fiebig overall responsibility for the airlift, (in itself a major challenge while he was trying to support hard-pressed troops on a wide front), *Fliegerkorps VIII* appears to have delegated responsibility to *Oberst* Hans Förster, the *Kommodore* of *KGzbV 1*, who had been controlling Fiebig's Ju 52 units since before '*Uran*' and who somehow shared responsibilities with his base commander *Generalmajor* Viktor Carganico, as well as *Oberst Dr* Ernst Kühl, *Kommodore* of *KG 55*, who controlled the *Kampfgruppen* used as transports. Within the pocket, Paulus washed his hands of his responsibilities and refused to organise either the reception or distribution of supplies. Instead he delegated responsibility for co-ordinating the airlift effort to *Oberst* Wolfgang Pickert, the *Flak* commander.

The airlift severely affected *Luftwaffe* operations in a more insidious way, for virtually all Richthofen's bombers were diverted to transport operations which meant that *Luftflotte 4* lost most of its Operational level capabilities and became a Tactical air force. Largely as a result of the transport operations, the *Luftwaffe* lost 165 He 111, as well as many student bomber crews, and Göring later observed:

'There died the core of the German bomber fleet.' [71] The diversion of the *Kampfgruppen*, the Tactical nature of air operations and the need to organise the airlift meant that on 2 January Fiebig transferred his single-engined aircraft to the new *Fliegerdivision Donez*, under *Generalleutnant* Alfred Mahnke and appears to have become *Lufttransportführer Luftflotte 4*.

Richthofen desperately juggled his aircraft from crisis to crisis in a vain attempt to influence the situation but could fly no more than 350 sorties a day. Pflugbeil's *Fliegerkorps IV* withdrew from the Caucasus to become his fire brigade, a few units being left behind under Dessloch on 25 November as *Luftwaffenkommando Kaukasus* to support the retreating *Heeresgruppe A*. Pflugbeil supported Manstein's relief operation launched on 12 December but it ran out of steam within 12 days and on 16 December, the Russians launched *Operatsiya 'Malyi Saturn'* ('Little Saturn') supported by 415 aircraft (a third of them Po-2s and R-5s), which ambitiously aimed to finish off *Heeresgruppe B* and to isolate *Heeresgruppe A*. It largely succeeded in its aims, although most of *Heeresgruppe A*'s mechanised forces escaped to join Manstein, whose command would be renamed *Heeresgruppe Süd* on 13 February when Weichs' headquarters was taken out of the line. It also wrecked any hopes of a successful airlift by overrunning the main bases and driving the *Luftwaffe* 350–400 kilometres westwards, leaving it in a desperate position by the beginning of February. Richthofen's total losses from November were 775 combat aircraft (excluding *Nachtschlacht* machines) of which 300 were in accidents leaving him, by 1 February, to support Manstein with 624 combat aircraft (excluding bombers on transport duties) of which 384 unserviceable. [72]

Then things improved for, with the fall of Stalingrad, the battered *Kampfgruppen* began to revert to their traditional role and replacements began to arrive while *Luftgau Rostov* rebuilt the infrastructure. In February Richthofen's combat units received 329 replacement aircraft which the *Generäle der Kampf-* and *Jagdflieger* (*Oberstleutnant* Peltz and *Generalmajor* Galland) helped distribute as they re-organised their forces and sent eight weak *Gruppen* back to the *Reich* to re-organise. Fiebig and *Fliegerkorps VIII* moved to the Crimea to support *Heeresgruppe A*, which covered the extreme south of the Ukraine, while Pflugbeil (with Mahnke) and Korten were to support Manstein, Korten's command becoming *Fliegerkorps I* on 17 February and moving to Poltava.

By now the Russians were driving towards the Dnieper taking Kharkov on 14 February but they were outrunning their supplies and exposing their southern flank. Manstein decided to exploit the situation and on 18 February launched a riposte northwards backed by Richthofen, with some 600 aircraft including 30 anti-tank aircraft operating under *Panzerjägerkommando Weiss*. Korten struck from the west but the main blow, with some 400 aircraft, was by Fiebig and Mahnke from the south and together they provided substantial support at both Tactical and Operational levels flying more than 1,000 sorties a day, compared to 350 a day in January. Even the thaw failed to halt the Germans driving through the mud and retaking Kharkov on 14 March and pushing the enemy across the Donetz in a campaign which restored German morale while leaving the *Wehrmacht* in almost the same positions it occupied a year earlier. For the *Luftwaffe* it was a good end to months of campaigning and probably cost about 150 aircraft, of which half were due to accidents.

In the Caucasus *Heeresgruppe A*'s *17. Armee* retreated westwards into the Taman Peninsula and from 6 February the dissolving of Dessloch's puny command saw

Fiebig made responsible for supporting them from the Crimea. Initially he focused upon an airlift which helped sustain the army by flying in 5,418 tonnes and withdrawing 15,500 men. [73] On 31 March he exchanged tactical areas with Korten's *Fliegerkorps I* which was immediately involved in a fierce battle as the Russians made a vain attempt to storm the Taman Peninsula with air support which almost doubled in April to 1,150 aircraft. Korten, whose strength rose from 244 combat aircraft with a couple of Rumanian squadrons, to 497 by the beginning of May, held his own losing less than 40 aircraft to enemy action. [74]

To the north the winter saw a renewed attempt by the Russians to take the Rzhev Salient in *Operatsiya 'Mars'* which some commentators have suggested was of equal importance to Stalin as Stalingrad. This was underlined by the deployment of the first of *Stavka's* air corps and 1,463 aircraft but as in the earlier battles, Greim's outnumbered airmen helped the defenders stop the attack, and to inflict Marshal Zhukov's worst defeat, even after the transfer of *Fliegerdivision 2* headquarters to France to command anti-shipping units. Greim's success came despite the need to support the towns of Kholm and Velikiye Luki which were isolated by a separate Russian offensive, but they fell in January. Despite the German success it was clear that the Rzhev Salient was clearly too exposed and Hitler authorised its abandonment in March. [75]

The spring rasputitsa closed down air operations almost everywhere and thoughts turned to the summer campaign. Hitler sought to regain the strategic initiative through a double envelopment of the Kursk Salient (*Unternehmen 'Zitadelle'*) originally scheduled for May and then continually postponed until 5 July. But with Russian industrial strength clearly resurgent, *ObdL* pondered a strategic bombing campaign. Some attacks were made during the lull, but the limited range and payload of the twin-engined bombers restricted their effects and it was clear that a four-engined force was required. [76]

Changes took place in the air in the East beginning with the upgrading of Greim's command to *Luftflotte 6* on 5 May. Greim received *Generalmajor* Josef Punzert's *Fliegerdivision 4* in June to control air operations in the north, while *Fliegerdivision 1*, now under *Generalmajor* Otto Zech, controlled those in the south. On 11 June Korten was appointed acting commander of *Luftflotte 1* in succession to the retiring Keller, leaving Mahnke as acting commander, his *Fliegerdivision* having been dissolved on 31 March. When Korten's long overdue promotion was confirmed on 26 June, Mahnke handed over to *Generalleutnant* Karl Angerstein. On 18 May Fiebig was transferred to *Fliegerkorps X* in the eastern Mediterranean and after a brief delay he was replaced on 22 May by *Generalmajor* Hans Seidemann, who had spent several years as Richthofen's chief of staff. The spring and early summer gave the *Luftwaffe* a chance to refit its Eastern Front units whose combat strength rose to 2,000 machines, the Fw 190 being more widely introduced and more *Panzerjäger* (anti-tank) units being formed with Hs 129 and Ju 87 G.

Meanwhile, in Berlin Göring was tiring of Jeschonnek and many thought of exchanging him for Richthofen. The first steps were taken and Jeschonnek came to Richthofen's headquarters to gain 'work experience', but it was not to be. Richthofen recognised a poisoned chalice when it was being handed to him and opted to take command of *Luftflotte 2* instead and on 13 June handed over to Dessloch. A disconsolate Jeschonnek lingered at *ObdL* enduring Göring's tongue-lashings as the aerial situation both over the Reich and in the Mediterranean deteriorated, and eventually he committed suicide on 18 August, to be replaced by Korten and Koller who were determined to reform the *Luftwaffe*.

The omens were not good for the skies over the Eastern Front had also become a maelstrom. '*Zitadelle*' was launched and the *Luftwaffe* provided its usual high level of support flying 28,264 sorties and losing 193 aircraft between 5 and 15 July but the *Landsers* were unable to break through the defences. The Allied landing in Sicily was the ostensible reason for ending '*Zitadelle*', but the Germans had no time to stand on their laurels before the Russians launched a series of offensives which exploded like firecrackers along the southern part of the front. [77]

Table 7-5: Luftwaffe Eastern Front Strength, June 1943–May 1944

Month	Lft 1	Lft 6	Lft 4	Total
Jun 1943	257	791	1,047	2,095
Jul 1943	60	872	1,070	2,002
Aug 1943	77	820	961	1,858
Sep 1943	112	528	968	1,608
Oct 1943	212	458	840	1,510
Nov 1943	144	561	924	1,629
Dec 1943	224	448	911	1,583
Jan 1944	332	714	874	1,920
Feb 1944	287	832	827	1,946
Mar 1944	363	795	893	2,051
Apr 1944	317	819	930	2,066
May 1944	311	788	931	2,030

Sources: BA MA RL 2 III/877–882.

Table 7-6: Luftwaffe losses in the East, June 1943–May 1944

Month	Lft 1		Lft 6		Lft 4		Total	
	EA	Accid	EA	Accid	EA	Accid	EA	Accid
Jun 1943	15	17	92	78	102	75	209	170
Jul 1943	16	22	276	148	262	113	554	283
Aug 1943	6	5	199	152	181	139	386	296
Sep 1943	7	8	78	54	222	143	307	205
Oct 1943	38	41	65	33	169	125	272	199
Nov 1943	3	2	43	54	133	86	179	142
Dec 1943	12	8	26	22	71	62	109	92
Jan 1944	31	30	41	51	163	135	235	216
Feb 1944	37	30	37	42	78	83	152	155
Mar 1944	41	32	13	44	143	152	197	228
Apr 1944	47	51	91	83	214	144	352	278
May 1944	22	47	40	85	146	125	208	257

Source: BA MA RL 2 III/877-882.

For the *Luftwaffe* '*Zitadelle*' marked a peak not only in effort but also in operations, for in the following months its strength in the East was steadily reduced. In July and August six *Gruppen* were withdrawn, two from *JG 3* to defend the *Reich*. The Eastern Front fighter force was so overstretched even at the beginning of July that *Heeresgruppe Nord* was shielded only by *4./JG 54* and overall fighter strength between then and 1 September dropped from 425 aircraft to 322 (excluding the Slovak *13./JG 52*) and even by the end of the year there were only 339 fighters available against a VVS growing in strength and quality. By contrast, the *Jagdwaffe* declined in quality as, for the first time, its endemic weakness became obvious. During the Great War the *Jagdwaffe* tradition was to encourage the heroic *Experten* (aces) who were feted and showered with awards. Perhaps the Germans instinctively recognised what became apparent through analysis half a century later: that only 5 per cent of fighter pilots became aces (five or more victories) but that these men accounted for 40 per cent of all victories. The average fighter pilot was a spear-carrier or bullet catcher for the *Experte* with little attempt to raise the overall quality of the average pilot in either the *Jagd-* or *Nachtjagdgruppe* and, unlike the Royal Air Force and US Army Air Force, no system for sending experienced pilots for a tour with training units both to rest and to pass their experience to the next generation. In the target-rich environment of the Eastern Front, many *Experte* built up scores running into three figures: 345 of Erich Hartmann's total of 352 were claimed in the East, 272 of Günther Rall's 275 and 255 of Walter Nowotny's 258 as well as all of Gerhard Barkhorn's 301 and Otto Kittel's 267. But from the summer of 1943 the war of attrition eroded the numbers of *Experten* and the *Jagdwaffe*'s overall effectiveness, *JG 51* losing 72 pilots killed and missing between August 1943 and April 1944. [78]

Fighter pilot casualties grew as the training organisation continued to bear the brunt of fuel cuts. A surge in operations in both the Russian and Mediterranean fronts saw consumption exceed supply in the first quarter and third quarters of 1943 by more than 20,000 tonnes each, savings in the last quarter of 1943 and the first of 1944 possibly reflecting the withdrawal of *Kampfgruppen* in the East (see Table 7-7). The impact on training was catastrophic with overall training hours dropping during the summer to 175 while fighter pilots would average only 25, with catastrophic results. [79]

Table 7-7: Luftwaffe fuel situation, January 1943–June 1944

Quarter	Production (*tonnes*)	Consumption (*tonnes*)
Q1 1943	407,000	429,000
Q2 1943	483,000	471,000
Q3 1943	515,000	538,000
Q4 1943	512,000	387,000
Q1 1944	535,000	413,000
Q 2 1944	386,000	541,000

Source: United States Strategic Bombing Survey, Overall report (European War), 30 September 1945. Chart No 16.

Like the VVS the *Luftwaffe* became largely a Tactical force, a point underlined in October. Close Air Support had been distributed between the dive-bombers (*Stukagruppen*), fighter-bombers (*Schlachtgruppen*) and anti-tank units (*Panzerjägerstaffeln*), but it was clear a rationalisation was required and on 18 October 1943 these units were organised into *Schlachtgeschwader*. SG 4 (formerly *Sch.G 2*) and SG 10 (formerly *SKG 10*) already had *Jabos*, while two *Jabo Gruppen* from *Sch.G 1* joined SG 2 and SG 77. The Hs 129 were concentrated in *IV/SG 9*. The remainder of the *Schlachtgruppen* had the Ju 87, although *II./SG 2* also retained a few Hs 123 B biplanes until May 1944, but they were gradually replaced by *Jabos* between April 1944 and December 1944, apart from *III./SG 2* and the *Panzerjägerstaffeln*. Many of the *Stukas* would be transferred to the *Nachtschlachtgruppen* which were organised at the same time from *Störkampfgruppen*. [80]

Even the *Kampfgruppe* were diverted away increasingly from interdicting communications to striking enemy concentrations in missions which often lasted only an hour. Worse still, they suffered the indignity of being used increasingly as transport units because only the bombers had the firepower to protect themselves and their precious cargoes from the packs of Russian fighters. The one area where they retained an Operational role was in interdicting the enemy rail system with dedicated rail-busting *Staffeln*. [81] The erosion of the bomber force was completed by the reformers Korten and Koller who strongly advocated the creation of a strategic bombing force and prevailed upon both Hitler and Göring to sanction the move which was authorised on 26 November. In December *Fliegerkorps IV*, under *Generalleutnant* Rudolf Meister since 4 September, was withdrawn from *Luftflotte 4* and was assigned most of the Eastern Front *Kampfgruppen*, spending most of the winter and spring re-equipping and training as *Auffrischungsstab Ost* and reverting to its original designation on 31 March when it began some strategic and operational missions [82]. Crises saw the temporary assignment of *Kampfgruppen* to the front, especially in April and May when 57 were lost to enemy action, but for the most part Korten and Koller succeeded in conserving their force whose strength grew from 286 aircraft on New Year's Day to 471 by 1 June despite the loss of 131 in accidents, and with the summer campaign imminent they eagerly anticipated its use after a dismal year.

During the late summer and autumn of 1943 the *Wehrmacht* was pushed back along most of the Eastern Front with the main effort in the Ukraine, where the Russians reached the Dnieper by the end of September. Greim and Dessloch were unable to influence events, their forces acting as little more than firemen flying from one crisis to another, Dessloch having to despatch *I./KG 55* because of the crisis in Italy where it arrived on 28 July and returned to *Luftflotte 4* on 19 August having failed to fly a single mission. [83] Seidemann supported Manstein's left and Pflugbeil, then Meister, was on his right, while Angerstein's *Fliegerkorps I* covered *Heeresgruppe A* which slowly evacuated the Taman Peninsula and finally abandoned it on 9 October. [84]

The late summer campaign saw the Russians stab deep into Dessloch's infrastructure, *Feldluftgaukommando XXV*, overrunning supply depots and work shops so that many of the 164 aircraft sent by Dessloch's units for overhaul in August were lost. The Russian advance also isolated the Crimea and while Angerstein was briefly transferred to the 'mainland' at Nikolayev on 14 October he returned a few weeks later, possibly on 7 November when *Generalmajor* Paul Deichmann relieved him, but his subsequent career suggests he had failed to gain *ObdL*'s confidence. The difficulties of directing the defence of the Crimea and support for *Heeresgruppe A* meant Deichmann did not remain long and during December he moved to Kirovograd, the remaining units on the peninsula being assigned to *Einsatzstab Fliegerkorps I*, as *Seefliegerführer Schwarzes Meer* under *Oberst* Joachim Bauer was renamed. To support *17. Armee* on the peninsula, an airlift was organised from 5 December and placed in the reliable hands of Morzik as *Transportfliegerführer 2 der Luftflotte 4* with some 200 aircraft.

Stalingrad and Tunisia had demonstrated that the *Luftwaffe* transport force could no longer consist of a few *Transportgruppen* for airborne operations augmented by ad hoc units during crises. Morzik's *LTF* had become a front-line command known as *Transportfliegerführer 1* or *Ost*, and served in this role during 1942, but a centralised administrative transport command to organise and to support the *Transportgruppen* was an urgent requirement. It was eventually formed on 15 May 1943 under Coeler as *Fliegerkorps XIV*, based at Tutow and organised from the airfield staff. It had five *Transportgeschwader* and three *Gruppen* comprising in total 673 aircraft but the majority were, and would continue to be, the 11-year-old Ju 52 when their enemies largely relied on the next-generation Douglas DC 3. [85]

ObdL assembled a substantial transport force in October just as the Russians crossed the Dnieper with 268 aircraft on 1 November. With the Russian drive westwards, air transport became key to the survival of isolated *Wehrmacht* formations, notably *1. Panzerarmee* under *Generaloberst* Hans Hube which was isolated in mid-March 1944 and faced the prospect of facing a 'mini-Stalingrad' when most of *Heeresgruppen Süd* and *A* withdrew into Rumania. Hube decided to strike out for Poland and fought his way to safety by mid-April greatly aided by a new air supply operation organised by Morzik again with some 200 aircraft which sometimes flew five sorties a night. The well-organised operation saw some 8,000 sorties being flown and some 3,500 tonnes of supplies being delivered, but between November and April Dessloch's *Transportgruppen* lost 238 aircraft destroyed or badly damaged, 129 to enemy action. [86] Despite this success, both Manstein and *Generalfeldmarschall* von Kleist, the *Heeresgruppe A* commander, were relieved and their commands renamed *Heeresgruppen Nordukraine* and *Südukraine*.

Morzik's airlift to the Crimea became an evacuation operation as the Russians prepared to storm the peninsula. Bauer had 127 combat aircraft at the beginning of April plus 20 seaplanes and some Rumanian aircraft while the Russians had 1,250. Fighting was fierce with the *Luftwaffe* flying 3,795 sorties from 8 to 22 April, but Hitler prevaricated about evacuation even as the Russians attacked. Between 12 April 1944 and 13 May, when the last Axis troops surrendered near Sevastopol, Morzik's men flew 765 sorties and brought out 14,120 troops, mostly wounded.

At the other end of the front *Luftflotte 1*, under Pflugbeil from 4 September 1943 following Korten's elevation to *ObdL*, had been a backwater since 1941. But the Russians, who had relieved the siege of Leningrad in January 1943, now decided to ensure the safety of the city. On 14 January 1944 they launched an offensive which pushed the Germans some 180 kilometres back, but fortunately the army group commander, *Generalfeldmarschall* Georg von Kuechler, had been granted permission to build a rear defensive position which stopped the advance. Pflugbeil had 294 combat aircraft on New Year's Day augmented by some 90 *Nachtschlachtflieger*, rising to some 400 aircraft by the beginning of March. He faced 1,300 aircraft, but he was still able to give a good account of himself by destroying 260 enemy aircraft for the loss of about 180 aircraft, 110 to enemy action. [87]

On 11 April 1944 *ObdL* and *RLM* were finally merged as *Oberkommando der Luftwaffe* (Luftwaffe Command) or *OKL*, bringing the *Luftwaffe* in line with the other services. [88] With the imminence of the 1944 summer campaign season, the *Luftwaffe* hoped to repeat this defensive success and to strike deadly blows but the omens were bad, for everywhere the *Luftwaffe* was on the defensive, even over the *Reich*.

Chapter Eight

The Shield cracks and the Sword breaks

In the summer of 1943 the *Reich*'s air defences suffered two crises as the British and American bomber crusades got into their stride. The former was largely contained, but just as the night defenders had their greatest success, the day defenders were brought to the brink of disaster.

By the summer of 1943 Kammhuber had 40,000 personnel (including 14,000 women) in *Fliegerkorps XII* and nearly 350 aircraft, excluding Sperrle's *Luftflotte 3* night fighter forces, with 76 per cent of interceptions leading to kills. But there were problems; RAF bomber streams, which were organised to ensure that targets were bombed within 40 minutes, were difficult to detect and to track, while the inflexibility of Kammhuber's defensive system made it impossible to concentrate the night fighter force against it. Not only was the *Nachtjagdwaffe* command and control too rigid, but also not all of Kammhuber's 28 bases were adequately equipped with night-landing aids. [1] Harris's Bomber Command was increasingly an instrument of retribution rather than retaliation. As more squadrons received four-engined heavy bombers with H2S on-board navigation radar and bombing support systems such as 'Oboe' and 'Gee' were perfected, the British were able to strike cities with a high degree of precision, delivering 1,000 tonnes of bombs per night, a figure doubled within a few months (see Table 8-1 for statistics of the British campaign).

Table 8-1: Night strategic bomber campaign, July 1943–June 1944

Quarter	Sorties	Lost	Percentage	N/F claims
Q3 1943	15,463	579	3.74	668
Q4 1943	11,804	485	4.10	444
Q1 1944	14,551	728	5.00	825
Q2 1944	15,493	318	2.05	856

Sources: Middlebrook/Everitt. UKNA Air 14/2666–75. UKNA Air 24/937–938.

Studies have shown that Harris' 'area attack' policy helped to restrict any German industry gains achieved through rationalisation. Facilities were destroyed and the random nature of the attacks (from the German perspective) disrupted the supply of components and materiel, forcing companies to carry larger stocks than they required and making them vulnerable. At a time when concentration was beginning to prove profitable, the authorities had to disperse industry, forcing a growing dependency upon transport and reliance upon skilled labour at small firms. By the beginning of 1945, Speer calculated that when compared with production which might have been achieved if his factories had been untouched, strategic bombing by both the Allies had caused a 35 per cent shortfall in tank production, 31 per cent in aircraft and 42 per cent in trucks. It was one reason why only half the aircraft scheduled in 1942 to be produced in 1944 emerged from the factories. Part of this shortfall was due to poor morale, displayed in high levels of absenteeism, among German workers (especially among female workers, who comprised half the industrial workforce in 1944). This increased from 4 per cent to 25 per cent between 1940 and 1944 in some (non-aviation) factories, compared to 3 per cent with foreign workers (these under-performed German workers by up to 80%), who could be more easily 'disciplined' [2].

The catalyst which changed the *Nachtjagdwaffe* from July 1943 was one for which the Germans should have prepared. Tests on the Düppel estate during the spring of 1940 showed *Würzburg* could be jammed by strips of metal chaff (which the Germans called '*Düppel*'), but Göring thwarted Martini's attempts to develop counter-measures because he feared this would alert the enemy to the sensors' vulnerability. Milch took a different view and chaired a conference on 16 July which reviewed the night-fighting situation and pushed for more flexible tactics concentrating forces upon the bomber streams. Milch was worried about the prospect of new Allied advances in electronic warfare, and the meeting led to the establishment of the *Reichsstelle für Hochfrequenz-Forschung* (Reich High-Frequency Research Establishment) with some 3,000 scientists [3]. To support flexible tactics, which were to complement *Himmelbett* (see Chapter Four), Milch on 21 July requested new airborne radars from Telefunken and hoped to inflict 20–30 per cent losses. [4]

The British had similar concerns about the use of chaff, which they called 'Window', upon their own radars but these concerns were allayed as centimetric (0.5 GHz and above) sensors were introduced and, after a *Luftwaffe* crew defected in a brand new Ju 88 R-1, and they were given the opportunity of evaluating *Lichtenstein* B/C radar, they decided to use 'Window', offensively. [5] A conference hosted by Churchill on 15 July , the day before the establishment of the *Reichsstelle für Hochfrequenz-Forschung*, authorised Bomber Command's use of 'Window' and from 24/25 July, the chaff supported devastating attacks upon Hamburg (Operation 'Gomorrah') and then the Ruhr, which continued until 2/3 August. The second Hamburg raid (27/28 July) created a firestorm which killed some 40,000 people, leading Göring to notify Milch that '...the (*Luftwaffe's*) main effort is to be focused forthwith on the defence of the Reich.' [6]

'Gomorrah' proved to be a catalyst for the German night fighters, accelerating changes which had already begun, but the speed of the recovery surprised Harris. The first use of 'Window' cut his loss rate to 1.5 per cent (12 aircraft), but the next night, when Essen was attacked, the rate doubled to 3.7 per cent (26 aircraft). In the short term, Bomber Command's overall losses on major missions dropped from 5.53 per cent to 3.29 per cent, but they then climbed rapidly and by September were 4.65 per cent in Main Force missions. This reflected the German success in adapting rapidly to the situation.

Within three days of the first Hamburg raid, Germany's leading aviation electronics scientist, *Dr* Hans Plendl developed 'de-lousing' (ECCM) systems for the air and ground radars, although these often cut sensor range. The *FuMG 404 Jagdschloss* (Hunting Lodge) panoramic radar with 120 kilometres range was also introduced, together with the *Egon* navigation system, exploiting 70 *Freya-Gemse* emitters to control fighters up to 200 kilometres (124 miles) away. Production of *Lichtenstein SN-2* (see Chapter Four) was slow (only 49 sets delivered by November 1943), but by May 1944 1,000 had been delivered to provide immunity to 'Window', improved short-range resolution and a simplified display. [7] Yet the growing effectiveness of the new flexible tactics did not depend just upon the new radars: the old *Lichtenstein* could be used to home in on 'Window' clouds which acted as trail for experienced pilots, while passive sensors were even more useful. The H2S navigation and *Monica* tail-warning radars carried by the bombers could be tracked by *Naxos-Z* and the new *FuG 227 Flensburg* at distances of 50 and l0 kilometres (30 and 6 miles) respectively. [8] By incorporating *Naxos* into *Würzburg* during the autumn to create *Naxburg*, the enemy bomber stream's progress could be followed from the ground at distances of up to 256 kilometres. Reports from *Naxburg*, code-named '*Flammen*' were intercepted by the British through 'Ultra', and it was calculated that between January and February they were responsible for the destruction of 42 per cent (210) of the 494 heavy bombers lost over Germany in the same period, yet the British refused to believe that the bombers could be tracked through H2S transmissions. [9]

Table 8-2: Luftwaffe night fighter statistics, July 1943–May 1944

Month	Strength	Reich sorties	Losses Enemy	Losses Accident	Total claims
Jul 1943	349/121	N/A	9/9	43/7	165 (46)
Aug 1943	409/127	N/A	45/17	35/16	276 (43)
Sep 1943	430/84	N/A	29/3	52/11	227 (85)
Oct 1943	442/82	1,381	37/2	58/18	174 (42)
Nov 1943	466/94	756	32/3	44/14	95 (2)
Dec 1943	524/90	771	35/7	48/5	175 (23)
Jan 1944	528/67	1,651	102/6	58/13	321 (25)
Feb 1944	497/73	1,243	70/5	37/15	187 (15)
Mar 1944	585/80	1,676	76/13	91/11	317 (34)
Apr 1944	357/94	1,640	66/21	53/25	212 (14)
May 1944	363/109	1,001	61/45	54/46	277 (8)

Source: Flugzeugbestand und Bewegungsmeldungen (BA MA RL 2 III/877-882). Figures Reich/Luftflotte 3. Claims in parenthesis are Wilde Sau units.

On 29 July the night fighter expert *Oberleutnant* Viktor von Lossberg, head of the night fighter section at *RLM*'s *Technische Amt* (see Chapter Four), presented proposals for new tactics at a conference chaired by Milch (for *Luftwaffe* night fighter statistics, see Table 8-2). The investment in *Himmelbett* could not simply be abandoned but it was adapted to meet Lossberg's tactical idea with spare fighters assembled behind the *Räume* and *Fühlungshälter* ('contact-keepers'), using *Y-Verfahren*, to detect the bomber stream leaders. These aircraft were not covered by 'Window', and *Himmelbett* paced them, broadcasting location and direction data over a common frequency to bring the rest of the night fighters into the stream. The new tactics dubbed *Zahme Sau* ('Pet Lamb'), depended upon the rapid introduction of new airborne radars for all night fighters but, co-incidentally, an interim measure was already taking shape. [10] In April, the inventive bomber ace, Hajo Herrmann (see Chapter Four), had persuaded the fighter general, Adolf Galland, to authorise experiments with an *ad hoc* force of pilots 'moonlighting' from the *Fluglehrerschule* (Flying Instructors' School) at Brandenburg-Briest. On 26 June this led to the creation of a *Nachtjagdversuchskommando* which claimed 12 victories (it was credited with six) on 3/4 July. Göring, with Milch's enthusiastic backing, ordered its expansion to a *Gruppe*, with Herrmann as *Kommodore* of the '*Stab/JG Herrmann*', which was redesignated *JG 300* on 20 August and whose tactics were dubbed *Wilde Sau* ('Wild Boar'). [11]

Kammhuber and *Generaloberst* Weise, commander of *Luftwaffe Befehlshaber Mitte*, remained sceptical about cutting the night fighters loose even after Lossberg made two presentations to them, but their objections were overruled by *Oberst* Bernd von Brauchitsch, Göring's adjutant and the son of the former Army Chief of Staff, who reminded them that the system was to be accepted '…on the *Reichmarschall*'s orders', and it was formally adopted on 1 August. [12] Lossberg's *Zahme Sau* system appears to have been used from 9/10 August, but its first real test was against a raid on Nuremberg on 27/28 August which suffered 4.9 per cent losses (33 aircraft, although 48 were claimed). Yet until the early winter, Hermann's *Wilde Säue* dominated the defence and helped inflict 6.7 per cent losses during an attack which wrecked the Peenemünde missile research base on 17/18 August, and 7.9 per cent upon bombers attacking Berlin on 23/24 August. At one point Göring impetuously informed Herrmann that he was making Kammhuber his subordinate, but Herrmann observed the proprieties while establishing his own command posts within the *Luftgaue* as his pilots, answerable to no one, rushed around the skies.

Their success led to Herrmann being given his own, autonomous *30. Jagddivision* on 26 September, to which were added two new *Geschwader*. But by the beginning of October they had only 58 aircraft, with four *Gruppen* having no aircraft at all, which meant they were forced to borrow from the *Jagdgruppen*. When aircraft were returned they were often badly damaged, usually by *Flak* fire, but even more frequently they were lost. *Nachtjagdgruppen* aircrew observed cynically that most of Herrmann's pilots had more parachute jumps than victories to their credit. In retaliation the *Jagdgruppen* began allocating the *Wilde Säue* worn-out, or even unserviceable fighters which pushed up the accident rate, especially when Herrmann demanded his men take off in conditions where, as one observed, '…even the birds were walking'. This led to a demoralising increase in casualties with enemy (or 'friendly') action accounting for 78 of the 119 *Wilde Sau* aircraft lost between 1 October 1943 and 1 March 1944. The effectiveness of *Wilde Sau* declined rapidly: the *Verbände's* claims of total night victories was 28 per cent in July and reached a peak of 37 per cent in September before dropping to 13 per cent in December and about 8 per cent in the next two months. With the *Reich* under growing threat from American heavy bombers and the *Jagdgruppen* ill-fitted for bad-weather operations, the *Wilde Säue* were absorbed by the day fighter force on 16 March 1944 and *30. Jagddivision* was disbanded, Herrmann being given command of *1. Jagddivision*. However, the *Wilde Säue* still flew occasional night missions notably on 22/23 April 1944 (nine victories claimed) and 22/23 May 1944 (eight) with the last two victories apparently claimed by *Oberleutnant* Karl-Heinz Seeler who was credited with two victories on the night of 22/23 May 1944. [13]

Wilde Sau tactics were widely adopted by the conventional *Nachtjagdgruppen* although *Himmelbett* continued to be used extensively, but against occasional individual targets such as minelayers, and had clearly outlived its usefulness. Its demise was accelerated by the decline in *Nachtjagdwaffe* serviceable strength during the autumn (390 aircraft on 20 September, 221 on 20 October and 244 on 20 November) which led to the decision to focus upon the Main Force early in November. Kammhuber's scepticism of *Zahme Sau* and his continued belief in *Himmelbett*, although it claimed only 48 of the 250 victories during August, meant his star was waning. [14] *Zahme Sau* was plagued by a shortage of airborne radars, while plans to provide a running commentary from *Fühlungshälter* were abandoned for fear of attracting intruders. However, as more airborne radars became available *Himmelbett*'s days were clearly marked and during the first three months of 1944 most of the *Nachtjagdraumführer* were disbanded, although Sperrle retained them until May.

The growing Eighth Air Force daylight threat helped undermine Kammhuber whose *Fliegerkorps XII* had also been responsible for daylight defence, tactical control being devolved to the *Jafü* staffs. The organisation inflicted heavy losses but was clearly inadequate and on 15 September Korten, who had *Gauleiter* support for improved defensive measures, renamed *Fliegerkorps XII* as *I. Jagdkorps* to become a day/night fighter command. Korten and Koller had wanted Lossberg as the new commander but he refused and they then selected *Generalmajor* 'Beppo' Schmid, possibly through Göring's influence. [15] Schmid returned to grace following a year in the wilderness after his intelligence organisation was found to be a major source of information for the *Rote Kapelle* ('Red Orchestra') Russian spy ring which was led by a well-connected *Luftwaffe* officer, Harro Schulze-Boysen. [16] Although Schmid was not directly involved, the discovery provided an excuse for moving him to a new appointment and he was relieved by *Oberst* Josef Kogel on 14 October 1942. [17] He had led the *Hermann Göring Division* in North Africa and before his new appointment had been working in the *RLM* and *ObdL* as an *Offizier zbV*. He would followed Kammhuber's precedent by using the new headquarters as a day fighter co-ordination centre, leaving tactical decisions to the newly formed *Jagddivisionen* which were also responsible for night fighters (for *I. Jagdkorps* night operations to mid-December, see Table 8-3).

Kammhuber was now *Kommandierender General der Nachtjagd* under Schmid and presided over a slow recovery of the arm, but Göring remained dissatisfied with him. The excuse to remove him arose when Harris began his new offensive, what became 'the Battle of Berlin', a series of deep penetration missions exploiting new navigation aids and reducing the length of the bomber stream; the first raid on the German capital on 18/19 November cost him only 2 per cent of his force and Kammhuber his job. [18] Galland reluctantly accepted responsibility for the night fighter force, but he relied heavily upon Herrmann until the appointment in March 1944 of *Oberst* Werner Streib, the *Kommodore* of *NJG 1*, as *General der Nachtjagd* and Galland's subordinate. Kammhuber became acting commander of *Luftflotte 5*, Stumpff having been assigned to the *Führer* reserve and sent on leave on 6 November for unknown reasons. Stumpff briefly returned to Norway to keep a watch on his replacement whose position was confirmed on 23 December, Stumpff himself then departing for Germany to command *Luftflotte Reich*.

Table 8-3: I. Jagdkorps Night Fighter weekly operations, 20 September–19 December 1943

Week	*Wilde Sau*	*Zahme Sau*	Sectors	Other	Losses
20–26 Sept	383	18	56	2	9
27 Sept-3 Oct	401	19	145	-	16
4–10 Oct	298		175	1	15
11–17 Oct	-	-	4	1	
18–24 Oct	310	56	82		17
25–31 Oct	38		20	-	1
1–7 Nov	33	25	31	_	2
8–14 Nov	-		L	2	-
15–21 Nov	83	3	53	21	11
22–28 Nov	284	78	118		7
6–12 Dec	-		14		
13–19 Dec	30	28	42	-	6

Notes: 'Other' includes *Freijagd* and *Y-Verfahren* missions. Data for 1–5 December is incomplete.

Source: BA MA RL 8/91–2.

From each *Jagddivision*'s *Grossgefechtsstand* ('main command post'), or 'battle opera houses' as Galland called them, and *Jagdkorps* headquarters came a running commentary on the location, altitude and direction of the enemy formations and the meteorological situation, as well as instructions to fighter formations which were given specific initial headings to avoid confusion with the enemy. The Anne-Marie forces' radio station was also later exploited, broadcasting music to indicate the areas under threat, for example dance music for Berlin and beer cellar songs for Munich. [19]

To disrupt this command and control system from the late summer onwards the British introduced diversionary raids and a series of electronic counter-measures to jam radar, communications and even *Y-Verfahren* signals. One of the most startling was 'Corona', first used on 22/23 October, in which a Canterbury-based transmitter provided a false commentary, in the middle of which the German pilots heard one man say, *'The Englishman is now swearing'*, whereupon the genuine controller retorted, *'It is not the Englishman who is swearing, it is me.'* The false commentaries were often provided by German emigrés, including women, to match the introduction of *Luftwaffehelferinnen* (female auxiliaries) and on occasion the women would exchange invective like fish-wives. As a result of these, and other activities, only 5 of 28 missions despatched by Bomber Command (joined on a few occasions by the Eighth Air Force) against Germany between 2/3 August and 17/18 November suffered losses in excess of 5.8 per cent, while losses in other major missions during October and November averaged 3.65 per cent. [20]

The winter saw the *Nachtjagdwaffe*'s effectiveness growing as Harris continued the Battle of Berlin, believing that the capital's destruction would cost him up to 500 bombers but cost Germany the war. The night fighter force had only 258 serviceable aircraft when the offensive started and 247 a month later, but the new sensors and tactics began making their presence felt. The first to suffer were Stirling and Halifax

II/V crews because their bombers' poor performance exposed them to the full fury of the defences. Within a week the Stirlings were withdrawn from Main Force operations followed by the older Halifaxes in late February, reducing Main Force strength by 250 aircraft. The defences gradually became deadlier, especially to deep-penetration raids, as *Zahme Sau* now came into its own, partly as more *Lichtenstein SN-2* sets became available and partly with the decline of the *Himmelbett* system. The main night fighter force now orbited radio and visual beacons like moths, until the *Fühlungshälter* made contact with, and trailed, the bomber stream, calling in the fighters to exact bloody retribution upon the so-called '*Terrorflieger*' and by 30/31 March 1944 13 (39%) of the 33 Main Force attacks upon Germany suffered losses in excess of 5.8 per cent. The increasing flexibility of the *Nachtjagdgruppen* meant they were no longer territorially bound, and on occasion Danish-based units inter-cepted bombers over Stuttgart.

Despite the growing 'butcher's bill', Harris remorselessly pursued his objectives, with losses in excess of 5 per cent inflicted in seven out of nine Main Force missions during January, although in the first quarter of 1944 the number of serviceable night fighters varied from 179 to 273 aircraft. [21] Dense cloud, diversions and counter-measures as well as a growing commitment to targets in France brought some relief to Harris's hard-pressed airmen during February, but on 30/31 March the defenders had their greatest success against a Nuremberg-bound mission, destroying 95 bombers, or 11.9 per cent of the force, to inflict Bomber Command's worst losses of the war. This forced Harris to end the Berlin campaign, ostensibly to pursue an operational role preparing for D-Day. The battle had cost Harris more than 1,000 bombers, and he had failed totally in his objectives.

Between December and April, the night fighters of *I. Jagdkorps* and *30. Jagddivision* flew 7,000 sorties and claimed 1,200 victories, but at a high price with 636 aircraft lost, 349 to enemy action; indeed losses during the first quarter of 1944 rose from 3.5–6 per cent of sorties, the victims including 18 *Experten*. The constant movement between beacons took its toll: between 15 and 26 March *I./NJG 6* lost six aircraft which ran out of fuel and two in action and there were further casualties due to bad weather, while an increasing number of aircraft were falling to intrud-ers, known to the *Luftwaffe* as *Indianer* ('Red Indians'), which prowled the bomber streams like wolves in sheep's clothing. The threat from intruders grew from October 1943 when long-range Mosquitos began operating over central Germany, leading to the development of the *FuG 216 Neptun-R* tail-warning radar as well as an ECCM system, *Freya-Halbe*, although most of the latter were assigned to *IV./NJG 5* protecting the U-boat pens in western France.

In April and May, Harris's Main Force visited German cities on 14 occasions, restricting themselves to targets in western Germany, yet the defences remained formidable. [22] During the spring Stumpff transferred four of his 24 *Nachtjagdgruppen* to Sperrle's Luftflotte 3, but in May two units were driven back into Germany by Allied air power, to give Schmid 320 serviceable night fighters by the end of the month (Sperrle later requested the transfer of *3. Jagddivision* to his command, but Stumpff refused). Meanwhile the Germans continued to improve their electronic defences, and by the summer development was well advanced on the wide-angle *FuG 228 Lichtenstein SN-3* and centimetric *FuG 240 Berlin N1a* airborne radars. However, ambitious plans for automated control and data links were abandoned at Milch's instigation in February 1944 to focus on more pragmatic technology.

One problem for which there was never any solution was the Mosquito bomber, which, although classified as 'light' by the British, could carry a similar bomb load to Berlin as the B-17 heavy bomber and was often used to mark targets as well as being deployed on harassing attacks. Night fighters lacked the performance and day fighters lacked the sensors to catch their irritating foe, making the destruction of a Mosquito at night almost an act of God. It was as difficult intercepting the Mosquito in daytime, and two units created for this purpose in July 1943 had so little luck that they were disbanded within four months. During 1944 Mosquito bomber units flew 11,690 night sorties against Germany. For its part, the *Nachtjagdwaffe* flew 1,836 sorties against the Mosquitos and lost 98 aircraft for little return because many of the 58 British bombers lost that year fell to *Flak*. [23]

Just as the *Nachtjagdgruppen* achieved their greatest success the daylight battle for Germany's skies became more desperate. [24] American heavy bombers first appeared over Wilhelmshaven on 27 January 1943 and their formations were veritable hedgehogs, for while European bombers were usually armed with rifle-calibre weapons the Americans had the 0.50 calibre (12.7 mm) Browning which had been designed as an anti-tank weapon and had similar ballistic characteristics to the *Luftwaffe*'s 2 cm Oerlikon, which had also been designed to stop tanks. [25] They flew in tight formations called 'boxes', which exposed the lower formations to 'friendly' bombs and a rain of spent cartridges, but the Americans were confident that their bombers would brush away opposition en route to their targets (see Table 8-4 for daylight operations against the *Reich*).

Table 8-4: The daylight assault on the Reich

Quarter	Sorties		Losses	
	Bombers	Fighters	Bombers	Fighters
Q3 1943	1,754	N/A	197	N/A
Q4 1943	7,726	10,759	394	100
Q1 1944	14,870	29,685	659	335
Q2 1944	23,394	35,038	340	371

Sources: Freeman, *Mighty Eighth War Diary*. UKNA Air 24/937 and 938.

The 'boxes', or '*Pulks*' as the *Luftwaffe* called them, posed a major tactical challenge to the *Jagdgruppen*, not only because of their formidable, interlocking firepower but also because they operated at 6,000–7,600 metres (20,000–25,000 feet), close to the limits of the Bf 109s' and Fw 190s' high-altitude performance. Worse still, fighter armament proved inadequate, an average 20 rounds of 2cm ammunition being required to shoot down a B-17, yet an analysis of gun camera film showed only 2 per cent of rounds aimed at a bomber actually hit it, so that 1,000 rounds of ammunition (23 seconds' firing time) were actually fired to achieve a result. [26] The introduction of 3cm MK108 cannon (augmented by 15mm MG 151 heavy machine guns) meant that only three hits were required to destroy an '*Ami Viermot*' (American four-engined bomber), but often the new weapons had to be installed in underwing gondolas ('Bathtubs'), which degraded performance.

Table 8-5: Luftwaffe day fighter force, April 1943–May 1944

Month	Single-engine fighters	Twin-engine fighters	Total
Jan 1943	234	1	235
Feb 1943	188	1	189
Mar 1943	190	1	191
Apr 1943	262	1	263
May 1943	274	1	275
Jun 1943	394	39	433
Jul 1943	419	38	457
Aug 1943	452	58	510
Sept 1943	615	171	786
Oct 1943	531	97	628
Nov 1943	565	123	688
Dec 1943	589	111	700
Jan 1944	455	80	535
Feb 1944	541	92	633
Mar 1944	513	59	572
Apr 1944	758	76	834
May 1944	691	110	801

Source: BA MA RL 2 III/877-882.

For three years the day bomber threat to the Reich had been confined to light attacks largely made on the periphery and when the first American raid was made there were barely 160 operational fighters (see Table 8-5 for day fighter strength). Night fighters augmented the defenders when the second American raid was made on 4 February 1943, the Bf 110s demonstrating, as they had in the first months of the war, that their formidable armament could be terribly effective against day bombers. But two of the eight night fighters fell to the Americans' equally formidable armament and the tactic of deploying *Alarmrotten* ('Alert Sections') threatened the loss of valuable night fighter crews and aircraft (see Table 8-6 for day fighter losses). *Hauptmann* Ludwig Bekker, *Kapitän* of 12./*NJG 1* and a 44-victory *Experte*, was lost on 26 February and *Hauptmann* Hans-Joachim Jabs who led the first mission, was also shot down during daylight, yet night fighter crews were still sent against the *Viermots* until the end of January. [27]

Following these early raids, Galland vainly asked Hitler to expand the *Jagdwaffe* which gradually gained the measure of the new threat. As Brigadier-General Ira C. Eaker's US Eighth Army Air Force pushed deeper into the Reich, the *Jagdwaffe* inflicted heavy losses on the so-called '*Dicke Auto*' or '*Möbelwagen*' ('Big Cars' or 'Furniture Vans') – 7 per cent on the first mission over the Ruhr on 4 March. The German fighters increasingly attacked the bombers from the front so as to exploit the bombers' poor nose armament. [28] Individual attacks by *Schwarm* were abandoned in favour of a 'wolf-pack' approach with co-ordinated *Staffeln* and on 17 April, this tactic destroyed almost 14 per cent of the bombers attacking Bremen, leading to the first doubts being expressed by the Americans about the ability of the heavy bombers to conduct unescorted missions successfully [29]. One solution was to have some bombers modified as dedicated 'escorts' with increased armament and ammunition, but experiments with the YB-40, a form of converted B-17 'gunship', over France were unsuccessful, as will be noted later. Meanwhile, the *Luftwaffe* also experimented with stand-off attacks to break up 'boxes' through bombs and modified *Nebelwerfer* rocket-launchers with unguided air-to-air rockets.

Table 8-6: Reich day fighter force losses

Month	Single-engine fighters		Twin-engine fighters		Total Losses	
	Enemy	Accid	Enemy	Accid	Enemy	Accid
Jan 1943	9	10	-	-	9	10
Feb 1943	8	17	-	-	8	17
Mar 1943	16	19	-	-	16	19
Apr 1943	12	22	-	-	12	22
May 1943	31	34	-	-	31	34
Jun 1943	37	40	5	1	42	41
Jul 1943	86	47	10	2	96	49
Aug 1943	56	39	-	5	56	44
Sept 1943	21	64	-	4	21	68
Oct 1943	106	80	20	9	126	89
Nov 1943	106	48	21	6	127	54
Dec 1943	127	68	27	18	154	86
Jan 1944	95	64	13	22	108	86
Feb 1944	158	42	49	11	207	53
Mar 1944	234	79	25	5	259	84
Apr 1944	388	122	20	14	408	136
May 1944	391	146	30	20	421	166

Source: BA MA RL 2 III/877-882.

In mid-August – under tremendous pressure – Eaker began deep penetration missions, although monthly loss rates over Germany had been climbing remorselessly since May, averaging 6.4 per cent and nearly 10 per cent per month in the first two quarters of 1943 (with peaks of nearly 9.5 per cent and 15 per cent in February and April respectively). In real terms 248 aircraft had fallen to an efficient, well-oiled defensive system which was exploiting the bombers' weakness. On the afternoon of 17 August Schweinfurt and Regensburg were struck by 315 bombers which were escorted across the German border by P-47 Thunderbolts, but the moment they departed, the *Jagdgruppen* struck. The Americans suffered a 19 per cent loss rate (64 bombers destroyed or damaged beyond repair) and losses might have been heavier had not part of the force flown south to North African bases rather than return to England. The *Luftwaffe* lost 42 aircraft (including nine night fighters and *Zerstörer*) and a score of aircrew killed, and Göring received another tongue-lashing from Hitler because of the damage inflicted, and he remained dissatisfied and blamed both the absence of a centralised day fighter organisation and 'skulking' fighter pilots. [30]

Three weeks later, on 6 September, a mission against Stuttgart by 111 bombers saw 16 per cent losses in what according to one historian '…proved to be one of the most costly fiascos in Eighth Air Force history.' [31]

In a crisis of confidence the USAAF toyed with converting to night operations and one squadron flew 27 shallow penetration night sorties from 15/16 September before reverting to leaflet missions, while 90 B-17s began conversion to night operations until confidence in day-bombing was restored. [32] The Americans also adopted British technology to deal with targets obscured by cloud, haze and smoke, and on 27 September a mission against Emden saw the first use of H2S (known to the Americans as H2X) radar. As more electronic aids were used for blind-bombing techniques, the Eighth Air Force also adopted, in all but name, the British policy of area attack. Electronic support was not ignored, and from October at least two groups in each combat wing carried 'Carpet' jammers for use against *Würzburg* radars, which cut *Flak* efficiency by half. [33]

It was against this background that the *I. Jagdkorps* was established on 15 September (see Table 8-7 for *I. Jagdkorps* operations). Schmid, like Kammhuber before him, hoped to establish a centralised fighter command but his hopes foundered on the rock of Sperrle's ego which was as substantial as his girth. Sperrle argued he was running a separate air theatre acting as a glacis to Fortress *Reich*. The best that Göring was able to do was to persuade him to transfer tactical control of *Luftflotte* 3's two *Luftgaue* (*Luftgaue VII* in Munich and *XII/XIII* Wiesbaden) to Weise's *Luftwaffe Befehlshaber Mitte* early in November. On New Year's Day Weise also received from *Luftflotten 1* and *4 Luftgaue I* (Königsberg), *VIII* (Krakow) and *XVII* (Vienna) but lost *Luftgau XI* (Hamburg) to *Generalmajor* Eduard, *Ritter* von Schleich's *Kommandierende General der Deutschen Luftwaffe in Dänemark* as fears grew of an invasion of Denmark (34).

Table 8-7: I. *Jagdkorps* operations, 15 September 1943–June 1944

Month	Sorties	Losses	Percentage
Sept 1943	497	11	2.2
Oct 1943	3,840	119	3.1
Nov 1943	2,531	102	4.0
Dec 1943	1,153	88	7.6
Jan 1944	3,315	177	5.4
Feb 1944	4,242	379	8.2
Mar 1944	3,672	347	9.4
Apr 1944	4,505	469	9.2
May 1944	3,805	446	11.7
Jun 1944	1,264	187	14.9

Sources: BA MA RL 8/91–2.USNA T971 Roll 2, fr.82–3.

In an echo of the Battle of Britain the tactical discussion drifted towards ever-larger attack formations or 'Big Wings'. The problem, as over England, was assembling them, but the first success was on 10 October when four *Gruppen* assembled into a *Gefechtsverband* ('battle formation') which intercepted a raid on Münster and played a major role in the destruction of 30 bombers, nearly 11 per cent of those despatched. Following this success each *Jagddivision* was assigned a *Jagdgeschwader* whose *Stab* was to control a *Gefechtsverband* although there was a shortage of suitable leaders. They were no panacea, for they were difficult to assemble (as were the British 'Big Wings') and to control in the air, while inexperienced pilots had difficulty staying with the formation. [35]

While effective against bomber formations, the *Gefechtsverband* also developed into a means of meeting the ever-more powerful bomber escorts. [36] The P-47 Thunderbolt had made its debut on 8 April but for the first three months its radius of some 200 nautical miles (370 kilometres) was little better than the Spitfire, although it could absorb a formidable amount of battle damage. [37] The P-38 Lightning had a radius of 260 nautical miles (480 kilometres) on internal fuel but the twin-engined fighter could not dog-fight and its introduction into north-west Europe was delayed allowing the Mediterranean and Pacific theatres to have priority for these aircraft.

But from 28 July expendable fuel tanks (drop tanks) were introduced, extending the P-47's range to 290 nautical miles (540 kilometres) and in rapid stages to 410 nautical miles (760 kilometres) by the end of the year, allowing them to reach central Germany. Galland had anticipated the new threat but when Göring heard in July that enemy fighters had entered German air space his response was, as usual, to disbelieve it. When told that wrecked American fighters had been found near Aachen, he claimed that they had glided eastward after receiving fatal damage. When Galland objected, Göring blustered, 'I hereby give you an official order that they weren't there!' and stormed off. [38] With drop tanks the Lightning's range extended to some 450 nautical miles (830 kilometres) by the end of the year and by February 1944 to some 500 nautical miles (935 kilometres) – or to Berlin. [39]

By extending the range of his fighters Eaker cut the bombers' loss rate to 3 per cent and encouraged the Americans to begin striking targets as far east as the Rhine from 4 October. [40] The presence of the Thunderbolts also forced Schmid to withdraw *Jagdgruppen* from western Holland to the German border and as confidence returned, the Eighth Air Force flew further into Germany with renewed pressure on Eaker for deep penetration missions. On 14 October he bowed to pressure and flew another catastrophic mission against Schweinfurt in which he suffered almost 19 per cent casualties (67 bombers shot down or damaged beyond repair), most to fighters which flew 567 sorties and lost 21 aircraft. [41] Despite the losses, between 31 August and 31 October Eighth Air Force heavy bomber strength rose from 907 to 1,138, including replacements and non-operational second-line aircraft, and the number of crews from 806 to 1,116 [42].

The disaster raised questions over Eaker's leadership and in January he was 'kicked upstairs' to become commander of the Mediterranean Allied Air Forces, being replaced by Major-General James H. Doolittle. The inability of short-range RAF fighters to help the American bombers caused Anglo-American friction while within the Eighth Air Force attention focused upon providing adequate escort. Much was expected of the P-38 Lightning, which entered the fray on 15 October, but deliveries were slow and unlike the Pacific theatre, it proved no match for nimble, single-engined fighters possibly because the cold, moist European air played havoc with its Allison engines; indeed, half the Lightning losses during the winter of 1943/44 were to engine failure. [43] The backbone of Eaker's fighter groups remained the Thunderbolt but then it was discovered that the P-51B Mustang should be able to fly close escort missions all the way to Berlin if fitted with two 75 US-gallon drop tanks. P-51 escort missions began on 5 December while Eighth Air Force missions continued strictly under fighter escort which meant they were limited to the Rhine valley although the monthly bomber loss rate fell to 3.78 per cent, compared with 9.16 per cent in October.

Throughout this period the Reich-based *Tagjagdwaffe* was expanded from 275 aircraft on 1 May to 700, including 111 *Zerstörer*, on 1 December but only by stripping the hard-pressed Eastern and Mediterranean fronts. Other aircraft had to be deployed to the Danube valley to shield the oil fields of Rumania and Hungary. Galland did not neglect the infrastructure and organised a network of camouflaged airfields away from the main bases where fighters could be refuelled, re-armed and repaired, but were there were also refreshment rooms and medical, meteorological and briefing facilities. The network ensured that pilots could pursue the enemy and still fly two or even three sorties a day. [44]

With the New Year Doolittle inherited a slowly improving escort situation as Mustang strength expanded and he was willing to exploit the technology to the hilt and destroy German fighters. [45] Yet in a mission against aircraft factories in Oschersleben and Halberstadt on 11 January he lost another 60 bombers (nearly 11%) against a fighter force which flew only 239 sorties, Schmid later commenting that this was the last *Luftwaffe* victory over the US Army Air Force. Yet in the process he lost 40 aircraft, representing nearly 17 per cent of the aircraft despatched. [46]

This success occurred as there was another re-organisation of the *Reich*'s air defences. The need for a commander with experience of directing air operations meant that on 6 January Stumpff replaced Weise as leader of *Luftwaffe Befehlshaber Mitte*, the latter being upgraded on 9 February to *Luftflotte Reich* and moving its headquarters to a more central location in Brunswick-Querum. [47] Stumpff's appointment partly reflected *Gauleiter* discontent over the *Luftwaffe*'s inability to protect the *Reich*. He was not tainted with this failure, he was an experienced commander and he was a trained staff officer who quickly reformed the *Flugmeldedienst*, centralising the observer system to provide simplified overland tracking under *I. Jagdkorps* control and upgrading comint facilities. Unfortunately, as Koller observed in his diary, Stumpff was well-known for his prima donna temperament, while night fighter pioneer and *Experte*, Wolfgang Falck, who was now a staff officer, noted that, while not necessarily timid, he did seem acutely aware of how important was his survival to the war efforts. Yet he did back Schmid's moves for greater central control and on 31 March Sperrle's air defence forces were integrated with *Luftflotte Reich*. [48]

Stumpff inherited a deteriorating situation with casualties steadily rising. In September 1943 21 pilots were lost in action and further 68 in accidents but by December the figures had risen to 154 and 86 respectively. The problem became increasingly acute as Koller, at Göring's behest, demanded *Jagdgruppen* move from one divisional area to another to pursue bomber formations, although this exhausted both man and machine. [49] Not only did few fighter bases have navigation aids, but fewer pilots, especially the newer ones, were experienced in instrument flying which meant fewer interceptions being made in poor weather or visibility and in the coming months led to a high accident rate. This problem was highlighted at a conference which Schmid attended on 4 November when it was noted that fighters were grounded even when enemy bombers were striking German cities. In the face of American fighter escorts Weise had believed that the *Zerstörer* should revert to their original bomber-destroyer role, while the single-engine fighters tackled the escorts, but most people recognised that this was only a short-term solution; indeed from October to January an average of 20 *Zerstörer* per month were lost to enemy action and the *Gruppen* were gradually moved eastwards beyond enemy fighter range. [50]

The growing desperation of the *Jagdwaffe* was highlighted early in 1943 when *Major* Hans-Günther von Kornatzki proposed forming a volunteer *Staffel* willing to ram American lead aircraft, and although rejecting this in principle, Galland agreed to the formation in June 1943 of *Sturmstaffel 1* under Kornatzki to press home attacks in tight formations. The unit's success on 7 November led to a proposal to form heavy and light single-engine units. [51] It was decided the following day to form five light *Gruppen* with Bf 109 Gs to engage the escorts while three heavy *Sturmgruppen* ('Assault Groups') flying heavily armed and armoured Fw 190s struck the bombers. This was not implemented until April 1944 when *IV./JG 3* was formed with the remainder of the *Gruppe's* parent *Geschwader* consisting of light *Gruppen*. The first mission was delayed until 7 July. Meanwhile on 29 December another *I. Jagdkorps* conference had concluded depressingly that the weather, but mostly German numerical inferiority, would neutralise new tactics to engage escorted formations. [52]

The impact of the American long-range fighters was felt gradually with monthly bomber losses averaging 4.5 per cent from January to April 1944, dropping to 3.11 per cent in May when Mustangs began to fly the majority of escort missions. The real success of the American long-range fighters was in forcing the *Jagdgruppen* into a battle of attrition they could not win, with loss rates rising alarmingly from February to undermine the *Luftwaffe's* plans for expansion. In the first four months of 1944 the *Reich's* daylight defence force lost 982 fighters to enemy action and 358 to accidents, but it was the erosion of quality which was even more serious; four *Experten* with more than 100 kills in March, two in April and another two in May. In April the *Jagdgruppen* throughout Europe lost 489 pilots, the majority over Germany, but they received only 396 replacements. The American long-range fighters also ended the participation of multi-engined fighters in the Reich's air defence when, following a series of air-massacres of *Zerstörergruppen*, the *Nachtjagdgruppen* were effectively stood down on 30 January. By the summer Galland stopped using *Fühlungshälter* in daytime, partly because the ground organisation now provided adequate tracking.

Worse still from the German viewpoint was that on 21 January Doolittle had informed his staff that the fighters of Major-General William E. Kepner's 8th Fighter Command were not to escort the bombers passively but were to take the war to the enemy. Three days later Kepner assigned long-range fighters to patrol areas and once the bombers had passed through, they were free to raise mayhem, with airfields a favourite target. [53] Harried in the air and on the ground, it is little wonder that the less experienced German *Jagdflieger* developed *Jägerschreck* ('Fighter Fear'), which pressured them to break off engagements upon spotting Thunderbolts or Mustangs. On 21 May the Mustangs began autonomous offensive sweeps against the overstrained German rail network, and on the first day of 'Chattanooga' operations they attacked 225 locomotives and claimed 91 destroyed (in fact 105 were damaged).

That day 36 airfields were also attacked: 57 aircraft were destroyed (38 of them trainers) and 52 were damaged. [54] The effect of enemy fighters upon training was profound, creating *Kindermord* ('Massacre of the Innocents') in the schools which lost many students and instructors to the marauders, which in turn contributed further to a declining standard in fighter pilots despite all Galland's efforts to raise them. [55]

A further threat appeared on 20 February when the Eighth Air Force began its campaign against the German aircraft industry: during 'Big Week' or Operation 'Argument' it dropped more than 8,300 tonnes and caused severe damage for the loss of 158 bombers (3.73%) and 37 fighters. [56] The *Jagdgruppen* could still bite deep, however, and on 6 March the bombers suffered their highest loss – 69 aircraft (10.26%) while on 11 April they suffered 6.97 per cent losses. Yet American confidence grew and from March olive green camouflage paint was increasingly removed from the bombers in favour of a bare metal finish. In May they were striking eastern Germany and western Poland. The *Jagdgruppen* tended to concentrate upon stragglers and 'winged birds' and the growing awareness of this among American crews meant that some sought sanctuary in neutral Switzerland or Sweden rather than fight the odds and make a solo journey home. Yet it was a sign of the deteriorating standard of *Luftwaffe* training that pilots found it difficult to intercept bomber formations in bad weather. From 16 December the *Wilde Säue* were committed to day operations which led to the transfer of all Herrmann's *Gruppen* with 170 aircraft on 16 March. [57]

Once again the Americans sought the Reich's most vulnerable spot and from 12 May began attacking the oil industry. While the bomber loss-rate for the first mission was 5 per cent, this was quickly halved, although a mission against Berlin on 24 May suffered 6 per cent losses. But the Americans could absorb these casualties, as Doolittle's strength rose from 2,647 bombers (2,496 crews) on 30 April to 3,137 (3,225) a month later and on 27 May he was able to despatch 1,000 bombers [58]. Another indication of the declining effectiveness of the *Jagdgruppen* is shown by the activities of the US Fifteenth Air Force which despatched only 12 per cent of its sorties from the south against the *Reich* between January and June, but these cost it 46 per cent of its losses (245 bombers). However, even here with more limited fighter escort, the monthly loss rate halved from 9.8 per cent in February to 5.5 per cent in May (on 30 April the Fifteenth Air Force had 1,375 heavy bombers [1,436 crews] and a month later 1,499 bombers [1,537 crews]). [59]

By contrast *Luftwaffe* aircrew losses continued to rise. In the first quarter of 1944, 453 were killed or missing and a further 148 were wounded. [60] Schmid was placing his hopes increasingly on new technology: *III./ZG 26* began to receive the jet-propelled Me 262interceptor while *I./JG 400*, formed in January, had 10 of the new Me 163 *Komet* rocket-propelled fighters. [61] Despite 'Big Week', improved production brought the prospects of expanding unit strength; on-paper *Staffeln* strength increased to 16 aircraft and a fourth *Staffel* was added to each *Gruppe*. From May, Galland began planning to exploit this in order to launch one great blow but the summer campaigns in the East and the West proved an unsurmountable obstacle. With the fighters increasingly held at bay, *Flak* returned to its own, and while Eighth Air Force records show that 30 per cent of monthly bomber losses were due to *Flak* up to May (including missions over Western Europe), subsequently the figure rose to 66 per cent. For the Fifteenth Air Force the figures were 36 per cent and nearly 71 per cent. [62]

While the *Luftwaffe's* defence of the *Reich* floundered, its attempts at strategic operations against Great Britain and Allied shipping were slowly sinking. Its offensive capabilities in the West had become terminally feeble and largely retaliatory, most missions being at night, although there were some unsuccessful *Pirätangriffe* exploiting cloud during 1943. Fewer than 4,000 bomber sorties were flown against Britain during 1943, and the *Jabo* offensive was curtailed in the summer by a mixture of higher casualties and the need to reinforce the Mediterranean Theatre. The real contribution was to force the British to maintain strong fighter patrols, for little significant damage was inflicted.

With Peltz' departure to the Mediterranean in the summer of 1943 Fröhlich, promoted *General der Flieger* on 1 July, took over responsibility for attacks upon the British Isles beginning on 21/22 June, but into August the night campaign involved less than 75 aircraft a night due to a shortage of aircraft. Although a *Luftwaffe* report of 6 July recognised that British war production was growing stronger, the bombers continued to strike ports and towns near the coast in an attempt to reduce exposure to the defences, although not always successfully (see Table 8-8 for Luftwaffe operations against Great Britain). There was the growing use of pathfinders and the reintroduction of intruder operations. The former would line up on a visual beacon, then make a low-level approach, dropping flares to mark turning points (as the RAF did at that time), while the *Zielfinder* would mark the target and a trio of *Beleuchter* (illuminators) would strike it with incendiaries and drop flares for the remainder of the bombers. Electronic support for the pathfinders included the use of *Knickebein*, *Elektra* and *Sonne*, but the British retaliated by switching from spot to area jamming with considerable success. [63]

Table 8-8 Luftwaffe night operations against Great Britain, July 1944–June 1944

Quarter	Sorties	Losses
Q3 1943	1,020	39
Q4 1943	1,051	41
Q1 1944	3,460	176
Q2 1944	1,193	77

Note: Night bomber includes *Jabo* sorties.

Sources. Balke, *KG 2 Band 2*, p.183. *UKNA* Air 41/49, p.187, Appendix 24.

Peltz returned on 3 September anxious to resume his campaign against Great Britain while Fröhlich departed for Vienna to command *Luftgau XVII*. Bomber strength in the West grew slowly from to 252 bombers on 1 November to 501 in mid-December but Peltz had barely enough fully qualified crews to man his serviceable aircraft. The desultory intruder campaign by the Me 410s of *V./KG 2* over Bomber Command bases claimed 10 aircraft (four were shot down) and during the autumn Peltz, fearing the dilution of his strike force, restored the *Gruppe* to bombing duties. *ObdL* had little interest in intruding, and when, in December, Schmid proposed pursuing a bomber stream across the North Sea with *Naxos*, then to strike its bases with every night-fighter and bomber available, he was rebuffed by Göring on the grounds that Peltz was responsible for intruders! Schmid tried again when Stumpff assumed command of the Reich defences, but fears of compromising *Lichtenstein SN-2* again led to rejection. [64]

Peltz's overworked crews continued to harass the British during the late summer and early autumn using '*Düppel*' chaff from 7/8 October, to little effect, but the attack upon London was renewed from 12/13 October using the new Ju 88S and Ju 188. [65] There were minor changes to tactics with the bombers now climbing directly to 4,500 metres (14,700 feet) to make a shallow-angle dive-bombing attack and most missions were against ports or targets near the coast to reduce exposure to night fighters, while, to confuse the enemy, aircraft would be frequently moved around bases. [66]

Peltz' objective was to emulate the British by delivering devastating, short-duration raids led by pathfinders, a policy supported by the *Reich*'s leadership, especially when Harris launched the 'Battle of Berlin'. On 3 December Göring issued orders for *Unternehmen* '*Steinbock*' ('Capricorn' or 'Ibex') so as 'to avenge the terror attacks of the enemy'. Richthofen provided Peltz (promoted to *Generalmajor* on 1 November) with six *Kampfgruppen* while *ObdL* provided another three which lifted *Fliegerkorps IX* strength to 524 aircraft (including 46 heavy and 27 light-bombers, as well as 25 *Jabos*) by 20 January of which 462 were serviceable (including 42 He 177 and 20 *Jabos*); it was the largest strike force assembled in the West since the Blitz. The bombers were to carry 'English Mixture' loads of 70 per cent incendiaries and 30 per cent high explosive, including one-tonne bombs and mines. The British use of electronic support was also a feature of the campaign with navigation beacons operated in pairs intended to beat meaconing, Germany's Oboe equivalent. FuSAn 730/731 *EGON* (*Erstling Gemse Navigations Verfahren* or Erstling Gemse offensive navigation system) was used in association with *Freya* and *Mammut* radars (but would fall prey to jammers) while Gee was also copied, with bombers using captured equipment (*Hyperbel*) and new systems (*Truhe*). [67] Koller and Korten, although supporters of strategic bombing, would have preferred to use this force in the East because the defences were weaker.

'*Steinbock*' began on 21/22 January 1944 with 10 major raids on London in the six weeks to mid-March involving nearly 2,000 sorties and the delivery of more than 2,600 tonnes of ordnance of which about half were incendiaries. The scale of the attacks, the use of heavy bombs and harassment attacks by *Hornisse* caused British civilian morale to plummet but had little effect upon war production. Yet Hitler was not impressed and was especially disappointed by the performance of the He 177 telling Korten on 28 January: 'This crap machine (*Dreckmaschine*) is obviously the biggest load of rubbish that has ever been built.' [68] The effort was also undermined by the transfer of four *Kampfgruppen* (one with He 177), or a fifth of his force, to *Luftflotte 2* following the Anzio landing which occurred on the night '*Steinbock*' opened. By mid-February the withdrawal of other units for conversion to more modern aircraft reduced Peltz to 387 bombers (271 serviceable) and 242 fully operational crews yet he tried to maintain the pressure against Britain.

The bombers now crossed the coast at 7,000 metres (23,000 feet) and released their ordnance from 6,000 metres (19,700 feet). Electronic aids were used to bring the strike forces to jump-off points outside British jamming range from where they could navigate to the target with *EGON* which was used to inform them when they reached the bomb-release point. '*Düppel*' had a major impact upon the CHL, GCI and gun-laying (GL) radars in the bombers' flight path but only a moderate effect upon CH, which had received 750 kW transmitters and improved receivers before the start of the offensive, but whose operators learned to distinguish between chaff clouds and targets. Augmented by jammer aircraft from May, the German ECM effort had no effect upon 10cm or F-band (3–4 GHz) sensors such as the AI Mk X, carried in the Mosquito NF.XVIII (which formed 15% of No 11 Group's night fighter force), the Type 21 GCI radars and the gunners' GL Mk III, but it did cause a 15.5 per cent failure in interceptions by night fighters with older radars, according to RAF figures. [69]

Peltz found it difficult to keep his strike force together, the arrival of three *Kampfgruppen* being offset by the departure of an equal number in mid-March to help occupy Hungary in *Unternehmen 'Margarethe'*. This left Peltz with 328 aircraft (232 serviceable) and 225 operational crews. Three more *Gruppen* departed the following month ending the campaign after a raid on 20/21 April. The remaining bombers switched from a strategic to an operational role for night photo-reconnaissance and on 25 April they brought in photographs of large shipping concentrations in Portsmouth. Peltz thus struck shipping assembled in the southern ports for the invasion of Western Europe. These missions would involve *III. /KG 100* from the Mediterranean carrying PC 1400X (*Fritz-X*) guided bombs, but each mission was weaker than its predecessor and by mid-May, *Fliegerkorps IX* was down to 186 aircraft (148 serviceable). '*Steinbock*', and its aftermath, was as bloody a failure against Britain's air defences as Bomber Command's had been against the *Reich*'s, with the proviso that Harris had more influence upon Germany's war production than Peltz had upon Churchill's. The cost was high with *Fliegerkorps IX* losing 591 aircraft (12.7%), between January and April, only 253 of them (5.5%) to the defences. [70] Losses to intruders may have encouraged Peltz, despite his doubts, to resume similar operations on 30/31 March 1944 using *Hauptmann* Herbert Voss' *II./KG 51* (formerly *V./KG 2*) which destroyed 13 British aircraft in 59 sorties for the loss of nine aircraft (three in accidents) to the beginning of June. Their greatest success was against the Eighth Air Force on 22 April, when the *Gruppe* met a returning mission over its bases and 14 bombers were either shot down or forced to crash land. [71]

'*Steinbock*' should have been joined by a new weapon, the ramjet-powered Fieseler Fi 103 or FzG 76 surface-to-surface missile. During the summer of 1943, *Oberst* Max Wachtel's *FlakR I55 (W)* had begun building an infrastructure of launchers and storage facilities in western France and hoped to have 96 launchers ready by the beginning of 1944. But from 5 December the sites came under remorseless attack, not only from the Allied tactical air forces, but also from the strategic ones, so disrupting preparations that it was not until mid-June that the first missiles were launched. [72]

With British factories becoming almost as free from aerial bombardment during 1943 as American ones, the *Luftwaffe*'s remaining strategic option was to prevent the transport and distribution of materiel by sea. From 1942 the Mediterranean was the main venue for *Luftwaffe*'s anti-shipping operations, although a substantial presence had been maintained in northern Norway. However, the Allies' capture of Tunisia in May 1943 meant the whole focus of mercantile interdiction was in these waters. This was because control of the entire North African coast allowed the Allies the opportunity to exploit the sea lanes, running convoys of more than 100 ships under land-based air protection, freeing thousands of tonnes of shipping which was no longer forced around the Cape of Good Hope. [73]

In preparation for anti-shipping operations the headquarters of *Fliegerdivision 2* was transferred from the central Eastern Front to southern France in November and placed under *Generalmajor* Johannes Fink, one time *Kanalkampfführer*, which was to have five torpedo-bomber and two air-to-surface missile *Gruppen*. For the first half of the year, Fink's airmen were engaged in Operational-level missions intended to disrupt enemy supply build-ups and amphibious operations. Then, during the summer there was a dispute between Fink and *Oberstleutnant* Werner Klümper, *Kommodore* of the torpedo-bombing *KG 26* over strategy, with Fink wishing to strike every eastbound convoy while Klümper advocated selective blows. Klümper took his campaign to Jeschonnek and threatened to resign his commission if Fink's views were accepted and despite his insubordination this policy was accepted (see Table 8-9 for merchant ship losses).

Table 8-9: Allied Merchantmen Losses due to the Luftwaffe, January 1943–May 1944

Month	Atlantic	Mediterranean	Arctic	Total
Jan 1943	-	5 (25,503)	-	5 (25,503)
Feb 1943	-	-	-	
Mar 1943	2 (25,150)	6 (45,785)	1 (7,173)	9 (78,108)
Apr 1943	-	-	-	
May 1943	2 (6,687)	3 (14,255)	-	5 (20,942)
Jun 1943	2 (5,274)	1 (813)	-	3 (6,087)
Jul 1943	6 (66,803)	8 (54,306)	-	14 (121,109
Aug 1943	1 (6,070)	3 (11,567)	-	4 (17,637)
Sep 1943	1 (7,135)	3 (15,770)	-	4 (22,905)
Oct 1943	-	3 (15,504)	-	3 (15,504)
Nov 1943	1 (4,405)	6 (58,047)	-	7 (62,452)
Dec 1943	-	17 (75,471)	-	17 (75,471)
Jan 1944	-	4 (24,237)	-	4 (24,237)
Feb 1944	1 (7,264)	2 (14,352)	-	3 (21,616)
Mar 1944	-	-	-	
Apr 1944	-	3 (19,755)	-	3 (19,755)
May 1944	-	1 (2,873)	-	1 (2,873)

Note: First figure number of ships, figure in parenthesis tonnage in gross registered tons. The Mediterranean total includes ships lost in harbour and those lost supporting amphibious operations.

Sources: UKNA Adm 186/804. UKNA Air 41/75, Appendix 30.

The offensive began on 13 August 1943 and lasted until the end of October during which Klümper flew 316 sorties, claiming to hit 64 ships (423,000 grt) and 10 warships for the loss of 55 aircraft (17%) and 31 crews. Torpedo-bombing was regarded as especially successful, and during August, 65 sorties were estimated to have sunk 88,000 grt while only 33,000 grt was sunk by 1,140 bomber sorties, although this activity attracted American heavy fighters which periodically struck Fink's bases, destroying 106 aircraft in late July and August alone. [74] New weapons were deployed against shipping from 4 October when the first *Fritz-X* (PC 1400 X) guided bombs were used by *III./KG 100* with some success, although the *Gruppe* was transferred to Greece to support operations against the British in the Aegean Islands, then held back for a planned surprise attack upon Scapa Flow before returning in January to support operations around Anzio. Luckily the He 177s of *II./KG 40* with Hs 293s air-to-surface missiles, made their Mediterranean debut on 26 November, sinking the liner *Rohna* (8,602 grt) with the loss of 1,000 servicemen, more than half the number embarked. Four of the 14 aircraft (28%) were lost, however, and two were wrecked on landing, leaving the *Gruppe* with seven serviceable machines. [75] Allied intelligence noted that He 177 crews were enthusiastic about their much-maligned engines, '... which appear to function smoothly and efficiently over incredibly long journeys.' [76]

But it was Klümper's torpedo-bombers which bore the brunt of the campaign and helped to ensure that airmen usually sank more ships in the Mediterranean than U-boats did. However, by December Allied ship movements in the Mediterranean had increased from 357 in June to 1,012 to exceed Atlantic traffic, and they were defended day and night by the Mediterranean Coastal Air Force under Air Vice-Marshal Sir Hugh Lloyd (the former Malta commander) with more than 50 squadrons, although the defenders were hamstrung by the lack of fighter-direction ships. [77] In response, from January 1944, the anti-shipping missions were often escorted by up to 24 Ju 88C *Zerstörer* of *ZG 1*, but *KG 26*'s losses were high.

Partly because of this, Fink was relieved on 10 February, promoted to *General der Flieger* and became *Kommandierender der Deutschen Luftwaffe in Griechenland*. He was succeeded 12 days later by *Generalmajor* Hans Korte, who had no anti-shipping experience and had spent a year with infantry units. Despite changing tactics, he had little success and his torpedo-bomber units suffered badly; even the new weapons had lost their advantage, *KG 100* sadly reporting on 30 April the decline of the missiles. Indeed, post-war analysis showed the *Fritz-X* sank a battleship and damaged three more warships while Hs 293s sank a cruiser and four other warships (three damaged) as well as three merchantmen for the loss of 38 aircraft (25,140 grt). [78]

The prime naval battleground was the Atlantic, where Dönitz came close to winning the battle in March by sinking 108 ships (627,377 grt), of which 8 per cent were with the assistance of Kessler's *FlFü Atlantik*. During the first quarter of 1943 only six convoys were shadowed, but of the 74,954 grt sunk in co-ordinated air/U-boat operations during the year, 85 per cent were sunk during this period, mostly in actions against two convoys during March. [79] But after March 1943, *FlFü Atlantik* detected only 14 convoys, while during June 1943 none was attacked in the North Atlantic, allowing Coastal Command to reinforce its anti-submarine sweeps in the Bay of Biscay, sinking or damaging many U-boats in the process. As his losses rose, Dönitz sought to abandon the Atlantic but was told unequivocally by Hitler on 31 May: 'There can be no let-up in the U-boat war. The Atlantic, Admiral, is my first line of defence in the West.' The Fw 200 *Condors* continued their tedious patrolling, but often flew in formation to and from their sectors for protection not only against Beaufighters, but also against Liberator, Fortress and Sunderland ASW aircraft.

Kessler's frustration mounted, and on 4 May he wrote to Jeschonnek that more than 3.75 million gross registered tons of shipping was escaping interception on the Gibraltar route. He requested the He 177, Hs 293 and *Fritz-X* with which he could sink up to 500,000 grt a month, but, while production supremo Milch was sympathetic, none of this equipment was available immediately. The *Condors* did receive the *Lotfe 7D* bomb sight, which assured accurate bombing from up to 4,000 metres (13,000 feet) and resumed the offensive role, with 42 attacks between 23 February and 1 October (26 upon convoys). Eleven ships (79,050 grt) were sunk including the liners *Duchess of York* and *California* (36,813 grt), carrying troops to the Middle East on 11 July. [80] But there were rarely more than six aircraft available and the cost was high, with 17 aircraft lost (13 to enemy action). Lacking He 177s, *ObdL* authorised the conversion of *Condors* to carry the Hs 293 and shortly after Christmas, *III./KG 40* flew a few fruitless missions until it was diverted to Anzio in January 1944.

The clouds lightened for Kessler during the summer when new long-range reconnaissance aircraft arrived, capable of reaching the central Atlantic. The Bv 222 *Wiking* flying boat began flying to 30°W, or 1,200 kilometres (650 nautical miles) west of the British Isles while the land-based Ju 290 could fly even further westward and took over the long-range reconnaissance mission from the *Condors*. Better air support with new sensors in his U-boats gave Dönitz hope of an autumnal renaissance in the Atlantic, but this quickly evaporated. There were not enough aircraft and during the last quarter of 1943 only 12 convoys were detected, from which the U-boats sank only one ship (2,968 grt); indeed their total successes in this period were only 67 ships (369,800 grt), yet 72 convoys with 2,218 vessels crossed the Atlantic without loss. [81]

Under Korten ambitious plans were produced on 26 August for prosecuting the maritime war, including upgrading Kessler's command to *Fliegerkorps III* with 42 *Staffeln* (19 with He 177s, 18 with *Zerstörer* and *Jabos*) but they were never implemented. [82] Kessler continued to seek more long-range aircraft – Hs 293 anti-ship missiles for his *Condors* and Ju 88H-2 *Zerstörer* to strike the anti-submarine aircraft escorting the convoys – but by mid-November he had only 111 aircraft (more than half of them Ju 88C fighters), although he could call upon Fink's *Fliegerdivision 2* which was under *ObdL* control, to attack shipping in either the Atlantic or the Mediterranean. He tried to remain optimistic and on Christmas Eve claimed that with some 500 aircraft he could sink 500,000 grt a month, but he admitted that his command was being increasingly marginalised, partly because the Allies were tightening their control over the Bay of Biscay; it reminded him of the North Sea in the Great War.

The matter was certainly being considered at the highest levels, and on 19 December, Dönitz's inconclusive conference with Hitler and Göring on the inadequate air support led him to interdict Gibraltar traffic, where Kessler could assist him, to recoup his losses. His hopes were again dashed, for each Gibraltar convoy now had an escort carrier and a fighter direction ship, and a disastrous attack upon MKS.30/SL.129 saw few U-boats able to exploit the convoy's detection while three were lost together with two reconnaissance aircraft.

Much was expected of stand-off weapons but the carrying units were diverted to the Stalingrad airlift and not re-formed until April 1943. They did not become operational until July and then not in the Atlantic as Göring hoped, but in the Mediterranean because of the landings in Sicily. [83] Only on 31 July was the Hs 293 unit II./KG 100 assigned to Kessler and between 25 and 27 August it flew 25 sorties against anti-submarine groups in the Bay of Biscay, severely damaging two ships and sinking the sloop HMS *Egret* which had a team of scientists embarked to study the Hs 293. [84] The Royal Navy hastily withdrew westwards but returned within a fortnight following the Allied landing in Salerno. Kessler finally received the long-awaited missile-armed He 177s in October 1943 and their first attack was on 21 November when 40 missiles were fired at a convoy in which a straggler (4,405 grt) was sunk for the loss of three aircraft (18%). After a brief sojourn in the Mediterranean, the *Gruppe* returned but had little success. However, on the evening of 12 February 1944 it joined *Condors* to attack a convoy in mid-Atlantic, but escort carrier fighters destroyed half the attackers in what proved to be *FlFü Atlantik*'s last strike mission.

Kessler was already on the defensive over the Bay of Biscay trying desparately to shield the U-boats from enemy ASW aircraft, using a *Gruppe* of Ju 88C *Zerstörer*. In 127 clashes the *Gruppe* shot down 69 and an airliner carrying British movie star Leslie Howard, but the Ju 88s soon found themselves outclassed first by the Beaufighter and then the Mosquito. Indeed during the year, the British lost only nine aircraft in 27 fighter-versus-fighter engagements while the *Zerstörer* lost 32, some to gunners in anti-submarine aircraft. [85] The Fw 190s of *JG 2* and its *Jagdkommando Brest* on the Brittany peninsula were the only fighters available and six of them, fitted with long-range tanks, were assigned to 5./BdF1Gr 196 (1./SAGr 128 from July 1943) for escort missions until early 1944, when they were absorbed by III./ZG 1. [86]

Yet Dönitz constantly complained to Hitler about inadequate *Luftwaffe* support, a point underlined in June when Sperrle informed *Marinegruppe West* that air-sea rescue of U-boat crews had priority over maritime reconnaissance. [87] Kessler did his best but of 86 U-boats which attempted the passage across the Bay between 1 July and 2 August, 16 (18%) were sunk, mostly by aircraft. Only by abandoning group surface sailings and relying on slower underwater transit did Dönitz end the slaughter in the Bay, and of 169 U-boats which crossed the Bay in the first quarter of 1944, only three were sunk and six damaged (5%) and in May 1944, the British ended their 41-month-old offensive, having sunk 50 boats at a total cost of 350 aircraft. [88]

Nevertheless, during the first five months of 1944 Coastal Command flew 4,439 anti-submarine and 796 fighter sorties over the Bay losing 10 anti-submarine aircraft to ZG 1 (U-boat *Flak* destroyed 12) while the *Luftwaffe* lost 66 aircraft, 28 to enemy action. However, Dönitz decided to conserve his strength from May in anticipation of the Allied invasion, depriving the *Geschwader* of its *raison d'etre*. [89] His decision was influenced by the *Luftwaffe's* failure to detect targets, despite the U-boats' returning to the Western Approaches in mid-January 1944 after a three-year absence in the hope of exploiting air reconnaissance. During the first months, four convoys were detected, but escort carriers and Beaufighter patrols prevented the *Luftwaffe* from maintaining contact and three Ju 290s were lost shadowing ONS.29 to 18 February, in what proved to be *FlFü Atlantik's* last success in locating convoys.

Dönitz briefly returned to the central Atlantic but was driven out within a month and he refused to return without improved air support. This reduced *Luftwaffe* long-range maritime reconnaissance to a token effort until the invasion in June, with missions often flown to acquire meteorological data. [90] Ironically, in January 1944 Kessler received a prototype six-engine Ju 390, which successfully completed a proving flight within 25 kilometres (15.5 miles) of New York City, while there was talk of using the Me 264 to bomb the port. But these plans were overtaken by events.

Kessler's failure was a growing embarrassment for Göring, especially as Hitler favoured Dönitz. Since the Munich Crisis, the *Reichsmarschall* had felt that Kessler was a 'moaning Minnie', and this view was reinforced by *FlFü Atlantik's* constant, but justified, demands for aircraft. In one of its first actions, the newly created OKL decided, on 7 February, to disband *FlFü Atlantik*, and did so as casually as it had activated the command. Indeed Kessler was not even informed. At the end of February, *Fliegerkorps X* commander *Generalleutnant* Alexander Holle ambled into Kessler's noon conference and informed him of the decision, although this was not confirmed by teleprinter for several embarrassing hours and Kessler officially retained his command until 15 March. [91] Holle, for his part, followed Dönitz's example and merely conserved his anti-shipping forces for the Allied invasion although with the deteriorating situation, the four-engined units were transferred to Norway on 7 July.

Even minelaying was a declining activity for the *Luftwaffe*. *Fliegerkorps IX* had gradually drifted to a conventional strike force during 1941 and 1942 but its bombers were engaged both in minelaying and coastal traffic interdiction. However, British estimates noted a sharp drop in minelaying activity in the second half of 1942, although there was some improvement in 1943 with about 1,000 sorties being flown. [92] This proved a disappointment, for the navy's hopes had been raised with the development of a pressure fuse to convert the LMB mine into the so-called *Druckdosenmine* ('Oyster mine'). In May 1943, Jeschonnek allocated two *Kampfgruppen* to lay them from August, but Hitler, fearing that the enemy would learn the mine's secrets and interrupt training of the new high-underwater-speed U-boats in the Baltic, vetoed the plan at the end of July, commenting, 'If the British should lay those mines in the Baltic we are finished.'

Korten returned to the matter within three weeks of his appointment as chief of staff supporting Navy pleas for a renewed minelaying offensive using acoustic and magnetic/acoustic weapons to coincide with the new moon in September, and on 26 August he published plans for a substantial expansion of the minelayer force to 11*Kampfgruppen* with Ju 188s and He 177s. [93] The campaign lasted from 15/16 September to 3/4 October, when it was abandoned after the previous night's mission suffered an 8 per cent loss rate, some 600 mines having been laid. With the focus on *Unternehmen 'Steinbock'* the bombers were diverted to conventional operations and the *Luftwaffe* ceased minelaying in the West apart from 80 sorties in April and May 1944, the Oyster mines being conserved for the Allied invasion. [94]

Chapter Nine

Endgame in the East and South

The summer of 1944 saw a sense of expectation along the Eastern Front (see Table 9-1 for Luftwaffe activity in 1944). Three years earlier Nazi Germany had treacherously struck at the Soviet Union, creating a great swathe of destruction and killing millions, but the Russians had fought back and were now ready for revenge. [1]

Table 9-1: Luftwaffe operations on the Eastern Front 1944.

	Luftflotte 1		Luftflotte 6		Luftflotte 4	
	Sorties	*Lost*	*Sorties*	*Lost*	*Sorties*	*Lost*
Day fighters	12,143	133	20,206	260	29,426	336
Night fighters	436	–	1,731	16	621	19
Day attack	29,932	260	48.416	458	88,057	582
Night attack	27,559		13,183		15,399	
Day reconn	9,649	67	19,519	171	19,313	118
Night reconn	1,086		4,159		1,648	

Source: IMW Tin 192 fr 1041.

Notes: Attack is both *Kampf-* and *Schlachtflieger*. Lost are totally destroyed by enemy action.

They first ended the potential Finnish threat to Leningrad with an attack on 10 June supported by 1,547 aircraft (741 VVS; 500 Navy and 300 medium bombers) which quickly broke through the defences on the Karelia Isthmus to advance on Vyborg (Viipuri). The Finns, with only 118 aircraft, sought German reinforcements. These included a division and some armour, but on 16 June *OKL* despatched *Oberst* Kurt Kuhlmey's *Stab SG 3* from *Luftflotte 1* which arrived at Imola with two *Schlachtgruppen* (46 *Stukas* and *Jabos*) augmented by two *Jagdstaffeln* and a *Nahaufklärung* detachment to form *Gefechtsverband Kuhlmey*. [2]

The strike force was committed from 19 June in a vain attempt to save Vyborg, but then delivered fierce attacks upon the Russians. It mounted 149 *Schlachtflieger* sorties on 26 June dropping 69 tonnes of bombs, which helped contain the threat, the Germans also claiming 200 tanks. Kuhlmey rarely had more than 50 serviceable aircraft, but aggressive operations helped the Finns and by mid-July the Russians were transferring forces southwards. Almost all the Eastern Front was by now ablaze and *OKL* needed *Gefechtsverband Kuhlmey* in the Balkan states, to which it was transferred from 21 July. A *Jabostaffel* remained and all of *I./SG 5* was briefly assembled there 3–14 August before being transferred to Estonia. Kuhlmey's men flew almost 2,000 sorties, lost 27 aircraft to enemy action and 10 to accidents, dropped 577 tonnes of bombs and the fighters claimed 100 victories. By contrast, the Russians flew 28,000 sorties, dropped 4,700 tonnes of bombs and lost 311 aircraft. Fearing further wrath from Moscow, the Finns signed an armistice on 4 September under which the Germans had to withdraw by 15 September. In the event there was some fighting between Finnish and German forces including some clashes in the air.

On the main battle front between the Baltic and the Black Sea *OKL* began the summer optimistically for on 27/28 March the strategic bombing force, *Fliegerkorps IV*, began a campaign, *Unternehmen 'Zaunkönig'* ('Wren'), involving 44 raids, all but five of them in the Ukraine. But this was an operational, not a strategic, campaign, aimed at rail marshalling yards which would support future Red Army offensives. The *Luftwaffe* built on the experience it had gained over England using electronic navigation and support systems with pathfinder target markers (usually dropped by *KG 4* crews) and flew 180–190 sorties a night to deliver 200 tonnes of bombs with the largest effort on 30 April–1 May involving involving 252 sorties. [3]

Its greatest success was against the US Army Air Force which had long been interested in 'shuttle bombing' – missions which took off from one country and ended in another. [4] With the Russian success in the Ukraine, Washington sought to establish bases there and with extreme reluctance on 4 February 1944 the Soviets agreed. Four airfields were established around Poltava and on 2 June these took in aircraft from a Fifteenth Air Force mission which returned on 6 June. On 21 June the Eighth Air Force flew its first shuttle mission, Operation 'Frantic'. *OKL* was alarmed by this new threat and determined to nip it in the bud. A He 177 had shadowed the Americans and radioed the location of their new bases. That night 200 bombers from *Fliegerkorps IV* struck the bases, which were poorly defended, destroying 59 aircraft (including 44 B-17) and damaging 26. Only two B-17s were left undamaged but the Americans hastily moved to Mirgorod and escaped a second attack upon Poltava. Although a few more missions were flown, the 'shuttle bombing' campaign never recovered and Meister's attack gave the Russians the excuse to shut down the bases. Some damaged B-17s and B-24s were repaired by the Russians and issued to a heavy bomber regiment although it is unclear whether or not they were used.

Meister's attack was never repeated because he was sucked into the key event of 1944 which took place on the central front. The southern flank of *Generalfeldmarschall* Ernst Busch's *Heeresgruppe Mitte* had been stretched to near breaking point after the Russians recovered almost all of the Ukraine, bringing them to the borders of Poland and most of Germany's Eastern Front allies. This political threat, and the fear of losing his Balkan oil fields, was uppermost in Hitler's mind and he convinced himself the next great blow would come in the south, a belief the Russians were careful to encourage. As a result Busch, who had to defend a front 700 kilometres (435 miles) long, lost most of his tanks in May to *Generalfeldmarschall* Walter Model's *Heeresgruppe Nordukraine* in southern Poland.

The Russians had decided to smash Busch's forces on the third anniversary of the German attack in Operation 'Bagration' (*Operatsiya 'Bagration'*). During May and early June their armies facing Busch's front saw manpower and armour increase by 62 per cent and 300 per cent respectively and their air forces were also substantially reinforced. On 1 June the VVS had 13,418 aircraft available for operations between the Baltic and the Black Sea (41% fighters) augmented by 1,266 medium and heavy bombers of the ADD and 3,436 PVO fighters. For 'Bagration' nearly 40 per cent of the VVS and 79.5 per cent of the ADD were committed; 5,327 VVS aircraft (2,318 fighters, 1,744 Il 2, 655 Pe 2, 431 Po 2) and 1,007 ADD. [5]

The VVS was now better trained at all levels; indeed Novikov had encouraged a more flexible form of command allowing the lower leadership echelons to use their initiative [6]. Production was exceeding losses and, from 1943, VVS regiments received a third squadron to bring their strength to 32 aircraft. The fighter force had aircraft equal or superior to the Germans and a new model, the Yak-3 would soon be introduced, while the Il-2 had been improved with all-metal wings, but the bomber arm remained weak. The Pe-2 remained the prime VVS day-bomber but lacked performance and range; it was augmented by some A-20 Bostons. The Po-2 (formerly U-2) night-bomber was little more than a sheep in wolf's clothing. Although the ADD was receiving greater numbers of excellent Tu-2, it remained a mix of the disappointing Yer 2, the elderly Il-4, the B-25 Mitchell and even converted Li-2 Dakota transports. Yet the need for replacement aircrew resulted in short training-courses which was reflected in the fact that a third of the 17,191 VVS combat aircraft lost in 1944 were due to accidents, partly due to operations in poor weather and from inadequate airfields, and this figure rose to 36 per cent with fighters. [7]

On 20 June 1944 the *Luftwaffe* had 2,085 combat aircraft (1,651 serviceable) in *Luftflotte 1, 6* and *4* (see Table 9-2) but on the central front Greim's *Luftflotte 6* had only 540 (371) augmented by Meister's strategic bomber force of *Fliegerkorps IV* with 389 (326). Greim split his forces in three; *Fliegerdivision 4* (*Oberst* Franz Reuss) in the east, at Orscha, supporting *3. Panzer* and *4.Armee*; *Fliegerführer 1* (*Generalmajor* Josef Punzert) at Minsk in the centre supporting *9.Armee* and anti-guerrilla forces (including three *Einsatzgruppen* of the *Fliegerschuledivision*), and *Fliegerdivision 1* (*Generalmajor* Robert Fuchs) at Biala Podlaska in the west supporting *2. Armee*. Greim's strike force of 100 *Jabos* and *Stukas* was with Fuchs and the fighters with *Oberst* Karl-Gottfried Nordmann's *Jagdabschnittsführer 6* which had been formed on 1 May and had 85 serviceable fighters, partly due to Dessloch's last-minute transfer of *III./JG 51* and *IV./JG 51*. Greim also retained a train-busting *Staffel* (*14./KG 3*) and some *Fernaufklärungsstaffeln*.

Table 9-2: Luftwaffe strength Eastern Front, June 1944–December 1944

Month	Lft 1	Lft 6	Lft 4	Total
Jun 1944	316	860	991	2,167
Jul 1944	383	1,135	772	2,290
Aug 1944	504	1,327	329	2,160
Sep 1944	411	1,391	405	2,207
Oct 1944	553	1,013	598	2,164
Nov 1944	251	965	589	1,805
Dec 1944	263	1,079	721	2,063

Source: BA MA RL 2 III/880 – 882.

Note: Figures in June and July exclude *Nachtschlacht*.

The *Schlachtflieger* were Greim's reserve which could be used against a threat to Busch's forces or to Model's but he was hamstrung because Hitler's strategy forced chief-of-staff Korten and operations chief Koller to support Dessloch's *Luftflotte 4* which was believed to face the main blow, making Dessloch the strongest commander with878 combat aircraft (695 serviceable), the majority (547) in Rumania with *Fliegerkorps I*. Shielding the Danube valley from Anglo-American bombing raids were another 420 German fighters of which 83 (70 serviceable) were in Rumania. [8]

The Russian campaign opened with probing and bombardments on 22 June but was preceeded by a 10-day air campaign involving 1,472 sorties against German communications. [9] The main blows came from 23 June: three of Busch's armies were rapidly enveloped as the VVS increasingly demonstrated its abilities at the Operational level, interdicting communications to turn retreat into Calvary and to paralyse every counter-attack in a mirror image of June 1941. Elements of the trapped armies escaped westwards but most were annihilated within a fortnight in a disaster which cost Germany 300,000 troops. Worse still not only were the Russians now driving west to Poland and the Vistula, after a brief pause to mop up Busch's isolated troops, but also heading north-west to the Baltic, threatening to isolate *Heeresgruppe Nord* which desperately tried to protect its right and prevent isolation. On 28 June Model took over what was left of *Heeresgruppe Mitte* to prevent the Red Army reaching the Vistula; he began by stripping forces from *Heeresgruppe Nordukraine*, which he continued to command.

The *Luftwaffe* responded with its usual vigour. On 22 June *Luftflotte 6* flew 1,633 sorties but the pace steadily increased to 2,162 the following day and, thanks to massed *Schlachtflieger* attacks, 5,319 on 24 June. [10] But against an enemy in overwhelming strength, it had little influence upon events and the rapid Russian advance compounded its problems, disrupting *Feldluftgau XXVII*'s infrastructure and forcing units to abandon airfields with their repair shops (*I./JG 51* moved seven times to 1 July and *1./NSGr 2* eight times to the end of July). Supply shortages, especially fuel, further restricted the *Luftwaffe* response (for casualties see Table 9-3). Nordmann's fighters could make little impression upon the enemy armada; *JG 51* flew 180 sorties and claimed 43 victories on 23 June, although he received some 170 reinforcements; two *Jagdgruppen* from the Reich and one each from his neighbours, but on 1 July he had only 259 fighters including the whole of *JG 51*. They fought desperately, and while achieving many victories, the continual loss of *Experten* gradually undermined *Jagdwaffe* effectiveness (see Table 9-4 for *Luftwaffe* fighter activity in the East).

Table 9-3: Luftwaffe losses in the East, June 1944–December 1944

Month	Lft 1	Lft 6		Lft 4		Total			
EA	EA	Accid	EA	Accid	EA	Accid	EA	Accid
Jun 1944	29	28	78	61	131	105	238	194
Jul 1944	87	92	267	170	208	156	562	418
Aug 1944	78	71	201	150	107	49	386	270
Sep 1944	62	14	85	61	62	46	209	121
Oct 1944	43	50	151	72	122	64	316	186
Nov 1944	9	15	18	16	52	77	79	108
Dec 1944	53	46	27	73	55	107	135	226

Source:, BA MA RL 2 III/880 – 882.
Note: Figures in June and July exclude *Nachtschlacht*.

Table 9-4: German fighter activity in the East 1944

Month	Sorties			Losses		
	Day	Night	Total	Day	Night	Total
January	2,306	1,436	3,742	122	59	181
February	2,861	1,115	3,976	299	53	352
March	2,226	1,334	3,560	240	87	327
April	4,522	1,884	6,406	395	76	471
May	3,618	1,266	4,884	384	41	425
June	1,310	1,159	2,469	179	56	235
July	2,652	2,701	5,353	341	58	399
August	2,241	500	2,741	293	32	325
September	2,547	1,131	3,678	371	54	425
October	783	824	1,607	59	49	108
November	2,168	956	3,124	404	61	465
December	2,114	1,440	3,554	265	112	377
Total	**29,348**	**15,746**	**45,094**	**3,352**	**738**	**4,090**

Source: IWM, Duxford, Tin 30 Frames K3312–3356.

Meister's bombers joined in and were initially used in their traditional role against rail targets and airfields, but their fuel consumption was a matter of growing concern at *OKL*. From 25 July having suffered 72 bombers shot down or severely damaged, Meister's operations began to be scaled down with the withdrawal of *KG 53* and *KG 55*, the former to become an air-to-surface missile unit. From the night of 24/25 July Meister's *Kampfgruppen* were used for Tactical-level night missions against troop concentrations advancing upon Warsaw. The bombers were also used to supply isolated garrisons and troops, for even with the arrival of a second *Transportgruppe*, Greim had only 66 transports available on 1 July. Daylight bomber missions were flown by the high-flying He 177 of *Stab* and *II./KG 1*, assigned directly to Greim rather than Meister, apparently largely for Tactical-level missions although no more than 30 were committed at any one time, two being lost, before fuel shortages caused them to be withdrawn on the morning of 29 July. [11] The fuel shortages were a result of the Allied strategic bombers pounding German production facilities at a time when consumption was growing. In the second half of 1944 the consumption outstripped supply by 55,000 tonnes leading to ever more stringent efforts to reduce usage with training necessarily reduced to 100 hours and fighter pilot training cut to 35 hours (see Table 9-5).

Table 9-5: Luftwaffe fuel situation, July 1944–December 1944

Quarter	Production (tonnes)	Consumption (tonnes)
Q3 1944	91,000	311,000
Q4 1944	105,000	138,000

Source: United States Strategic Bombing Survey, Overall report (European War) 30 September 1945. Chart No 16.

Most of Greim's reinforcements (he had 1,109 aircraft on 26 June) were *Schlachtflieger* who flew four or five sorties a day when fuel was available. However it seems extremely unlikely that Greim's airmen ever reached their potential of 3,000 sorties a day. [12] The *Schlachtflieger* were in the vanguard of the defence and received substantial reinforcements; *SG 4* with 141 aircraft arrived on 1 July, mostly from Italy, although it was an indication of Hitler's strategic priorities that *III./SG 4* came from attacking the Normandy beachhead in France. The *Gruppe's* arrival gave Greim 395 *Schlachtflieger*, but while they inflicted casualties they could not stem the tide alone. Worse still, other crises reduced his force; 90 aircraft were sent to help out Pflugbeil's *Luftflotte 1*, who was supported by Reuss, as the Russians neared the Gulf of Riga in mid-July and then returned as the Russian advance on the Vistula was renewed.

Heeresgruppe Nordukraine was struck on 12 July, the Russians quickly pushing the Germans back to the Vistula and the Carpathians. The reaction of Seidemann's *Fliegerkorps VIII* was handicapped by his loyal support of Model in sending some 80 aircraft, including half of his *Panzerjägerstaffeln*, to Greim. *Fliegerkorps VIII* received some 30 *Jabos* (*II./SG 10*) and 20 fighters (*II./JG 52*) from Rumania in compensation, but Seidemann still had barely 350 aircraft (plus some Hungarian and Slovak units) facing 2,800 Russian machines. The Red Army attack actually began a day early and caught the Germans withdrawing to new positions. Uncertain of the situation, Seidemann delayed his response and on 13 July only 123 sorties were flown. He was soon reinforced and the pace increased with 2,604 sorties on 14 July and 2,282 the following day, but even with support from Meister's *Fliegerkorps IV*, air operations had little impact upon the ground battle. When Model's counter-offensive on 15 July was smothered by the VVS which flew 3,288 sorties, the Germans were in full-scale retreat. [13] This led to a *Luftwaffe* reorganisation in which Greim became responsible for holding Poland; he was assigned *Fliegerkorps VIII* which continued to support forces in the south while Fuchs defended the centre around Warsaw.

On 25 July the Russian spearheads reached the Vistula and within a few days were across but they had suffered heavy losses and were outrunning their supply lines. The *Luftwaffe's* supply situation was easing but continued fuel shortages were reducing it to 500–600 sorties a day in favourable weather. On 29 July alone, the *Schlachtflieger* claimed 71 tanks. Yet the situation was grave and on 14 July Greim reported he had only 256 fighters (140 serviceable) and only enough fuel for three days of major operations. [14] At the end of July Model began a counter-offensive which drove the Russians back, aided by some 200 aircraft mostly under Fuchs, Greim's limited bomber force being used in night attacks upon enemy bridges, although *KG 4* was used to support the suppression of the Warsaw Uprising. The front had stabilised by mid-August although the Russians retained a bridgehead south of Warsaw at Magnuszew and at Sandomierz/Baranow. The effort exhausted the Germans, *JG 51* being left with 19 serviceable aircraft at the end of July. Russian air superiority was such that fighters sometimes had to fly tactical reconnaissance missions. Between 22 June and 31 August JG 51 lost 43 pilots killed and missing with another 14 wounded.

Desultory air combat continued through the late summer and autumn with Greim's airmen flying an average 300 sorties a day. Some 240 combat aircraft were lost in September and October and there was no hope of gaining air superiority. A *Luftwaffe* report noted that units in the East lost 136 aircraft in September of which

75 (55%) were over enemy territory. Only one aircraft was destroyed on the ground while 808 victories were claimed together with 295 by *Flak* on the ground. [15] Another measure of the fighting in October may be taken from the fact that *IV./JG 51* flew 330 sorties and claimed 102 victories (see Table 9-6 for details of the Luftwaffe in the East and South during 1944).

Table 9-6: Luftwaffe activity in the East, Balkans and Italy, October 1944

Command	Sorties		Losses		Victories (Night)		
	Day	*Night*	*Day*	*Night*	*Fighter*	*Flak*	*Ground*
Lftfl 1	2,773	1,464	21	1	306 (4)	166 (-)	-
Lftfl 6	5,980	425	104	4	422 (10)	202 (7)	8 (-)
Lftfl 4	5,483	485	80	-	64 (-)	10 (-)	38 (-)
LwKdo Südost	1,176	98	33	10	-	51 (-)	-
Italy	291	158	6	1	2 (-)	6 (-)	2 (-)

Source: IWM, Duxford, Tin 30 Frames K3312–3356.

Increasingly the fighting in the East took on a mediæval quality with the knights replaced by heavy armour and the infantry little more than poorly-trained peasants. Consequently, the destruction of heavy armour had a high priority and during the latter months of 1944 the *Luftwaffe Panzerjäger* forces received new weapons. Until now tank-busting depended upon either the 30mm cannon of the Hs 129 B or the 37mm guns of the Ju 87 G, whose most formidable exponent was *Oberst* Hans-Ulrich Rudel. But during the late autumn the Hs 129 B-3/Wa with a 75mm gun was introduced into *10. and 14./SG 9*, providing a weapon which could stop even the heaviest Russian tank, although the aircraft was ponderous and vulnerable to ground fire. [16] Less accurate, but almost as effective, were anti-tank rockets which were issued to the *Jabos* from September; firstly the 88mm *Panzerschreck* which was a modified bazooka-style missile and on 16 November, the 81mm *Panzerblitz* had its combat debut with *III./SG 3*, a six-rocket salvo having an excellent chance of destroying a tank. [17] But there were never enough to equip all units; indeed by 20 April of 61 *Schlachtstaffeln* only 12 had *Panzerblitz* and two had *Panzerschreck*, leaving the *Schlachtgruppen* relying upon bombs which were best used against 'soft' targets such as enemy troops and trucks. [18]

A feature of operations during July was the dwindling use of bombers which consumed precious fuel. Around 25/26 July 1944 *Fliegerkorps IV* was withdrawn to the *Reich* and most *Kampfgruppen* were grounded permanently. On 16 September *Fliegerkorps IV* was disbanded and Meister became *Kommandierenden General der deutschen Luftwaffe in Dänemark*. *KG 27* and *KG 55* would be assigned to *Fliegerkorps IX (J)* on 13 November to convert to fighter units while *KG 53* flew West to launch V-1 missiles at the British Isles. The remaining *Kampfgruppen* were now used more for transport than bombing missions. The scale of Meister's operations may be gauged from a report on *KG 55*, a *Geschwader* that was withdrawn from the Eastern Front on 12 August. During 1944, the *Geschwader* flew 3,164 sorties out of 4,250 (74.4%) in the East against marshalling yards, during which it dropped 3,782 tonnes of bombs and lost 49 aircraft. Another 602 sorties (14%) were in support of the army, *KG 55* dropping nearly 750 tonnes of bombs and losing eight aircraft while 535 sorties (12.6%) were supply drops delivering 619 tonnes for the loss of 17 aircraft. Total losses from 1 January to 31 July 1944 were 107 aircraft of which 45 were to enemy action. During operations until October 1944, *14 (Eisen)./KG 55* flew 1,126 sorties, dropping 1,982 tonnes of bombs on rail targets and nearly 28 tonnes of supplies. It lost 17 aircraft, 10 to enemy action. [19]

The decision on *Fliegerkorps IV* was probably taken by Göring in the aftermath of the July bomb plot in which an attempt to assassinate Hitler saw Korten mortally wounded on 20 July. Koller was away on the fatal day, possibly visiting *Luftflotte 3* where he is reported to have thwarted attempts by the plotters to seize power in France, and he may not have returned until Korten died on 22 July, to find the reins firmly in Göring's hands. Koller appears to have remained in post as operations chief until the end of August and to have acted as interim chief-of-staff for nearly a fortnight. He held his old position until replaced by *Oberst* Eckhard Christian at the end of August but could not reverse the *Fliegerkorps IV* decision. Once Hitler had recovered, he quickly sought a successor to Korten for he had no confidence in his deputy's abilities and his preference was for Greim.

With political rather than operational acumen, Göring pre-empted the decision by appointing *Generalleutnant* Werner Kreipe, a training specialist, as acting chief of staff on 2 August. Although he had some operational experience, most of Kreipe's war had been spent organising training, but he had taken part in the 1923 Munich Beer Hall *Putsch* which probably earned him some kudos. Hitler may well have accepted him as a stopgap and in September he met Greim and discussed making him de facto *Luftwaffe* commander, the conversation leading Göring to throw a tantrum and bully the *Generalfeldmarschall* into rejecting the offer. [20]

Kreipe's appointment saw no improvement in the air situation as crises grew on each flank. From Belorussia the Russians drove into Lithuania then thrust northwards to the Baltic at the Bay of Riga and westward towards East Prussia. Reuss and Pflugbeil's *Luftflotte 1* struggled to contain the threat with the latter receiving 140 aircraft from Greim including a substantial number of his *Schlachtflieger*. They were especially active, but they were unable to prevent the enemy reaching the Baltic near Riga on 30 July, isolating *Generalfeldmarschall* Ferdinand Schoerner's *Heeresgruppe Nord* which promptly received an infantry division flown in from Königsberg by a fleet of 86 Ju 52s. Pflugbeil had 321 combat aircraft (excluding *Nachtschlachtflieger*) on 1 August including all of *SG 3* and *SG 4*, but nine days later he faced a new threat when the Russians attacked Schoerner from the east.

A relief operation was imperative and Reuss received reinforcements, including a *Jagdgruppe* from Fuchs and a *Nahaufklärungsstaffel* from Greece, giving him some 140 aircraft. Model began the relief operation, *Unternehmen 'Doppelkopf'* ('Twin Head') on 16 August but almost immediately was transferred to the West and replaced by *Generaloberst* Hans Reinhardt as Russian spearheads approached East Prussia, whose defence diluted some of Reuss' efforts. Greim reinforced Reuss with one of Seidemann's *Jagdgruppen* and two of his *Schlachtgruppen* including most of *IV./SG 9* while Fuchs had to surrender a *Schlachtgruppe* and a *Nahaufklärungsstaffel* which gave Reuss 301 aircraft including a *Schule Einsatzstaffel* together with 1,152 tonnes of fuel. [21] With their support Reinhardt linked up with Schoerner on 20 August and within a week had established a

30-kilometre-wide coastal corridor [22]. Many wished to evacuate Schoerner's troops, but Hitler refused because they shielded the training grounds for the new generation of Walter U-boats with which Hitler hoped to regain control of the Atlantic.

During midsummer Dessloch's *Luftflotte 4* was untroubled and was steadily milked of units before losing *Fliegerkorps VIII* to Greim. By mid-August *Luftflotte 4* was down to 232 combat aircraft including most of *SG 2*, mainly under Deichmann's *Fliegerkorps I*, and augmented by 436 serviceable Rumanian aircraft and 40 German fighters defending the oil fields. [23] Just before the Russian blow fell, Dessloch was sent to the West to bring order out of the chaos and was replaced on 17 August by *Generalleutnant* Alexander Holle who had been serving in the Balkans for more than a year.

While Hitler's fears of a Red Army assault on the oil fields were partly allayed, his oil supplies were nevertheless under a constant pounding by the US Fifteenth Army Air Force, augmented by the RAF's long-range heavy bombers of 205 Group, which reduced the fields to a blackened wreck. The Russians had been biding their time and on 20 August they struck, supported by 1,756 VVS aircraft. The *Luftwaffe* flew 246 sorties on the first day of the assault while the Rumanians collapsed, allowing most of *Heeresgruppe Südukraine*, including *6.Armee*, to be enveloped. The *Luftwaffe* was again overwhelmed, despite 60 aircraft sent down by Greim, with the VVS losing only 111 aircraft to 29 August. [24] The situation was compounded when the Rumanians sought an armistice on 23 August and the young King Michael arrested the Rumanian Fascist dictator, Ion Antonescu. *Generalleutnant* Alfred Gerstenberg, *Kommandierende General der deutschen Luftwaffe in Rumänien* and the man responsible for defending the oil fields, convinced Hitler he could rescue Antonescu and seize the King, and on 24 August drove to the capital with some 6,000 *Flak* troops.

Almost immediately Gerstenberg's troops were pinned down in the suburbs and later driven out, even after Ju 52s dropped an SS paratroop battalion which was quickly destroyed. In supporting Gerstenberg, Holle compromised his own operations; on 24 August he flew 376 sorties of which 254 were over Bucharest and during the next two days the figures were 233 (95) and 267 (130) while the bombing of the palace and government buildings provided the Rumanians with an excuse to declare war on Germany. Most of Holle's staff were transferred to Hungary on 25 August but he remained with Deichmann's staff at Catesti for a few days until it became obvious the situation could not be salvaged, a fact emphasised by the fall of Ploesti two days later when *Luftflotte 4* flew only 79 sorties. [25]

Holle's outnumbered airmen now faced not only the VVS but also the Rumanian Air Force, many of whose squadrons had German aircraft. The *Luftwaffe* often replaced its losses with former Rumanian aircraft, *I./SG 2* using some Rumanian *Stukas* to attack Bucharest which the Russians entered on 31 August. The *Luftwaffe* was now fighting a desperate rearguard action to cover the flight into Hungary, transport aircraft dropping supplies to isolated forces having evacuated 2,050 personnel, 300 wounded and 412 tonnes in 297 sorties from 22–28 August. From 30 August to 4 September there were 43 Ju 52 sorties delivering 43 tonnes to isolated units with three landings which evacuated 42 wounded and 22 German women. [26] By the end of August, Holle and Deichmann had moved to Hungary with the Russians hard on their heels, the *Luftwaffe* using the last of its fuel to fly to brief safety in Hungary. It had lost 16,130 personnel, more than half of them *Flak* troopers, but most of the *Luftwaffehelferinen* escaped in one of the first convoys across the border. On 25 August *Oberstleutnant* Joachim Bauer, *Seefliegerführer Schwarzes Meer*, was ordered to organise the evacuation of the *Luftwaffe* units and personnel on the south bank of the Danube. His seaplanes had already flown to Varna in Bulgaria and on 26 August they flew to Salonika while Bauer apparently moved to Yugoslavia where his command was disbanded on 5 September. [27]

The Russians first secured Rumania then drove south into Bulgaria which they entered on 8 September and Sofia promptly defected to the Allied camp. The *Luftwaffe* presence in the country had been confined to *Major* Karl Rammelt's *Jagdabschnittsführer Bulgarien*, part of *Jafü Balkan* defending the eastern Danube valley, and the personnel appear to have withdrawn into Hungary unhindered. However, a few days earlier, on 30 August, the German Air Attaché, *Oberst* Clemens *Graf* von Schönborn, the former *Kommodore* of *St.G* 77, was killed in a crash while flying to the *Reich*. The Bulgarian Air Force had 186 serviceable aircraft, but the Germans were worried less by these than by the hundreds of VVS aircraft which soon appeared on Rumanian airfields ready to support a thrust into Hungary.

At the beginning of September, *Heeresgruppe Südukraine* (*Heeresgruppe Süd* from 24 September) had only 20 battalion-sized battlegroups supported by 284 combat aircraft (excluding *15./SG 151*) and some 25 *Nachtschlachtflieger*, the *Luftwaffe* having to commit student crews of *IV (Erg)./KG 2* to both reconnaissance and bombing missions. [28] In addition there were some 150 Hungarian aircraft under their own command, *Fliegerführer 102 (ungarische)*, which was now placed under Deichmann who faced some 1,600 Russian aircraft supported by 390 from Rumania and Bulgaria. Fuel shortages and the need to rebuild the infrastructure meant that *Luftflotte 4* flew an average 125–150 sorties a day during this period, but luckily the Russians had again outrun their supplies and for a month there was an uneasy calm. This remained the situation when Holle and Dessloch exchanged places on 22 September.

However, this did not save Kreipe whose mild manner and querulous approach led to him being referred to as '*Fräulein* Kreipe'. His relations with Hitler were poor, a combination of the former being headstrong and the latter increasingly interfering in *Luftwaffe* matters such as operations by the Me 262 jet which the *Führer* wanted to use as a strike aircraft rather than a fighter. The issue had led to Milch's fall in May and by the time of the Bomb Plot he had no role in the *Luftwaffe* but Kreipe had worked as a staff officer under him and potentially could have used him as a consultant. [29] Hitler first met Kreipe on 11 August but by the end of the month the *Führer* was accusing Kreipe of betrayal and the *Gestapo* was watching him [30]. With Milch in disgrace for ignoring Hitler's instructions to produce Me 262s as bombers, his previous association with Kreipe was another black mark against him in the eyes of both Hitler and Göring and the latter banned his Chief of Staff from any contact with his former deputy. On the night of 11/12 September a Bomber Command raid on Darmstadt so infuriated Hitler than he banned Kreipe from his headquarters and with Göring absenting himself to escape tongue-lashings from his leader, only the Operations officer, *Oberst* Christian, represented the *Luftwaffe*. On 18 September, Kreipe was told to resign and was replaced by Koller, although Göring would have preferred Pflugbeil, who preferred the perils of the Russian Front to those of Hitler's headquarters. [31]

A potential source of reinforcements for Hungary was in the Balkans where the Russian advance and the defection of Bulgaria threatened to isolate 900,000 troops (including 'volunteer' Italians) in Yugoslavia, Albania, Greece and the islands of the Aegean and eastern Mediterranean. The rapidly deteriorating situation in the East led Hitler to fear that Turkey would enter the war on the Allied side and on 31 July he moved *Fliegerkorps II* under *Generalleutnant* Kurt Kleinrath from Chartres to Niš in Serbia to control the *Luftwaffe's* response. With the collapse of Rumania, this problem was less pressing than the exposure of Löhr's *Heeresgruppe F* in Greece and the islands, where there were also thousands of civilians and military non-combatants who were essentially holidaymakers. Hitler ordered their evacuation from 25 August, the same day *OKW* authorised a covert evacuation of the 90,000 troops on the various islands. Two *Transportgruppen* were assembled under *Stab TG 4* (probably under *Oberst* Richard Kupschus), augmented by two floatplane *Staffeln* to give a strength of 109 aircraft (20 floatplanes) of which 107 were serviceable on 20 August.

The evacuation began 10 days later and during the first week the transports flew 308 sorties but the pace doubled as more units were brought in and in the next week up to 101 sorties a day were flown. The Allies made no attempt initially to interfere, but on 1 September began Operation 'Ratweek' to cut the mainland exit routes from Greece and Yugoslavia. Attacks upon the transports and their bases cut activity in the third week to as little as 38 sorties a day and although the force had grown to four *Gruppen* by 20 September its strength had declined to 90 aircraft (55 serviceable). The transports were later augmented by *Staffel*-sized *Kommandos* of KG 4 and KG 27 and the four-engined aircraft of *Lufttransportstaffel 5*. The airlift continued at a declining rate as fuel stocks were reduced and ended on 31 October after 2,050 sorties which had brought back 30,740 troops and 1,000 tonnes of materiel from the islands at the cost of 100 transports destroyed or severely damaged by enemy action and seven in accidents. Nearly 23,000 German troops remained on Crete and in the Dodecanese Islands and a four-engined unit equipped with Fw 200 and Ju 352 flew urgent supplies and mail to Rhodes and Crete. By the end of the war they had received 10 sorties and about 9 tonnes of supplies, some redistributed by a lone Ju 52 based on Crete. [32]

Once on the mainland Löhr's troops marched northwards through Albania and Yugoslavia joining those of *Heeresgruppe E*, both these groups being harassed by Communist guerrillas and Allied air attacks from Italy. The Germans were supported by Fröhlich's *Luftwaffenkommando Südost* which was being milked for aircraft but which rose in strength from 111 combat aircraft (77 serviceable), mostly *Nachtschlacht* and *Nahaufklärungsflieger*, on 20 September to 145 (94 serviceable). On 10 October *Luftwaffenkommando Südost* was aided by the transfer of *I./KG 4* for transport duties, supporting *Sonderkommando Major Augst* which operated out of Vienna-Aspern with some 40 transports. [33] But 12 days later Fröhlich's command was disbanded and its aircraft absorbed by *Kommandierende General der Deutschen Luftwaffe in Nordbalkan* which had been formed on 29 August from *Fliegerkorps II* headquarters and *Feldluftgau XXX* under *General der Flieger* Bernhard Weber. Weber had *Generalmajor* Walter Hagen's *Fliegerführer Nordbalkan*, created from *Fliegerführer Kroatien* also on 29 August.

Weber was subordinated to Dessloch and remained so until 1 November when the command reverted to its old title of *Fliegerkorps II* and was transferred to *Luftflotte 4* under Fink to support *Heeresgruppe E* which had moved into southern Hungary. Hagen's command (now under Dessloch) continued to support German forces in northern Yugoslavia, where there was a brief fear the two *Heeresgruppen* would be isolated following the Red Army's entry into the country on 4 October. Fortunately the Russians were content to take Belgrade a fortnight later and leave the liberation of the country to Tito's partisans, supported by Allied air forces in Italy and a Russian force of some 300 aircraft including Yugoslav communist squadrons. But these were not strong enough to prevent the German withdrawal in good order, still covered by Hagen whose command, based at Agram, had between 90 and 100 aircraft and became *Fliegerdivision 17* on 1 February 1945.

As *OKL* struggled to rebuild its forces in Hungary and the former Czechoslovakia, a new threat emerged in the north as *Luftwaffe* resources were stretched ever thinner. Three months bitter fighting had cost the *Luftwaffe* 1,186 combat aircraft destroyed or severely damaged by enemy action (excluding *Nachtschlachtflieger* and training units) and 882 by accidents while the *Transportverbände* had lost 43 and 26 aircraft respectively. Russian losses in the same period were more than 1,200 aircraft but the Soviets could more easily replace both men and machines as the quality pendulum had swung firmly in favour of the Soviet Union. [34]

The exposure of *Heeresgruppe Nord* was too tempting a target for Stalin and he prepared a new attempt to isolate it. The *Aufklärungsstaffeln* charted the slow build-up of men and supplies and the Russian attack was no surprise when it came on 14 September. Schoerner, the army group commander, had anticipated the threat and was prepared to abandon Estonia and retreat into Latvia, and within two days he secured Hitler's reluctant approval. While Reinhardt held open the corridor, Schoerner's troops began to fall back covered by Pflugbeil's trouble-shooter, *Generalmajor* Sigismund *Freiherr* von Falkenstein and his *Fliegerdivision 3* which controlled some 400 aircraft including 160 *Jabos*. This force repeatedly struck the advancing Russians inflicting heavy casualties and losing about 50 of its own aircraft. Some idea of the scope of air activity on this front may be gauged from a report of *III./SG 4* which noted that the *Gruppe* had flown 363 sorties on 73 days between 4 July and 27 October and had dropped more than 709 tonnes of bombs to destroy 2,179 vehicles (including 16 tanks), 54 guns and 10 bridges. [35]

But on 5 October a new Russian offensive drove towards the Baltic at Memel. While the port did not fall until 27 January, Schoerner had become isolated and his troops concentrated on the Courland Peninsula in north-eastern Latvia. They would remain there until the end of the war supported by Pflugbeil, whose command was rapidly milked as the threat to East Prussia grew. By mid-October half the *Jabos* and *SG 3's Panzerjägerstaffel* had gone south. Even Falkenstein departed, his *Fliegerdivision* being transferred to the Western Front and its return to the East in January 1945 benefited Greim, not Pflugbeil. [36]

The crisis also saw the disbandment of two Baltic State *Nachtschlachtgruppen* which had contributed some 50 aircraft to the defence and had flown some 12,600 sorties to that point. *Sonderstaffel Buschmann*, was created by Gerhard Buschmann, an Estonian of German descent, in February 1942. Within a year it had expanded into a seaplane unit (*SAGr 127*) and was converted to the night harassment role as *NSGr 11 (Est)* in

October 1943 encouraging the development of a similar Latvian unit, *NSGr 12 (lett)*. But the new Russian invasion hit Estonian morale and several crews defected to Sweden. On 4 October *NSGr 11* was disbanded and it was followed, despite the best efforts of *Luftflotte 1* chief-of-staff *Generalmajor* Klaus Siegfried Uebe, by *NSGr 12* on 17 October, which had been tarred with the same brush although none of its personnel had fled. A few pilots would join *JG 54* to defend their homeland, but for the majority their only contact with aircraft was either dismantling *Luftwaffe* bombers for scrap or guarding them until they were scrapped. [37]

Luftflotte 1 was quickly reduced to a pair of *Jagdgruppen*, a *Jabogruppe*, *NSGr 3* and *NAGr 5*. At the beginning of December this force totalled 263 aircraft but by 20 December this number had dropped to 189 (146 serviceable) while *III./SG 3* was briefly detached to *Luftflotte 6*. Its subsequent return brought the strength of *Luftflotte 1* to 237 (214 serviceable) on 10 January when there were some 20,500 *Luftwaffe* personnel including *Flak* crews while the Russians had 2,063 aircraft on 1 January. [38]

The *Luftwaffe* provided valuable air support to the *Landsers*, warning them when enemy attacks were imminent and striking enemy concentrations when fuel and ammunition was available, but the VVS had air superiority. *OKL* fed Pflugbeil enough resources to keep alight the flame of resistance, including a *Staffel* of *Panzerblitz*-equipped *Jabos* in January, but not enough to even scorch the enemy and on 17 April, *Luftflotte 1* was downgraded to *Luftwaffenkommando Kurland*, still under Pflugbeil, whose chief of staff since 25 December had been Mediterranean *Stuka* ace *Oberstleutnant* Paul Hozzel. By 9 April they were down to 170 aircraft (153 serviceable) but they struggled on until Germany surrendered on 9 May, a few pilots escaping Russian captivity by flying to Sweden, the *Jabos* of *III./SG 3* cramming up to three of their '*Schwarzmänner*' in each aircraft! There was also a last-minute attempt to evacuate wounded soldiers and fathers of large families with 35 Ju 52 flying in from Norway, but 32 of them were shot down. [39]

If the strategic rationale for holding Courland was to give the German Navy the opportunity to regain control of the Atlantic, from *OKL*'s viewpoint the bridgehead offered the last remaining prospect for attacks upon Russian industry. With the loss of the last Russian bases and the He 177s being consigned to scrap the only prospect was to use the *Mistel* ('Mistletoe') composite aircraft – Ju 88 bombers packed with explosives guided to their targets by attached fighters which separated from their charges after aiming them. [40] Throughout 1944 the Germans tinkered with plans for strategic bombing of Russian industry and on 6 November *Unternehmen 'Burgund'* ('Burgundy') was authorised using 10 He 177 but later abandoned due to lack of fuel. On 7 January 1945 however, Koller produced a new plan, *Unternehmen 'Eisenhammer'* ('Iron Hammer') which would use *Mistel* against targets up to 2,100 kilometres east of Berlin, with the pilots returning to Courland. The task was assigned to *KG(J) 30*, acting under *Oberstleutnant* Werner Baumbach's special operations force, *KG 200*, but the deteriorating situation meant that on the brink of being launched it was 'postponed' on 30 March 1945. A new plan, *Unternehmen 'Gertraud'* ('Gertrude'), called for an attack by Ju 290s, but the destruction of half the aircraft by Allied fighters meant Koller cancelled the operation on 14 April. [41]

The Russian advance to the Baltic in October also brought them to the borders of East Prussia, where Reuss' *Fliegerdivision 4* supported the defence with some 350 aircraft. However, with the Western Front falling apart, some 50 aircraft including those of *Stab SG 4* were sent westward during October followed by two *Jabogruppen* as soon as the crisis had passed in early November although the arrival of *NAGr 3* was some compensation. Fighting was fierce with Reuss' men losing some 75 aircraft, while *Fliegerdivision 4* claimed 264 enemy aircraft and 189 tanks between 16 and 28 October alone. [42] *JG 51* suffered especially badly losing 50 aircraft to enemy action during October but only 15 pilots killed, and the scale of operations may be judged from the fact that *IV./JG 51* flew 330 sorties that month and claimed 102 victories. [43]

Heavy rain drowned the air battles north of the Carpathians from November and the onset of winter prevented them returning to their former intensity. But south of the mountains the front flared into life again when the Russians entered Hungary in early October. They were checked by Friessner's *Heeresgruppe Süd* staged bold counter-attacks supported by *Fliegerkorps I* and the *Fliegerführer 102* which briefly stabilised the front in the second half of the month in operations which cost Dessloch at least 122 aircraft to enemy action. For Dessloch the air battle was one of considerable confusion, for not only did he face more than 1,500 Russian aircraft, but also attacks upon his forces in the Balkans from Allied aircraft in Italy, including those from the US Fifteenth Air Force mounting raids on Hungarian oil and industrial targets. These fully absorbed the attentions of both *Jagdfliegerführer Ungarn*, incorporated into the *Reich*'s air defence force *I. Jagdkorps* on 1 September, and *8. Jagddivision* operating in Bavaria and Austria. So confused did the situation become that on 7 November a fierce air battle developed between Russian and American fighters over Yugoslavia with each side's fighters shooting down two of their allies. [44]

Friessner's success in October was aided by severe supply problems for the Russians who had to convert the Rumanian and Bulgarian railway lines to their gauge. On 29 October they struck again and drove towards Budapest, but although they reached the Hungarian capital on 3 November they were too weak to storm it and slowly isolated it as driving rain turned the battlefield to mud. By 26 December they achieved their objective. Deichmann's *Fliegerkorps I* with some 600 aircraft fought valiantly despite the handicap of low fuel supplies which reduced operations to 150–200 sorties a day which could not prevent the gradual isolation of Budapest where the *Korps*' own headquarters were located from 1 December. Dessloch's problems grew as a new threat developed in southern Hungary, which was attacked from Bulgaria and Yugoslavia, but some relief also came from the south for *Heeresgruppe E* sent *2. Panzerarmee* to plug the gap and in support came the reformed *Fliegerkorps II* under Fink who moved his headquarters to Pecs (Fünfkirchen) and had some 120 aircraft, half of them *Nachtschlachtflieger*, most of which were drawn from Deichmann.

This was a minor matter for Deichmann who was trapped in Budapest with 70,000 troops, of whom 33,000 were German under *SS Obergruppenführer* Karl Pfeffer von Wildenbruch, and 800,000 civilians, whose fate was a matter of indifference to the German high command. [45] On 27 December, *General der Infanterie* Otto Wöhler, who replaced Friessner on 22 December, demanded an airlift of 80 tonnes a day (20 tonnes by parachute) into the besieged city, although the prospects were bleak, especially after the Russians managed to take most of Pferrer-Wildenbruch's supplies on the day they isolated the city. [46] *Generalleutnant Dipl.Ing* Gerhard Conrad, a transport expert on Dessloch's staff, created *Luftversorgungsstab Budapest* which was subordinated to Fink and had two transport and one glider *Gruppen* as well as a Hungarian transport squadron with some 80 transports (a figure which had dropped to 60 by 10 January). Additionally, Conrad could also call on 85 He 111 of *KG 4* (70 by 10 January) to drop supplies, although some of its aircraft were still based in Austria.

Main roads and a park within the city were used as landing grounds for both aircraft and gliders, the latter's pilots recovered by Fi 156, and this allowed the withdrawal of Deichmann's staff to Veszprém a few days after the siege began. But fuel shortages meant an average of only 36 tonnes of supplies were flown each night and the last airfields were lost on 9 January. The city did not fall until 12 February, the civilian population having suffered terribly. The *Luftwaffe* had flown in more than 1,515 tonnes of supplies and lost 45 aircraft and 48 gliders and suffered 138 aircrew casualties of whom 109 were dead or missing. [47]

The vain two-month battle for Hungary cost Dessloch 291 aircraft and the poor weather meant that 184 of them were in accidents but such were the efforts of the *Reich*'s factories that he received 336 replacements (37.6% of the total sent to the East). The ease with which replacement aircraft could be obtained meant that during its last months the *Luftwaffe* became a throw-away organisation, for it was easier to acquire the latest aircraft than send older ones for overhaul. *Luftwaffe* combat strength in the East in the first two months and last two months of 1944 was some 3,860 aircraft but in the first two months 271 (excluding *Nachtschlacht*) were sent for overhaul compared with 162 (including *Nachtschlacht*) in the last two months representing 7 per cent and 4 per cent of overall strength respectively. Even within the *Reich* there was a noticeable decline in single-seat piston-engined day fighter overhaul rates which amounted to 38 per cent of overall strength in the first two months of 1944 and 34 per cent in the last two months. [48]

Throughout the siege of Budapest *Fliegerkorps I* supported vain attempts to relieve the city, but it was outnumbered and lost most of *SG 2* to *Luftflotte 6* during December. By 10 January it was down to 168 combat aircraft (excluding *14./SG 9*) of which 132 were serviceable, while to the south Fink had 129 aircraft (106 serviceable), all the fighters being concentrated under *Major* Ernst Düllberg's *Stab JG 76* during January, while Dessloch had 40 aircraft, mostly reconnaissance, under his direct command. He faced 1,896 Russian aircraft on 1 January plus 385 Rumanian and Bulgarian aircraft. [49] With the fall of Budapest an uneasy lull fell on the Hungarian battlefield but this merely heralded a new storm, for both sides were planning offensives. Hitler wanted *Unternehmen 'Frühlingserwachen'* ('Spring Awakening') to create a greater buffer zone between the Russians and his last oil field at Nagykanizsa and he brought over *6. SS Panzerarmee* from the Ardennes to north of Lake Balaton. The attack began on 5 March and was quickly contained, exhausting Germany's last reserve so that when the Russian counter-offensive began in snow and fog on 16 March, it quickly drove the Germans westwards into Austria, taking Vienna on 13 April but the Germans then rallied in the eastern Alps and the Red Army switched most of its forces northwards. [50]

For Dessloch these final battles were extremely frustrating. The battles north of the Carpathians had priority and for '*Frühlingserwachen*' he appears to have received few reinforcements and probably little extra fuel yet he faced 965 Russian aircraft which helped smother the attack. Fink's headquarters was transferred to *Luftflotte 6* on 3 February and *KG 4* began migrating north to doom any lingering hopes of operational bombing missions [51]. He was also under pressure from the West with the US Fifteenth Air Force flying 603 heavy bomber and 286 fighter sorties against Hungarian targets, mostly communications, in which it lost three bombers and a fighter. [52] Dessloch covered the retreat during March and took over Hagen's *Fliegerdivision 17* to increase his strength to 430 aircraft (328 serviceable) by 9 April together with 60 Hungarian, but there were major changes in the wind.

On 4 April *Fliegerkorps I* was renamed *Fliegerdivision 18* to support *8.Armee* and *6. SS Panzerarmee* and on 21 April *Luftflotte 4* was redesignated *Luftwaffenkommando 4* and placed under *Luftflotte 6*. Dessloch remained in command for nearly a week, but on 27 April took over *Luftflotte 6* and handed over to Deichmann who was himself replaced by *General der Flieger* Paul Weitkus. Weitkus had joined the *Luftflotte* staff after his *FlFü Albanien* was disbanded on 29 August. Harassed from Italy and from the East, Deichmann could offer only token resistance; although he did receive *Jagddivision 8* from the *Reich*'s defence force but he was having to abandon hundreds of aircraft for lack of fuel and by the war's end he was disbanding four *Gruppen*.

In Austria he encountered *Luftwaffe* refugees from Italy where *Luftflotte 2* was drained dry following the loss of Rome. Richthofen, who had been in ill-health for months, advocated re-organising the *Luftwaffe* command and on 6 September Pohl, the first *Luftwaffe* representative in Italy as *Italuft* and now head of the *Nahkampffliegerkorps* was made *Kommandierende General der Deutschen Luftwaffe in Italien* in a remarkable display of continuity. The sequence of subsequent events is unclear, but *Luftflotte 2* headquarters was withdrawn to Vienna and apparently disbanded on 27 September as Richthofen went on sick leave. He was diagnosed with a brain tumour and an operation proved only a partial success. He never returned to command and died shortly after the war ended. [53]

Pohl's resources were sparse and the foundation of German air operations in Italy during the last year of the war was the Italian *Aeronautica Nazionale Repubblicana* (*ANR*) which had 120 aircraft by the end of the war. [54] The *Luftwaffe*'s presence was confined to *Aufklärung-* and *Nachtschlachtstaffeln* which, in total, had 76 aircraft (59 serviceable) on 10 October (including a suicide unit *Sonderkommando Einhorn*). Relations between the two allies were sometimes tense but they fought together and by the end of the war German air strength had actually risen to 96 including a detachment of Ar 234 reconnaissance jets. [55] A *Luftwaffenführenstab* report noted that between February and July 1944 12,769 fighter sorties were flown but during the rest of the year only 637. [56]

The prime *Luftwaffe* command in the East remained Greim's *Luftflotte 6* covering the sector from the Baltic to the Carpathians, including the former Czechoslovakia. A relative lull had seen some rationalisation of command under Greim with Fuchs' *Fliegerdivision 1* transferred to Stolp on the coast, and Seidemann's *Fliegerkorps VIII* responsible for the defence of Poland, while *Fliegerdivision 4*, temporarily under former *Luftflotte 1* chief of staff, *Generalmajor* Uebe from 25 December, defended East Prussia assisted by the night fighters of *Hauptmann* Egbert Belau's *Jagdfliegerführer Ostpreussen*. Mention should also be made of *Fliegerführer 6* created by Wild on 9 December to control anti-submarine and mine destruction units on the coast and from 24 December under the command of *Oberst* Karl Stockman.

Luftflotte 6 had 1,079 combat aircraft on 1 December and by 10 January it had 998 (811 serviceable) supported by 94 (76 serviceable) night fighters; the *Luftflotte's* importance was so great that it received 397 replacement aircraft in the last two months of 1944, or nearly 45 per cent of those sent to the East. It was a purely tactical force lacking any medium bombers but in anticipation of a major Russian offensive, Greim had been able to assemble 461 ground-attack aircraft and kept *SG 2* in reserve with 89 of them. But he was weak in fighters with only 204 single-engined aircraft compared with the VVS' 4,650 on 1 January out of 10,809 aircraft which could be reinforced by about 1,000 medium and heavy bombers of the 18th Air Army, as the ADD was redesignated on 26 December. [57]

The Russians' grand design was to thrust out of their bridgeheads on the Vistula and drive westwards to the Oder and Neisse lines to clear Poland, then turn north to isolate and overwhelm East Prussia. [58] The offensive began in fog and low cloud on 12 January and smashed through the Germans to take Warsaw on 17 January and Cracow two days later, with the spearheads reaching the Oder on 22 January. The VVS interdicted German communications, mercilessly destroying motor and equine transport and blasting any attempts to counter-attack or any bottlenecks of men and transport. The Russians were soon entering Silesia which was now the backbone of German war industry and while January ended with a thaw which halted the Russian advance on most fronts, they were able to isolate Breslau by the middle of February. After a brief pause in late February they struck north towards the Baltic and after fierce resistance occupied the coast between the Oder and Danzig (Gdansk) which fell on 30 March. Throughout this period the Russians were also pushing into East Prussia and stormed the capital, Königsberg, on 9 April.

Seidemann and Fuchs faced the main blow which was supported by 7,800 aircraft. Greim had conserved his resources and did not commit them until 12 January when his day units flew 167 sorties and dropped 16.5 tonnes of bombs. The following day his units flew 602 sorties, dropping more than 90 tonnes of bombs and firing 24 *Panzerschreck* anti-tank rockets, while the cannon-armed tank-busters of *10.(Pz)/SG 9* claimed their 500th tank (see Table 9-7). During this period 70 night sorties were flown and nearly 19.75 tonnes of bombs were delivered. The *Schlachtflieger*, operating in groups of 20 to 50 aircraft, desperately struck enemy spearheads, destroying a few tanks here and some vehicles there, but overall it was like trying to stop a tidal wave with a stone and the cost was heavy. Seven *Ritterkreuz*-holders were killed in January alone and on 20–22 January *SG* 77 lost 26 aircraft. On 8 February the tank-busting ace *Oberst* Hans-Ulrich Rudel, who had destroyed 12 tanks that day alone, was shot down and had to have a leg amputated. [59]

Table 9-7: Luftflotte 6 operations, January 1–21 1945

Date	Day (*lost*)	Night (*lost*)	Total
Jan 1–7	180 (-)	29 (-)	209
Jan 8–14	809 (22)	70 (5)	879
Jan 15–21	3,477 (91)	259 (11)	3,736

Source: BA MA RL 7/526 & 529.

As the front collapsed, Fuchs' *Fliegerdivision 1* was given four of Uebe's *Gruppen* to defend Pomerania and the northern Oder while Falkenstein's *Fliegerdivision 3* returned from the Western Front to defend the mountain approaches into the Sudetenland and Moravia. *Fliegerdivision 3* was given a *Gruppe* each from Uebe and Seidemann together with two *Reichs* air defence *Jagdgruppen* (a third was briefly given to Seidemann before joining Falkenstein), reducing Uebe's force by 16 January to a *Jagdgruppe* and a *Nahaufklärungsstaffel* while facing more than 2,900 VVS aircraft. Curiously, while the enemy had air superiority and inflicted losses on the *Luftwaffe* between 8 and 21 January, the day loss rate was an average 2.6/2.7 per cent including accidents. On 21 January (when detailed reporting became impossible) Greim's airmen flew 424 day sorties (253 by the *Schlachtflieger*) dropping more than 62 tonnes of bombs while the *Nachtflieger* flew 32 sorties. The desperate need for ground-attack aircraft meant that possibly as early as 13 January, night fighters and long-range reconnaissance aircraft were pressed into this role for which they were totally unsuitable, while the small numbers of Fw 189 in the *Nahaufklärungsgruppen* augmented the *Nachtschlachtgruppen*. [60]

The threat to Berlin led to a major transfer of units from the West to the East involving 16 *Jagdgruppen* of *JG 3, 4, 6, 11* and 77 with some 460 fighters and 100 *Jabos* of *SG 4* augmented by 90 fighters from *Luftflotte Reich*'s *JG 1* giving Greim some 1,300 combat aircraft by 1 February and a day fighter force of about 750 aircraft. [61] He had the advantage of using many pre-war air bases with concrete runways while the VVS operated from muddy and flooded fields, leading to numerous accidental losses. But only slightly more than half of the Russian machines – 750 aircraft – were serviceable, as the rapid Soviet advance forced units to abandon airfields and aircraft, while the loss of supply depots and the general disruption of transport starved units of supplies. Furthermore, the loss of major ferrying points hindered the replacement of aircraft. [62]

Retreats exacerbated fuel problems, with limited stocks scattered to protect them from air attack forcing petrol bowsers to travel long distances, picking up a few tonnes here and a few there, so that even home defence units found difficulty assembling the 20 tonnes they needed for a mission. [63] Ferrying aircraft from airfield to airfield wasted fuel and was another reason why the *Luftwaffe* was unable to influence events on the ground. On 27 January 1945 the 2,000 aircraft on the entire Eastern Front flew only 1,403 sorties with 608 the following day, mostly by *Luftflotte 6*. Another indication of the ineffectiveness of the *Luftwaffe* comes from the fact that the Russians lost only 343 aircraft in this offensive to 3 February. [64] Incomplete data from the *OKW* war diary indicated that *Luftwaffe* activity in the East dropped from 7,300 sorties per week in the first half of February to 5,100 in the second half, 2,900 in the first half of March and 2,600 in the second half. [65]

The *Fliegerschule* of *Luftflotte 10*, formed under *General der Flieger* Seidel on 1 July as the training command, had been driven by prowling US fighters to seek sanctuary in Poland, but with their bases under threat they now dispersed to the Leipzig area and to Denmark, with an inevitable disruption in training (Fröhlich replaced Seidel on 27 February). Then the Russian advance into Silesia caused the loss of aircraft assembly plants and the supporting facilities for producing components, the impact in the East being especially bad as there was a 25 per cent cut in Fw 190 production.

This type formed the backbone not only of the *Jagdgruppen* but also the *Schlacht-* and *Nahaufklärungsgruppen*; the situation was mitigated in the short term by the large stock of reserves assembled previously. [66]

The Russian advance also caused major changes in the Eastern Front command structure north of the Carpathians. On 3 February Fiebig, who had been in command for barely two days, was ordered to take *Fliegerkorps II* headquarters north from Hungary to support the newly created *Heeresgruppe Weichsel* (Vistula) defending Pomerania (Fuchs) and the approaches to Berlin together with the newly arrived *Fliegerdivision 4*. Seidemann's *Fliegerkorps VIII* was driven into Silesia and from 25 January to 2 February was briefly designated *Luftwaffenkommando Schlesien* with Falkenstein's *Fliegerdivision 3* on his right. But the greatest change was in East Prussia where Uebe's rise in command status occurred as his tactical area was steadily reduced, for on 24 January he was given the newly formed *Luftwaffenkommando Ostpreussen* with his own *Fliegerdivision 4* (until it was transferred to *Fliegerkorps II* on 3 February), *Jafü Ostpreussen* and the maritime support units of *FlFü 6*. Uebe also received a *Schlachtgruppe*, but by 1 March he was down to some 70 aircraft and could do little to prevent the remorseless Russian advance. Reinforcements during March raised Uebe's strength to 147 aircraft (96 serviceable) by 9 April and after the fall of Königsberg, he continued the struggle from Pillau-Neutief, facing the usual problems of supply shortages as well as difficulties in finding suitable airfields yet despite the problems his forces destroyed 1,450 Russian aircraft from January to 2 May. [67] Uebe was replaced on 24 April but his successor, *Generalmajor* Günther Sachs, could do nothing to prevent constant attacks upon the *Landsers*, and with the loss of Danzig he had to support troops with a fingerhold on the coast between Danzig and Königsberg.

Elsewhere on Greim's front the thaw at the end of January provided the Germans with a brief opportunity to regroup and to contain the enemy. The thaw forced Russian transport onto the handful of highways running through Poland and they thus proved vulnerable to attack, with 800 vehicles being claimed on 28 February alone. Even Berlin's aerial shield, comprising the units of *1. Jagddivision*, was committed and on 6 February most of its 445 aircraft, including 46 *Jabos* under *SG 104*, were committed to attacking the Russians with three Ju 88 night-fighters being lost to ground fire. [68] The Russian advance beyond the Oder was contained by counter-attacks supported by every aircraft Seidemann could find but on 24 January this meant only 280 sorties. In attacks upon the Oder bridgeheads Greim's airmen flew 3,300 sorties between 31 January and 2 February, losing 107 aircraft but claiming up to 2,000 vehicles.

Fuchs supported a brief counter-offensive, *Unternehmen 'Sonnenwende'* ('Solstice'), in mid-February which ended in the rain on the 18th of the month. Two days later fuel shortages led *OKW* to order that aircraft were to be used only in decisive points of the front and when nothing else was practical, and by mid-March Greim was down to 64–72 tonnes of fuel per day. [69] The effects of *Panzerblitz* missiles may be judged by the fact that on 3 March *1./SG 2*, operating under *SG 3*, claimed 74 tanks while *III./SG 4* claimed 23 tanks in 16 days of operations between 21 January and 16 March. [70] In late February, in an effort to make the most effective use of scarce fuel, Greim organised tank-detecting *Panzeraufklärungsschwarme* with Fi 156 *Storch* and by 1 March he had four such units with 25 aircraft on strength; they evidently proved successful, for a month later he had five *Schwarme* with 33 aircraft.

Following their Polish success, the Russians frantically rebuilt their communications (each of the three fronts in Poland required up to 25,000 tonnes of supplies a day) which would have offered the German *Kampfgruppen* an excellent opportunity to disrupt their preparations, but they had largely abandoned their strike role and had become de facto transport units. There was a brief resurgence during this period when Hitler appointed Baumbach his plenipotentiary for the destruction of the enemy-held bridges over the Oder on 1 March. Although Baumbach (later *FlFü 200*) would report his progress in this mission to Hitler, he was also planning '*Eisenhammer*', organising the escape of leading Nazis and conducting a variety of special operations, so *OKL* quietly assigned the task to *LG 1*'s *Kommodore*, *Oberst* Joachim Helbig, without bothering to worry the *Führer* about such minor details. [71] *Gefechtsverband Helbig*, the last long-range strike command formed to support the Western Front, moved east on 5 March with a bomber unit (*II./LG 1*), a minelayer unit (*III./KG 53*), which was soon replaced by *II./KG 200*, and *Versuchskommando 200* with bombers carrying Hs 293 missiles, to execute the *Luftwaffe*'s part in the mission.

Operations began the following day with four Hs 293 sorties (one aircraft was badly damaged) and on 24 March Helbig had 78 bombers (46 serviceable) and 29 *Mistel* [12] and he could also call on the *Schlachtgruppen*. Until mid-April some 550 sorties were flown against the bridges, 200 by bombers which delivered a variety of ordnance including 1-tonne bombs and Hs 293 missiles, together with some 40 *Mistel* which had the greatest successes. In addition to attacks upon the bridges *14.(Eis)/KG 55* tried to pick off trains until transferred to transport duties on 29 March. These missions continued until the end of April with some success, but there was never sufficient fuel for a sustained attack which might have ensured traffic did not cross the Oder. American air attacks gradually reduced the *Mistel* force. [72]

Most of the surviving bomber force was used for transport operations with two gruppen of *KG 4* attached to Morzik's *Lufttransportchefs der Wehrmacht beim OKL* with eight *Transportgruppen* and the *Grossraumtransportsgruppe* with some 150 aircraft. They were used to support major units escaping westwards and isolated garrisons flying more than 900 sorties between mid-January and the end of March. [73] Priority was given to the support of Breslau, to which the Germans flew some 3,500 sorties between 15 February and 1 May to deliver up to 3,000 tonnes of food and ammunition together with some 500 soldiers, while evacuating around 12,000 wounded and civilians at the cost of 165 Ju 52s. [74] Initially these missions were largely flown by Ju 52s, production of which had ceased in July 1944, but as the Russian air defences improved and fighters were moved forward, the He 111 had to be used, increasingly together with *Stukas* and, from 16 March, even Bf 109s! Landings ceased after 7 April and supplies had to be dropped in but on the night of 1/2 May two Fi 156 managed to land and take out glider crews and the garrison commander, *SS Obergruppenführer* Karl Hanke. [75]

Meanwhile, Fuchs' *Fliegerdivision 1.* was fully engaged in meeting a major new thrust into Pomerania starting on 24 February and reaching the coast on 1 March, driving the German troops in western Pomerania across the Oder and those in eastern Pomerania towards Danzig. Fuchs had 468 aircraft (367 serviceable) on 1 March, but with little fuel he was again unable to influence events and was pushed back westwards. However, the Russians noted their losses to 4 April as 1,073 aircraft, although many of these were to *Flak*. [76] Yet shortages of fuel and poor weather meant that the 2,700 German aircraft on the Eastern Front flew 285–621 sorties daily in the first week of March peaking at 1,718 on 9 March. Fuchs' arrival bolstered the defence of Berlin where *Fliegerkorps II* already had 1,141 aircraft (875 serviceable) on 1 March, while in Silesia Seidemann's *Fliegerkorps VIII* had 524 (395) and Falkenstein's *Fliegerdivision 3* had 336 aircraft (266). Greim also had a force of 100 transport aircraft. Despite the fuel shortages, Fuchs' *Fliegerdivision 1* flew 2,190 sorties defending Pomerania during March and claimed 172 tanks and 250 trucks while *Fliegerdivision 4*'s SG 1 dropped 295.5 tonnes of bombs. [77] Reconnaissance activity was also maintained during the month with Greim's *FAG 3* flying 53 sorties and losing three aircraft, while Seidemann's *1./NAG 15* flew 71 sorties, usually in *Rotte* strength, of which only 13 were photographic reconnaissance sorties the others being fighter and ground-attack. [78]

With no threats to their rear the Russians prepared a final assault upon Berlin which began on 16 April. [79] The Germans were aware of the threat and *Luftwaffe* preparations included moving most of Berlin's mobile *Flak* batteries to the front while Fiebig's *Fliegerkorps II* was renamed *Luftwaffenkommando Nordost* with Fuchs' *Fliegerdivision 1* and Reuss's *Fliegerdivision 4*. Fiebig had 1,355 aircraft (plus 68 seaplanes) including 622 fighters and 451 *Schlachtflieger* facing 4,548 VVS aircraft augmented by 800 bombers of the 18th Air Army and 297 Polish aircraft, while Seidemann and Falkenstein had 791 aircraft including 206 fighters and 339 *Schlachtflieger* facing 2,150. [80] The VVS fighter forces were now supported by radar and the service carefully co-ordinated its operations with those of the ground force. The 16th Air Army supporting the Russian centre had even targeted the enemy's headquarters in an attempt to decapitate his command. The intense battles of March had drained *Luftwaffe* fuel stocks leaving sufficient for only 300 aircraft, forcing Greim to disband six *Jagdgruppen*. Such was his desperation of *OKL* that a suicide unit, *Sondergruppe A*, was created to attack the Oder bridges and it would reportedly fly 60 sorties on 16 April.

The direct attack upon Berlin across the Oder proved a bloody shambles which made little progress, but the attack across the Neisse was more successful and swiftly began to encircle Berlin from the south. On 16 April the *Luftwaffe* flew 891 sorties on the entire Eastern Front of which 453 were by *Luftflotte 6*, including 195 fighter and 224 attack, the latter expending 74 tonnes of bombs and 408 *Panzerblitz* with 19 aircraft lost (a 4% loss rate), but on the Berlin front only 165 sorties were flown. [81] With radar support the VVS provided an effective shield and eventually sheer weight of numbers carried the Russian centre through the German lines. From 20 April, Hitler's birthday, Soviet forces began to encircle Berlin from the north, capturing 144 aircraft at Jüterbog; the two arms met east of the city on 25 April, the same day the Russians met the Americans at Torgau.

The air battles often took place in poor visibility and the *Schlachtflieger* flew valiantly trying to stem the tidal wave but without success and at heavy cost, 19 *Ritterkreuz*-holders falling in April, while the destruction of the *Luftwaffe*'s infrastructure inevitably followed the Russian advance. [82] The vulnerability of even Eastern Front air units to attacks from the West was underlined on 16 April when *III./SG 2* and *FAG 3* lost 10 aircraft to American *Jabos* at Klentschang, while the next day Mustangs which had completed a heavy bomber escort mission caught *III./SG 77* at Kamenz north of Dresden as it prepared to take off to strike the Red Army. Nine *Jabos* were shot down while six more were destroyed or severely damaged on the ground. [83]

Hitler decided to remain in the isolated city which was now suffering storms of shells and Göring sent him a telegram asking whether or not he was now *Der Führer*. [84] The paranoid Hitler saw this as a coup; he dismissed Göring as the supreme chief of the *Luftwaffe* and summoned Greim to his presence, the *Luftflotte 6* commander being flown in to the city by the aviatrix, *Flugkapitän* Hanna Reitsch, but he was wounded on landing. His wounds were barely dressed when Hitler fulfilled a long desire and appointed him commander of an ever-decreasing *Luftwaffe*. Greim was then flown out in an Ar 96 trainer to do what he could and was replaced at *Luftflotte 6* by Dessloch. [85]

As the Russians began to storm Berlin there was little the *Luftwaffe* could do apart from almost random fighter and *Jabo* operations in support of the 91,000 defenders. Russian air superiority was such that the VVS flew 92,000 sorties during the campaign and lost 917 aircraft, mostly to ground fire whereas, for example, *SG 1* was forced to fly at night with up to 20 sorties. [86] Aerial resupply of the German capital had been planned since mid-March and there had been amibitious plans for 250 transport sorties a day, to bring in 500 tonnes of supplies, but by mid-April there was simply not enough fuel. By 20 April the city centre was under artillery fire and city airports quickly fell. The supply task was assigned to *Transportfliegerführer Luftflotte Reich* possessing only about 115 transports, including Ju 352s, which brought in troops and munitions and evacuated important personnel using roads and parks as airstrips until these either came under fire or were taken. [87]

Supply drops were then organised but dust, smoke, and fog made it difficult to find the dropping zones and the vulnerability of Ju 52s to ground fire meant Bf 109s and Fw 190 dumped supply containers into the burning ruins from 26 April until 1 May. The transport mission involved some 200 sorties and cost up to 30 transports, ultimately achieving nothing. A few Fi 156 *Storchs* were used after most of the main roads had fallen, but even this became too hazardous. By the time Hitler committed suicide (appointing *Grossadmiral* Karl Dönitz as leader) and the city surrendered on 2 May, any form of air support had been abandoned. South of the city, 9. *Armee* was in a moving pocket, fighting its way westwards with thousands of civilian refugees and *KG 4*, which had been supporting Breslau, was ordered to drop supplies to the pocket from 28 April. However, the *Geschwader* was unable to locate dropping zones although the army managed to reach sanctuary in the west before the war's end.

With Germany split in half, Fiebig's *Luftwaffenkommando Nordost* (which was given *FlFü 6* on 21 April) directed what air operations it could in the north while Dessloch's *Luftflotte 6* commanded the forces in the south, including Seidemann's *Fliegerkorps VIII* which absorbed *Luftgau VIII* and became *Luftwaffenkommando VIII* on 12 April. But it was driven out of Silesia into Moravia. Such were the fuel shortages that when *Major* Gerhard Barkhorn's *JG 6* received 150 brand-new Fw 190 D-9 from a local Focke-Wulf factory, there was only enough fuel for patrols by four fighters. [88]

It was a measure of German desperation that Dessloch also commanded *Luftwaffenkommando West* which was placed under *Luftflotte 6* on 1 April. But this was akin to shuffling the deckchairs on the Titanic, for the *Luftwaffe* no longer had any industrial support, its infrastructure was in tatters and fuel was desperately short. By the time the *Luftwaffe* surrendered on 8 May it was eating its young, disbanding units wholesale in an attempt to fan the flames of resistance. On the afternoon of 8 May, *Oberleutnant* Friedrich 'Fritz' Stehle, flying an Me 262 of *JG* 7, shot down an Airacobra in what was probably the last *Luftwaffe* victory in the East, although the last air combat appears to have taken place the following day over Czechoslovakia. [89]

OKL did not climb onto the *Führer's* funeral pyre – in fact it began moving out of Berlin into the so-called Bavarian redoubt in March, a tactical headquarters having been established in a lunatic asylyum at Wasserburg near Munich on 21 February. From 4 March the majority of the staff departments began moving to the Weimar area but then went to Wasserburg, Koller departing Rechlin on 28 April. With the Franco-American advance into Bavaria, Koller moved his staff to Berchtesgaden, although his small organisation of 90 personnel then moved across the border to the little Austrian village of Thumersbach where he joined them on 6 May, followed by Greim two days later, and together they surrendered to the Americans. [90]

Chapter Ten

Endgame in the West

The successful Allied invasion of Europe in June 1944 followed the defeat of the U-boats in March which allowed men, supplies and raw materials to flood across the Atlantic while in the air the Allies began to gain air superiority over Western Europe.

The success reflected the benefits of American industry and in particular medium bombers such as the North American B-25 Mitchell, the Douglas A-20 Havoc and the Martin B-26 Marauder – which made its debut on 14 May, collectively superior to almost any European design except the Mosquito in performance, payload and defensive capability. The exception was the Lockheed Ventura, a development of the Hudson: on 3 May an unescorted British squadron of 11 was wiped out over the Netherlands by *Jagdgruppen* leaders who were taking a break from a conference in Amsterdam-Schiphol. [1]

Allied bombers lacked escorts because most of the Allied fighters in 1943 were short-range British types, although the RAF's aircraft flew 86 per cent of all Allied fighter/fighter-bomber sorties over Western Europe in 1943. The majority were Spitfire IX and XII whose limited combat radius was some 170 nautical miles (320 kilometres) which confined them to a relatively narrow belt along the west European coast. However, their performance now matched that of both the Fw 190 A and the Bf 109 G which equipped the outnumbered and increasingly outclassed *Jagdgruppen*, and partly for this reason plans to exchange *JG 26* and *JG 54* during the spring – owing to the fact that the *JG 54* pilots were more used to low-level (under 15,000 feet or 4,500 metres) operations – would have required complete retraining.

The *Jagdgruppen* continued their hit-and-run tactics, withdrawing eastwards if pressure grew too great; but this strategy was steadily undermined by the arrival of the new generation of American fighters. The P-47 Thunderbolt made its debut on 8 April 1943 but for the first three months of its deployment its radius of some 200 nautical miles (370 kilometres) was little better than the Spitfire, although it could absorb a formidable amount of battle damage. [2] The P-38 Lightning had a radius of 260 nautical (480 kilometres) on internal fuel but the twin-engined fighter could not dogfight and its engines proved unreliable in the cold, humid European air which is why the Mediterranean and Pacific Theatres had priority for these aircraft.

Using drop tanks from late July 1943, the range of the American fighters was steadily extended until they reached central Germany and France. The tanks were originally deployed to strengthen the escorts for the Eighth Air Force's heavy bombers which were used against French targets, usually U-boat bases, during the first quarter of 1943. Although the bombers were unescorted they were a serious tactical problem for *JG 2* and *JG 26* who even tried dropping bombs on their formations on 16 February. The *Luftnachrichtentruppe* preferred the 'soft kill' option and turned back the US 305th Bomb Group with a bogus recall message on 27

February when it was within sight of its Brest target. [3] During the first four months of 1943 the Americans' average monthly loss rate of bombers which crossed the French coast was 5.72 per cent, shaking confidence in the belief that the bombers would blast their way to and from a target. Some B-17s were converted into escort aircraft known as YB-40s with heavier armament and increased ammunition. Examples of these flew with a mission to St Nazaire on 29 May, but their charges suffered 12.5 per cent losses. The Americans persevered, flying 47 sorties with the YB-40, but there was no benefit and the last YB-40 mission was flown against Le Bourget airfield on 16 August. [4]

By now the USAAF was flying the majority of its bomber missions over Western Europe and planning for the invasion was moving from the theoretical to the practical, reflected in the creation of the RAF's Second Tactical Air Force on 1 June from elements of Fighter, Bomber and Army Co-operation Commands. [5] On 16 October the Eighth Air Force transferred its light and medium bomber squadrons and tactical reconnaissance units to Lieutenant-General (later Major-General) Lewis H. Brereton's Ninth Air Force, although this organisation did not receive any fighter squadrons until 11 December, but these would be P-51Bs which claimed their first victories five days later. [6] Now bombers could be escorted throughout the operational zone in France, the Low Countries and even Germany, while fighters swept through most of these areas (for Allied operations over Western Europe to May 1944, see Table 10-1 and Table 10-2 and 10-3 for defensive operations). Daytime flying of all sorts became increasingly hazardous for the *Luftwaffe*; *3./KG 2* lost eight of 11 Do 217 during a formation training flight near Eindhoven on 4 December. [7]

Table 10-1: Allied air operations over Western Europe, January 1943–May 1944

Month	Fighter/fighter-bomber (day)		Light/medium bomber		Heavy bomber		Total
	RAF	USAAF	RAF	USAAF	RAF	USAAF	
1943							
Jan	3,102 (24)	192 (1)	324 (8)	-	186 (15)	692 (13)	4,496 (61)
Feb	2,995 (29)	212 (1)	444 (10)	-	146 (10)	1,505 (21)	5,302 (71)
Mar	2,325 (28)	180 (1)	223 (4)	-	388 (12)	1,089 (4)	4,205 (49)
Apr	4,589 (49)	515 (6)	314 (12)	-	245 (12)	146 (2)	5,809 (81)
May	5,467 (41)	2,084 (11)	341 (17)	11 (-)	675 (35)	104 (-)	8,682 (104)
Jun	5,974 (52)	1,834 (9)	251 (7)	-	372 (17)	455 (4)	8,886 (89)

Month	Fighter/fighter-bomber (day)		Light/medium bomber		Heavy bomber		Total
	RAF	USAAF	RAF	USAAF	RAF	USAAF	
Jul	8,204 (65)	2,208 (13)	267 (6)	184 (2)	777 (22)	293 (5)	11,933 (113)
Aug	10,612 (62)	2,250 (10)	409 (16)	637 (3)	1,129 (21)	205 (1)	15,242 (113)
Sept	14,900 (80)	2,859 (14)	783 (6)	2,009 (6)	1,704 (58)	1,069 (8)	23,324 (172)
Oct	7,046 (44)	– (14)	334 (-)	1,070	–	127 (-)	8,577 (58)
Nov	8,644 (48)	–	709 (6)	1,568 (6)	388 (10)	605 (5)	11,914 (75)
Dec	6,922 (32)	415 (7)	837 (1)	2,067 (2)	1,137 (34)	288 (1)	11,666 (77)
Total	**80,780 (554)**	**12,749 (73)**	**5,236 (107)**	**7,546 (19)**	**7,147 (246)**	**6,578 (64)**	**120,036 (1,063)**
1944							
Jan	7,618 (54)	370 (4)	1,137 (2)	1,711 (3)	1,232 (21)	554 (-)	12,622 (84)
Feb	8,291 (41)	1,966 (16)	1,167 (5)	3,881 (14)	1,842 (23)	205 (2)	17,352 (101)
Mar	4,885 (32)	5,080 (36)	833 (7)	4,067 (10)	2,346 (21)	2,138 (8)	19,349 (114)
Apr	6,831 (26)	7,914 (39)	1,166 (2)	7,346 (30)	3,001 (28)	4,501 (68)	30,759 (193)
May	17,495 (97)	21,074 (78)	11,947 (2)	1,399 (43)	5,874 (53)	7,526 (155)	65,315 (428)
Total	**45,120 (250)**	**36,404 (173)**	**5,702 (18)**	**28,952 (100)**	**14,295 (146)**	**14,924 (233)**	**145,397 (920)**

Note: RAF heavy bomber are all night but exclude minelaying and leaflet sorties and this figure includes Eighth Air Force.

Sources: UKNA Air 40/1096. UKNA Air 41/49 Appendices 19, 28. UKNA 24/1496. UKNA Air 24/1101. Freeman, *Mighty Eighth War Diary*. Middlebrook/Everitt.

As the defence weakened, British fighter and fighter-bomber loss rates declined steadily throughout 1943, from a quarterly average of 0.94 per cent to 0.54 per cent, but the British day bombers (which attracted more *Flak* and fighter attention) suffered heavier losses, although the average monthly loss per quarter also fell, from a peak of

3.97 per cent in the second quarter to 1.11 per cent in the last – an indication of growing Allied air superiority. The American medium/light day-bomber force had a far lower casualty rate despite flying twice as many sorties during this same period.

During the year the Allies flew more than 120,000 fighter and bomber sorties over Western Europe and more than 2,100 reconnaissance sorties. Some idea of the scale of operations may be gauged from the fact that during 1943 *JG 26* claimed a total of 385 victories in the West but lost 151 pilots killed. Pressure on *Luftflotte 3's Jagdgruppen* was eased during the last quarter of 1943 as the fighters of the Eighth Air Force focused upon supporting the strategic bombing campaign at a time when the Ninth Air Force was still being formed. Nevertheless, Sperrle's *Jagdgruppen* came under increasing pressure from the summer with mounting casualties; 134 aircraft in the second quarter of the year and 222 the following quarter (Table 10-1), and it became increasingly difficult to shield *OB West's* communications and installations (Table 10-2). An added complication was the air defence of the *Reich* which not only took units from Sperrle, but also saw *Jagdgruppen* roaming like gypsies to meet both Strategic and Operational threats.

Table 10-2: Luftflotte 3/Luftwaffenkommando West, day-fighter force 1944

Date	Fighter strength (first day of month)	Monthly losses (destroyed or badly damaged)	
		Enemy action	Accident
January	199	23	18
February	204	18	23
March	248	15	39
April	291	32	42
May	314	54	44
June	322	48	40
July	251	66	64
August	168	55	38
September	163	101	47
October	276	61	32
November	225	27	40
December	208	26	31

Source: BA MA RL 2 III/876–879.

Sperrle lacked the resourceful and dynamic leadership needed to meet the challenge of the Allied threat. The good life in Paris appears to have drained him of energy and while angry at the chaos of *ObdL*, he was too vain or too lazy to make a stand, descending into bitter sarcasm and increasingly turning to the pleasures of the table. His mood was exacerbated by misogyny as women were increasingly employed for second-line duties, and if a female telephone operator answered on a military line he would throw a tantrum. [8] But he retained sufficient political clout to oppose *I. Jagdkorps* commander Schmid's attempts to create a *Luftwaffe* equivalent of Fighter Command. When *I. Jagdkorps* was created in the *Reich*, a *II. Jagdkorps* was created in France and Belgium with

4. Jagddivision(*Oberst* Carl Vieck) covering southern Belgium and northern France from Metz, while *5. Jagddivision* (*Oberst* Harry von Bülow-Bothkamp) covered western France from Paris. [9] The re-organisation saw a brief increase in *Jagdgruppen* strength to more than 200 aircraft but this dropped to 177 by the beginning of the year (Table 10-3).

Table 10-3: Luftflotte 3 fighter force, January–May 1944

Date	Total sorties	Strength *(first day of month)*		Monthly losses *(destroyed or badly damaged)*	
				Enemy action	Accident
January	3,239	Day	177	59	33
		Night	67	6	13
February	2,142	Day	207	81	62
		Night	73	5	15
March	1,349	Day	157	82	60
		Night	80	13	11
April	1,192	Day	110	67	46
		Night	94	17	25
May	1,704	Day	220	100	67
		Night	109	43	39

Sources: BA MA RL 2 III/880–882. US NA T971, Roll 32, Fr. 3330. IWM, Duxford, Tin 30 Frames K3312–3356.

Over the next five months the pace of air warfare increased, with the Allies flying more than 145,000 fighter and bomber sorties together with 6,083 tactical reconnaissance sorties, the USAAF bearing the lion's share of the burden with more than 80,000 sorties in an unremitting campaign both day and night. Not only were the 'Tactical' air forces committed but also the strategic squadrons, albeit reluctantly as from the spring Bomber Command was unable to strike deep into Germany. Factories, communications, fortifications and the *Luftwaffe* infrastructure (including that of the V-1 missiles) were attacked systematically with daylight rail movements in France ceasing on 26 May while Normandy was gradually isolated.

The *Luftwaffe* was overwhelmed and from 16 March to 2 June the Allies blinded the Germans by targeting the radar network, the sites being easy to identify because they had been fortified after the Dieppe landing in August 1942. By 6 June, 76 of 92 radar sites identified had ceased operations, including all 46 of the long-range *Wassermann* and *Mammut* whose narrow beams were difficult to jam. Sperrle's *Jagdgruppen*, whose average strength was 174 aircraft, struggled in vain, losing 154 aircraft to enemy action and another 166 in accidents. *JG 26* lost 106 pilots, including 11 *Staffelkapitäne*, between January and May. [10]

British Comint reported that the pilots of *II./JG 26* seemed nervous of enemy fighters which were now encountered almost everywhere; on 31 May, for example, US fighters swept fighter bases in western Germany, driving the *Luftwaffe* eastwards to airfields which offered the illusion of security. Increasingly, the *Wehrmacht*'s shield was based upon *Flak* batteries which comprised 10,481 guns (1,502 heavy) by June. Even two of Sperrle's *Nachtjagdgruppen* were forced back to Germany and the intruder *Gruppe* of *KG 51* and the *Jabos* of *I./SKG 10* had to fly *Wilde Sau* missions with some success from 3/4 May to 5/6 June during which period they were credited with 15 victories. History was also made in the night skies over France on 19/20 May when a Mosquito of No 605 Squadron shot down a He 219 of *1./NJG 1* near Floerennes, but its crew of *Leutnant* Otto Fries and *Feldwebel* Arthur Staffa were the first aircrew to be saved by ejector seats. [11]

The *Kampfgruppen* suffered badly and with their airfields under attack they were driven ever further from the potential beachheads. Fighter-bombers cost *KG 2* four Do 217 at Hesepe and Achmer on 8 March and another to fighters near Cologne, while *KG 100* lost five Do 217 to fighter-bombers at Toulouse-Francazal on 15 April and a He 177 to fighters at Aalborg-East on 17 May. [12] On 29 May the headquarters of *Fliegerkorps X* at Angers was bombed and it had to be transferred to Château Serrant, 15 kilometres outside Angers with its *Gruppen* in south-western France while *Fliegerdivision 2*'s were in southern France. By 6 June only 300 aircraft were west of the Seine with the rest scattered around France or the Low Countries.

The problem was aggravated by the fragmentation of Sperrle's forces; the largest concentrations were the eight *Kampfgruppen* under Peltz' *Fliegerkorps IX* and *Generalleutnant* Werner Junck's *II. Jagdkorps* with three *Jagdgruppen* and eight *Nachtjagdgruppen* divided between two *Jagddivisionen*. Junck also commanded *Jafü Bretagne*, *Jafü Süd* as well as *Jagdabschnittsführer Bordeaux* – each with a *Jagdgruppe*. The four-*Gruppen* anti-shipping force was under *Fliegerdivision 2*, commanded by *Generalmajor* Hans Korte since 22 February but it excluded the U-boat-support force (*KG 40*, *FAGr 5*) under Fiebig's *Fliegerkorps X*, although the *Zerstörergruppen* shielding the U-boats were assigned to Bülowius' *Fliegerkorps II* which also had a *Schlachtgruppe* and was to control operations west of the Seine.

Plans were made to transfer *Jagd-* and *Kampfgruppen* from the *Reich* the moment the code-word (*Dr Gustav Wilhelm* for *Drohende Gefahr West*, or 'Imminent Danger, West') for the invasion was received, and many airfields were prepared with supplies, communications and accommodation, some reportedly having dispersal bays up to five kilometres from the runway. [13] On 1 June *Luftflotte 3* had 1,021 combat aircraft with 49 maritime support and 53 transports while *Luftflotte Reich* had 815 day fighters (of which only 55% were serviceable), 94 *Zerstörer* and 259 strike and reconnaissance aircraft, some in units which were being re-equipped. By contrast, the RAF's Second Tactical and the US Ninth Air Forces had 4,029 aircraft, while the strategic air forces and the Air Defence of Great Britain (ADGB) had another 5,514.

ADGB secured the British Isles not only from bombs but also from prying German eyes. The German threat had declined so much that the British had closed 24 radar stations in less threatened areas but updated the 10cm radars covering the invasion ports with 500kW transmitters. [14] When *Oberstleutnant* Hans Wolff assumed command of *FAGr 123* on 24 September 1943, he learned that British fighters had largely prevented his *Fernaufklärungsstaffeln* from daylight photographic-reconnaissance for a month and high-altitude reconnaissance sorties, probably by Ju 86, had to be abandoned in October leaving only low-level missions on cloudy days or images acquired at night. Under intense pressure from *Führer* headquarters, Sperrle was demanding by spring of 1944 reports and photographs of inland England but this task was especially hazardous from mid-April 1944, when the RAF began standing fighter patrols over ports and even the Bf 109 H of *5.(F)/121*, which could operate at 12,200 metres (40,000 feet), were encountering Spitfires, so that most photographs were of targets within 40 kilometres of the coast. [15]

The whole of the *Wehrmacht* was blinded in the days before 6 June because of a storm which threatened to prevent the Allied landing. [16] The landing was heralded by a massive airborne attack involving 1,487 transports and 868 gliders, the transports losing 34 to flak. Throughout the day Allied air power dominated the Normandy battlefield from the beaches to deep into France, flying 12,351 combat sorties and losing 86 aircraft (0.7%) with 42 damaged. [17] Confirmation of the landings was made by *Leutnant* Adalbert Bärwolf of *3./NAGr 13* in the first of 24 reconnaissance sorties, but the *Luftwaffe's* reaction was, slow for German aircraft were far from the beachheads. [18]

The *Jagdgruppen* were dispersed all over France to assure their survival and while Normandy was covered by *Hauptmann* Erich Hohagen's *I./JG 2* at Cormeilles-en-Vexin, 60 kilometres from the coast, the initial response on 6 June was a quick pass along 'Sword' Beach by the *Kommodore* of *JG 26*, *Oberst* Josef 'Pips' Priller, and his *Rottenhund*, *Unteroffizier* Heinz Wodarczyk, who flew 320 kilometres (200 miles) from Lille-North. [19] Hohagen was unable to attack immediately because he was ordered to Creil, north of Paris, to fit bomb racks but by exploiting thick cloud he was able to make a *Jabo* attack upon 'Gold' Beach at 09:30. The *Schlachtflieger* were in action from 1100 hrs when *I./SKG 10* sent four aircraft against the British beaches but *III./SG 4* had to fly to Le Mans, losing six *Jabos* to the Allied fighter screen, and by the end of the day only 51 *Jabo* sorties had been flown. [20] The *Jagdgruppen* flew 121 sorties (eight were lost), with 35 flown by the *Nachtjagdgruppen*, while the *Kampfgruppen* flew 88, 64 against ships, but were also hampered by having to deploy to new airfields closer to the front. [21]

The *Dr Gustav Wilhelm* code-word was issued to 13 *Jagdgruppen* in the *Reich*, including the whole of *JG 1* and *JG 3*, and soon 450 fighters with some 110 night-fighters from five *Nachtjagdgruppen* began deploying into France assembling by 10 June. But their arrival went neither unnoticed nor unchallenged night and day; two of *JG 1's* Ju 52 were intercepted on the night of 6/7 June and one was shot down while the following morning the transports of *I./JG 1* were strafed by American fighters and 10 exhausted *Schwarzemänner* sleeping in them were killed. [22] The move was chaotic, for some airfields lacked adequate support such as petrol bowsers while some were swamped when units had to divert from bombed airstrips. The shortage of earth-moving equipment meant that bomb craters had to be filled in laboriously by hand and some airfields were out of action for six days. Even when the units arrived, their supplies, equipment, personnel and kit often took days to arrive. [23] There was some air transport assistance, the move from Germany being supported by some 40 aircraft of *Luftverkehrsgruppe (Mot)* while *TrGr 30* deployed with 33 He 111 to support isolated troops.

Allied air power had disrupted the French rail network, causing significant problems especially with moving and distributing fuel supplies to the *Luftwaffe* and the army. Enemy aircraft also significantly affected the battlefield (see Table 10-4) interdicting transport and helping to reduce the German vehicle fleet by 20 per cent in 10 days. Movement by daylight was hazardous and on 17 July Typhoons strafed the staff car of the commander of *Heeresgruppe B, Generalfeldmarschall* Rommel, who commanded all forces along the Channel coast. He was severely wounded and had to be replaced by *Generalfeldmarschall* Kluge. A key element of Rommel's plan had been to launch a prompt counter-attack by *Panzergruppe West* under Russian Front veteran *General der Panzertruppen* Leo Geyr von Schweppenberg. Schweppenberg's headquarters was promptly detected by Ultra, but RAF tactical reconnaissance aircraft were sent to 'discover' it, an easy task since it was poorly camouflaged and officers in distinctive staff uniform came out to see the aircraft. On 10 June the site was heavily bombed, killing many of the staff and putting Schweppenberg's command *hors de combat* for a fortnight.

Table 10-4: Allied 'Tactical' air force operations over Western Europe, June 1944–April 1945

Month	Fighter/fighter-bomber (day)		Light/Medium bomber (day)		Night operations		Total
	RAF	USAAF	RAF	USAAF	Bomber	Fighter	
June	37,957 (222)	47,253 (254)	3,117 (26)	11,687 (20)	2,059 (15)	1,586 (16)	
Jul	29,605 (150)	32,494 (55)	1,282 (7)	8,008 (15)	2,105 (16)	1,774 (5)	
Aug	34,282 (223)	34,293 212)	1,514 (13)	9,192 (15)	2,435 (23)	902 (3)	
Sep	23,446 (147)	23,135 (72)	1,616 (9)	5,431 (9)	874 (7)	1,648 (9)	
Oct	25,241 (99)	19,494 (39)	988 (6)	3,692 (9)	667 (4)	1,510 (13)	
Nov	17,520 (81)	18,579 (71)	1,170 (4)	5,176 (8)	630 (13)	1,507 (5)	
Dec	15,289 (123)	30,288 (199)	963 (3)	6,868 (28)	1,113 (7)	1,302 (12)	
Jan	10,768 (89)	21,603 (111)	646 (4)	4,192 (18)	1,109 (13)	610 (3)	
Feb	19,373 (156)	24,373 (246)	1,740 (26)	8,974 (12)	1,686 (17)	957 (3)	
Mar	20,557 (121)	53,727 (221)	2,510 (10)	17,022 (24)	1,587 (9)	1,715 (7)	
Apr	27,636 (193)	46,283 (200)	1,102 (-)	10,270 (24	2,096 (17)	1,286 (10)	

Sources: UKNA Air 16/1036. Air 40/1096. UKNA Air 40/1097. Freeman, *War Diary*. No information available on French operations.

By contrast the German ground-attack force was tiny: on 1 July the two available *Schlachtgruppen* had only 75 aircraft, forcing *OKL* to press-gang the *Jagdgruppen*.

Aircraft conversion kits arrived and were hastily installed while pilots, many of whom had barely mastered formation flying, were given a crash course in fighter-bomber operations and often sent to their deaths with no effect upon the battle. The Allies steadily expanded their bridgehead during June, aiming to take ground around Caen as bases for their tactical air power as well as the port of Cherbourg as an entry point for American reinforcements and supplies. The Allied strategy was for the British Empire forces to act as an anvil while the US Army formed the hammer which would eventually break out of the bridgehead, but there was fierce fighting.

The *Luftwaffe* played its part and despite bad weather on many days, it flew 13,982 sorties between 6 June and 1 July of which 10,061 (nearly 72%) were by fighters, *Jabos* and reconnaissance aircraft while 1,101 night-fighter sorties were flown. By contrast, estimated enemy sorties were 96,000, of which 83,000 were during the day including 35,000 by fighters, a figure which proved a reasonably accurate estimate. The *Luftwaffe* bomber force flew 2,667 sorties divided evenly between land and sea targets with 384 torpedo-bomber and 954 minelayer sorties, the latter laying 1,906 mines against a fleet of 137 major and 1,073 minor warships, 4,000 landing vessels and 864 merchantmen. In June and July the *Luftwaffe* sank three destroyers (one already damaged by a mine), an anti-submarine trawler and two freighters (9,008 grt) while two cruisers, a frigate and two freighters (14,299 grt) were damaged. Mines laid by both the *Luftwaffe* and the *Kriegsmarine* sank a cruiser, eight destroyers, three small warships and 10 merchantmen (37,760 grt) while a battleship, three destroyers and frigates, two small warships and 11 merchantmen (54,343 grt) were damaged. But the Hs 293s were neutralised by barrage jamming from the fleet and air attacks failed to sink a single ship on the first night. [24]

Luftwaffe losses were heavy: 689 in the air, including 224 bombers and seven transports, while 137 aircraft were destroyed on the ground and a further 212 damaged, 86 severely. [25] Sperrle's five original *Jagdgruppen*, which had 140 fighters at the beginning of June, lost 131 aircraft to enemy action. *II.* and *III./JG 3* started the month with 60 aircraft and lost 134 of the original aircraft and their replacements while *III./JG 54* started with 23 and lost 27. In the first six days of the invasion 15–20 per cent of day sorties saw losses or badly damaged aircraft but in the last fortnight up to 95 per cent of aircraft failed to return and claims of 1,305 victories (414 by day fighters, 219 by night fighters and 672 by *Flak*) were small compensation. [26] There were 153 transport sorties and, as the American grip on Cherbourg tightened, *TrGr 30* flew 188 tonnes of supplies to the city and some other isolated garrisons from 20–30 June. [27]

The *Luftwaffe's* impact upon the battlefield steadily declined under the weight of Allied air power. During July the *Luftwaffe* flew 15,345 sorties with losses of 738 aircraft although unit records show the loss of 631 combat aircraft (excluding transports and seaplanes) during July with another 397 lost to accidents. [28] The bomber effort included 1,953 bomber sorties over land (expending some 1,860 tonnes of ordnance including illumination ordnance), with 90 bombers lost to enemy action. 1,837 sorties were over the sea of which 1,357 were minelaying operations involving 2,683 mines. The decline in the effectiveness of the anti-ship force is notable with only 480 sorties including the expenditure of 171 torpedoes, 64 Hs 293 and 14 FX 1000 guided bombs, the *Gruppen* losing 44 aircraft to enemy action and 16 to accidents. [29] It was the fighter force which bore the brunt of the losses, however, with 412 aircraft and 221 pilots lost to enemy action, including at least 289 fighters in the air, while some were certainly shot down making ground attacks to augment the *Schlachtgruppen* which lost only 12 aircraft. Yet one of the *Schlachtgruppen Gruppe* was sent to the Russian Front! [30]

On 25 July the Americans began Operation 'Cobra', the beginning of the break-out. Junck flew 506 sorties, losing nine aircraft, without effect, and in a desperate attempt to recoup the situation, the Germans counter-attacked at Mortain on 6 August. With barely 40 sorties in support, the effort was blotted out by Allied air power. Two days later the British began their break-out, Operation 'Totalise', and on 16 August they entered Falaise to isolate the Germans in Normandy. Although some were able to break out, by the 19 August the German defeat was obvious and the Allies fanned out across France, heading for the Belgian and German borders.

The Allied strategic bomber force played a significant part in the victory, flying 48,800 sorties in June and July not only at the Operational level but also at the Tactical one, being used as substitute artillery to blast a way forward for the troops. [31] Neither Doolittle nor Harris were enthusiastic at what they regarded as the misuse of their bomber fleets, but the night skies remained perilous to Harris' airmen who flew only 4,119 main force strategic sorties and 1,474 by the nimble Mosquitos, while, by comparison, the Eighth Air Force had mastered the German defences and was able to fly 16,248 strategic bomber sorties in the same period (and 120 against Danube valley targets). [32] Consequently, when the Allies decided to bite the German jugular vein of synthetic oil production, from May it was the Americans who were first over the targets (see Tables 10-5 and 10-6).

Table 10–5: Strategic Bombing Force operations, June 1944–April 1945

Month	Strategic (against Reich)		Operational		Total
	Day	Night	Day	Night	
June	5,333	942	18,531	11,737	
	(137)	(98)	(96)	(214)	
Jul	15,222	3,253	13,535	4,997	
	(354)	(169)	(54)	(146)	
Aug	11,937	3,955	18,476	2,905	
	(203)	(147)	(112)	(18)	
Sep	13,151	3,250	12,960	362	
	(261)	(72)	(56)	(3)	
Oct	19,132	6,601	6,818	-	
	(258)	(44)	(44)		
Nov	17,205	6,699	8.715	-	
	(275)	(96)	(34)		
Dec	8,770	8,703	15,168	212	
	(243)	(86)	(69)	(1)	

Month	Strategic (against Reich)		Operational		Total
	Day	Night	Day	Night	
Jan	3,858	6,487	13,355	893	
	(72)	(119)	(62)	(10)	
Feb	17,927	21,435	13,181	1,676	
	(100)	(142)	(70)	(12)	
Mar	26,901	7,008	19,860	1,065	
	(156)	(155)	(79)	(5)	
Apr	3,098	4,799	20,378	648	
	(14)	(35)	(130)	(2)	

Sources: Freeman. Middlebrook/Everitt. UKNA Air 24/937–939, 945–948, 996–999.

Table 10-6: Strategic force other operations, June 1944–April 1945

Month	RAF			USAAF fighter	Electronic warfare		Total
	Day bomber	*Night bomber*	*Fighter*		*Day*	*Night*	
Jun	1	743	764	4,724	1	252	
		(8)	(5)	(21)		(2)	
July	-	731	806	9,299	-	457	
		(7)	(4)	(57)		(3)	
Aug	-	808	582	7,259	12	444	
		(6)	(3)	(74)	(-)	(2)	
Sep	-	1,022	604	8,045	129	486	
		(6)	(3)	(103)	(-)	(4)	
Oct	18	1,841	495	10,360	96	768	
	(-)	(7)	(3)	(87)	(-)	(-)	
Nov	159	1,632	717	11,364	91	716	
	(20)	(6)	(4)	(127)	(-)	(5)	
Dec	80	1,287	559	6,191	156	683	
	(-)	(4)	(2)	(63)	(-)	(2)	
Jan	145	1,183	458	3,280	145	533	
	(-)	(12)	(6)	(33)	(-)	(4)	
Feb	72	1,954	687	8,551	190	816	
	(1)	(7)	(3)	(65)	(-)	(8)	
Mar	185	2,790	687	11,012	284	881	
	(1)	(13)	(5)	(67)	(-)	(12)	
Apr	106	1,982	668	1,463	153	733	
	(2)	(15)	(2)	(5)	(-)	(6)	

Sources: Freeman. Middlebrook/Everitt. UKNA Air 24/937–939, 945–948, 996–999.

From August until the end of the year, Doolittle focused upon the strategic war against both oil and communications targets. He flew 39,900 bomber sorties losing just 610 aircraft, the majority to flak, for they were accompanied by 30,583 fighter sorties (with 331 lost). A feature of Doolittle's operations from November was the increasing importance of ECCM; 295 night electronic-warfare sorties were mounted between August until January with a separate chaff force used from 2 November, Mandrel and Dina jammers from 18 November and VHF jammers from 25 November.In addition, Eaker's Fifteenth Air Force flew 18,900 bomber and 12,676 fighter sorties, losing 522 bombers and 123 fighters. The American bombers ranged across the *Reich* as far east as Silesia and Czechoslovakia, wrecking the synthetic oil production facilities, slashing production and forcing the *Wehrmacht* to ration consumption.

This meant doom for the *Luftwaffe* bomber force and from 24 August *Kampfgruppen* were either disbanded or began converting either to fighters or to jet units. *Inspekteur der Jagdwaffe* Galland and his subordinates could only watch in impotent fury as the American armadas flew overhead. The fighter escorts usually kept the *Jagdgruppen* at bay, although occasionally they had some luck, and although a Me 262 fighter unit had been formed under the Eastern Front ace and Nazi Party member, Walter Nowotny, his lacklustre leadership prevented it achieving much. Galland increasingly became obsessed with delivering a morale-boosting 'Big Blow' (*Grosse Schlag*) and sought to build up his forces for such a move, although the inadequacy of the *Jagdgruppen* was now arousing Hitler's ire.

From August Harris also returned to deep penetration missions aided by the disruption of *II. Jagdkorps'* night-fighter organisation which deprived the *Reich* of its glacis, allowing the bomber streams to approach many German targets almost undetected. Harris also improved electronic support for his squadrons, flying 2,814 sorties. Having realised that *Naxos* could home-in on H2S, he ensured stricter controls on its use while the more extensive deployment of intruders (2,957 sorties) also helped shield the bombers by harassing the *Nachtjagdwaffe* bases and beacons to erode numbers. In June and July night-fighter losses to enemy action averaged 37 aircraft a month, but in September, October and November it was 64 a month rising to 159 in December, while from August to December 369 night-fighters were lost in accidents. Consequently, the British main force suffered only 1.5 per cent casualties (437 aircraft), flying 29,016 strategic sorties. But from 27 August, daylight missions became a growing feature of Bomber Command strategic bombing and with 11,395 sorties, involved 28 per cent of strategic main force bombing missions. While the Lancasters and Halifaxes were far more vulnerable to German fighters than their USAAF equivalents (see Table 10-7 for *Luftwaffe* fighter activity), strong fighter escorts ensured that losses were confined to 0.94 per cent (108 aircraft).

The heavy bombers continued to be used for Operational-level tasks, usually against communications and as the Allies approached and entered Germany the distinction 'strategic' and 'operational' became increasingly blurred. More than 26,500 Bomber Command sorties were flown from August, increasingly during daylight hours, and 38,750 Eighth Air Force bomber sorties (supported by 24,400 fighter sorties) in addition to the Tactical Air Force operations. Collectively, attacks throughout the Strategic and Operational levels disrupted the *Luftwaffe's* supply lines to deprive it of fuel and spares, although not aircraft. Its bases were frequently attacked and many of the newer ones not only lacked facilities and key equipment, but also adequate *Flak* protection.

Table 10-7: Luftwaffe day and night fighter activity, 1944

Month	West	Reich	Total
January	3,239	5,300	8,539
February	2,142	4,874	7,016
March	1,349	4,275	5,624
April	192	6,085	6,277
May	1,704	6,889	8,593
June	9,471	3,644	13,115
July	6,159	5,533	11,692
August	7,131	4,681	11,812
September	3,118	4,749	7,867
October	3,006	2,700	5,706
November	2,076	4,703	6,779
December	7,468	5,600	13,068
Total	**47,055**	**59,033**	**106,088**

Source: IWM Duxford, Tin 30 Frames K3312–3356.

The collapse of France was accelerated by the Allied landings on the Riviera (Operation 'Dragoon') on 15 August where the *Luftwaffe* had *Oberst* Friedrich Vollbracht's *Jafü Südfrankreich* and Korte's *Fliegerdivision 2* which had 122 combat aircraft (79 serviceable) and 11 seaplanes (eight) at the time of the landings. [33] The *Luftwaffe's* prime concern had been counter-insurgency operations, especially after an uprising in the Vercors Plateau, south of Grenoble, which was suppressed with the aid of the ad hoc *Geschwader Bongart* as well as airborne troops using both parachutes and gliders. [34]

The *Luftwaffe* gave early warning to the local *19.Armee* of the imminent threat, but the defenders were too weak to offer more than nominal resistance and within four days were retreating northwards. Between them Vollbracht and Korte had only three *Gruppen* and four *Staffeln* (reinforced by *II./JG 77* from Italy) and they flew some 250 sorties to 19 August, losing some 15 aircraft in the air. There were some reconnaissance and fighter escort sorties, and there was some bombing of the beach head, while the anti-shipping aircraft struck ineffectively although they did record the last Hs 293 success, sinking *LST 282* off St Raphael. [34] *Luftwaffe* airfields were under constant attack, and the Allies discovered the wrecks of 72 aircraft. On 18 August Korte was transferred to *Luftflotte 2*, moving his headquarters to Bergamo but this command was disbanded on 6 September to form *Kommandierende General der deutschen Luftwaffe in Italien*. The *Luftwaffe* began its withdrawal on 19 August with Vollbracht moving to Metz and over the next few days most units followed apart from *II./JG 77* which returned to Italy.

Vollbracht joined a *Luftflotte 3* which by 20 August had a nominal 998 combat aircraft of which a third were unserviceable and they were scattered throughout Western Europe from the Zuider Zee to central France. [35] Apart from the occasional daylight hit-and-run raid on enemy columns and night-bombing on targets which were difficult for the crews to find, *Luftflotte 3* was as impotent as *Luftflotte Reich*. The only brief rays of hope were the small number of jet units entering service, with the Me 262 used as a light bomber while the Ar 234 bomber was used for reconnaissance, providing much-needed information of the Allied progress. Sperrle departed his beloved Paris for Arlon in August but had little time for regret for Göring made him the scapegoat for the *Luftwaffe's* failure, relieved him on 23 August and never employed him again to Sperrle's great bitterness. *Generaloberst* Otto Dessloch replaced him, but there was little he could do apart from moving the headquarters to Mannheim-Sandhofen on 2 September (see Table 10-8). However, on 22 September he, in turn, was relieved by *Generalleutnant* Alexander Holle but within a week, on 26 September, the *Luftflotte* was down-graded to *Luftwaffenkommando West* with Bülowius' *II. Jagdkorps*. *Jagddivision 4* had been disbanded however on 8 September.

Table 10-8: Luftflotte 3 activity, August 28–September 30 1944

Week	Fighter	Strike	Recon	Transport	Total
Aug 28-Sep 3	390 (26)	297 (7)	9	39 (2)	735 (35)
Sep 4–10	422 (41)	65 (2)	24	24	535 (43)
Sep 11–17	920 (35)	138 (1)	37	32	1,127(36)
Sep 18–24	929 (17)	219 (6)	51 (5)	25 (3)	1,224 (31)
Sep 25–30	678	147 (3)	31 (7)	45 (4)	901 (46)
Total	**3,339 (151)**	**866 (19)**	**152 (12)**	**165 (9)**	**4,522 (191)**

Source: USNA T971 Roll 3
No data 28 August. No JK II sorties for 25 September.

Note: Strike includes day and night bombers and *Nachtschlacht*. Fighters includes *Jabo*.

Dessloch's departure followed a new crisis, for on 17 September the Allies sought to cross the lower Rhine in a *coup de main*, Operation 'Market Garden', another massive airborne assault intended to take the bridges at Nijmegen and Arnhem. Ironically, the area was defended by SS and airborne troops of *Generaloberst* Student's *1. Fallschirmjägerarmee*. In what was *Luftflotte 3's* swansong, most of the effort was diverted to supporting the defenders, especially by *5. Jagddivision*. Attacks were made on the bridges with more than 1,000 sorties, and 30 aircraft were lost, but the Arnhem bridge was held. A few days later, on 28 September, Student's son, Hans-Dietrich, a *Leutnant* with *I./JG 77*, was shot down and killed. [36]

Luftwaffe reports noted that in September *Luftflotte Reich* lost 436 aircraft in the air, 128 (29%) over enemy territory while 221 aircraft (including 47 fighters and 113 bombers) were destroyed on the ground during attacks upon 155 airfields. Another 176 aircraft were severely damaged (70 bombers, 46 fighters) and 102 damaged (27 bombers, 22 fighters). *Luftflotte 3/Luftwaffenkommando West* lost 240 aircraft, 235 (98%) over enemy territory, but only four (all bombers) were destroyed on the ground, while two (one bomber) were severely damaged and three suffered minor damage. [37]

The defensive victory on the lower Rhine provided the *Reich* with continued use of the western Netherlands as a base for ballistic missile (V-2) attacks on England which had already been under cruise missile (V-1) bombardment since June. In the face of powerful air attacks during the winter of 1943–1944, *Oberst* Max Wachtel's *FlakR 155 (W)* rebuilt its launcher network which was left unmolested. On 12 June, Wachtel began his offensive and in the first month launched 4,200 missiles. [38] The bombardment saw a major re-organisation of the British air defences, with a belt of 800 guns and 1,000 barrage balloons being established south-east of London, augmented by fighters which would include the new Meteor jets. British GL Mk 3 fire control radars were augmented by US SCR 584 sensors whose accuracy was such that by the end of August up to 82 per cent of missiles were being shot down. [39]

The V-1 pulse-jet was as devastating as the aerial mines dropped during the Blitz, but after four years of aerial conflict the *Luftwaffe* was still unable to project its daylight striking power beyond London because range posed an insurmountable hurdle. In 1940 the problem was with the Bf 109 fighter escorts, while in 1944 it was because the V-1 had a range of only 250 kilometres (155 miles). Whatever its impact upon civilian morale, it was incapable of threatening Great Britain's industrial heartland and at best might disrupt the Allied assault upon Europe, making it an Operational-level weapon. The rudimentary guidance system meant it was a very inaccurate missile (only 25% reached their targets) and while some 5 per cent of V-1s carried a radio transmitter in the 340–450 kHz range to help the Germans track them, this failed to help because the the British 'meaconed' the signals to produce false readings. [40]

Some 8,000 missiles had been launched by August when the Allied advance forced Wachtel to new sites in Germany and the Netherlands from where he began launching missiles at Brussels, Liège and Antwerp from 21 October, firing 5,750 missiles by the New Year. [41] The threat to Antwerp was especially serious for it was a major conduit of supplies for the Allies and suffered a rain of missiles – 2,448 V-1 and 1,261 V-2 rockets. Only 5.4 per cent of the V-1s landed in and around the city centre, but they caused heavy casualties; indeed the Allied Anti-Flying Bomb Command established under Brigadier-General Clare H. Armstrong lost 32 dead, but the port continued to operate. In March Wachtel resumed his bombardment of London and between 3–29 March launched 275 of the longer-ranged F1 missiles, but only 37 succeeded in running the gauntlet, of which a mere 13 fell in the greater London area.

The surface-launched V-1 campaign against England was augmented by air-launched missiles from 7/8 July 1944. In March *Hauptmann* Martin Vetter's *III./KG 3* began converting from conventional bombing to missile-launching operations and targeted ports on the British South Coast to disrupt the Allied build-up of supplies into Normandy until mid-September. Vetter started with 30 aircraft but lost 16 to accidents in the first month and another three to September, while losses to enemy action were two bombers (only two to ADGB). [42]

On 9 September the *Gruppe* was absorbed by *Oberstleutnant* Friedrich 'Fritz' Pockrandt's *KG 53* which became the main missile-launching formation, steadily expanding to about 100 aircraft which launched 1,287 missiles until the beginning of March, of which only 235 broke through the defensive belt (Table 10-9). The aircraft made a low-level approach at night towards the English coast, launching their missiles at distances of 50–70 kilometres, stand-off launches being essential because production of *Düppel* chaff had ceased. Accuracy was poor because the Allies were jamming and meaconing much of the radio navigation system, while accidents took a steady toll with 36 aircraft lost to the end of the year many because missile warheads exploded prematurely.

Table 10-9. Air-launched V1 operations, September 1944–January 1945

Month	Strength	V1			Aircraft losses	
		Launched	Aborted	Evade defence	Enemy action	Accident
Sept	106	156	78	57	12	–
Oct	81	283	80	61	8	10
Nov	104	316	128	46	16	16
Dec	96	188	71	52	3	8
Jan	115	85	34	20	3	2

BA MA RL 2 III/880–882. Smith, Appx II; Kiehl, p.359, notes the numbers serviceable on 20th day of each month were October 24, November 58, December 85 and January 79.

Note: *KG* 53 strength on first day of month.

The British deployed low-flying Mosquito night-fighters (although this was such a strain on crews that operational tours were limited to three months), assisted by the frigate HMS *Caicos* in the North Sea acting as a night fighter controller. Late in 1944 she was augmented by trials with a Wellington bomber fitted with centimetric 'Vapour' radar, an anti-ship sensor modified to detect low-flying aircraft over the sea and with an on-board night fighter controller position. The aircraft had a 'Eureka' radar beacon so night-fighters of the Fighter Interception Development Unit with AI Mk VIII/X radars could detect it and it flew along the Dutch coast, although there is little information about its effectiveness. [43] The campaign began to decline due to fuel shortages and in March the bombers either reverted to their conventional role or were disbanded, *KG 53* having lost 78 aircraft of which 42 were on operations including 16 to night fighters.

The V-1 and V-2 represented a desperate desire within the German leadership to strike back at their foes. One flight of fancy which almost took wing was *Unternehmen 'Drachenhöhle'* ('Dragon's Cave'), a *Mistel* and *Jabo* attack by *KG 200* upon the Royal Navy at Scapa Flow which would regain Göring's prestige and for which both fuel and aircraft were assembled in Denmark. The *Kommodore* of *KG* 200, *Oberstleutnant* Werner Baumbach, came to believe this was a useless suicide mission and after being postponed several times it was abandoned on 16 February. [44]

The strike-back envisaged by Galland and his associates in the *Jagdwaffe* was a 'Big Blow' involving a holocaust of the American bomber force over the Reich by deploying 11 *Gefechstverbände*. He carefully conserved his forces in preparation, although fuel remained limited and serviceability hovered at about 70–75 per cent. [45] His hopes were raised when, on 23 November, he won a turf war with Peltz (who became commander of II. *Jagdkorps* on 15 October) to convert 11 *Kampfgruppen* into *Jagdgruppen*, although they remained under *Fliegerkorps IX* which had become

Fliegerkorps IX (Jagd) 10 days earlier. [46] Galland also hoped to use the Me 262 fighters, but operational development of these new aircraft proved frustratingly slow until Nowotny was killed on 8 November, when a more dynamic leadership improved results.

But while Galland planned his 'Big Blow', Hitler had his own plans, having noticed that the Allied line was very weak in the Ardennes. *Unternehmen 'Wacht am Rhein'* ('Guarding the Rhine'), renamed '*Herbstnebel*' ('Autumn Fog') in December, envisaged breaking through the American lines in the Ardennes, then isolating the Allied left by driving north-west across a series of major geographical obstacles, including ranges of hills and the River Meuse, to Antwerp. '*Herbstnebel*' was launched under snow-filled clouds and in icy fog on 16 December, gaining some 65 kilometres, but it was unable to overcome the terrain obstacles, while American paratroops held the key crossroads at Bastogne. When the weather cleared from 24 December, the full force of Allied air power fell upon the *Wehrmacht*, driving it back to its start line by early January.

In the months preceeding '*Herbstnebel*' the *Luftwaffe* went through the motions but, despite the heroism of its aircrew, it could achieve little (Table 10-10). By 10 October, with the Allies now on Germany's borders, *Luftwaffenkommando West* had only 729 aircraft (590 serviceable) and it was a reflection on the Allies' dominance of the daylight skies that it had replaced its *Schlachtgruppen* with *Nachtschlachtgruppen* (*I./SKG 10* became *III./KG 51* on 20 October). Me 262 bombers of *Kommando Schenck* (to become *3./KG 51*) were largely immune to enemy fighters, but there were barely 12 of the jet-bombers available. OKL insisted they operate at only 4,000 metres (13,100 feet) to reduce the risk of them falling into enemy hands. This prevented accurate bombing so that they were confined to striking airfields with bomblets until 7 November when they were ordered to strike towns and villages designated by *Heeresgruppe B* defending the lower Rhine and the Ruhr. Meanwhile conventional bombers mined the Scheldt estuary and occasionally attacked convoys. [47]

Table 10-10: Luftwaffe statistics, October 1944

Command	Sorties	Losses		Victories			
		Air	Ground	Fighter	Flak		Ground
Reich	2,700	116	206	103	211		-
	(1,357)	(57)	(3)	(48)	(15)		
West	4,843	229	-	103	120		-
	(1,413)	(54)		(-)	(-)		
Totals	**7,543**	**345**	**206**	**206**	**331**		-
	(2,770)	**(111)**	**(3)**	**(48)**	**(15)**		

(Figures in parentheses are night sorties.)

Source: IWM Duxford, Tin 30 Frames K3312–3356.

After August the only *Luftwaffe* aircraft crossing France were Heinkels of *TGr 30* augmented from September by *KG 55*, and two *Transportgruppen*. Based in Strasbourg and later Frankfurt-am-Main, they flew supplies to isolated garrisons on the Biscay coast as well as in the Channel Islands and, briefly, the islands in the Scheldt Estuary. Until August some 50 tonnes a night was delivered, but afterwards this dropped to 20 tonnes as *Transportgruppen* were disbanded to fill out new 'parachute' divisions. The garrisons continued to be supplied by a dwindling force – six aircraft by 25 April, with the last mission taking place on 16 April 1945 to La Pallice. [48]

A month before the Ardennes offensive began, Schmid was given command of *Luftwaffenkommando West* with the former bomber leader, Peltz, of *II. Jagdkorps (4. and 5. Jagddivisionen)*, as his prime subordinate. Peltz would now win his last turf war with Galland. Galland had launched a full dress-rehearsal of the 'Big Blow' on 2 November and it went badly, for although 56 aircraft were destroyed, 30 were claimed by *Flak* and Galland lost 120 fighters and 70 pilots. Hitler brooded on the figures and decided the fighters could best be used to support '*Herbstnebel*' and on 20 November Galland was ordered to start moving his fighter reserve west, but was not informed why. It soon became clear Galland was yesterday's man and just before the offensive was launched, Koller informed him that Hitler wanted the fighter *Experte*,Oberst Gordon Gollob, to be the new *General der Jagdflieger* and that the Big Blow would be delivered by Peltz, not over the *Reich* but against enemy airfields. At the same time Galland came under the scutiny of the *Gestapo*. [49]

Schmid began to receive substantial reinforcements and by 10 December had received seven *Jagdgruppen* (including *JG 4* and most of *JG 27*), *SG 4* from the Eastern Front (three *Gruppen*) and by 20 December another 19 *Jagdgruppen* (*JG 1, JG 3, JG 6, JG 11, JG 53, JG 77*). Nominally this gave Schmid a formidable force of 2,354 combat aircraft (1,830 serviceable) and 116 transports, although 117 He 111 were *KG 53*'s V-1 force, leaving a bomber force of 109 aircraft of which half were Me 262 and Ar 234 jets. For close-support the 117 *Schlachtflieger* (91 serviceable) were augmented by 172 (127) *Nachtschlacht* aircraft although these included Fw 190 *Jabos* and Ju 87 *Stukas*. On 14 December Peltz assembled his unit commanders and informed them they would attack 16 airfields in *Unternehmen* '*Bodenplatte*' ('Base Plate') as '*Herbstnebel*' began, but ultimately the weather kept most of the airmen on both sides on the ground for several days. [50]

The operation was preceded by an airborne operation, *Unternehmen* '*Stösser*' ('Bird of Prey'), involving some 800 troops to be dropped near the crossroads of Malmedy. The troops were formed of a mixture of veterans and raw recruits and were to be guided to the drop zone by *NSGr 20*, but the whole operation was a shambles with the men dropped by two *Transportgruppen* in the wrong position. They fought a brief guerrilla battle before trying to regain their lines but only a third succeeded.

To provide offensive support for '*Herbstnebel*', *Generalmajor* von Falkenstein's *Fliegerdivision 3* was brought in from *Luftflotte 1* to control all the *Kampf-* and *Nachtschlachtgruppen*. When the weather improved, the fighters engaged in desultory combat which cost them 55 pilots killed and 24 wounded while the *Kampfflieger* bombed targets in the battle area and its approaches, Falkenstein's men flying up to 300 sorties a night. The jets became more prominent, Peltz authorising the Me 262 to make low-level approaches from 21 December, while Christmas Eve saw the first Ar 234 bombing mission against rail targets in Liège and Namur. That night the *Luftwaffe* tried bombing the Americans out of Bastogne, but it was in vain.

The *Luftwaffe* effort from 17 December was extensive with 600 *Jabo* sorties, but hopes of screening the spearheads with up to 150 fighter sorties an hour proved impossible due to the weather. When conditions improved from 24–27 December, Allied aircraft roamed the battlefield in overwhelming strength and while the *Luftwaffe* was flying some 600 day and up to 250 night sorties it could make no impact. The poorly trained fighter pilots reportedly displayed a lack of resolution, there was little attempt to challenge the Allied heavy bombers as they smashed rail marshalling yards and the disruption of supplies meant that spares were not getting through, causing a drop in serviceability. In desperation a third of the night-fighter force was sent on ground-attack missions and the 124 aircraft lost to enemy action during December reflected the desperate stupidity of this decision.

By the end of December the *Luftwaffe* was exhausted, having lost 7,957 dead and missing (1,280 in non-operational missions) with another 3,260 injured (687 in non-operational missions) on all fronts from July to the end of December 1944. During the same period it lost 10,362 aircraft destroyed (1,698 in accidents) and 6,787 damaged (2,919 in accidents). The training units lost 1,314 dead and 672 injured while their material losses were 2,052 aircraft destroyed and 1,986 damaged and 1945 would start with another bloodbath. [51]

Those fighter pilots in the West who had anticipated a wild celebration to end the year were ordered by commanders to go to bed and be ready for an early start. [52] The objective of '*Bodenplatte*' was to make a morning attack using *Jagd-* and *Schlachtgruppen* with *Nachtjagdgruppen* providing pathfinders upon 17 airfields, many of them having been *Luftwaffe* bases barely three months earlier. But the obsession with secrecy meant that *Flak* units were not forewarned, and especially those in the dense concentrations protecting the V-weapon sites. The attack forces, already eroded by engine failures at take-off, suffered further losses en route to their targets. Success varied, with major damage inflicted at Brussels-Evere, Brussels-Melsbroek, Eindhoven, Ghent-St Denis and Maldegem but the poor training of the younger pilots meant they inflicted little damage. The Allies lost more than 300 aircraft destroyed and badly damaged on the ground and 27 in the air (at least one the victim of friendly fire), although *Luftwaffe* claims were for 52–65 enemy aircraft shot down, while some 150 Allied machines suffered minor damage. But a high proportion of these victims were transports (including most of the RAF's fleet of Harrows) or light aircraft including both the Dakota transports of Air Marshal Sir Arthur Coningham, commander of Second Tactical Air Force, whose Mosquito also was damaged.

Although the *Luftwaffe* achieved surprise, and at many airfields found the enemy recovering from New Year parties, not only did the Allies often react promptly, but one or two bases had actually anticipated such a move and had fighters ready. The V-1 attacks upon Belgium meant that light anti-aircraft batteries were also on full alert and inflicted a steady stream of casualties while poor reconnaissance meant that some of the target airfields were minor ones. The *Luftwaffe* was reported to have flown 1,035 sorties of which some 920 were by the *Jagd-* and *Schlachtgruppen* and they lost 279 aircraft, a third of their number, while 43 were damaged by enemy action and a further 22 in accidents. Worse was the loss of pilots, of whom 217 were killed or missing with a further 21 injured, and these numbered three *Kommodore*, four *Kommandeure* and 18 *Kapitäne*, the dead *Kommodore* including *Oberst* Alfred

Druschel, the former *Inspizient der Tag-Schlachtfliegerverbände* who had been appointed to *SG 4* only three days earlier. He fell to flak fire. [53]

'*Bodenplatte*' was quickly recognised as a Pyrrhic victory and Peltz returned to *Fliegerkorps IX (J)* on 12 January but he remained highly regarded by Hitler and on 26 January his command replaced the disbanded *I. Jagdkorps* as the *Reichs* defence force. Simultaneously while *II. Jagdkorps*, in which *Generalmajor* Karl-Eduard Wilke had been acting commander, was also disbanded and the new organisation reflected the declining fortunes of the *Luftwaffe* which was now simply an army support force. The *Jagdkorps* was replaced by *Fliegerdivision 14* (*Oberst* Lothar von Heinemann) supporting *Heeresgruppe H* along the lower Rhine, and *Fliegerdivision 15* under Wilke supporting *Heeresgruppe B* in the central Rhine, while *5. Jagddivision* was renamed *Fliegerdivision 16* (*Generalmajor* Karl Hentschel) to support *Heeresgruppe G* on the upper Rhine, thus aping German air power organisation in the Great War. But *Luftwaffenkommando West*, which had some 1,691 combat aircraft (1,206 serviceable) and 111 transports (99) on 10 January, was hard put to fly 250 sorties a day and the Russian offensive in Poland a few days later saw up to half its force transferred eastwards. [54]

As fuel shortages grew more desperate, Schmid was forced to conserve his forces, ensuring that only half his fighters were ready for action, but ordering the pilots not to cross the lines, to avoid combat and to defend the lines of communication. Yet there was some offensive action, with shipping being attacked in the approaches to Antwerp while a minelaying effort, *Unternehmen 'Ziesig'* ('Siskin'), involved some 20 aircraft, of which a third fell to night fighters. Jet bombers continued to strike, and on 25 January four Ar 234 bombed the port of Antwerp. [55]

In mid-February the British spearheaded a drive into the Rhineland towards the river, the Reich's last great natural defensive barrier. The jet bombers played a major part in the resistance; there were 28 sorties on 8 February and 90 on 14 February, but as as one *Luftwaffe* historian has observed, the revolutionary, war-winning weapons probably dropped most of their bombs on German towns and villages. Conventional fighters were reduced to shielding the jets' vulnerable bases with 80–90 sorties a day, but on 25 February 125 fighters swept over the Allied lines. [56]

Yet nothing could stop the remorseless Allied advance and by early March they had reached the Rhine across much of the Rhineland. [57] On 7 March troops of Major-General Courtney H. Hodges' First US Army seized a rail bridge across the river at Remagen and began driving into central Germany, while on 23 March the British crossed in the area of Wesel and Major-General George S. Patton's Third American Army crossed the upper Rhine at Oppenheim.

On 8 March the *Luftwaffe* created *Gefechtsverband Kowalewski* from *Stab KG 76* (*Oberstleutnant* Robert Kowalewski) and this formation used jets and *Jabos* to attack the Remagen bridge sometimes under Egon control. Partial demolition of the bridge as the Americans crossed combined with the impact of the bombs to cause the bridge's collapse on 17 March, although by then the Americans were well established on the eastern shore and had established pontoon bridges. [58]

By now *Luftwaffenkommando West*'s front had again been split into two following the disbandment of Hentschel's *Fliegerdivision 16* and it was *Fliegerdivision 15's* Wilkewho vainly sent out jets to stop the advance upon Oppenheim. However attacks on *KG 76*'s base saw the destruction of 16 Ar 234 bombers and the unit later rarely reached a level of double-digit sorties. Other jet units and *Fliegerdivision 16*'s *Nachtschlachtflieger* harassed the advance on Oppenheim supported by with 150 *Jagdgruppe* sorties on the day of the crossing, but casualties were so heavy that the figure dropped to 60 the following day while during the intervening night 50 *Stuka* sorties were flown against the bridgehead. [59] The Americans were undeterred and overran Wilke's bases on 25 March leading to a collapse of *Luftwaffe* activity.

To the north the British crossing produced what the British Official History described as a 'mediocre' reaction because for the previous two days Allied air forces had struck the *Luftwaffe's* airfields, concentrating upon the jet bases which also provided the only reliable reconnaissance. [60] Once across the river they drove into northern Germany and the Netherlands, supported by the 2nd Tactical Air Force. Simultaneously, the Americans, supported by Ninth Air Force, isolated *Heeresgruppe B* in the Ruhr and the *Luftwaffe* tried desperately to send in supplies from 8 April as its fuel seeped away, but barely 50 sorties had been flown by the time the army group surrendered on 17 April. [61] Even as the Ruhr Pocket was being squeezed, the Americans were driving through central Germany towards the Elbe while their 6th Army Group, supported by the First Tactical Air Force (the latter created on 1 November to support forces on the upper Rhine) drove into southern Germany, a move which led to Schmid's *Luftwaffenkommando West* receiving 7. *Jagddivision* under Hentschel from 10 April. But without support from Stumpff's *Luftflotte Reich* Schmid never achieved more than 150 sorties a day. [62]

By 9 April he had 698 aircraft (413 serviceable); *Fliegerdivision 14* faced the British with 301 aircraft (153 serviceable), *Fliegerdivisionen 15* and *16* faced Ninth Air Force with 228 (133) while 7. *Jagddivision* faced First Tactical Air Force with 169 (127) including 44 jets. [23] Schmid's squadrons were driven into central Germany, their efforts undermined by constant moves which soaked up precious petrol while the infrastructure collapsed, making the delivery of any supplies a problem. The Allies had, in fact, linked up five days earlier when an Eighth Air Force reclamation and repair squadron engineer, Second Lieutenant John R. Campbell, looking for a wrecked aircraft, met Russian scouts. [63]

During early April *Luftwaffe* commands were switched around as if in a maniacal game of chess. Eventually, on 14 April, Stumpff was assigned the air defence of northern Germany while Schmid was assigned the south-west under Greim's *Luftflotte 6*, retaining *Fliegerdivision 16* and 7. *Jagddivision*. Stumpff had *Fliegerdivisionen 14* and *15* (the latter under *Generalmajor* Walter Grabmann from 30 April) facing west while facing east were *1.* and *2. Jagddivisionen* together with Fiebig's *Fliegerkorps II* which had become *Luftwaffenkommando Nordost* on 12 April with *Fliegerdivisionen 1* and *4* as well as the maritime aircraft of *Fliegerführer 6*. In the game of command musical chairs Schmid became one of the last casualties, Greim replacing him on 28 April with *Generalleutnant* Martin Harlinghausen. Koller (who personally flew him to his new headquarters) stated cryptically: 'The reasons are evident' [for the move] without elaborating. [64] Yet *Luftwaffe* resistance was collapsing and with Hitler's suicide on 30 April the end was clearly in sight. Stumpff had some 1,000 aircraft while Harlinghausen had around 380, a transport force of some 150 aircraft being scattered between them. But serviceability was probably only 25 per cent and in order to maintain a token operational capability units were being cannibalised to provide men and machines. Such was the desperation that light training aircraft were modified to carry *Panzerfaust* rocket-propelled anti-tank grenades and bazooka (*Panzerschreck*) rockets in *Unternehmen 'Bienenstock'* ('Beehive'). They flew several missions against American tanks, with mixed results. [65]

The retreat in the West caused the boundaries between *Luftwaffenkommando West* and *Luftflotte Reich* to overlap, then become blurred, then disappear altogether. The winter of 1944–1945 saw the air defence of the Reich slowly collapse, its demise accelerated by *'Bodenplatte'* which further weakened the day fighter force. [66] In the aftermath of the abortive air offensive, senior *Jagdwaffe* leaders, including Günther Lützow and Johannes Trautloft, concerned about Galland's fall from grace, met Greim on 13 January to seek his opinion about approaching Hitler directly about the fighter crisis. Greim refused to get involved, but Göring quickly learned of the meeting and summoned all the senior *Jagdwaffe* personnel – except Galland – to a conference on 19 January. Lützow was the spokesman and protested at both Galland's dismissal and Peltz' latest appointment as well as dismissing the *Reichsmarschall's* frequent accusations of fighter pilot cowardice. Göring stormed out of the room threatening to court-martial and shoot Lützow and the *Kommodore* for mutiny, but Koller played a leading part in cooling the situation. Yet he could not prevent Lützow being banished to Italy or Gollob's appointment as *Inspekteur der Jagdflieger* on 23 January. A Party witch-hunt followed which saw Galland placed under house arrest until the armaments supremo and minister, Albert Speer, learned of the situation and contacted Hitler who crushed the conspiracy. [67]

As compensation for his travails Galland was given command of an outcast jet-fighter unit, *Jagdverband 44*, as Germany's daytime shield increasingly turned to the Me 262. The piston-engined fighters were swamped by the Mustangs and Thunderbolts. One alternative use for the conventional fighters was proposed by Herrmann, who had been promised Galland's job by Göring. He had long advocated ramming American four-engined bombers. Such was the desperation of the *Luftwaffe* that this unit, *Schulungslehrgang Elbe* (often called *Sonderkommando Elbe*), was formed in early March and flew its lone mission on 7 April with 143 aircraft. Some 40 aircraft attempted to ram the Americans, bringing down 13 bombers for the loss of 21 aircraft and 24 pilots, although the Fortresses proved to have more robust airframes than their attackers: total American losses for the day were 17 bombers. [68] Three days later the Eighth Air Force struck jet bases and were attacked by 63 Me 262 which destroyed 10 bombers, but the 900 escorts shot down some 32 jets while others were destroyed on the ground.

The night-fighter arm was also collapsing, its demise accelerated by demands for ground-attack missions; 10 machines were lost supporting *'Bodenplatte'*, while there were ever-demanding restrictions on fuel. [69] The British were also increasingly attacking during the day, a third of their 38,885 strategic sorties flown during the first four months of 1945, but their nocturnal casualties remained high with 448 (82%) of their 545 losses being at night. Many were to *Flak*, for British electronic counter-measures continued to degrade the night defences with 2,961 electronic support sorties to the end of April.

Bizarrely, at this desperate time, the *Luftwaffe* conducted its largest intruder mission, *Unternehmen 'Gisela'*, on the night of 3/4 March. The *Nachtjagdwaffe* used

142 aircraft which shot down 21 bombers while three crash-landed and six were damaged, but 23 night fighters and their precious crews were lost, a third of them running out of fuel. [70] The lack of fuel meant this effort was never repeated and the *Nachtjagdgruppen* gradually faded into oblivion.

With fuel almost non-existent, the *Luftwaffe* died not with a bang but a whimper. The government, under Dönitz following Hitler's death, was so deluded it believed it could negotiate an armistice with the Anglo-Americans and persuade them to join the fight against the Russians. On 3 May it sought to surrender its forces in the north to the British and capitulated on 4 May, but *Luftwaffe* units were ordered (it is unclear whether these orders came from *OKL* or Stumpff), to prepare to move either to Prague or to Norway in an attempt to preserve them for the forthcoming fight against the Russians. Many pilots were unhappy, and in *II./JG 26* they were forced to fly at gunpoint. During 5 May some 114 aircraft flew through storms to Norway where they would end the war. [71]

Born on Bastille Day 1932, the *Luftwaffe* had overshadowed Europe for a decade, but within a year of the Second World War breaking out the fault lines were becoming apparent. At the heart was the Nazi regime it served with its 'divide and conquer' philosophy preventing coherent strategic and industrial decision-making. This was exacerbated by the lack of adequately trained *Luftwaffe* staff officers and a leadership which usually thought only in the short-term, gradually giving away the Operational-level birthright which was the foundation of its reputation and effectiveness for the mess of potage which was Tactical Air Support. Yet this in turn had overtones of the German air power experience gained in the First World War and suggests that, ultimately, the *Luftwaffe* leadership, whatever its claims, was not air-minded and thus doomed the Third Reich. Thousands of German airmen would perish bravely doing their duty in the belief, shared by their enemies, that such endeavour would lead to a better world. Truly, as the English saying has it: 'Never did a better servant have a worse Master.'

End Notes

Chapter One

1. For German air power between 1918 and 1936 see Schliephake; Völker, *Dokumente*; Völker, *Entwicklung*. For officers who would become *Luftwaffe* generals the best and most accessible source of information is Collins and Miller's website *Axis Biographical Research: Luftwaffe*. I would also like to express my profound thanks to Mr Hans-Eberhard Krüger and his unstinting generosity in supplying information and material. See also his articles in *Jägerblatt*.

2. Morrow, *German Air Power in World War I*, pp. 92, 126, 146, 150,154, 236 f/n 13; UKNA Air 9/24.

3. For air operations see *Darstellungen aus den Nachkriegskämpfen deutscher Truppen und Freikorps.4.Band* and *5. Band 4*.

4. For the *Freikorps* squadrons see Hooton, *Phoenix*, pp. 20–22; Schliephake, pp. 11–16; Völker, *Entwicklung*, pp. 124–125, f/n 2, 4.

5. For air operations, *Official History. Band 2*; Hooton, pp. 22–23; Krüger, *Jagdstaffeln über Kurland und Oberschlesien*; Wendel, *Axis History Factbook*, Germany and Austria, Freikorps 1918–1923. Kampfgeschwader Sachsenberg, Website axishistory.com.

6. His predecessor had been transferred to Estonia.

7. Hooton, p. 24.

8. Hooton, pp. 29–31; Völker, *Dokumente*, pp. 51–52, 55–57; Official History, *Band 9*; Krüger, *Die Reichswehr-und Polizeiflieger-Staffeln*; SHAD 7N2611.

9. See *Official History, Band 2*; Hooton, pp. 22–23; Krüger, *Jagdstaffeln über Kurland und Oberschlesien*; Wendel, *Axis History Factbook*, Germany and Austria, Freikorps 1918–1923. Kampfgeschwader Sachsenberg. Website axishistory.com.

10. For Seeckt and his influence see Corum, *Blitzkrieg*, pp. 31, 148–149; Carsten, pp. 104–108, 115, 213. Seaton, pp. 6–10.

11. See his entry in Collins and Miller's website *Kriegesmarine*.

12. For the German aero-industry Homze is indispensable. For the post-war industry see, pp. 3–4.

13. Homze, pp. 10–15; Suchenwirth, pp. 8–10, 14–16.

14. For the Ruhr Crisis see Carsten, pp. 154–155; Völker, pp. 133–134, 138, 200. Also Lennart Andersson's article *Secret Luftwaffe*.

15. Corum, *Blitzkrieg*, p. 170.

16. For the negotiations see Carsten, pp. 67–68, 70–71, 116, 135–138, 142–143, 147, 234, 362; Erickson, *The Soviet High Command*, pp. 92, 109–110, 144–163; Homze, pp. 7–9, 8–11; Lennart Andersson, *Junkers Two Seaters*.

17. For Lipetsk see Braatz, pp.53ff.; Carsten, pp. 236–237; Homze, p. 9; Hooton, pp. 44–49; Schliephake, pp. 14, 17–18, 21, Appendix B; Suchenwirth, pp. 11–13; Völker, pp. 134–135, 140–142, 156, 158–159; Articles by Anderson and Speidel; website worldatwar.net Johnson, *Planting the Dragon's Teeth*. Website feldgrau.com article by Vercamer and Pipes.

18. For *Sportsflug* and its successors see Hooton, pp. 57–59; Völker, pp. 137–140, 145–146, 149–151, 154.

19. The future *Lufttransportchef* Friedrich 'Fritz' Morzik flew for the rival Russian airline Dobrolet during the 1920s – Alexandrov, *Junkers Planes in Russia*.

20. UKNA Air 2/1353: report 0160/1825 of 5 July 1933, Appendices A–F; SHAD 7N2620. Information kindly supplied by Mr Richard Smith.

21. For Milch and *Lufthansa* see Irving's biography. See also Corum, pp. 150–151, 153; Völker, pp. 152–153.

22. UKNA Air 2/13889.

23. Carsten, p. 27, Homze, pp. 30–31, 43; Völker, pp. 159–160, 166–169.

24. Corum, p. 149, 162–163.

25. Völker, p. 171. Useful information on clandestine German air activity may also be found in Nowarra, *Verbotenen Flugzeuge* and Ries, *Maulwürfe*.

26. Völker, pp. 159–160.
27. For this debate see Corum, *Luftwaffe*, pp. 86–88; Völker, pp. 173–180; Hooton, pp. 71–74.
28. Hooton, pp. 73–74; Völker, pp. 171–172, 188–189.
29. For naval aviation see Corum, *Luftwaffe*, pp. 78–81; Hooton, pp. 59–61, 65–66; Suchenwirth, pp. 41–45. Völkers, pp. 135–136, 139, 145, 151, 156–158, 164–165.
30. For Austrian aviation see Gabriel, pp. 230–232; Hooton, pp.79–80; Mitcham, p. 133; Green, *Aerial Alpenstock*.
31. He also provided Hitler with a *Lufthansa* Ju 52 during the 1932 elections. For Göring see biographies by Irving, Manvell and Fraenkel.
32. O'Niell, Appendix A.
33. Irving, *Milch*, p. 32, 357 n.16 and *Göring*, p. 113; UKNA Air 118/33.
34. For the *Luftwaffe* 1933–1936 see Corum, *Luftwaffe*, pp. 124–181; Homze, pp. 46–138 (the definitive work on the aero-industry and production); Hooton, pp. 94– 119; Schliephacke, pp. 31– 40, 44–47, Appendix G; Suchenwirth, pp. 57–60, 74–80, 84–90; Völker, *Entwicklung*, pp. 201–230, while the definitive work on Luftwaffe pre-war organisation is Völker, *Luftwaffe*, pp. 11–158. For aircraft see Green's *Warplanes* and for units see both Rosch and Holm's website. See also Nowarra, *Verbotenen Flugzeuge* and Ries, *Die Maulwürfe* and *Luftwaffen-Story*.
35. Corum, p. 157; Völker, *Luftwaffe*, p. 52.
36. Irving, *Milch*, p. 359/n.46.
37. For Wever see Deichmann, p. 69; Faber, pp. 23–24; Homze, pp. 60, 99–100, 133/n.4; Mason, pp. 183–184; Völker, *Luftwaffe*, pp. 31–32.
38. For *Luftwaffe* doctrine the definitive work is Corum's *The Luftwaffe*, especially pp. 124–154.
39. The texts are in Corum/Muller, pp.72–76, 86–90.
40. For Richthofen in Italy see Corum, *Richthofen*, pp. 94–97.
41. For the bomber debate see Homze, pp. 33–34, 56; Völker, *Luftwaffe*, pp. 28–31.
42. Corum and Miller, pp. 91–115.
43. Corum, pp. 152–153, Deichmann, p. 53, Mason, p. 212, Völker, *Luftwaffe*, pp. 32–33.
44. For the text of the Regulation and further details see Corum, pp. 140–144; Corum/Muller, pp.118–157.
45. Hooton, pp. 101–106.
46. Faber, pp. 160–162. Green, *Warplanes*, pp.127–129, 483–484; Homze, pp. 121–123; Mason, pp. 191–192.
47. Corum, p. 107.
48. For dive-bombing see Faber, pp. 149–155; Homze, p. 127; Ishoven, pp. 289–290, 295–298, 306; Smith, pp. 8–10.
49. Greene and Massignani, p. 11.
50. For the Austrian air force see Gabriel and Green, *Alpenstock*.
51. Corum, pp. 157–161; O'Niell, p. 126.
52. For *Luftwaffe* training see Ketley and Rolfe. Also Faber, pp. 141–148; Hooton, pp. 110–111; Rosch, pp. 384–413.
53. UKNA Air 2/1353. See Schipephake, Appendix C.
54. For Rowehl's early career see website Aerodrome Forum, www.theaerodrome.com, entries of Gunnar Soderbaum 5 and 6 November 2004. For the evolution and development of *Kommando Rowehl* see Axis History Forum website, www.forum.axishistory.com, information from L.V.Arvo 22 October 2006.
55. For *Winterübung* see Hooton, p. 115; Schliephake, p. 41; Völker, p. 148

Chapter Two

1. For the *Luftwaffe* 1936–1939 see Corum, *Luftwaffe*, pp. 224–270; Homze, pp. 139–256; Hooton, *Phoenix*, pp. 146–174; Schliephacke, pp. 49–51, 53–58, Appendix G; Suchenwirth, pp. 61–73, 82–90; Völker, *Luftwaffe*, pp. 71–147, 159–214 (Hereafter Völker). Again for aircraft see Green's *Warplanes* and for units see both Rosch as well as Holm's website. See also Ries, *Luftwaffen-Story*.
2. Corum, pp. 154, 235.

3. Macksey, pp. 52–54;Völker p. 158.
4. Corum, *Richthofen*, pp. 111–116.
5. Corum, pp. 225–6; Hooton, pp. 151–153.
6. Deichmann, p. 87.
7. Goulding and Moyes, pp. 50–59.
8. For German air operations during the Spanish Civil War the essential sources are Laureau, Proctor and Ries and Ring. See also Hugh Thomas' classic history, Howson, Mombeek, Smith and Creek, Salas Larrazabel, and Schliephake, pp. 41–44. BA MA RL 35/7–8, 39–41.
9. Hermann, pp. 25–26; Proctor, pp. 3–23; Ries/Ring, pp. 12–14. It should be noted that Germans at this time referred to sexual liaisons as achieving strength through joy, a parody on the State holiday organisation.
10. For the airlift see Laureau, pp. 7–8; Proctor, pp. 20–22, 25–33; Ries/Ring, pp. 14–16; Green, *Warplanes*, p. 407. The first airlift was by the RAF who flew 586 people out of Kabul, Afghanistan, over a two-month period during the winter of 1928–1929. See Baker.
11. Proctor, pp. 28–29; Ries and Ring, p. 17. See also Dr Osborne's essay.
12. Proctor, pp. 53–70; Ries and Ring, pp. 35, 37–41.
13. Mombeek et al., pp. 136, 138. Ries/Ring, pp. 170–171.
14. For the Madrid campaign Hooton, pp. 125–129; Mombeek et al., p. 107; Proctor, pp. 80–116; Ries/Ring, pp. 42–49.
15. For Lützow see Braatz, pp. 148ff. It should be noted that the term '*Kettehunde*' was also an uncomplimentary term for the Military Police.
16. For *Luftwaffe* ground attack operations in Spain see Weal, pp. 8–16.
17. For the Bilbao campaign see Proctor, pp.116–144; Rie/Ring, pp. 56–67. See also Martínez Bande.
18. For Guernica see Kappe-Hardenberg, Martínez Bande (with excellent sketch maps), Thomas and Witts. Also Proctor, pp. 127–130; Ries/Ring, pp. 62–64; Thomas, pp. 624–629; Richthofen diary. The French Général Maurice Duval, who commanded the French Air Force in 1917–1918, perceptively described Guernica as '…an experimental bombardment by the Condor Legion on a communication centre and an army in retreat.' Quoted Martínez Bande, p. 111 n.174.
19. For Brunete see Howson, p. 233; Proctor, pp. 145–155; Ries/Ring, pp. 68–82.
20. For the northern campaigns see Proctor, pp. 157–169,171; Ries/Ring, pp. 87–104.
21. Proctor, pp. 157–158.
22. The French evaluation is in SHAD, 2B78 Dossier 2.
23. For Teruel see Laureau, p. 194; Mombeek, Smith, Creek, p. 138; Proctor, pp. 170–186; Ries/Ring, pp. 110–127; BA MA RL 35/39.
24. For the Spring-summer 1938 campaigns see Proctor, pp. 187–219; Ries/Ring, pp. 127–178; Thomas, p. 801.
25. For AS/88 operations see Hooton, pp. 138–141; Ries/Ring, pp. 135–142; Thiele, pp. 11, 14. Articles by Dr Osborne and Torroba. *K/88* and *VB/88* sank 11 ships (27,335 grt) attacking ports.
26. For the Battle of the Ebro see Henry. For air operations see Hooton, pp. 140–142; Proctor, pp. 221–236; Ries/Ring, pp. 178–200. IWM Microfilm Ger/Misc/ MCR./19 (1A).
27. For the last air operations of the Spanish Civil War see Proctor, pp. 237–249; Ries/Ring, pp. 201–224.
28. Proctor p. 253; Ries and Ring, Appendix L and M; Salas, p. 206. Westwall in *Axis History Fact Book* website.
29. Proctor, pp. 251–266.
30. Corum, pp. 223, 234; Murray, *Effectiveness*, pp. 104–105.
31. Blandford, pp. 11–37; Völker, pp. 120, 122, 125.
32. Corum, *Richthofen*, p. 20.
33. Steinhilper, pp. 108–109; *HJ Quex* [*Hitlerjunge Quex*] was a Goebbels propaganda movie about a son of Communist parents who joins the *Hitlerjugend* (Hitler Youth) organisation and betrays dastardly Bolshevik plots to his new friends only to perish in the final reel.
34. For flying training see Corum, p. 223; Hermann, pp. 44–45; Hooton, pp. 158–159; Ries, *Fliegerführerschulen*; Völker, p. 145–146.

35. For the *Anschluss* air operations see Haubner and Tuidor. Also Hooton, pp. 160–162; Schliephake, pp. 47–48; Völker, p. 154.
36. For the Austrian air force orbat in March 1938 see Wendel's website Österreichische
37. See UKNA FO 371/21710, C 2354. There were only 77 qualified staff officers in the *Luftwaffe*. Völker, p. 124 f/n 240.
38. Information kindly supplied by Dr Erich Gabriel of the Heeresgeschichtliches Museum
39. SHAD 2B97.
40. Homze, pp. 149, 158–159, 229–230; Hooton, pp. 163–169; Schliephake, p. 48; Völker, p. 154–156. Murray's article and BA MA RL7/1.
41. Weal, pp. 15–16. At this time the Spanish Nationalist Air Force were already using He 45s in the *Schlacht* role. Green, *Warplanes*, p. 260.
42. Corum, pp. 236–238; Kuhn, pp. 9, 14, 16.
43. Jones, pp. 129–130; UKNA Air 9/90.
44. Christienne and Lissarague, p. 300. Hooton, pp. 164–165; Patric Façon's article. SHAD, 2B61.
45. A similar conclusion was reached at about the same time by Group Captain John Slessor of the British Air Ministry; UKNA Air 9/90.
46. Hooton, p. 170; Irving, *Göring*, pp. 244–245; Schliephake, p. 52; BA MA RL7/85; Schliephake, p. 52.
47. The most detailed account is Price's article 'Watching the Detectives' but see also Pritchard, pp. 55–56; Wood and Dempster, pp. 17–21. The *Graf Zeppelin* flew some 30 missions for the *Luftwaffe* before being laid up on 20 August 1939. I would also like to thank Mr Martin Streetly of Jane's Radar and Electronic Warfare for his advice.

Chapter Three
1. For the Poland air campaign see Speidel, Monograph 151:*The German Air Force in Poland*; Bekker, pp. 19–59; Blandford, pp. 47–53; Belcarz and Pęczkowski, pp. 112, 147–221, 247–250; Cynk, pp. 134–139; Hooton, pp. 175–189; BA MA RL 2 II/51, RL 7/2, RL 8/102. For planning and preparation see USNA Microfilm, T971, Roll 18. For German units see Balke, Dierich, Gundelach, Schmidt and Smith. For the ground campaign see Zaloga, Zaloga and Madej.
2. BA MA RL7/2.
3. Belcarz and Pęczkowski, p. 200.
4. Report by *Oberst* Wilhelm Speidel, IWM AHB6/158, Tin 148. The RAF used similar tactics in the autumn of 1918.
5. Monograph 151, pp. 134–137, 147–149. See also Deichmann's *Spearhead for Blitzkrieg*.
6. Richthofen diary.
7. Weal, p. 19.
8. Murray, pp. 108–109; BA MA RL 7/2.
9. Rosch, p. 277.
10. Bekker, p. 57. Boog, p. 373–404; *Fliegerdivision 1* war diary and Richthofen diary entries for 11 September and 13 September.
11. Monograph 151.
12. Richthofen's diary for September 25. Rundstedt's Saxon accent meant that he actually said '*Sie oller Gokelfritze*'.
13. Green, pp. 449–450; Windrow, p. 4; Speidel, Monograph 152, pp. 89–91.
14. Schmidt, pp. 302; Shores, p. 28; Zaloga/Madej, p. 148.
15. For the *Sitzkrieg* see Hooton, *Blitzkrieg*, pp. 5–25 and *Phoenix*, pp. 189–211; Speidel, Monograph 152: *The German Air Force in France and the Low Countries*; Shores et al., *Fledgling Eagles*; BA/MA RL 7/2.
16. Frieser, p. 146.
17. This is based upon Gottschling's Monograph 191.
18. For *Weserübung* planning see Claasen, pp. 22–61; Taylor, pp. 82–101.
19. Claasen, p. 40.

20. For air operations over Norway the most detailed descriptions are Claasen, pp. 83–140; Hooton, *Blitzkrieg*, pp. 27–43 and *Phoenix*, pp. 218–238; Shores, pp. 213–351. See also Balke, *KG 100*, pp. 31–46; Goss, pp. 18–22; Gundelach, *KG 4*, pp. 62–67; Hümmelchen, pp. 76–81; Isby, Kesseler's article. Morzik/Hümmelchen, pp. 82–96; Niehaus, pp. 124–137; Prien, pp. 196–242; Radtke, pp. 22–26; Schlaug, pp. 27–35; Schmidt *KG 26*, pp. 53–62; Anlage 11–14; Smith, *Stuka* pp. 27–31; Smith/Creek, pp. 76–86; Vasco, pp. 18–19; Weal, *Bf 109*, pp. 35–39; BA MA RL 2 II/47–49; UKNA HW 5/1.
21. UKNA HW5/1.
22. Claasen, p. 89; IWM AHB 6/4.
23. IWM EDS 229.
24. UKNA Air 22/477.
25. See Kessler's article in Isby. Collins and Miller's website is confusing but Mitcham's biography of Harlinghausen, p.111, fills the gap.
26. Claasen, pp. 131–132, 135–136; Isby p. 223.
27. Air operations over Western Europe are based upon Bingham. Hooton, *Phoenix*, pp. 239–271 and *Blitzkrieg*, pp. 45–92 and Monograph 152. They are augmented by Aders/Held, pp. 51–55; Balke, *KG 2*, pp. 71 -108; Cull, Lander and Weiss, pp. 15–305; Dierich *KG 51*, pp. 68–103; Dierich *KG 55*, pp. 36–46; Fast, pp.31–33; Goss, pp.22–25; Gundelach, *KG 4* pp.68–80; Hooton, pp. 239–271; Hümmelchen, p. 81; Kiehl, pp. 58–92; Niehaus, pp. 138–164; Mombeek, Smith and Creek, pp. 344–370; Morzik/Hümmelchen, pp. 52–53, Anlage, 11; Pegg, pp. 11–16; Smith, *Stuka*, pp. 32–42; Smith and Creek, pp. 87–96; Prien, pp. 269–310; Radtke, pp. 26–41; Ring/Gerbig, pp. 21–43; Vasco, pp. 28–30; Weal, *Bf 109D/E* pp.40–50 and *Schlachtgruppen*, pp. 21–26; BA RL 8/45; UKNA Air 22/32, and France 1940 website.
28. Frieser, p. 108.
29. Frieser, pp. 108, 131.
30. Freiser, p. 296; UKNA HW5/1.
31. UKNA HW 5/2.
32. Christienne and Lissarague, pp. 352–353, 359–360; UKNA Air 35/197.
33. See Dierich, *KG 51* p. 103; Dierich, *KG 55* p. 56; Gundelach, *KG 4* p. 80; Radtke, p. 40.
34. For the Battle of Britain see Bungay, Collier, Goss, Mason, Wood and Dempster. Price, *Blitz*, has much valuable information and is especially perceptive over a number of key issues and Ray, *Battle of Britain*, is also interesting. See also Aders/Held, pp. 60–83; Balke, *KG 2*, vol. 1, pp. 127–181; Caldwell, pp. 43–80; Dierich, *KG 51*, pp. 103–120 and *KG 55*, pp. 57–96, 108–127; Hooton, *Eagle*, pp. 13–31; Kiehl, pp. 94–103; Prien, pp. 329–404; Priller, pp. 66–92; Radtke, pp. 41–50; Ring and Gerbig, pp. 47–56; Smith and Creek, *Kampfflieger*, vol. 2, pp. 98–122; Schmidt pp.69–70; USNA, T321, Roll 176.
35. For the text see Wood/Dempster, pp. 225–226.
36. Mason p. 131. The excellence of these telephone lands is mentioned by *Oberleutnant* Klaus Ostmann of *St.G 1*. Goss, *Bombers*, p. 55.
37. UKNA HW 5/3, 14 July, 1 July, 9 July.
38. UKNA HW 5/3UKNA HW 5/3 31 July CX/JQ/199. See also entries for 6, 8 and 14 July.
39. UKNA HW 5/3, CX/JQ/199.
40. Osterkamp, pp. 324–327.
41. For Dowding's pre-war plans see UKNA Air 16/260; Price, *Blitz*, pp. 5, 32–33.
42. Price, *Blitz*, p. 29, 33; UKNA Air 24/526 Fighter Command War Diary July 1940, Appendix.
43. Price, *Blitz*, pp. 48, 55, 71, 85, 86.
44. M. Svejgaard in website Gyges.dk/Funkaufklaerungsdienst.htlm.
45. See SHAAir 1D37.
46. Estimates of *Luftwaffe* bomb tonnage during August vary widely from 2,317.25 to 4,522 tonnes. UKNA Air 41/16, Appendices 23 and 32; USNA, T321, Roll 176. IWM Misc/McR19(2).
47. UKNA Air 41/16, Appendix 23.
48. Bungay, pp. 162–164, 297.

Chapter Four
1. For the Blitz, see Price, *Blitz* and *Instruments*; Ray, *Blitz*, Ramsey, Wakefield, *Blitz* are the best general accounts. Balke, *KG 2, vol. 1*, pp. 161–228 and *KG 100*, pp. 48– 77, Anlage, 2–3, 18; Dierich, *KG 51*, pp. 120–131and *KG 55*, pp. 104–108, 136– 150, 151–154, 162–167; Gundelach, pp. 90–110; Kiehl, pp. 104–129; Radtke, pp. 50–65; Schmidt, pp. 68–86; Smith/Creek, pp. 122–130; UKNA 14/17.
2. Gundelach, p. 92; Neitzel, pp. 71, 110, n.281.
3. For details of the German electronic systems and British counter-measures see Balke, *KG 100*, pp. 48, 52, Anlage 3; Price, *Instruments*, pp. 20–22, 24–25, 32–49, 95–99, 126, 136, maps, p. 137,170 and *Blitz*, pp. 39–43, 41, 95, 99, 126, map p. 137, 170; Schmidt p. 68. 357; Wakefield, *Pathfinder*.
4. Balke, *KG 100*, p. 55; Anlage, 2, 3; Price, *Blitz*, p. 115; BA MA RL 8/65. For details of German bombs see Fleischer, p. 95.
5. Clayton, p. 79, quoting UKNA Air 20/2419.
6. Ray, p. 76.
7. Goss, *Bombers*, p. 52; Mason, pp. 146–147; Wright, p. 74. The first German airborne radar 'kill' was a year later.
8. John Ray, *Battle of Britain*, pp.145–169; Wright, pp. 209–258.
9. Price, *Blitz*, pp. 112–114.
10. For Coventry see Balke, *KG 2*, vol. 1, pp. 195–197 and *KG 100*, p. 60; Price, *Instruments*, pp. 43–45; Radtke, p. 56; UKNA 14/17.
11. Ramsey, vol. II, pp. 2801–1; Ray, *Blitz*, pp. 162–164.
12. Price, *Blitz* p. 117; Smith/Creek p. 124.
13. Delve, p. 90, Table 1.
14. Price, *Blitz*, pp. 130–134.
15. Stahl, pp. 164–165.
16. UKNA Air 40/288; UKNA 14/17, Appendix 1.
17. Poston, pp. 124, 164–165, Table 22. UK NA Air 40/288.
18. WAAF Iris Price flew an unofficial mission with No 153 Squadron on 13/14 March 1945 while the dog Antis flew semi-officially with Czech aircrew from 1941 *(Daily Mail*, May 1994 and 9 October 1995).Thomas Dobney, aged 15, flew several missions as a pilot in Whitleys until his real age was discovered and he was discharged.
19. Brookes, p. 101.
20. For the air defence of the *Reich* see Aders, Caldwell and Muller; Delve; Hinchcliffe; Isby, *Fighting the Bombers*; Price, *Instruments*.
21. Caldwell/Muller, p. 44; Koch, p. 427.
22. Hinchliffe, pp. 40–1.
23. Aders, p. 18; Middlebrook/Everitt, pp. 63, 66.
24. Aders, pp. 28–9.
25. Aders, p. 24; Middlebrook/Everitt, p. 89.
26. Caldwell/Muller, p. 44.
27. IWM Duxford, Tin 14, frames H9440–9480.
28. Middlebrook/Everitt, pp. 168, 217–218.
29. I am indebted to Alex Vanags-Baginskis for this information and for a copy of his article 'Red Stars Over Berlin'.
30. Aders, p. 54.
31. The arrogant *Experte Major* Heinrich, *Prinz* zu Sayn-Wittgenstein (usually called Wittgenstein), who was the *Nachtjagdwaffe's* top-scorer at the time of his death on 21/22 January 1944 with 83 victories, was one of those who pulled rank to increase his score. When a raid was imminent he would fly to the most favourable beacon and if another fighter was orbiting would radio: 'Wittgenstein here – bugger off' – Hinchliffe, p. 142, but with my translation.
32. Aders, p. 47; Bungay, p. 162–164; Hinchliffe, p. 82.
33. Aders, pp. 57–8, Appendix 10; Hinchliffe, pp. 64–5, 6870, 98; Price, *Instruments*, pp. 65–70; Streetly, pp. 214–16, Appendix 1.

34. In 1938 Harris was scheduled to take over No 11 Group but swapped assignments with Park; Probert and Cox, p. 37.
35. By contrast a *Krokodil* stream tended to be less than 15 kilometres wide.
36. Aders, p. 56; Middlebrook/Everitt, pp. 269–73.
37. UKNA Air 22/79 Weekly Intelligence Summary 214 (9 October 1943). In his diary Knocke, who was given a rocket by Kammhuber for bombing American bombers in 1943, described him as a 'poisonous little twerp.' Knocke, p. 96.
38. British Air Ministry History, Rise and Fall of the German Air Force. Hereafter BAM, pp. 185, 278.
39. *Hauptmann* Ludwig Bekker was lost on 26 February 1943 during a daylight mission against US heavy bombers. He should not be confused with another night-fighter *Experte, Hauptmann* Martin 'Tino' Bekker, who survived the war with 58 victories.
40. Aders, p. 135. Figures based upon BA MA RL 2 III/874–879.
41. Aders, pp. 75–9.
42. Kozhevnikov, pp. 87, 123; BA MA RL 8/84.
43. *Deutschen Reich und der Zweite Weltkrieg* Band 7, pp. 147,215.
44. Isby, pp. 80–81, 97.
45. Aders, pp. 127–8.
46. *Würzburg* was not jammed because the Allies did not wish to alert the enemy until after the invasion of Sicily. Yet, according to Aders, pp. 79–81, *Würzburg* radars in western France reported jamming from March 1943. The *Freya* solution was similar to that used by the British with CH sensors in 1940; Bragg, pp. 259–260.
47. Parry has the most detailed picture of *Luftwaffe* intruder operations. See also Foreman, Matthews and Parry, *Luftwaffe Night Fighter Victory Claims*.
48. Foreman et al.
49. For *Luftwaffe* bombing operations from July 1941 to June 1943 see Balke's *KG 2* Band 2. Collier; Price, *Blitz* and *Instruments*; Wakefield, *Blitz*; USNA, T321, Roll 176; IWM, Tin 29, frames 2826.
50. Balke, *KG 100*, pp. 77–81.
51. Price, *Blitz*, p. 141, and *Instruments*, p. 50; Balke, pp. 53–54 for meaconing.
52. Balke, *KG 2*, pp. 21–67; UKNA 14/17, p. 119.
53. UK NA Air 41/49, p. 14/n. 1.
54. Balke, *KG 100*, pp. 91, 93.
55. Price, *Blitz*, pp. 149–154.
56. For the night offensive see UK NA Air 41/49, pp. 39–67; Balke, *KG 2*, pp. 103–83, Anlage, 10; Collier, pp. 305–8; Wakefield, 'The Baedeker Raids'.
57. Balke, *KG 2*, p. 429.
58. Price, *Blitz*, p. 144, 147–149.
59. Wakefield, 'The Danger by Day'; Bowyer, 'High-Flying Raiders'.
60. Price, *Blitz*, p. 167.
61. For the 1943 campaign see UKNA Air 41/49, pp. 171–228; Balke *KG 2*, pp. 215–242, 262–286; Wadham/Pegg, pp. 89–91; Wakefield, 'The Fiasco of 1943.'
62. Price, *Blitz*, p. 169.
63. Op. cit., p. 173.
64. Op. cit., pp. 164, 169–170, 175.
65. Balke, *KG 2*, pp. 215–242.

Chapter Five
1. This chapter has greatly benefited from Neitzel's exhaustive study on the *Luftwaffe's* operations in the Atlantic and North Sea and its relations with the Navy. See also Hooton, *Eagle*, pp. 42–76; Thiele.
2. As Horst Boog has pointed out, the German Navy never produced an aviation doctrine. Howarth and Law, p. 304.
3. See Shores, *Eagles*, pp. 77, 85, 88–90; Bekker, pp. 65–71.

4. Naval Staff Operations Division War Diary, IWM EDS 229.

5. BA MA RL 2 II/25.

6. See Harlinghausen's report, quoted in Schmidt, Anlage, 10, and IWM, EDS 229.

7. See Roskill, pp. 137–43. Thiele, pp. 20–22 is the best source for torpedo-bomber operations.

8. IWM, EDS 229.

9. BA MA RL, 2 *II/25*.

10. For *Luftwaffe* minelaying to the summer of 1940 see Marchand and Huan's article.

11. For anti-shipping operations over the Channel see Balke, *KG 2*, pp. 129–46; Mason, pp. 108–76.

12. Thiele, p. 22–24.

13. UKNA Air 24/364. However, in July 1943 Spanish fishing boats in the Bay of Biscay suspected of passing information to U-boats were warned by Coastal Command to stay out of operational areas or be attacked on sight.

14. For the Do 26 story see Neitzel, pp. 74–6.

15. The most comprehensive description of Condor operations is by Ehrhardt and Benoit.

16. Neitzel, pp. 76–8.

17. Poolman, pp. 27–34. Jope became the last *Kommodore* of *KG 100* in September 1943.

18. During the last two quarters of 1940 the *Luftwaffe* accounted for an average 12.5 per cent of shipping lost in the Atlantic and British waters, excluding ships sunk in harbour, or 2 per cent of total shipping losses.

19. Jeschonnek's brother Gert became an admiral in the post-war West German Navy, while his half-brother Wolf served in U-boats.

20. Neitzel, pp. 80–3.

21. Boog, op. cit., p. 308.

22. Neitzel, Appendix 1, provides details of U-boat/Luftwaffe cooperation in the Atlantic.

23. Neitzel, Appendices 2a, 2d. The Royal Navy had similar problems with Coastal Command during the 1943 Bay of Biscay offensive.

24. The *Luftwaffe* was responsible for 15 per cent of total British shipping losses in the Atlantic and British waters in this period, a figure it never equalled. On 25 March 1941 *Hauptmann* Fritz Fliegel, who became *Kommandeur of 1./KG 40* when Peterson became *Kommodore of KG 40*, was awarded a *Ritterkreuz* because his *Gruppe* was officially credited with sinking 39 ships (206,000grt).

25. To provide meteorological support for this operation, Jope flew a 17-hour mission from Stavanger along the Greenland coast on 24 March to find suitable sites for a covert meteorological station; Ehrhardt and Benoit.

26. Neitzel, p. 136.

27. The *Kommando* appears to have returned to France in mid-September.

28. Based on Neitzel, p. 90 and Appendix 1. This figure excludes the *Empress of Britain*. In the second half of 1941, *Luftflotte 3* flew 4,878 anti-shipping sorties.

29. See Brutting, *Kampfflieger*, pp. 129–30.

30. Schmidt, *KG 26*, pp, 160–70; Poor tactical planning meant that *KG 26* lost 22 crews in November alone.

31. Neitzel, pp. 168, 169, 211/n.81, 90; Pritchard, pp. 136–42.

32. USNA, T971, Roll 16, frames 325ff.

33. USNA, T971, Roll 37, frames 902ff; UKNA AIR 20/1101 (translation).

34. On 11 June Dönitz's War Diary noted: 'The Bay of Biscay had become the playground of the British air force.'

35. Neitzel, pp. 166–7.

36. During 1943 Kessler's men claimed to have sunk 13 ships (98,000grt) and two destroyers; USNA, T971, Roll 16, frames 325ff.

37. On 8 December 1942, a Sunderland shot down the first Fw 200 carrying Hs 293.

38. For these operations see Claasen, pp. 187–249; Schmidt, pp. 133–147, 212–234, Thiele, pp. 34–47.

39. In addition to maritime reconnaissance, until the autumn of 1943 these aircraft were also involved in supporting covert meteorological stations in Greenland; Ehrhardt and Benoit.

40. Schmidt, pp. 133–47.

41. Mason, p. 105, and Neitzel, pp. 70–4, Appendix 5, based upon BA MA RM71826. These figures differ from Table D. See Marchand and Huan, *Achtung Minen!*

42. Roskill, III/I, pp. 96, 289; Balke,*KG 2*,vol. 2, Appendix 7. During this period 26 fishing vessels and sailing barges as well as four small warships were also sunk by mines. It was claimed that between July 1940 and December 1943 *Luftwaffe* mines had sunk 42 ships (167,000grt). USNA, T971, Roll 16 Frames325ff.

43. These figures exclude fishing vessels.

44. Bv 138 and Ju 88 aircraft were also used later.

45. See Hoffman, vol. III, map 6.

46. For *JG 26* see Caldwell. The name 'Shrike' or 'Butcher Bird' was only briefly allocated to the Fw 190, which remained anonymous for the remainder of the war.

47. Caldwell, pp. 106–8, for a typical day in 1942.

48. See Price, *World War II Fighter Conflict*, pp. 106–107.

49. UKNA Air 41/49, p. 88; Caldwell, pp. 93, 103, 105.

50. For *'Cerberus/Donnerkeil'* see USNA, T971, Roll 16, frames 325; Aders, p. 50; Baker, pp. 181–90; Balke, *KG 2*, pp. 84–90; Caldwell, pp. 110–13; Galland, pp. 91–116; Middlebrook/Everitt, pp. 234–5.

51. Caldwell, p. 113.

52. Price, *Instruments*, pp. 88–9.

53. For air operations over Dieppe see Franks, *Greatest Air Battle*. Balke, *KG 2*, vol. 2, pp. 147–57; Caldwell, pp. 124–129; Freeman, *War Diary*, p. 11; Website fw190.hobbyvista.com ' Focke-Wulf 190s Over Dieppe.'

54. For RAF offensive operations in 1942 UKNA Air 41/49, pp. 87–134, 50.

55. For early USAAF operations see Freeman, *War Diary*, pp. 6–7.

56. Head-on attacks were made against German bombers by Nos 111 and 132 Squadrons in July 1940 and often forced the bombers to swerve out of formation, but they were an extremely risky tactic which required both experience and courage. There were several collisions with German aircraft and Fighter Command largely abandoned the tactic. Mason, p. 121; Freeman, *War Diary*, p. 15; Caldwell, pp. 133, 139.

57. Freeman, *The US Strategic Bomber*, pp. 153–4, and *War Diary*, pp. 19–22.

58. UKNA Air 41/49, p. 132.

59. For the *Jabo* campaign the most comprehensive source is Goss, Cornwell and Rauchbach but also see UKNA Air 41/49, pp. 16–36; Caldwell, pp. 135–136; Wadham/Pegg, pp. 29, 32, 62–65, 89–91; Saunders, '*Jabo Attack*'.

60. Balke, *KG 2*, vol. 2, pp. 197.

Chapter Six

1. Gundelach, *Mittelmeer*, is the best source for the *Luftwaffe* in the Mediterranean to the summer of 1944. See also Hooton, *Eagle*, pp. 77–91, 210–249.

2. For *Luftwaffe* activity in the Balkans between October 1940 and March 1941 see Axworthy et al., p. 278; Gundelach, Band 1, pp. 147–158; Hoffmann Band 2, pp. 65–69, Band 3 p. 108; Koch, Schindler, Tessin, pp. 144–145; Ring/Gerbig, pp. 61–62; Shores/Cull, *Yugoslavia, Greece and Crete* (hereafter Shores/Cull, *Balkans*), pp. 1–172.

3. For Italian air power see Neulen, pp. 26–29.

4. See Morzik/Hümmelchen, pp. 98–103.

5. Gundelach, pp. 38–39, 73, 81–83, 88–102; Irving, *Milch*, pp. 111–112.

6. For operations over Malta January to May 1941 see Gundelach, pp. 92–109, 110–125; Hermann, pp. 71–100, 121–128; Shores/Cull, *Malta: The Hurricane Years* (hereafter Shores/Cull, *Hurricane*), pp. 109–111, 114–115, 119–136.

7. British fighters flew 366 sorties between March and May losing 19. UKNA Air 24/908.

8. *Luftwaffe* operations in North Africa in this period see Gundelach, pp. 105–106, 109–110, 125–138; Hoffmann Band 2, pp. 233–238; Koch et al., pp. 160–166; Playfair, vol. II p. 6; Ring /Gerbig, pp. 77–94.

9. Hinsley, *British Intelligence*, vol. I, pp. 390–392.
10. Ring/Gerbig, p. 77.
11. Playfair, vol. II, p. 35.
12. Foreman, 1941–1, p. 296. USNA, T971, Roll 3, frames 751ff.
13. Deichmann, *Spearhead*, p. 144. Shores, *Balkans*, pp. 173–174, 177, 187–191.
14. For air operations in Yugoslavia and Greece see Gundelach, pp. 160–198; Koch et al., pp. 150–152; Neulen, pp.38, 122–123, 157–159; Prien, *Teil 1*, pp. 482–555; Ring/Gerbig, pp. 62–66; Shores, *Balkans*, pp. 173–311, 405; USNA, T971, Roll 3, frames 751ff.
15. *Das Deutschen Reich und der Zweiten Weltkrieg*. Band 3 p. 492.
16. Prien, *Teil 1*, pp. 491–498.
17. *Deutschen Reich* et al., p. 498.
18. *JG 27* personnel took five days to reach Rumania from Greece by train; Ring/Gerbig, p. 66.
19. For '*Merkur*' see Bekker, pp. 184–200; Gundelach, pp. 198–221; Ireland, pp. 83–88; Prien, *Teil 1*, pp. 556–619; Shores, *Balkans*, pp. 307–403.
20. Gundelach, pp. 123, 233.
21. UKNA Air 24/908.
22. Ireland, p. 95
23. Op. cit., pp. 95–102.
24. *Deutschen Reich*, p. 712.
25. Thiele, p. 31.
26. *Deutschen Reich*, p. 716.
27. Op cit, pp. 711–719.
28. Kesselring had commanded *Regia Aeronautica* units attached to *Luftflotte* 2 in the winter of 1940/1941.
29. Ireland, p. 107.
30. Gundelach, pp. 329–338.
31. Army Air Force Historical Studies No 30. The Ninth Air Force in the Western Desert Campaign to 23 January 1943.
32. UKNA Air 22/212.
33. For *Luftwaffe* operations in North Africa from May 1941 to January 1942 see Gundelach, pp. 142–146, 270–272, 300–326; Hoffmann Band 2, pp. 233–242 and Band 3, pp. 191–198; Niehaus, p. 179; Neulen, pp. 48–49. Ring/Gerbig, pp. 86–148.
34. BAM, p. 138
35. For Malta in 1942 the best account is Shores and Cull, *Malta: The Spitfire Years*; Gundelach, pp. 338–365, 373–386, 399–408, 431–437; Gundelach, Anlage, 29; IWM Duxford, Tin 14, frames H9289–9306.
36. For operations over Malta to mid-May and '*Herkules*' see Gundelach, pp. 338–366, 373–386. Radtke, pp. 100–120. Shores/Cull, pp. 29–266.
37. UKNA Air 24/908.
38. Op. cit.
39. For '*Herkules*' see Shores /Cull, Appendix IV; Bekker, p. 244.
40. Shores/Cull, pp. 195–206, 242–251.
41. UKNA Air 22/186 and Air 22/187.
42. For the July offensive see Gundelach, pp. 399–406; Radtke, p. 2126; Shores/Cull, pp. 379–447.
43. Shores/Cull, pp. 45–56, 82–84, 138–144, 324–359.
44. For Pedestal see Gundelach, pp. 374–375, 406–407; Radtke, pp. 126–130. Shores/Cull, pp. 45–46, 82–84, 138–144, 318–360, 449–455.
45. For this offensive see Gundelach, pp. 423–437; Scutts, pp. 34–35; Shores/Cull, pp. 569–643.
46. Shores/ Cull, pp. 645–646. Some 65 British fighters were also destroyed on the ground.
47. The term '*pulk*', which is Russian for 'regiment', was used by the *Luftwaffe* from 1941 onwards as a generic term for large formations because the Soviet Air Force had fought in large, unwieldy regimental size formations.
48. Morzik/Hümmelchen, p. 113; Ring/Gerbig, pp. 184–185; Shores/Ring, pp. 109–110.

49. For air operations see Gundelach, pp. 347–350; Hoffmann Band 2, pp. 242–246; Koch et al., pp. 160–166; Ring/Gerbig, pp. 148–186.
50. See IWM Duxford, Tin 2, frames K7769–7784. The document begins on 28 May and was apparently in British hands by 20 July.
51. For air operations from May to August see Gundelach, pp. 366–373, 376–398; Ring/Gerbig, pp. 187–221; Shores/Ring, pp. 107–155.
52. Statistics from UKNA Air 22/186.
53. Shores/Ring, p. 153.
54. UKNA Air 22/212.
55. For air operations from October to December see Gundelach, pp. 437–472; Hoffmann, Band 3, pp. 207–210; Ring/Gerbig, pp. 240–248; Shores/Ring, pp. 182–216.
56. Ireland, pp. 165–167.
57. For transport operations UK NA Air 41/50, Appendix 1; BAM, pp. 153–155, 158–159; Gundelach, pp. 409–412; Morzik/Hümmelchen, pp. 112–117. Also information provided by Mr Dave List.
58. For 'Stockdorf' see Balke, *KG 2*, pp. 172–8; BAM, pp. 147–8, map 10; Caldwell, pp. 136–7.
59. Far operations in Tunisia see Aders/Held, *JG 51*, pp. 126–32; BAM, pp. 145–9, 152, 159, 220, 249–54, map 10; Galland, pp. 152–3; Gundelach, pp. 450–472; Mark, pp. 21–50; Prien, pp. 1328–565; Radtke, pp. 160–81; Ring/Gerbig, *JG 27*, pp. 254–66; Scutts, pp. 55–8; Schmidt, *KG 27*, pp. 160–70; Shores, *Tunisia*. Gundelach, pp. 455–584; BA MA RI. 7/30–33; BA MA RL 7/632–5; IWM Duxford, Tin 19, K334–86; UKNA Air 40/2437.
60. In late April *II./JG 27* had only one petrol bowser which could provide each Bf 109 with just 300 litres of fuel for each mission when each fighter had a 400-litre internal tank; Shores, pp. 344–5.
61. Brütting, *Kampfflieger Asse*, p. 60.
62. Gundelach, p. 593, from correspondence with Deichmann. For Richthofen in the Mediterranean in 1943 see Corum, *Richthofen*, pp. 318–348.
63. Richthofen's diary, 22 June 1943.BA MA N67119.
64. Baker, p. 197; Gundelach, pp. 592–3.
65. The new appointments are inaccurately given in BAM, pp. 254, 257 and Molony, p. 47/n. l.
66. For operations over Sicily see Galland, pp. 153–154; Gundelach, pp. 585–651; Mark, pp. 53–79; Molony, vol. V, pp. 128–9, 169–70; Prien, pp. 1570–1704; Radtke, pp. 179–89; Scutts, pp,59–61; Shores, *Pictorial History of the Mediterranean War*, p. 107; Neetzow, pp. 187–90 and UKNA Air 41/75, Appendix 15.
67. Gundelach, p. 616–618; and Molony, V, pp. 48/n.1, 51, 74–75, 127–128.
68. Baker, p. 218; Gundelach, pp. 614, 617–18, 1062/n.92, 1063/n.98; Richthofen diary, 11 June, 25 June. In July the *Luftwaffe* lost 321 fighters to enemy action in the western Mediterranean and 123 to accidents, receiving 310 replacements; BA MA RL 2 III/875–881.
69. BAM, pp. 258–9.
70. Gundelach, pp. 670–1.
71. Balke, *KG 100*, pp. 259–60. For airborne operations in Italy see Kuhn, pp. 194–202.
72. For the Salerno campaign see Balke, *KG 100*, pp. 205–66; Gundlach, pp. 653–687; Mark, pp. 81–108; Radtke, pp. 191–3; Schmidt, *KG 26*, pp. 181–2, and Scutts, p. 61.
73. Gundelach, pp. 734–5.
74. Between July and October *Luftwaffe* combat strength in the Mediterranean dropped by 59 per cent.
75. For the Sardinia-Corsica operations see Balke, *KG 100*, p. 267; Gundelach, pp. 687–694. Morzik/Hümmelchen, p. 119; Neetzow, pp. 195–7; UKNA Air 41/75, Appendices 20 and 21.
76. Gundelach, p. 1092/n.67.
77. Radtke, *KG 54*, pp. 196–7; Roskill, vol. III, pt 1, p. 210.
78. Richthofen diary; BA MA N671/12.
79. Dörffel became *Nahkampfführer der Luftflotte 2* in January 1944.
80. Gundelach, pp. 765, 766.
81. BAM, p. 267.

82. Gundelach, pp. 779, 781, 1106/n.103.
83. Op. cit., p. 772.
84. UKNA Air 24/949 Summary 63; IWM Dixford, Tin 195, frames 3385–9 Interrogation of Hitschold.
85. Gundelach, pp. 804, 807.
86. The previous day Richthofen's son Wolfram was lost in Romania. Weal, *Fw 190 Aces of the Russian Front*, p. 44.
87. The British naval historian is especially critical of the campaign, which repeated the mistake of trying to operate when the enemy had air superiority. For Kos and Leros see Holland, '*The Aegean Mission*'. Balke, *KG 100*, pp. 270–3; Gundelach, pp. 694–710; Ring/ Gerbig, *JG 27*, pp. 275–9; Roskill, vol. III, pt 1, pp. 203–5.
88. Koch, p. 156; Tuider, p. 166.
89. For Allied operations see Neulen, pp. 110–116, 135–142, 162–168; see also Axworthy, pp. 313–315; Bateson, '*Bulgaria at War*', p. 177; Green/Swanborough, '*Balkan Interlude*', pp. 71–3; Sarhidai, Punka and Kozlik, pp. 35–6, 40.

Chapter Seven
1. See Kuhn, p. 133.
2. Irving , *Göring*, pp. 307–309, 317–319.
3. Leach, pp. 145–149.
4. Irving, *Milch*, pp. 114–117.
5. For the VVS see Andersson, pp. 23ff; Gordon, pp. 5–45; Hardesty, Appendices 3, 11, 12; Kopanski 5–20; Kozhevnikov, pp. 13, 18, 20–23; Shukman, p. 161; Tyushkevich, pp. 231, 242.
6. Bergstrom, *Barbarossa* p. 12.
7. Bergstrom op. cit.; Hoffmann, vol. II, p. 81; Reinhardt, p. 8.
8. Braithwaite, pp. 147–149; Shukman, pp. 97, 161–2, 362; Volkogonov, p. 375.
9. *Deutschen Reich*, Band 4, p. 307.
10. In May 1940 the *Luftwaffe* had 1,760 bombers and in June 1941 1,338; Murray, pp. 76–77.
11. Leach, pp. 99, 129–130.
12. For operations in 1941 see Bergström, *Barbarossa*, pp. 14–114; Hooton, *Eagle*, pp. 94–104; Plocher, *1941*, pp. 38–253.
13. Fleischer, p. 98.
14. USNA, T971, Roll 26. Another German source, Der Luftkrieg in Osten, says the *Luftwaffe* lost 160 aircraft in the first week and destroyed 4,017 aircraft. USNA, T971, Roll 18 frames 793.
15. Muller, pp. 48–51.
16. Bergström, p. 22.
17. BAM, map 15.
18. Balke, *KG 2*, pp. 406–419; Bergstrom, pp. 14, 25, 26, 28.
19. Bekker, pp. 223–224; Muller p. 51.
20. Plocher, pp. 79–116.
21. Bergstrom, p. 60; Plocher, 1941, pp. 146n, 157–177; Rohwer /Hümmelchen, pp. 69–81; see Arvo L. Vercamer's article 'Naval War in the Baltic Sea 1941–1945' Website. Feldgrau.com/baltsea.html.
22. Serviceable aircraft from Halder's diary for 12 September 1941.
23. Bergstrom, p. 85; Brütting, p. 252; Rohwer/Hümmelchen, p. 87.
24. Murray, p. 84; Plocher, pp. 136–158.
25. UKNA Air 40/2037; Murray, pp. 83–84.
26. Pegg, p. 33.
27. Gundelach, vol. 1, p. 275. See also Chapter 4, Note 218.
28. Halder diary entry for 12 September 1941.
29. Plocher, pp. 117–135; UKNA Air 40/1925; UKNA Air 40/2037.
30. USNA, T971, Roll 26.
31. Muller, pp. 57–58.BA MA RL8/49; Halder's diary, entry for 8 October 1941.

32. For operations during the Moscow and winter campaigns see Bergström, *Barbarossa*, pp. 89–119 and *Stalingrad*, pp. 16–35; Hooton, pp. 101–104, 170–171; Plocher, *1941*, pp. 202–253 and *1942*, pp. 68–73, 101–114, 151–171.
33. See Hooton, p. 102, Table 24.
34. USNA, T311, Roll 288.
35. Murray, Table XIII; Reinhardt, p. 370.
36. Baker, Galland, p. 174.
37. Bergström, *Stalingrad*, pp. 13–15; Morzik/Hümmelchen, pp. 121–150; Pegg, pp. 34–36; Plocher, *1942*, pp. 97–100.
38. USNA, T971, Roll 26; UKNA Air 40/1207.
39. Wadman, *Aufklärer*, vol. 2, pp. 2–29.
40. An *Armeegruppe* was a task force of two or three armies, one of which was often an allied army.
41. United States Strategic Bombing Survey, Chart 16, p. 21.
42. Plocher, *1942*, p. 97.
43. The account of the summer campaign in the south is based upon Bergström, *Stalingrad*; Plocher *1942*; and Hayward, *Stopped at Stalingrad*; Hooton, *Eagle*.
44. Bergström, pp. 29–35; Plocher, pp. 177–184; Hayward, pp. 65–94.
45. BAMA RL 10/102
46. Bergström, pp. 36–41; Plocher, pp. 171–177; Hayward, pp. 120–128; Hooton, pp. 174–175.
47. Bergström, pp. 42–46; Plocher, pp. 184–206; Hayward, pp. 95–119.
48. Bergström, p. 54.
49. Details of Soviet air forces from Tyushkevich, pp. 66, 271; Ziemke/Bauer, pp. 302, 308. For Germany's allied air forces Axworthy, pp. 289–307; Neulen, pp. 63–66, 99–109, 126–135, 173–175, 188–191, 280–285.
50. For '*Kreml*' see Ziemke/Bauer, pp. 328–30.
51. This analysis follows research by the author using Boevoi sostav Sovetskoi armii vols 2 and 3 and website allaces.ru.
52. See Bergström, *Bagration*, pp. 14–20; Plocher, *1942*, pp. 120–122, 130–134.
53. For air operations from late June 1942 see Bergström, pp, 60–66; Hooton, pp. 176–177; Plocher, pp. 212–23, 338.
54. Between 2 July and 25 August the *Luftwaffe* in the East lost 647 aircraft while 536 were damaged. USNA, T971, Roll 26. IWM Duxford, Tin 20, frames K14 78–503.
55. Murray, Table XXV.
56. Hayward, pp. 150–151.
57. BAM, p. 178; Plocher, pp. 231–2, 245, 340–2.
58. BA MA N 671/9.
59. Muller, pp. 90–1.
60. Axworthy, p. 293 and his article 'Flank Guard: Rumania's Aerial Advance on Stalingrad.'
61. Muller, p. 88; Ziemke/Bauer, p. 381.
62. For air operations in the Caucasus see Bergström, pp. 67–71; Hayward, pp. 152–182; Dierich, *KG 51*, pp. 185–6; Plocher, pp. 223–30, 337–8, 343–4; IWM Duxford, Tin 21, frames K1604–61.
63. BAM, p. 182.
64. For air operations during the German Stalingrad offensive see Axworthy, pp. 293–295; Balke, *KG 100*, pp. 117–25; BAM, p. 179; Bergström, pp. 72–87; Dierich, *KG 51*, pp.186–90; Hayward, pp. 183–221; Hooton, pp. 178–180; Kozhevnikov, pp. 81–94; Muller, pp. 89–91; Plocher, pp. 231–42, 337–8, 348–51; Prien, pp. 1080–221; Sarhidai, Punka and Kozlik, pp. 20–7; Ziemke/Bauer, pp. 460, 463, 464; BA MA RL7/482; IWM Duxford, Tin 20, frames K 1478503 and Tin 21, frames K1604–61.
65. See Russian archive-based website avia-hobby.ru/publ/soviaps/soviaps.html. and sample entries 45, 46, 50 and 92 IAP.
66. Bergstrom, *Bagration*, Appendix 6; Gordon, *Soviet Air Power*, p. 54.
67. See Weal, '*A Nocturnal Miscellany*' and *Schlachtflieger*, pp. 64–67; Plocher, pp. 137,145,147. For later *NSGr* operations see Beale, *Ghostbombers*; Smith, *Stuka*, pp. 102–3.

68. For air operations in Stalingrad from November 1942 to April 1943 see Aders/Held *JG 51*, pp. 122–125; Bergström, *Stalingrad*, pp. 88–126 and *Kursk*, pp. 13–16; Dierich, *KG 51*, pp. 198–202 and *KG 55*, pp. 286–303; Gundelach, *KG 4*, pp. 223–233; Hayward, pp. 251–310; Hooton, pp. 187–191; Kozhevnikov, pp. 95–101; Irving, *Milch*, pp. 183–96; Morzik/Hümmelchen, pp. 150–66; Anlage, 15; Muller, pp. 91–101; Pegg, *Transporter*, vol. 1, pp. 53–58; Plocher, *1942*, pp. 243–330 and *1943*, pp. 1–66; Rudel, pp. 81–8; Weal, *Schlachtflieger*, pp. 48–51; BA MA RL30/1–7; US NA, T971, Roll 18, Morzik.
69. Plocher, p. 261, quoting Fiebig's diary.
70. After the catastrophe Göring blamed both men and threatened them with courts martial, but Seidel retained his post until promoted commander of the training *Luftlotte 10* at the end of June 1944.
71. Price, *Kampfflieger*, vol. 3, p. 246.
72. Bergstrom, p. 122.
73. Pegg, *Transporter*, vol. 1, pp. 68–69.
74. The Russian 812 IAP lost 25 Yak 1 fighters and 17 pilots between 19 April and 29 June 1943. See entry on website allaces.ru
75. Bergström, *Bagration*, pp. 15–20; Plocher, *1942*, pp. 122–123; Glantz, *Zhukov's Greatest Defeat*.
76. Bergström, *Kursk*, p. 20.
77. For *Zitadelle* see Bergström, *Kursk*, pp. 17–81, 116–121; Hooton, pp. 193–196; Aders/Held, *JG 51*, pp. 133–138; Beal, *Kampfflieger* vol. 4, pp. 291–294; Dierich, *KG 55*, pp. 304–310; Gundelach, *KG 4*, pp. 233–241; Plocher, *1943*, pp. 75–97; Scutts, *JG 54*, pp. 95–97; Weal, *Schlachtflieger*, pp. 52–55.
78. Bergstrom, *Kursk*, p. 118 and *Bagration*, pp. 16, 34; Aders/Held, *JG 51* p. 140; Bungay, pp. 163–164, 238.
79. United States Strategic Bombing Survey, Chart 16, p. 21.
80. Bergstrom, *Bagration* p. 28; Weal, *Schlachtgruppen*, pp. 81–82.
81. Dierich, *KG 55*, pp. 335–338.
82. Bergström, *Bagration* p. 33; Gundelach, *KG 4*, pp. 270–283; Hooton, pp. 192, 202–203; Plocher, *1943*, pp. 221–229. BA MA RL7/521.
83. BAMA RL 10/120; KTB I/KG 55.
84. For Greim's operations see Aders/Held *JG 51*, p. 138; Bergström, *Kursk*, pp. 82–95, 102–115 and *Bagration*, pp. 24, 31–44; Gundelach, *KG 4*, pp. 241–251; Hooton, pp. 196–197; Plocher, *1943*, pp. 98–119; Weal, *Schlachtflieger*, pp. 55–56. For Dessloch's operations see Aders/Held, *JG 51*, pp. 138–139; Beale, *Kampfflieger* vol. 4, pp. 300–301; Bergström, *Kursk*, pp. 96–101 and *Bagration*, pp. 25–30, 38–44; Dierich, *KG 55*, pp.310–314; Gunbdelach, *KG 4*, pp. 255–270; Hooton, pp. 197–201; Plocher, *1943*, pp. 119–171; Weal, *Schlachtflieger*, pp. 56–58, 88–90; IWM Duxford, Tin 21, frames K2126–2169.
85. Green, *Warplanes*, pp. 491–493, 512–514; Morzik/Hümmelchen, p. 11; Anlage, 7, 8; Pegg, *Transporter*, vol. 2, pp. 113–114.
86. For airlift operations see Bergström, *Bagration* p. 42; Dierich, *KG 55*, pp. 315–316; Gundelach, *KG 4*, pp. 265–266; Morzik/Hümmelchen, pp. 176–205; Pegg, *Transportflieger*, vol. 2, pp. 130–136, 143–144.
87. See Bergström, *Bagration*, p. 37; Hooton p. 202.
88. Caldwell/Muller, pp. 144–145.

Chapter Eight
1. Aders, p. 60.
2. Based upon Overy, *War and Economy*, pp. 280/n.71, 373.
3. The British had created the equivalent Telecommunications Research Establishment some three years earlier. For changes in night fighting see Aders, pp. 61–3, 85–7, 101; Herrmann, pp. 160–70; Hinchliffe, pp. 127–33; Price, *Instruments*, pp. 145–8.
4. Hinchliffe, p. 159.
5. For the electronic warfare situation see Aders, pp. 79–81; Hinchliffe, pp. 135–6; Price, *Instruments*, pp. 128–42; Price, *Ju 88 Night Fighters*, p. 6.

6. See Hinchliffe, pp. 143–58. Irving, *Goring*, pp. 395–6. Middlebrook/Everitt, pp. 411–416; Middlebrook, *The Battle of Hamburg*; Price, *Instruments*, pp. 151–65.

7. The *I. Jagdkorps* war diary reports the first *Lichtenstein SN-2* victory on 13 December 1943. For the new generation of sensors see Aders, pp. 122–8.

8. The Germans also created radar decoys on the ground to confuse the H2S.

9. Hinsley, Appendix 21.

10. The exact translation of *Zahme Sau* is 'Tame Boar', but the colloquial English translation would be 'Pet Lamb'.

11. *Wilde Sau* literally means 'Wild Boar' or 'Savage Boar' but the colloquial English equivalent is 'Rogue Elephant'.

12. Aders, pp. 101–2; Herrmann, pp. 176–7; Hinchliffe, pp. 159–60.

13. For *Wilde Sau* see Aders, pp. 97–101, 106–7, 141–2, 147; Foreman, Matthews, Parry, pp. 168–169, 178–179; Herrmann, pp. 177–214; Hinchliffe, pp. 150–1, 166–7, 179–92, 211–15; Middlebrook/Everitt, pp. 422–4.

14. Aders, p. 104.

15. Caldwell/Muller, pp. 115, 118–119. *II. Jagdkorps* was also formed to perform a similar function under *Luftflotte 3* and there were plans for a *III. Jagdkorps* covering Bavaria and Austria but these were later abandoned.

16. For Schulze-Boysen see Hooton, *Phoenix Triumphant*, pp. 113, 125.

17. Kogel would be succeeded first by *Oberst* Rudolf Wodrag then *Oberst* Walter Kienitz. Information on this matter came via the *12 o'Clock High Forum* from Mr Bruce Dennis.

18. For the Battle of Berlin see Aders, pp. 111–14, 148–58; BAM, pp. 277–9; Hinchliffe, pp, 203–57; Hinsley, Appendix 21; Middlebrook/Everitt, pp. 446–88; Middlebrook, *Berlin Raids* and *Nuremberg Raid*; Price, *Instruments*, pp. 179–98; Streetly, pp. 35–50; BAMA RL8I91–3.

19. For a detailed description of the headquarters and commentaries see Hinchliffe, pp. 163–6, 191; Hooton, *Eagle* p. 258.

20. For operations from July to November 1943 see Aders, pp. 146–7; Hinchliffe, pp. 1879, 196–7, 200; Middlebrook/Everitt, pp. 415–43.

21. *Jagdkorps I* war diary, BA MA RL 8/93.

22. Middlebrook/Everitt, p. 552.

23. IWM Duxford, Tin 30, frames K3312–3356.

24. For German day fighter defence the best source is Caldwell and Muller and Isby, *Fighting the Bomber*. Also Baker, pp. 225–9; Feist, pp. 66–77; Hooton, *Eagles*, pp.263–273; IWM Duxford, Tin 195, frames 3296–311, 3443–5, 3525–7.

25. A B-17F carried 4,430 rounds or more than half a tonne. Freeman, *Strategic Bomber*, p. 120.

26. Price, *Fighter Conflict*, p. 83.

27. Caldwell/Muller, pp.75, 84, 86.

28. See notes of Brigadier-General Frank A. Armstrong, then commander of the 10lst Provisional Combat Wing and later of the 1st Bombardment Wing, published in Freeman, *Mighty Eighth War Diary* (henceforth Freeman, *Diary*), pp. 50–51. Middlebrook points out that while all the other gunners in the bomber were professionals, those in the nose tended to be the bombardier and navigator who had no gunnery training. *Schweinfurt-Regensburg*, pp. 101–2. For *Jagdgruppe* tactics see Baker, pp. 211–212.

29. Freeman, *Diary*, p. 54.

30. For the first Schweinfurt-Regensburg mission see Aders, p. 110; Bekker, pp. 320–1; Caldwell, pp. 184–91; Caldwell/Muller, pp. 113–114; Freeman, *Diary*, pp. 89–95. Irving, *Goring*, p. 397; Middlebrook, *Schweinfurt-Regensburg*. Middlebrook's excellent account indicates that *Flak* shot down only four bombers and damaged eight which were finished off by fighters; Appendix 1.

31. Freeman, *Diary*, pp. 106–7.

32. Freeman, pp. 112–13, 116, 119.

33. Caldwell/Muller p. 129.

34. *Das Deutschen Reich* Band 7 p. 215. On New Year's Day Schleich was relieved by *Generalmajor* Andreas Nielsen.

35. Caldwell/Muller, pp. 132–134, 147–148, 154–156.

36. Caldwell/Muller, p. 147.

37. Caldwell, p. 175.

38. Baker, p. 235; Murray, p. 231.

39. For drop tanks see McFarland/Newton, pp. 103–106, 146–147.

40. Freeman, pp. 118–21, 239.

41. Caldwell, pp. 200–2; Caldwell/Muller, pp. 134–137; Freeman, *Diary*, pp. 126–9; McFarland/Newton, pp. 129–30.

42. Freeman, *Strategic Bomber*.

43. Freeman, *Diary*, pp. 123–5, 173–4, 183.

44. Caldwell/Muller, pp. 82, 94,129–131.

45. For the issue of US fighter escorts see McFarland/Newton, pp. 140–1, 144–50,160–237.

46. Freeman, *Diary*, p. 165; McFarland/Newton, p. 158; BAMA RL 8/93.

47. Weise spent most of the war as a *General zbV* with *OKL*.

48. Caldwell/Muller, pp. 146–147; Falck, Erinnerungen, p. 267 ff; Koller War Diary, Entry 27 April 1945 p. 63; Isby p. 189. According to Falck, Stumpff brought to Germany from Finland a log cabin alongside a concrete garage built to protect his motor car.

49. Baker, pp. 220–1.

50. Caldwell/Muller, p. 140.

51. Mombeek, Forsyth and Creek, *Sturmstaffel 1*; Caldwell/Muller, pp. 138; Weal, *Fw 190 Aces*, pp. 52–3, 77–8; Murray, pp. 231–2.

52. BAMA RL 8/93.

53. Caldwell/Muller, pp. 150–151.

54. Freeman, *Diary*, p. 246; USNA, T971, Roll 2, frames 1.

55. *Kampfergänzungsgruppen* lost 58 aircraft to enemy action between January and May 1944. BA MA RL 2 III/880–881.

56. Freeman, *Diary*, pp. 169, 183ff; McFarland/Newton, pp. 141–2, 157–92.

57. Caldwell/Muller, pp. 141, 156, 176.

58. For Eighth Air Force and the *Luftwaffe's* reactions see Caldwell/Muller, pp. 190–207; Freeman, Diary, pp. 248–9, 252–4; McFarland and Newton, pp. 193–237.

59. Freeman, *Strategic Bomber*.

60. BAMA RL 8/91–2.

61. In August *ZG 26* was redesignated *JG 6*, while the following month *III Gruppenstab* became *Kommando Nowotny* under *Major* Walter Nowotny. The *Komet*-equipped *EK 16* flew individual sorties against American bombers from 13 May, but without success. See Spate and Bateson.

62. Freeman, *Strategic Bomber*, pp. 155–6.

63. For operations under Fröhlich see Balke, *KG 2*, pp. 242–62; Hinsley, Appendix 21.

64. Schmid's plan sowed the seed for *Unternehmen 'Gisela'* in March 1945. For intruder operations see Parry, pp. 87ff.

65. Bragg, pp. 300–301 on the impact of *Düppel*.

66. For offensive operations against Britain in 1943 see Balke, *KG 2*, pp. 262–86; Hooton, *Eagles*, pp. 275–276; Wakefield, *'The Fiasco of 1943'*; UKNA Air 41/49, pp. 171–228.

67. Navigation beacons had operated in quartets during 1943, but this proved too complicated for the *Kampfgruppen*; UKNA Air 24/949 Intelligence Summary 66; Hinsley, Appendix 23.

68. Price, Blitz, p. 187; my translation of *Drekmaschine*.

69. For electronic warfare see Bragg, pp. 300–301, 304; Price, *Blitz*, pp. 180–181, 191–192; Radtke p. 203; Kenneth Wakefield, *The Blitz Then and Now vol. 3*, p. 320.

70. For *'Steinbock'* see Balke, *KG 2*, vol. 2, pp. 287–342 and *KG 100*, pp. 174–190, Appendix 14; Beale, pp. 312–320; Brooks, p. 171; Delve, pp. 159–61; Hooton, *Eagles*, pp. 276–279; Neitzel, pp. 205–7; Price, *Blitz*, pp. 180–183, 191–192, Appendix E; Radtke, pp. 203–209; Ramsey, vol. III; Wakefield, *'The Steinbock Raids'*; UKNA Air 41/49, pp. 208–28.

71. All based upon Parry, Beale p. 320; Dierich, *KG 51*, pp. 220–3.

72. For FzG 76 see Koch, p. 129; Price, *Luftwaffe Handbook*, pp. 85–9; UKNA Air 22/8 Intelligence Summary 265.
73. For maritime operations see Neitzel, pp. 158–220; Hooton, *Eagles*, pp.66–73.
74. USNA, T971, Roll 16, frames 325ff
75. For the anti-shipping campaign in the Mediterranean see Gundelach, pp. 752–4. Between May 1942 and October 1943 *KG 26* flew 2,139 torpedo-bomber sorties, during which it launched 1,653 torpedoes. It was claimed that 21 per cent of these weapons had hit their targets, sinking 77 ships (552,000grt). USNA, T971, Roll 16, frames 325ff.
76. UKNA Air 24/ 949 Intelligence Summary No 65.
77. Roskill, III/I, p. 210.
78. Balke, *KG 100*; Anlage, 13.
79. During 1943 Kessler's men claimed to have sunk 13 ships (98,000 grt) and two destroyers. USNA, T971, Roll 16, frames 325ff.
80. Neitzel, Table 17. Kessler's airmen had damaged the *Duchess of York* on 14 March.
81. Roskill, vol. III/I, p. 54.
82. USNA, T971, Roll 37, frames 1078ff.
83. For development of the weapons and their units see Balke, *KG 100*, pp. 236–8, 245–51; Smith/ Kay, pp. 673–8, 679–83, 696–9; Dr Carlo Kopp's article on the Airpower Australia website.
84. Poolman, p. 176.
85. For details of these operations see Franks, *Conflict over the Bay*; Figures from Neitzel, Appendix 3.
86. Hümmelchen, p. 129; Neitzel, p. 217/n.300.
87. Boog, p. 315.
88. Roskill, III/I, pp. 30, 262.
89. Neitzel, Appendix 3.
90. Since 1941 many *Condor* crews included a 'weather frog', partly to support their own operations and partly to provide vital meteorological data to the *Wehrmacht* in the West.
91. Neitzel, p. 215/n.240.
92. Balke, *KG 2*, Appendix 10; Roskill, vol. III/I, Table 3, estimates the effort at 825 sorties.
93. USNA, T 971, Roll 37, frames 1078
94. Neitzel, pp. 203–4.

Chapter Nine
1. This chapter is based upon Beale, *Kampfflieger*, vol. 4; Bergström, *Bagration to Berlin*; BAM; Forsyth, *Mistel*; Griehl, *Luftwaffe '45*; Morzik/Hümmelchen, *Transportflieger*. Pegg, *Transporter*, vol. 2; Price, *Last Year of the Luftwaffe*; Weal, *Schlachtgruppen*.
2. For these Finnish operations see Stenman's article in Air Enthusiast; Bergström, p. 59.
3. For the bombing campaign see Bergström p. 33; Dierich, *KG 55*, pp. 354–359; Gundelach, *KG 4*, pp. 272–283, 293; Kiehl, *KG 53*, pp. 269–271; IWM Duxford, Tin 21, frames K2126–2169.
4. For Poltava see Beal, p. 328; Bergström, p. 33; Dierich, op. cit., pp. 359–368; Gundelach, op. cit., pp. 283–292; Kiehl, op. cit., pp. 271–274; Price, p. 73.
5. Data from Bergström, p. 58; Kozhevnikov, pp. 153–154; Boyevoy ee cheeclyenny sastav vazdooshych armee frontov website http:/ilpilot.narod.ru/vvs_tsifra/gl_2/2.11 and 2.15 and 2.16.html. The *Luftwaffe* had only 350 fighters in the East with another 64 defending the Rumanian oil fields.
6. Hardesty, pp. 178–179, 191–192.
7. Gordon, pp. 54–55.
8. Dispositions are courtesy of order of battle information kindly supplied by Mr J. Richard Smith to whom I am deeply indebted. BAM p. 358, para 4, claims Greim has lost a *Jagdgruppe* to *Reich* defence but the last *Jagdgruppe* he lost was *IV/JG 51* transferred to *Luftflotte 4* on 1 April.
9. For air operations north of the Carpathians June–December 1944 see Aders/Held *JG 51*, pp. 146–147, 161–167; BAM, pp. 358–362; Bergström, pp. 55–82, 84–89; Gundelach, *KG 4*, pp. 294–300; Price, pp. 71, 73–77; Scutts *JG 54*, pp. 137–138, 141– 144.
10. IWM Duxford, Tin 21, Frames K2126–2169.

11. Beal, p. 329; Bergström, p. 77, Appendix 1; Gundelach, *KG 4* p. 295.Unit records show *KG 1* had 72 He 177 on 1 July.
12. Bergström, Appendix 1.
13. *Luftwaffe* sorties from IWM Duxford, Tin 21, frames K2126–2169.
14. BA MA RL 7/522.
15. GAF sorties and losses. IWM Duxford, Tin 30, frames K3312–3356.
16. Green, *Warplanes*, pp. 396–397.
17. Griehl, p. 46.
18. Griehl, pp. 42–49; Weal, pp. 109–110.
19. BA MA RL 10/106; RL 2 III/880–882.
20. For the change in leadership see below, pp. 219–220; Caldwell/Muller, p. 219; Irving, *Milch* p. 288; Mitcham, pp. 278–279; Price p. 99. There is some confusion over Koller's activities after the July Bomb Plot and the exact date Kreipe was appointed, some sources saying 24 July.
21. BA MA RL 7/522.
22. Bergström, p. 76.
23. Kissel, pp. 83–85. According to Kissel *Luftflotte 6* had 982 aircraft on 20 August while there were 164 in the Balkans. There were another 50 maritime support aircraft under *Seefliegerführer Schwarzes Meer*.
24. For Rumania see Aders/Held *JG 51*, pp. 147–148; BAM, pp. 359, 363; Bergström, pp. 83, 87; Gundelach, *KG 4*, pp. 301–317; Kissel, pp. 83–85, 109ff.
25. USNA, T971, Roll 1 Frames 482.
26. Op. cit.
27. UK NA HW5/581 CX/MSS/T297/25; Holmes, Luftwaffe website.
28. Beal, p. 328.
29. Irving, *Milch*, pp. 281–288.
30. Below, p. 216.
31. Middlebrook/Everitt, pp. 580–581; Mitcham, pp. 256.
32. For the airlift see Griehl, pp. 200–201; Gundelach, *KG 4*, pp. 318–319; Morzik/Hümmelchen, pp. 77–79; Pegg, 1943–1945, p. 152. A Fw 200 landed in Crete on 8 May 1945.
33. Gundelach, *KG 4* p. 319; Morzik/ Hümmelchen, p. 79.
34. Russian losses from Glantz and House, Table B.
35. Haupt, *Heeresgruppe Nord*, p. 214.
36. For *Luftflotte 1* operations see Bergström, pp. 84–85; Griehl p. 266.
37. Neulen, pp. 286–312.
38. Bergström, *Bagration*, Appendix 5.
39. For Courland battles see Bergström, p. 103, 123; Scutts, *JG 54*, p. 143; Weal, p. 115.
40. For the development of *Mistel*, also called *Beethoven*, see Forsyth, pp. 39–84, 175–200.
41. For the last strategic planning see Beale, pp. 376–377; Forsyth, pp. 153–168.
42. Haupt, *Heeresgruppe Mitte*, pp. 236–237.
43. Aders/Held, *JG 51*, pp. 165–167.
44. Bergström, p. 87. A third American fighter fell to ground fire.
45. Ziemke, p. 385.
46. Op. cit., p. 433.
47. For the Budapest airlift see Bergström, p. 102; Griehl, pp. 182–183; Gundelach, *KG 4*, pp. 320–323; Morzik/Hümmelchen, pp. 206–213; Pegg, pp. 165–166; Ziemke, pp. 433–437, 448–449.
48. Analysis based upon RL 2 III/880–882.
49. Bergström, *Bagration*, Appendix 5.
50. For *Luftflotte 4*'s last operations see BAM, pp. 388; Bergström, p. 106; Neulen, pp. 145–148.
51. BAM claims that 60 *Jabos* and 20 bombers were sent to *Luftflotte 6* in February actually refer to *KG 4* and *14. (Eins)/KG 27*; BAM, p. 387.
52. UKNA Air 24/998.appendices.
53. Corum, pp. 367–369; Beale et al., *Air War Italy*, p. 97. Beale is the best source for air operations in Italy from June 1944.

54. For the ANR see Neulen, pp. 76–88. For air operations see BAM, p. 385; Beale, pp. 97–207; Griehl, pp. 41–42.
55. According to Griehl the *Luftwaffe's* last photo-reconnaissance mission was over Italian harbours on 11 April; Griehl p. 130.
56. IWM Duxford, Tin 30, frames K3312–3356.
57. Bergström, Appendix 5.
58. For air operations north of the Carpathians January to early April see Aders/Held *JG 51*, pp. 167–181; BAM, pp. 386–387; Bergström, pp. 89, 93–106, 110–111, 116; Griehl, pp. 30–34, 39–41, 44–47, 59–67, 78–82, 119–121, 128–129, 130–132, 183–188, 209–210, 229–233; Price, pp. 142–144.
59. Bergström, p. 98; Weal, p. 110–111.
60. Night fighter sorties were flown from 13 January but it there is no indication whether these were conventional or ground attack missions; BA MA RL 7/526. Nightfighters were used for ground attack during the Ardennes offensive; Griehl, pp. 104,121,129–130.
61. Figures based upon from Smith orbat for 10 January. *II./JG 3* followed in the first half of February. *JG 77* would lose 69 fighters destroyed or badly damaged in the East with 42 pilots killed or missing and 11 wounded. For *JG 4* operations see Price, p. 142.
62. The Russian 1st Guards Tank Army captured 700 aircraft in the Kleineichen area during its advance to the Oder. Bergström, p. 98.
63. For the problems of *II./JG 301* see Price, p. 130.
64. Glantz/House, Table B.
65. Schram, p. 987 ff
66. BAM, p. 387.
67. Glantz/House, Table B.
68. Griehl, p. 30–31.
69. Ziemke, pp. 449–450.
70. Griehl, pp. 45, 49.
71. *I./KG 200* was assigned the task of flying leaders to Spain and was later joined by the Ju 290 of *Transportstaffel 5*. Hitler's personal transport, a Ju 290A-6 was eventually flown to Spain on 26 April 1945. Green, *Warplanes*, p. 508. *KG 200* continued to be responsible for dropping spies with the last mission, using a captured B-17, taking place over Algeria on 2 May; Griehl, pp. 196–198.
72. For attacks upon the bridges see Beale, pp. 379–380. Bergström, pp. 109, 116. Forsyth, pp. 203–244. Griehl, pp. 59–67, 78–82. Some 50 Hs 293 sorties appear to have been flown.
73. Beale p. 377–379; Griehl, pp. 183–184, 187–188; Morzik/Hümmelchen, pp. 224–230, 232.
74. For the Breslau airlift see Griehl, pp. 184–187; Gundelach *KG 4*, pp. 324–326; Morzik/Hümmelchen, pp. 217–224; Pegg, pp. 169–170. Data for 25 March to 6 April is missing.
75. Hanke fled to Czechoslovakia where he was shot while trying to escape. Pegg, p. 170. The claim that Hanke was flown out by a Flettner Fl 282 *Kolibri* helicopter is dismissed by Mr Steve Coates who has produced the definitive *Helicopters of the Third Reich* and was kind enough to advise me.
76. Glantz/House, Table B. The Pomeranian campaign also saw the first use of a helicopter in a military search-and-rescue mission on 6 March. Griehl, pp. 209–210.
77. Griehl, p. 34.
78. Griehl, pp. 119, 129.
79. For the last campaigns see Aders/Held *JG 51*, pp. 181–184; BAM, pp. 388–389; Bergström, pp. 109–124; Griehl, pp. 34–36, 40–41, 47–49, 119–122, 132, 188, 190–193, 195, 202–207, 231, 233. Morzik/Hümmelchen, pp. 230–233; Pegg, pp. 176–179; Price, pp. 161–173; Prien, *JG 77* Band 4, pp. 2336–2365; BA MA RL 7/542–543.
80. Bergström, p. 117.
81. RL 7/543.
82. Weal, p. 112.
83. Schlachtgeschwader 77 Massacre at Kamenz 17 April 1945. Fw190.hobbyvista.com/kamenz.htm
84. It is claimed that Fl 282 *Kolibri* helicopters acted as artillery spotters during this battle, but Mr Steve Coates states he has seen nothing to substantiate this. Correspondence with the author.
85. Griehl, pp. 205–206.

86. Griehl, p. 36.
87. The total transport force in mainland Europe on 26 April was 235 transport aircraft, 76 bombers, 6 helicopters, 29 glider tugs and 19 gliders. Griehl, p. 188, 190–193, 195, 202–207; Morzik/Hümmelchen, pp. 248–249.
88. For fighter operations Griehl, pp. 262–264.
89. Bergström, pp. 123–124. For jet operations in the East see Griehl, pp. 266–267.
90. BAM, pp. 398–399; Griehl, p. 206.

Chapter Ten
1. Middlebrook/Everitt, p. 383.
2. Caldwell, p. 175.
3. Freeman, *War Diary*, pp. 39, 41.
4. Freeman, pp. 64–89.
5. For the Allied air offensive from 1943 to D-Day, and the German reactions, see Bowyer; Caldwell, pp. 150–241; Hoffmann, vol. III, pp. 253–63; Lacey Johnson; Mark, pp. 211–63; Mombeek, pp. 113–240; Price, *Instruments*, pp. 199–201; Priller, *JG 26*, pp. 226–238; Weal, *Fw 190 Aces*; UKNA Air 22/8 Intelligence Summaries 252, 254, 256, 259, 262; UKNA Air 41/49, pp. 255–98; USNA, T97l, Roll 5l, frame 273.
6. I am grateful to Mr Horst Weber for providing me with this information on the 12 o'Clock High forum.
7. Balke, *KG 2*, pp. 282–3.
8. Mitchell, pp. 249–50.
9. *Generalmajor* Werner Junck briefly commanded *Jagddivision 4* until the end of September. *Generalleutnant* Joachim-Friedrich Huth succeeded Bülow-Bothekamp on 11 November and was himself replaced by *Generalmajor* Karl Hentschel in 5 February 1944. Collins and Miller's website.
10. USNA, T971, Roll 2, frames 82–3 gives *Luftwaffe* losses in April and May as 102 and 119 compared with 74 (including accidents) and 98 based upon BA MA RL 2 III/876–879 and probably include more minor damage. For *JG 26* see, pp. 236, 241.
11. Foreman, Matthews, Parry, pp. 173–182.
12. Balke, *KG 2*, p. 318–319, 325; Balke, *KG 100*, pp. 292, 296.
13. UKNA Air 22/8 Intelligence Summary 250.
14. Bragg, p. 305
15. Bushby, pp. 168–9; Brooks, p. 171; Air 41/49, pp. 171–88. Claims the *Luftwaffe* used a captured Thunderbolt for photographic reconnaissance in Hooton, p. 284 (based upon UKNA Air 22/8 Intelligence Summary 247), are dismissed by Mr Dave Wadman who has written two books on *Luftwaffe* reconnaissance, has excellent contacts with survivors of the western *Aufklärungsgruppen* and states he has seen no authoritative evidence to support the claims.
16. For the Normandy air campaign to the end of August see Buffetaut, Frappé and UKNA Air 41/67 as well as Balke, *KG 2*, pp. 343–364; Balke, *KG 100*, pp. 301–315; BAM, pp. 329–334; Beale, *Kampfflieger*, pp. 336–344; Forsythe, *Mistel*, pp. 93–115; Mombeek, *JG 1*, pp. 241–256; Morzik/Hümmelchen, pp. 241–245; Neitzel, pp. 221–226; Pegg, *Transporter*, pp. 156–159; Price, *Last Year*, pp. 57–69; Priller, pp. 238–257; Schmidt, pp. 194–212.
17. Buffetaut, p. 36.
18. Frappé, p. 266.
19. Priller, pp. 242–243.
20. Frappé, pp. 252–253, 262.
21. Buffetaut, p. 37.
22. Some *SG 4* pilots took a *Schwarzmann* in their cockpit. At least one was killed when his Fw 190 was shot down.
23. See Mombeeck, pp. 241–243.
24. Neitzel, p. 224. Price, p. 58.
25. BA MA RL 2 III/880–882 records show 874 aircraft lost to enemy action by *Luftflotte 3* in June excluding seaplanes and transports while 186 were lost to accidents.

26. BA MA ZA 3/156.
27. Pegg, p. 157.
28. BA MA RL 2 III/880–882.
29. BA MA ZA 3/155 and RL 2 III/880–882.
30. Frappé, Annex II; BA MA RL 2 III/880–882.
31. For strategic operations from June 1944 see BAM, pp. 333, 365–368, 370–373; Caldwell/Muller, pp. 190–262; Price, *Last Year*, pp. 91–96.
32. The Fifteenth Air Force flew 4,307 bomber and 2,156 fighter sorties against the *Reich*, mostly against targets in the south and east.
33. The best description of *Luftwaffe* operations during 'Dragoon' is in Nick Beale's website Ghostbombers.com 'Operation Dragoon'. The Ghostbomber site establishes standards of research which should be followed by many others on the web. See also BAM, p. 336; Frappé, pp. 266–273, 282–290; Pegg, *Transporter*, p. 157.
34. Immediately after the war one of the LST survivors drove Göring's captured limousine.
35. For air operations from September to December see UKNA Air 41/68; BAM, pp. 339–341, 365, 368–370, 373–374; Beale, pp. 348–35; Morzik/Hümmelchen, pp. 245–246; Pegg, *Transporter*, vol. 2, pp. 158–159, Price, *Last Year*, pp. 97–111.
36. See 12 o'Clock High forum, comment by John Manrho on 18 January 2009 under the heading *Luftwaffe* generals' sons and Prien, *JG* 77, vol. 4, p. 2166.
37. IWM Duxford, Tin 30, frames K3312–3356.
38. The missiles also damaged five merchantmen (23,915 grt) and three tugs. One of the merchantmen was the SS *Fort McPherson* on 26 July, having earlier been hit by a Hs 293. She was the first merchant ship to survive two missile attacks.
39. Bragg, p. 306.
40. Bragg, p. 307.
41. Patzwall, p. 107.
42. For the air-launched V-1 campaign see Smith, *Air-launched Doodlebugs*. Also Beale, pp. 345–347; Collier, Appendix XLV; Kiehl, pp. 285–291, 356–360; Anlage VI; Price, *Blitz*, pp. 194–202 and *Last Year*, pp. 87–89. The references to electronic navigation aids, counter-V1 missions and airborne early warning owe a very great debt to the generosity of Mr Martin Streetley who allowed me to use material from his unpublished book on electronic warfare aircraft 'On Watch.'
43. To counter suspected V2 rocket external guidance systems the British prepared an extensive land-based jamming organisation with 44 transmitters, while the Eighth Air Force deployed Fortresses and Liberators fitted with jammers. No 100 Group RAF had aircraft orbiting suspected launching sites seeking radio guidance signals until it was learned the missiles had an internal autonomous navigational system while some CH stations were modified to detect missile launch sites; Bragg, p. 308.
44. Beale, *Kampflieger*, vol. 4, p. 365; Forsyth, *Mistel*, pp. 132–151.
45. Baker, pp. 271–273.
46. Beale, op. cit., p. 356; Griehl, pp. 248–251.
47. Beale, pp. 351–352, 359.
48. Morzik/Hümmelchen, pp. 241–246; Griehl, 1945, p. 20; Pegg, pp. 157–159. *KG* 55 flew 32 missions and 96 sorties but delivered only 126 tonnes for the loss of 27 aircraft; BA MA RL 10/106.
49. Baker, pp. 272–278; Caldwell/Muller, pp. 249–251.
50. For '*Wacht am Rhein/Boddenplatte*' see BAM, pp. 374–381; Beale, *Kampflieger* vol. 4, pp. 359–361. Morzik/Hümmelchen, pp. 233–24; Pegg, *Transporter*, vol. 2, pp. 159–162; Price, pp. 112–118.
51. IWM Duxford, Tin 192, frames l071-85. Figures extrapolated from Einsatzbereitschaft der fliegende Verbände.
52. For *Bodenplatte* Manrho and Pütz are the best source. See also BAM, pp. 379–381. Mombeek, *JG 1*, pp. 289–290; Price, pp. 116–118; Prien, *JG* 77, vol. 4, pp. 2243–2259; Ring/Gerbig, *JG* 27, pp. 306–307; Scutts, *JG 54*, pp. 125–130; Weal, *JG* 2, pp. 114–115 and *Schlachtflieger*, p. 99.
53. Weal, *Schlachtflieger* p. 99.

54. The figure includes 101 V1 (79) launchers of KG 53.
55. Beale, *Kampflieger*, pp. 362–363.
56. Op. cit., p. 363.
57. For the *Luftwaffe*'s last weeks in the West see BAM, pp. 389–392; Beale, *Kampfflieger*, vol. 4, pp. 371, 374–375; Morzik/Hümmelchen, p. 247; Pegg, *Transporter*, vol. 2, p. 162; Price, pp. 140–142.
58. Griehl, pp. 67–75.
59. Griehl, p. 38–39, 42,104–105, 265.
60. BAM, p. 390; Griehl, pp. 122–127,133–136.
61. Griehl, pp. 188, 201.
62. Griehl, pp. 159–165,262–263.
63. Freeman, *War Diary*, p. 479.
64. Koller, p. 61.
65. Griehl, 1945, pp. 259–261; Weal, *Schlacht*, pp. 113–114.
66. For strategic air defence Caldwell/Muller, pp. 262–285; Price, pp. 129–140.
67. Baker, pp. 280–282; Caldwell/Muller, pp. 263–264.
68. The most detailed account of this bizarre unit is in Weir. See also Caldwell/Muller, pp. 279–281; Freeman, *War Diary*, pp. 482–483; Griehl, pp. 157–159.
69. For nightfighter operations see Griehl, '45, pp. 90–102, 106–108, 113–117.
70. For 'Gisela' see Griehl, '45, pp. 103–104; Parry, Appendix VI, VII.
71. Griehl, pp. 198–200, 254–258, 268–269. For the flight to Norway see Axel Urbanke's article.

Sources and Bibliography

ARCHIVES

Bundesarchiv, Militärarchiv (BA–MA), Freiburg
N 671 Richthofen Tagesbuch.
MSG 1/1 1410. Hoffman von Waldau Tagesbuch.
RL 2 II/25. Beschränkte Luftkriegführen gegen England.
RL 2 II/47–49 Generalstab 1.Abt, laufende Meldungen May 1–20, 1940.
RL 2 II/25 1 Einsatzzum Schütze der Deutschen Westgrenze/Beschränkte Luftkriegführung gegen England.
RL 2 II/51 Führung des Luftkriegs gegen Polen.
RL 2 III/874–882:Flugzeugbestand und Bewegungsmeldungen, 3.42 – 12.44 (on Holms' Luftwaffe web site.).
RL 7/1 Planstudie Grün.
RL 7/2 Einsatz im Feldzug gegen Polen.
RL 7/30–33 Einsatz Afrika,Mittelmeerraum, FdL Tunis. 11 November 1942–10 Februar 1943.
RL 7/85 Ensatz Tschechoslowakei Marz 1939.
RL 7/88 Einsatz gegen England.
RL 7/482 Luftflotte 4 vor Stalingrad unter Verwendigung des Tagebuchs Gen.Obst. Frh. v. Richthofen.
RL 7/521 Einsatz, Luftflotte 6, June 1943–June 1944.
RL 7/522 Anlagen zum KTB Luftflotte 6 Juli bis Oktober 1944.
RL 7/526–529Anlagen zum KTB Luftflotte 6 January 194.
RL 7/542–543 Anlagen zum KTB Luftflotte 6, April 1945.
RL 7/632–5 Einsatz Afrika, Mittelmeerraum, Lft 2. 28 Marz–11 Mai 1943.
RL 8 I/91–3 Geschichte des I. Jagdkorps.
RL 8/45 Fliegerkorps VIII. Einsatz im Feldzug gegen Frankreich 11.5–26.5 40.
RL 8/49 Fliegerkorps VIII Einsatz Russland–Mittelabschnitt.
RL 8/65 Fliegerkorps IX: Einsatz gegen England.
RL 8/84 Fliegerkorps XII: Organisation der Nachtjagd Juni 1943.
RL 8/91–93 Kriegestagesbuch Jagdkorps I.
RL 8/102 *Fliegerdivision 1* war diary.
RL 10/102 III/KG 55 Einsatz in Osten 7.5 42/10.7.42.
RL 10/106 KG 55 29.11.42–03.02.43.
RL 10/120 Kriegestagesbuch I/KG 55.
RL 30/1–7 Sonderstab GFM Milch Kriegestagbuch.
RL 35/7–8 Kriegstagbuch, Legion Condor.
RL 35/39–41 Legion Condor–1938.
RM71826. Die Luftmine als Kriegsmittel im Rahm.en der Belagerung Englands.
ZA 3/155 Luftflotte 3 Monatsübersicht Juli 1944.
ZA 3/156 Die Lage im Westen von April 1944 bis Juni 1944, 8. (Kriegswissenschaftlichen) Abteilung, 23.Juli 1944.

Imperial War Museum, London
EDS 229, Part A, vol. 6. War Diary of the German Naval Staff Operations Division (February 1940).
EDS 229, Part A, vol. 7. War Diary of the German Naval Staff Operations Division (March 1940)E.
Ger/Misc/MCR./19 (1A).Lagebericht Spanien ab Juli 6 1938.
AHB6/158 Tin 148. Report by Oberst Wilhelm Speidel, Die Einsatz der Luftwaffe im Polnischen Feldzug, December 1 1939.

Imperial War Museum, Duxford

Tin 14, frames H9440–9480, Denkschrift über die Luftverteidigung Herbst und Winter 41/42.

Tin 29, frame 2826, Einsatz gegen England: Übersicht zur der Zeit vom 26.8.1941 bis 3.4.1943.

Tin 14, frames H9289–9306, Der Einsatz der Luftwaffe im Mittlemeer. Ihre Taktik und die Lehren 1941–1943.

Tin 2, frames K7769–7784, Operational diary and notes of *Hauptmann* Gerd Kleedehn, Air Liaison Officer, HQ Afrika Korps.

Tin 19, K334–86, Ablauf des Krieges im Mittelmeer 1.1–31.3 1943.

Tin 195, frames 3385–9, Interrogation of Hitschhold, 20 September – 4 October 1945.

Tin 20, frames K1478–503, Der Einsatz der Luftwaffe vom 1. Juli 1942.

Tin 21, frames K1604–61, Der Luftkrieg in Osten.

Tin 21, frames K2126–2169, Kriegschauplatz Fernost.

Tin 30, frames K3312–3356, Zusammenstellung der Ersätze und Verluste der Luftflotten.

Tin 192, frame 1041, Luftwaffe Activity, vol. 1.

Tin 192, frame l07l–85, Air Staff Post-Hostilities Studies, Book 21: 'Luftwaffe Activity I'.

Tin 195, frames 3296–311, Fighter Operations of the German Air Force.

Tin 195, frames 3443–5, Interrogation of *Oberstleutnant* Dahl.

Tin 195, frames 3525–7, Tactical Regulations for Fighters in Home Defence, 3 September 1943.

Service Historique de Défence (Armée de Terre), Vincennes

4N80–I 2e Bureau, Allemand.

4N96–I 2e Bureau, Allemand.

4N96 2e Bureau, Allemand.

4N105 Commission Militaire Interallié de Control en Austriche. Juillet 5, 1922.

7N2611 2e Bureau, Allemand.

7N2620 2e Bureau, Allemand.

Service Historique de Défence (Armée de l'Air), Vincennes

2B78 Dossier 2: Guerre en Espagne.

2B97 Aviation, Pologne et Tchequeslovakie.

1D37 Opérations 1939–1940.

1D41 Forces Aérienne britaniques.

1D44/1& 2 GQG Aérienne Journaux des Eventements. Opérations 11 september 1939–23 juin 1940.

1D45 Opérations.

1D51 Material aérien 30 août 1939–24.juin 1940.

2D2 Grand Quartier Général Aérien journaux de marches.

2D17 ZOAN journal de marche.

2D27 ZOAE journal de marche.

United Kingdom National Archives (UK NA)

Adm 186/804 British and Foreign Merchant Ships lost or damaged by enemy action during the Second World War.

Adm 53/111432–111434 Ship's log, HMS *Ark Royal* April–June 1940.

Air 1/522/16/12/5 Trenchard to Robertson, Air Policy OB 1837S1.

Air 2/1353 Preparations for the Formation of a German Air Force.

Air 2/13889 Annual report of Commander, Air Defence of Great Britain 1934.

Air 8/863 Battle of Britain: despatch by Sir Hugh Dowding.

Air 9/24. Director of Plans. Germany 1921–1938.

Air 9/90 Group Captain Slessor's collection of special papers in connection with the.

German emergency.

Air 41/17 Air Historical Branch. The Air Defence of Great Britain, vol. III. Night air defence June 1940 to December 1941.

Air 14/91. Exchange of reports on air operations between CinC Home Fleet and Bomber Command.

Air 14/2666–2680 Night Bombing Raid Sheets.

Air 14/3361–3368 Day Bombing Raid Sheets.

Air 16/260 Air Officer Commanding in Chief Fighter Command: Lecture on employment of the Fighter Command in Home Defence 24th May 1937.

Air 16/1036 Monthly operational summaries of Fighter Command, ADGB and 2 TAF January 1941–May 1945.

Air 16/1037 Fighter Command Summary of sorties.

Air 20/2419 Enemy aircraft: night interception. September 1940–June 1941.

Air 22/8 War Room Daily Summaries 256–285.

Air 22/32 Air Ministry Daily strength returns.

Air 22/71 Air Ministry Weekly Intelligence Summary, vol. 3.

Air 22/186 Tables of Operations: Middle East February– June 1942.

Air 22/187 Tables of Operations: Middle East June–July 1942.

Air 22/477 Air Ministry W/T (Wireless Telegraphy) Intelligence Service Daily Summaries. March–June 1940.

Air 22/478 Air Ministry W/T (Wireless Telegraphy) Intelligence Service Daily Summaries, vol. 3 Nos. 296–363 (June–August 1940).

Air 22/212 Weekly State (Middle East) Aug '41–Dec 42.

Air 22/478 WT Intelligence Summaries 25 June–31 August 1940.

Air 24/21 Advanced Air Striking Force Operations Record.

Air 24/364 Coastal Command Operations Record Book to December 1943.

Air 24/100 Army Co–operation Command Operational Year Book 1942.

Air 24/507 Fighter Command Operations Record.

Air 24/526 Fighter Command War Diary July 1940.

Air 24/679 Operational Record Book. The RAF in France 1939–1940.

Air 24/908 RAF Operations Record Book Malta 1940–August 1942.

Air 24/937–941. Mediterranean Allied Air Forces operational record January–August 1944.

Air 24/945–948 Mediterranean Allied Air Forces operational record September–December 1944.

Air 24/996–999 Mediterranean Allied Air Forces operational record January–May 1945.

UKNA Air 24/949 Mediterranean Allied Air Force Intelligence Summaries January–April 1944.

Air 24/101 Army Co-operation Command Operational Year Book January–May 1943.

Air 24/1496 2nd Tactical Air Force operations record.

Air 25/390 Operations Record Book No 18 Group April 1940 Appendices.

Air 35/284 Air Component Diary of Operations September 1939 to January 1940.

Air 35/339 Unfinished draft of report being prepared by the late A/V/M C.H.B.Blount.

Air 40/1096 Statistical Summary of 9th Air Force Operations 16 October 1943 to 8 May 1945.

UKNA Air 40/1097 First Tactical Air Force (prov) summary of operations of American units 1 November 1944 through 8 May 1945.

Air 40/1925 German Air Force operations against the USSR.

UKNA Air 40/2037 Russian Campaign Papers.

Air 40/2437 German Air Force Activities in the Mediterranean.

Air 40/288 Air Intelligence 9 (Air Liaison) report and appendices: 'The Blitz' August–October 1941.

Air 41/15 Air Historical Branch. The Air Defence of Great Britain, vol. II. The Battle of Britain.

Air 41/16 Air Historical Branch.The Air Defence of Great Britain, vol. II. Appendices and maps.

Air 41/17 Air Historical Branch.The Air Defence of Great Britain, vol. III. Night Air Defence, June 1940 – Dec. 1941.

Air 41/49 Air Historical Branch, The Air Defence of Great Britain, vol. V. The Struggle for Air Supremacy, January 1942–May 1944.

Air 41/50 Air Historical branch. The Middle East Campaign, vol. IV. Operations in Libya, the Western desert and Tunisia. July 1942 to May 1943.

Air 41/75. Air Historical Branch. The RAF in the Maritime War, vol. VII, pt I. Mediterranean Re-conquest and the Submarine War, May 1943–May 1944.
Air 118/33. Report of British Air Attaché 1933.
FO 371/4752 C12077 IACC Reports.
FO 371/4757 C11056 IACC Reports.
FO 371/4872 IACC Reports.
FO 371/21710 Austrian Crisis. Air Attaché's report.
HW5/1–703 Government Code & Cypher School, German section. Reports of German Army and Air Force High Grade Machine Decrypts.

United States National Archives (US NA)
T311, Roll 288, Heeresgruppe Mitte Kriegestagbuch.
T32, Roll 176, Luftkrieg gegen England–Gefechtskalender.
T971, Roll 1, Luftflottekommando 4/Führungsabteilung I–Bericht über Verrat und Rückzug aus Rümanien. Der Luftkrieg gegen England 1940/1941.
T971, Roll 2, frame 1 Bericht über den Allierten Luftkrieg gegen das Reich.
T971, Roll 2, frames 82–3 Luftwaffenkommando Führungsabteilung: Bericht über den Allierten Luftkrieg gegen das Reich (incomplete report).
T971, Roll 3, Fall 'Marita'–Wehrmachtberichte über die Tätigkeit der Luftwaffe in Jugoslawien und Greichenland.
T971, Roll 3, Luftflotte 3 KTB 27.8–30.9.44.
T971, Roll 4, Vorstudie zur Luftkriegsgeschichte Heft 10.
T97, Roll 8, Materialsammelung für Buch von Rohden 'Die Schlacht um England.
T971, Roll 16, frames 325ff Studien zum Luftkrieg: gedanken zum Einsatz der Luftwaffe im Luftkrieg über See.
T971, Roll 18, Der Luftkrieg in Osten. The planning and preparations for the Air War against Poland 1939.
T971, Roll 18, Lufttransportführer Oberst Morzik, 'Erfährungsbericht Stalingrad'.
T971, Roll 32, frame 3330 Zusammenstellung der Ersätze und Verluste der Luftflotten.
T971, Roll 37, Ausbildung der Luftwaffe für die Belange des Seekrieges für den Einsatz der Luftwaffe im Kampf gegen England.
T971, Roll 37, frames 1078ff Ausbildung der Luftwaffe für die Belange des Seekrieges. Planung für den Einsatz der im Kampf gegen England.
T97l, Roll 5l, frames 273ff Befehl des Luftflottenkommandos 3 für die Kampfführung in der Küstenverteidigung.

PUBLISHED BOOKS

Absalon, Rudolf (ed.). *Rangliste der generale der deutschen Luftwaffe den Stand von 20.April 1945*, Podzun Verlag, Freiburg, 1984.
Adams, Jack. *The Doomed Expedition: The Campaign in Norway 1940*, Leo Cooper, London, 1989.
Aders, Gebhard. *History of the German Night-Fighter Force 1917–1945*, Arms & Armour Press, London 1979.
Aders, Gebhard, and Held, Werner. *Jagdgeschwader 51 'Molders'*, Motorbuch Verlag, Stuttgart 1993.
Andersson, Lennart. *Soviet Aircraft and Aviation 1917–1941*, Putnam, London, 1994.
Axworthy, Mark (with Scafes, Cornet, and Craciunoiu, Cristian). *Third Axis, Fourth Ally: Romanian Armed Forces in the European War 1941–1945*, Arms & Armour Press, London, 1995.
Baker, Ann. *Wings Over Kabul. The First Airlift*, Kimber, London, 1975.
Baker, David. *Adolf Galland: The Authorised Biography*, Windrow & Greene, London, 1996.
Balke, Ulf. *Der Luftkrieg in Europa: Der operatives Einsätze des Kampfgeschwader 2 im Zweiten Weltkrieg*, 2 vols, Bernard & Graefe Verlag, Coblenz, 1989.
Balke, Ulf. *Kampfgeschwader 100 Wiking*, Motorbuch Verlag, Stuttgart, 1981.

Bateson, Richard. *Junkers Ju 87 D Variants*, Profile Publications, Windsor, n.d.

Baumbach, Werner. *Broken Swastika*, Robert Hale, London, 1986.

Beale, Nick. *Kampfflieger, vol. IV. Bombers of the Luftwaffe 1943–May 1945*, Classic Publications Ltd, Crowborough, 2005.

Beevor, Antony. *Crete: The Battle and Resistance*, John Murray, London, 1991.

Bekker, Cajus. *The Luftwaffe War Diaries (Angriffshöhe 4000)*, Macdonald, London, 1967, and Gerhard Stallingverlag, Hamburg, 1964.

Belcarz, Bartlomiej and Pęczkowski, Robert. *White Eagles: The Aircraft, Men and Operations of the Polish Air Force 1918–1939*, Hikoki Publications, Ottringham, 2001.

Below, Nicolaus von (translated by Geoffrey Brooks). *At Hitler's Side: The Memoirs of Hitler's Luftwaffe Adjutant 1937–1945*, Greenhill Books, London, 2004.

Bennett, Ralph. *Ultra and Mediterranean Strategy 1941–1945*, Hamish Hamilton, London, 1989.

Bergström, Christer and Mikhailov, Andrey. *Black Cross Red Star, vol. 1: Operation Barbarossa 1941*, Pacifica Military History, Pacifica, California, 2000.

Bergström, Christer. *Barbarossa–The Air Battle: July–December 1941*, Midland Publishing, Hinckley, 2007.

Bergström, Christer. *Kursk–The Air Battle: July 1943*, Midland Publishing, Hinckley, 2007.

Bergström, Christer. *Stalingrad: the Air Battle–1942 through January 1943*, Midland Publishing, Hinckley, 2007.

Bergström, Christer. *Bagration to Berlin–The Final Air Battles in the East 1944–1945*, Midland Publishing, Hinckley, 2008.

Bickers, Richard Townsend. *The Desert Air War 1939–1945*, Leo Cooper, London, 1991.

Bingham, Victor. *Blitzed: The Battle of France May–June 1940*, Air Research Publications, New Malden, 1990.

Blandford, Edmund. *Target England: Flying with the Luftwaffe in World War II*. Airlife Publishing, Shrewsbury, 1997.

Bloemertz, Gunther. *Heaven Next Stop*, William Kimber, London, 1953.

Boog, Horst, (ed.). *The Conduct of the Air War in the Second World War: An International Comparison*, Berg Publishers, Oxford, 1992.

Boog, Horst. *Die deutsche Luftwaffenführung 1935–1945* Deutsches Verlags–Anstalt, Stuttgart 1982.

Boog, Horst; Krebs, Gerhard; Vogel, Detlef. *Das Deutschen Reich und der Zweiten Weltkrieg. Band 7: Das Deutsche Reich in der Defensive – Strategischer Luftkrieg in Europa, Krieg im Westen und in Ostasien 1943 bis 1944/45*, Deutsche Verlags-Anstalt, Stuttgart, 2001.

Bowyer, Michael J. F. *2 Group RAF*, Crecy Books, London, 1992.

Braatz, Kurt. *Gott oder ein Flugzeug: Leben und Sterben des Jagdfliegers Günter Lützow*, Neunundzwangsig Sechs Verlag, Moosburg, 2005.

Braithwaite, Rodric. *Moscow 1941: A City and its People at War*, Profile Books, London, 2006.

British Air Ministry, *The Rise and Fall of the German Air Force*, (Air Ministry Pamphlet 248), London, 1948/49 (All references from reproduction by WE Inc., Old Greenwich, Conn 1969).

Brookes, Andrew. *Photo-Reconnaissance: An Operational History*, Ian Allan, Shepperton, 1975.

Brookes, Andrew. *Bomber Squadron at War*, Ian Allan, Shepperton, 1983.

Brütting, Georg. *Das waren die deutschen Kampfflieger Asse 1939–1945*, Motorbuch Verlag, Stuttgart, 1981.

Brütting, Georg. *Das waren die deutschen Stuka-Asse 1939–1945*, Motorbuch Verlag, Stuttgart, 1995.

Buffetaut, Yves. *La Bataille Aérienne de Normandie: juin–août 1944*, Hors Série Avions No 2, Editions Lela Presse, Boulogne sur Mer, 1994.

Bungay, Stephen. *The Most Dangerous Enemy: A History of the Battle of Britain*, Aurum Press, London, 2000.

Bushby, John R. *Air Defence of Great Britain*, Ian Allan, Shepperton, 1973.

Cain, Anthony Christopher. *The Forgotten Air Force: French Air Doctrine in the 1930s*. Smithsonian Institution Press, Washington DC, 2002.

Caldwell, Donald L. *JG 26: Top Guns of the Luftwaffe*, Orion Books, New York, 1991.

Caldwell, Donald. *The JG 26 War Diary: vol. 1 1939–1942*, Grub Street, London, 1996.

Caldwell, Donald and Muller, Richard. *The Luftwaffe over Germany: Defense of the Reich*, Greenhill Books, London, 2007.

Campbell, John. *Naval Weapons of World War Two*, Conway Maritime Press, London, 1985.

Carsten, F. L. *The Reichswehr and Politics 1918–1933*, Oxford University Press, Oxford, 1966.

Chorley, W. R. *Bomber Command Losses*, Midland Counties Publications, 1992/1993.

Christienne, Charles and Lissarrague Pierre (trans. Frances Kianka). *A History of French Military Aviation*, Smithsonian Institution Press, Washington DC, 1986.

Claasen, Adam R. A. *Hitler's Northern War: The Luftwaffe's Ill-Fated Campaign 1940–1945*, University Press of Kansas, Lawrence, 2001.

Clayton, A. *The Enemy is Listening: The Story of the Y Service*, Hutchinson, London, 1980, and Crecy Books, London, 1993.

Coates, Steve with Carbonel, Jean Christophe. *Helicopters of the Third Reich*, Classic Publications, Crowborough, 2002.

Collier, Basil. *The Defence of the United Kingdom*, HMSO, London, 1957.

Cooke, R. C., and Nesbit, R. C. *Target: Hitler's Oil*, William Kimber, London, 1985.

Cooksley, Peter G. *1940: The Story of No 11 Group, Fighter Command*, Robert Hale, London 1983.

Cooper, Alan W. *Bombers Over Berlin*, Patrick Stephens, Wellingborough, 1989.

Corum, James S. *The Roots of Blitzkrieg: Hans von Seeckt and German Military Reform*, University Press of Kansas, Lawrence, Kansas, 1992.

Corum, James S. *The Luftwaffe: creating the Operational Air War 1918–1940* University Press of Kansas, Lawrence, Kansas, 1997.

Corum, James S. *Wolfram von Richthofen: Master of the German Air War*, University Press of Kansas, Lawrence, Kansas, 2008.

Corum, James. S. and Muller, Richard R. *The Luftwaffe's Way of War: German Air Force Doctrine 1911–1945*, The Nautical & Aviation Publishing Company of America, Baltimore/Charleston, 1998.

Craven, W. F., and Cate, J. L. *The Army Air Forces in World War II*, 7 vols, Chicago University Press, Chicago, 1948.

Cull, Brian and Lander, Bruce with Weiss, Heinrich. *Twelve Days in May: The Air Battle for Northern France and the Low Countries, 10–21 May 1940 as seen through the eyes of the fighter pilots involved*, Grub Street, London, 1999.

Cynk, Jerzy B. *History of the Polish Air Force 1918–1968*, Osprey Publishing, London, 1972.

Daniel, Raymond. *The Potez 63 Series*. Profile Publications, Leatherhead, 1967.

Davies, R. E. G. *Lufthansa*, Paladwr Press, Rockville, 1991.

Deichmann, Paul. *Der Chef im Hintergrund: Ein Lebel als Soldat von der Preussischen Armee bis zur Bundeswehr*, Stalling Verlag, Hamburg, 1979.

Deichmann, General der Flieger Paul (ed. by Dr Alfred Price). *Spearhead for Blitzkrieg: Luftwaffe Operations in Support of the Army 1939–1945*, Greenhill Books, London, 1996.

Deist, W. *The Wehrmacht and German Rearmament*, Macmillan, London, 1981.

Delve, Ken. *Nightfighter: The Battle for the Night Skies*, Arms & Armour Press, London, 1995.

Dickfeld, Adolf. *Footsteps of the Hunter*, J. J. Fedorowicz Publishing, Winnipeg, 1993.

Dierich, Wolfgang. *Kampfgeschwader 51 Edelweiss*, Motorbuch Verlag, Stuttgart, 1973.

Dierich, Wolfgang. *Kampfgeschwader Edelweiss*, Purnell Book Services, London, 1975.

Dierich, Wolfgang. *Kampfgeschwader 55 'Greif'*, Motorbuch Verlag, Stuttgart, 1975.

Dierich, Wolfgang (ed.). *Die Verbände der Luftwaffe*, Motorbuch Verlag, Stuttgart, 1976.

Doolittle, Gen. James H. (with Glines, Carroll V). *I Could Never Be So Lucky Again*, Bantam Books, New York, 1991.

Edmonds, Brigadier-General Sir James E. *Military Operations in France and Belgium, 1918, vol. II*. Macmillan, London, 1937.

Ellis, John. *Brute Force: Allied Strategy and Tactics in the Second World War*, Andre Deutsch, London, 1990.

Erickson, John. *The Soviet High Command*, Macmillan, London, 1962.

Erickson, John. *The Road to Stalingrad*, Weidenfeld & Nicolson, London, 1977.

Erickson, John. *The Road to Berlin*, Weidenfeld & Nicolson, London, 1983.

Ethell, Jeffrey, and Price, Alfred. *Target Berlin: Mission 250–March 6 1944*, Book Club Associates, London, 1981.

Faber, Harold (ed.). *Luftwaffe: An Analysis by former Luftwaffe Generals*, Sidgwick & Jackson, London, 1979.

Faber, Harold (ed.) *The Luftwaffe: A History*, New York Times Book Company, New York, 1977.

Falck, Wolfgang. *Erinnerungen 1910–2003*, NeunundzwanzigSechs Verlag, 2004.

Fast, Niko. *Das Jagdgeschwader 52. I.Band*, Bensberger Buch-Verlag, Bergisch Gladbach, 1988.

Feist, Uwe. *The Fighting Me 109*, Arms & Armour Press, London, 1988.

Fleischer, Wolfgang *German Air-Dropped Weapons to 1945*, Midland Publishing, Hinckley, 2004.

Foreman, John. *Battle of Britain: The Forgotten Months, November and December 1940* Air Research Publications, New Malden 1988.

Foreman, John. *1941. Part 1: The Battle of Britain to the Blitz* Air Research Publications, Walton-on-Thames 1994.

Foreman, John. *1941. Part 2: The Turning Point* Air Research Publications, Walton-on-Thames 1994.

Foreman, John; Matthews, Johannes; Parry, Simon. *Luftwaffe Night Fighter Victory Claims; The Individual Combat Victory Claims of the Luftwaffe Nightfighter Pilots 1939–1945*, Red Kite, Walton-on-Thames, 2004.

Forschungsanstalt für Kriegs-und Heeresgeschichte. *Darstellungen aus den Nachkriegskämpfen deutscher Truppen und Freikorps 2. Band (1937).Der Feldzug im Baltikum bis zur zweiten Einnahme von Riga.Januar bis Mai 1919*, Verlag von E.S.Mittler & Sohn, Berlin, nd.

Forsyth, Robert. *Mistel: German Composite Aircraft and Operations 1942–1945*, Classic Publications, Crowborough, 2001.

Franks, Norman. *Conflict Over the Bay*, William Kimber, London, 1986.

Franks, Norman L. R. *Royal Air Force Fighter Command Losses of the Second World War, vol. 1. Operational Losses: Aircraft and Crews 1939–1941*, Midland Publishing Ltd, Leicester, 2000.

Franks, Norman. *The Battle of the Airfields*, William Kimber, London, 1982.

Franks, Norman L. R. *Valiant Wings: The Battle and Blenheim squadrons over France*, William Kimber, Wellingborough, 1988.

Franks, Norman. *The Greatest Air Battle*, Grub Street, London, 1992.

Frappé, Jean-Bernard. *La Luftwaffe face au débarquement allié 6 juin au 31 août 1944*, Editions Heimdal, Bayeux, 1999.

Freeman, Roger. *The US Strategic Bomber*, Macdonald & Jane's, London, 1975.

Freeman, Roger (with Crouchman, Alan, and Maslen, Vic). *The Mighty Eighth War Diary*, Arms & Armour Press, London, 1990.

Friedman, Norman. *Naval Radar*, Conway Maritime Press, London, 1981.

Frieser, Dr Karl-Heinz (trans. John T. Greenwood). *The Blitzkrieg Legend: The 1940 Campaign in the West*, US Naval Institute Press, Annapolis, 2005.

Frieser, Karl-Heinz; Schmider, Klaus; Schönherr, Klaus; Schreiber, Gerhard; Ungváry, Krisztián; Wegner, Bernd. *Das Deutschen Reich und der Zweiten Weltkrieg. Band 8 Die Ostfront 1943/44 – Der Krieg im Osten und an den Nebenfronten*, Deutsche Verlags-Anstalt, Stuttgart, 2007.

Gabriel, Erich. *Flieger 90/71. Teil 1. Militärluftfahrt und Luftabwehr in Österreich von 1890 bis 1971*, Heeresgeschichtliches Museum, Vienna, 1971.

Galland, Adolf. *The First and the Last*, Methuen, London, 1970.

Gander, Terry, and Chamberlain, Peter. *Small Arms, Artillery and Special Weapons of the Third Reich*, Macdonald & Jane's, London, 1978.

Geust, Carl-Fredrik. *Under the Red Star*, Airlife Publications, Shrewsbury, 1993.

Girbig, Werner. *Jagdgeschwader 5 'Eismeer'*, MotorbuchVerlag, Stuttgart, 1975.

Girbig, Werner. *Six Months to Oblivion*, Ian Allan, Shepperton, 1975.

Glantz, David M. and House, Jonathan. *When Titans Clashed: How the Red Army Stopped Hitler*, University of Kansas Press, Lawrence, 1995.

Gordon, Yefim. *Soviet Air Power in World War 2*, Midland Publishing, Hinckley, 2008.

Goss, Chris. *The Luftwaffe Bombers' Battle of Britain: The inside story July–October 1940*, Crécy Publishing Ltd, Manchester, 2000.

Goss, Chris. *The Luftwaffe Fighters' Battle of Britain: The inside story July–October 1940*, Crécy Publishing Ltd, Manchester, 2000.

Goss, Chris; Cornwell, Peter; Rauchbach, Bernd. *Luftwaffe Fighter-Bombers over Britain: The Tip and Run Campaign 1942–1943*, Crecy Publications, Manchester, 2004.

Goss, Chris. *Luftwaffe Colours. Sea Eagles, vol. 1. Sea–Strike and Maritime Units 1939–1941*, Classic Publications, Crowborough, 2006.

Gottschling, Kurt. *The German Air Force Radio Interception Service in World War II*, USAF Historical Studies, Monograph 191, US Air Force Historical Division, Maxwell AFB, Alabama, 1955.

Goulding, James, and Moyes, Philip. *RAF Bomber Command and its Aircraft 1936–1940*, Ian Allan, Shepperton, 1975.

Goulding, James, and Moyes, Philip. *RAF Bomber Command and its Aircraft 1941–1945*, Ian Allan, Shepperton, 1978.

Goulter, Christina J. M. *A Forgotten Offensive: RAF Anti-Shipping Operations*, Frank Cass, London, 1995.

Green, William. *Warplanes of the Third Reich*, Galahad Books, NewYork, 1990.

Greene, Jack and Massignani, Alessandro. *The Naval War in the Mediterranean 1940–1945*, Chatham Publishing, London, 1998.

Griehl, Manfred. *Junkers Ju 88: Star of the Luftwaffe*, Arms & Armour Press, London, 1990.

Griehl, Manfred. *Do 217–317–417: An Operational History*, Airlife, Shrewsbury, 1991.

Griehl, Manfred. *Luftwaffe '45: Letzte Flüge unde Projekte*, Motorbuch Verlag, Stuttgart, 2005.

Gundelach, Karl. *Kampfgeschwader 'General Wever' 4*, Motorbuch Verlag, Stuttgart, 1978.

Gundelach, Karl. *Die deutsche Luftwaffe im Mittelmeer 1944–1945. Band 1: 1940–1942. Band 2: 1943–1945*, Verlag Peter D. Lang, Frankfurt aM, 1981.

Halder, Franz (ed. Burdick, Charles, and Jacobsen, Hans-Adolf). *The Halder War Diary 1939–1942*, Presidio Press, Novato, 1988.

Hardesty, Von. *Red Phoenix: The Rise of Soviet Air Power 1941–1945*, Smithsonian Institution Press, Washington, 1995.

Harvey, Maurice. *The Allied Bomber War 1939–1945*, Spellmount, Tunbridge Wells, 1992.

Haubner, F. *Die Flugzeuge der Österreichen Luftstreitkräfte vor 1938 (Österreichs Luftfahrt in Einzeldarstellung, Band 2 & Band 5)*, H. Weishaupt Verlag, Graz, 1982.

Haupt, Werner. *Heeresgruppe Nord 1941–1945*, Verlag Hans–Henning Podzun, Bad Nauheim, 1966.

Haupt, Werner. *Heeresgruppe Mitte 1941–1945*, Verlag Hans–Henning Podzun, Dorheim, 1968.

Hayward, Joel S. *Stopped at Stalingrad: The Luftwaffe and Hitler's Defeat in the East. 1942–1943*, University of Kansas, Lawrence, 1998.

Hecks, Karl. *Bombing 1939–1945*, Robert Hale, London, 1990.

Held, Werner, and Obermaier, Ernst. *The Luftwaffe in the North African Campaign 1941–1943*, Schiffer Military History, West Chester, 1992.

Henry, Chris. *The Ebro 1938: Death knell of the Republic*, Osprey Military Campaign Series No 60, Osprey Publishing, Oxford, 1999.

Hermann, Hajo. *Eagle's Wings: The Autobiography of a Luftwaffe Pilot*, Airlife Publishing, Shrewsbury, 1991.

Hildebrand, Karl-Friedrich. *Die Generale der deutschen Luftwaffe 1935–1945*, 3 vols, Biblio Verlag, Osnabrück, 1990–93.

Hinchliffe, Peter. *The Other Battle: Luftwaffe Night Aces versus Bomber Command*, Airlife Publishing, Shrewsbury, 1996.

Hinsley, F. H., with Thomas, E. E.; Ransom, C. F. G; Knight, R. C. *British Intelligence in the Second World War*, vol. 1–3, HMSO, London, 1974–1979.

HMSO. *Statistical Digest of the War*, HMSO, London, 1951.

Hoeffding, Oleg, *German Air Attacks Against Industry and Railroads in Russia 1941–1945*, Rand Corporation, Santa Monica, 1970.

Hoffmann, Karl Otto. *Geschichte der Luftnachrichtentruppe*, 3 vols, Kurt Vowinckel Verlag, Neckargemüind, 1965–1973.

Holland, Jeffrey. *The Aegean Mission: Allied Operations in the Dodecanese 1943*, Greenwood Press, London, 1988.

Homze, Edward L. *Arming the Luftwaffe: The Reichs Air Ministry and the German Aircraft industry 1919–1939*, University of Nebraska Press, Lincoln, Nebraska, 1976.

Hooton, E. R. *Phoenix Triumphant*, Arms & Armour Press, London, 1994.

Hooton, E. R. *Eagle in Flames*, Arms & Armour Press, London, 1997.

Hooton, E. R. *Luftwaffe at War: vol. 1 Gathering Storm 1933–1939*, Midland, Hersham, 2007.

Hooton, E. R. *Luftwaffe at War: vol. 2 Blitzkrieg in the West 1939–1940*, Midland, Hersham, 2007.

Hough, Richard, and Richards, Dennis. *The Battle of Britain: The Jubilee History*, Hodder & Stoughton, London, 1989.

Howard-Williams, Jeremy. *Night Intruder*, David & Charles, London, 1976.

Howarth, Stephen, and Laws, Derek, (eds). *The Battle of the Atlantic 1939–1945*, Greenhill Books, London, 1994.

Howson, Gerald. *Aircraft of the Spanish Civil War 1936–1939*, Putnam Aeronautical Books, London, 1990.

Hümmelchen, Gerhard. *Die deutschen Seeflieger 1935–1945*, J. F. Lehmanns Verlag, Munich, 1976.

Irving, David. *The Destruction of Convoy PQ.17*, Transworld Publishers, London, 1970.

Irving, David. *The Rise and Fall of the Luftwaffe: The Life of Erhard Milch*, Weidenfeld & Nicolson, London, 1973.

Irving, David. *Göring*, Macmillan, London, 1989.

Isby, David (ed.). *The Luftwaffe and the War at Sea 1939–1945: As seen by the officers of the Kriegsmarine and Luftwaffe*. Chatham Publishing, London, 2005.

Ishoven, Armand van. *Messerschmitt Bf 109 at War*, Ian Allan, Shepperton, 1977.

Ishoven, Armand van. *Ernst Udet: Biographie eines grossen Fliegers*, Manfred Pawlak Verlagsgeselischaft, Herrsching, 1977.

Ishoven, Armand van. *The Luftwaffe in the Battle of Britain*, Ian Allan, Shepperton, 1980.

Jackson, Robert. *Fighter: The Story of Air Combat 1936–194*, Arthur Barker, London, 1979.

James, John. *The Paladins: A Social History of the RAF up to the Outbreak of World War II*, Macdonald, London, 1990.

Jones, Neville. *The Beginnings of Strategic Air Power: A History of the British Bomber Force 1923–1939*, Frank Cass, London, 1987.

Kappe-Hardenberg, Siegfried. *Ein Mythos wird Zerstört: Der Spanische Bürgerkrieg, Guernica und die Antideutsche Propaganda*, Kurt Vowinkel Verlag, Neckargemünd, 1987.

Kaufmann J. E. and Kaufmann H. W. *Fortress Third Reich: German Fortifications and Defence Systems in World War II*, Greenhill Books, London, 2003.

Kesselring, Albert. *The Memoirs of Field Marshal Kesselring*, Purnell Book Services, London, 1974.

Ketley, Barry, and Rolfe, Mark. *Luftwaffe Fledglings 1935–1945*, Hikoki Publications, Aldershot, 1996.

Kiehl, Heinz. *Kampfgeschwader 'Legion Condor' 53*, Motorbuch Verlag, Stuttgart, 1983.

Kissel, Hans. *Die Katastrophe in Rumänien 1944*, Wehr und Wissen Verlagsgesselschaft, Darmstadt, 1994.

Klink, Ernst. *Das Gesetz des Handedns: Die Operation 'Zitadelle' 1943*, Deutsches Verlags Anstalt, Stuttgart, 1966.

Knocke, Heinz. *I Flew for the Führer*, Evans Bros, London, 1954.

Koch, Hannsjoachim W. *Der deutsche Bürgerkrieg: Ein Geschichte der deutschen und österreichischen Freikorps 1918–1923*, Ullstein, Berlin, n.d.

Koch, Horst-Adalbert. *Flak: Die Geschichte der deutschen Flakartillerie und der Einsatz der Luftwaffenhelfer*, Podzun Verlag, Bad Nauheim, 1965.

Koch, Horst-Adalbert, Schindler, Dr Heinz, Tessin, Dr Georg. *Flak: Die Geschichte der deutschen Flakartillerie und der Einsatz der Luftwaffehelfer*, Podzun Verlag, Bad Nauheim, 1965.

Kopański, Tomasz J. *Barbarossa Victims*, Mushroom Model Publications, Redbourn, 2001.

Kozhevnikov, M. N. *The Command and Staff of the Soviet Army Air Force in the Greater Patriotic War 1941–1945*, US Government Printing Office, Washington, 1977.

Kriegsgeschichtlichen Forschungsanstalt des Heeres.

Darstellungen aus den Nachkriegskämpfen deutscher Truppen und Freikorps.

4. Band (1939). Die Niederwerfung der Räteherrschaft in Bayern 1919.

5. Band (1939). Die Kämpfen in Südwestdeutschland 1919–1923.

6. Band (1940). Die Wirren in der Reichshauptstadt und im nördlichen Deutschland 1918–1920.

9. Band (1943). Erretuung des Ruhrgebiets 1918–1920.

Band 17 (1941). Freiheitskämpfe in Deutschösterreich. Kärntner Freiheitskampf. Erster Teil: 1918 bis 28. April 1919, Verlag von E. S. Mittler & Sohn, Berlin.

Kucera, Pavel; Bernad, Denes; and Androvic, Stefan. *Focke-Wulf Fw 189*, MBI, Prague, 1996.

Kuhn, Volkmar. *Der Seenotdienst der deutschen Luftwaffe*, Motorbuch Verlag, Stuttgart, 1978.

Kuhn, Volkmar. *German Paratroops in World War II*, Ian Allan, Shepperton, 1978.

Kurowski, Franz (trans. Johnston, David). *Luftwaffe Aces*, J. J. Fedorowicz Publishing, Winnipeg, 1996.

Kurowski, Franz. *The Brandenburger Commandos: Germany's elite warrior spies in WW I*, Stackpole Books, Mechanisburg, 2005.

Lacey Johnson, Lionel. *Point Blank and Beyond*, Airlife Publishing, Shrewsbury, 1991.

Laureau, Patrick. *Condor: The Luftwaffe in Spain 1936–1939*, Hikoki Publications, Ottringham, 2000.

Leach, Barry A. *German Strategy Against Russia 1939–1941*, Clarendon Press, Oxford, 1973.

Longmate, Norman. *Air Raid: The Bombing of Coventry 1940*, Hutchinson, London, 1976.

Longmate, Norman. *The Bombers: The RAF Offensive Against Germany 1939–1945*, Hutchinson, London, 1983.

MacDonald, Callum. *The Lost Battle*, Macmillan, London, 1993.

McFarland, Stephen L., and Newton, Wesley Philips. *To Command the Sky: The Battle for Air Superiority over Germany 1942–1944*, Smithsonian Institution, Washington, 1991.

Macksey, Kenneth. *Kesselring: The Making of the Luftwaffe*, Batsford, London, 1975, and Greenhill Books, London, 1996.

Manrho, John and Pütz, Ron. *Bodenplatte – The Luftwaffe's Last Hope: The attack on Allied airfields New Year's Day 1945*, Hikoki Publications, Crowborough, 2004.

Manvell, Roger and Fraenkel, Heinrich. *Göring*, NEL Books, London, 1968.

Mark, Eduard. *Aerial Interdiction in Three Wars*, Center for Air Force History, Washington, 1994.

Martínez Bande, José Manuel. *Monografías de la Guerra de España Numero 6: Vizcaya* Libreria Editoral San Martin, Madrid, 1971.

Mason, Francis K. *Battle over Britain*, 2nd edn, Aston Publications, Bourne End, 1990.

Mason, Herbert Molloy. *The Rise of the Luftwaffe, 1918–1940*. Cassell, London, 1975.

Middlebrook, Martin. *The Nuremberg Raid*. Allen Lane, London. 1973.

Middlebrook, Martin. *The Battle of Hamburg*. Allen Lane, London, 1980.

Middlebrook, Martin. *The Schweinfurt-Regensburg Mission*. Allen Lane, London, 1983.

Middlebrook, Martin. *Berlin Raids* Viking, London, 1988.

Mitcham, Samuel W. *Men of the Luftwaffe* Presidio Press, California 1988.

Molony, Brig. C. J. C. *The Mediterranean and Middle East, vol. V* HMSO, London 1973.

Mombeek, Eric. *Defending the Reich: The history of Jagdgeschwader 1 'Oesau'*, Jac Publications, Drayton, 1992.

Mombeek, Erik (trans. Vasco, John J.). *Defending the Reich: The History of Jagdgeschwader 1 'Oesau'*, JAC Publications, Norwich, 1992.

Mombeek, Eric with Forsyth, Robert and Creek, Eddie J. *Sturmstaffel 1: Reich Defence 1943–1944. The War Diary*, Classic Publications, Crowborough, 1999.

Mombeek, Eric with Smith, J. Richard and Creek, Eddie J. *Luftwaffe Colours: Jagdwaffe, vol. 1, Section 2: The Spanish Civil War*, Classic Publications, Crowborough, England, 1999.

Mombeek, Eric with Smith, J. Richard and Creek, Eddie J. *Luftwaffe colours: Jagdwaffe. Attack in the West May 1940*, Classic Publications, Crowborough, 2000.

Mortensen, Daniel R. *A Pattern for Joint Operations: World War II Close Air Support, North Africa*, Office of Air Force History and US Army Center of Military History, Washington, 1987.

Morzik, Fritz, and Hümmelchen, Gerhard. *Die deutschen Transportflieger im Zweiten Weltkrieg*, Bernard & Graefe Verlag, Frankfurt aM, 1966.

Muller, Richard. *The German Air War in Russia*, The Nautical & Aviation Publishing Company of America, Baltimore, 1992.

Murray, Williamson. *Luftwaffe: Strategy for Defeat 1933–1945*, Air University Press, Maxwell Air Force Base, Alabama, 1983.

Murray, Williamson. *German Military Effectiveness*, The Nautical and Aviation Publishing Company of America, Baltimore, Maryland, 1992.

Neetzow, Klaus. *Geschichte einer Transportfliegergruppe im II.Weltkrieg; Die II.Kampfgeschwader zur besonderen Verwendung 1 1938–1943 umbennant in II.Transportgeschwader 1*, Kameradschaft ehemaliger Transportflieger, Ronnenberg/Hannover,1989.

Neitzel, Sönke. *Der Einsatz der deutschen Luftwaffe über dem Atlantik und der Nordsee 1939–1945*, Bernard & Graefe Verlag, Bonn, 1995.

Nesbitt, Roy C. *The Armed Rovers: Beauforts and Beaufighters over the Mediterranean* Airlife Publishing, Shrewsbury 1995.

Neulen, Hans Werner (trans. by Alex Vanags-Baginskis) *In the Skies of Europe: Air forces allied to the Luftwaffe 1939–1945*, The Crowood Press, Marlborough, 2000.

Niehaus, Werner. *Die Nachrichtentruppe: 1914 bis heute*, Motorbuch Verlag, Stuttgart, 1980.

Nielsen, Andreas. *The German Air Force General Staff (USAF Historical Study 173)* Arno Press, New York, 1968.

Nissen, Jack (with Cockerill, A. W). *Winning the Radar War*, Robert Hale, London, 1987.

Nowarra, Heinz. *Die Verbotenen Flugzeuge 1921–1935*, Motorbuch Verlag, Stuttgart, 1980.

Nowarra, Heinz. *Nahaufklärer 1910–1945*, MotorbuchVerlag, Stuttgart, 1981.

Nowarra, Heinz. *Fernaufklärer 1915–1945*, MotorbuchVerlag, Stuttgart, 1982.

Orenstein, Harold S. (trans.). *Soviet Documents on the Use of War Experience, vol. 1* Frank Cass & Co, London 1991.

O'Neill, Robert J. *The German Army and the Nazi Party*, Corgi Books, London, 1968.

Osterkamp, Theo. *Durch Höhen und Tiefen jagt ein Herz*, Vowinckel Verlag, Heidelberg, 1952.

Overy, R. J. *The Air War 1939–1945*, Europa Publications, London, 1980.

Overy, R. J. *War and Economy in the Third Reich*, Clarendon Press, Oxford, 1994.

Pallard, Jean-Paul. *Blitzkrieg in the West: Then and Now*, After the Battle, London, 1991.

Parry, Simon W. *Intruders over Britain: The Luftwaffe Night Offensive 1940–1945*, Air Research Publications/Kristall Publications, Surbiton, 1987.

Patzwall, Klaus D. *Vergeltung-Das Flak-Regiment 155 (W)*, Verlag Militaria–Archiv Klaus D.Patzwall, Hamburg, 1985.

Pegg, Martin. *Luftwaffe Colours: Transporter, vol. 1: Luftwaffe transport units 1939–1943, vol. 2 Luftwaffe Transport Units 1943–1945*, Classic Publications Ltd, Crowborough, 2006.

Perret, Geoffrey. *Winged Victory: The Army Air Forces in World War II*, Random House, New York, 1993.

Playfair, Major General I.S.O. *The Mediterranean and the Middle East, vol. II*, HMSO, London, 1956.

Playfair, Major General I.S.O. *The Mediterranean and the Middle East, vol. III*, HMSO, London, 1960.

Pletschacher, Peter. *Die Königlich Bayerischen Fliegertruppen*, Motorbuch Verlag, Stuttgart, 1978.

Plocher, Generalleutnant Hermann. *The German Air Force versus Russia 1941*, (USAF Historical Studies No 153), USAF Historical Division, Aerospace Studies Institute, Air University, Arno Press, New York, 1965.

Plocher, Generalleutnant Hermann. *The German Air Force versus Russia 1942*,(USAF Historical Studies No 154), USAF Historical Division, Aerospace Studies Institute, Air University, Arno Press, New York, 1966.

Plocher, Generalleutnant Hermann. *The German Air Force versus Russia 1943*, (USAF Historical Studies No 155), USAF Historical Division, Aerospace Studies Institute, Air University, Arno Press, New York, 1967.

Poolman, Kenneth. *Focke-Wulf Condor: Scourge of the Atlantic*, Macdonald & Jane's, London, 1978.

Postan, M. M. *British War Production*, HMSO, London 1952.

Price, Alfred. *Heinkel 177*, Profile Publications, Windsor, 1972.

Price, Alfred. *Battle over the Reich*, Ian Allan, Shepperton, 1974.

Price, Alfred. *World War II Fighter Conflict*, Macdonald & Jane's, London, 1975.

Price, Alfred. *Blitz on Britain*, Ian Allan, Shepperton, 1976.

Price, Alfred. *The Bomber in WorldWar II*, Macdonald & Jane's, London, 1976.

Price, Alfred. *Instruments of Darkness* Macdonald & Jane's, London, 1977.

Price, Alfred. *Aircraft versus Submarines*, Jane's Publishing Co., London, 1980.

Price, Alfred. *The Luftwaffe Handbook*, 2nd edn, Ian Allan, Shepperton, 1986.

Price, Alfred. *Battle of Britain Day: 15 September 1940*, Sidgwick & Jackson, London, 1990.

Price, Alfred. *The Last Year of the Luftwaffe: May 1944–May 1945*, Arms & Armour Press, London, 1991.

Price, Alfred. *The Luftwaffe Data Book*, Greenhill Books, London, 1997.

Price, Alfred. *Kampfflieger, vol. III. Bombers of the Luftwaffe January 1942–September 1943*, Classic Publications Ltd, Crowborough, 2005.

Price, Alfred. *Messerschmitt Bf 110 Night Fighters*, Profile Publications, Windsor, n.d.

Prien, Jochen. *Geschichte des Jagdschwaders 77, Teil 1 (1934–May 1941); Teil 3 (July 1942–December 1943); Teil 4 (Januar 1944–Mai 1945*, privately printed, Hamburg, 1991–96.

Priller, Josef. *J.G.26 Geschichte eines Jagdgeschwader: Das J.G.26 (Schlageter) 1937–1945*, Motorbuch Verlag, Stuttgart, 1980.

Pritchard, David. *The Radar War: Germany's Pioneering Achievement 1904–1945*, Patrick Stephens, Cambridge, 1989.

Probert, Air Commodore Henry, and Cox, Sebastian. *The Battle Re-Thought: A Symposium on the Battle of Britain*, Airlife Publishing, Shrewsbury, 1991.

Proctor, Raymond R. *Hitler's Luftwaffe in the Spanish Civil War*, Greenwood Press, Westpoint, Connecticut, 1983.

Quarrie, Bruce. *Airborne Assault*, Patrick Stephens, Sparkford, 1991.

Radtke, Siegfried. *Kampfgeschwader 54. Von der Ju 52 zur Me 262*, Schild Verlag, Munich, 1990.

Ramsey, Winston (ed.). *The Blitz Then and Now, vol. 1: September 3 1939–September 6 1940* and vol. 2: *September 1940–May 1941*, Battle of Britain Prints International, London, 1987–88.

Ray, John. *The Battle of Britain: New Perspectives*. Arms & Armour Press, London, 1994.

Ray, John. *The Night Blitz 1940–1941*, Arms & Armour Press, London, 1996.

Reinhardt, Klaus. *Moscow: The Turning Point*, Berg Publishers, Oxford, 1992.

Richey, Paul. *Fighter Pilot*, Pan Books, London, 1969.

Ries, Karl. *Die Maulwürfe: Geheimer Aufbau 1919–1935*, Verlag Dieter Hoffmann, Mainz, 1970.

Ries, Karl. *Luftwaffen-Story 1935–1939*, Verlag Dieter Hoffmann, Mainz, 1974.

Ries, Karl. *Deutsche Fliegerführerschulen und ihre Maschinen 1919–1945*, Motorbuch Verlag, Stuttgart, 1988.

Ries, Karl and Ring, Hans (trans. by David Johnston). *The Legion Condor: A history of the Luftwaffe in the Spanish Civil War 1936–1939*, Schiffer Military History, West Chester, Pennsylvania, 1992.

Ring, Hans, and Gerbig, Werner. *Jagdgeschwader 27*, Motorbuch Verlag, Stuttgart, 1971.

Roell, Werner P. *Laurels for Prinz Wittgenstein*, Independent Books, Bromley, 1994.

Rosch, Barry C. *Luftwaffe Codes, Markings and Units 1939–1945*, Schiffer Publishing, Atglen, 1995.

Roskill, Capt, S. W. *The War at Sea, vol.* II, HMSO, London, 1956.

Roskill, Capt, S. W. *The War at Sea, vol. III, pt 1* (June 1943–May 1944) HMSO, London, 1960.

Rothnie, Niall. *The Baedeker Blitz*, Ian Allan, Shepperton, 1972.

Rohwer, Jürgen, and Hümmelchen, Gerhard. *Chronology of the War at Sea*, Greenhill Books, London, 1992.

Rudel, Hans-Ulrich (trans. Hudson, Lynton). *Stuka Pilot*, Transworld Publishers, London, 1957.

Rumpf, Hans. *The Bombing of Germany*, Frederick Muller, London, 1961.

Sarkar, Dilip. *Angriff Westland*, Ramrod Publications, Yeovil, 1994.

Salas Larrazabel, Jésus. *Air War over Spain*, Ian Allan, Shepperton, 1974.

Sarhidai, Gyula; Punka, Gyorgy; and Kozlik, Viktor. *Hungarian Eagles: A Magyar Kirklyi Honved Legiero 1920–1945*, Hikoki Publications, Aldershot, 1996.

Saward, Dudley. *'Bomber' Harris: The Authorised Biography*, Cassell, London, 1984.

Schliephake, Hanfried. *The Birth of the Luftwaffe*, Ian Allan, London, 1971.

Schmidt, Rudi. *Achtung–Torpedos los!: Der strategische und operative Einsatz des Kampfgeschwaders 26*, Bernard & Graefe Verlag, Coblenz, 1991.

Schramm, Percy Ernst (ed). *Kriegstagesbuch des Oberkommandos der Wehrmacht. Band IV 1.January 1944–22.Mai 1945. Erster Hallband*, Bernard & Graefe Verlag für Wehrwesen, Frankfurt aM, 1961.

Schreiber, Gerhard; Stegemann, Bernd; Vogel, Detlef. *Das Deutschen Reich und der Zweiten Weltkrieg. Band 3 Der Mittelmeerraum und Südosteuropa – Von der »non belligeranza« Italiens bis zum Kriegseintritt der Vereinigten Staaten*, Deutsche Verlags-Anstalt, Stuttgart, 1984.

Scutts, Jerry. *Bf 109 Aces of North Africa and the Mediterranean*, Osprey Publishing, London, 1995.

Scutts, Jerry. *JG 54: Jagdgeschwader 54 Grünherz. Aces of the Eastern Front*, Airlife Publishing, Shrewsbury, 1992.

Searby, Air Commodore John. *The Bomber Battle for Berlin* Airlife, Shrewsbury, 1991.

Seaton, Albert. *The Russo–German War*, Arthur Barker, London, 1971.

Seaton, Albert. *The German Army 1933–1945*, Wiedenfeld & Nicolson, London, 1982.

Shores, Christopher F. *2nd Tactical Air Force*, Osprey Publishing, London, 1970.

Shores, Christopher F. *Pictorial History of the Mediterranean Air War*, 3 vols, Ian Allan, Shepperton, 1972–1974.

Shores, Christopher. *Dust Clouds in the Middle East: The Air War for East Africa, Iraq, Syria, Iran and Madagascar*, Grub Street, London, 1996.

Shores, Christopher, and Cull, Brian (with Malizia, Nicala). *Malta: The Hurricane Years, 1940–1941*, Grub Street, London, 1987.

Shores, Christopher, and Cull, Brian (with Malizia, Nicala). *Air War for Yugoslavia, Greece and Crete*, Grub Street, London, 1987.

Shores, Christopher, and Cull, Brian (with Malizia, Nicala). *Malta: The Spitfire Year, 1942*, Grub Street, London, 1991.

Shores, Christopher with Foreman, John; Ehrengardt, Christian-Jacques; Weiss, Heinrich; Olsen, Bjorn. *Fledgling Eagles: A Complete Account of Air Operations during the 'Phoney War' and Norwegian Campaign 1940*, Grub Street, London, 1991.

Shores, Christopher, and Ring, Hans. *Fighters over the Desert*, Neville Spearman, London, 1969.

Shores, Christopher; Ring, Hans; and Hess, William. *Fighters over Tunisia*, Neville Spearman, London, 1975.

Short, Neil. *Hitler's Siegfried Line*, Sutton Publishing, Stroud, 2002.

Shukman, Harold, (ed.). *Stalin's Generals*, Weidenfeld & Nicolson, London, 1993.

Smith, J. Richard. *The Focke-Wulf Fw 200*, Profile Publications, Leatherhead, 1966.

Smith, J. Richard (ed.). *The Koller War Diary*, Monogram Aviation Publications, Sturbridge, Massachusetts, 1990.

Smith, J. Richard and Creek, Eddie J. *Luftwaffe Colours. Kampfflieger, vol. 1. Bombers of the Luftwaffe 1933–1940*, Classic Publications, Crowborough, 2004.

Smith, J. Richard and Creek Eddie J. *Me 262, vol. One*, Classic Publications, Crowborough, 2000.

Smith, J. R., and Kay, Antony. *German Aircraft of the Second World War*, Putnam & Co., London, 1972.

Smith, Malcolm. *British Air Strategy between the Wars*, Clarendon Press, Oxford, 1984.

Smith, Peter C. *Stuka at War*, Ian Allan, Shepperton, 1980.

Smith, Peter C. *Stuka Squadron: Stukagruppe 77 – The Luftwaffe's Fire Brigade*, Patrick Stephens, Cambridge, 1990.

Smith, Peter J. C. *Air-Launched Doodlebugs*, Pen and Sword, London, 2007.

Smith, Peter C. *Luftwaffe Colours: Stuka Dive–Bomber Units, vol. 1 1935–1940*, Classic Publications Ltd, Crowborough.

Soviet Defence Ministry (trans. Fetzer, Leland). *The Soviet Air Force in World War II: The Official History*, David & Charles, Newton Abbot/London, 1974.

Späte, Oberstleutnant Wolfgang, and Bateson, Richard P. *Messerschmitt Me 163 Komet*, Profile Publications, Windsor, 1971.

Spick, Mike *Luftwaffe Fighter Aces*, Greenhill Books, London, 1996.

Speidel, General Wilhelm. *The German Air Force in Poland*, USAF Historical Studies, Monograph 151, US Air Force Historical research Association, (Microfilm K1026-U).

Speidel, General Wilhelm. *The German Air Force in France and the Low Countries*, USAF Historical Studies, Monograph 152, US Air Force Historical Research Association, 1958.

Stahl, Peter. *The Diving Eagle: A Ju 88 Pilot's Diary (1940–1941,)* William Kimber, London, 1984.

Steinhilper, Ulrich and Osborne, Peter. *Spitfire on my Tail. A view from the other side*, Independent Books, Bromley, 1990.

Steinhoff, Johannes. *The Straits of Messina*, Andre Deutsch, London, 1971.

Streetly, Martin. *Confound and Destroy: 100 Group and the Bomber Support Campaign*, Jane's Publishing Co., London 1985.

Suchenwirth, Professor Richard. *The Development of the German Air Force 1919–1939*, USAF Historical Studies, Monograph 160, US Air Force Historical Division, Maxwell AFB, Alabama, 1968.

Taghorn, Peter. *Hors–Série Avions No 18: L'Aéronautique Militaire Belge en mai–juin 1940*, Éditions Lela Presse, Outreau, 2006.

Tarrant, V. E. *Stalingrad*, Leo Cooper, London, 1992.

Taylor, Telford. *The March of Conquest: The German Victories in Western Europe 1940*, Edward Hulton, London, 1959.

Taylor, Telford. *The Breaking Wave: The German Defeat in the Summer of 1940*, Weidenfeld & Nicolson, London, 1967.

Terraine, John. *The Right of the Line: The Royal Air Force in the European War 1939–1945*, Hodder & Stoughton, London, 1985.

Tessin, Georg. *Verbände und Truppen der deutschen Wehrmacht und Wqffen SS 1939–1945. Band 14 (Die Luftstreitkräfte)*, Biblio Verlag, Osnabruck, 1980.

Thomas, Gordon and Morgan-Witts, Max. *The Day Guernica Died*, Hodder & Stoughton, London, 1975.

Thomas, Hugh. *The Spanish Civil War*, 3rd edn, Penguin Books, London, 1986.

Thomas, Lowell, and Jablonski, Edward. *Bomber Commander*, Sidgwick & Jackson, London, 1977.

Tieke, Wilhelm. *The Caucasus and the Oil*, J. J. Fedorowicz Publishing, Winnipeg, 1995.

Thiele, Harold. *Luftwaffe Aerial Torpedo Aircraft and Operations in World War Two*, Hikoki Publications, Crowborough,2004.

Toliver, Raymond F., and Constable, Trevor J. *Das waren die deutschen, Jagdflieger Asse 1939–1945*, Motorbuch Verlag, Stuttgart, 1986.

Tuider, Dr Othmar. *Die Luftwaffe in Österreich 1938–1945*, Österreichischen Bundesverlag, Vienna, 1985.

Tyushkevich, S. A. *The Soviet Armed Forces: A History of Their Organizational Development*, US Government Printing Office, Washington, 1978.

United States Army Air Force. *Army Air Force Historical Studies No 30. The Ninth Air Force in the Western Desert Campaign to 23 January 1943*.

United States Strategic Bombing Survey. *Overall report (European War) 30 September 1945*.

Vasco, John J. *Luftwaffe colours: Zerstörer. Luftwaffe Fighter-Bomber and Destroyer Units, vol. 1 1936–1940*, Classic Publications, Crowborough, 2006.

Villa, Brian Loring. *Mountbatten and the Dieppe Raid*, Oxford University Press, Oxford, 1989.

Vogt, Harold. *Schlachtsfeld Luftfahrzeug: Der Einsatz der Schwarzen Manner im II Weltkrieg*, Flugzeug-Publikations, 1994.

Völker, Karl-Heinz. *Die Entwicklung der Militärischen Luftfahrt in Deutschland 1920–1930*, Beiträge zur Militär-und Kriegsgeschichte, Dritter Band Deutsches Verlags–Ansalt, Stuttgart, 1962.

Völker, Karl-Heinz. *Die Deutsche Luftwaffe 1933–1939: Aufbau, Führung und Rüstung der Luftwaffe sowie die Entwicklung der deutschen Luftkriegstheorie*. Deutsche Verlags-Anstalt, Stuttgart, 1967.

Völker, Karl-Heinz. *Dokumente und Dokumentarfotos zur Geschichte der Deutschen Luftwaffe*, Deutsches Verlags–Ansalt, Stuttgart, 1968.

Volkogonov, Dmitri. *Stalin: Triumph and Tragedy*, Prima Publishing, Rocklin, 1992.

Voroshilov Academy of the General Staff. *Boevoi sostav Sovetskoi armii, vol.s 1–5*, Moscow, 1963 (CD version Eastview publications, Minneapolis, Minesota, 2004).

Wadman, David. *Luftwaffe colours. Aufklärer: Luftwaffe reconnaissance aircraft and units*, 2 vols, Midland Publishing, Hersham, 2007.

Wadman, David and Pegg, Martin. *Jagdwaffe, vol. 4 Section 1; Holding the West*, Classic Publications, Crowborough, 2003.

Wakefield, Kenneth. *The First Pathfinders*, Crecy Books, London, 1992.

Wakefield, Kenneth (ed.). *The Blitz Then and Now, vol. 3: May 1941–May 1945*, Battle of Britain Prints International, London, 1990.

Warner, Graham. *The Bristol Blenheim. A Complete History*, Crécy Publishing, Manchester, 2002.

Weal, John. *Focke-Wulf Fw 190 Aces of the Russian Front*, Osprey Publishing, London, 1996.

Weal, John. *Focke-Wulf Fw 190 Aces of the Western Front*, Osprey Publishing, London 1996.

Weal, John. *Luftwaffe Schlachtgruppen*, Osprey Publishing, Botley, 2003.

Weal, John. *Bf 109D/E Aces 1939–1941*, Osprey Publishing, Oxford, 2005.

Weal, John. *Junkers Ju 87 Stukageschwader of the Russian Front*, Osprey Publishing, London, 2008.

Weal, John. *Jagdgeschwader 2 'Richthofen'*.

Weir, Adrian. *The Last Flight of the Luftwaffe: The Fate of Schulungslehrgang Elbe, 7 April 1945*, Arms & Armour Press, London, 1997.

Whiting, Charles. *The Three Star Blitz: The Baedecker Raids and the Start of Total War*, Leo Cooper, London, 1987.

Williamson, Gordon. *Aces of the Reich*, Arms & Armour Press, London, 1989.

Windrow, Martin. *The Junkers Ju 88A*, Profile Publications No 29, London, 1965.

Wood, Derek and Dempster, Derek *The Narrow Margin*, Arrow Books, London, 1967.

Woodman, Richard. *Arctic Convoys*, John Murray, London, 1995.

Wright, Robert. *Dowding and the Battle of Britain*, Corgi Books, Ealing, London, 1970.

Wynn, Humphrey, and Young, Susan. *Prelude to Overlord*, Airlife Publishing, Shrewsbury, 1983.

Young, Richard Anthony. *The Flying Bomb*, Ian Allan, Shepperton, 1978.

Zaloga, Steven J. *Poland 1939: The Birth of Blitzkrieg*, Osprey Publishing, Botley, Oxford, 2002.

Zaloga, Steve and Madej, Victor. *The Polish Campaign*, Hippocrene Bools, New York, 1985.

Ziemke, Earl F. *Stalingrad to Berlin: The German Defeat in the East*, Office of the Chief of Military History, US Army, Washington, 1968.

Ziemke, Earl F., and Bauer, Magna E. *Moscow to Stalingrad: Decision in the East*, Military Heritage Press, NewYork, 1988.

ARTICLES AND ESSAYS

Argyle, Christopher J. *The Liverpool Blitz*, Air Pictorial, October, 1975.

Alexandrov, Alexander. *Junkers Planes in Russia*, Skyways: The Journal of the Airplane 1920–1940, No 25.

Andersson, Lennart. *Secret Luftwaffe: German Military Aviation between the Wars*, Air Enthusiast, vol. 41.

Arthy, Andrew. *Luftwaffe Anti-Partisan Operations in France, June–September 1944*. Geschwader Bongart web site.

Arthy, Andrew. *A History of 5./B.F.Gr.196, 1./S.A.Gr.128, 10./Z.G.1, and Geschwader Bongart*. Geschwader Bongart web site.

Axworthy, Mark. *Flank Guard: Romania's Aerial Advance on Stalingrad*, Air Enthusiast, Nos 64, July–August 1996 and 65 September–October 1996.

D'Amico, E, andValentini, G. *La Legione Croata in Guerra*, JP 4, April 1993.

Bateson, Richard P. *Georg Sattler–Mediterranean Bomber Pilot*, Aircraft Illustrated, August 1970.

Bateson, Richard P. *Bulgaria at War*, Air Pictorial, March 1972 (pt 1) and April 1972 (pt 2).

Bowyer, Michael. *High-Flying Raiders*, Aviation News, 18–31, October 1974.

Boyne, Walt. *Missiles Against the Roma*, Flying Review, February 1968.

Brooks, Robin J. *When the Luftwaffe Landed in Britain*, The Blitz Then and Now, vol. 3.

Brown, Pete *KG 200: Fact and Fiction*, Aeroplane Monthly, November 1994.

Chamberlain, Peter *Bombs and other missiles dropped on the United Kingdom*, The Blitz Then and Now, vol. I.

Collis, Bob. *Jabos over Suffolk*, The Blitz Then and Now, vol. 3.

Collis, Bob. *The First of the Ks*, The Blitz Then and Now, vol. 3.

Collis, Bob. *Mosquito versus Hornet*, The Blitz Then and Now, vol. 3.

Collis, Bob. *The First Junkers 188 Down on British Soil*, The Blitz Then and Now, *vol*. 3.

Collis, Bob. *Escape to Britain*, The Blitz Then and Now, vol. 3.

Ehrhardt, P and Benoit, M. *La Guerre de Condor*, La Fanta de l'Aviation, Nos 256–259, March June 1991.

Cockburn, Sir Robert. *The Radio War*, IEE Proceedings, vol. 132, Part A, No 6, October 1985.

Daniel, Raymond. *La Conquête de la Hollande:Opération secondaire?* Icare No 79, vol. IX.

Façon, Patric. *La Visite du Général Vuillemin en Allegmagne*, Recueil d'Articles et Études 1981–1983, Service Historique de l'Armée de l'Air Fatutta, Francesco.

Operazione Rosselsprung, Revista Italiana Difesa, November 1989.

Frka, Daniel. *Croatian Air Force in WW 2*, Scale Models International, June 1993.

Giessler, Capt. Helmuth Giessler. *The Breakthrough of the 'Scharnhorst': Some Radio–Technical Details*, IRE Transactions on Military Electronics, January 1961.

Green, William. *Aerial Alpenstock*, Flying Review, December 1969.

Green, William. *Finland's Modest Air Arm*, Flying Review, January 1969.

Green, William. *Magyar Air Cover*, Flying Review, September and October 1969.

Green, William. *Sentinel over the Fiords*. Flying Review, April 1969.

Green, William, and Swanborough, Gordon. *Balkan Interlude*, Air Enthusiast, No 39, May–August 1989.

Hartmann, Ernst. *Einsatz Kubangebiet: Weitere Einsatze der KGrzbV 23/TGr 30*, Luftwaffen-Revue, 3/93, September 1993.

Hartmann, Ernst. *Eine Fluzeugführerausbildung im 2.Weltkrieg*, Luftwaffen-Revue. 4/94, December 1994.

Huan, Claud, *La bataille aéronavale de l'artique*. La Fanatique de l'Avion, Nos 198–201, May–August 1986.

Huan, Claude and Marchand, Alain. *La Bataille Aéronaval de Dunkerque 18.Mai–3. Juin 1940*. Revue Historique de l'Armée, vol. 172, September 1988.

Johnson, Robert Craig. *The White Falcons: The white air forces*. World at War web site.

Johnson, Robert Craig. *Planting the Dragon's Teeth: the German Air Combat School at Lipetsk (USSR) 1925–1930*. World at War web site.

Kirk, Peter and Felix, Peter. *Attack on GB 73 19*, The Blitz Then and Now, vol. 3.

Kirkland, Lieutenant Faris R. *The French Air Force in 1940. Was it defeated by the Luftwaffe or politics?* Air University Review, September–October 1985.

Kopp, Dr Carlo. *The Dawn of the Smart Bomb*, Air Power Australia web site.

Krüger, Hans-Eberhard *.Jagdstaffeln über Kurland und Oberschlesien*, Jägerblatt, April–May 1989, pp 18–27.

Krüger, Hans-Eberhard. *Die Reichswehr-und Polizeiflieger-Staffeln*, Jägerblatt, August 1989, pp 8–9.

Lutz, Fritz. *Mein griechisches Abenteuer*, Luftwaffen–Revue, 2/94, June 1994.

Marchand, Alain, and Huan, Claude. *Achtung Minen!* pt III, La Fanatique de l'Avion, No 211, June 1987.

Munday, Eric. *Chain Home Radar and the Blitz*, The Blitz Then and Now, vol. 1.

Murray, Williamson. *German Air Power and the Munich Crisis*, War and Society: A Yearbook of Military History, vol. 2, Croom Helm, London, 1977.

Osborne, Dr Richard. *Naval Actions of the Spanish Civil War*, Warships Supplement: Proceedings of Naval Meetings. World Ship Society, Kendal, Cumbria, 1989.

Philpott, Brian. *The Luftwaffe's Night-Fighter Force*, Aviation News, 18–31 March 1988.

Price, Alfred. *Watching the Detectives*, Aeroplane, vol. 35 No 10, October 2007.

Price, Alfred, and Smith, Richard. *The Heinkel He 177*, Archiv, vol. 3, No 9.

Saunders, Andy. *Jabo Attack*, The Blitz Then and Now, vol. 3.

Schlaug, Georg. *Luftversorgung eingekesselter Verbande der 2. Armee durch Lastensegler Go 242 des Luftwaffenkommandos Don Januar/Februar 1943*, Luftwaffen-Revue, 1/94, March 1994.

Schreiber, *Generalmajor Dr* Jürgen. *Fliegerische Grundausbildung und Jagdfliegerschulung 1935–1945*, Luftwaffen-Revue, 4/92, December 1992.

Schreiber, *Generalmajor Dr* Jürgen. *Luftwaffen– und Marinehelfer (Flak)*, Luftwaffen–Revue, 3/93, September 1992.

Schuh, Prof. Horst. *Bomber und Jager–Ein Kampftag im Jahre 1944*, Luftwaffen-Revue, 3/96, September 1996.

Schumann, Ralf. *Ritterkreuztrager der Kampfflieger: General der Flieger Ulrich O.-E. Kessler*, Luftwaffen-Revue, 2/97, June 1997.

Scott, Ben. *The origins of the Freikorps. A re-evaluation*. University of Sussex Journal of Contemporary History, 1, 2000.

Soumille, Albert. *L'Aviation Slovaque*, Fanatique, July 1970.

Speidel, Helm. *Reichswehr und Rote Armee*, Vierteljahrshelte für Zeitgeschichte, vol. 1, 1953.

Spencer, Flt Lt Michael. *Lessons Learned from the First Operational Air-Launched Anti-Ship Missiles*, Maritime Patrol Aviation, September 1991.

Stenman, Kari. *The Short Saga of Battle Unit Kuhlmey*, Air Enthusiast, No 34, September–December 1987.

Terlinden, Lieutenant Colonel Michel. *L'Aéronautique Militaire Belge en 1940*, Icare No 74, Autumn 1975.

Toll, Karl. *Storm Bird*, Airpower, *vol. 23*, No 2, March 1993.

Torroba, César O'Donnell. *Las Perdidas de Buques Mercantes Republicanos Causadas por Hidroaviones de la Legión Cóndor durante la Guerra Civil Española (1936–1939)*, Revista de Historia Naval, No 43, 1993.

Urbanke, Axel (tr. Dave Roberts). *The Luftwaffe's Last throw of the Dice: last-minute relocation: May 1945*, Aeroplane, vol. 33, No 7, July 2005.

Vercamer, Arvo L. *Naval War in the Baltic Sea 1941–1945*. Feldgrau web site.

Vercamer, Arvo, and Pipes, Jason. *German Military in the Soviet Union 1918–1933*, in Feldgrau web site.

Verton, Hendrik C. *Erstes Fluglebnis für Grenadiere 1941*, Luftwaffen-Revue, 2/95, June 1995.

Wakefield, Kenneth. *The Baedeker Raids*, The Blitz Then and Now, vol. 3.

Wakefield, Kenneth. *The Danger by Day: Fighter-Bomber and High Altitude Attacks*, The Blitz Then and Now, Vol, 3.

Wakefield, Kenneth. *The Fiasco of 1943*, The Blitz Then and Now, vol. 3.

Wakefield, Kenneth. *The Knickebein Effect*, Aviation News, 4–17, March 1988.

Wakefield, Kenneth. *The Steinbock Raids*, The Blitz Then and Now, vol. 3.

Watson-Watt, Sir Robert. *Battle Scars of Military Electronics–The Scharnhorst Breakthrough*, IRE Transactions on Military Electronics, March 1957.

Weal, John. *A Nocturnal Miscellany*, Air International, vol. 48, No 3, March 1995.

Westwall, Ian. *Condor Legion: The Wehrmacht's Training Ground*, Axis History web site.

Widfeldt, Bo. *German Aircraft Landed/Crashed in Sweden, WW II*, Archiv, vol. 3, Nos 10–12.

Wixey, Ken. *Incidental Combatant*, Air Enthusiast, No 67, January/February 1997.

WEBSITES

Aerodrome Forum. the aerodrome.com.

(US) Air Force Historical Research Agency. Numbered USAF Historical Studies: Au.af.mil.

Air of Authority–A history of RAF organisation: Personnel-Air officer biographies. Rafweb.org/Biographies.

Axis Biographical Research: Luftwaffe (Gareth Collins and Michael Miller). Geocities.com/~orion47.

Axis History Factbook Axishistory.com.

Deutsches Atlantikwall Archiv. Research by Harry Lippmann on German air defence system. Deutschesatlantikwallarchive.de/radar.

France 1940. France1940.free.fr.

Feldgrau. The German Armed Forces 1919–1945. feldgrau.com.

Ghostbombers (Nick Beale). Ghostbombers.com.

Soviet air units in the Second World War (V.V.Kharin). allaces.ru.

The Luftwaffe 1933–1945 (Michael Holm) Ww2.dk.

The World at War: worldatwar.net.

Web.genealogie. Le site de la génealogie historique. Généraux d'armée aérienne: http://web.genealogie.free.fr/Les_militaires/2GM/France/Air/Generaux_Armee.

Geschwader Bongart, a history. fw190.hobbybista.com/geschwaderbongart.doc.

Index

Vercors Plateau 237
Versailles conference and
  Treaty 14, 17, 21-22, 24,
  30
Veszprém 216
Viazma 159
Vichy France 103, 140
Vienna 155, 194, 216-217
Vienna-Aspern 212
Vigo 48
Vistula 59, 205, 207, 218,
  220
Viterbo 150
Vitoria 42
Voronezh 19, 166-167
VVS (Peasants Red Army)
  153-154, 156, 160, 164,
  166, 169, 175-176, 203-
  205, 207, 210, 214, 218-
  219, 222-223
Vyborg 202

Wangerooge naval air base
  23
Warsaw 57, 59-60, 206-207,
  218
  Uprising 207
Wasserburg 24
Weimar 224
Wesel 244
West Wall 62
Western Approaches 110-
  112, 200
Western campaign, 1940
  68-73
Western Desert Air Force
  135, 140-141
Western Front 215, 219
Wiener-Neustadt 147
Wiesbaden 93
Wilhelmshaven 186
Wilhelmshaven-Rüstringen
  naval air base23
Wolverhampton 87
World Disarmament
  Conference, 1932 28

York 102
Yugoslav Air Force 130
Yugoslav Army 131

Yugoslavia 15, 130-132,
  151, 211-213, 215

Aircraft

Aero engines
  Allison 123, 190
  Junkers Jumo 205 30, 50
  Napier Lion 20
Airship *Graf Zeppelin II* 76
Albatros 18
  D.Va 13
  L 75a/L82 21
  L.76/78 19
Arado
  Ar 64/65 29
  Ar 68 53
  Ar 196 112, 116
  Ar 234 217, 238, 242, 244
Armstrong-Whitworth
  Whitley 83, 94
Avia B.71 52
Avro
  Anson 106
  Lancaster 38, 94, 236
  Manchester 38, 94

Bell Airacobra 224
Boeing
  B-17 Flying Fortress 117,
    123, 186, 188-189, 198,
    203, 226, 246
  YB-40 Flying Fortress
    188, 226
Blohm & Voss Bv 222
  Wiking 116, 199
Boulton-Paul Defiant 75-76
Brandenburger C.1 24
Bristol
  Beaufighter 86, 88, 100,
    102, 116-117, 139, 147,
    198, 200
  Blenheim 123, 131; IVF
    86

Caproni Ca 133 32, 51
Consolidated B-24
  Liberator 117, 151, 198,
    203
Curtiss Hawk 31

de Havilland
  Mosquito 102, 104, 125,
    185-186, 200, 225, 230,
    240, 243; NF.XVIII 196
  Tiger Moth 65
Dietrich DP IIa 16
Dornier 16
  Do 11C 29; Do 11D 29
  Do 13 (DO 23) 29
  Do 17 30, 44, 50, 86; Do
    17 E 52; Do 17 E-1 42;
    Do 17F 44; Do 17M/P
    53; Do 17 Z 108;
    Do 17Z-6/10 92
  Do 19 30
  Do 23 118
  Do 26 110
  Do 215B 97
  Do 217 108, 122, 226,
    230; Do 217E-2 102; Do
    217M 04
  R *Superwal* 23, 28
Douglas
  A-20 Boston 123, 204;
    Havoc 225
  DC 3 Dakota 177, 243

Fairey
  Albacore 170
  Fulmar 112
  Swordfish 128, 170
Fiat
  CR 20bis 51
  CR 30 51
  CR 32 51; CR 32bis 32
Fiat-Ansaldo A120 24, 51
Fieseler
  F 103 (FzG76) – see V-1
  Fi 156 *Storch* 59, 69, 216,
    220-221, 223
Focke-Wulf 223
  Fw 58 170
  Fw 189 219
  Fw 190 *Jabo* 103-104, 116,
    122-124, 141, 144-146,
    148, 166, 173, 176, 186,
    192, 195, 200, 208, 219,
    223, 223, 231, 240, 242-
    244; Fw 190A 120, 225;